For Rebecca Jill

If you marry, you will regret it; if you do not marry, you will also regret it; if you marry or do not marry, you will regret both; whether you marry or do not marry, you will regret both.

Søren Kierkegaard, "Diapsalmata," *Either/Or*, vol. 1

SEX, LOVE, AND FRIENDSHIP

Studies of the Society for the Philosophy of Sex and Love 1977-1992

VIBS

Volume 45

a volume in
Histories and Addresses of Philosophical Societies
HAPS
Richard T. Hull, Editor

Rebecca Jill Soble
(1976)

(photograph: Alan Soble)

SEX, LOVE, AND FRIENDSHIP

Studies of the Society for the Philosophy of Sex and Love 1977-1992

Edited by

Alan Soble

Amsterdam - Atlanta, GA 1997

Cover design by Chris Kok based on a photograph, © 1984 by Robert Ginsberg, of statuary by Gustav Vigeland in the Frogner Park, Oslo, Norway.

♾ The paper on which this book is printed meets the requirements of "ISO 9706:1994, Information and documentation - Paper for documents - Requirements for permanence".

ISBN: 90-420-0001-5 (bound)
ISBN: 90-420-0227-1 (paper)

Printed in The Netherlands

Contents

List of Illustrations

Credits

Chapter One, "Sexual Desire" by Jerome A. Shaffer, was previously published in *Journal of Philosophy* 75:4 (1978): 175-89, and is reprinted with the kind permission of the journal.

Chapter Two, "The Definition of Love in Plato's *Symposium*" by Donald Levy, was previously published in *Journal of the History of Ideas* 40 (1979): 285-91, and is reprinted with the kind permission of The Johns Hopkins University Press.

Chapter Three, "The Language of Sex and the Sex of Language" by Hugh T. Wilder, was previously published in Alan Soble, ed., *The Philosophy of Sex*, 1st ed. (Totowa, N.J.: Littlefield, Adams, 1980), 99-109, and is reprinted with the kind permission of Littlefield, Adams and Co.

Chapter Five, "Why Are Sex and Love Philosophically Interesting?" by Ann Garry, was previously published in *Metaphilosophy* 11 (1980): 165-77, and is reprinted with the kind permission of Blackwell Publishers.

Chapter Seven, "Are There Gay Genes? Sociobiology and Homosexuality" by Michael Ruse, was previously published in *Journal of Homosexuality* 4 (1981): 5-34, and is reprinted with the kind permission of Haworth Press.

Chapter Nine, "Are Androgyny and Sexuality Compatible?" by Robert Pielke, was previously published in Mary Vetterling-Braggin, ed., *"Femininity," "Masculinity," and "Androgyny"* (Totowa, N.J.: Littlefield, Adams, 1982), 187-96, and reprinted by kind permission of Littlefield, Adams and Co.

Chapter Twelve, "Gay Civil Rights: The Arguments" by Richard D. Mohr, was previously published in Richard D. Mohr, *A More Perfect Union* (Boston: Beacon Press, 1994), 77-96, and is reprinted with the kind permission of Beacon Press. ©1994 by Richard D. Mohr.

Chapter Thirteen, "What Is Wrong With Treating a Woman As a Sex Object?" by Linda LeMoncheck is, in part, derived from Linda LeMoncheck, *Dehumanizing Women* (Totowa, N.J.: Littlefield, Adams, 1985), 7-8, 11-14, 17-19, 24, 27, 29-30; 92-3, and is reprinted with the kind permission of Littlefield, Adams and Co.

Chapter Seventeen, "Sex, Love, and Friendship," is published here by the kind permission of John McMurtry. ©1997, John McMurtry.

Chapter Twenty-Three, "Abortion and Sexual Morality" by Roger Paden, was previously published in *Diálogos* 50 (1987): 145-54, and is reprinted with the kind permission of *Diálogos*. ©1987, Universidad de Puerto Rico.

Chapter Twenty-Nine, "The Symbolic Significance of Sex," is published here with the kind permission of Claudia Card. ©1997, Claudia Card.

Chapter Thirty-One, "Sex, Time, and Love: Erotic Temporality" by M. C. Dillon, was previously published in *Journal of Phenomenological Psychology* 18 (1987): 33-48, and is reprinted with the kind permission of Humanities Press International, Inc.

Chapter Thirty-Three, "Friends as Ends in Themselves" by Neera Kapur Badhwar, was previously published in *Philosophy and Phenomenological Re-*

search 48 (1987): 1-23, and is reprinted with the kind permission of *Philosophy and Phenomenological Research*.

Chapter Thirty-Four, "Irreplaceability" by Alan Gerald Soble, was previously published in Alan Soble, *The Structure of Love* (New Haven: Yale University Press, 1990), 290-3, and is reprinted with the kind permission of Yale University Press. ©1990, Yale University.

Chapter Thirty-Five, "The Structure of Sexual Perversity" by Russell Vannoy, was previously published in *Philosophy and Theology* 2:5 [disk supplement no. 1] (1988): 30-44, and is reprinted with the kind permission of *Philosophy and Theology*.

Chapter Thirty-Six, "Romantic Love: Neither Sexist Nor Heterosexist" by Carol Caraway, was previously published in *Philosophy and Theology* 1 (1987): 361-8, and is reprinted with the kind permission of *Philosophy and Theology*.

Chapter Thirty-Seven, "Love Without Sex" by Dana E. Bushnell, was previously published in *Philosophy and Theology* 1 (1987): 369-73, and is reprinted with the kind permission of *Philosophy and Theology*.

Chapter Thirty-Eight, "The Unity of Romantic Love" by Alan Soble, was previously published in *Philosophy and Theology* 1 (1987): 374-97, and is reprinted with the kind permission of *Philosophy and Theology*.

Chapter Thirty-Nine, "Romantic Love: A Patchwork" by Carol Caraway, was previously published in *Philosophy and Theology* 2 (1987): 76-96, and is reprinted with the kind permission of *Philosophy and Theology*.

Chapter Forty-Two, "AIDS and *Bowers v. Hardwick*" by Christine Pierce, was previously published in *Journal of Social Philosophy* 20:3 (1989): 21-32, and is reprinted with the kind permission of *Journal of Social Philosophy*.

Chapter Forty-Four, "Love at Second Sight" by Alan Soble, was previously published in Alan Soble, *The Structure of Love* (New Haven: Yale University Press, 1990), 31-47, and is reprinted with the kind permission of Yale University Press. ©1990, Yale University.

Chapter Forty-Five, "Is *Works of Love* a Work of Love?" by Gene Fendt, was previously published in Gene Fendt, *Works of Love? Reflections on Works of Love* (Potomac, Md.: Scripta Humanistica, 1990), 9-21, and reprinted with the kind permission of Scripta Humanistica.

Chapter Forty-Seven, "Kierkegaard on Despair in *Works of Love*" by T. F. Morris, is, in part, derived from T. F. Morris, "Kierkegaard on Despair and the Eternal," *Sophia* 28:3 (1989): 21-30, and is reprinted with the kind permission of *Sophia*.

Chapter Forty-Eight, "Which One Is the Real One?" by Anthony J. Graybosch, was previously published in *Philosophy and Theology* 4 (1990): 365-84, and is reprinted with the kind permission of *Philosophy and Theology*.

Chapter Fifty, "The Style of Sade: Sex, Text, and Cruelty," is published here with the kind permission of Timo Airaksinen. ©1997, Timo Airaksinen.

Chapter Fifty-Two, "The Attractions of Gender" by Steven G. Smith, was previously published in Steven G. Smith, *Gender Thinking* (Philadelphia: Temple University Press, 1992), 139-203, and is reprinted with the kind permission of Temple University Press. ©1992, Temple University.

Chapter Fifty-Six, "Romantic Love" by Joseph Kupfer, was previously published in *Journal of Social Philosophy* 24:3 (1993): 112-20, and is reprinted with the kind permission of *Journal of Social Philosophy*.

Chapter Sixty, "Desire and Love in Kierkegaard's *Either/Or*" by Sylvia Walsh, was previously published in Sylvia Walsh, *Living Poetically: Kierkegaard's Existential Aesthetics* (University Park: Pennsylvania State University Press, 1994), and is reprinted with the kind permission of Pennsylvania State University Press. ©1994, Pennsylvania State University.

The artwork by Sir Viggo Bang (on the postage stamp issued by the Danish Post on 11 November 1955 to commemorate the 100th anniversary of the death of Søren Kierkegaard; p. 475) is reproduced with the kind permission of Sven Bang.

Material quoted in the "Introduction" from "Semantics, Paradigms, Ontology . . . Love," by Henry Allen, *Washington Post* (28 December 1978), B1, B3, is reprinted with the kind permission of the author and the *Washington Post*. ©1978, Washington Post Writers Group.

Editorial Foreword

Histories and Addresses of Philosophical Societies (HAPS), a special series in the **Value Inquiry Book Series (VIBS)**, aims to preserve and present to the world-wide audience of philosophers and others interested in value inquiry the best materials aired in the give and take of presentations and commentaries that constitute the content of meetings of philosophical associations.

As early as 1902, James Edwin Creighton, one of the founders and first President of The American Philosophical Association, articulated "The Purposes of a Philosophical Association." Creighton held that

> the history of philosophy is only intelligible when read in the light of present-day problems. . . . [I]t is only one who has pondered on philosophical problems for himself who can intelligently study the history of philosophy. . . . [P]hilosophy, of all species of scientific inquiry, is that which demands, in order to be fruitfully prosecuted, the closest and most intimate intellectual relations between a number of minds. . . . The task which seems too hard for the individual appears in a different light when he regards himself as a member of a body of organized workers. The sense of comradeship, or working with others for a common end, which is brought home to one most forcibly by personal contact, arouses enthusiasm and friendly emulation that issue in a courageous determination on the part of individuals to play their rôle and contribute in some way to the accomplishment of the common task. It is the development of this feeling of intellectual fellowship and coöperation that is the most hopeful sign of all scientific work at the present day. It is also to a large extent the source of the inspiration which animates all modern investigation and scholarship. . . . The main purpose which we *should* conscientiously set before us . . . is to promote and encourage original investigation and publication.[1]

This century has seen an enormous proliferation of philosophers, philosophies, and philosophical associations. And, those associations have for the most part served precisely the functions and aims set out by Creighton at the beginning of the century. But in an important sense, philosophical associations and their activities have remained, historically at least, invisible to future historians of philosophy. For, the activities of philosophical associations—their meetings, their members' conversations, the reflections and reconsiderations evoked in those meetings and conversations—are in danger of being lost, as are the contents of those meetings and conversations.

The **HAPS** special series **VIBS** is dedicated to recovering important content and elements of the activities of philosophical associations throughout the twentieth century. It seeks to preserve the stuff, substance, and process of philosophical inquiry into the problems of our age; to assemble our rethinking of the history of philosophy through our investigations of today's problems; to record the remarkable (to the "disciplined" mind of today) phenomenon of persons from different disciplines finding common ground in mutual inquiry. Its aim in short, is historical: to write, as the decade closes, the history of our activities that those who follow us may know our processes with an intimacy approaching that of we who have lived them.

Creighton would have found this record of the presentations given over a fifteen-year period at the Society for the Philosophy of Sex and Love (SPSL) to be the record of a philosophical association *par excellence*. The genius of Creighton's vision of a philosophical association's function is well realized in SPSL's annals of explorations and exchanges about contemporary problems and historical figures. The ability of philosophical inquiry to probe the most basic of human activities in a manner that is intellectually respectable, enlightening, expansive, evolutionary, at once socially conservative and critical, is magnificently exemplified in this collection.

The Preface to the present volume by Carol Caraway, who has taken up the leadership of SPSL and the preparation of the next volume of its annals, makes clear that the focus of the Society's attention will move to new dimensions of sex, love, and friendship. This illustrates another theme implicit in Creighton's remarks but known to all serious philosophers, that the business of philosophy, its work, its tasks, are not to be finished and completed but constantly taken up in the thought, research, teaching, and lives of those who practice it. We look forward to the Society's further development under Caraway's careful and inspired leadership and to the sharing of the fruits of that leadership in future volumes of the Society's proceedings.

A word of thanks is in order to the Executive Director of **VIBS**, Robert Ginsberg, and to the publisher of the series, **Rodopi**, for making possible the pursuit of the aims of **HAPS**. Their commitment to the preservation of scholarship that might otherwise remain inaccessible is admirable and rare in this time of market-driven publishing decisions.

Finally, a personal note of enormous satisfaction at Alan Soble's undertaking this volume. Soble was the founder of SPSL and its director during its first fifteen years. It came into being but a few months after he had left graduate school, and he sustained it resolutely as the vagaries of the job market of the late 1970s and the early 1980s saw him without a steady and permanent home. The constancy of his vision, its power to attract adherents from across the disciplines and around the world, and its ability to inspire "original investigation and publication" are celebrated in these pages. The profession owes Alan Soble a great debt for his leadership and commitment.

Richard T. Hull
Editor, **HAPS**

Note

1. J. E. Creighton, "The Purposes of a Philosophical Association," *The Philosophical Review* 11:3 (May 1902): 219-37.

Carol Caraway
(photograph: James Wakefield)

President
The Society for the Philosophy of Sex and Love
1992-

Preface

Carol Caraway

1.

The twenty-first century is upon us. Soon it will be time for historians to write the complete history of twentieth-century American philosophy. *Sex, Love, and Friendship* is a contribution to that history.

During the past quarter century, numerous small philosophical societies have come into existence to support scholarship in specialized areas of philosophy. The Society for the Philosophy of Sex and Love is one such society. Founded in 1977 by Alan Soble, this Society is devoted to the philosophical exploration of love, human sexuality, friendship, marriage, and related topics. Membership in the Society is open to anyone and varies between fifty and seventy members. Most members of the Society are philosophy professors or students in the United States. The Society also has members who live in Canada, Israel, Australia, New Zealand, and Russia, as well as members who teach and do research in fields other than philosophy, including psychology, sociology, education, and medicine.

In the 1970s, love and human sexuality were discussed and portrayed widely in the popular media and investigated extensively by the humanities, the social sciences, and biomedicine. Yet, love and sex had received scant attention from contemporary philosophers. In founding the Society, Soble's guiding idea was that philosophers can make an important contribution to our understanding of these topics; they only needed a forum for presenting and discussing work in this area. The Society was founded to provide that forum. The central activity of the Society from its inception has been to sponsor meetings at which scholarly papers on love, human sexuality, and related topics are presented, with subsequent critical commentary and audience discussion. The Society meets twice a year in conjunction with The American Philosophical Association; before these meetings, papers and commentaries are mailed to members of the Society. The Society is supported by member dues adequate only to cover costs of producing and mailing a newsletter and the papers to be presented at its meetings. In such a small, strictly voluntary organization, the leadership of the president and other officers is vital to its continued existence. The Society's success from 1977 to 1992 is due primarily to the vigorous leadership of Alan Soble, who planned and announced its programs; reviewed paper submissions; secured program chairs and commentators; wrote, edited, and published the newsletter; and handled the finances. Lee Rice of Marquette University also deserves credit for maintaining the Society's mailing lists.

This volume contains most of the papers presented at Society meetings from 1977 through December 1992, when the directorship passed from Soble to myself. This book inaugurates a sustained effort to preserve the history of the Society for its members and for other scholars in the humanities and the sciences who work on love and sex. As is evident from the range of approaches and topics of the papers in this volume, the Society is not a doctrinaire group: essays from various philosophical perspectives are considered, encouraged, and promoted. This commitment to philosophical pluralism is fitting, since the Society arose partly in reaction to the narrow view of logical positivists and other analytic philosophers (and some congressmen) that, while exploring love and sex might be fun, this activity yields no real knowledge and is therefore not a particularly worthwhile pursuit for philosophers.

2.

Love and sex are important aspects of human life. Historical giants in philosophy from Plato through Bertrand Russell wrote on these topics. Nonetheless, before 1970, twentieth-century Anglo-American philosophers seldom wrote on love and sex. As a student in the 1970s, I never encountered these topics in a philosophy course. During my first job, I finally discovered that these topics were being covered in philosophy courses: my colleague, Marshall Missner, taught a course in the philosophy of love. At my second appointment, I had the opportunity to offer that kind of course; while preparing for it, I discovered and joined the Society, which provided me with syllabi, a bibliography, and other useful information.

Why were Anglo-American philosophers ignoring such important topics? I believe this neglect was due partly to the logical positivist dogma that areas of study other than science, mathematics, and logic are nonsense. It was also due partly to the lack of fit between personal relationships and traditional ethical theories.[1] Personal relations involve particularity and partiality; traditional deontological and consequentialist ethical theories and their off-shoots, such as social contract ethics and rights theory, emphasize impartiality. Deontology requires universalizable reasons for action that do not mention logically proper names. But we do not treat everyone as we treat our friends and lovers, and affectionate or sexual feelings can interfere with impartiality. Indeed, a moral justification of such personal relations seems to require justifying partiality with impartial reasons—an apparently paradoxical project. Consequentialism maintains that love is valuable only if it produces the greatest benefit for all concerned. This appears to instrumentalize love and to make the beloved, in some objectionable sense, replaceable.[2]

Since 1970, philosophers have become more interested in sex and love. Two reasons for this are Bernard Williams's personal point of view criticism of traditional ethical theories, and the revival of virtue ethics. Williams argues that traditional ethical theories do not take account of our personal values and projects.[3] Thus, the study of friendship, love, and sex became more legitimate because philosophers realized that exploring such topics could not only expose problems with traditional ethical theories, but might also provide insights into and solutions to those problems. Indeed, exploring such topics might provide the key to a different approach to ethics altogether (for example, the ethics of care of Carol Gilligan).[4] Alasdair MacIntyre, Elizabeth Anscombe, Philippa Foot, and others have revived Aristotelian virtue ethics as an alternative to deontology and consequentialism.[5] In an ethics of virtue, the basic judgments are not about acts but about character, and the ability to choose well depends on courage, benevolence, generosity, and other character traits. Some versions of virtue ethics start, logically, with the individual's concern to live well; they make personal relations crucial to explaining the social character of morality.

In the past few years, there have been many significant publications in the area of the philosophy of love and sex. In *Love and Friendship in Plato and Aristotle*, A. W. Price explores the idea, common to Plato and Aristotle, that one person's life may overflow into another's, so that helping the other is a way of serving oneself.[6] Price argues that their views on love and friendship promise to resolve the old dichotomy between egoism and altruism. Thus, friendship is central to Plato's and Aristotle's social philosophy. In *The Structure of Love*, Alan Soble distinguishes eros-style love from agape-style love by their structures: erosic love is based on the admirable or valuable qualities of the beloved, whereas agapic love is not a response to any merit perceived by the lover in the beloved.[7] Soble defends erosic love from accusations that it lacks the exclusivity and constancy of "genuine" love, and shows that agapic love may also lack these features. He also argues that under certain conditions, erosic love is both more moral and more rational than agapic love. In *Good Sex: Perspectives on Sexual Ethics*, Raymond Belliotti examines the field of sexual ethics historically and provides his own modified libertarian theory of sexual morality.[8] And in *Sexual Investigations*, Alan Soble examines pornography, masturbation, healthy sexuality, perversion, date rape, prostitution, and the beauty and ugliness of the sexual body.[9]

More numerous than the recent monographs in this area are the many recent anthologies, which include Alan Soble, *Eros, Agape, and Philia*, a revised second edition of Alan Soble, *The Philosophy of Sex: Contemporary Readings*, Robert Solomon and Kathleen Higgins, *The Philosophy of (Erotic) Love*, Robert Stewart, *Philosophical Perspectives on Sex and Love*, Clifford Williams, *On Love and Friendship: Philosophical Readings*, and a second edition of D. P. Verene, *Sexual Love and Western Morality*. Anthologies on friendship include Neera Badhwar, *Friendship: A Philosophical Reader* and Michael Pakaluk, *Other Selves: Philosophers on Friendship*.[10]

In addition to many books and articles on the philosophy of love and sex, another indication of the flourishing and increased respectability of this area of philosophical investigation was the 29 December 1993 meeting of the Society for Lesbian and Gay Philosophy. This was the first time the Society for Lesbian and Gay Philosophy met with the Eastern Division of The American Philosophical Association. It had met previously with the other two divisions, but never with the Eastern, the largest and most prestigious division. At this important meeting, a panel discussion entitled "Why Sexuality Matters to Philosophy" took place, co-sponsored by the Society for Women in Philosophy and the Society for the Philosophy of Sex and Love. Edward Stein, President of the Society for Lesbian and Gay Philosophy, chaired the session; the speakers were Helen Longino, Martha Nussbaum, Cass Sunstein, and Michael Tanner, and the discussant was Morris Kaplan. Longino discussed what biological research on homosexuality assumes about the notions of persons and gender;

Nussbaum stressed the importance of restoring acceptance of sexuality and the body; and Sunstein demonstrated how laws against same-sex relationships reinforce patriarchy. Well-attended and well-received, the session marked a new level of recognition of the importance of sexuality to philosophy, and the discussion suggested new and interesting lines of research.

3.

Important world events and social problems suggest other topics for philosophical investigation. In particular, three recent incidents have focused public attention on love, sex, and marriage: (1) the trial of O. J. Simpson, (2) the separation and divorce of Prince Charles and Princess Diana, and (3) the Hawaii Supreme Court decision on same-sex marriage. Each event raised issues philosophers can and should explore.

(1) The trial of O. J. Simpson for the murder (in 1994) of Nicole Brown Simpson transformed spousal battery from a private, obscure, and underreported "dirty little secret" into a matter of public debate and national concern.[11] Spousal battery is physical violence intentionally inflicted by intimate partner (or ex-partner) on another. It might also involve emotional, psychological, or sexual violence. According to the U. S. Department of Justice, more than 90% of the victims of spouse or partner abuse are female. This figure is disputed; some researchers claim that the rate is lower—50% or less—but most agree that male violence produces many more serious injuries and deaths than female violence. The Justice Department reported that in 1992, 383 wives killed their husbands, whereas 913 husbands killed their wives.[12]

Philosophers have generally ignored this issue. Why? One explanation is that since everyone condemns spousal battery, philosophers do not need to talk about it. But this is inadequate; universal condemnation or approval has not stopped philosophical discussion. Almost everyone in our culture condemns sex between adults and children, yet two papers on this issue, one supporting intergenerational sex, the other critical, were presented in 1980 at a meeting of the Society for the Philosophy of Sex and Love.[13] Indeed, much of what philosophers discuss (for example, "Can we really know anything?") is what everyone agrees on. In the past, philosophers may have believed that spousal abuse was so rare it did not warrant philosophical investigation. That belief is no longer tenable, for partner battery is now reported to be shockingly common. In 1992, the American Medical Association warned that one in three American women will be assaulted by an intimate male partner in her lifetime.[14] According to information from the National Coalition Against Domestic Violence, between four and six million American women are assaulted by their male partners, one every fifteen seconds.[15] For certain groups, the estimates are considerably higher. One study reported that 77% of women whose immigration status depends on their marriage are victims of partner battery. Both the rates and the severity of violence are reported to be higher in military families, where use of weapons is twice as frequent as among civilians, and three-fourths of the cases are life-threatening (compared to one-third of cases involving civilians).[16] Estimates vary from study to study, and obtaining accurate estimates is notoriously difficult; many cases are never reported or discovered. (This may be especially true when the victim is male, and when the battery occurs in a gay or lesbian relationship.) Nonetheless, it is clear that partner battery is not as rare as we once imagined.

Finally, not everyone condemns partner battery. Batterers often believe that their attitudes and behavior are justified and give reasons for them. What types of reasons? They often commit the fallacy of unjustified appeal to force. Some psychological research studies indicate that some male batterers believe they are rightfully entitled to dominate and control their partners through violence. "She provoked me; she had it coming," a batterer argues. In some cases, spousal battery by men may be supported by patriarchal notions of love and marriage. For much of the history of Western culture—especially in ancient Rome and medieval Europe—a husband had the (legal) right to beat his wife if she was disobedient or unfaithful; despite current legal prohibitions, some men believe that beating their wives into submission is their moral right, perhaps even their moral obligation: spare the rod, spoil the wife! Moreover, in military families, domestic violence is believed to result primarily from the carryover into the home of the aggressive values of combat; the soldier, trained to use weapons on the enemy, sees his partner as an enemy to be subdued and, if necessary, destroyed. Thus, it seems that the more dependent the partner and the more aggressive and violent the man, the greater the potential for partner-beating and homicide.[17] These analyses are, at best, a part of the explanation of domestic violence. There are also women who batter their husbands, and women who beat their lesbian partners. Is their reasoning supported by feminism, or is feminism better seen as providing an egalitarian view that opposes all domestic violence? And what about gay men who batter their male partners?

Let's proceed to the next logical question: How do victims of partner battery reason? Do they commit certain fallacies? Some psychological research indicates that the victim (whether female or male) often blames herself for her partner's violence.[18] The victim's perspective may include denial, minimizing, disassociation, low self-esteem, shame, guilt, passivity, depression, and fear (often warranted) of serious physical injury or death. To this psychological analysis, we must add the realities of economic dependence, fear of losing custody of children, social isolation, and ignorance about, or the absence of, shelters and other sources of support.[19] Patriarchal notions of love and marriage may underlie not only the reasoning of male batterers, but also the reasoning of their female victims. The wife may believe that her husband comes first and that, as a woman, she is responsible for his emotional well-being. Thus, if he becomes angry and beats her, it is her fault; she provoked him. If she were a better wife, it would not have happened; and if she can improve, it will not happen again. In many Asian-American communities, saving the honor of the family from shame deters immigrant women from reporting domestic violence.[20] Saving themselves from shame may also deter male victims from reporting abuse or seeking aid. The greatest difference between female and male victims seems to be that since males typically earn twice as much as females, they can more easily afford to leave an abusive relationship.[21]

How can philosophy shed light on the phenomenon of partner battery? First, philosophers can clarify the concept of partner battery and how its definition affects the reported rate of violence. Second, we can advise the public on how to assess the widely divergent and apparently conflicting statistics about partner battery. Third, we can explore the extent to which partner battery is supported by patriarchal notions of love and marriage and develop alternative egalitarian notions of personal relationships. Fourth, we can investigate the concepts of human action, emotion, and responsibility that support battering, and offer alternatives. A Sartrean philosopher, for example, might argue that each individual is totally free, and therefore batterer is fully responsible for his emotions and actions; he cannot rightfully blame them on his partner. Moreover, the female victim who remains with a batterer is responsible for that decision. Feminists might discuss the harm done to women, children, and men by patriarchal marriage and offer alternative conceptions of marriage. Logicians might point out the fallacies committed by batterers and victims and help them to reason more critically. Psychologists working with batterers and victims are already attempting to use these approaches. Their attempts would benefit significantly from philosophical clarification. These are some ways philosophy can help assess and address the social problem of partner battery and thereby aid psychology, law, and public policy in this area.

How might studying the problem of partner battery contribute to philosophy? Doing so might yield new insights into the relative merits of traditional ethics (deontological and consequentialist), virtue ethics, and an ethics of care. How does each type of ethics characterize the immorality of partner battery; which characterization is most apt? Maybe such an investigation would lead us to better conceptions of action, emotion, and responsibility. Certainly, it would reinforce and clarify feminist critiques of patriarchal marriage. This project is open-ended, like some loves and lovers: we won't know exactly how such an investigation will benefit philosophy until we have carried it out.

(2) On 9 December 1992, Buckingham Palace announced that the Prince and Princess of Wales had decided to separate. The royal separation and the revelations of Charles's and Diana's extramarital affairs focused public attention on questions of marriage, adultery, and divorce. In our profession, where divorce is common, that little has been written on the subject of divorce is surprising. When is divorce morally justified? What count as good reasons for divorce? What duties do former intimates have to each other? What duties do non-custodial parents have to their children? What constitutes a just divorce settlement? The law addresses these issues; however, legally "just" settlements have typically significantly lowered the standard of living of former wives and children, but not of former husbands. Custodial arrangements, on the other hand, have typically awarded primary custody to the mother and limited the father's access to his children in ways that may have been harmful to them and him. Philosophers can and should contribute something toward solving these problems. They have shown great interest in biomedical ethics, but little interest in what might be called "family ethics," so little that this area of study does not even have a name. The situation is changing. Some philosophers have

begun to look at children's rights,[22] and an issue of *Hypatia* (Winter 1996) was devoted to "The Family and Feminist Theory."

Adultery is difficult to discuss openly because it carries social stigma. Defending divorce is often socially acceptable, but defending adultery seldom is.[23] Some assume there is nothing new for philosophers to say about adultery, but this assumption is incorrect. Much of what twentieth-century philosophers have written on adultery assumes a simple Kantian or Rossian view that adultery is always wrong (except, perhaps, in open marriages) because, or when, it involves the breaking of the promise to be sexually faithful to one's spouse. More work needs to be done on this topic by philosophers. How do we define "adultery" after the electronic explosion of the 1990s? Do phone sex and cybersex constitute adultery? What, indeed, is a sexual act? What is the nature of the marriage commitment, and under what circumstances is it morally justified to break such a commitment? How do consequentialism, virtue ethics, feminism, and an ethics of care conceive of and assess adultery? Do any of them give us a better understanding of adultery than deontological theories, or do we lose something important if we abandon a deontological account?[24]

(3) In 1991, three same-sex couples in Hawaii tried to get marriage licenses. Their requests were denied, and they later filed a discrimination suit against the state. Later, in 1993, the Hawaii Supreme Court ruled that Hawaii's not permitting same-sex marriage is sex discrimination: it presumptively violates Hawaii's Equal Rights Amendment.[25] The Supreme Court's reasoning was that if X is a woman, then a man Y can marry X, but a woman Z cannot, and that is discrimination against Z on the basis of sex. The Court required the state, under "strict scrutiny" analysis, to justify such discrimination by demonstrating that the state has a compelling interest in not allowing same-sex marriage (or in not issuing marriage licenses to all same-sex couples otherwise qualified). This was the first time a state has been required to justify discrimination against same-sex marriage. During the June 1994 hearings, one of the three grounds cited by the state was that the purpose of marriage is reproduction, and since two persons of the same sex cannot reproduce, they should not be allowed to marry.[26] This argument is problematic. Two women can have a child by one of them undergoing artificial insemination by a donor, as do some married heterosexual women. Two men can have a child by contracting with a surrogate mother or by adoption. Further, many heterosexual couples are either incapable of reproduction or never intend to have children. By 1997, the Hawaii Supreme Court should issue a new ruling. A ruling that the state must allow same-sex marriages would break new ground, and many commentators are optimistic because "strict scrutiny" generally leads to death for a statute or state action. Moreover, if the outcome favors the plaintiffs, only a constitutional amendment could allow the continued denial of same-sex marriage licenses. Nonetheless, as one commentator has pointed out, "both sides will undoubtedly appeal all the way to the [U. S.] Supreme Court, and no one knows what it will do."[27]

Currently, some religious groups (for example, Unitarians) perform same-sex marriage ceremonies,[28] but no state or country recognizes same-sex marriage. Hawaii's allowing same-sex marriage would strike a blow against patriarchal marriage and open the door for other nontraditional forms of family. In anticipation of this decision, supporters of patriarchal marriage have filed bills against same-sex marriage in most states. Utah was the first to pass such a bill. (President Bill Clinton promised to sign a federal version of such a bill, and the House recently passed it.) Utah's reaction is ironic; Joseph Smith, the founder of the Mormon religion, left New York where polygamy was illegal, and moved west so he could practice polygyny.[29] Indeed, even though the arrangement is now illegal, some Mormons still practice it informally. Contemporary Mormons see no contradiction between their founder's practicing polygyny and their opposing same-sex marriage. This seems paradoxical, but can be explained. Mormon polygyny serves the purpose of reproduction and can be seen as an extreme form of patriarchal marriage in which the man rules over several women. Same-sex marriage, in contrast, challenges patriarchal assumptions about marriage and gender roles. (There is still the problem of battery in those homosexual relationships that mimic patriarchal patterns.)

The Hawaii same-sex marriage case raises many conceptual and ethical issues. What is marriage? What is its purpose? Who has a right to marry whom? What is the constitutional relationship between discrimination against nonheterosexuals and discrimination against women or blacks? Do states have the right to restrict marriage to one man and one woman? If not allowing same-sex marriage is unjustified, then is requiring that marriage be between only two persons also unjustified? If three persons (for example, three women) wanted to marry each other, why shouldn't the state recognize that marriage?

4.

There are, then, many areas in which philosophers can advance our understanding of love, sex, and marriage. As the second president of the Society for the Philosophy of Sex and Love, I have maintained Soble's original purpose and format: the Society continues to be devoted to the philosophical exploration of love, sex, and related topics and to meet bi-annually in conjunction with The American Philosophical Association. I have continued to foster philosophical pluralism within the Society and to see that both genders are represented on the program at every meeting. The Society's presentations since 1992 have included studies of classical historical figures and movements (Kierkegaard, Spinoza, Stoicism), conceptual analyses of love and friendship, a postmodernist investigation of the future of romantic love, explorations of gender issues (feminism and promiscuity, date rape, the gender politics of cross-dressing), and investigations of specific ethical issues (sex education, homosexual ethics).

I anticipate optimistically that philosophers will continue to carry out significant research in these areas. My hope for the Society is that it will provide an ongoing forum for the philosophical investigation of love and sex. International interest in presenting papers at the Society meetings is increasing. In Spring 1996, our speaker came from Australia and, in December 1996, from Germany. It would be pleasing for this trend to continue, for our area of study would benefit greatly from a multicultural perspective. Anthropologists have investigated marriage practices in various cultures; sociologists have investigated various aspects of contemporary marriage, including the effects of dual careers on marriage. Sociologists have found, for example, that males in dual-career marriages were less willing to move from one city to another and got smaller raises than men whose wives did not have careers. They also found that when there is a significant difference in income, the partner with the larger income tends to dominate the relationship (even in same-sex relationships).[30] These studies provide empirical data that have implications for philosophical theories of love, marriage, adultery, and divorce. Psychologists' studies of attraction, communication, and relationships, and neuroscientists' studies of brain anatomy, emotions, and hormones should also be taken into account by philosophers. In short, philosophers interested in love and sex should become better educated about this relevant scientific research.

The Society must continue to examine the views on love, sex, and friendship of the historically important male philosophers, but also the views of long-neglected women authors. The only woman author whose work has standardly been included in anthologies on love and sex is Simone de Beauvoir. Throughout history there have been other women with interesting views on love and sex (Sappho, Heloise, Emma Goldman, Karen Horney), and these need to be explored. I also want to see investigations of innovative topics; the politics of cross-dressing is a good example. Another gender area to study further are the implications of sex-change operations for gender identity, marriage (same-sex or not), and parental rights.[31] The Society should encourage submissions on what cognitive science can tell us about sex and love. Other matters worth investigating further are the relative roles of reason and emotion in sex and love; institutional policies concerning sexual harassment, sexual consent, and acquaintance or date rape; and Catharine MacKinnon's sharp critique of sexuality in our culture.[32]

Philosophers have written about how love can be egoistic, jealous, and unreciprocated, and about pornography, rape, prostitution, and the so-called sexual perversions. But we have generally ignored partner battery, child abuse, anger, and hate. We strive to teach our students the importance of a balanced view, that they should consider all the relevant evidence and look at an issue from all sides. Yet, those of us (myself included) who have written on love and sex—even those who have taken a realist perspective—have largely ignored these negative aspects of relationships. We have thus failed to present a balanced view. Anger, hate, and abuse are aspects of intimate relationships. The person you love and enjoy sex with today may be, tomorrow, your attacker or the target of your most intense anger. Moreover, neurobiological research shows that perception and memory are affected in similar ways by both anger and love. Both are characterized by selective memory, for example. When angry, we remember inflammatory incidents and repress positive ones; when falling in love, we do the reverse.[33] We need to expand the range of the emotions that we investigate.

Why are philosophers neglecting these important topics? In discussing the O. J. Simpson trial, I sketched and responded to several possible reasons. Allow me to mention three others. First, perhaps philosophers think anger, hate, and abuse are issues for psychology and criminology, not philosophy. But, historically-speaking, psychology and criminology grew out of philosophy and have often benefitted from the conceptual clarification philosophy provides. Second, perhaps partner battery and child abuse are too physical or bodily for philosophers, who traditionally have wanted to focus on consciousness, the mental, the rational. We should take a hint from those contemporary feminist post-structuralists and others who have written a good deal on the philosophy of the body and why it is important.[34]

Finally, I fear that many philosophers simply do not want to look at the harsh reality of domestic life in America; it is too ugly and unpleasant. Let me share one personal experience that may illustrate this situation. In February 1996, my institution (Indiana University of Pennsylvania) hosted a month-long Marriage Project consisting of two art exhibits, a lecture series, and films on marriage, broadly construed to include same-sex relationships. As a member of the planning committee for this project (consisting primarily of university professors from a variety of disciplines), I suggested that we include a lecture on domestic violence and incest. The committee's initial reaction was favorable, and I was asked to contact a speaker. At the next meeting, I reported my successful results and requested that the committee choose a date for the lecture. But this time, the reaction was different: "We do not want someone speaking on that! That's not what this project is about." The implication seemed to be that the Marriage Project was about only the nice aspects of marriage, the parts we enjoy thinking and talking about and remembering. Inconsistently, the works of art exhibited in the Project were not all about the nice parts of marriage: one was a visually violent depiction of interracial jealousy, another was a set of wedding rings with spikes on the inside to pierce the flesh of the wearers. We had violent works of art, but no lecture on the taboo topics of domestic violence and incest.

In addition to exploring long-neglected negative aspects of love and sex, philosophers should investigate overlooked positive aspects, for example, intimacy. Psychologists have written a great deal on this topic; twentieth-century Anglo-American philosophers have written hardly anything.[35] What is intimacy? What role does it play in the good life? Is it a virtue? What acts foster intimacy, and what acts prevent or inhibit it? Does romantic love generate or interfere with intimacy? Does marriage? What is the relationship between intimacy and sexuality? These are good questions for philosophical reflection.

The philosophical exploration of love and sex should be self-reflective, leading us to think critically about our own lives. When undertaken in a spirit of open-minded inquiry and not merely to rationalize our behavior or to blame others for our shortcomings or failures, critical reflection can increase our awareness and understanding of our love relationships and sexual experiences. This heightened awareness should—as the best philosophy is supposed to do—make us better persons and enrich our lives.

Notes

1. See Jesse Kalin, "Lies, Secrets, and Love: The Inadequacy of Contemporary Moral Philosophy," *Journal of Value Inquiry* 10 (1976): 253-65.

2. See Neera K. Badhwar, "Friends as Ends in Themselves," *Philosophy and Phenomenological Research* 48 (1987): 1-23; reprinted, revised, in Alan Soble, ed., *Eros, Agape, and Philia* (New York: Paragon House, 1989), 165-86; and, further revised, in this volume, 333-52, below.

3. Bernard Williams, "Ethical Consistency," in *Problems of the Self: Philosophical Papers, 1956-1972* (Cambridge, Eng.: Cambridge University Press, 1973), 166-86. See also Williams's *Moral Luck: Philosophical Essays, 1973-1980* (New York: Cambridge University Press, 1982); *Ethics and the Limits of Philosophy* (Cambridge, Mass.: Harvard University Press, 1985); "Persons, Character, and Morality," in Amélie O. Rorty, ed., *The Identities of Persons* (Berkeley: University of California Press, 1976); and J. J. C. Smart and Bernard Williams, *Utilitarianism: For and Against* (Cambridge, Eng.: Cambridge University Press, 1973).

4. See Carol Gilligan, *In A Different Voice* (Cambridge, Mass.: Harvard University Press, 1982); Nel Noddings, *Caring: A Feminine Approach to Ethics and Moral Education* (Berkeley: University of California Press, 1984); and Virginia Held, *Transforming Culture, Society, and Politics* (Chicago: University of Chicago Press, 1993).

5. Alasdair MacIntyre, *After Virtue*, 2nd ed. (Notre Dame: University of Notre Dame Press, 1984); Philippa Foot, *Virtues and Vices* (Berkeley: University of California Press, 1978); and Elizabeth Anscombe, "Modern Moral Philosophy," *Philosophy* 33 (1958): 1-19.

6. *Love and Friendship in Plato and Aristotle* (Oxford: Oxford University Press, 1989).

7. *The Structure of Love* (New Haven: Yale University Press, 1990).

8. *Good Sex: Perspectives on Sexual Ethics* (Lawrence: University Press of Kansas, 1993).

9. *Sexual Investigations* (New York: New York University Press, 1996).

10. *Eros, Agape, and Philia* (New York: Paragon House, 1989); *The Philosophy of Sex*, 2nd ed. (Savage, Md.: Rowman and Littlefield, 1991); *The Philosophy of (Erotic) Love* (Lawrence: University Press of Kansas, 1991); *Philosophical Perspectives on Sex and Love* (New York: Oxford University Press, 1995); *On Love and Friendship: Philosophical Readings* (Boston: Jones and Bartlett, 1995); *Sexual Love and Western Morality* (Boston: Jones and Bartlett, 1995); *Friendship: A Philosophical Reader* (Ithaca: Cornell, 1993); *Other Selves: Philosophers on Friendship* (Indianapolis: Hackett, 1991).

11. Bonnie M. Flynn, President and chief executive officer of Women in Distress, reported that following the Simpson hearings, calls to the shelter increased by 40 to 50%. Jan Marie Werblin, "When Black and Blue Are the Colors of Christmas," *Changes* (December 1994): 52-60, at 56.

12. V. Michael McKenzie, "Beating Spousal Battery," *Professional Counselor* (April 1996): 15-51; Tish Durkin, "Domestic Violence Affects Both Men and Women," in Scott Barbour and Karen L. Swisher, eds., *Violence: Opposing Viewpoints* (San Diego: Greenhaven Press, 1996), 151-7, at 153.

13. These papers, by Robert Ehman and Marilyn Frye, were published in Robert Baker and Frederick Elliston, eds., *Philosophy and Sex*, 2nd ed. (Amherst: Prometheus, 1984), 431-46 and 447-55, respectively.

14. Jill Smolowe, "When Violence Hits Home," *Time* (4 July 1994): 12-13.

15. Christina Hoff Sommers has challenged these figures in *Who Stole Feminism?* (New York: Touchstone, 1995), esp. ch. 9.

16. Uma Narayan, "Male-Order Brides: Immigrant Women, Domestic Violence, and Immigration Law," *Hypatia* 10:1 (1995): 104-19, at 106-7.

17. McKenzie, "Beating Spousal Battery," 49-51; and Narayan, "Male-Order Brides," 107.

18. McKenzie, "Beating Spousal Battery," 16, 48-51.

19. Narayan, "Male-Order Brides," 108; and Werblin, "When Black and Blue," 56.

20. Narayan, "Male-Order Brides," 106.

21. Durkin, "Domestic Violence Affects Both Men and Women," 156-7.

22. See Susan Moller Okin, *Justice, Gender, and the Family* (New York: Basic Books, 1989); and Laura Purdy, *In Their Best Interest? The Case Against Equal Rights for Children* (Ithaca: Cornell University Press, 1992).

23. For an exception, see Richard Taylor, *Having Love Affairs* (Buffalo: Prometheus, 1982).

24. For good discussions of adultery, see Raja Halwani, "Virtue Ethics and Adultery," paper presented at a meeting of the Society for the Philosophy of Sex and Love, Atlanta, December 1996; and Laurie Shrage, *Moral Dilemmas of Feminism* (New York: Routledge, 1994).

25. Hawaii Supreme Court No. 15689 (1993); originally Baehr v. Lewin, renamed Baehr v. Milke.

26. For a more complete account of the state's arguments, see K. Anthony Appiah, "The Marrying Kind," *New York Review of Books* (20 June 1996), 48-54.

27. Gabriel Rotello, "To Have and To Hold: The Case for Gay Marriage," *Nation* (24 June 1996), 11-18, at 16.

28. Gay marriage ceremonies have long been carried out in Christianity. See John Boswell, *Same-Sex Unions in Premodern Europe* (New York: Villard Books, 1994).

29. John Krajnak, "The Roots of the Mormon Religion," paper presented at a meeting of the State System of Higher Education Interdisciplinary Association for Philosophy and Religious Studies, 23 March 1996, held at Edinboro University of Pennsylvania.

30. Pepper Schwartz, Ph.D., "Quality and Equality in Diverse Relationships," presented at Indiana University of Pennsylvania, 15 February 1996. See her book, *Love Between Equals: How Peer Marriage Really Works* (New York: Free Press, 1995).

31. See Norman Daniels, *Am I My Parents' Keeper?* (New York: Oxford University Press, 1988).

32. See her *Feminism Unmodified* (Cambridge, Mass.: Harvard University Press, 1987), and *Toward a Feminist Theory of the State* (Cambridge, Mass.: Harvard University Press, 1989).

33. Daniel Goleman, "How to Get a Grip on Anger," *New Woman* (December 1995): 103-24, at 104-5. Goleman is the author of *Emotional Intelligence* (New York: St. Martin's Press, 1995).

34. The Fall 1991 issue of *Hypatia* is devoted to "Feminism and the Body."

35. But see Hugh Lafollette, *Personal Relationships* (Oxford: Blackwell, 1996).

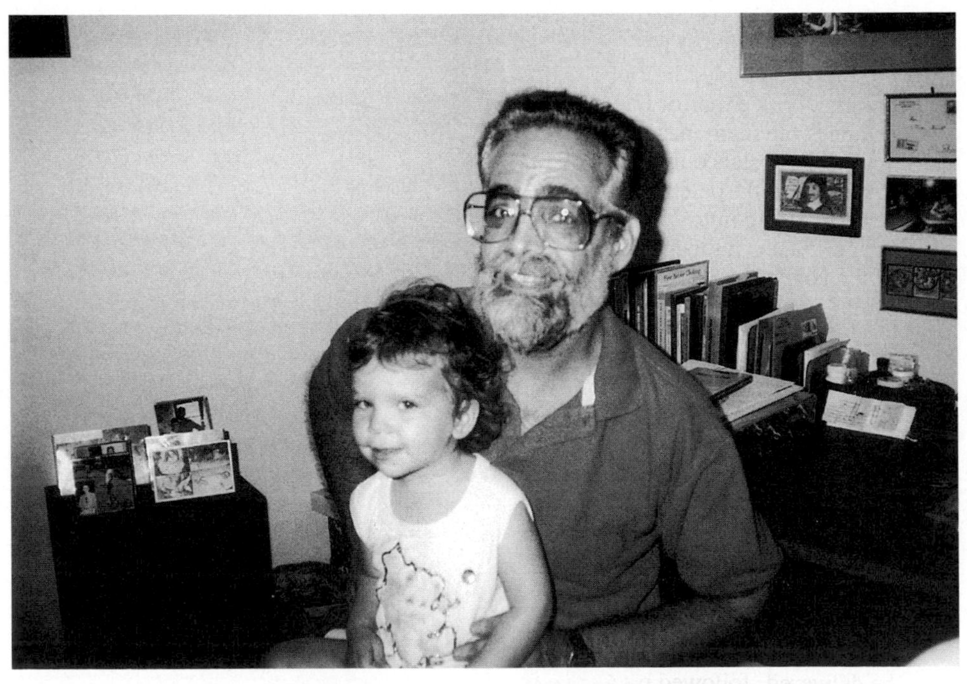

Alan Soble and Rachel Emőke Soble
(photograph: Sára Szabó Soble)

Alan Soble, President
The Society for the Philosophy of Sex and Love
1977-1992

Introduction

Alan Soble

> This, my present love, is my first true love, but the true love is the first, *ergo*, this third love is my first love.
>
> Kierkegaard, "The First Love," *Either/Or*, vol. 1

1.

In this introduction, I later provide some very brief remarks on just a few of the essays included in this book that I find especially provocative or noteworthy. My task here, as I see it, is primarily to record the important and interesting parts of the history of the Society for the Philosophy of Sex and Love (SPSL), without making too many substantive comments on or judgments about the content or quality of the essays that follow. For one thing, I authored six of the pieces included in this volume; that seems to be plenty of substance for one tiny-boss editor of one large book. For another thing, so much substance occupies the many pages of this enormous book already that no reader needs yet more substance in a mere introduction to the substance. Volumes such as this one should be entered lightly, in anticipation of and preparation for the heaviness to come. I advise examining the photographs of the authors first, taking in their humanity, character, and beauty, followed by a bit of stroking of the covers and smelling the book's paper. *Pace* Italo Calvino, the sensuous should proceed and accompany the philosophy of the sensuous.

2.

In 1977, I decided to attempt to establish a professional organization that would devote itself to the philosophical exploration of love, human sexuality, friendship, marriage, sexual reproduction, and related matters. The central activity of the planned organization, which I eventually named the Society for the Philosophy of Sex and Love—over the objections of members (mostly women, but also some men) who preferred the reverse order—was anticipated to be the sponsoring of meetings, held concurrently with meetings of the three divisions of The American Philosophical Association, to be attended by professionals in various fields, at which papers examining the topics mentioned above would be delivered, followed by a critical commentary and audience discussion. The guiding idea was that love and sex, subjects widely talked about outside the academy, had received insufficient (or insufficiently competent) attention from philosophers, and that contemporary philosophy, when done well, had worthwhile contributions to make to our understanding of this constellation of items. The ambition of the Society was to encourage, among both philosophers and professionals in other fields who had an interest in philosophical questions and methods, a sustained, pluralistic, and expert investigation into this area of human life.

In December 1977, right after Christmas (as has long been the habit with the Eastern Division of The American Philosophical Association), SPSL held its first meetings, in Washington, D. C., at which were presented, first, an analytic essay on the nature of sexual desire by Jerome Shaffer and, second, a historical essay on homosexuality and epistemology in Plato by Ellen Shapiro. The attendance at these meetings, as well as the number of membership subscriptions, convinced me that the formation of SPSL had been a satisfactory idea: there was enough interest in love, sex, marriage, and related topics among philosophers and scholars in other fields to justify proceeding further with the Society. During the fifteen years of my administration of SPSL (1977-1992), the Society held twenty-eight meetings in eighteen cities—from Philadelphia and New York to San Francisco, from Detroit to Atlanta and New Orleans—at which over fifty main papers were presented, along with about an equal number of brief, adversarial commentaries. I attended most of these meetings, as many as my personal budget would allow (university travel money has always been difficult to come by), and over the years found myself out of necessity either chairing more than my rightful share of them or too often commenting on the main paper. I did get to see the States.

I have gathered together in this volume many of the papers and commentaries presented at meetings of SPSL during this fifteen-year period, thereby providing a record of the activities of the Society and making this material available to members, both old and new, of SPSL and to other scholars in the humanities and the sciences working in the area of love and sex. My original goal of including every SPSL paper and commentary turned out to be unrealistic; some authors and participants could not be located and others declined, for various good and bad reasons, the invitation to participate in this project. The final table of contents lists sixty chapters. Twenty-five of these essays have been previously published elsewhere (see "Credits") and have been revised, sometimes importantly, for this volume; the remaining thirty-five appear in print for the first time here. A glance at the table of contents will show that this collection is at the same time both eclectic and unified. (Chapter Thirty-Nine, Carol Caraway's essay "Romantic Love: A Patchwork," was not written for or presented at any meeting of SPSL. It is included here for the sake of completeness, since it is a reply to Chapter Thirty-Eight, my "The Unity of Romantic Love," which was a commentary on Caraway's 1986 SPSL paper, Chapter Thirty-Six, "Romantic Love: Neither Sexist Nor Heterosexist.")

One question that I have been repeatedly forced to answer by callous and inquiring minds, not only about my founding the Society but also about my long string of publications in this area of philosophy, needs to be broached once again, this time publicly: "Why the philosophy of sex and love (of all things)?" The short answer, which must suffice, is that I love sex, in all its myriad forms (nearly); I love love, in many of its energizing and even agonizing forms; I love the two together and I love the two apart. So much for confessing the obvious. (Can the epistemologist say this about knowledge, or the metaphysician about relations?) Sex and love were (are) my first loves, along with the unattainable and unforgettable trio consisting of knock-out Sharon down-the-street, my ugly, large-nosed Latin teacher Mr. Feingold, and Bertram, my handsome, much older cousin from Boston. But philosophically dissecting, in a society and in publications, that which one loves—does it not amount to murder? So claim the critics. Here is a poem that was sent anonymously to me, *qua* director of SPSL, in the early 1980s:

"Weirdo" Groups #37

Soble's seems doubly oxymoronic
Causing a boom that's visibly sonic.
Conjoining sex and love is bad enough,
Achieving tenderness is really tough.
While sex produces that in-bedward leap,
Philosophy's Drone just puts folks to sleep.
Eros' reversal makes everyone sore;
Philos and Sophos (once wed) merely bore.
That tangled web that lovers weave while *hot*
Tends to unravel mind's Gordian knot.
Can thinking clearly be the catalyst
Which turns Brute Rape into a Tender Tryst?
Society/Philosophy/Sex/Love:
Can anyone have all of the above?

Maybe, if supermoms exist.

3.

For the sake of the historical record, I thought it appropriate to include in this introduction yet another introduction, the opening speech (not nearly as good as Phaedrus's opening speech) I gave at the first meeting of the Society, which was held on 28 December 1977 during the Eastern Division Meeting of The American Philosophical Association. Instead of rewriting the text, I added, in 1996, some corrective notes, resisting the powerful impulse to change the historical and embarrassing record. I reproduce this ancient document in its entirety:

The Philosophy of Sex and Love:
A Subject with a Great Future

Alan Soble
Department of Philosophy
University of Texas at Austin

I am pleased to see you here this afternoon, and I welcome you to the first meeting of the Society for the Philosophy of Sex and Love. I do not want to take much of your time, as we are looking forward to an interesting paper and discussion, but I would like to make a few remarks about what I take to be the dual focus of the philosophy of sex and love.

One focus was introduced by Professor Thomas Nagel in his paper on sexual perversion, which I did not discover until late in 1974.[1] Many philosophers were impressed by Nagel's attempt to approach philosophically a topic that had been dealt with previously primarily only by psychoanalysts and the sociologists of deviance. I was personally impressed by Nagel's courage in writing about a subject the discussion of which would almost necessarily expose his own conscious or unconscious sexual attitudes. (We know that Robert Solomon found humor in Nagel's sexual use of mirrors[2] and that Janice Moulton, in turn, caught Solomon on some of the absurdities of sex as communication.)[3] I was less impressed, however, by Nagel's particular analysis of sex.[4] Allow me to explore, for a moment, a relatively neglected feature of Nagel's account.[5]

Often I have tried to work out intellectually and to experience emotionally[6] the higher levels of sexual awareness that this theory says are possible, but unless I am, mysteriously, overtaken by brilliance I cannot with any great success pass beyond the second or third iteration.[7] On occasion I have had what I like to think of as an experience of infinity, which does include an accelerating ascent through levels of awareness, but when this happens I am usually tired and alone, and my feet seem to expand and to fill the void of the universe.[8] This feeling does remind me, however, of the oceanic feeling described by Sigmund Freud in the opening section of *Civilization and Its Discontents*.[9] Freud was describing some kind of religious experience, and therefore one might suggest that Nagel's infinite levels of awareness are helpful if we combine his theory with Wilhelm Reich's idea that during *true* orgasm a pair of persons comes to mesh, religiously, with the energy of the universe.[10] Similarly, we might also note the orgiastic sexual merging of Krishna with 16,000 Indian cowgirls on the banks of the Ganges, a merging that created the Oneness, the Union of Love that was God.

Of course, Nagel's thesis proposes to be an analysis of mundane sex and not a theological doctrine, and as a piece of analysis it is a noteworthy attempt. We have followed with considerable admiration how philosophers have developed, refined, modified, and complemented both the questions and the answers introduced by Nagel, and the high quality of the debate, as documented in part in the Baker and Elliston collection,[11] was a very important consideration in the formation of this Society. Indeed, this afternoon Professor Shaffer is going to make a contribution to this analytic progression by presenting his paper on sexual desire.[12]

The second focus is provided by the increasing attention paid to the feminist perspective within philosophy. In the late 1960s the contemporary independent feminist viewpoint was developed, and this movement has had significant impact only among academics but also on the administration and formation of law, on business and the economy, and on our personal lives—although one wishes that its impact in these latter areas did not encounter so many obstacles. For our purposes, the interesting contribution made by the feminist movement is its re-emphasizing and re-analyzing the ways in which sexuality, the family and marriage, and the socialization of the sexes are central to the rest of the political, economic, cultural, and social order. This consciousness of the widespread and reciprocal relationship between gender, sexual identity, and personality, on the one hand, and, on the other, politics and economics, must certainly be a major concern for the philosophy of sex and love.

Whereas with Nagel and his successors philosophers have become concerned with trying to understand the basic concepts of sexuality and love, with the leadership provided by the feminist movement philosophers have become attuned to the promise of understanding sexuality in terms of its connections with the whole range of human social experience. In Nagel's tradition, the philosophy of sex and love pursues conceptual and linguistic matters; in the feminist tradition the philosophy of sex and love attacks the broader and, to some, the more urgent ethical, social, and political questions surrounding sexuality. The philosophy of sex and love, then, as I see it, is both analytically oriented in clarifying the language[13] of sexuality, and at the same time continues the interdisciplinary investigations begun by Freud, Reich, Erich Fromm, Herbert Marcuse, Betty Friedan, Simone de Beauvoir, Shulamith Firestone, Kate Millett, and Juliet Mitchell.[14] I am optimistic that a workable alliance can exist under the general rubric of the philosophy of sex and love, an alliance between the analytic and the nonanalytic.[15] Indeed, on Thursday evening Ellen Shapiro, in presenting her paper on homosexuality in Plato, will show us what exciting things can be done within the nonanalytic framework.

At the very start I heard comments about a society for the philosophy of sex and love that are by now trite; I imagine that Havelock Ellis, Alfred Kinsey, and Virginia Johnson and William Masters heard similar remarks.[16] I was told, for example, that my proposal to establish a society for the philosophy of sex and love was nothing more than a proposal to have sex. Or we are to believe that the process of analyzing sexuality is symptomatic of our inability to lead fully satisfying sexual lives, or that our intellectual "preoccupation" with sexuality is just the manifestation of the repression and sublimation of our sexual energy. Indeed, the very ink on the pages I'm reading from has been given an astonishing sexual interpretation. Such accusations or innuendos can be safely ignored. Even if they had some truth, it is also true that an ultimate goal of this society and of our other philosophical and political activities is to make it possible for persons to live in such a way that needless repression is eliminated, and to make it possible to abandon talk about sexuality simply because there would no longer be any sexual problems to talk about.[17] If this society is born out of repression, then, at least the way in which the energy has been sublimated creates the attempt to exorcise the repression that makes this society both useful and necessary. Finally, it is often lamented that the philosophy of "X" (for example, art) is much less exciting, if not terribly boring by comparison, than "X" itself.[18] Certainly the philosophy of sex and love will be in some ways less exciting than sex and love themselves, but in other ways it will be more exciting. We would expect sex and the philosophy of sex to be exciting in the same ways only if, which is false, a society for the philosophy of sex were a society for sex. I should mention that when I first read Professor Shaffer's paper on sexual desire, my immediate gut-level reaction was to get very hungry.[19]

I think it is realistic to say that the philosophy of sex and love is a subject with a great future; that it is also a subject with a great past is made clear for us by Ellen Shapiro. The formation of the Society comes at a time when the study of sexuality is proceeding full-steam ahead in the other disciplines, including psychology, sociology, physiology, and medicine. And it is quite appropriate that philosophers should bring their talents to bear not only on specifically philosophical questions but also on the methodological and theoretical questions that arise from the investigations done within these other disciplines. There is much interesting work to be done, and I am pleased that there are so many philosophers who have accepted the challenge.

Let me introduce to you now Professor Jerome Shaffer, from the philosophy department at the University of Connecticut, who will read his paper on sexual desire.

Were I now, twenty years later, to deliver an opening speech of this sort for the same purpose, it would be much different. I would, for example, mention (which is today *de rigueur*) the ideas of the polar opposite thinkers Camille Paglia and Catharine A. MacKinnon, and I would ask the audience to ponder why, in January 1995, a philosopher of the caliber of Christina Hoff Sommers would make an appearance—albeit fully dressed—in the pages of *Penthouse*.

4.

Jerome Shaffer's essay on sexual desire soon appeared in print in the *Journal of Philosophy*, and fittingly is the opening piece (in that later version) in this volume. Ellen Shapiro's essay on Plato could not be included here; locating her after so many years, in order to ask permission, proved impossible. I am also sorry not to be able to include, as a result, L. A. Kosman's comments on Shapiro's paper. A year later, in December 1978, the Society held its next meeting, again in Washington, D. C., and featured a paper by Donald Levy on the concept of love in Plato's *Symposium*, later published in the *Journal of the History of Ideas*, and one by Jacqueline Kinderlehrer (later Jacqueline Fortunata) on masturbation and female sexuality, which was published in my first book, an anthology, the first edition of *The Philosophy of Sex: Contemporary Readings*. Levy's essay is included here, as Chapter Two, but not Kinderlehrer's, another author I could not locate.

The first meetings of SPSL, in 1977, were reviewed for the popular press by the journalist/model Suzanne Felzen, who was sent to cover The American Philosophical Association convention (including both receptions) by New York's *Cheri* magazine. Her observations were pungent, showing philosophers at work and at play in an interesting light. In late 1995, I wrote to G. J. Clique, the managing editor of *Cheri*, asking permission to reprint Felzen's account of her experiences at a philosophy convention (and for at least one photograph of her stunning beauty). Clique did not reply, not even when prompted by a follow-up request a few months later. I have misplaced, I suspect forever, my copy of the issue of *Cheri* that contained Felzen's review. Its loss saddens me primarily because it was a gift from Richard Hull (who threatened to send another copy to the Society for Women in Philosophy).

The next meetings of the Society, in 1978, were covered by an arguably more respectable publication. The *Washington Post* was represented at the Eastern Division of The American Philosophical Association by Henry Allen, who wrote a news article about the convention, a substantial part of which was devoted to panning the Society. In "Semantics, Paradigms, Ontology . . . Love,"[20] Mr. Allen wrote:

> One noted attraction was the meeting of the Society for Philosophy of Sex & Love, at 11:30 a.m. ("Don't they usually meet at night?" asked John Brough, chairman of the department at Georgetown.)
>
> If the prurient itch had driven anyone to the meeting, the reading of a paper entitled "The Definition of Love in Plato's Symposium" elicited no immoderate chuckles at the more telling phrases: "Ordered hierarchy" or "Plato's ontology" or "horns of a dilemma."
>
> One woman even wrote a postcard. In aqua ink, beneath the oratory on the intrinsic worth of love, regardless of its object, she began: "Thanks so much for the leather purse."
>
> Another young woman seemed to be turning boredom into an amatory art form with her small sighs, surveys of the ceiling and an occasional pout that made her look as if she just might be whistling to herself.
>
> Her companion, in beard and lumberjack shirt, even slipped his arm around her when the speaker, Donald Levy of Brooklyn College, got to the part about how all human activity is motivated by love.
>
> "Everything was valid, I suppose, and the statements were cogent, but perhaps more was being made of it than necessary," she said afterwards in the hallway, being Susan Muller, a Long Island pianist who "takes an interest in philosophy, but more usually analytic philosophy."
>
> Down by registration, Charles Stevenson, one of the great ethicists of the University of Michigan, emeritus, now teaching at Bennington in his retirement, said he'd seen the sex and love business but "I thought it was crackpot. Maybe I was wrong." . . .
>
> Just down the hall from the philosophy of sex and love gang was the child-care center. Three young women looked after . . . Paul Tong . . . and his brother John.

I guess you had to be there.

5.

When a great deal of material is written on a subject, some things that are asserted about it will be silly; to reverse a well-known story, one of a bunch of monkeys will sooner or later type a Shakespearian sonnet. This principle holds, as it should, for the topics of love, human sexuality, friendship, and marriage. In a book that contains sixty essays, that several sentences here and there will strike some readers as absurd is unavoidable. For example, in one essay we find the claim that after two people marry and begin their daily lives together, their personalities are fully revealed and, as a result, "idealizations give way to a better understanding of what's really admirable about one's partner." This generalization receives the "syrup-of-the-book" award. I should have thought, in the spirit of Søren Kierkegaard, that matters were quite the reverse: after marriage, or by living together, we find out how rotten the other person really is. By its nature, idealization, as pointed out by innumerable theorists of love, *collapses* (into disgust) instead of *convalescing* (into admiration). This is why, for Kierkegaard, allegiance to God (or the Party) is required of both partners, in order to keep the dyad from falling apart out of boredom or incessant annoyance. When *eros* is gone, *agape* is the cement. Or the dyad is doomed.

But even the best of philosophers has been known to say nearly moronic things about sex and love, and we need not turn to the long and disturbingly sexist history of Western philosophy of sex and love to make that point. The contemporary Harvard philosopher Robert Nozick, well-known for his award-winning explorations in social and political theory, opines that sexuality is "metaphysical exploration, knowing the body and person of another as a map or microcosm of the very deepest reality, a clue to its nature and purpose"[21] —as if investigating the pimples on our partner's bottom provides a reflection of cosmic order. Nozick also exaggerates the uniqueness of sexuality when he writes that "the most intense way we relate to another person is sexually."[22] Bursts of mutual hatred or anger can be just as if not more intense. And in the dull coitus routinely performed by long-married couples, there is not much intensity. Would Nozick remind us that, on his view, sexual activity is a metaphysical exploration, an examination of the minutiae of the other's body? The cosmic significance of the vaginal lips or the glans of the penis compensates for the loss of passion. What *I'd* like to see (instead of, or in addition to, papers on O. J. and Charles and Di, as recommended by Carol Caraway in her "Preface" to this volume) are serious philosophical studies of the death of sexual desire in marriage and other long-term relationships, and hardnosed investigations of sexual bargaining between partners, both heterosexual and homosexual, in and out of marriage. Another recent notable event about which philosophers should cogitate, that is, is the purported appointment between Bill Clinton and Paula Jones (who appears, semi-nude, a few pages after the Christina Hoff Sommers interview in *Penthouse*).

This volume, nevertheless, contains a great deal of superb material, else I would not have spent almost three years doing all the tedious things required preparing the manuscript for publication. (I beg of you not to think more than once: having sunk so much time and energy into the project, Soble is here rationalizing.) I beseech you to read carefully, as evidence of my proposition, the following essays (my favorites), after leisurely browsing through the whole book. First and foremost is Jerome Shaffer's brilliant essay on sexual desire (Chapter One), which is not only a paradigm of the philosophy of sex, but a paradigm of philosophy *simpliciter*. I wish Shaffer, before retiring, had turned his acute analytic skills and sound perceptions of the human condition to other questions in the philosophy of sex. Neera Badhwar's skillful and comprehensive treatment of loving a person as an end is another magnificent contribution

(Chapter Thirty-Three), despite the fact that I take issue with her view (Chapter Thirty-Four). The exchange between Natalie Dandekar and Carol S. Gould on Phaedrus's speech in Plato's *Symposium* (Chapters Fifty-Four and Fifty-Five) is a fascinating discussion of an underexplored portion of that rich dialogue. Gene Fendt's essay on Kierkegaard as a tricky fellow indeed (Chapter Forty-Five) is provocative, even if Steven Emmanuel is right (Chapter Forty-Six) that Fendt's thesis about Kierkegaard's deceptions is unfalsifiable. Justin Leiber's speculations about the origins of the pornographic impulse are refreshing (Chapter Fifty-Nine), and deserve to be taken into account as feminist philosophers (and others) continue to toss around this hot potato. Donald Levy's analysis of Plato's concept of love in the *Symposium* (Chapter Two)—even if, as observed by Henry Allen, some nonphilosophers in the audience were bored to tears, or to writing postcards, by it—is an insightful addition to Plato scholarship. David Mayo's essay, in which he denies that HIV-positive persons have a moral duty to warn potential sexual partners of that fact (Chapter Forty-Three), is the most outrageous piece in the book; but Mayo, the philosopher that he is, argues for his thesis vigorously. Steven Smith and Nancy Snow (Chapters Fifty-Two and Fifty-Three) fruitfully examine the relationship between sex and gender (with Kant and Carol Gilligan in the foreground), an issue probed explicitly or implicitly by many essays in this book (see, for example, the exchange among Carol Caraway, Dana Bushnell, and me in Chapters Thirty-Six through Thirty-Nine). Finally, I have always been impressed by the originality and seductiveness of Russell Vannoy's account of sexual perversity (Chapter Thirty-Five), and hope that he soon finishes writing the book in which he develops further his intriguing ideas on this topic.

6.

The Society began in 1977 with about fifty members. Throughout my tenure as its director, membership never fell below fifty but also never rose above seventy in any of the years from 1977 through 1992. The turnover rate, in my judgment, was on the high side: perhaps as many as twenty members let their subscriptions lapse each year, while the Society added roughly the same number of new members. That's an annual turnover rate of about 30%, which suggests that there has not been much continuity in the membership. (But I'd like to see the membership figures and turnover rates of other small societies.) Nineteen members, however, were with me from the very beginning, joining SPSL in 1977, and were still members in 1992, when I turned the directorship over to Carol Caraway. These nineteen members, the core membership of SPSL, deserve to be thanked for their initial support of the newly-formed society and for staying the course with me: Ed Abegg, Joseph Aieta, W. M. Alexander, Bernard (Stefan) Baumrin, Donald Blakeley, Richard Hull, Edward Johnson, Rolf Johnson, John Kleinig, Brendan Liddell, Pat McGraw, John McGraw, Lee Rice, R. C. Richards, Irving Singer, Art Stawinski, John Sullivan, Ed Vacek, and Russell Vannoy.

John Sullivan, one of the most distinguished members of SPSL, died in Santa Barbara, California, on 9 April 1993. His essay on sexual objectification

(Chapter Fifteen) is published here for the first time, with the permission of his wife, Judy Godfrey, who also supplied the biographical information comprising Sullivan's entry in "Contributors." Two other deaths should be noted. Fred Berger was a loyal member of SPSL from the beginning, but did not make it into the fifteen-year club; Berger died on 20 November 1986. I recommend to you his excellent essay "Gratitude."[23] Fred Elliston, although he was not a member of SPSL, participated generously in its meetings, presenting two commentaries for the Society, one in 1978 (on Chapter Two, Donald Levy's paper on love in Plato's *Symposium*), the other in 1985 (on Chapter Thirty, Charles Johnson's "Body Language"). Elliston died in an automobile accident on 17 May 1987. I could not locate Elliston's wife or any other appropriate party to get permission to publish his commentaries.

Special thanks are due to Richard T. Hull—my migrainous mentor years ago, and still my migrainous mentor—who has been, *qua* my **HAPS** editor, a medium-size boss with a huge-size amount of patience and words of encouragement. Others who assisted in various and sundry ways, and whom I here thank, include, in no coherent order, Kris Lackey and Terry Coverson (Deparment of English, University of New Orleans); Barbara Kirshner, who worked for a year with me on the project; Lee C. Rice (Marquette University); Lynn Hankinson Nelson (editor of the SWIP newsletter; Rowan College of New Jersey); Janet Sample (of The American Philosophical Association); Eric van Broekhuizen (my editor at **Rodopi**); Robert Ginsberg (executive editor of **VIBS**); the University of New Orleans Research Council and College of Liberal Arts, for release time from teaching; Irving Singer (Massachusetts Institute of Technology); Stephen Posey, Jim Wentzel, Gwen Burda, and Dennis McSeveney, for technical computer, printer, and word-processing advice; Kimberley Arrington (at the *Washington Post*); Judy Godfrey, for her help with John Sullivan's contribution and biographical note; and Sára Szabó Soble, my spouse, for performing many time-consuming library tasks for me. The "Introduction" was gone through carefully by Edward Johnson (my chairperson), Richard Hull, and Robert Ginsberg. I thank each for spotting my mistakes and bringing them to my attention, and for allowing me to incorporate (when I did) their suggestions for modifying the penultimate version. Others who contributed in diverse ways to this project and my life are L. Sacks, S. N. Moyer, B. Albright, V. Wu, R. Robbins, R. Cutlin, C. Bleier, K. Marshall, J. Grey, S. Taylor, J. Wick, S. McBeth, R. Schmidt, K. B. Craig, G. Castellano, A. Pirruccello, D. Ragsdale, and the now-deceased B. Sonia, J. Trautwein, K. Avegno, and Norton Nelkin.

My opening address at the first meeting of the Society for the Philosophy of Sex and Love is the only piece in this volume that is absolutely unchanged. Because I prepared the manuscript of the entire book on the top of my desk, it was both possible and necessary to edit (in either a weak or a strong sense, depending on the nature and provenance of the essay occupying the screen of my monitor at the time) every other essay contained in this volume. Further, most authors had the opportunity (and took it) to revise their original contributions. In some cases, the author and I settled on a new title as well. This explains the several discrepancies between the title given directly below the author's photograph—the title of the original SPSL live presentation—and the title that appears at the beginning of the author's essay and in the "Contents."

At first I used WordPerfect 5.1 on the entire manuscript, but later, in light of severe formatting and printing problems, I converted everything into WordPerfect 6.0 (at the suggestion of Richard Hull). In many ways, that decision proved wise, but I soon discovered that WordPerfect 6.1 for Windows 3.1—even though I was equipped with limited hard drive space and only 8 megabytes of RAM—was the best choice. The final manuscript was printed 600x600 dpi on a Hewlett-Packard LaserJet 4Plus, an HP LaserJet 5P, and an HP LaserJet 5L Xtra (which three printers gave nearly visibly identical results, even if not at the same speed: the workhorse 4Plus is the fastest).

The photographs were the occasion for additional headaches and expense. Although most of the contributors supplied photographs of excellent quality and appropriate size and color, others, unfortunately for me, could not do so. Of these photographs new negatives had to be made, and if the final results are acceptable, I will owe a great deal to luck and to the efforts of the professionals at **Rodopi**. A word about the photographs of the editor: since a history of me and a history of the Society are inseparable (although not seamlessly), I have chosen to show my face, body, and clothing at various stages of their predictable development. (There are no nudes of me in *Penthouse* or *Cheri*.) *In mitn derinnen*, I share with the readers of this book another part of my history and development: the reader will find photographs of my two wonderful daughters (Rebecca Jill Soble and Rachel Emőke Soble), my two loving parents (Sylvia and William Soble), my two terribly-missed grandmothers (Gertrude Bronsweig Ratener and Rose Goldberg Soble), my two strong and successful sisters (Phyllis Ellen Soble and Janet Marlene Soble), and my second, but number one, wife (Sára Szabó Soble).

Notes

1. Thomas Nagel, "Sexual Perversion," *Journal of Philosophy* 66:1 (1969): 5-17; reprinted in Alan Soble, ed., *Philosophy of Sex*, 1st ed. (Totowa, N.J.: Littlefield, Adams, 1980), 76-88, and *Philosophy of Sex*, 2nd ed. (Savage, Md.: Rowman and Littlefield, 1991), 39-51.

2. Robert Solomon, "Sexual Paradigms," *Journal of Philosophy* 71:11 (1974): 336-45; reprinted in Soble, *Philosophy of Sex*, 1st ed., 89-98, 2nd ed., 53-62.

3. Janice Moulton, "Sexual Behavior: Another Position," *Journal of Philosophy* 73:16 (1976): 537-46; reprinted in Soble, *Philosophy of Sex*, 1st ed., 110-18, 2nd ed., 63-71.

4. I am more impressed now with the subtlety and beauty of Nagel's account of psychologically natural human sexuality; see my sympathetic discussion in *Sexual Investigations* (New York: New York University Press, 1996), 71-4, 81-3.

5. What follows was meant as a joke; the large and possibly apprehensive audience (I wore my uniform—jeans and a dungaree jacket—and my hair was tied back in a long ponytail) did not take it that way. Or maybe they were concentrating on their postcard-writing.

6. Today I would replace "emotionally" with "phenomenologically."

7. I have trouble comprehending "x is aroused by sensing that y is aroused by sensing that x is aroused by sensing that y is aroused by sensing that x is aroused by sensing y." So do my philosophy of sex and love students.

8. I am sad to report that I no longer experience this infinity feeling, which is odd, since I am more exhausted these days than I ever have been.

9. *Civilization and Its Discontents*, in James Strachey, ed. and trans., *The Standard Edition of the Complete Psychological Works of Sigmund Freud*, vol. 21 (London: Hogarth Press, 1964), 64-5.

10. Today I would replace "religiously" with "ontologically."

11. I was referring to the first edition of Robert Baker and Frederick Elliston, eds., *Philosophy and Sex* (Buffalo: Prometheus, 1975), which later appeared in its second edition (1984). Not too long after this meeting, I put together the first edition of my *Philosophy of Sex* (Totowa, N.J.: Rowman and Littlefield, 1980). The second edition (much revised) came out in 1991 and the third (again largely a new book) in 1997.

12. A longer version was published as "Sexual Desire" in *Journal of Philosophy* 75:4 (1978): 175-89, and is included in this volume as Chapter One.

13. And "logic."

14. More writers must be added to the list of significant earlies: Ti-Grace Atkinson, Susan Brownmiller, Andrea Dworkin, Germaine Greer, Sheila Rowbotham, and Eli Zaretsky, to name a few.

15. This optimism has nearly been shot to heck by Catharine MacKinnon and the more recent work of Andrea Dworkin, as well as by postmodernist and French feminism. But note the existence, if not popularity, of the Society for Analytic Feminism, which also meets with the three divisions of The American Philosophical Association.

16. Robert Solomon quipped, in the prestigious pages of the *Philosophical Review*, that "the program committee of the APA . . . delights in assigning the newly formed Society for the Philosophy of Sex and Love to the 'Thoroughbred Room' of its convention hotel" (review of *Sex Without Love: A Philosophical Exploration* by Russell Vannoy, 91:4 [1982], 653-6, at 654). Cute, but false. A glance through the *Proceedings of The American Philosophical Association* reveals that the Society has dwelled in such distinguished locations as "Monroe West," "Holmes," "Independence East," "Commonwealth," "Consulate," and "Cabinet."

17. ☺

18. Said to me by the late Thomas D. Perry, who might have thought that the philosophy of law was less exciting than law itself.

19. At least Shaffer laughed at this from the podium, and added before reading his paper that he got hungry writing it. (As the young Woody Allen might have said, the best part of sex is the fettuccine alfredo that comes afterwards.)

20. Henry Allen, "Semantics, Paradigms, Ontology . . . Love," *Washington Post* (28 December 1978), B1, B3.

21. Nozick, *The Examined Life* (New York: Simon and Schuster, 1989), 67. Not much life-examination on this page, at least.

22. *Ibid.*, 61.

23. *Ethics* 85:4 (1975): 298-309.

Jerome A. Shaffer

Author of "Sexual Desire"
Paper presented at the Society for the Philosophy of Sex and Love
during the
Eastern Division Meeting of The American Philosophical Association
Washington, D. C., 28 December 1977

One

SEXUAL DESIRE

Jerome A. Shaffer

What is *sexual desire*? In the recent philosophical literature on sex, there is very little discussion of this important element in sexual behavior. Thomas Nagel claims to develop "a specific psychological theory of sexual desire and human sexual interactions," but he never does provide a theory or even any discussion of sexual desire as such. In presenting his primary example, the cocktail lounge patrons Romeo and Juliet, he takes "X regards Y with sexual desire" as the undefined, unanalyzed, and undiscussed first state in a series of successive, increasingly complex, mutual perceptions of each other's desire, desire that the other desire, and so forth,[1] and he goes on to offer a specific theory not of sexual desire but of some conditions for what he calls a "full-fledged" and "complete" sexual relationship.

Robert C. Solomon correctly objects to Nagel's account as "sexuality without content," and points out that Nagel's Romeo and Juliet "arouse each other, but there is no indication to what end."[2] On Solomon's account, the end or goal of sexual desire is "interpersonal communication" in which, by "body language," we express various emotions, such as "tenderness and trust, domination and passivity . . . , possessiveness, mutual recognition, 'being-with,' and conflict."[3]

Janice Moulton, in criticizing Solomon's account, points out correctly that there is nothing particularly sexual about these emotions, that they are often expressed nonsexually and even better expressed nonsexually, and that "even if some attitudes and feelings (for example, prurience, wantonness, lust) are best expressed sexually, it would be questionable whether the primary aim of sexual activity should be to express them."[4] We might add that the desire for "interpersonal communication" via "body language" seems neither necessary nor sufficient for sexual desire, nor even widely conjoined with it, although one might find this fact regrettable. But Moulton does not provide an account of sexual desire either.

Alan H. Goldman, attempting to introduce a more robust sense of reality into these abstruse accounts, claims that "sexual desire is desire for contact with another person's body and for the pleasure which such contact produces."[5] But anyone who has seen a parent and child warmly hugging or two old friends enthusiastically shaking hands knows that this is not a *sufficient* condition; and he or she will reject, as highly implausible, Goldman's suggestion that either sex is at the bottom of such contact or the physical contact is not really desired for itself.[6] Nor is it a *necessary* condition, as voyeurism and exhibitionism show. If, with Goldman, we say these cases involve abnormal or perverted sexual desire, we still need to be told why they are called sexual desire at all, and Goldman fails to do that. Nor is the desire for contact with an *animal's* body necessarily abnormal sexual desire; it would be ludicrous to accuse the myriad of those who have had the pleasure of petting a cat of engaging in sexual abnormality.

These various accounts of sexual desire, though differing in detail, present a common general formula, namely, that sexual desire is *desire for* something, let us say desire for sex, or, alternatively, *desire that* one engage in something, let us say desire that one engage in sexual activity. Let us call this *the propositional theory* of sexual desire. We can express it this way. Taking our situation to be a case in which a person S at some time t sexually desires O, the propositional theory holds the following:

At t, S sexually desires O $=_{df}$ At t, S desires that S have sex with O.

To keep the theory general, we leave open what is to count as "having sex." Although this theory has the merit of simplicity, unfortunately it is false. Neither side of the purported equation entails the other.

(1) Desiring to have sex does not entail having sexual desire. A person might desire that sex occur for any number of reasons without having sexual desire. The person might desire sex because he or she believes that it would be a valuable experience, be good for the health or the nerves, bring in some money, result in a desired pregnancy, be required by obligation or duty, provide pleasure for the other, or even induce sexual desire, without it being the case that he or she actually has sexual desire. Even where sex is desired just for the fun or enjoyment or satisfaction it will produce, there might be no sexual desire: if S is informed that sex with O will be enjoyable, S might desire sex with O just for the fun of it without sexually desiring O (who might be unknown to S). If we were to allow meaning to talk of S's desiring sex with O "intrinsically" or "for its own sake," it still would not follow that S sexually desires O; S might have been informed that sex with O would be "intrinsically" good or good "for its own sake" and, thereby, come to desire sex with O "intrinsically" or "for its own sake" without sexually desiring O.

(2) Nor does having sexual desire entail desiring to have sex. Suppose a person sexually desires someone but finds it unthinkable that he or she actually have sex with that individual. Perhaps it is an adult who sexually desires some child or close relative (or both). In some such cases, there is a conflict of desire, ambivalence, repressions, and so forth, but cases exist in which there might be absolutely no real desire that sex occur, no conceivable circumstances under which the adult would have sex with the other, but, to the contrary, an unambivalent desire that sex not occur and a total horror at the idea of its occurring. Or could not a widow find herself thinking with sexual desire of her late husband? She might well *wish* he were alive so that she could have sex with him, but she knows he is dead and therefore knows that sex with him is impossible. A person cannot *want* what she believes to be impossible, although she might *wish* for it. Therefore the widow cannot want to have sex with her husband, although she might still sexually desire him. Suppose a person is extremely

naive sexually, having had neither sexual experience nor sex education, so that he or she has no concept of what sexual behavior or sexual activity is. Such a person would be incapable of forming the desire that a certain form of activity take place, because he or she would have no notion of such activity. Yet it is not impossible that such a person should have sexual desires. Many sheltered adolescents are undoubtedly in such a situation.[7] If it is difficult to imagine such sexual innocence, consider a confirmed heterosexual who suddenly and unaccountably finds himself or herself for the first time sexually desiring someone of the same sex. Such a person might have no idea of what sort of sexual activity would be appropriate and, therefore, would not even know what to desire.

In pointing out that sexual desire is not a case of *desiring that*, I am saying that sexual desire as such has no necessary connection with any goal, aim, or end in view. It does not consist in the envisaging of some state of affairs toward which one has a positive attitude. Of course, a sexually experienced person will often have very specific things in mind, precise aims, goals, or ends, some clearly envisioned outcome that is indeed desired. My point is that such specific desires that certain states of affairs occur are *logically independent* of sexual desire. Sexual desire does not entail any *desirings that*, nor do any *desirings that* entail sexual desire. They do often accompany each other. But, as is well known, there is enormous variety in the desirings that accompany sexual desire; there are the various so-called "perverted" and "normal" desires that vary so from culture to culture, the desires of the comparatively mature and immature, the sane and insane, the imaginative and unimaginative, poetic and prosaic, romantic and unromantic, sexually passive and active, and so on. A person experiencing sexual desire might, as in Eric Rohmer's movie, desire only to touch Claire's knee, or might have in mind an elaborate scenario, or might simply be assailed with sexual desire and not a glimmering of a desire that some state of affairs occur.

In this respect, sexual desire differs markedly from the standard case of desire. Ordinarily, to desire something is necessarily to envisage favorably some future state of affairs that is one's goal or aim; so it makes sense to ask, of someone who expresses a desire, *what* is it you desire? This is obviously true of *desiring that*. It is a strength of the propositional theory that its generalized version also accounts for cases of *desiring to*. To *desire to* be a doctor is to *desire that* one become a doctor. It also accounts for many cases where "desire" takes a direct object, as in desiring a new car; to desire a new car is to desire that one should have a new car. But sexual desire is the exception. One might try the view that when S sexually desires O, S desires to "have" O, that is, S *desires that* he or she "have" O. But I think one can see that the objections we raised earlier to the propositional theory would apply to this variant as well.

In his account of desire, Anthony Kenny proposes a generalized version of the propositional theory. He summarizes his position as follows:

> *Wanting X* is always *wanting to get X*; and a description of *getting X* describes a state of affairs. . . . An analysis of a report of a desire should display the same structure as the analysis of a report of judgement.[8]

In elaborating this position, Kenny says:

> We can, therefore, it seems, lay down some restrictions on possible objects of desire. Where X is a tangible object we may say:
>
> (1) For "I want X" to be intelligible at all as the expression of a desire, the speaker must be able to answer the question "what counts as *getting* X?"
>
> (2) For "I want X" to be a complete specification of a desire, the speaker must be able to answer the question "what do you want X for?"[9]

How odd this all seems when applied to sexual desire. When S sexually desires O, who in a typical case is a person and therefore would be acknowledged by Kenny to be a tangible object, there is a certain inappropriateness in asking S what counts *as getting O* and what S wants O *for*. It is not merely indelicate for us to ask. S might have no idea what counts as getting O, and anything we might suggest to S to might strike S as repugnant. As for what S wants O for, the question might well be utterly incomprehensible to S. I certainly would not want to be the person to raise these questions with S, and S's inability to answer them would hardly rule out O as an object of desire. To the contrary, it would be evidence that the desire was indeed sexual. Again, to avoid misunderstanding, let me stress that, although sexually experienced people will often have pretty definite ideas concerning what counts as getting X and what they want to do with X, these plans are not essential to sexual desire.

It is not simply that Kenny failed to think of the case of sexual desire when he put these restrictions on possible objects of desire. In a footnote on the same page, he refers to "Faustus's desire for Helen" and claims Faustus "could answer the questions 'what counts as getting Helen?' and 'what will you do with Helen when you get her?'", adding that "in . . . case Faustus [is] unable to specify what counts as 'getting Helen' his want will be ruled out by condition (1)."[10] Perhaps Faustus could answer these questions, for he had sold his soul to the Devil for knowledge and power. But some, in the grips of sexual desire, are not so clear about things; at any rate, there seems to be no *necessity* for being so clear about such things.

If Kenny is right in taking desire to be necessarily propositional, then one would have to conclude that sexual desire is not a species of desire or not a case of desire in its standard or fundamental sense. This is not so paradoxical as it might at first appear. After all, dry ice (frozen CO_2) is not a kind of ice (frozen H_2O). In fact, if *sexual* desire were a kind of desire, it would be in contrast with other kinds of desire. But there is no set of alternative terms that in natural language occupy the place of "sexual" in "sexual desire." One might introduce artificial expressions like "nutritional desire" or "nutriental desire" or simply "food desire" as analogues of "sexual desire." The most natural construal of such expressions would be as "desire for (say) food," that is, *desire that* one have or eat food. Since, as we have seen, S's sexual desire for O cannot be construed as a *desire that*, sexual desire does not come close to paralleling our artificial construction, "food desire." If sexual desire is not a species of desire to be contrasted with *x desire*, *y desire*, and so forth, it might be because it is not a case of desire at all. But then what is it?

Progress in answering this question can be made by turning to an important feature of sexual desire: that it is *directed toward* an object. At t, S sexually desires O. Of course, there is such a thing as *undirected* sexual tension, feeling "horny," as it is called, an objectless state that is related to sexual desire as anxiety is related to worry. Being horny falls into the category of moods, such as being depressed, happy, restless, or in a frivolous or gloomy mood.[11] But in our paradigm of sexual desire, and probably for sexual desire in general, there is a particular object of desire. How are we to understand this object?

Is the object of desire the *cause* of desire? A drawing or piece of music might cause me to feel sexual desire without my desiring the drawing or the music. An aphrodisiac could be the cause of desire without being the object of desire. So, being the cause of desire is not a sufficient condition for being the object of desire. But is it a necessary condition? Let us consider the following case. S is fooled by a *trompe l'oeil* painting into thinking that there is a very attractive person in the doorway, and S reports desiring the person in the doorway. If we allow that this is a case of sexual desire, then, since the object of desire is nonexistent, the object cannot be the cause, and, therefore, being the cause of desire is not even a necessary condition of being the object of desire. But is S reporting truly or is S mistaken? Does S feel sexual desire and, if so, for what? Not for the painting. This much can be said. So far as S's subjective condition is concerned, that is, S's frame of mind or emotional state, it is just what it would be if there had been in the doorway a real person just like the person portrayed in the painting. But is this really a case of sexual desire. I do not think our language makes it clear whether we should say in such a case that it is or is not really sexual desire. If it is not sexual desire, however, there is no nonawkward alterative description for it either. We would have to make up some expression, say, "illusional sexual desire," to cover such cases. Perhaps the best thing to say is that sexual desire is somewhat extensional.

A related question concerns whether the substitution of coextensive terms for the object of desire preserves truth. It would seem so. If S desires O and O is identical with the person who just had certain secret thoughts, then necessarily S desires the person who had certain secret thoughts. Oedipus unwittingly sexually desired his mother. A person might unwittingly desire a dummy or a transvestite. If we allow that there is sexual desire in the case of the *trompe l'oeil* painting, then it might be true that S desires the attractive person in the doorway but false that S desires the dowdy person in the doorway, even though "the attractive person in the doorway" and "the dowdy person in the doorway" will be coextensive terms by virtue of the fact that each has no extension at all. But if we require that, for the feeling to be sexual desire, the object must exist, then substitutability *salva veritate* does obtain.

It is a further weakness of the propositional theory that it has difficulty accommodating this somewhat extensional feature of sexual desire. We can easily add to "At t, S desires that he or she have sex with O" a *de re* element, as follows: "At t, S desires of O that he or she have sex with O." And the awkwardness of desire for nonexistents will properly reappear in this analysis. But the substitutability of coextensive expressions does not obtain in the analysis. It might well be *false* that Oedipus desired that he have sex with his mother and it might well be false that the person who (unwittingly) desired the dummy or the transvestite desired that he or she have sex with the dummy or the transvestite. *Desiring that* does not admit of substitutability *salva veritate*.

This somewhat extensional feature is present in many sorts of *emotion*. If S hates O and O is the person who had certain secret thoughts, then S hates the person who had those thoughts, so substitutability does obtain. However, there is the same awkwardness about nonexistent objects. If a person falsely believes that someone is plotting his ruin and says, sincerely, "I hate that person plotting my ruin," can that person be truly said to hate? The subjective state is just what it would be if the belief were true, but there is no individual who is the object of the subjective state. If we call this "delusive hate," then (true) hate will be not just somewhat extensional but fully so and will admit of coextensional substitutability.

There are so many similarities between sexual desire and the emotions that one might be inclined to think of sexual desire as an emotion. Both are typically *directed toward* an object. Both are *attitudes* or ways of regarding an object; S can think of O with sexual desire, or with anger, pity, envy, fear, or love. Both involve *feelings*; one can feel a twinge of desire and one can burn with desire, just as one can feel a twinge of pity or burn with anger. Both can have *bodily expressions*; one's heart can pound with desire or with anger, and one's hands can tremble with either. Both can have behavioral *consequences*; pity can lead, motivate, incline, or dispose one to seek out another, and so can sexual desire. Furthermore, both can be "*agitations*,"[12] states or conditions that interfere with our voluntary, intentional, or deliberate behavior; we can be transfixed, overcome, gripped, carried away, flustered, or distracted by desire or by fear. Finally, both appear, at least to Kenny, to be necessarily connected with desiring that. We have already seen his position on desire. On emotions he says:

> One emotion differs from another because of the different sort of things it makes one want to do. Fear involves wanting to avoid or avert what is feared; anger is connected to the desire to punish or take vengeance on its object. . . . These connections are not contingent: a man who was unaware of them would not possess the concept of the emotions in question.[13]

I would want to make the same point here that I made for desire. There is no contradiction in saying that S feared O but wanted to confront O or seek O out rather than avoid O. Such desires might be unusual but they cannot be ruled out conceptually. Not everyone who is angry desires to punish or take vengeance. One can grieve for a dead one without necessarily having any desires (although one might have *wishes*, for example, that the person were alive again). Kenny's point does indeed apply to *motives*, such as greed, which involves the desire to acquire, and malice, which involves the desire to do harm. Emotions, however, are not motives; one would not say that the murderer's *motive* was anger.

Despite the similarities between sexual desire and emotions, there are important differences. Emotions are tied to our rationality in a way that sexual desire is not. One can always ask what a person's *reason* was for feeling some emotion. One's reason for pitying O might be that O has lost his or her job and one's reason for fearing O might be that O has made threats. Sometimes we hate or fear without reason. In such cases our hatred or fear is unreasonable. In other cases it is unreasonable because our reason is a bad one. Because of this connection with reasons, emotions can be reasonable or unreasonable, well-founded or ill-founded, appropriate or inappropriate, justified or unjustified. We say, "There is no reason for you to fear him" or "Your pity is misplaced; feel sorry for S, not for O," or "His grief was more than the situation warranted; he hardly knew him." But sexual desire does not admit of such evaluations. If S sexually desires O, it makes no sense to ask for S's reasons for sexually desiring O, and it makes no sense to judge S's desire as reasonable or unreasonable, well or ill-founded, justified or unjustified. We might not understand what S sees in O, we might not share S's taste in these matters, we might think S is doomed to frustration, we might even think that S's desire is neurotic, sick, or self-destructive, but we cannot say that S has bad reasons or even that S has no reason for desiring O.

There is another important difference between sexual desire and emotions, which will lead us back to the idea that sexual desire is, after all, a case of desire (although not a case of desiring that) and explain why it is called sexual *desire*. The idea of desiring something is necessarily connected with the idea of *satisfaction*. The conceptual connection is clearly present in the case of sexual desire. Sometimes sexual desire just goes away, but sometimes it gets satisfied, and sometimes it gets frustrated or remains unsatisfied. This tie is not present in the case of emotion; there is no such thing as satisfying one's grief, anger, or pity, nor are these emotions doomed to frustration either.

In this respect, sexual desire is like the feelings of longing, craving, yearning, pining, hungering, and thirsting. Unlike emotions, these are connected with the idea of satisfaction. However, like emotions, they have a strong introspectable component of sensation ("He wanted it so much he could taste it"). Nevertheless, these feelings differ from sexual desire; they are amenable to the propositional theory; to have a longing for the old homestead is to have a *longing that* one be there.

Sexual desire is like *desiring that* in its tie to satisfaction or frustration. But the idea of satisfaction is to be distinguished from the ideas of attaining, getting, fulfilling, or realizing. These ideas, in suggesting *a pre-envisaged state* that is to be attained, got, fulfilled, or realized, are thus appropriate to *desiring that* but are not appropriate to sexual desire. One can attain, get, fulfill, or realize one's desires (that) but one can only satisfy one's sexual desires. Kenny, in claiming that the desirer *must* have some idea of what counts as getting what he desires is right about *desiring that* but wrong about sexual desire. At the time of sexual desire, S might have no particular pre-envisaged idea of what getting O will consist of.

But, one will ask, if there is no goal, how can there be satisfaction or lack of satisfaction? Here one might resort to metaphor, speaking of "blind desire" to emphasize the lack of a pre-envisioned goal, or of sexual desire as a "drive" to emphasize the way we are pushed or carried toward the satisfaction, rather than motivated by our picture of what form the satisfaction will take. There is satisfaction of desire, but the desire is not for the particular state that will constitute satisfaction nor is it a desire merely for satisfaction. It is for this reason that there is often a sense of novelty that characterizes sexual behavior even where one knows pretty well how it will end; the particular way in which sexual desire will be satisfied might be entirely predictable, but it is not spelled in the desire itself how it should be satisfied. The novelty is logical, so to speak; the form of the satisfaction is not contained in the context and nature of the desire itself. And, for the sexually inexperienced, it might be a complete surprise.

One is tempted to say that in sexual desire the specifics of how the desire is to be satisfied must be there from the beginning, perhaps in unconscious form. On this view, if and when I am satisfied, then I discover what I was looking for all along, what I had wanted from the beginning. But why should one have to bring in unconscious desire? To succumb to this way of thinking is to fall back into the mistake of thinking that sexual desire is *desiring that*, and, if it is not conscious, it must be unconscious. The fact is that there might be no desired outcome, not even an unconsciously desired outcome, which is necessarily present in sexual desire. As things unfold after sexual desire rears its head, what we have is satisfaction or frustration without prior determination of any specific satisfaction state. This is not so weird. It is often the case that we search for satisfaction and finally find it in a particular form without its being the case that what we found was what we were really searching for all along.

There is *some* specification after all. It lies in the fact that it is O who is desired by S. S sees O as the source of the satisfaction. But the particular form the satisfaction will take if it occurs is not entailed by the fact of desire nor contained in the nature of the sexual desire.

If we have accounted for what makes sexual desire a case of desire, we have still to account for what makes it *sexual*. Obviously it cannot be the nature of the object. When S sexually desires O, O can be of any sex or age, living or dead, human or animal. Perhaps O must be a spatiotemporal particular, perhaps even animal rather than vegetable or mineral, but such restrictions might reflect my own lack of experience or imagination. The most tempting theory of what makes it sexual is a kind of James-Lange account in which desire is sexual because it is accompanied by certain bodily events or bodily sensations in various areas of the body that are called "sexual," and these areas are called "sexual" because they are the areas that distinguish the two sexes, male and female, from each other (mainly the genital areas). Unfortunately, this theory is objectionable for the same sort of reason that makes it an objectionable account of emotions; people who have suffered loss of relevant parts or sensations of those parts still continue to have the correlated emotions. In the case of sexual desire, male paraplegics, who have become paralyzed and unfeeling from the trunk down, seem still to have sexual desire.[14]

But these bodily phenomena do come in to the story in an essential way. If what is definitory of sexual *desire* is the prospect of satisfaction or frustration, then what is definitory of *sexual* desire is *sexual* satisfaction or frustration. And what makes satisfaction or frustration *sexual*? It is what desire often leads to, and what satisfaction or frustration follows, namely, sexual arousal, sexual excitement, "turning on." Sexual arousal is a distinctive state, not to be identified with sexual desire. There can be arousal without sexual desire; fantasy, pictures or music, or physical stimulation can produce arousal without there being sexual desire directed at some object. It is, perhaps, uncommon for there to be sexual desire without some degree of arousal, but in cases where desire is incipient or lacking in intensity, there can be desire without arousal. It is with arousal that bodily phenomena come into the picture, for sexual arousal is a state of the body in which the sexual areas, the parts of the body that distinguish the sexes, undergo certain typical changes and the subject has typical sensations that are the awareness of these events. These bodily events are just beginning to be studied in detail,[15] but we have long known of the sensations that are correlated with them, as well as some of the more obvious bodily events, such as erection and lubrication. They are centered in the genital area and radiate out from them. Certain subsequent bodily events and the sensations that are the awareness of them often follow arousal; these subsequent events constitute the *satisfaction* or *fulfillment* of desire. Often satisfaction consists in orgasm and the sensations involved in it, and there is a felt sense of the resolution of the earlier stages in the later ones. But this sense of resolution, which is the mark of satisfaction, can be accomplished in ways other than orgasm. For example, the awareness of the orgasm of the other, holding or being held, or, in more pathological cases, the exhibition of one's naked body or the infliction of violence might be the culmination of sexual arousal in which the satisfaction or fulfillment of sexual desire consists. What makes the touching of Claire's knee the *sexual* satisfaction of *sexual* desire is the occurrence of the intervening sexual excitement and the sense of resolution of that excitement in which satisfaction consists. Otherwise, it would be merely the desire to touch her knee and the eventual fulfillment of that desire. What makes desire and satisfaction *sexual* is the intervening state of sexual arousal, which is directly sexual in that it involves the sexual parts, *viz*., the genital areas.

Let us now proceed to give our account of sexual desire. Sexual desire is a state of a subject which is directed toward an object but does not necessarily involve any *desiring that* concerning the object and which is such that, if it is followed by sexual arousal, then certain subsequent events will be felt as constituting the satisfaction or frustration of that original state. On this account it is not necessary that the original state (sexual desire) actually lead to sexual arousal, but it is necessary that, if it does lead to sexual arousal, then succeeding events will count as the satisfaction or frustration of that original state.

Sexual desire is often classified with hunger and thirst, as a bodily desire, drive, or appetite, although it differs from them in that its satisfaction is not necessary to keep the body alive or even healthy. It is instructive to note how sexual desire compares with hunger. Hunger, like sexual desire, has no simple relation to desiring that. It is obvious one can desire to eat without being hungry. But, since hunger is so often accompanied by the desire to eat, it is not so obvious that one can be hungry without desiring to eat. Still, it is the case. If people were not assailed with hunger until, say, puberty and at that time knew little about eating, if hunger could be satisfied in lots of ways besides eating (say, by touching food, gazing at it, whipping it, exhibiting oneself before it, or, more realistically, by injecting it), if most of the edible objects around us had strong taboos attached to eating them, then it would be easier to see how there could be hunger without the desire to eat. Like sexual desire, hunger is necessarily connected with the idea of satisfaction, and we quickly become experienced in the relativity limited ways (primarily, eating) of achieving that satisfaction. Hence where there is hunger there is usually also the desire to eat.

Hunger, however, is more like horniness than sexual desire; it is typically not directed at a particular object. It is either objectless (one is just hungry) or directed toward a class of objects, any one of which will do, for example, a (any) thick, juicy steak. It is more like S's desiring a man (or a woman) but not any particular one, rather than S's desiring O. One can want *that* piece of pie, but, if no other will do, it would seem to be more (or less) than just a case of hunger. If life were like a cafeteria and we wandered around surrounded by edible portions of food, each different from the others, perhaps hunger, like sexual desire, would be more apt to focus on particular objects. Mencken said that love is the illusion that one woman differs from another; childhood might be said to be the illusion that one piece of cake differs from another.

In a typical case of hunger, the body is in a specific state of deprivation, and also there are familiar sensations usually associated with that state. However, it is clear that there can be deprivation without sensation, and sensation without deprivation. We could mark this distinction as the difference between *being* hungry and *feeling* hungry, although this would probably constitute a refinement of our present language. But such a distinction makes no sense at all for sexual desire. For S to sexually desire O is for S to *feel* sexual desire for O. Furthermore, the term "feel" here is less like a sensation word and more like an emotion word, as in "feeling glad for O" or "feeling pity for O." There often are sensations that accompany sexual desire but, as we have seen, they are the sensations of sexual arousal, a state distinguishable from sexual desire.

Sexual *arousal* has its counterpart in hunger. The bodily mechanisms involved in eating go through a preparatory phase, as in salivating, and there are sensations of those processes. We do not make a sharp distinction in the case of hunger between the sensations associated with the bodily state of deprivation and the sensations associated with the bodily processes of preparing to eat, because we are dealing with processes and sensations that are fairly continuous; we just as well say, "That makes me (feel) hungry," when we look at a picture of food that starts our juice flowing. But we do need to make such a distinction in the case of sexual desire, because sexual desire and sexual arousal are different sorts of phenomena. Sexual desire consists in an attitude toward an object, and sexual arousal consists in identifiable, locatable physiological processes and the sensations concomitant with them. I claim that it is the special features of the arousal stage that serve to define sexual desire as *sexual*, even though they might not be present in every case of sexual desire. But in the case of hunger, the sensations in the deprivation state or in the preparatory-to-eating state are each sufficient for hunger.

Finally, hunger is, like sexual desire, necessarily connected not with the ideas of getting, attaining, fulfilling, or realizing one's hunger but with the allied idea of *satisfying* one's hunger. Again, it is not spelled out in the hunger precisely what particular object will satisfy the hunger (not even in the case of hungering for a food of a certain sort). Nor is it plausible to claim in every case of satisfaction that all along there was the (perhaps unconscious) desire for that particular object that gave satisfaction. The form the satisfaction takes might be a complete surprise and yet still be the satisfaction of that original hunger. But there is one important difference between hunger and sexual desire here, although it is a purely contingent difference between them. As things are, the satisfaction of one's hunger requires transforming the object that provides the satisfaction in such a way that one cannot use the same object again for that purpose. "One cannot have one's cake and eat it too" is a (contingent) truth. Sexual desire is not like that. Ordinarily when S's desire for O is satisfied, O is not so transformed that S could not satisfy a new desire for O. But it is easy enough to imagine a world in which these different situations for hunger and sexual desire were reversed, where one and the same object could repeatedly satisfy one's hungers but could not repeatedly satisfy one's sexual desires. It is not so easy to decide whether such a world would be a better world. I leave that to the reader.[16]

Notes

1. Thomas Nagel, "Sexual Perversion," *Journal of Philosophy* 66:1 (1969): 5-17, at 6, 10-11.
2. Robert C. Solomon, "Sexual Paradigms," *Journal of Philosophy* 71:11 (1974): 336-45, at 336, 337.
3. *Ibid.*, 338, 344.
4. Janice Moulton, "Sexual Behavior: Another Position," *Journal of Philosophy* 73:16 (1976): 537-46, at 544.
5. Alan H. Goldman, "Plain Sex," *Philosophy and Public Affairs* 6:3 (1977): 267-87, at 268.
6. *Ibid.*, 269, 270.
7. Jean-Paul Sartre points this out in his remarks on sexual desire in *Being and Nothingness*, trans. Hazel E. Barnes (New York: Washington Square Press, 1966), 501:

> Desire is not a desire of *doing*. The "doing" is after the event, is added on to the desire from outside and necessitates a period of apprenticeship; there is an amorous technique which has its own ends and means. . . . Desire can not posit its suppression as its supreme end nor single out for its ultimate goal any particular act.

Sartre's emphasis here on *doing* reflects an aggressive or active sexuality that has been typically associated with a masculine approach to sex. The more passive the individual, the less likely it is that he or she will have a clear or even a vague desire that specific events transpire. We need to add to Sartre's claim that desire is not a desire of doing that it is not a desire that something *be done* nor, in general, a *desire that* something should occur.

8. Anthony Kenny, *Action, Emotion, and Will* (London: Routledge and Kegan Paul, 1963), 206-7.

9. *Ibid.*, 115.

10. *Ibid.*, footnote. What Marlowe's Faustus seemed to have in mind was innocent enough: "Sweet Helen, make me immortal with a kiss."

11. For a discussion of moods, see Gilbert Ryle, *The Concept of Mind* (New York: Barnes and Noble, 1949), ch. 4.

12. This term is used by Ryle to pick out an important kind of emotion.

13. Kenny, *Action, Emotion, and Will*, 100.

14. "Paraplegics who were incapable of receiving genito-pelvic signals did continue to experience erotic dreams, daydreams and plans. . . . In a psychological evaluation of impotent male paraplegics [it was] found that there was little cessation of sexual drives, although the sources of satisfaction often underwent considerable change." Lawrence I. Kaplan, *Comprehensive Follow-up Study of Spinal Cord Disfunction and Its Resultant Disabilities* (New York: N. Y. U. Medical Center, 1966), 101.

15. See William H. Masters and Virginia E. Johnson, *Human Sexual Response* (Boston: Little, Brown, 1966).

16. Earlier versions of this essay were presented to my own department on Valentine's Day, 14 February 1977, to that of Dartmouth College on 30 September 1977, and to the Society for the Philosophy of Sex and Love at The American Philosophical Association meeting on 28 December 1977. I am indebted to participants at those meetings, plus Lawrence Shaffer, John Troyer, and Thomas Nagel.

Donald Levy
(photograph: Tom Dickson)

Author of "The Definition of Love in Plato's *Symposium*"
Paper presented at the Society for the Philosophy of Sex and Love
during the
Eastern Division Meeting of The American Philosophical Association
Washington, D. C., 27 December 1978

Two

THE DEFINITION OF LOVE IN PLATO'S *SYMPOSIUM*

Donald Levy

For anyone who wants to think philosophically about love, the only way to begin is to reflect on the problems first raised in Plato's *Symposium*. The dialogue is original in at least two ways. In that it exposes the presuppositions of Greek sexual morality to the sort of critical scrutiny practiced by Socrates, there is nothing like it by anyone else before. Second, the new theory of love and the new ideal of it developed in Diotima's speech appear to be Plato's own equally original advance over Socrates' philosophy.

The dialogue records the brilliant conversation at a dinner party at which Socrates is a guest. Those who speak before Socrates mainly share the typical Greek tendency to glorify the instinct of sex rather than its particular objects.[1] For them, love (*eros*) is a god whose beauty and goodness they compete with one another in praising. Even Pausanias, who takes care to distinguish noble from base love, claims that "it is always honorable to comply with a lover to attain excellence" (*Symp*. 185b); even if the lover turns out to be bad, it does the boy credit to have been so deceived! It is this almost universally held belief in the intrinsic value of sexual love against which Socrates sets himself from the start; love, he says, is neither beautiful nor good (though he does not mean it is ugly or bad). Love cannot be beautiful because it is the desire to possess what is beautiful, and one cannot desire that which one already possesses, Socrates argues. That love is not good in itself, but is merely a means to the attainment of things that *are* good in themselves, is emphasized again at the end of Socrates' recital of Diotima's speech when he says, "human nature can find no better helper than love" (*Symp*. 212b). Socrates' own love of testing the opinions of others is not exempt from this new test; just as Socrates had surprised Agathon by claiming love is not beautiful, so Diotima bewilders Socrates with the idea that "the object of love is to procreate and give birth in the presence of beauty" (*Symp*. 206e). It is not enough, she seems to say, for a philosopher, a lover of wisdom, merely to assist at the birth of ideas in others, playing the midwife, herself barren (to which Socrates often compared himself), examining the new-born ideas for soundness. Such activities have no intrinsic worth; they are of value only if they lead the philosopher to bring forth theories of his own. The genuine lover of wisdom must himself conceive.

The new account of love introduced in the final part of Diotima's speech is one she is not certain Socrates can understand, she says. This appears to be Plato's way of signaling the radical shift in what follows from the comparatively simple attempt to define love by finding the element common to all types of love (typical of Socrates' method), when no distinctions of value among types of love are made (*Symp*. 202d-209e), to Plato's new approach. Now the different types of love are ordered hierarchically, one being judged superior to another because its object is inherently better. Further, the hierarchy of love objects involves another non-Socratic idea: one ultimate object of love exists to which all others must be tending in order for them to be objects of love at all. For those who seek to understand love, this absolute beauty, existing apart and alone, is the final goal of all their previous efforts. To achieve the vision of absolute beauty one progresses from love of physical beauty in an individual to love of all physical beauty; then, love of beauty in the soul leads to awareness of the beauty of acts, institutions, and sciences. On surveying all these different kinds of beauty, one is led to glimpse the science whose object is absolute beauty.

This theory of love has appeared defective in at least two ways to Gregory Vlastos, whose "The Individual as an Object of Love in Plato"[2] is the most important recent discussion of Plato's views. According to Vlastos, the defects in Plato's account of love can be seen by comparing it with the definition of love Vlastos accepts, and which Vlastos adopts from Aristotle: "Love is wishing good things for someone for that person's sake." Vlastos's first objection is that since Plato has already defined love as the desire for oneself to possess what is beautiful, Plato's idea of love, however spiritualized it might be, remains essentially egocentric.[3] Secondly, Plato does not see that love fundamentally and primarily has persons as its object; for Plato, the love of persons is placed far below the love of an abstract entity, absolute beauty. "What we are to love in persons is the 'image' of the Idea in them."[4] In a note, Vlastos says: "this is all love for a person could be, given the status of persons in Plato's ontology."

> We are to love the persons so far, and only insofar, as they are good and beautiful. . . . [T]he individual . . . will never be the object of our love . . . in Plato's theory. . . . [It] does not provide for love of whole persons, but only for love of that abstract version of persons which consists of the complex of their best qualities.[5]

So, for Plato, our affections for concrete human beings are "lesser loves," as Vlastos paraphrases it,[6] to be used "as steps" (*Symp*. 211c) to the attainment of absolute beauty. Vlastos concludes his criticism by noting the emphatic frequency of this idea.[7]

Without trying to deal with the entire array of evidence Vlastos presents to support these criticisms, it is enough to point out in reply to the first objection that Vlastos's definition of love, compared to which he finds Plato's defective, seems a definition not of what love is, but of what love ought, perhaps, to be. Clear examples of love abound which do not always conform to our moral ideals of love; the love of children and parents for one another—often negligent, selfish, confused, slow to develop—is one. So it is probably wrong, in defining love, to lay down as a necessary condition of one's loving a person at all that one seeks what is good for the other for the other's sake. At least some of the time when we love, we might be seeking what is good for others for our own sake, not theirs, as Aristotle recognizes;[8] and we must also consider the possibility that we might not even be seeking what is good for the other at all: smothering mothers and murderously jealous husbands.[9] If these examples are granted, Vlastos's definition of love does not state a necessary condition of love. Accepting his definition would make it impossible to distinguish between a person's loving well and that person's being a genuine instance of a lover.

Vlastos's definition seems also not to state a sufficient condition of love, since persons do seek what is good for others for the sake of the others (that is, because the others need or deserve it), when love for them is not the motive and might not even be present. Nurses, firemen, and teachers seek to do what is good for others, even if love for the others is wholly absent. It might be, as Diotima argues, that love motivates us whenever we achieve anything good; the nurse, fireman, and teacher might love the science, art, or skill to which each is devoted. But granting this does not narrow the distance between Plato's theory and the requirement laid down by Vlastos.

I have restricted myself to arguing here that Vlastos's definition of love is defective; whether Vlastos is right to suppose that his definition is the same as Aristotle's is a separate question. Most scholars have agreed with Vlastos's interpretation of the definition of love in the *Nicomachean Ethics*.[10] But even if Vlastos's definition were accepted, his conclusion that Plato's idea of love is egocentric does not directly follow. For his argument to work, Vlastos must show that desiring for oneself to possess what is beautiful never consists in wishing good things for someone for the person's sake; Vlastos must show that the first *cannot* consist in the second. But suppose the beautiful thing one desires for oneself to possess is the good (*Symp*. 204e). Further, suppose that some of the time the good one desires for oneself to possess is virtue. At least some of the time, then, desiring to possess virtue for oneself *consists* in wishing good things for someone for that person's sake. It would not be correct to say that wishing good things for someone for that person's sake is merely a *means* to acquiring virtue for oneself. For the good one seeks to possess for oneself is precisely to be the cause of what is good for another person for that person's sake.

One obstacle to seeing that there is nothing essentially egocentric about Plato's definition of love probably comes from our imagining an incompatibility between it and Paul's "Love seeketh not its own" (1 Corinthians 13:5). If Paul is interpreted to mean "Love consists in seeking only what is good for others, never for oneself," perhaps there is something to fear here. But as modern translations make clear, what Paul meant to say was, "Love does not insist on its own way" (*Revised Standard Version*), "Love is . . . never selfish" (*New English Bible*). To be selfish means to ignore or neglect the needs and wishes of others in pursuit of one's own good. Not being selfish, then, consists in not ignoring or neglecting others; it need not consist in not pursuing any goods of one's own at all. It would be an error to make it a necessary condition of love that the lover not be seeking what is good for himself. If this point seems obvious, the reader might consult Anders Nygren's *Agape and Eros*[11] to see the crucial role played in the minds of some scholars by the interpretation of Paul's remark I have criticized.

Vlastos's second objection is three tied together: (1) Plato ranks love of persons far below love of other things, such as absolute beauty; according to Vlastos, Plato does so because (2) Plato takes love of individuals in themselves to be impossible (only their good qualities can be loved); and partly because (3) Plato understands love of persons to consist in nothing more than love of absolute beauty by way of individual persons. The person we love is merely of use as an image of beauty, as a means to it.

It should be noted, in reply to (3), that Diotima does in a sense speak of using particular objects of affection, for example, other persons, to gain knowledge of absolute beauty; but the use to which they are to be put is as examples, instances of beauty, as Walter Hamilton's interpretive translation (*Symp*. 210d and 211c) suggests. If we use a person in this way, it does not follow that that person cannot really be loved by us, any more than our using Thomas Jefferson as an example of a great president implies that we do not really admire him. To use a person in that way implies that we do really admire or love him or, in Plato's case, that we do regard the person as a genuine instance of beauty.

Besides, when Diotima speaks of using examples of beauty, she is speaking of those who seek to be initiated into love's mysteries, who seek to learn what love really is. For that, a person must understand absolute beauty, and to achieve that, one must use the objects of one's love as examples, images of absolute beauty. In saying these things, Diotima seems to be thinking of a distinctive imaginative process, one people might engage in without being obliged to treat the objects of their affections merely as examples of something else. Certainly, a person might engage in such an activity without necessarily believing that all anyone is ever doing in loving is using the objects of love as examples of something else, or that using the objects of love as examples of something else is all we ought to do with them. Diotima's recommendation of this imaginative process does imply that if (and when) we wish to understand the mysteries of love, we must go about it by thinking of the beautiful objects to which we have formed attachments as examples of absolute beauty, leading us onward. But not everyone is always engaged in seeking this, and when not so engaged it would be absurd to treat others merely as instances of something else. It does not appear correct to attribute to Plato the view that we cannot love individual persons, or that we can love them only instrumentally, or that we ought to love them only instrumentally. Diotima does say, "this above all others . . . is the region where a man's life should be spent, in the contemplation of absolute beauty" (*Symp*. 211b). But that region is not the only region in which we can spend our lives, or even the only region in which we ought to spend our lives. Of all the regions in which life should be spent, it is the highest, Diotima says; so there are others.

If Vlastos's objections do not reveal any basic flaws in Plato's theory, this does not mean it is free of problems. The real trouble might be, not as Vlastos thought, that Plato ranks the love of persons far below other sorts of love, but that love itself, regardless of its object, has no intrinsic value for Plato, and so ranks below things that do. The value of love is entirely dependent on the worth of its object, Socrates emphasizes at the beginning of his discussion; love is at best a mighty helper to human nature, but nothing more.

The oddness of this cannot be avoided, though the logic of the argument might seem good; knowledge, virtue, and beauty seem to be inherently superior to the love we have for them. Whereas they are inherently good, our love for them seems to be good only insofar as it helps us to acquire them. As plausible and insightful as this might sound, it is nevertheless natural to protest that a life devoid of love would be worthless, and that love itself must therefore have some great inherent worth. Perhaps Pausanias was not so wrong after all to judge the deceived lover as he did.

But it would be a mistake to suppose that the only alternative to Plato's treatment of love as merely instrumental in value is the typical Greek view Socrates reacted against. That view saw value in love, but merely because it was pleasurable in itself and productive of excellence. Is there no intrinsic value to love higher than mere pleasure? One solution is to argue that the intrinsic value of love is to be found in its being constitutive of the soul; that is, to claim that love is the fundamental activity (or one of them) all souls are necessarily always engaged in, whatever else they might be doing. Then, the worth of love is established if the worth of the soul is. Such a claim is not part of Pausanias's commendation of love, nor is it part of any of the praises of love pronounced by the speakers in the *Symposium* before Socrates. Such a view of love as constitutive of the soul might seem to be the one Diotima expresses when she says

> Now do you suppose that this desire [for what is good] and this love are characteristics common to all men, and that all perpetually desire to be in possession of the good, or what? (*Symp*. 205a; see 205c)

But Socrates' response leaves it unclear whether he accepts the whole of this view: "That is exactly what I mean; they are common to all men." Diotima made two distinct claims, and Socrates, it seems, assented only to the weaker of the two, that is, to the claim that all persons love (at some time or other, we might add). This view is associated with the idea that every person has a master passion, love of money, physical prowess, or wisdom, that are all expressions of the desire for the good and for happiness, according to Diotima (*Symp*. 205d). This view requires that (1) all persons love at some time or other and (2) each person loves some one thing more than any other thing. It is consistent with these conditions that much of what people do is not done out of love at all. We must keep separate the stronger thesis that all human activity is motivated by love, as well as the thesis that love is the essential activity of the soul. These three are not equivalent, and Plato does not accept the last one. This we know from the *Phaedrus*, where the essential activity of soul is said to be eternal motion, self-motion (*Phaed*. 245e), of which love is perhaps a resemblance. True, love is "the greatest benefit that heaven can confer on us" (*Phaed*. 245b); but it is not constitutive of soul. Indeed, that love is said to be a type of madness conferred on us implies that we are able to exist without it. Does the claim that love is the greatest benefit that heaven can bestow on us imply that love must be greater than knowledge or justice, which are inherently good? The implication would succeed only if it were possible for knowledge or justice to be conferred. However, if we take seriously Plato's doctrine that knowledge is recollection, then even heaven cannot confer knowledge on us. It must be recollected. That justice cannot be conferred either follows from another of Plato's views, that virtue (hence justice) is a kind of knowledge.

J. M. E. Moravcsik considers, but dismisses, the idea that when the soul reaches the higher stages of the *Symposium*'s ascent "it no longer has passions or aspirations."[12] He is forced to consider this possibility because there is an evident absence of emotion steps in the higher stages of the ascent, in contrast to the lower ones. He concludes that though

> eros is still at work in the soul in the later stages, it no longer functions as a guide, thus not appearing in the sequence of steps described. No change in over-all aspiration is needed in order to lead the soul from the contemplation of the sciences to the comprehension of the Forms. Like Virgil in the "Divine Comedy" eros helps as a guide only until we reach the final stages; there contemplation becomes self-sufficient.[13]

But how eros can still be at work in the soul when contemplation becomes self-sufficient is not clear, since Moravcsik noted earlier that "in general one can say about the causal influence of eros on the mind that eros is what pushes the mind to new investigations."[14] Presumably, when contemplation becomes self-sufficient, eros ceases to be that which "pushes the mind to new investigations." (The Virgil analogy seems unsuited to Moravcsik's point, since Virgil vanishes when he ceases to serve as a guide [*Purgatorio*, Canto 30]; he does not continue to accompany Dante in some nonguidance role.)

A resolution of Plato's doubts about the role of love in the soul would have to take up and reply to his view of the emotions (and therefore of love) as alien to intellect, "the best part of the soul" (*Phaed*. 248b). Part of the answer might also draw on features of his theory of knowledge as recollection. That is, if there were something which, to be known at all, must be loved, it would be difficult to deny that loving it was intrinsically good if knowing it was held to be good in that way. Even if it were granted that knowing it was intrinsically better than loving it, the intrinsic value of loving it would not be undermined. Whether there are any such objects of love and knowledge is a question lying outside the scope of this essay, though it is at least plausible to say that God is such a being, since it is hard to make sense of the claim that someone knows God but does not love God.

Perhaps a different type of case of the following sort illustrates the same point. Suppose that the only way, the only conceivable way, to gain self-knowledge (or any other kind of knowledge) is through loving others. Further, suppose that loving others well is sufficient for self-knowledge. It would then be hard to deny that love was intrinsically valuable, if the knowledge depending on it was assumed to be intrinsically good. These cases suggest that Plato's worry about love's inherent worth rests on a presupposition hard to justify, namely, that any knowledge or other good reached as a result of love necessarily can be obtained or possessed without love. This presupposition must be false if, as I suggest, love is at least sometimes a necessary condition of recollection.

The subsequent history of philosophizing about love reflects some of these concerns; it is not until Plotinus, I believe, that love is conceived to be constitutive of the soul. He writes, "This being, Love, has from everlasting come into existence from the soul's aspiration toward the higher and the good, and he was there always, as long as Soul, too, existed."[15] Such an idea seems wholly absent in Aristotle's psychology; love is purely an ethical problem for him. Augustine's famous remark, "love is the weight by which I act. To whatever place I go, I am drawn to it by love,"[16] implies both that love is constitutive of soul (as he takes weight to be constitutive of body), as well as that whatever good he achieves, including knowledge, is the result of that love. Both of these thinkers can be seen as struggling with a problem inherited from Plato: of understanding love in such a way that its intrinsic as well as its instrumental value is made clear.

Notes

1. Jeffrey Henderson, *The Maculate Muse* (New Haven: Yale University Press, 1975), 205. Throughout, I employ Walter Hamilton's translation of Plato, *Symposium* (Harmondsworth, Eng.: Penguin, 1951) and Plato, *Phaedrus* (Harmondsworth, Eng.: Penguin, 1973).

2. Gregory Vlastos, "The Individual as an Object of Love in Plato," *Platonic Studies* (Princeton: Princeton University Press, 1973), 3-34.

3. *Ibid.*, 30.

4. *Ibid.*, 31.

5. *Ibid.*

6. *Ibid.*, 32.

7. *Ibid.*

8. *Nicomachean Ethics*, bk. 8, ch. 1.

9. This matter is discussed in detail by Alice Balint, "Love for the Mother and Mother Love," in Michael Balint, *Primary Love and Psycho-analytic Technique* (New York: Liveright, 1965), 91-108.

10. An excellent opposing interpretation can be found in W. W. Fortenbaugh, "Aristotle's Analysis of Friendship: Function and Analogy, Resemblance, and Focal Meaning," *Phronesis* 20:1 (1975): 51-62.

11. Anders Nygren, *Agape and Eros*, trans. Philip S. Watson (London: S. P. C. K., 1957).

12. J. M. E. Moravcsik, "Reason and Eros in the Ascent Passage of the *Symposium*," in J. P. Anton and G. L. Kustas, eds., *Essays in Ancient Greek Philosophy* (Albany: State University of New York Press, 1971), 285-302, at 294.

13. *Ibid.*

14. *Ibid.*, 292.

15. *Ennead* III.5.9, in *Plotinus*, vol. 3, trans. A. H. Armstrong (Cambridge, Mass.: Loeb Classical Library, 1967), 203.

16. Augustine, *Confessions,* trans. R. S. Pine-Coffin (Harmondsworth, Eng.: Penguin, 1961), 317 (bk. 13, ch. 9).

Hugh T. Wilder

Author of "The Language of Sex and the Sex of Language"
Paper presented at the Society for the Philosophy of Sex and Love
during the
Pacific Division Meeting of The American Philosophical Association
San Diego, Cal., 23 March 1979

Three

THE LANGUAGE OF SEX AND THE SEX OF LANGUAGE

Hugh T. Wilder

It has long been popular to compare sex with language. The comparison is plausible and suggestive: sexual activity and linguistic activity both seem to be intentionally communicative, both foster interpersonal intimacy and understanding, both have a grammar of sorts, and so on. Robert Solomon has recently given a philosophical defense of this comparison,[1] to the detriment, I believe, of both sex and language. Both deserve better treatment, which I hope to provide in this paper. I will explore the comparisons between sex and language through a close reading of Solomon's phonocentric view of language, which results, I will argue, in a repressive and sexist view of sex. This view of sex is clear in two claims made by Solomon that we will look at closely: that heterosexual intercourse is the "paradigm of sexual activity,"[2] and that masturbation is a "deviation."[3] Through this study of Solomon's treatment of sex and language, I will be offering a richer understanding of the comparison between sex and language.

1.

In his writing on sexuality, Solomon is attempting to develop a theory of "natural" or "paradigmatic" sex. He says that his

> starting point will be that human sexuality has its own "natural purpose," its own "nature," apart from any *further* purposes attributed to our creator, and apart from any biological function of increasing the numbers of an already too numerous natural kind.[4]

Natural or paradigmatic sex is sex that serves this natural purpose; perverted sex is sex that does not.

The natural purpose of sex is, according to Solomon, interpersonal communication. Interpersonal communication is also the essential purpose of language. Therefore, he claims, sex is a language: communication is the aim, the body is the medium.[5] Sex that does not serve the purpose of interpersonal communication is deviant sex, just as language not serving the same purpose is deviant language. Communication essentially involves more than one person; therefore, natural sexual activities essentially involve more than one person. Masturbation is not interpersonal communication; therefore, Solomon argues, masturbation is "borderline"[6] sex, a deviation, sex misfired.

2.

Granting Solomon's major thesis, that sex is a language, we can learn about the nature of sex by studying the nature of language. More immediately, we might learn about Solomon's conception of sex by studying his conception of language. Solomon gives an instrumentalist analysis of language: language is an instrument serving the end of interpersonal communication, and it has succeeded in serving this end when mutual understanding is produced. Since sex is language, Solomon not surprisingly also endorses an instrumentalist analysis of sex.

But the essential purpose of language is *not* interpersonal communication. Claims about the essential purposes of language can be interpreted in either of two ways: according to the stronger interpretation, language not serving the putative essential purpose is not even language; according to the weaker, language not serving the putative essential purpose is deviant or abnormal language. While which interpretation Solomon intends is not clear, this is relatively unimportant; the thesis, that the essential purpose of language is communication, is false on both readings. If it were true, many perfectly good, nondeviant uses of language would be marked as deviant or even nonlinguistic, as not serving the putative essential purpose of language. The issue here is twofold: does language have an essential purpose and, if it does, what is it? Although the issues obviously cannot be resolved here, I will argue that, especially in the context of comparing language with sex, language is best understood as having *no essential* purpose.

Those who believe that language does have an essential purpose fall roughly into two traditions: the instrumentalist and formalist. Instrumentalists (Solomon, Searle, Austin, and many other post-Wittgensteinians) claim that language is an instrument, essentially used for communication. The formalists (Descartes, Humboldt, Chomsky) claim that language is essentially a means of thought and self-expression.[7] As Chomsky points out, when the instrumentalists limit normal, nondeviant communication to *interpersonal* communication, as Solomon does, they are wrong. To say that soliloquies are nonlinguistic or deviant is absurd; thinking out loud, talking to express and clarify one's thoughts, whether or not anything is communicated, are normal linguistic activities.

A second argument against the instrumentalist view is that even if the concept of communication is extended to include communication with one's self (that is, thinking in words), still, the intent of normal language is not always to communicate.[8] Sometimes we use language to deceive, sometimes to fill embarrassing silences, sometimes to play a part in a ritual (to use Chomsky's examples);[9] in these and countless other normal, nondeviant cases, language is being used, while nothing is communicated and there is not even an intention to communicate anything.

The last argument could be used (although it is not by those I have called linguistic "formalists") to support the view that language has no inherent purpose. Our uses of language have as wide a variety of purposes as human beings can have, and none of these purposes is inherent in language; none is more normal, in either a normative or statistical sense, than any other. The linguistic formalists are just as wrong as the instrumentalists. To cite just a few examples: to speak a part in a verbal ritual, to read aloud, to transcribe, summarize, and even write a text are all perfectly good "uses of language," but are hardly ever expressions of one's thoughts, as the formalists might have us believe. We have many different reasons for saying and writing what we do; sometimes our reasons are so vague and amorphous as to be nonexistent. Language has no one purpose to the exclusion of others, unless one so general could be found that it was utterly trivial.

The rubric "sex is language" takes on new significance in this noninstrumentalist and nonessentialist view of language. One traditional support of the phallocentric view of sex is knocked out. On the phallocentric view, sexuality in general is understood as "normal" (Freudian) male sexuality: that is, sex with a direction, a point, a central thrust, a purpose; sex that has results, sex with a clear criterion of success and completion; sex modeled on male ejaculation.[10] This theme will be further developed in the next few pages; the way has already been opened, however, for a nonsexist, nonphallocentric conception of sex. Sex is still language, but perhaps aimless language. The concepts of directionality, thrust, goal, success, and completion drop out, or at least lose potency. Sex is no longer necessarily productive: perhaps, to be extreme, not even productive of male ejaculate.

The language of sex, as any language, can have any number of different purposes, but it has no essential purpose. Therefore no one sexual activity can be said to serve the putative purpose of sex/language, and no activity can be said to be deviant because it does not serve the putative purpose.[11] In particular, conceiving sex as language no longer provides support to those, including Solomon, who elevate heterosexual intercourse to paradigmatic sex while derogating masturbation as a "borderline case" of sexual activity.

3.

The second main problem with Solomon's conception of language is that language is assumed to be entirely spoken and never written. This "phonocentrism" leads to a narrow, repressive conception of the language of sex. It also leads to a sexist conception because, as Jacques Derrida has shown, linguistic phonocentrism is one aspect of philosophical phallocentrism that becomes apparent once philosophy has made the linguistic turn.

Solomon is not alone among philosophers in valuing speech over writing and in conceiving of language exclusively in terms of speech; as Derrida has shown, Western philosophers from Plato to Austin have, with few exceptions, shared this bias.[12] The bias in favor of speech is traced by Derrida to "the doctrine of presence," the pervasive search for Being, which has animated Western philosophy from the beginning. Being is truth, beauty and goodness; the closer we are to it and the clearer we are about it, the better. Intuition, immediacy, and clarity are valued in the search; opacity, indirection, and inference are risky; aimlessness is anathema.

The doctrine of presence is hierarchical. Being is at the top: the really real, the object of all inquiry. Thought is (better or worse) representation of Being, speech is representation of thought, and writing is representation of speech. If proximity to Being is good, writing is bad. This hierarchy is explicit in Aristotle:

> Spoken words are the symbols of mental experience and written words are the symbols of spoken words. Just as all men have not the same writing, so all men have not thc same speech sounds, but the mental experiences, which they directly symbolize, are the same for all, as also are those things of which our experiences are the images.[13]

The doctrine of presence dictates a program for scientific and philosophical writing. Science is the attempt to represent Being correctly, and philosophy is the metascientific attempt to represent representation correctly. Both scientific and philosophical writing aspire to the lucidity of speech and to proximity with Being. Such writing-as-speech is self-destructive, in the sense that good scientific and philosophical writing is clear, invisible, transparent; it denies its existence as writing in its attempt to let Being shine through.

Normal scientific language is phallocentric.[14] Such language, whether speech or writing-as-speech, is used as an instrument, to get something or to get somewhere else. It is not important or pleasurable in itself; it is important as a means to the end of mirroring Being. It is language with a point. It is a way of "getting off": getting off *itself*, getting onto or closer to Being. The language that has the best chance of getting off is spoken language. If one's goal is Being, to begin with writing is risky and dangerous; the path through representations of representations of representations is too easy to miss.

If normal scientific language is phallocentric, writing-as-writing (writing without aspirations to speech) is masturbatory. It is not nonsexy masturbation for quick orgasm, but masturbation as aimless self-pleasuring.[15] Writing-as-writing is opaque and dense rather than transparent; it is nonself-destructive; it is writing content with its status as writing; it is playful and indirect rather than serious and direct; aimless and pointless, never finished, infinitely readable and interpretable rather than definitively communicative.

If this discussion, invited by Solomon, of the sex of language seems extravagant, one only need read for justification the phallocentric writers on language cited by Derrida. The terms of their elevation of speech and derogation of writing are the same as philosophers' elevation of heterosexual intercourse (which is described, all too often, as male evacuation lust coupled with female submissiveness) and derogation of masturbation. Plato: writing is a drug. Levi-Strauss: writing is perfidy. Saussure: writing is to speech as a photograph is to reality (compare Sartre's "masturbation counterfeits intercourse").[16] Rousseau: "languages are meant to be spoken, writing serves only as a supplement to speech"; writing is "dangerous," "scandalous," "perverse," even "a sin."[17] Writing is a cheat: writing-as-writing makes no pretense of representing Being. (Compare Sartre's "dishonest masturbator": the masturbator by choice, the one who can get away, *off*, without the real thing, that is, without intersubjectivity.) Speech carries the burden of purpose; writing-as-writing is light and free. It is therefore too easy, seductive, and dangerous.

4.

With this Derridean understanding of the sex of language, we can return to Solomon. For him, sex is language, language is speech, good ("natural") sex is speech, and masturbation as far from "natural" sex as writing is from speech. Solomon's probably unwitting censure of writing parallels his censure of masturbation.

Solomon assumes that language is essentially spoken language and that sexual language is the sexual equivalent of speech. He writes: "sexuality is primarily a means of communicating with other people, a way of *talking* to them."[18] The language of sex has its own "phonetics," but no alphabet.[19] The language of sex is "*essentially* an activity performed with other people."[20] It is plausible (but false, I believe) to think that spoken language is essentially interpersonal; it is obviously false that *written* language is essentially interpersonal. In fact, an argument could be given showing that writing is best understood as a private activity, not surprisingly, on the model of masturbation: both are done by oneself for oneself, and are perhaps shared and observed by others, but usually not.

Solomon's treatment of sexual perversion and aberration, as well as of refined and offensive sex, provides further illustrations of his phonocentric view of the language of sex. Consider, first, masturbation: a "borderline case" of sex, for Solomon. Solomon explains masturbation mostly in terms of verbal analysis: masturbation "is essentially speaking to oneself," "muttering to oneself," the sexual equivalent of a soliloquy, "an inability or a refusal to say what one wants to say."[21] No wonder masturbation is not quite sex: neither is refusal to say what one wants to say speech. Solomon does use one writing metaphor: masturbation is like writing a letter and not mailing it. This metaphor is intended to support the claim that masturbation is a borderline case of sexual language. But in this the metaphor fails; writing a letter and not mailing it, not even intending to mail it, is a fine case of *written* language.

Consider also Solomon's treatment of sexual aberrations. Fetishism is "talking to someone else's shoes," bestiality is "like discussing Spinoza with a moderately intelligent sheep;"[22] a voyeur is "someone with nothing to say;" in sexual promiscuity "one risks carrying over from one conversation gestures that are appropriate to another," and group sex "creates the serious danger of simultaneous incoherent polylogues," but "offers the rare possibility of linguistic forms unavailable with fewer voices."[23] Sexual aberrations are *verbal* aberrations.

Further, refined sex, for example, communicative, nonanimalistic sex,[24] is always compared to verbal language; one of the few times Solomon switches to sex-as-written language is when he is describing offensive sex:

> blatant sexual propositions and subway exhibitionism are offensive . . because they are vulgar, the equivalent of an antipoetry poet who writes an entire poem consisting of a single vulgar word, or a comedian who, unable to handle condensation and understatement, has to spell out his obscene jokes explicitly.[25]

Solomon also writes (admittedly, to lift a line out of context): "The cry of perversion with regard to body language is very much like that of censorship with regard to the written word."[26] This is precisely my complaint: Solomon's probably unwitting censorship of the written word from his conception of language has as its sexual analogue his own censorship of masturbation from the realm of the sexual.

Solomon also equates what he thinks are the genuine sexual perversions with the Austinian verbal "infelicities" of lying and insincerity.[27] Perversions *are* sexual, and they need not be vulgar or bad in any sense;[28] hence they receive treatment as *verbal* infelicities. For example, on Solomon's view to entertain private fantasies while having sex with another is a perversion, because this is a form of insincerity in the language of sex. But fantasizing while having sex, whether fantasizing other partners, other situations, other kinds of sex, and so forth, is not a perversion, especially not the central case of perversion it turns out to be on Solomon's view. The problem is, again, that Solomon's phonocentric view of language is too narrow: in this case, it leads him to classify as perverse something that is not. Lying and insincerity are fairly straightforward notions in spoken language; not so in written language, however. As Derrida has written in response to Austin,[29] the idea that lying and insincerity are infelicities in written language is nonsense; most literature depends essentially on what would be lying and insincerity in verbal contexts. Had Solomon compared sex with *language*, spoken and written, instead of speech, he might have been able to develop a less repressive and nonsexist view of sex and its aberrations.

5.

Solomon's instrumentalist and phonocentric conception of the language of sex leads to a conception of sex that is peculiarly nonsexy. Sex is a language with communication as its aim; further, normal sex is restricted to communication with others, and some communications are evidently taboo. Solomon writes: sexual communication "is *essentially* an activity performed with other people";[30] the messages communicated in sexual language are "*limited to* interpersonal attitudes and feelings."[31] These limitations on sex and on language generally only make sense on the assumption that Solomon has some sort of grudge against diaries, journals, any manner of self-expression of personal (as opposed to interpersonal) feelings, as well as against masturbation. It might seem extravagant to be defending the writing of diaries as genuine linguistic activity, as extravagant, as I hope it seems, to be defending masturbation as genuine sex. After reading Solomon, both seem to be necessary.

Solomon begins "Sexual Paradigms" with the announcement that heterosexual intercourse is "the paradigm of sexual activity"; toward the end of the paper he offers his "linguistic" derogation of masturbation. The point of sex, for Solomon, is to communicate messages. While refinement is good, anything that inhibits communication is bad. As with male sexuality, success in Solomon's verbal sexual encounters is well defined and easily recognizable: reception and comprehension of the message is all that counts. Incomprehension is sex misfired; deliberate obfuscation of the message is perverse.

Not only is sex not important in itself, or at least not as important as the messages communicated; Solomon even argues that it is tasteless to think that the aim of sex is enjoyment.[32] It might well be misleading to think that the aim of sex is enjoyment; but when this view is combined with Solomon's instrumentalist view of sexual language, one is left with a repressive, stereotypically male view of sex: straight heterosexual intercourse, little dallying around, finished when the man comes, and if the proceedings are pleasurable at all, the pleasure is in the coming. If one insists that sex is language, then sex must be seen as including noninstrumental written language (Derrida's writing-as-writing) if one is to allow oneself to see the sexiness of dalliance, indirection, softness, pointlessness, density, playfulness, and endless incompletion. Masturbation, among other things, happily turns out to be real sex.

Solomon's instrumentalist analysis of sexuality is repressive: any activity not serving the interests of interpersonal communication is stigmatized as deviant. For some unexplained reason, heterosexual intercourse is claimed to be a paradigm case of interpersonal communication. Obviously, cases of heterosexual intercourse are not always cases of interpersonal communication. And other actions and practices (forms of dyadic homosexual lovemaking, for example) are often perfectly good cases of interpersonal communication. Further, in denying the validity of masturbation as sex, Solomon is denying to both men and women a primary source of sexual self-discovery and independence. This denial weighs most heavily on women: in celebrating heterosexual intercourse at the expense of masturbation, Solomon is defending exclusively a kind of sex in which traditionally the shots are called by the man.

Notice that from the instrumentalist point of view heterosexual intercourse and masturbation are equally effective *for men*: both virtually always result in male ejaculation. Masturbation is often a reliable source of orgasms *for women*; a much more reliable source, at least in our culture, than heterosexual intercourse. Further, male masturbation is also perceived by men as dangerous *for men*: it is linked in most men's thoughts with castration fears. Most importantly, female masturbation is also perceived by men as dangerous *for men*, for a different reason: it restores sexual power and independence to women. To glorify heterosexual intercourse while derogating masturbation turns out to be a subtle kind of sexism.

To give up instrumentalist analyses of language and sex is not to deny all similarities between the two. Sex is still comparable with language in many ways. For example, language can be used to communicate, to express ideas and feelings, to produce ideas and feelings, to fill silences, to start conversations, to end conversations, to inform, to entertain, to deceive; it can be an instrument of pleasure, of pain, of goodness, of vice; it can be refined and offensive, boring and exciting, pointed and pointless. So, too, can sex. To limit sex to one kind of thing, serving one kind of purpose, degrades sex and degrades the language with which it is being compared.

Notes

1. Robert Solomon, "Sexual Paradigms," *Journal of Philosophy* 71:11 (1974): 336-45; reprinted in Alan Soble, ed., *Philosophy of Sex* (Totowa, N.J.: Littlefield, Adams, 1980 [1991]), 89-98 [53-62]. Subsequent page references are to the 1980 reprint. See also Robert Solomon, "Sex and Perversion," in Robert Baker and Frederick Elliston, eds., *Philosophy and Sex* (Buffalo: Prometheus, 1975), 268-87.

2. Solomon, "Sexual Paradigms," 90.

3. Solomon, "Sex and Perversion," 283.

4. *Ibid.*, 271.

5. *Ibid.*, 279ff. and "Sexual Paradigms," 96.

6. Solomon, "Sex and Perversion," 280. Solomon specifically writes in this passage that "autoeroticism . . . is at best . . . a borderline case" of sex. Later in the same essay Solomon distinguishes between "masturbation as autoeroticism" and "masturbation as narcissism" (283). Both are deviations, secondary to or derivative from interpersonal communicative sex. [Note added 1995.]

7. Noam Chomsky, *Cartesian Linguistics* (New York: Harper and Row, 1966). See also his *Reflections on Language* (New York: Random House, 1975), 55ff., and *Problems of Knowledge and Freedom* (New York: Random House, 1971), 19.

8. Janice Moulton makes this same point against Solomon without herself giving up the instrumentalist analysis of language and sex: "Solomon's comparison of sexual behavior with linguistic behavior is handicapped by the limited view he has about their purposes. Language has more purposes than transmitting information. . . . [It] has a phatic function to evoke feelings and attitudes. Language is often used to produce a shared experience" ("Sexual Behavior: Another Position," in Soble, *Philosophy of Sex*, 110-18 [1991, 63-71]).

9. Chomsky, *Problems of Knowledge and Freedom*, 19.

10. Richard Rorty, "Derrida on Language, Being and Abnormal Philosophy," *Journal of Philosophy* 74 (1977): 673-81. My understanding of "the sex of language" is borrowed from Jacques Derrida; Rorty's article is an excellent introduction to this aspect of Derrida's writing.

11. However, charges of deviance might be sustained on other, nonteleological grounds.

12. Jacques Derrida, "Signature Event Context," in Samuel Weber and Henry Sussman, eds., *Glyph I* (Baltimore: Johns Hopkins University Press, 1977), 172-97.

13. Aristotle, *De Interpretatione,* in Richard McKeon, ed., *The Basic Works of Aristotle* (New York: Random House, 1941), I/16a/3 (p. 40). See also Jacques Derrida, *Of Grammatology*, trans. Gayatri Chakravorty Spivak (Baltimore: Johns Hopkins University Press, 1974), 11.

14. Rorty, "Derrida on Language," 681.

15. This important distinction is developed by several contemporary writers on masturbation. See, for example, Bernie Zilbergeld, *Male Sexuality: A Guide to Sexual Fulfillment* (Boston: Little, Brown, 1978), 139; Barry McCarthy, *What You (Still) Don't Know About Male Sexuality* (New York: Crowell Press, 1977), ch. 3.

16. See R. D. Laing, *Self and Others*, 2nd ed. (Middlesex, Eng.: Penguin, 1969), 59.

17. The examples are from Michael Wood, "Deconstructing Derrida," *New York Review of Books* 24 (3 March 1977), 27-30, and Derrida, *Of Grammatology*, 141-64.

18. Solomon, "Sex and Perversion," 279 (emphasis added).

19. Solomon, "Sexual Paradigms," 96.

20. Solomon, "Sex and Perversion," 279 (emphasis added).

21. *Ibid.*, 283.

22. Solomon, "Sexual Paradigms," 97.

23. Solomon, "Sex and Perversion," 286.

24. *Ibid.*, 285.

25. *Ibid.*

26. *Ibid.*, 284.

27. Solomon, "Sex and Perversion," 286, and "Sexual Paradigms," 98.

28. Solomon, "Sexual Paradigms," 98.

29. Derrida, "Signature Event Context," 191.

30. Solomon, "Sex and Perversion," 279.
31. Solomon, "Sexual Paradigms," 96 (emphasis added).
32. *Ibid.*, 94.

Flo Leibowitz
(photograph: Wendy Madar)

Author of "Professor Wilder on Sexuality"
Paper presented at the Society for the Philosophy of Sex and Love
during the
Pacific Division Meeting of The American Philosophical Association
San Diego, Cal., 23 March 1979

Four

"SEXUAL PARADIGMS" TWENTY YEARS LATER

Flo Leibowitz

According to Hugh Wilder,[1] the model of human sexuality that Robert Solomon provides in "Sexual Paradigms" is phallocentric, puritanical, and sexist. The source of these flaws, Wilder thinks, is the essentialism in the model, which assumes that the purpose of sexual behavior is communicative and makes deviant any form of sexuality whose purpose is different. Further, these flaws are a consequence of Solomon's model of language, which is systematically biased against writing and unduly elevates the spoken word. Wilder is particularly concerned with the lack of attention to the ritual functions of language and, primarily, of linguistic play, and with the consequences this has for models of sexuality. It seems to me that these objections go wrong from the start.

First, goal-directed sex is not phallocentric and sexist merely because it is goal-directed, since not all goals are phallocentric and sexist. In fact, personal expression for its own sake is phallocentric in Wilder's sense, in that the expresser emits and the response of the audience matters not. Yet this is what he fears is lost. Solomon's language of sex is goal-directed, but that is a strength of the model, not a weakness, since goal-directed activities are associated with complex intentions. The ritual functions of language are not emphasized because the ritual aspects of sexuality are not what Solomon's theory is about. He is concerned with interpersonal authenticity. And social rituals typically are communicative as well as constitutive. For example, the rituals of knighting and of marrying change a person's social and legal standing in complex ways, yet their associated ritual utterances are also public proclamations. The ritual utterances of knighting proclaim that this person is worthy of respect, and the ritual utterances of marrying proclaim that these two people are no longer sexually available to others.

Solomon's model assigns a purpose to sexuality, and this is what it is intended to do. The question is, what purposes are being privileged, and is this privilege justified? Early in "Sexual Paradigms," Solomon tells us what the project is: to characterize and criticize the sexual ideology of social liberals in order to improve it and make it more timely. This ideology had elevated individual gratification to the point of obscuring the interpersonal dimensions of liberal sexual behavior, or so the project assumes, and that is why it needs reformulation. He writes:

> There was a time, and it was not so long ago and it may come soon again, when sexuality required defending. It had to be argued that we had a

> right to sex, not for any purpose other than our personal enjoyment. But that defense has turned stale, and sexual deprivation is no longer our problem. The "swollen bladder" model of repressed sexuality may have been convincing in sex-scared bourgeois Vienna of 1905, but not today, where the problem is not sexual deprivation but sexual dissolution. The fetishism of the orgasm, now shared by women as well as men, threatens our sex lives with becoming antipersonal and mechanical, anxiety-filled athletic arenas with mutual multiple orgasms its goal. Behind much of this unhappiness and anxiety, ironically, stands the liberal defense of sexuality as enjoyment.[2]

It is easy to laugh this off as yet another baby boomer finally getting wisdom, but, as usual, the easy course is not the right one. Sexual tastes typically change with a person's age, just as David Hume thought artistic tastes do, and for many of the same kinds of reasons. But there is a deeper basis to Solomon's analysis. It assumes that the sexual practices of social liberals are genuinely different from those of conservatives (sexual authoritarians) and from those of sexual libertarians, and it assumes that the liberal practices are or ought to be preferable. Second, it assumes that forms of sexuality are constituted by the sentiments they express. This is, incidentally, an insight that Solomon shares with Catharine MacKinnon,[3] whose feminist analysis also emphasizes the role of sentiments about the other in the constitution of sexuality. MacKinnon's analysis is different in aiming to present a real, rather than an ideal, sexual sentiment, and the paradigm sexual sentiment in her model is a desire to dominate the other. This is a sentiment that Solomon's picture would associate with conservative forms of sexuality, and not with sexuality generally.

Wilder says that this authoritarian sentiment, or something unwholesomely like it, is ultimately the basis of Solomon's paradigm. But it is not. Pushing someone around wouldn't merely be communication on Solomon's model, it would be outright aggression, and that is not his model of sexuality. On his model, sexuality is paradigmatic when it expresses the model sentiment, which is a desire to *discover* the other. This model is not sexist, it is partnerist and, as a result, the model is open to important forms of sexual diversity. On this picture, homosexuality is not a perversion, and ethically its status is no different from heterosexuality. Thus construed, neither of these major forms of sexuality is intrinsically superior to the other; you judge the ethics of a sexual practice by whether it is conversation or exploitation. Hence, the concerns in "Sexual Paradigms" about the insincere.

Solomon's emphasis on discovering the other makes self-pleasuring sexuality deviant, but this is not the problem Wilder says it is. Masturbation is deviant because it is self-absorbed sex and, as such, it is not based on curiosity about the other, which is the model sentiment. Incidentally, this is why keeping a diary is not a good analogy on Solomon's model even for playful sex: the purpose of keeping a diary is self-discovery, but the purpose of sex, in Solomon's liberalism, is not. People keep diaries to satisfy their curiosity about their own thinking, not to discover someone else's. A person might *read* Samuel Pepys's diary to find out about Samuel Pepys's England, but that is the difference between writing your own diary and reading the diary of someone else. Reading a diary is intrinsically voyeuristic. Writing a diary is not. And, according to Solomon, neither is sex. On Solomon's model, sexuality is paradigmatically conveyed in person, hence the privileging of spoken language. Letters and notes are a part of sexual relationships, and they have their own enjoyments, as a minimal literary or cinematic imagination will tell you. But they are typically a prelude to a further development, or a placeholder in times of absence, as the books and movies tell you, too.

Wilder objects that play is not accommodated in Solomon's sexual paradigm; but it *is* accommodated, in the context of discovering-the-other. Solomon's model of sexuality appears to reflect a romantic ideal much like the one that Stanley Cavell later attributed to the comedies of remarriage.[4] Discovering the other is a basic theme in these films, and in romantic comedies generally; not incidentally, they depict the discovery business with special attention to its verbal and playful dimensions. Still, the classic film analogy brings with it a new worry: you wonder whether the picture of discovery in Solomon is overly innocent and sentimental, just as you wonder about the films themselves. In the end, there is a basis for concern about the role of play in Solomon's model. The discovery of the other is serious business in some contexts, for example, when it is part of institutionalizing diversity and pluralism as the basis of a society. So, romantic comedy notwithstanding, there might be an irreducible gravity in the concept of discovering others that makes the role of play in social relations, and by extension in sexuality, more complicated and more vexing than it initially appears to be.

"Sexual Paradigms" first appeared more than twenty years ago, and you wonder whether the times that Solomon referred to have come around again, and whether the enjoyment of sex again requires defending. In some respects, they have and it does. Homosexuality requires defending, especially in areas of the country where antigay ordinances and ballot measures are the fashion, and the defense that is called for goes deep. Liberals are being called upon to defend not "merely" gay sex but the legitimacy of personal intimacy in same-sex couples. Even the Victorians supported families, marriage, and monogamy, yet gay couples who subscribe to these familiar ideals are regarded by sexual conservatives as depraved. Such is the climate that the conservative beachhead in value theory has created. In justifying gay monogamy and gay parents, Solomon's model is still timely.

How well does this sexual paradigm address the issues of the day for heterosexual women? Its relevance is mixed, because deprivation of sexuality is not the issue today. When a woman is sexually harassed on the job or in school, it is not a suppression of her sex; rather, this is her reduction to nothing but her sex in a context where she is engaging in other forms of social expression. Sexual violence is like this, too; insofar as it is sexual, it is not a suppression of sex, it is being drowned in it. To widen the scope of concern somewhat, Naomi Wolf might be right about the beauty myth,[5] and discovery of the other, Solomon-style, is not likely to happen until the myth falls away. Solomon's paradigm addresses the emotional satisfactions of sexual relationships for and with persons of any gender, and it assumes that this satisfaction depends on mutuality. In this way, it presents an ideal that is still appealing, if anyone out there in men-from-Mars-and-women-from-Venus-land still believes it is possible. It is an ideal that has probably been paid more lip service than carried out in practice, but that might be why "Sexual Paradigms" was written in the first place.

Notes

1. Hugh Wilder, "The Language of Sex and the Sex of Language," this volume, 23-31.

2. Robert Solomon, "Sexual Paradigms," *Journal of Philosophy* 71:11 (1974): 336-45; reprinted in Alan Soble, ed., *Philosophy of Sex* (Totowa, N.J.: Littlefield, Adams, 1980 [1991]), 89-98 [53-62]; at, in [1991], 55-6.

3. See, for example, Catharine MacKinnon, *Feminism Unmodified* (Cambridge, Mass.: Harvard University Press, 1987).

4. Stanley Cavell, *Pursuits of Happiness: The Hollywood Comedy of Remarriage* (Cambridge, Mass.: Harvard University Press, 1981).

5. Naomi Wolf, *The Beauty Myth: How Images of Female Beauty Are Used Against Women* (New York: William Morrow, 1991).

Ann Garry
(photograph: California State University at Los Angeles)

Author of "Why Are Love and Sex Philosophically Interesting?"
Paper presented at the Society for the Philosophy of Sex and Love
during the
Eastern Division Meeting of The American Philosophical Association
New York, N.Y., 28 December 1979

Five

WHY ARE LOVE AND SEX PHILOSOPHICALLY INTERESTING?[1]

Ann Garry

1. Introduction

Love and sex interest most philosophers as part of their personal lives, some philosophers in their therapy, and a few philosophers as subjects worthy of serious philosophical attention. To use one's philosophical energy thinking and teaching about love and sex has obvious benefits. One's life seems more integrated than usual: it is pleasant when one's work concerns problems about which one spends time and emotional energy in daily life. Because students as well as professors use their time and energy in this way, teaching issues concerning love and sex is worthwhile and enjoyable.[2] We all have experience to draw on to test our philosophical theories and analyses; we can tell more easily (than we can with problems of reference or certainty) when important philosophers have gone wrong, are not addressing themselves to the hardest questions, or are simply saying silly things; we can see political, cultural, and religious biases; and we can appreciate that we hold philosophical opinions and understand why clarity about these subjects is useful to us.

In addition, fascinating methodological problems arise concerning the ways one deals with love and sex in philosophy, in psychology (as well as in psychotherapy), and in feminist theory (as well as in feminist consciousness raising). A related benefit of teaching love and sex is evident here: one can include feminist writings as an integral part of a course. Feminist philosophers not only question some of the traditional methodological assumptions (such as the possibility of doing value neutral philosophical analysis; and the differences among the philosophical, the political, and the personal in these matters), but also consider the political assumptions and values underlying our personal relationships and the institutions surrounding them.

Given all these benefits, why do philosophers shy away from writing and teaching about love and sex? The following are some of the replies I have received. Why are *these* benefits? I do not want my life integrated; how can I escape from my personal problems if my philosophical work is not removed from my everyday life? And even if I want to deal with my own problems concerning love and sex, it would be a mistake for me to believe that philosophical thinking about them can replace confronting my emotions and dealing with the problems on that level. Why divert my attention by thinking about the conceptual relationship between love and commitment when what I really want is to get a divorce? Furthermore, I've been told, philosophy classes should avoid the danger of engaging in pseudo-therapy or consciousness raising: separate problems should be kept separate. Personal/emotional problems about sex or love should be kept separate from political problems about how love has been institutionalized and used to keep women "in their place," which in turn should be kept separate from conceptual points about love.

Finally, why would I want to undertake a course in which the methodology is unclear and in which personal feelings create problems in the classroom? Breaking new ground methodologically is never easy, and is especially troublesome in messy, touchy areas such as love and sex. How can we tell the difference between a philosophical and a psychological claim about the relationship between sexual fidelity and jealousy? What are philosophical criticisms of the institution of marriage, what are political ones? And to discuss these subjects in a classroom will stir up students' feelings: they will be upset, angry, excited, depressed, want to tell personal stories, be tempted to invade my privacy, and who knows what else. Are the philosophical issues about love and sex so interesting that I should want to deal with all these problems?[3]

I think so. After I give the reasons for this answer, which constitute most of the paper, I will make some suggestions for dealing with some of the practical problems that arise when teaching this kind of subject matter.

2. Philosophy, Psychology, and Feminism

In order to determine what is *philosophically* interesting about love and sex, it would help to distinguish what would traditionally interest us as philosophers from what would interest us personally or as feminists or as psychologists. One way to try to distinguish these categories, if it is possible at all, is to utilize some of Wittgenstein's remarks: "The work of a philosopher consists in assembling reminders for a particular purpose." Something of which we need to remind ourselves is "something that we know when no one asks us, but no longer know when we are supposed to give an account of it . . . (and it is obviously something of which for some reason it is difficult to remind oneself)."[4] To talk about assembling reminders seems appropriate not only for some philosophers' work on love and sex, but also for the work we do as feminists or psychologists. We can assemble many kinds of reminders about love and sex for many different purposes. We need to look at what the purposes are for feminists, psychologists, and philosophers, and why assembling these reminders is difficult. Talk about reminders is further appropriate because much of the work about love and sex is done piecemeal, in fragments; we often can remind ourselves of only a few things at a time. Especially where methodological problems are difficult and emotions are easily stirred, it helps to make progress where one can.

I will discuss feminist theorists and consciousness raising groups, psychologists and psychotherapy groups, and philosophers, in that order. To do this requires me to generalize and oversimplify in ways that make me very uncomfortable. People within each category vary tremendously; in addition, some people fit in at least two categories, for example, feminist and philosopher. For ease of comparison, I am emphasizing groups' activities rather than the work of individuals. The questions I will ask about each category are these. What kinds of things are the theorists saying? What kind of activity is going on in the groups (what kind of reminders are they assembling)? What purpose does the group have? What impact does the group have in terms of personal, political, or intellectual change?

3. Feminist Theorists and Consciousness Raising Groups

Although feminist theory can be more or less empirical, conceptual, or speculative, any feminist theory about love and sex would deal in some way with the political and institutional underpinnings of love and sex. "Sexual politics" and "the personal is the political" are not just catchy phrases: personal relationships have political bases and implications. In addition, it is important to feminists to call attention to biases and sexist assumptions in traditional academic methodologies. An example of a largely speculative feminist issue is what might happen to sexual attraction between people (of any combination of sexes) if society were radically different: if people did not have traditional sex roles, if inequalities were erased, and if the sex or gender of one's lover were irrelevant to one's attraction. An empirical problem might be whether there is any change in sexual behavior or emotional patterns in families in which there have been abrupt changes in roles performed by men and women (for example, wage earning, housekeeping, child care).

Although some of the same kinds of topics could come up in a consciousness raising group, participation in such a group is not the same as discussing feminist theory or teaching a class in feminist theory. The purposes differ, though they overlap. In each case, feminists want to improve the position of all women; theorists work on the theoretical foundations for action, realizing that neither theory nor action exists alone. A consciousness raising group attempts to put feminist theory into practice. In it, women aim to develop trust in and respect for themselves and the others in the group. It is a small structured group whose discussion is focused not on personal "coping" solutions to individual members' problems, but on the common problems of women and the shared political, social, economic, and emotional circumstances from which our experiences arise. Because one woman's problems are not solved until the condition of all women is improved, consciousness raising groups discuss experiences for the purpose of fostering social change, and function as a microcosm of such change.[5]

Suppose both a consciousness raising group and a group discussing feminist theory were assembling reminders on the subject of the possibility of nondestructive heterosexual love relationships in a situation of economic and political inequality. Although both would be doing it for the purpose of bettering the condition of women, the procedures differ. In a consciousness raising group, individual women would recount their experiences in love relationships, thinking about what impact inequality or economic dependence had on them. The group would look for generalizations from these experiences or for their political as well as emotional bases. To assemble these reminders might be difficult: women have been isolated from each others' experiences; other people close to the women in the group (for example, their lovers) might find newly expressed anger or other feelings hard to accept and might not see the validity of some of the reminders. This kind of pressure makes it hard to assemble reminders and makes the support of the group all the more important.

When feminist theory groups assemble reminders they need not proceed from specific experiences to generalizations, but they do think it important that the theoretical claims be linked repeatedly to experience. If, after careful analysis, a woman is sure that her current long-standing love relationship with a man is healthy and non-destructive, she cannot very well deny that such a thing is possible, though it might be very rare and almost never "permanent." The reminders assembled in this context can concern our own experience or be about theoretical points. The kinds of theoretical reminders would vary greatly; feminist theorists have first received some kind of traditional training, for example, in biology, sociology, or philosophy, which often influences the nature of their reminders. Although the purpose here is to produce theory for social change, not specifically to raise consciousness or to develop trust in oneself and other women, such discussion tends to produce all these results. They come to be expected and valued by feminists.

4. Psychological Theorists and Psychotherapy Groups

I use "psychological theorist" very broadly to include those who take human psychology to be their field; for example, psychoanalysts, psychiatrists, therapists, and psychologists. Yet, within psychologists I want to focus on humanistic psychologists and clinically-oriented psychologists. I use "psychologist" here to refer to those psychological theorists whose theories about love and sex tend to be supported by case studies and anecdotes rather than systematic empirical research and statistical data. By choosing to discuss this group of psychologists, I am making it more difficult to distinguish psychologists from philosophers. But the fact is that many psychologists writing on love and sex, particularly on the relation between them, tend to take this approach. And one can find differences in philosophers' and psychologists' uses of anecdotal data. Only psychologists apologize for having mere anecdotes to support their theories. Philosophers are often glad to have an anecdote to provide an interesting test case or object for analysis.

The sort of psychotherapy I am discussing here would fall midway between classical psychoanalysis and radical therapy.[6] It can be practiced in groups or individually; it emphasizes getting in touch with one's current feelings (with some encouragement to understand the present by reference to the past); and it wants to look at recurrent behavior patterns in order to see to what extent a person contributes to the perseverance of her/his problems.

If we look at the purposes for which reminders are assembled in therapy groups and by psychologists, it is easier to distinguish these two groups from feminists than to distinguish philosophers from psychologists. For the political commitments of a feminist are clearly different from those of a psychologist. A feminist's reminders are assembled for a political purpose. The purpose of some psychologists would be to construct and support theories about love and sex that not only are good theories but can, when applied, help people to fulfill their potentialities for satisfactory sexual experiences and love relationships. The fact that psychologists (including therapists) need not have a commitment to social change has brought them criticism from feminists. Feminists have said that psychologists who believe they have no political commitment *qua* psychologists do, in fact, assume society's standards for health, including the notion that the individual should adapt to current social arrangements (or perhaps to the most moderate of feminist reforms, such as shared housework or the ability of each partner to make sexual overtures). Feminists would be skeptical of the reply that psychologists do work for social change by trying to increase love in the world.

A similar contrast is present between therapy groups and consciousness raising groups: only the latter has a commitment to a political analysis of problems, not just "personal solutions." A therapy group (like a consciousness raising group) seeks to build trust among its members in order for its members to express their feelings and to interact openly with each other. In a therapy group, however, the purpose is not to foster a commitment to social change or to see the ways in which institutions contribute to our problems, but to see the ways we as individuals contribute to our problems and can free ourselves to solve our problems. This is not to say that feminist-inspired political points do not arise in therapy groups (or for that matter that therapy-inspired points do not arise in consciousness raising groups); however, in my experience, it is feminists in therapy groups who make such political points, and it is not part of the process of therapy itself that these points be made.

The reminders that emerge in therapy groups are sometimes difficult to assemble. Although we have admirable purposes such as self understanding or personal growth, we have built up defenses against recognizing and appreciating the reminders; they are sometimes painful or hard to face. For example, suppose a man tells his therapy group that he cannot get close to one woman because she is too dependent, he cannot get close to the next one because she whines, the third one because she's too aggressive. He and his group might assemble some reminders about what worries him about women, what fears he has of closeness, of women, of dependency, or of loss of control. There is no easy way to spell out the causal connections between what "clicks" with him and whether it leads to different feelings or changed behavior. (Similarly, in a consciousness raising group, there is no clearly defined causal chain between first sharing experiences and giving political analyses, and the members' subsequent changes in feelings, political attitudes, and commitments.) In both kinds of groups our feelings are stirred up and, in fact, people sometimes change. When asked about the change, they sometimes see important influences from the interactions and discussion in their groups.

5. Philosophers

Because the traditional view of analytic philosophy is that the purpose of philosophy is solely intellectual, not to produce emotional or political change, it might be hard to see the value of a comparison between philosophy and either consciousness raising or therapy. For example, there is no institutionalized group doing philosophy that corresponds to therapy groups or to consciousness raising groups. The group activity of doing philosophy, whether in classes, discussion groups, or among friends, would correspond to discussions of theory by feminists or psychologists. And philosophers usually do not have political change or emotional growth as the goal of theorizing. The similarity among these discussion groups is that the purpose of each group is to produce theory or analysis but, as a by-product of the discussion, people are sometimes stirred up either emotionally or politically. The more emotionally-charged the topic the easier it is to be stirred up, to have points "click," which in turn sometimes leads to other changes. I think we should be pleased, not distressed, by the idea that philosophical discussions can have this effect and accept philosophy as another useful approach for thinking about our emotional and political lives.

The kind of philosophy I discuss here is analytical, broadly construed. It includes not only analysis of "ordinary" and "ideal" concepts, but also such tasks as criticizing the foundation of work in other fields and constructing certain kinds of philosophical theories. Since analytic philosophy is thought to be among the most dry, detached, aloof forms of philosophy, if *it* can have an impact on our lives, surely most any philosophy can.

I want to tamper a bit with a characteristic that is commonly attributed to analytic philosophy: that it is "value-neutral" or "objective." (I believe that we are still left with analytic philosophy after my tampering, but in case we are not, we can think of it merely as acceptable philosophy.) It does not make sense to think that philosophers are indifferent onlookers (not to mention ideal observers) when they discuss love and sex. Philosophers speak from a time and place, a race, a sex, and an economic and social class. We have many explicit and implicit theoretical assumptions, not the least of which is "common sense." But given this, there are still degrees of fairness and impartiality we can exhibit. For example, a philosopher might analyze the concept of sexual perversion or the connection between sexual perversion and morality not for the purpose of recommending action or making a political statement, but wanting the analytical chips to fall where they may. But the chips may, in fact, fall in a path leading toward concrete action. Perhaps the law governing sexual activities in one's city or state is based on a confused concept of sexual perversion. It does not detract from the philosophical merit of someone's paper if it finds its way into the hands of a state assembly representative. Nor is it inappropriate to have begun the analysis in the first place because of a hunch about the conceptual confusion in the law.

In addition, "objectivity" does not require that we isolate philosophy from social reality. Instead, we should try to distinguish the features of each. For example, what part of the relation between love and dependency is conceptual and what part is the empirical fact that between men and women there is frequently an important economic basis for psychological dependency? I do not mean to minimize the difficulty in drawing these distinctions. How we talk and think about love and sex is set within complex institutions that have social, economic, and psychological components. But it seems to me that philosophers who have not hidden their heads in the political sand are well equipped to sort out these components.

It is especially important to sort out the empirical from the conceptual in developing new theories. Suppose one is analyzing sexual attraction in the context of developing a theory of sexuality. It would be important to separate features of sexual attraction that are "necessary" from those that happen to exist currently. For some of the current features surely stem from the combination of the use of a heterosexual model for sexual attraction and the fact of inequality between men and women. One hopes that factors such as these do not produce key features of a concept of sexual attraction in a new theory.

Other philosophers have asked me, at least partially seriously, whether good philosophy leads to better sex or more love. I want to discuss briefly two questions that underlie an inquiry about the value of doing philosophy about love and sex. (1) Of what use and interest is it philosophically? (2) What impact can it have on us personally or politically?

(1) Philosophy about love and sex leads to the same things to which any other philosophy leads. The goal might be truth, plausible theories, clearer concepts, or uncovering nonsense (as one finds appropriate). Take conceptual clarity as an example. No one denies that the concepts in the area of love and sex are interesting and of importance in human existence. Such concepts are worth analyzing. (The worry one has is that philosophers will produce boring analyses of interesting concepts.) Furthermore, the analyses are useful to counteract the rampant popular (and theoretical) confusions about love. Think of "Love means never having to say you're sorry" or Lee Marvin's courtroom distinctions about the types of love that began "Love is like a gas tank." Conceptual clarity is especially important for concepts such as love, dependency, sex, need, autonomy, and trust, which come in clusters and are overlaid with emotion. Not only do the concepts form a complex cluster, but different people's input on their meaning is important. For we look at trust and need in importantly different ways.

Also of philosophical interest are the moral problems that arise when analyzing concepts in this area. For example, application of moral concepts such as self-interest and self-respect to the context of personal relationships is extremely interesting. How do self-interest and self-respect fit in with loving other people, being committed to them, and acting in their interests?

But what about less "pure" questions that seem to require more empirical content to their answers or that seem to be filled with loaded psychological terms? Are these *philosophically* interesting? For example, a philosopher might be interested in an issue I mentioned previously: are all heterosexual love relationships in our society destructive dependency relationships (or worse)?[7] A philosopher can proceed to think about what it means to be dependent on a lover, what the difference between healthy and destructive dependency might be, what notion of health we tend to use in this context, and what all this has to do with love, which, in turn, needs elucidation, too. There is much empirical content here, some psychologically loaded terminology, and many underlying political questions (for example, in this society is it *prima facie* worse for women to be dependent than for men to be?). However, it is also interesting philosophy. One is certainly mapping conceptual relations; the concepts just happen to be ones that have bearing on our emotional lives.

It is easy to overlook one factor that leads people to think mistakenly that investigations such as the above are not really philosophical: when nonphilosophers write more about a subject than philosophers, we forget that the subject can still be philosophical. Not only have humanistic psychologists and the "human potential movement" flooded the popular market with material about love, personal growth, and sex, but social scientists and feminists have been doing much more than have philosophers in criticizing the institutions surrounding personal relations. It sometimes does not look like philosophy; the jargon is funny; however, social scientists and feminists are sometimes functioning as philosophers when they offer this kind of criticism. This kind of philosophy is in addition to the more obviously philosophical approach of those who set about analyzing the nature of love (or even the essence of love), making distinctions with which philosophers feel comfortable, talking about what is necessary and universal. For example, consider Erich Fromm: "In contrast to both types of love [brotherly and motherly] is erotic love; it is the craving for complete fusion, for union with one other person. It is by its very nature exclusive and not universal."[8] Even Masters and Johnson do philosophy. Their discussion of commitment in *The Pleasure Bond* is budding philosophical analysis.[9] My point is that because nonphilosophers do philosophy of love and sex, it does not follow that philosophers should not do it, too (and, one hopes, do it better). It is philosophically interesting material.

I have already touched on the answer to question (2). What impact does philosophy about love and sex have on us personally or politically? I cannot agree with the position that philosophy "leaves everything as it is,"[10] but neither can I believe that philosophy solves our emotional problems. The impact that philosophy can have on us depends largely on us. First, we have to overcome the common assumption that philosophy is divorced from what is personally or politically useful. Then, if we are emotionally open to thinking about the implications that a view could have for our lives, it might, in fact, have an impact. We react to philosophical points at different levels. Suppose I am reading an analysis of the conflict between commitment and autonomy; I might find useful comments that explain some of the conflicts I have felt myself; I might also find puzzles that intrigue me philosophically.

I do not want to claim that reading some philosophical remark or discussing philosophy is likely to cause significant, longstanding behavior patterns to change; I am saying, instead, that when philosophical discussion is directed toward areas of life in which emotions play an important role, it stirs up people, triggers certain changes in feelings, raises doubts about their previous beliefs, and leads them to change some of their beliefs. What people do as a result of change in beliefs or feelings depends on the person. Suppose a man reads an analysis of the meaning of "respect for a person" in the context of a sexual relationship. He sees what his lover has been complaining about (which he had previously denied he was doing at all), and feels bad about the way he has treated her. Regardless of what happens next, it was a philosophical reminder that made him see the problem.

Another, more general, way in which philosophy is of use to us personally and politically is in the way we are trained to think. This is such an obvious point that we overlook it. It applies far beyond the issue surrounding love and sex. We can apply our methodologies in a clearheaded way to any problem.

When discussing therapy groups and consciousness raising groups, we noted that the purposes for which reminders are assembled are, respectively, emotional growth and social change. They both share with philosophy the assumption that improvement of some kind is possible. In philosophy, although our purposes are intellectual, we have a long tradition of thinking that the examined life is better than the unexamined life. Constructing good theories and clarifying our concepts are part of the process of examining our lives. Other parts of the process deal more directly with political and emotional factors. Philosophy contributes indirectly to other changes for the better in our lives because it does, in fact, stir up feelings. We should look not only at the indirect, contingent benefits, but also at the direct one: philosophy is one useful tool for thinking about our lives.

6. Practical Suggestions

At the beginning of this paper I stated what I consider to be the benefits of teaching a course on love and sex, realizing that some people would not see them as benefits at all, but as problems to be dealt with grudgingly, or to be avoided entirely by not teaching the course at all. I now want to offer some common sense suggestions for some of the typical problems that arise because of the subject matter.

I feel strongly that it is a mistake to try to gear one's course to avoid arousing students' feelings. Something would be sorely missing from such a course; it might well be impossible anyway. It is much harder to dismiss issues about love and sex as having bearing for one's life than it is to dismiss the question whether moral judgments are relative or absolute. If one fears that loving a person deeply always means loss of identity or the necessity to subject oneself to the will of another, then it will be hard not to be affected by even the most abstract discussion of love and autonomy. We should not deny to ourselves or to students that we might feel uncomfortable or threatened by some of the discussion; but discomfort is not always bad and can be profitable in getting us to think about the issues differently.

We should think through the responsibilities we feel we have as instructors. People's extra-philosophical training varies; I do not see why someone without training in "facilitating" groups should be reluctant to teach this course, as long as one has confidence in one's basic human judgment and sensitivity. Much of the responsibility I feel in a course of this kind differs only in degree from that which I always feel: to treat students' views and feelings with respect, to listen carefully to what people say, to balance the need to pursue the issues as they arise with the need to follow through "on the point." The difference in degree stems from the difficulty in understanding what people are trying to say: for not only does the usual obscurity exist, but sometimes people either do not realize, or deceive themselves about, what their feelings and views are in sensitive areas. A libertarian might oppose marriage because it is an unwarranted intrusion of the state into people's lives; he or she might also fear commitment; he or she might have both these feelings and views simultaneously and not know it. One must not only think about what is underlying the words spoken, but be sensitive enough not to allow someone to be pressed beyond comfortable limits. This task is not impossible or even very difficult, for it is not solely the responsibility of the instructor.

Groups of students seem to regulate themselves very well; people tend not to pursue what they see someone cannot handle. Although students argue vigorously and with anger, I have found that when someone seems to need support or encouragement, people give it readily. This is especially true when a common commitment or ideology, such as feminism, binds people together. But even between women and men with radically different and equally intense political commitments about sexism and sexual issues, there is a bond between them, as members of the group, that leads them to be supportive. Of course, the instructor can encourage this behavior, explicitly by suggesting it and implicitly by doing it.

Another responsibility that is easy to exercise is to remind students that their lovers, families, or roommates have not been reading or discussing what the class has and might not be wholly sympathetic to abrupt behavior changes.

Privacy is a two-faceted problem: how to keep enough privacy about one's own life and how not invade the privacy of students. In one's own case, it is a matter of personal taste whether one wants to answer questions such as "How do you, as a woman, feel about anal sex?" or "Do you have an open marriage?" I do not consider areas of privacy to include important political commitments such as feminism. I would find it very difficult to teach the course in a sincere manner without making these commitments explicit.

In order to avoid invading the privacy of students and at the same time encourage them to deal with the feelings and attitude changes that discussions stir up, I ask students to keep journals or notebooks. They write entries for each class, describing their reactions to the reading and to the discussion. The style and content of the journals reflect the choice of the students: some are more purely intellectual than others; some are self-analytical; some students spend time expressing anger toward people in the class with whom they were afraid to disagree openly. They may block out parts of their journals that I am not to read. In addition to obtaining valuable information about student reaction to the material and discussion, and spotting people with unusual problems, the journals have obvious virtues; for example, they help people to keep up with the reading and to think about the discussions between sessions; they also provide opportunities to tell about relevant conversations they have had at home. When possible I avoid grading the journals, but make comments on them.

One can utilize other centers on campus to fill different kinds of needs of people in the class. Women's centers often operate consciousness raising groups that women and sometimes men can join. Counseling centers sometimes have special focus groups. (Our counseling center has had "Sexual Concerns Discussion Groups"; several students attended such a group while participating in my class and found the combination beneficial. One woman noted an important difference between them: in class they are not criticized for intellectualizing.) In addition, students tend to their own emotional needs; for example, they continue their discussion long after class. If possible, it is good to arrange the time of the class to facilitate this natural, emotional-overflow group.

If someone has serious emotional problems, one can obviously refer him or her to a professional of the sort with whom the student would feel compatible: campus counseling centers, traditional therapists, radical therapy collectives, feminist therapists, or others.

7. Summary

I have both talked about assembling reminders in this paper and have been doing it. I have called attention to some of the benefits of thinking and teaching about the philosophy of love and sex and to a few ways of handling a class. I have discussed feminist theory and consciousness raising, psychology and psychotherapy, and philosophy, thinking about the purpose for which we assemble reminders in each. Although the purpose of philosophy is intellectual, philosophical reminders can produce results similar to those aimed for in feminism and psychology: political change and personal growth, respectively. Love and sex are philosophically interesting both for their own sake and because they are central in the lives and happiness of human beings.

Notes

1. This paper grew out of a workshop presented with Sharon Bishop in the Philosophy and Feminism section of the National Workshop Conference on Teaching Philosophy, Schenectady, New York, August 1976. Sharon Bishop's influence on this paper is great; we have discussed most of the issues in it, and I have used several examples from her paper "Love and Dependency" (in Sharon Bishop and Marjorie Weinzweig, eds., *Philosophy and Women* [Belmont, Cal.: Wadsworth, 1979], 147-54). I also want to thank William Winslade, Naomi Scheman, and the participants in the workshop, especially Sandra Harding.

2. I have been told, only partly in jest, that my generalizations about students and professors are based on a skewed sample of divorced Southern Californians. I doubt this, but even if there is something to it, can the rest of the country be far behind?

3. See Laurence E. Winters, "Danger of Teaching Philosophy of Love Courses," *American Philosophical Association Newsletters* 94:1 (Fall, 1994): 152-55. [Noted added by A.S., 1995.]

4. *Philosophical Investigations*, trans. G. E. M. Anscombe (New York: Macmillan, 1953), Part I: §127, §89. The reader should not expect to find a Wittgensteinian view of philosophy in this paper. I consider a much wider view of philosophy than Wittgenstein's, but find his remarks about assembling reminders a good way of thinking about the work that goes on concerning love and sex. I further stray from Wittgenstein in the sort of reminders I assemble. I do not, as Wittgenstein usually does, restrict my reminders to those about the uses of language.

5. This is as good a point as any to answer a few questions that might have come to mind. (1) Do feminists want to improve the position of women at the expense of men, or will everyone be better off? Feminists differ about the extent to which men will benefit from women's liberation; men will lose some of their current power; they will gain more options for their lives. (2) Can there be male feminists? Yes. (3) What does "consciousness raising" mean and must consciousness raising groups include only women? There are groups for men; there are some that are mixed sexually. But most are only for women, and it is an important part of the theory that this be true. To raise one's consciousness is to become more aware of the many, varied forms of sexism and how they affect us. For detailed information, see Gay Abarbanell and Harriet Perl, *Guidelines to Feminist Consciousness Raising* (Los Angeles [1835 S. Bentley]: prepared for the National Organization for Women, 1976). A philosophical discussion of how collective autonomy works in consciousness raising groups can be found in Larry Blum, Marcia Homiak, Judy Housman,

and Naomi Scheman, "Altruism and Women's Oppression," in Carol C. Gould and Marx Wartofsky, eds., *Women and Philosophy* (New York: G. P. Putnam's Sons, 1976), 222-47.

6. Radical therapists see the purpose of therapy not as adjustment but as social, political, and personal change. They would agree with most of the criticisms of traditional therapy and therapists that I attribute to feminists or feminist therapists. See, for example, a journal, *The Radical Therapist*. I do not include radical therapists in my use of "psychologist" here.

7. For an affirmative answer to this question, see Shulamith Firestone, *The Dialectic of Sex* (New York: Bantam, 1970) and Ti-Grace Atkinson, *Amazon Odyssey* (New York: Links, 1974). Atkinson thinks lesbian and male homosexual relationships are not healthy either.

8. Erich Fromm, *The Art of Loving* (New York: Harper and Row, 1956), 44.

9. William H. Masters and Virginia E. Johnson, *The Pleasure Bond* (Boston: Little, Brown, 1970), ch. 12, "Commitment."

10. Wittgenstein's point that philosophy "leaves everything as it is" (in *Philosophical Investigations*, §124) is harder to interpret than it sounds when used as a slogan. He made the remark in the context of leaving mathematics and language as they are, not leaving one's life as it is. One way to interpret Wittgenstein, suggested to me by Naomi Scheman, is that we are not to try to show that our concepts are mistaken, but show how they function in our lives. Once we see this, it might lead us to make changes in our lives (or not).

Sandra Harding
(photograph: University of Delaware)

Author of "Why Are Love and Sex Philosophically
Interesting? A Response to Ann Garry"
Paper presented at the Society for the Philosophy of Sex and Love
during the
Eastern Division Meeting of The American Philosophical Association
New York, N.Y., 28 December 1979

Six

WHY LOVE AND SEX ARE REALLY INTERESTING

Sandra Harding

1.

Love and sex are often regarded as shoddy, or at least shady, topics for philosophic inquiry. But Ann Garry[1] proposes that love and sex can be made as philosophically interesting and philosophically respectable as the traditional topics addressed under such headings as "the problems of philosophy." And she finds the analytic framework especially useful for this purpose. Furthermore, she points out that there are personal pleasures and enjoyments for philosophers and for their students to be gained from such inquiry.

In contrast, I regard as somewhat shady, perhaps even shoddy, both the traditional definition of "the problems of philosophy" and the analytic approach to these issues. I regard love and sex, or their near relatives about which I am going to talk, as philosophically interesting precisely because a critical examination of these topics can be used, first, to reveal the shadiness of, the cultural biases in, the approach to these problems. Second, such an examination can show us how to formulate a new and important set of philosophical problems. And third, a truly critical inquiry forces philosophers and their students to the often painful struggle out of which not a "liberated personal life style," but more liberating social structures, can emerge.

In this brief response to Garry's paper, let me fill in what I have in mind. My alternative proposal amounts to applause for Garry's bringing into focus a crucial area of human life too long relegated to the fringes of philosophical attention; and to applause for her respect for the tradition of critical inquiry into the deepest foundations of our beliefs and actions that marks philosophy itself as a uniquely valuable fringe of social life. But my alternative also questions whether her proposals do justice either to the social and intellectual importance of these topics or to the courageous tradition of critical philosophical inquiry within which I, for one, want to work.

2.

Shift of scene. The theater lights are dimmed. In the darkness we feel alone with ourselves and separated from each other, though we are huddled together in this small space. We are exhausted or exhilarated, as the case may be, from the day's efforts to figure out what our knowledge claims correspond to, if anything; to discover the relationship of the observer to the external world, if there is an external world; to understand whether or not science coincides with rationality, should rationality be humanly possible; and to construct arguments showing of what justice consists, if any social models for such a concept are even in principle detectable. This was *our* labor during the day. For 95% of our species through history, their labor, day and night, has been more intimately connected with sheer physical survival.

From the orchestra pit emerge the soothing strains of violins and the throbs of the cello; our attention is alerted only peripherally to an occasional unidentifiable tinny sound. The curtain rises. Love and Sex, misshapen little puppets decked out in gaudy costumes, move on stage and sing a series of catchy tunes from down through the ages. Now they are Socrates and his handsome lad; now the Virgin Mary and her son; now Tristan and Isolde; now Shakespeare and his dark lady (or lord, as the case may be); now Jeanette MacDonald and Nelson Eddy; now "O" and her owner. Finally they are begging each other for "some hot stuff tonight." The curtain falls. We applaud. Ah, at last. Here is what life is really about, though not, we reassure ourselves, what philosophy has been about.

3.

From this quasi-anthropological perspective, love and sex appear as much more intriguing heralds to unexamined and underlying philosophical issues than Garry gives them credit for being. But in order to see what those issues are, we have to ask a different set of questions than Garry's proposals directly suggest.

Who owns the theater in which these misshapen puppets called "love" and "sex" prance each night? Whose hands direct their movements? Why is the audience for the evening's performance the same people who, with their patrons, for 2,500 years have had such problems understanding the relationship between mind and body, between reason and emotion, between the observer and the external world, between our descriptions of the world and the way the world is, between how we should live and how we in fact live? What is the *system* we have had, for at least two and a half millennia, of relating to ourselves, to other people and to nature, and of *understanding* these relationships, which forces the traditional "problems of philosophy" to the center of our attention in the daytime but relegates to the darkness of the theater Love and Sex's stories of our relationship to ourselves, to other people, and to nature?

Let me spell out a couple of the challenges we face in trying to address this set of questions about love and sex. And let me note that in significant ways it is the writings of nonphilosophers, thinkers refusing to work within the great tradition of Western culture of which philosophy is a part, that have alerted me to how to formulate these challenges. In particular, I am indebted to Nancy Hartsock, Gayle Rubin, Dorothy Dinnerstein, Adrienne Rich, Audre Lorde, and (especially) Jane Flax.[2]

4.

In the first place, we need a *causal* account of the connections between our daytime activities and the night time performances of Love and Sex. We are the same people twenty-four hours a day. But the conceptual scheme that structures the performances of Love and Sex, and also our day time philosophy, is designed to make it difficult to provide a causal account of these connections. We need a more adequate conceptual scheme. As a start, it is not "sex" (badly named) that should be the focus of our attention, but instead the "sex/gender system," as the anthropologist Gayle Rubin has named it.[3] Sex is a biological category, more or less given by nature, to which a wide variety of cultural roles have often been attributed. But culture, which includes both philosophizing and the performances of Love and Sex, is a social construct. Thus we need a social category such as "the sex/gender system" to understand the underlying causal connections among the social behaviors in which we are interested.

We are conscripted into particular positions in the sex/gender system at an early age, probably by the time we are three; and this conscription has virtually nothing to do with our awareness of biological sex differences. Our position in the system shapes (though it does not irretrievably determine) not only whether we will get to sing the Tristan tune or the Isolde tune, or to play "O" or her owner, but also what our roles will be in *all* the economic, political, psychological, and ideological institutions that have structured societies through history. For instance, as Rubin has pointed out, in pre-state societies, the sex/gender system was used to *create* the rules for conducting economic life and the rules for who ruled whom.[4] More modern traces of this ancient system for structuring the social life of the species maintain men's unique rights to themselves, to their children, to women, and to nature's resources, and their unique right to construct the forms of our mental life that justify this gender-unique relationship of men to themselves, to others, to nature. Freud, in a way that was often obscuring and misleading, was at least looking in the right direction when he tried to show how in the Viennese middle class, individuals were psychologically conscripted into the nineteenth-century remnants of the sex/gender system before the age of three, and prior to their emergence into what we have been pleased to call the beginnings of the life of reason. The point is that personhood, as we have known it for 2,500 years, is inseparable from gender categories. The transformation from a biological human infant to a social person is simultaneous with, and intimately connected with, the transformation from androgyne to a distinctively gendered person. No one passes through the roughly three-year process of "psychological birth" without also becoming distinctively gendered. And to be distinctively gendered is only partially to know how or with whom to use one's genitals. More important, it is to adopt gender-distinctive ways to relate to one's body, one's mind, one's emotions, to relate to others, and to relate to nature.

Thus if we would follow Garry's lead and try to understand how "sex" functions in our lives, we need a conceptual scheme that will allow us to understand how the traces of that original sex/gender system still function today. We must understand how men and women have different roles in the system, and how the distinctive patterns of the system both underlie and mediate many other aspects of both our actual social practices and our ways of understanding those practices. All these aspects are discernible in the nature of and division between our day time and night time activities.

Similarly, "love" is an inadequate and misleading focus for our philosophical attention. As the label under which the personal and collective tragedies and comedies of the sex/gender system are played out (reflected in the ditties sung by our puppets) we can see "love" as the red herring that prevents us from critically examining the nature and workings of the sex/gender system. Instead we could turn our attention to the underlying nature and causes of our emotional relations with self and others. What kinds of emotional relations do men and women have? What kinds do men and women want? Are the kinds of emotional relations wanted by men likely to be satisfied by the stereotypical relations with women institutionalized in our society? By the stereotypical relations with other men institutionalized in our society? Are those wanted by women likely to be satisfied by the stereotypical relations with men sanctioned in our society? By those sanctioned with other women? What kinds of changes in the social structure within which "psychological birthing" takes place—early child care—must we make to allow healthy emotional wants to be satisfied? What kinds of changes in the institutional structures of adult social life would support healthier emotional lives? What kinds of changes in our social *practices* must we make if we are to have the nourishing and emancipating emotional lives we each feel we so richly deserve?

So, just as in the history of science where concepts such as "the humors" and "the ether" were replaced by concepts with greater explanatory power, we need a more powerful explanatory conceptual scheme than that in which the terms "love" and "sex" are traditionally embedded. Here is one challenge for those who undertake critical philosophical inquiry into these areas of our lives.

5.

In the second place, the kind of understanding I am here suggesting of the sex/gender system leads to a new understanding of the relationship between epistemology, metaphysics, ethics, and political theory. On the one hand, what we know and can know about ourselves, others, and nature are in part consequences of what we do with ourselves, others, and nature. They are in part consequences of our practices, of how we interact as infants and adults with physical and social environments, where these interactions are themselves structured by political institutions and systems of morals. On the other hand, what we *do* changes the world with which we interact. From this perspective, metaphysics and epistemology merge, and their particular, historical forms are understandable only when seen in the context of particular political institutions and particular systems of morals. Both we and the "reality" we seek to understand take shape through historically particular interactions with each other. Theory gives form to social practices, and social practices give characteristic form to theory.

This brings us back to the striking fact that a certain range of questions about knowledge, reality, and social relations has held the collective social spotlight for 2,500 years and that other ranges of questions have been relegated to the intellectual darkness of only our personal attention, our solitary despair or joy, now often shared with our therapist or other confidantes engaged in "personal growth." Should we not examine what it is that those who shape intellectual life have been doing that makes one range of questions collectively important and the other only appropriately asked "in personal life"?

What leaps to the eye, from this perspective, is the fact that those who shape intellectual life have held easily identifiable positions in the sex/gender system, the system we noted was in part justified by the performances of our puppets "Love" and "Sex." Philosophers have been men. Becoming a male person is a different experience from becoming a female person. Becoming a man requires a distinctive set of interactions with self, others, and nature from those required if one is to become a woman. The first person males individuate and separate from as infants is, cross-culturally and through history, a devalued woman. It is a devalued woman in interaction with whom they first came to know the pleasures and travails of the body, of emotional life, of relations with "others." Should we be surprised if we begin to discern that the process of becoming gendered persons leaves men intellectually puzzled about their relationship to their body, to their emotional life, to "others," to nature? Should we be surprised if the stories about nature and social life constructed by men echo the crucial life problems of male children learning to individuate themselves and separate from socially devalued women? Should we be surprised if we are burdened with a conceptual scheme that isolates personally painful thoughts about love and sex from intellectually pleasant and enjoyable ones about the "problems of philosophy"?

6.

One need not accept the particular theoretical explanatory scheme I have been sketching out for understanding the relationship between the traditional problems of philosophy and the traditional issues of personal life. And I certainly do *not* mean to suggest that the problems of philosophy are nothing but the problems of overgrown male toddlers (unless, that is, you would also be willing to consider how the entire species has not yet emerged into fully adult ways of constructing social relations, and relations to nature, and of understanding those relations). Our conscious and unconscious structuring of our relations to ourselves, others, and nature are and always will be social projects for the species, since it is our species' gift to be able to construct these relations consciously: we are animals who not only "evolve" but also historically change. I am suggesting that the problems of philosophy reflect only a particular part of that social history. There are reasons why the sex/gender system hides as love and sex, as gaudy little creatures constructed so as not to be worthy of philosophical examination.

With respect to Garry's proposals, from my perspective she has tried to do the impossible: to adopt love and sex into "the problems of philosophy." As I have been stressing, on the one hand love and sex, and on the other hand "the problems of philosophy," are both social constructs designed to be considered separately. Failure to recognize this fact creates further problems. For instance, why try for intersubjective philosophical agreement about "conceptual clarity" about love and sex when what is needed is an explanatory scheme adequate to capture the regularities of nature and their underlying determinants? If you think of yourself as an analytic philosopher, you probably think these are identical projects. But they aren't, since we know we can be perfectly clear about a concept that has little explanatory power. "The humors," "ether," "phlogiston," and "environmental stimuli" are all examples of concepts that respectable scientists and philosophers have thought perfectly clear, yet they lack genuine explanatory power. Furthermore, should any substantive claims unexamined from the perspective of a more adequate conceptual scheme be accepted? Should we pass over without comment the claim that "erotic love is by its nature exclusive"? Maybe it is, maybe it isn't. Shouldn't we critically examine the social conditions under which as emerging persons we first have erotic experience? Should we accept any claims to know the "true nature" of phenomena that might in part be social constructs, such as "erotic attraction"?

7.

I could go on, but perhaps you can see why I think that love and sex are much more interesting philosophically than Garry does, and why I think the critical inquiry into the most fundamental aspects of our beliefs and practices, which characterizes philosophy, is much more powerful than Garry does.

We face a final and more basic challenge in choosing to address (or not to address) these issues as philosophers and in the classroom. As Adrienne Rich noted in her commencement address at Smith College this year,

> we live in a society leeched upon by the "personal growth" industry, by the delusion that the alienation and injustice experienced by women, by black and Third World people, by the poor, in a world ruled by white males, in a society which fails to meet the most basic human needs, and which is slowly poisoning itself, can be mitigated or solved by Transcendental Meditation. . . . It is important for each of you . . . that you discriminate clearly between "liberated lifestyle" and feminist struggle, and that you make a conscious choice.[5]

I think the responsibility for making that choice *wisely* falls even more heavily on those of us who believe we have an important role in helping to shape the way people think about themselves and their lives. Our choice might not be a popular one with our listeners and readers, but it could be the choice that offers them the possibility of making history rather than of wandering through 2,500-year-old scripts they can't even read.

Postscript (1995)

Rereading, after more than a decade, this response to Ann Garry, I was struck mainly by its arrogant self-righteousness, and by Ann's graciousness in continuing to be willing to know me after such a performance. Thank goodness some things get better as we get older. (Or, at least, I would like to think I am a little more respectful of other philosophers.)

Of course, there is much in the response I would change today: sexuality, that is, sexual desire and sexual identity, is a far more complex and interesting phenomenon than I could have dreamed then; there is more to be said about love than I intimated; object relations theory has its limitations; "personal life" is just where we enter theoretical discussions, whether we admit it or not; where in my paper is the cultural and historical variation, the differences, that shape how sex and love occur? And so forth. But I decided the response was a historical document and should be left that way.

Notes

1. Ann Garry, "Why are Love and Sex Philosophically Interesting?" this volume, 39-50.

2. Nancy C. M. Hartsock, "The Feminist Standpoint: Developing the Ground for a Specifically Feminist Historical Materialism," in S. Harding and M. Hintikka, eds., *Discovering Reality: Feminist Perspectives on Epistemology, Metaphysics, Methodology, and Philosophy of Science* (Dordrecht: Reidel, 1983); Gayle Rubin, "The Traffic in Women: Notes on the 'Political Economy' of Sex," in Rayna Rapp Reiter, ed., *Toward an Anthropology of Women* (New York: Monthly Review Press, 1975); Dorothy Dinnerstein, *The Mermaid and the Minotaur: Sexual Arrangements and Human Malaise* (New York: Harper and Row, 1976); Adrienne Rich, *On Lies, Secrets, and Silence: Selected Prose 1966-1978* (New York: Norton, 1979); Audre Lorde, *The Black Unicorn* (New York: Norton, 1978); Jane Flax, "Political Philosophy and the Patriarchal Unconscious: A Psychoanalytic Perspective on Epistemology and Metaphysics," in Harding and Hintikka, *Discovering Reality*.

3. Rubin, "The Traffic in Women."

4. *Ibid*.

5. Adrienne Rich, "On Privilege, Power, and Tokenism," *Ms*. (September 1979), 42-4, at 44.

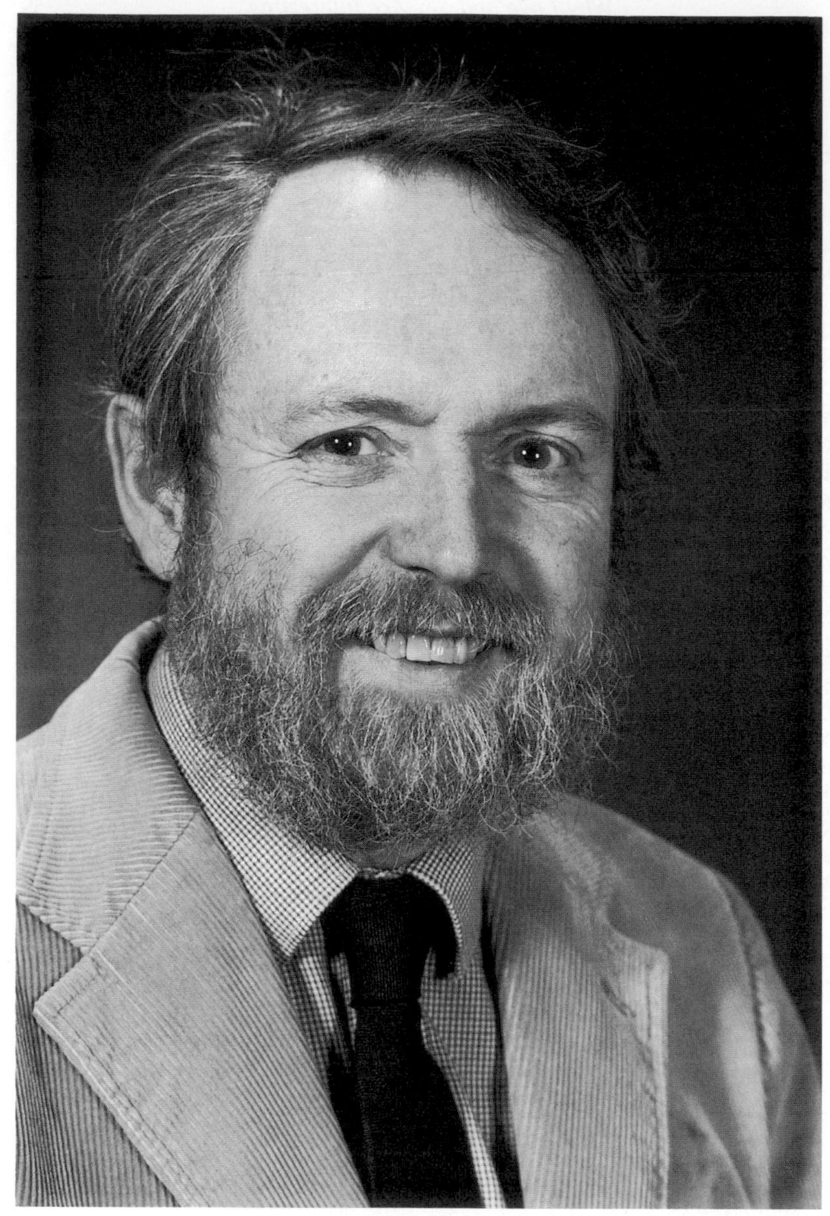

Michael Ruse

Author of "Are There Gay Genes? Sociobiology and Homosexuality"
Paper presented at the Society for the Philosophy of Sex and Love
during the
Eastern Division Meeting of The American Philosophical Association
New York, N.Y., 28 December 1979

Seven

ARE THERE GAY GENES? SOCIOBIOLOGY AND HOMOSEXUALITY

Michael Ruse

Interest in human sociobiology, the study of human social behavior from a biological viewpoint, continues at a high level. Although the controversy and bitterness sparked by the publication of *Sociobiology: The New Synthesis*[1] seem now to be somewhat muted, the ideas and applications of sociobiology receive increasing coverage in learned journals, conferences, and even in the popular press. Indeed, sociobiology was awarded that ultimate American accolade, an expository article in *Playboy* magazine advertised as "Why Modern Science Says You Need to Cheat on Your Wife," or some such nonsense.[2] Surely the time has come to stop general defenses of or onslaughts on human sociobiology and to start considering in detail specific claims made by the sociobiologists.[3] It is at this level that the real battle must be fought if sociobiology, and particularly human sociobiology, is to prove of lasting value. Following my own prescription, the present paper will consider sociobiologists' various claims and suggestions about an aspect of human behavior that has attracted quite as much interest and controversy in recent years as sociobiology itself: human homosexual inclinations and practices. An exploration of sociobiologists' explanations of human homosexuality will be followed by a critical evolution of these ideas.

1. The Hypotheses

Sociobiologists do not have an "official line" on homosexuality, nor at this stage is such a position even to be desired. Instead, the literature contains a number of suggestions and hints proffered with varying degrees of confidence and evidence. Four possible explanations of human homosexuality put forward by sociobiologists will be discussed here, although the reader is warned that at least one of these explanatory hypotheses is at this point so tentative it might be no more than half an explanation. The extent to which any or all of these explanations should be seen as excluding rival explanations is a matter to be left for later discussions.

First Hypothesis: Balanced Superior Heterozygote Fitness

The first of the sociobiological explanations sees human homosexuality as a function of balanced superior heterozygote fitness.[4] Since this explanation, like those to follow, presupposes some biological background knowledge, a sketch of such background is in order. Readers unfamiliar with biological theory might be well advised to consult M. W. Strickberger.[5]

For evolutionary biologists, the crucial unit is the *gene*, which is carried on the chromosomes, passed on from generation to generation, and responsible in some ultimate sense for the physical characteristics of the organism. The gene's random mutation is the raw stuff of evolution.

The chromosomes of organisms, including humans, are paired. Each gene, therefore, has a corresponding gene on the other paired chromosome. Such genes are said to occupy the same *locus*; the genes that can occupy the same locus are known as *alleles*. If the alleles at some particular locus are absolutely identical, then, with respect to that locus, the organism is said to be *homozygous* (the organism is a *homozygote*). If the alleles at some particular locus are not absolutely identical, then, with respect to that locus, the organism is said to be *heterozygous* (*heterozygote*). An organism might be heterozygous with respect to one locus but homozygous with respect to another.

Organisms pass on to their offspring a copy of one, and only one, allele from each locus. The selected allele is chosen at random. In sexual organisms like humans, therefore, each parent contributes one of the alleles at any locus. This fact about transmission, known as Mendel's first law, can be generalized to groups. When applied to groups it is referred to as the Hardy-Weinberg law, after its codiscoverers. The law can be stated succinctly as follows: in the case of a large, randomly mating group of organisms, if there is no external disturbing influence, and if at some particular locus there are two alleles (A_1 and A_2) in overall proportion $p{:}q$, then for all succeeding generations, the proportion will remain the same. Moreover, whatever the initial distribution, over the next and all succeeding generations the alleles will be distributed in the ratio

$$p^2 A_1A_1 : 2pq A_1A_2 : q^2 A_2A_2$$

where A_1A_1 is a homozygote for A_1, and so forth.

Now let's introduce the Darwinian element into our discussion. Organisms have a tendency to multiply in number; think, for instance, of the millions of eggs that one female herring lays. However, this tendency is necessarily curbed; there is just not sufficient space or food for unlimited growth. The result is the struggle for existence or, more precisely, since passing on characteristics to the next generation is what counts in the evolutionary scheme of things, a struggle for reproduction. The genes must cause physical characteristics that will help their possessors in the struggle; otherwise, the genes' progress through the ages will be halted abruptly, and their organisms will be supplanted by organisms whose genes confer more helpful characteristics. Hence, we get a continual "selection" for organisms with better "adaptations" than others. Such organisms are said to be "fitter," because they are better at reproduction. In the long run, selection for reproductive fitness, when combined with mutation, is what biological evolution is all about.

Although selection normally implies change in gene ratios, with the fitter replacing the less fit, under special circumstances selection can act to hold gene ratios constant and can even ensure that less fit organisms are maintained in a population. This is where balanced superior heterozygote fitness comes in. Consider a pair of alleles at a locus, and suppose the heterozygote is much fitter than either homozygote. Although the homozygotes might contribute little or nothing to each future generation, homozygotes will keep reappearing simply because, by the Hardy-Weinberg law, some of the offspring of heterozygotes are homozygotes. In certain circumstances, one can get a balance with the same ratios always holding.

Suppose that one has two alleles, A_1 and A_2, in equal ratio and that, on the average, each of the heterozygotes produces two offspring, whereas each of the homozygotes produces none (that is, the population number remains the same). With each generation, therefore, half the genes will be A_1 and half A_2 (because by definition heterozygotes have an equal ratio of genes and thus will contribute an equal ratio). However, by the Hardy-Weinberg law, the new distribution will be

$$1/4A_1A_1 : 1/2A_1A_2 : 1/4A_2A_2.$$

In other words, as long as the situation continues, 25% of the new population will always be totally unfit A_1A_1s and 25% will be totally unfit A_2A_2s, a situation maintained by natural selection.

The application of this theory to the phenomenon of homosexuality is not that hard to see, but first let us note that balanced superior heterozygote fitness is not merely a theoretical possibility, it does have empirical confirmation. The best known case occurs in the human species. In certain black populations, as many as 5% die in childhood from sickle-cell anemia, a genetic disease. The apparent reason for the persistence of this disease is that heterozygotes for the sickle-cell gene have a natural immunity to malaria, also widespread in these populations. Because the heterozygotes are fitter than either homozygote, the sickle-cell genes stay in the populations, and in each generation, a number of children die from anemia.[6]

What about homosexuality? Two points must be noted. First, although I have been writing of genes causing physical characteristics, orthodox biological theory defines physical characteristics sufficiently broadly to cover all aspects of an organism's makeup, including its behavior and inclinations. Just as the structure of a worker bee's wings is genetically caused, so is its ability to make a perfectly hexagonal cell. Second, remember that when a biologist talks of an organism being very unfit, this does not necessarily imply that the organism dies before reproducing, as does the child affected with sickle-cell anemia. A mule, although it might be tougher than either parent, is regarded as unfit by an evolutionary biologist simply because it cannot reproduce. Despite the example of the mule, however, many, if not most, of the cases of biological unfitness imply or entail unfitness at all levels.

Thus, biological principles dictate to organisms a sort of reproductive imperative. When this is applied to the human organism, conflicts with traditional ethical systems are virtually unavoidable. Quite simply, what we "ought" to do often runs counter to the biologically fittest course of action. Much of our current ethical thinking stems from two major sources, Kantian and utilitarian moral systems. Often, these two influences are mingled, as in the generally accepted belief that we ought to treat human beings as ends in their own right and not simply as means to the achievement of our goals and that we should attempt to maximize happiness and minimize unhappiness for as many people as possible. Practical application of such belief systems leads to the conclusion that there are times when one ought to limit one's family size. For instance, it is immoral to have ten children in India (or anywhere else, for that matter).

From a biological viewpoint, however, if one can successfully raise ten children, this is a much better (that is, fitter) thing to do than to raise a planned two children. (The claim that society will benefit more from two than from ten children and that two is therefore fitter than ten is not pertinent or well-taken; remember, biological fitness centers on the individual, not on the group.) In other words, what is moral and what is biologically fit are two different notions; the biological unfitness of homosexual persons has no implication for the moral desirability of a heterosexual life style over that of a homosexual, or vice versa. Indeed, given the present population explosion, it is easy to argue for the moral acceptability of homosexuality. (I am not arguing for the elimination of homosexuality; neither am I arguing that heterosexual persons ought to become homosexual. Vasectomies are just as efficient a method of birth control as switches in sexual orientation.)

In light of this, one can think of a possible explanation for human homosexuality. Homosexual individuals are by definition attracted to members of their own sex. (I am going to rest with this fairly undefined notion of homosexuality: the homosexual individual is attracted to her/his own sex and most probably has sexual relations with her/his own sex.) Homosexual couplings, of whatever nature, cannot lead to offspring. Hence, someone who is exclusively homosexual cannot have offspring and is therefore effectively sterile, that is, biologically unfit. (Obviously, I exclude here the relatively rare phenomenon of a homosexual person achieving parenthood through artificial insemination.) One might be tempted to conclude that if homosexual men and women fail to reproduce (or reproduce less than their heterosexual counterparts), homosexuality could not possibly be inherited. However, as we have just seen, the mechanism of balanced heterozygote fitness provides a means whereby homosexual genes could be passed on even if homosexual individuals left no offspring at all.

Let us see how this might work. Suppose that homosexuality is a function of the genes and that possession of two "homosexual genes" makes a person homosexual. Let us also suppose, however, that heterozygotes, possessors of one "homosexual gene" and one "heterosexual gene," were fitter than homozygotes for "heterosexual genes"; in other words, that by one means or another, heterozygotes reproduce more than heterosexual-gene homozygotes. It then follows naturally that the existence and persistence of homosexuality is a function of superior heterozygote fitness. Moreover, the theory can easily accommodate the fact that sometimes homosexual persons reproduce. All that is necessary for the theory to work is that they reproduce less often than heterosexual individuals. Also note that if one chooses from among the many estimates of the incidence of homosexuality a reasonable figure of about 5% of the total population, this can be accommodated by the theory, for 5% is the approximate figure suggested for sickle-cell anemia. (Needless to say, I draw this analogy not as proof, but simply to show that we are talking about a mechanism that could, in theory, handle the phenomenon of homosexuality.)

Second Hypothesis: Kin Selection

This is undoubtedly the most exciting of the new theoretical ideas of sociobiology, whether applied to animals or humans. It has been shown that, from a biological evolutionary viewpoint, reproduction is the crucial factor, but what precisely does this mean? First, while recognizing that ultimately everything comes back to the genes, it is important to ask what unit of reproduction above the level of the genes is most significant.[7] Until very recently, the majority of scientists, including most biologists, would have argued that in some important sense it is the species, the reproductively isolated interbreeding group, that is the basic unit of evolution. However, without disputing the species' very special position in the evolutionary scheme, scientists are stressing increasingly that the crucial unit of selection is the individual, that is, the reproduction of the individual organism is the cornerstone of evolutionary biology. Even if a characteristic is detrimental to the species, if it is advantageous to the individual in the short run, then selection will preserve it.[8]

A second question now arises: wherein lies the essence of the individual's reproduction? Obviously, it lies in the passing on of the individual's genes, the units of heredity. Note, however, that an individual is not going to pass on its own genes physically. Rather, it is going to pass on copies of its genes. The key fact behind the notion of kin selection is that it really does not matter where these copies come from. What does matter is that an organism be more efficient at perpetuating copies than its fellows.

Remember, however, that organisms are related to other organisms (brothers, sisters, cousins, and so forth) and that by Mendel's law, an organism and its relatives will have identical instances of alleles. Whenever an individual's relative reproduces, copies of the individual's own genes are being perpetuated. In theory, there is no reason why, under certain circumstances, selection should not promote characteristics that make an individual cut down or forego its own reproduction, so long as those same characteristics make the individual "altruistic" toward its relatives, in the sense that the individual increases the relatives' reproductive chances. This is kin selection.[9]

There is actually a little more to the story. With the exception of identical twins, a person is more closely related to her/himself than to anyone else. One has 100% of one's own genes; one's parents, siblings, and offspring have 50% of one's genes; grandchildren, 25%; first cousins, 12.5%. Hence, under normal circumstances one will prefer the reproduction of oneself even over close relatives. Simple arithmetic shows, for instance, that if by foregoing one's own reproduction one thereby increases a sibling's reproduction by over 100%, then it is in one's own reproductive interest to do so, for more copies of one's own genes are thereby transmitted. More generally, if k is the ratio of gain to loss in fitness and r is the coefficient of relationship of benefiting relatives

($0<r<1$), then, for kin selection to work $k>1/r$ (that is, if C is cost and B benefit, $C<rB$).

Kin selection is not only exciting theoretically. Its application to the social insects, although still controversial in some respects, is one of the triumphs of sociobiology. The Hymenoptera (wasps, bees, ants) show a distinctive, tight social structure, with hordes of sterile females altruistically raising their mother's (that is, the queen's) offspring; the males, incidentally, do no work at all. It is now believed that this is a function of kin selection.[10]

It is easy to see how an analysis like this would tempt sociobiologists faced with the phenomenon of human homosexuality.[11] Assuming that homosexual individuals have fewer offspring than heterosexual individuals, their apparent loss of reproductive fitness could be "exonerated" in terms of the increased fitness of close relatives. All one needs to do is to postulate that homosexuals take altruistic or high prestige jobs such as the priesthood, act as unpaid nannies to the children of siblings, etc. Thus, the siblings (or other relatives) gain in reproductive power and so, indirectly, do the homosexual individuals. If this explanation were true, homosexual humans would be analogous to sterile worker bees in that they reproduce through relatives rather than directly.

Simple and obvious though this explanatory hypothesis might be, it raises even more simple and obvious queries, not the least being those concerning the imputed altruistic motives and actions.

Third Hypothesis: Parental Manipulation

The key to kin selection is that it does not really matter how one's genes get passed on; what is evolutionarily important is that one increase or at least maintain one's genetic representation in future generations. Parental manipulation presupposes a similar attitude to the workings of natural selection and, likewise, serves to explain human homosexuality in terms of genetically caused altruism. The difference, however, is that whereas the kin-selection explanation regards homosexuality as a form of altruism ultimately of benefit to the nonreproducing homosexual individual, parental manipulation sees homosexuality as a form of altruism that ultimately benefits others, namely, the homosexual individual's parents.[12] Richard Alexander has most strongly endorsed the general mechanism of parental manipulation,[13] but, as I will show, he seems to prefer a different primary mechanism for (male) human homosexuality.

Speaking generally and as yet unconcerned with homosexuality specifically, let us first examine the essentials of the supposed mechanism of parental manipulation. Consider an organism with a number of offspring. It is in the organism's reproductive self-interest to have its offspring reproduce as efficiently as possible. Although the organism's reproductive interests depend on its offspring as whole, it is not necessarily true that these interests are identical with any one of the offspring taken individually. Indeed, if an organism has more than one offspring, then the parent's interest will not be the same as any individual offspring, for remember that even a parent and its child have only 50% of their genes in common. (The relationship is no closer if one has only one child; but in that case, kin selection apart, all of one's reproductive hopes rest on that child.) Consequently, considering a parent organism with a number of offspring, there might be occasions when it is in the parent's reproductive interest to sacrifice one or more of its offspring for the benefits that would accrue to the other offspring. Suppose, for example, that if all the offspring were to pursue their own interests, then only one would survive and in turn reproduce. Suppose also, however, that if one of the offspring no longer competed for itself, then, as a result, two of its siblings would survive to reproduce. This latter situation is not in the interests of the noncompetitive offspring, which is substituting a zero chance of reproductive success for what had been at least a minimally positive chance. (The qualification "under normal circumstances" is required because kin selection might also come into play.)

It would seem, therefore, that if the genes could give rise to behavior in one or both parents that would in some way and under special circumstances cause one offspring to become a nonreproducer, and this were in the parent's reproductive interests, such genes would be preserved and even multiplied by selection. Obviously, the circumstances would have to be rather special. Normally, if a parent would be better off with fewer potentially reproductive children, its best reproductive strategy would be not to have surplus offspring in the first place. However, another way to bring about the same situation would be for the parent's genetically caused behavior to force one offspring not merely not to compete with its siblings, but to aid the siblings in their reproductive quest. If the behavior could induce such altruism, it might well pay a parent to have an extra offspring, even though the offspring would never itself reproduce. This, then, is the essence of parental manipulation, although it must be pointed out that, despite the language, sociobiologists do not mean to imply conscious manipulative intent on the part of the parent. Indeed, the mechanism might well be more effective if both parent and child were unaware of what was going on.

The mechanism of parental manipulation has not met with unqualified enthusiasm, even from otherwise committed sociobiologists.[14] Nevertheless, there seem to be at least some cases in the animal world where parental manipulation actually occurs. The phenomenon of so-called trophic eggs, where, at times of drought or famine, some offspring are fed to others, would seem to qualify as an example.

At this point, and without concerning ourselves too greatly with the question of evidence, let us turn to the more specific question of how parental manipulation might be proposed as a mechanism for human homosexuality. One has merely to suppose that in some way, when it is in a parent's reproductive interests, this parent's behavior could cause a child to switch from developing into an exclusively heterosexual adult to developing into a person with at least some homosexual inclinations and practices. In our era, soaked as we are in Freudian and neo-Freudian speculations, to suppose that a parent can "make a child homosexual" does not require much of a leap of the imagination; to many, it is almost common sense. One must assume, of course, as in the case of kin selection, that the homosexual individual is indeed aiding its siblings or close relatives.

According to this view, therefore, homosexual men and women are not born, they are made, by the *parents*. There are, of course, genetic requirements, too: the parent must have genes that cause homosexuality-producing behavior; the offspring must have genes that permit it to be diverted into a homosexual role.

Fourth Hypothesis: Homosexuality as a By-Product

The fourth and final hypothesis hardly merits the title "explanation"; it is simply an unpublished speculation by one of the leading sociobiologists. However, given the fact that one philosopher of science has responded warmly to the idea and given that it does rather complete a list of the obvious possible ways in which homosexuality could be explained biologically, it seems worthwhile and legitimate briefly to consider the idea. It must be remembered that here we really are in the realm of speculation.[15]

Basically this explanation, credited to Alexander, understands homosexuality (or more particularly, male homosexuality) as a by-product of, or as incidental to, normal heterosexual development. Alexander writes: "It seems to me that an inadequately explored angle, in terms of immediate causes, is the idea that something that selected powerfully for heterosexual success (that is, reproduction) incidentally renders us all capable of homosexual preference, given particular circumstances especially during development."[16] He goes on to suggest that males compete very intensely for females (more so than females for males) and that just as one of the effects of this competition is that males have higher mortality than females and are more prone to disease and aging ("maladaptive, inevitable concomitants of the higher-stakes, higher-risk male strategy"),[17] so, too, "novel or extreme circumstances might be more likely to yield behavior (like homosexuality) that actually prevent (reproductive) success."[18]

Rather than postulating genes directly linked with homosexuality, as was the case in each of the first three hypotheses discussed, Alexander suggests that some feature that ordinarily would enhance an individual's ability to compete in the struggle to reproduce could, in special circumstances, also divert that individual into homosexuality.

Now what could such a feature be? What sort of attribute might usually lead to reproductive success but occasionally sidetrack one into homosexuality? Alexander's candidate is the propensity to masturbate! (Many nineteenth-century sexologists must be happily nodding approval in their graves.) Alexander points out that for most people, and particularly for boys, initial sexual experiences are autosexual: that is to say, boys masturbate a lot. The point here is that, absolutely, boys masturbate a fair amount and, relatively, masturbate more than do girls. Masturbation in adolescence seems normally to be of adaptive significance: one is learning about sex. For boys, however, there lurks the possibility of being switched towards homosexuality. After all, the masturbator is playing with organs of his own sex, and the visual stimuli are much more obvious for males than females. An erect penis, even if it is one's own, catches the eye far more than an erect clitoris, especially if it is one's own. Thus the male, as part of normal heterosexual development, treads a fine line between heterosexuality and homosexuality.

> We know that males masturbate more than females (both very likely are concomitants of more intense sexual competition). Moreover, male masturbation provides visual as well as tactual stimuli that are very similar to those involved in some homosexual activities. If one is stimulated sexually a great deal by seeing his own erect penis, then to be sexually stimulated by seeing someone else's is not such a great leap. Even if tactual and other stimuli are not greatly different between the sexes (and they may actually be), the great difference in visual feedback seems to be potentially quite significant.[19]

Does our society have idiosyncracies that push males towards homosexuality? Indeed it does: the fact that because so many males must wait so long before they can have heterosexual experiences, their only sexual relief is masturbation. By the time full heterosexual possibilities are available, it might be too late: the masturbating males prefer penises to vaginas. Thus, as a result of changes in society unrelated to sexuality, males are pushed towards homosexuality.

Alexander writes:

> Now, given the above sexual differences, and the likelihood (again, somewhat speculative) of enormous importance of *initial sexual experience*, what's going to happen if society creates a situation in which practically all boys masturbate for years before they have a real heterosexual experience? It seems to me that, for *incidental* reasons, many of them will become predominantly or solely homosexuals, and another large complement may continue to rely on masturbation as a sexual outlet, and may actually teeter on the edge of homosexuality as well. Females would not be so greatly affected.[20]

Concluding this discussion, he suggests that women have more trouble grasping the possible connection between masturbation and homosexuality, presumably because no such connection obtains in women's sexual development.

2. The Evidence

It is now time to ask: are any of these four possible sociobiological accounts of homosexuality true? How much evidence is there for or against each of them at present? What new data should be collected in order to test them?

Because the sociobiology of homosexuality is so new, many of the pertinent studies remain undone. Empirical science is not a question of simply gathering information, but rather of gathering information in the light of some hypothesis. Until recently, we did not have the sociobiological hypotheses. Now that we do, we can begin empirical studies in earnest, although for the time being we might have to make theoretical bricks with very little empirical straw.

Balanced Superior Heterozygote Fitness

This is still very much a hypothesis and appears to have been proposed for no better reason than because it describes one way to generate less than biologically fit humans. As yet, no study has shown that over a number of generations the ratios and distributions of homosexual to heterosexual offspring match those to be expected were a balanced superior heterozygote fitness mechanism at work. Indeed, it is questionable just how biologically unfit homosexuality actually is. It might be logical to suggest that a man who is attracted to other men will have fewer children than one who is exclusively heterosexual, but many homosexual men have fathered children. How reproductively unfit are homosexual men in our society? How unfit are they in preliterate societies?

Another problem is raised by the existence and nature of women. Fairly central to sociobiological theorizing is the claim that females (excluding fish but including humans) have little command over whether or not they will reproduce.[21] Males must compete for females and, hence, many males do not reproduce. Females, however, although they can use certain strategies to get a good mate, tend to be fertilized come what may. Does this imply, as there is empirical evidence to suggest, that lesbians are biologically as fit as their heterosexual sisters? This would not mean that, overall, homosexuality could not be biologically deleterious; the situation would approximate that of a sex-associated characteristic like hemophilia, which appears almost invariably in the male. It would mean, however, that theoretical ratios would change, and one would expect to find empirical evidence thereof.

In short, the balance hypothesis for homosexuality seems little more than a hypothesis, but before abandoning it altogether, one other area of possible evidence should be examined, evidence that might provide some necessary, albeit insufficient, conditions for the truth of the balance hypothesis. I refer to evidence that might be expected to show whether or not homosexuality is a genetic trait.

It is commonly thought (by nonbiologists) that there is a rigid dichotomy between genetically caused traits or characteristics and environmentally caused traits. Much of the controversy over the causes of intelligence has resulted from the belief that I.Q. is either a matter of *nature*, something one inherits, or a matter of *nurture*, something one is educated to or otherwise environmentally forced into. As biologists now realize, however, this sharply conceived dichotomy is misleading. All characteristics are in some sense a function of the genes in interaction with the environment. There is virtually nothing that could not be changed by a change in the genes; similarly, there is virtually nothing that could not be changed by a change in the environment. Why am I taller than my father? Partially because my mother's family members are taller than my father's. Partially because (English) children were better fed during the Second World War than they were during the First.

Nevertheless, some characteristics, such as human eye color, are controlled more by the genes in the sense that these characteristics develop on certain pathways, regardless of the normal environmental fluctuations. Conversely, some characteristics, such as speaking English rather than French, are more under the control of the environment in that they are very sensitive to variations in the normal environment, especially during development. If genetic and environmental traits are understood in these qualified senses, it would seem that a presupposition of the balance hypothesis for human homosexuality is that homosexuality falls fairly close to the genetic end of the spectrum. The hypothesis supposes that almost inevitably a homozygote for the homosexual gene will be homosexual and not otherwise.

The question to be asked, therefore, is whether homosexuality is genetic in this sense. Note that a positive finding only provides a necessary condition for the truth of the hypothesis. A characteristic can be essentially genetically controlled in many ways other than through homozygosity for a recessive gene. One could have straightforward dominance of a homosexual gene. Even if it were established that the pertinent causative gene is recessive, this does not prove, as the balance hypothesis claims, that the heterozygote is superior in fitness to all of the homozygotes.

To discover if homosexuality is genetic, one needs to observe situations where one might hope to distinguish genetic from environmental conditions. An experimental situation of growing popularity, particularly with those concerned with the genetics of I.Q., is provided by adoption.[22] If one can trace adopted children and their biological and adoptive parents, then one can observe if the children are more like their biological parents, in which case the genes seem to be playing the crucial role, or more like their adoptive parents, in which case the environment seems to be reigning. Unfortunately, in the case of homosexuality, it is not that easy to know to what extent studies of adoption would be applicable. Certainly many homosexual men and women have reproduced; but, as explained earlier, by the very nature of the case the data will be limited because homosexual individuals will tend to be less than fully reproductive. Also, I would imagine that gathering the required information would not be easy. A woman giving up a child for adoption might be prepared to answer questions about the education and jobs of herself and her lover. She might be far less willing to tell all about their sexual inclinations and practices. (Would a pregnant teenager know or admit that her boyfriend was homosexual? Even if she or her boyfriend had had homosexual encounters, how reliable a guide would that be to their adult sexual orientation?)

Much more promising are twin tests. There are two kinds of sets of twins: monozygotic twins, who share the same genotype, and dizygotic twins, who do not and are therefore no more closely related than normal siblings (that is, 50%). If one finds a significant divergence between the differences between monozygotic twins and the differences between dizygotic twins, then, since generally both twins experience the same environment, a reasonable inference is that genetic factors are involved. There is one major study of this kind, and the results, taken on their own, are astoundingly impressive.[23] In a study by Kallmann of 85 sets of twins where at least one twin showed homosexual behavior, in all 50 monozygotic cases, both twins were homosexual and, moreover, homosexual to much the same intensity. In the dizygotic cases, on the other hand, most of the twins of homosexual individuals showed little or no homosexual inclination or behavior. One could not ask for stronger evidence of a genetic component to human homosexuality. Indeed, the evidence is so strong one is reminded of Mendel's too perfect figures confirming his pea plant experiments.

Against Kallmann's study, it must be noted that cases of monozygotic twins with different sexual orientations have been discovered.[24] It certainly seems that homosexuality has some genetic basis, that it is not exclusively a function of environmental factors. Apart from anything else, it is almost inconceivable that the basic human sex drive, whatever its orientation, would have no genetic causal component. Humans would very soon die out if none of us cared a fig for sex or if we were attracted to cabbages rather than fellow humans. So at a maximum it would seem that, given our genetic sexuality, the environment could establish our preference for members of the same sex or the opposite sex, although no doubt the environment might increase or decrease the strength of our sexuality.

The counterfindings suggest two, not necessarily incompatible, possibilities. The first is that there are multiple causes of homosexuality. Perhaps some forms of homosexuality are essentially a function of the genes, whereas other forms or manifestations require a significant environmental input. Genetically speaking, this is quite plausible. Suppose homosexuality were a function of the number of genes, that is, if one had more than a certain number, then homosexuality would inevitably appear, but if one had less than that number, then a specific environmental input would be required to cause homosexuality. A person with none of the genes would not be homosexual whatever the input. This is a well-known phenomenon.[25] The second possibility is that at least one form of homosexuality has a genetic base but still requires some kind of special environmental input. Without it, one is heterosexual. (Alternatively, some form or manifestation of heterosexuality might require some kind of special environmental input; without it, one is homosexual.)

It should be added that some of the reported counterexamples to Kallmann's study (that is, monozygotic twins with different sexual orientations) lend plausibility to one or the other of the above possibilities, both of which require some specific environmental input to produce homosexuality. In the reported cases, there is evidence that within each pair, the twins were treated differently, with the later-to-be-homosexual twin generally getting more mothering, being treated more like a girl (nearly all the cases are of males), and so forth.[26]

In short, the evidence from twin tests provides fairly strong support for the belief that the genes play some role in homosexuality, although there is also evidence that the environment plays an important role. This brings us full circle back to Freud, for this was precisely his belief.[27] As pointed out, however, this conclusion does not support the balanced superior heterozygote fitness hypothesis as such, although the evidence is certainly compatible with other genetic mechanisms. Moreover, there are findings of another sort that cast doubt on the balance hypothesis. There are statistical findings about birth orders and parental ages at birth of child. In particular, there are significant correlations between male homosexuality and birth order (younger sons have a greater tendency to be homosexual) and between male homosexuality and age of parent at birth (older parents have more homosexual sons). At one point it was thought that the main correlation was between older mothers and homosexual sons, but now it seems that the age of the mother is a function of the age of the father, although indeed mothers are older.[28]

Now, if homosexuality were a simple case of balanced superior heterozygote fitness, these findings should not obtain. There is nothing in normal Mendelian theory, on which the balance hypothesis rests, to account for them. Indeed, an older child would be just as likely to be a homosexual homozygote as would older parents. At the very least, the findings suggest either that there are causes of homosexuality other than a balance mechanism or that the balance mechanism is complicated by other factors, genetic or environmental. At this point, given the lack of positive evidence for the balance mechanism and given the existence of other hypotheses, judicious use of Occam's razor is in order.

One might think that these findings about parental age and so forth would be fatal to any genetic hypothesis about the etiology of homosexuality, but this is not necessarily so. First, as has been noted, there might be multiple causes of homosexuality. Some homosexuality could be fairly directly controlled by the genes, and some not so. Although the above correlations point to significant connections between homosexuality, low birth order, and high parental age, they certainly do not deny that some homosexual men and women are first-born or that some have young parents. Second, it is well established that some genetic phenomena are a function of parental age (which is possibly not entirely unconnected with birth order, although not directly causally connected). In particular, the ova and sperm of older people are much more likely than those of younger people to have mutated in certain ways. For instance, older mothers are much more prone to having children afflicted with Down's syndrome (mongolism), caused by an extra chromosome, and older fathers are more prone to children with hemophilia.[29] There is, however, no cytological evidence for this hypothesis as it might apply in the case of homosexuality.[30]

Third, and perhaps most likely, the correlations are compatible with a genetic hypothesis if the environment also plays a significant causal role. The correlations suggest a more protective attitude of the parents (particularly the mothers) than is usual and also a child who feels cowed and dominated (and perhaps protected) by older siblings. Furthermore, an older father might play a less active role than usual. It is easy to see how environmental input of this kind could trigger a homosexual orientation in a child who already has the requisite genes. This would also explain why not all younger children or children of older parents are homosexual; indeed, most are *not*. For that matter, we would then have an explanation for why all children of dominant mothers (or whatever the environmental input might be) are not homosexual; they, too, lack the required genes.

I suggest, therefore, that our discussion so far has shown that at least some homosexuality could have a genetic component in the sense explicated above, that it is highly improbable that the environment does not play an important role, that the environmental input might be connected to familial factors such as parental age and birth order, and that while the balance hypothesis has not been proven false, it is unlikely to be the exclusive source of human homosexuality. Indeed, its only recommendation is that it is one way to get reduced fertility (which, it is assumed, homosexual individuals have).

Kin Selection

The key equation for the operation of kin selection, it will be remembered, is $C<rB$, where C is the reproductive *cost*, or loss of one's own personal reproductive success; r is one's degree of *relatedness* to the person who benefits; and B is the reproductive *benefit* conferred on the recipient of altruism. Thus, for instance, one's full siblings ($r = ½$) must benefit more than twice as much as one loses. There are a number of ways in which this inequality might obtain or be made more likely: if one's personal chances of reproduction are low, if the relationship to the recipient is high, and if the benefits obtained are high.

When applying this theory to homosexuality, it is assumed that homosexual individuals reduce their own reproductive fitness in order to boost the fitness of close relatives, especially siblings. There need not be anything intentional about this, but the effect is that in being homosexual, offspring become altruistic towards close relatives in order thereby to increase their own overall "inclusive fitness." This explanation is genetic in that the homosexual potential exists, but environmental in that the potential requires some reason to be triggered. (Since we are not Hymenoptera, there is no a priori advantage to being homosexual.) In verifying this hypothesis, we would look for some environmental reason suggesting that heterosexuality would be a bad reproductive strategy. In this, the kin selection hypothesis differs from the balance hypothesis. It differs also in expecting the homosexual individual to be altruistic: family members must breed better because of a relative's homosexual life style.

A number of sociobiologists have suggested that a major key to the causes of human homosexuality might lie in this theory of kin selection, and recently James Weinrich has argued the thesis at some length, basing his study on a far more detailed and extensive search of the empirical literature than had ever been undertaken before.[31] In line with another position taken by many sociobiologists and described above, Weinrich believes that the most unbiased sources of evidence for possible genetic foundations of human homosexuality lie in "primitive" or preliterate societies, for these most closely approximate early societies when natural selection was having its fullest effects on humans. With respect to homosexuality, Weinrich believes some suggestive extrapolations between preliterate societies and our own are possible.

Now, there are many reports in the anthropological literature of homosexuality of various forms in preliterate societies. One reads of various kinds of cross-dressing involving homosexual intercourse and even, in some societies, of certain forms of homosexual marriage. Unfortunately, because many of the reports concern adulthood almost exclusively, there is little information on whether something had occurred during the childhood of the homosexual adult that would make adult homosexuality an attractive reproductive strategy.

What information there is, however, suggests that adopting a homosexual life style frequently follows or is accompanied by phenomena that would indeed lower the reproductive cost. For instance, at one time among the Araucans of South America, all ritualized homosexual males "were men who had taken up the role of women, who took 'the passive role' in homosexual relations, and who were chosen for the role in childhood, due to their feminine mannerisms or certain physical deformities."[32] Among the Nuer, a "woman who married another woman is usually barren."[33] Among the Toradjas, the male homosexual life style and women's work occurred "primarily because of cowardice or some harrowing experience."[34] Generally, ritualized homosexual roles seem "to be attractive to individuals who have undergone some trauma, regardless of whether this involves a change of sex,"[35] although there certainly are exceptions. From a biological point of view, if such individuals have a low expectation of having offspring anyway, they have little to lose by becoming homosexual. In fact, if their siblings have more children as a result, they have much to gain.

Our own society provides some evidence to back up low *C* (reproductive cost) or low probability of *C* for homosexual individuals. "In accounts of modern male-to-female transsexuals, it is very common to read of some sort of childhood trauma immediately preceding the appearance of femininity."[36] A study of a group of effeminate boys (who apparently have a much higher probability of turning out homosexual than do average boys) "showed an above average incidence of certain physical defects."[37] Two other pieces of information might be pertinent, although Weinrich does not argue from them directly. First, a careful study implied that there are fairly significant physical differences between adult homosexual and adult heterosexual males. On the average (that is, there are definite exceptions), heterosexual males are heavier, although not taller, by 6.25 kilos, and they are stronger. As a statistical ensemble, homosexual males "had less subcutaneous fat and smaller muscle/bone development and were longer in proportion to bulk. Their shoulders were narrower in relation to pelvic width, and their muscle strength was less."[38] Given the fairly strong links between child development and the adult state, one might suppose that as a group, future homosexual males comprise the slighter, weaker children who face the possibility of reduced *C*, making a homosexual strategy more attractive from a biological viewpoint. (This would be especially true in preliterate societies.) Incidentally, lesbians tend to be taller than heterosexual females; would it make sense to suggest that this reduces their *C* also? Second, it should be remembered that homosexual children tend to be lower down in birth order. A lower birth order might not be so significant in our own society, but elsewhere this could be a reproductive handicap. By the time the youngest child comes along, most of the family resources, for example, a family farm, might already have been appropriated, significantly lowering the child's potential reproductive cost. Simply out of reproductive self-interest, it would pay the youngest child not to enter into heterosexual competition. All in all, therefore, it would seem that there is some evidence of lowered *C* or potential *C* for homosexual individuals.

At this point, there must be grumblings (or shrieks) of discontent from some readers. "Homosexuals are being presented as sickly, reedy little runts, unable to measure up to their heterosexual siblings! If this is not stereotypic thinking, nothing is." In reply to this objection, two points can be made. First, thanks to modern medicine, someone in our society who has had a childhood disease can be as perfectly physically fit as an adult. Second, there is nothing vilifying of homosexual men and women in the facts just related. If heterosexual men are indeed heavier and stronger than homosexual men, that is simply a fact. (Before accepting it as a universal truth, however, I would need the evidence of many more empirical studies.) Moreover, if sociobiologists want to seize on such a fact and use it to explain human sexual orientation, that is their right. After all, homosexuality must have some cause, and in terms of logic, having smaller body weight seems on a par with having a dominant mother, to cite a cause favored by many analysts. Certainly, smaller body weight is just the sort of thing that would attract evolutionists, which is what sociobiologists are, after all. If evolutionists found two races of the same species of animal with significant body weight differences, they would feel an explanation was in order and would search for other differences and consequences. (Indeed, the fact that members of different races have different body sizes has been of great interest to evolutionists. It is the basis of the evolutionary rule, Bergmann's principle, that members of races in colder climates tend to be larger than conspecifics in warmer climates. Various explanations have been sought.)[39]

So far we have considered only one side of the equation. The crucial inequality for kin selection is $C<rB$. Although this can be achieved by lowering C, raising B also helps. (I assume we are dealing with a fairly high r.) If a kin selection hypothesis for human homosexuality is to have any plausibility, then we might very reasonably expect to find that B, the amount one can help one's relatives, will be higher than normal. If one persists in linking facts to values, the values here would seem to elevate the status of homosexual men and women.

Again, consulting the example of preliterate societies, Weinrich argues that in such societies, homosexual persons tend to have high status that presumably would redound to the credit of close relatives. Weinrich documents the fact that in society after society, certain individuals adopt the dress and roles of members of the opposite sex, perform tasks appropriate to that sex, and engage in relations with members of their own sex. Moreover, with very few exceptions, homosexual persons have high status within their societies and, because they are considered to have certain special magical or religious powers, they often act as priests or "shamans." Weinrich catalogues their dignity thus: among the Inoits, "advice always followed"; the Araucans, "advice required for every important decision"; the Cheyenne, "goes to war; matchmaker; supervises scalps and scalp ceremonies"; the Illinois, "required for all important decisions"; the Navaho, "wealthy; leaders, mediators; matchmakers; unusual opportunity for material advancement"; the Sioux, "extraordinary privileges"; the Sea Dyaks, "rich; persons of great consequence; often chief."[40] In short, being homosexual and taking on a homosexual role in such societies often led to very high status and consequent opportunity to advance the cause and comforts of close relatives; that is, homosexual offspring were specially suited to raising the reproductive chances of those who shared their genes, for they could confer a high B on their relatives, which is something else required for the efficient operation of kin selection.

Of course, in our own society it is hardly true to say that homosexual men or women have an elevated status. Indeed, they tend to be despised and persecuted.[41] There does seem to be some evidence, however, that they have special abilities that would fit well in the roles that they would have been expected to play in preliterate societies where, according to sociobiologists, natural selection would have been having its crucial influence. Indeed, the abilities might even be such as to raise the *B* of homosexual persons in our own society, despite their apparent low status.

For one thing, there is evidence that they tend to have greater acting ability than heterosexual people.[42] Of course, it is notorious in our society that the stage (as do the arts generally) has a far higher proportion of homosexual participants than, say, the teaching profession. It could be that they are attracted to the stage precisely because this is one area where they will be accepted as normal. (Indeed, there are cases of heterosexuals who behave homosexually for the sake of professional advancement within the theater.) There is evidence that homosexuality has an even more complex causal relationship with the dramatic flair. For instance, effeminate boys, a group with proportionately more future homosexual adults than average, "are unusually adept at stage-acting and role-taking—at an age long before they could know that the acting profession has an unusually high incidence of homosexuality."[43] In other words, there is at least the possibility of a genetic link between homosexuality and acting ability, that is, between some homosexuality and some acting ability. It is obvious that the ability to act would be of value to a priest or shaman, given that so much of their work centers on magic, mysteries, and ceremonies.

The other pertinent piece of information is that homosexual individuals tend to have a higher I.Q. than their heterosexual peers. Several studies support this claim.[44] Of course, the whole question of intelligence and I.Q. tests gets one into some very murky areas, and some of the more grandiose and pernicious claims have been very properly criticized. Nevertheless, three pertinent points can be made. First, increasingly there is evidence that intelligence of some form exists and that this shares some kind of causal link with the genes, but not, I rush to say, independent of the environment; indeed, this kin selection argument rather invokes the environment.[45] Second, the justifiable criticisms of I.Q. studies, on the grounds that many are sexually or racially biased, are irrelevant to homosexual studies for which the comparison groups were drawn from similar social, sexual, and racial groups.

Third, and most importantly, the fear that I.Q. does not really represent some absolute quality of "brightness," but more an ability to get on in society (and to do well on things that teachers value, like I.Q. tests!) supports the kin selection hypothesis rather than detracts from it. Apparently, almost anyone can raise children, although some do it better than others. What homosexual persons must do, given the kin selection hypothesis, is raise themselves in society to such an extent that they win benefits for their kin, for example, through influence, find good jobs for nephews and nieces. In other words, homosexual men and women need to possess just those abilities and attitudes that critics fear are reflected on I.Q. tests. If society demands conformity rather than ingenuity, if the tests measure the former rather than the latter, if homosexual individuals shine on the tests, so much the better for the kin selection hypothesis.

Weinrich suggests that the increased abilities of homosexual people might be the effects of modifier genes. Perhaps a child has a physical injury. This affects its potential *C*. The child's genes then switch the child towards a homosexual orientation, and modifier genes come into play to increase the child's potential *B*. It would seem, however, that things could also work the other way, that children with certain superior abilities would be switched towards homosexuality in order that their inclusive fitness might be increased. It is important to emphasize that genes are pretty "ruthless." The case of the Hymenoptera clearly illustrates that there is nothing biologically sacred about parenthood. If it is in the reproductive interests of an organism to breed vicariously, then so be it. It is biologically possible that in humans, with their newly evolved factor of high intelligence, such reproduction by proxy could be a very attractive option.

How convincing is the evidence for the kin selection hypothesis for human homosexuality? Although most nonbiologists, and for that matter a good many biologists, find it difficult to take seriously any kind of kin selection hypothesis, I think that our experience with the Hymenoptera shows kin selection to be sensible and a crucial tool in causal understanding of animal sociality. Furthermore, since humans are animals, we ought at least to consider kin selection as working, or as having worked, on the human genotype. I suggest, therefore, that a case has been made for taking seriously the hypothesis that at least some human homosexuality might be a causal function of the operation of kin selection, if not in our own society, then in the societies of our ancestors.

On the other hand, no definitive case has been made for the hypothesis as yet. For instance, no proof has yet been offered showing that homosexual offspring really do increase the fitness of their relatives and thus, indirectly, increase their own inclusive fitness. Is it indeed the case that siblings of homosexual individuals successfully rear more offspring than they would have otherwise? It would be interesting to know, even in our own society, what attitudes homosexual men and women have towards their siblings and their nephews and nieces. Is there evidence, say, in the form of money left in wills, that they help their relatives to reproduce? Similarly, much more work needs to be done on the nature of homosexual people themselves. Do we systematically find that their *C* or potential *C* is reduced in childhood? In short, the case seems "not proven." Conversely, it ought to be taken seriously by anyone interested in the etiology of human homosexuality.

Parental Manipulation

In certain respects, this hypothesis overlaps the kin selection hypothesis, and much of the evidence garnered for one applies equally to the other. For instance, if a child has reduced *C* or potential *C*, it might be in the interest of the parents, and the child, to direct the child towards homosexuality. Similarly, if the homosexual offspring can and do benefit their relatives, this will help the parents as well as the children. Weinrich's evidence about the causes of shamanism and the status of shamans applies to this hypothesis as well as to the kin selection hypothesis.

The two hypotheses, however, are not identical and can lead to different predictions. What is in the reproductive interests of the parents might not be in the reproductive interests of the child. If a parent has three children and each child raises two children, there will be six grandchildren. Suppose, however, that one child were a nonreproductive altruist, then the others could raise three more children between them. Such altruism would benefit the parent, who would then have seven grandchildren instead of six, but would not benefit the altruist, who would exchange two children for three nephews and nieces, that is, 2 x 50% of its own genes for 3 x 25% of its own genes. More generally, conflict arises between parent and child over help to siblings, at a C to the child, whenever $C<B<2C$. Therefore, by identifying cost/benefit ratios, one ought to be able to distinguish between the operation of kin selection and parental manipulation or to recognize the presence of both.

Unfortunately, because we as yet have no quantified statistics on the benefits of having a homosexual sibling, there is presently no direct way to distinguish between kin selection and parental manipulation. What we can do, however, is ask if there is evidence that parents actively mold or influence their children, consciously or unconsciously, into homosexual lifestyles. This must occur if the hypothesis of parental manipulation is to have any truth at all.

In fact, the anthropological evidence is very strong that parents do play such a positive role. In case after case of homosexuality in preliterate societies, as listed by Weinrich, the parents play a part in encouraging or permitting the child to move towards the status of a member of the opposite sex. For instance, among the Sea Dyaks, in order to take on the cross-gender role of a *manang bali*, "one's father must pay a series of increasing fees to initiate the grown son into the role, and all three investigators (of the phenomenon) agree that the *manang bali* are invariably rich (often chiefs) as a result of their fees for shamanizing."[46] Similarly, in societies where a high bride price is demanded, parents will sometimes shift sons toward a female role, thereby changing an economic liability into an asset.

One might protest that the very opposite is the case in our own society. Most parents recoil from the thought of having a homosexual child. However, apart from the fact that our society might be atypical and inconsequential to long-range evolutionary considerations, it must be remembered that conscious manipulation is not demanded by sociobiology; indeed, control might be more effective if it occurs unrecognized. It is certainly tempting to speculate that when faced with a child who suffers some illness, parents become extraordinarily protective, thus triggering or aiding a switch in future sexual orientation. Again, if there is indeed anything to this whole question of birth order and the age of parents, it is not difficult to see how this might support parental manipulation. As the family gets larger and larger and, coincidentally, as the parents grow older, it becomes more in the parents' interest to raise a child to be altruistic towards the other children, rather than as yet another competitor. So, unwittingly, the mother smothers her youngest with affection, thus turning the child to homosexuality. Conversely, the father might start to lose interest, with the same effect occurring. This, of course, is all very speculative, intended merely to suggest that the parental manipulation hypothesis, like the kin selection hypothesis, deserves further study.

By-Product of Intense Male Heterosexual Competition

This is but a speculative and hitherto unpublished idea, and, as might be expected, it is not yet supported by much hard evidence. How could one test Alexander's suggestion that male homosexuality is a function of intense selection for heterosexual ability gone haywire? Certainly one could test the initial, crucial premise that competition among males is more intense than among females. Moreover, if the premise were true, then by implication there would be significant measurable differences between female homosexuality and male homosexuality. These differences would transcend fairly obvious physiological differences; for example, because males do not have vaginas but do have penises, almost necessarily homosexual males are going to be more anally oriented than lesbians. (In pornography, one sees lesbian encounters involving enemas and the like but, presumably, these magazines are directed primarily toward the male market. A survey of homosexual literature designed and read by males and of homosexual literature designed and read by females would be informative here.)[47] One could also test whether homosexual males are in some way more aggressive, perhaps more promiscuous, than homosexual females. Alexander's suggestion does not tackle female homosexuality. One must first invoke some other explanation for lesbianism and then see what the various implications for the possible differences between the female and male homosexualities would be.

The other significant way in which Alexander's suggestion seems to open itself to test rests on the differences one might expect to find between heterosexual and homosexual males. Alexander proposes that homosexuality is somehow a side effect of intense selection for heterosexuality and that masturbation might be a key factor here. At least two hypotheses seem worth checking. First, there seems to be an implication that homosexual males masturbate longer or more frequently or more intensely than do heterosexual males before they have the opportunity of having heterosexual relations. Might one expect to find that if within a certain period after a boy or adolescent starts masturbating he is initiated into heterosexuality, not necessarily actually going as far as intercourse, he will "turn heterosexual," but if there is not such heterosexual contact, he will "turn homosexual." Of course, how long he masturbates before heterosexual contact will be a function of both the age at which the boy starts masturbating and the age at which he first meets girls as girls. Tests certainly seem possible here: are homosexual males earlier masturbators than heterosexual counterparts? Do males brought up in the fashion of English public school boys, who live until eighteen in an all male, anti-female environment, really have greater tendencies towards homosexuality?

Second, given Alexander's suggestion, one might expect some physical differences between homosexual and heterosexual males. For instance, one might expect homosexual males to be able to sustain an erection longer and to have bigger penises. This last point might be particularly relevant, especially if one couples it with the claim that human penis size is key in human sexuality. The fact that human males have much larger penises than other primate males might be a factor in sexual attractiveness. After all, because of their upright stance, humans tend to copulate face to face rather than by the male mounting the female from behind. Face to face, the penis is much more visible to the female. It has also been suggested, by Desmond Morris, that the size of the human penis might be a function of the loss of body hair, something else that makes the penis more obvious.[48] Since the crux of Alexander's suggestion is that homosexuality is a function of adolescent masturbation, it is easy to see how having a somewhat larger penis might lead to an increased "penis fixation." One might think that if very large penises were causing homosexuality, natural selection would quickly step in to control the situation. Recall, however, that in Alexander's hypothesis, the crucial factor must be something that normally helps the individual in the reproductive struggle. It is the "super male," frustrated by lack of heterosexual outlets, who seeks satisfaction elsewhere.

It would be very interesting to know how significant a factor penis size really is in sexual attraction. Western males seem to think that a large penis is a desirable attribute. Many Western females must have picked up similar ideas, if only because magazines like *Playgirl*, aimed at women but produced by men, emphasize features prized by men. This, of course, has been going on for some time. Think of *Fanny Hill*, written by a man, where the women remain unmoved by anything less than a maypole. Are women really aroused by large penises, or, more pertinently, are women in preliterate societies aroused by large penises? Where does this particular attribute stand on a list of sexually attractive features?

Another fruitful area of inquiry concerns the question of whether delay of heterosexual relations leads to homosexuality. I know of no firm evidence that it does. Being cut off from heterosexual relations in adolescence can lead to homosexual practices when one is an adolescent. English public schools attest to the fact. Whether prolonged autosexuality causes homosexuality is another matter. However, does the denial of heterosexuality, and perhaps the indulgence in homosexuality, during adolescence really increase the chances of adult homosexuality? Do societies that bar adolescent heterosexuality, and perhaps also adolescent homosexuality, produce a higher proportion of homosexual adults than societies that allow or perhaps encourage adolescent heterosexuality? In short, all one can say is that Alexander's suggestion deserves investigation, but that at this point, it remains only a suggestion. (Studies by the Kinsey Institute suggest that male homosexuality is more common than lesbianism by 3:1, and that homosexual males tend to be more promiscuous than lesbians. Both these facts add to the plausibility of Alexander's hypothesis, but we could evaluate their full significance only if we had some likely hypothesis about the causes of lesbianism. In many ways, a detailed study of the differences between homosexual females and males would be most valuable in the search for causes.)

3. Biological Science, Social Science, and Homosexuality

By this point, my own feelings about the present state of the science must be fairly obvious. I think that the sociobiology of homosexuality is a viable source for scientific hypotheses and well worth investigation; I believe that all who concern themselves with the etiology of homosexuality should take sociobiology seriously. As yet, however, the sociobiology of homosexuality lies more in the realm of the hypothetical than the proven.[49] That the genes do play some role in homosexuality seems to be almost certain, that the environment plays some role in homosexuality seems just as certain, but we are still a long way from sorting out the respective components.

What more needs to be said? Perhaps a few words of comfort and encouragement to the social scientists. Social scientists tend to be horrified of and hostile towards biological science. Insecure at the best of times, they spend troubled nights dreaming of the bogey "reductionism," the rape of the social sciences as biologists move into the human domain. Of course, social scientists are not alone in their fear of reductionism. Those same, very arrogant biologists have much the same fears when faced with the physical sciences; "every biologist suffers from physics envy." In fact, social scientists can take comfort from what has happened to biology as a result of the reductionist impact of physics and chemistry. Although, in the 1950s, eminent biologists feared that molecular biology spelled their redundancy, precisely because of the coming of the physical sciences, biology flourishes today as never before. Molecular concepts and techniques have opened up whole new areas of discovery and theory in the biological world. As so often happens, the would-be conquerors have been assimilated to the mutual benefit of all.

What about the interaction between the biological and the social sciences? Can we expect to see the same kind of fruitful interaction and melding? My own feeling is that we can and that the sociobiology of homosexuality illustrates this point perfectly. Modern genetic thinking, more specifically, genetic thinking about homosexuality, emphasizes that it is not the genes alone that cause physical characteristics, including social behavioral characteristics. Rather, the genes *in conjunction with the environment* cause these characteristics. I believe the second half of this conjunct, the environment, leaves full scope for the legitimate and fruitful working of social science.

Let me illustrate my argument by reference to the causes of homosexuality. At this point, I am not particularly concerned about the absolute truth of the explanations I shall be considering: I use them to make a theoretical point. Doubtless, what I have to say will be generalizable to other situations and to other putative explanations that still await convincing confirmation.

Probably the most famous of all theories of homosexuality is the Freudian explanation for male homosexuality. All young boys are in love with their mothers. If they are to mature into heterosexual adults, at some point in their psychosexual growth they must learn to transfer this love to other females. Some boys, however, find it impossible to break from their mothers; the emotional links are too strong. This might well be a function of the mother being overinvolved and the father being withdrawn or hostile. These boys sense that there is something wrong with this situation: they are caught in an incestuous relationship, and humans have a universal horror of and aversion to incest. Unable to break from their mothers, they transfer their feelings of distaste for an incestuous relationship with a female to the rest of the female sex. Such boys and, when grown, such men are unable to respond sexually to females and, consequently, direct their sexual affections and behaviors to males. Significantly, homosexual males usually retain a very close bond with their mothers and often have very friendly nonsexual relations with other women, inasmuch as they can be seen as mother figures.

The Freudian explanation is drawn from the social sciences. Now consider an explanation drawn entirely from the biological sciences, namely the sociobiological explanation of homosexual behavior as the result of parental manipulation (where, remember, this need not be conscious manipulation). Are the two explanations rivals, in the sense that one excludes the other? No, rather they complement each other. The biological explanation sets certain parameters and limits, indicating gaps that can then be filled by the psychoanalytic explanation. The biological explanation does not, however, uniquely demand the psychoanalytic explanation. The biological explanation says that parents manipulate their offspring into homosexuality, while the psychoanalytic explanation tells how this manipulation takes place, namely, through mothers being overprotective and fathers withdrawn.

Without suggesting a unique relationship between the parental manipulation hypothesis and the Freudian story, and without presupposing the absolute truth of either explanatory account, I would add that the putative facts about parental ages and birth orders of homosexual offspring are highly suggestive. If, indeed, the parents are older and homosexual children tend to be somewhat low on the birth order, as pointed out above, this would fit in well with a parental manipulation explanation. As the parents' family grows, and coincidentally, the parents grow older, their reproductive strategy might favor an altruistic homosexual offspring over a competing heterosexual child. It is easy to imagine the form their manipulation might take: the father becoming indifferent and the mother becoming overprotective, just what the Freudian account supposes. It is worth emphasizing again that none of this need occur at the level of consciousness.

I suggest, therefore, that social scientists need not fear the coming of sociobiology. Specifically, conventional sexologists need not fear the sociobiology of homosexuality: the two disciplines can interact fruitfully. This being so, perhaps one final comment of a more philosophical nature might be permitted. Philosophers analyzing scientific change have tended to see it as falling into one of two camps. When a new theory comes along, some believe that the new theory *replaces* the existing theory, in the sense that the new theory proves the old theory wrong. Alternatively, some believe that a new theory absorbs the older theory or *reduces* it to a deductive consequence of the more general newer theory.[50]

I suggest that in the interaction between the biological and social sciences, we should look more for a process of reduction than replacement, at least as regards the explanation of human sexuality. Nevertheless, and this might mitigate the grumblings by social scientists that they no more want their work to be called the deductive consequences of biology than to be replaced by it, I would argue that the prospective absorption of social science would be something at once weaker and less threatening than straight deduction. Consider, for a moment, the way in which parental manipulation is supposed to work. As can be seen, although a place is created for the operation of parental manipulation, its exact nature is left blank. One cannot deduce how this parental manipulation will work. In the case of homosexuality, for instance, mothers could just as easily be hostile as loving. In short, rather than the deduction of the theories of social science, what we have is a need for social science to complement biological science and to explain what is going on at the phenotypic level about which the biology is silent. I do not imply that biology is always silent about the phenotypic level, far from it. I mean, rather, that in the human social context, biologists are as yet ignorant of much of the workings at the phenotypic level. Social scientists have worked at this level and, consequently, are already far ahead in a field that biologists would otherwise need to explore all by themselves.

I conclude, therefore, that the causes of homosexuality point to a more subtle relationship between the biological and social sciences than conventional philosophy might lead one to expect. More importantly, the future for both areas of scientific inquiry looks exciting and stimulating as they now begin to work together.

Notes

1. E. O. Wilson, *Sociobiology: The New Synthesis* (Cambridge, Mass.: Belknap Press, 1975).

2. Desmond Morris, "Darwin and the Double Standard," *Playboy*, August 1978, 108.

3. Full details of the sociobiology controversy and of general claims made by sociobiologists and their critics can be found in my "Sociobiology: Sound Science or Muddled Metaphysics?" in Frederick Suppe and Peter Asquith, eds., *PSA 1976*, vol. 2 (Lansing, Mich.: Philosophy of Science Association, 1976), and *Sociobiology: Sense or Nonsense?* (Dordrecht: Reidel, 1979).

4. George E. Hutchinson, "A Speculative Consideration of Certain Possible Forms of Sexual Selection in Man," *American Naturalist* 93:869 (1959): 81-91.

5. Monroe W. Strickberger, *Genetics* (New York: Macmillan, 1968). See also T. Dobzhansky, F. J. Ayala, G. L. Stebbins, and D. W. Valentine, *Evolution* (San Francisco: Freeman, 1977).

6. For more details, see my *The Philosophy of Biology* (London: Hutchinson, 1973) and Richard Lewontin, *The Genetic Basis of Evolutionary Change* (New York: Columbia University Press, 1974).

7. I trust that I am not prejudging issues by ignoring the fact that one of human sociobiology's most vocal critics, Richard Lewontin, has argued in *The Genetic Basis of Evolutionary Change* that the chromosome is more crucial than the gene.

8. See George C. Williams, *Adaptation and Natural Selection: A Critique of Some Current Evolutionary Thought* (Princeton: Princeton University Press, 1966); Wilson, *Sociobiology*.

9. See David P. Barash, *Sociobiology and Behavior* (New York: Elsevier, 1977); Richard Dawkins, *The Selfish Gene* (Oxford: Oxford University Press, 1976); W. D. Hamilton, "The Genetical Theory of Social Behavior. I," *Journal of Theoretical Biology* 7 (1964): 1-16 and "The Genetical Theory of Social Behavior. II," *Journal of Theoretical Biology* 7 (1964): 17-32; and E. O. Wilson, "Human Decency is Animal," *New York Times Magazine*, 12 October 1975, 38-50.

10. See George F. Oster and E. O. Wilson, *Caste and Ecology in the Social Insects* (Princeton: Princeton University Press, 1978).

11. See James D. Weinrich, *Human Reproductive Strategy. I. Environmental Predictability and Reproductive Strategy: Effects of Social Class and Race. II. Homosexuality and Non-reproduction: Some Evolutionary Models* (doctoral dissertation, Harvard University, 1976); Wilson, *Sociobiology*.

12. Robert L. Trivers, "Parent-offspring Conflict," *American Zoologist* 14 (1974): 249-64.

13. Richard D. Alexander, "The Search for an Evolutionary Philosophy," *Proceedings of the Royal Society of Victoria Australia* 84 (1971): 99-120; "The Evolution of Social Behavior," *Annual Review of Ecology and Systematics* 5 (1974): 325-84; "The Search for a General Theory of Behavior," *Behavioral Science* 20 (1975): 77-100.

14. See Dawkins, *The Selfish Gene*.

15. This idea comes in a letter written by Richard Alexander (University of Michigan) to Frederick Suppe (University of Maryland), 13 February 1978. In a letter to me, Suppe says that he thinks the idea has considerable merit.

16. Alexander, letter to Suppe.

17. *Ibid.*

18. *Ibid.*

19. *Ibid.*

20. *Ibid.*

21. Robert L. Trivers and Dan E. Willard, "Natural Selection of Parental Ability to Vary the Sex Ratio of Offspring," *Science* 179 (1973): 90-2.

22. I discuss conceptual and empirical questions surrounding the genetics of I.Q. in my *Sociobiology*.

23. Franz J. Kallmann, "Comparative Twin Study on the Genetic Aspects of Male Homosexuality," *Journal of Nervous and Mental Diseases* 115 (1952): 283-93; Leonard L. Heston and James Shields, "Homosexuality in Twins: a Family Study and a Registry Study," *Archives of General Psychiatry* 18:2 (1968): 149-60.

24. For example, J. D. Rainer, A. Mesnikoff, L. C. Kolb, and A. Carr, "Homosexuality and Heterosexuality in Identical Twins," *Psychomatic Medicine* 22 (1960): 251-58.

25. Conrad H. Waddington (*The Strategy of the Genes* [London: Allen and Unwin, 1957]) discussed this phenomenon extensively in the context of fruit-fly wing deformities. Whether, as he thought, this is the key to an important evolutionary mechanism is moot. See Williams, *Adaptation and Natural Selection* and my *Philosophy of Biology*.

26. Rainer *et al.*, "Homosexuality and Heterosexuality in Identical Twins."

27. Sigmund Freud, *Three Essays on the Theory of Sexuality*, in J. Strachey, ed. and trans., *The Standard Edition of the Complete Psychological Works of Sigmund Freud*, vol. 7 (London: Hogarth Press, 1953), 123-245.

28. Kutao Abe and Patrick A. P. Moran, "Parental Age of Homosexuals," *British Journal of Psychiatry* 115 (1969): 313-17; Eliot Slater, "Birth Order and Maternal Age of Homosexuals," *The Lancet* 1:7220 (13 January 1962): 69-71. See also John Birtchnell, "Birth Order and Mental Illness: A Control Study," *Social Psychiatry* 7 (1972): 167-79; Marvin Siegelman, "Birth Order and Family Size of Homosexual Men and Women," *Journal of Consulting and Clinical Psychology* 41 (1973): 164-73; and Weinrich, *Human Reproductive Strategy*.

29. B. Hilton, D. Callahan, M. Harris, P. Condliffe, and B. Berkley, *Ethical Issues in Human Genetics* (New York: Plenum, 1973).

30. See Judd Marmor, *Sexual Inversion: The Multiple Roots of Homosexuality* (New York: Basic Books, 1965).

31. Weinrich, *Human Reproductive Strategy*; see also E. O. Wilson, *On Human Nature* (Cambridge, Mass.: Harvard University Press, 1978).

32. Weinrich, *Human Reproductive Strategy*, 170.

33. *Ibid.*, 171.

34. *Ibid.*

35. *Ibid.*, 173.

36. *Ibid.*

37. *Ibid.*

38. *Ibid.*, 129.

39. See my *Philosophy of Biology*.

40. Weinrich, *Human Reproductive Strategy*, 203-5.

41. A matter on which Weinrich does not speculate is the possible pertinence to his case of a phenomenon in our own society, the Roman Catholic clergy. They have considerable influence, particularly in southern and rural Europe and in South America, and this influence obviously comes from their priestly roles. Is it significant that they abstain from heterosexual relationships and wear clothing which is far closer to that of women than men? It would be interesting to have answers to a number of questions. Does having a priest in the family raise the family's status? Do priests actively aid their siblings and their nephews and nieces? Why do men become priests? Are they often sickly children, are they down the birth order, are their mothers highly instrumental in their career choices? The one question that will probably never be answered is this: what connection, if any, is there between the priesthood and homosexuality? Was Voltaire's Jesuit the exception or the rule? Of course, one difference between Catholic priests and homosexual shamans is that priests are not supposed to have any sexual relations, homosexual or heterosexual.

42. Weinrich, *Human Reproductive Strategy*, 175.

43. *Ibid.*

44. *Ibid.*, 176.

45. I review some of the evidence for this claim in my *Sociobiology*.

46. Weinrich, *Human Reproductive Strategy*, 169.

47. See Donald Symons, *The Evolution of Human Sexuality* (New York: Oxford University Press, 1979).

48. See Wilson, *Sociobiology*, 554.

49. As a race, modern philosophers, as most people in the arts, tend to fear and be hostile towards science. It will therefore come as no surprise that eminent philosophers have already started pontificating on the conceptual impossibility of human sociobiology; see, for example, Stuart Hampshire, "The Illusion of Sociobiology," *New York Review of Books*, 12 October 1978, 64-9.

50. David Hull, *Philosophy of Biological Science* (Englewood Cliffs, N.J.: Prentice-Hall, 1974).

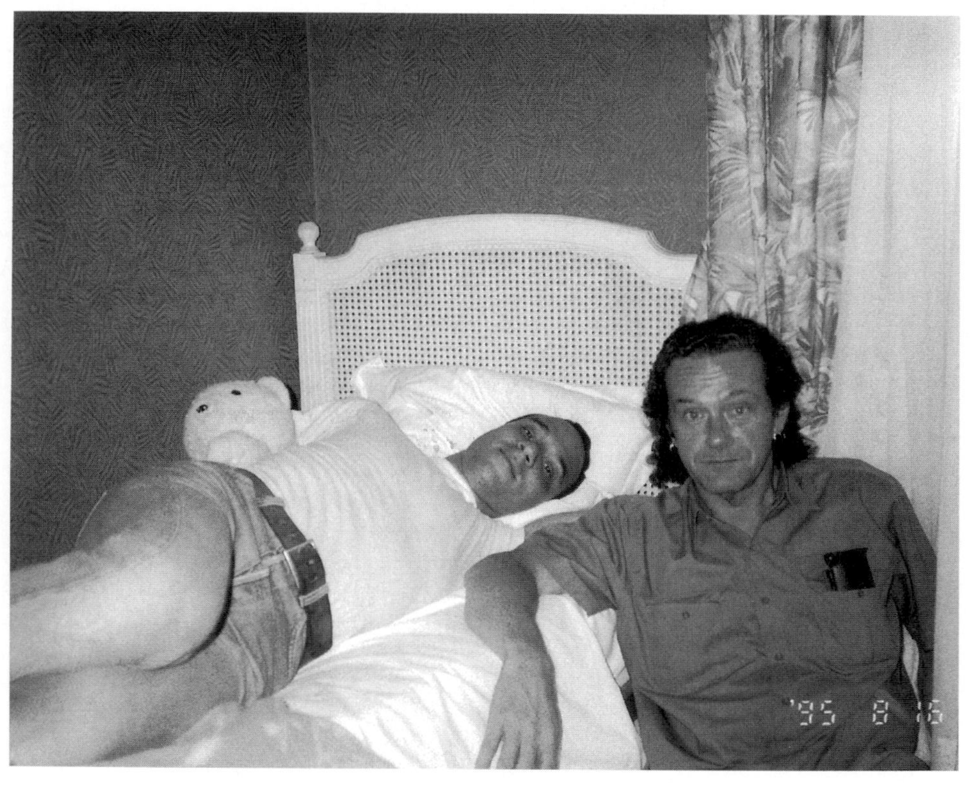

Steven Barbone (center), Lee Rice (right), and Lance (left)
(photograph: John Jenders)

Lee Rice, author of "Hatching Your Genes Before They're Counted"
Paper presented at the Society for the Philosophy of Sex and Love
during the
Eastern Division Meeting of The American Philosophical Association
New York, N.Y., 28 December 1979

Eight

HATCHING YOUR GENES BEFORE THEY'RE COUNTED

Lee Rice and Steven Barbone

1. Homosexuality and Sociobiology

Interest in sociobiology no longer continues at the high level prescribed by Michael Ruse in his 1981 paper.[1] The bitterness sparked by the publication of E. O. Wilson's *Sociobiology* gave rise to a wave of defense and counter-defense; but, as so often happens in the history of science, the positive aspects that the sociobiologists had to make to the study of human behavior have become incorporated into mainstream sociology and biology, and their excesses have been relegated to the dusty museum of the history of philosophy and science. The battle, of course, rages on about the related contributions of environment and heredity to human behavior. This battle is often one of ideology or philosophy rather than science. One has only to consider the more recent flurry of ideological charges concerning claims that I.Q. is hereditary.[2] The majority of scientists working in the relevant fields, however, would probably agree with Skinner's claim that the evidence for a crude environmentalism in accounting for a great deal of human behavior is overwhelming. The sociobiological hypotheses, however, remain as a reminder to us that, just as there is an outer world determining human behavior to a great extent, so the inner world (that is, inside the periphery of one's skin) is certainly a codeterminant. Where the "credit" (in Skinner's terms) is to go for a particular mode of behavior must be answered on a case by case basis for each such mode, general answers being as imprecise as they are empirically suspect.

Ruse remarks early in his paper that it is time for philosophers "to start considering in detail specific claims made by the sociobiologists" (61) and we should take this claim to heart in dealing with the four hypotheses that he joins the sociobiologists in offering (and that are treated *singulatim* in succeeding sections). Any proposed explanation, however, is embedded within a context of presuppositions, and part of the job of the philosopher of science is to isolate and to analyze just those principles on which the explanation rests, especially since they are so often unstated within the scientific literature. While Ruse notes that sociobiologists, with due scientific humility, have no present "official line" on homosexuality, he fails to note that they do presuppose a rather clear idea of what it is that they are setting out to explain. Perhaps he feels, as most social scientists do not, that everyone knows what homosexuality is, or that the world is neatly divided into homosexual and heterosexual components. This assumption is worth questioning, since so much else relies on it.

Due to his decision to follow the sociobiologists in not providing a specific characterization of their explicandum, the reader is left guessing whether the underlying criteria are behavioral or attitudinal. For either option, however, many researchers prefer a continuum model. One need only think back on Kinsey's behavioral scale (whose influences are still present)[3] or on more recent attempts to characterize human sexuality as essentially polymorphous and only socially object-specific.[4] How we distinguish "genuine" homosexuals from those who are "opportunists" in the area of same-sex relations (for example, prisoners, or anyone mindful of the dictum that any sex might be better than no sex at all) will much depend on our presuppositions of identification, and Ruse has no help to offer here.

If the scientific community is agreed on little else in dealing with sexual deviance, there is at least considerable agreement on the fact that "homosexuality" does not designate a single class of dispositions; or, to put the same point in another way, that "homosexual" is not keyed to a single or unique set of properties among individuals.[5] The most frequently used taxonomies for sexual deviance involve distinguishing biological sex, gender identity, social sex-role, and sexual orientation,[6] a procedure more complicated than Kinsey's seven-stage continuum, but which appears to have solid psychometric foundations. In short, one might argue against Ruse that homosexuality does not admit of a single explanation, since it fails to denote a class of behavior, persons, or dispositions with any real common property. Asking where bisexuals fit into his schemata of explanation might be one way to ferret out his presuppositions in more detail.

The four hypotheses Ruse discusses as examples of sociobiological explanatory schemata do little to allay our reservations about inattention to presupposition, however, since, while these hypotheses are certainly scientific in the broad sense (as opposed to pseudoscience), we shall now argue that they are just as certainly disconfirmed by most of the available evidence.

2. Balanced Superior Heterozygote Fitness

The first hypothesis Ruse presents is that of balanced superior heterozygote fitness, and it is even here in the beginning of his paper that one might well ask what exactly it is that sociobiology purports to bring to light regarding the etiology of male homosexuality. His explanation (mis)applies the Hardy-Weinberg law to account for the fact that homosexuals just don't die out. In the most simplistic terms, he proposes that it is a homozygotic pairing that causes a person's homosexuality, and that the incidence of this pairing, according to Ruse, can be predicted using a version of Hardy-Weinberg. Despite the apparent precision of terminology, a major problem arises in this section if one bothers to analyze the mechanisms at work. Calculations show that his application of the Hardy-Weinberg law predicts an incidence of homosexuality that is quite beyond even the most exaggerated estimation of percentage of gays in the general population. More exactly, using the Hardy-Weinberg law as Ruse suggests would predict an outcome of 25% of gays for each generation; this surpasses any accepted incidence of homosexual orientation in contemporary society. Attempts at correcting the model only lead to further discrepancies with available statistics. Even if it were assumed that homosexuals do not produce offspring (whether among themselves or though liaisons with heterosexuals) and that homozygous heterosexuals do reproduce (although, as homozygotes, they would be less "fit"), the mean incidence of homosexuality would work out to roughly a proportion of 1:5 for gays to nongays, a level that is not supportable by any available empirical evidence. Though the predictive value of his application of the Hardy-Weinberg law is not consistent with available empirical evidence, Ruse is not anxious to give it up so quickly; he suggests adding other variables and assumptions that, as he himself notes, still do not bring his predictive output in line with available data.

Despite the failure of the superior heterozygote fitness hypothesis as a single and simple explicans using the Hardy-Weinberg law, Ruse attempts to save this assumption by looking at cases of monozygotic twins. Though the Kallmann study[7] seems to indicate, as Ruse suggests, extremely strong evidence for a purely genetic cause of homosexuality, it would offer little support to the present hypothesis if any single instance of monozygotic twins who were not both heterosexual were documented. Unfortunately for those who would like to posit a unique genetic determinant to explain homosexuality, such cases have been found and studied, and Ruse, to his credit, does cite a major study that disconfirms this hypothesis (72). Rather than taking the data to discredit a possible genetic explanation for homosexuality, Ruse argues the contrary, that these instead provide *support* for this theory. At this point, however, one wonders what it is that this hypothesis means to explain, since if there were a unique genetic determinant for any trait or characteristic whatsoever, then that trait would necessarily manifest itself in each member of every set of monozygotic twins; any deviation signals causes other than genetic to account for the trait.[8] One way of saving the hypothesis, with which Ruse seems to flirt later in his paper, is that of introducing higher-level multigene interactions. The introduction of higher-level interactions will fit any hypothesis whatever, but it is legitimate if (and only if) the incidence one is attempting to predict is independently known (which it is not), and (not "or") there is some independent evidence for such interactions (which there is not).

This brings us to our major complaint against sociobiology, or at least the version that Ruse presents in his paper. Given the failure of any genetic theory to provide a full etiological explanation of homosexuality, Ruse adds that while the "right" genes are necessary, certain environmental factors are also required. The obvious problem here is that this is just plain bad science; having the "right" genes that require some sort of environmental activation almost smacks of Aristotelian forms waiting to be actualized in matter. One here wonders what role sociobiology claims for itself: if it requires another explanation to make it cogent, why not dispense with it altogether? It is not that, as members of that "race" of modern philosophers (86, note 49), we object to science; rather, we give our highest accolades to scientific theories that give us more bang for the buck, that is, those that offer explanations that are relevant, empirically testable, simple, and elegant. Our "hostility" to Ruse's sociobiology as science arises because it fails to meet these basic criteria for science. But perhaps we are being too hasty here; Ruse does offer other possibilities and hypotheses, and it is to one that he labels "most exciting" that we now turn.

3. Kin Selection

Ruse contends that the hypothesis of kin selection is the "most exciting of the new theoretical ideas" proposed by sociobiology (65), and it has met with limited success in genetic applications to simpler organisms, so that what is at issue here is whether we can reasonably hope for success in applying it to gays, or even to *homo sapiens* in general. The basis of the notion is that the individual is the critical unit in the evolutionary selection process, and that losses in passing on genes must be offset by gains. The "simple arithmetic" offered (65) is as simple as it is wrong. If foregoing all of my reproductive prospects increases a sibling's prospects by 100%, then no gain from my perspective is achieved unless my sibling's prospects were at least twice mine. This is teleologism with a vengeance, and it is not eliminable using any of the standard devices for casting functional explanations as short-hand expressions for longer mechanical ones. Despite the mathematical formulation of a few cost-benefit relationships, what counts as a gain and how one should project the coefficient of benefit remains obscure. Its obscurity is fairly close to the surface due to the manner in which Ruse switches between causal explanations and teleological ones. The notion of a coefficient of benefit sounds blatantly teleological in just the wrong sense and is begging for some clarification. In the absence of such clarification, we might not even have a genuine explanation, whether or not it should be even plausible.

Suppose, following Ruse, that such a coefficient could be extrapolated. We are then faced with explaining why gays don't just simply die out. "All one needs to do," he suggests, "is to postulate that homosexuals take altruistic or high prestige jobs" (66). While somewhat prophetically (in light of current publicity and litigation) he does mention the priesthood, he fails to mention hairdressers or ballet dancers;[9] but, regardless of their standing in his implicit metricization for altruism, not only is such a postulate *ad hoc*, but (once again) recent research tends to disconfirm it. The Weinberg and Williams study[10] provides as random a sample of homosexuals as we are likely to have for some time. If we discount the fact that some professions remain closed to open gays and concentrate on distributions for relatively "closeted" gays into various kinds of employments, we find a pattern nearly random. In short, gays are just as diverse in their personality features and in their choices of vocations as their nongay counterparts. Granted that there are more *open* gays in some professions, but that fact is explained by the crudest of environmental hypotheses: bringing sociobiological hypotheses to bear on it is a classic case of an answer looking for a question.

Added to the above considerations is the existence of evidence[11] that gays tend to be more egocentric than heterosexuals: hence the frequently leveled charge of narcissism more often imputed to gay males. How to square the psychological evidence for these claims with Ruse's hypothesis of inherent altruism as a means of applying kin selection we leave to greater minds.

Ruse's analogy of gays to "sterile worker bees" (66) is also misleading. Any social scientist (or gay, for that matter) who has made the rounds of cruising areas, bars, baths, and the like would be able to inform Ruse that gays are notoriously productive of offspring in our society. Many persons come to recognize or understand their gayness only rather late in life when they are married and already have (heterosexually produced) families. If gayness were teleologically driven by some mechanism such as kin selection, it would assuredly be an example of nature at its lowest state of efficiency. Some initial credibility for kin selection would be forthcoming if it could be shown that people with gay siblings had a significantly higher reproductive output than persons with nongay siblings, but even this evidence, if available (which it is not), would be ambiguous for reasons to be given shortly.

This second hypothesis, like its predecessor, presupposes some single set of properties, genetically determined, that will characterize all and only gays. In the first hypothesis, the set comprised sexual object choice; for the second, the set consists of subsidiary (that is, nonsexual) personality traits. Here again, however, psychometric evidence provides warrantable disconfirmation for any such conceivable set of hypotheses. Gays are running a close second to laboratory rats in the amount of testing being done on them. The literature offers countless studies of personality and attitudinal features of gay psychodynamics. All attempts to isolate a correlation, linear or not, between homosexuality and these features have ended in failure. The gay subculture displays as wide and variegated a class of attitudinal types as almost any other.

It would be unfair, however, not to mention one factor that, while it reduces somewhat the impact of the above critical remarks, does nothing positive to enhance the status of the hypothesis of kin selection. This is the sampling problem. Social scientists doing research on gay behavior will naturally begin with raw data from places where gays are likely to be both most accessible and most identifiable: gay bars, baths, and urban cruising areas. If we place the incidence of exclusive homosexuality at somewhere between 2% and 10% of the population, we simply have no way currently of estimating bias introduced by sampling error, even if the incidence were as low as 2%. We conclude that Ruse's second hypothesis, at least as applied to gays, is far from "exciting."

4. Parental Manipulation

Of the four hypotheses presented, this one is the most incredible, but it is unbelievable only in the sense that it defies logic and is almost magical. Though it is close to the second, it differs from it in that kin selection focuses on the particular offspring's success at maintaining its genes in the gene pool while parental manipulation focuses on the parents' success at safeguarding for posterity their own proper genetic material. "Without concerning ourselves too greatly with the question of evidence" (67),[12] we will suppose, for the sake of argument, that parental manipulation is a viable explanation to account for homosexuality; and, we will go further and grant that it is genetically caused. The situation with which we are faced is, then, that a parent or the parents, acting under the influence of their genetic makeups, somehow coax, lead, train, or fashion an offspring to become homosexual so that other offspring might better reproduce and increase the gene pool. The cause of homosexuality, according to this hypothesis, is now no longer related to the homosexual's genes, but to those of at least one of his/her parents. What we find troubling with this account is how it is supposed that the parent(s) should "know"[13] which of the offspring to "turn" gay. Ruse would have us believe that this too is genetically programmed, but what exactly is programmed? Is it that the last child is to be molded into a homosexual, or is it some complex formula? How does the parent organism compute (albeit unconsciously) which of the children is (are) the one(s) to be pushed into sexual deviance? Again, we venture to say that what Ruse presents is more teleology than science.

As evidence to support this hypothesis, Ruse does cite the anthropological literature to demonstrate that societies exist in which parents quite openly manipulate their offspring into taking homosexual roles. Even if we were to agree that the parental behavior is genetically caused, we are faced with a presupposition, not stated and one with which we would hazard few would agree, that a gay person is merely one who has homosexual encounters whether for love, money, or marbles. Speculating about the roles of contemporary smothering mothers or distracted fathers does not enhance Ruse's arguments.

Of course, Ruse does realize that the above description is, quite frankly, incredible, and so he is quick (once again) to add that environmental factors be required in addition to the genetic dispositions. Why must the parents' behavior be interpreted as being caused genetically? Would it not be simpler to posit that the parents who push their children into homosexuality are acting solely from environmental factors? Why couldn't the parents, on Ruse's account, after somehow mystically sensing which of their offspring have the best genes to pass on and thereby knowing which offspring to sacrifice to deviance, have learned that in their society it is best to rear some offspring as homosexual? This could have been learned and, as Ruse himself suggests, it is not necessary that behavioral mechanisms be conscious. Perhaps parents of gays, if they do lead their offspring down the garden path of homosexuality, do so because deep down they have learned, unconsciously, *pace* Ruse, that having a gay child is better for them as parents (materially, psychologically, socially). If we apply Occam's razor, as Ruse suggests we do (73), there is no need to drag genetics into the picture. Our major complaint against the superior heterozygote fitness hypothesis was that it required importing conditions or factors, which alone could be sufficient to explain the phenomena, in order to make them cogent; we have the same situation in the case of parental manipulation. Like innate ideas of the past waiting to be brought out by experience, this hypothesis, as Nelson Goodman once quipped about aesthetic qualities, should be dropped onto the dormitive virtue pile.

If one were still inclined, however, to consider seriously the sociobiological account of parental manipulation, some concerns would need to be addressed. One immediate query would be how this theory could possibly account for the fact that there are some gay offspring who have no siblings. Obviously, that this occurs would be a sign of genetics gone awry. Furthermore, evidence that sexual orientation is more or less determined early in the organism's existence[14] would also disconfirm the hypothesis. Given that much empirical evidence disconfirms the hypothesis, that evidence given in support of it is based on unaccepted presuppositions, and that the nature of the explanation tends towards teleology, we judge the hypothesis, like the previous ones, to have little merit or scientific interest.

5. Homosexuality as a By-Product

Ruse concedes that his fourth and last hypothesis is less an explanation than a speculative suggestion. In his original presentation, from which the paper was developed, the hypothesis made much of penis size as one factor that might explain homosexual development as a deviation from the heterosexual norm. In the paper, we are left only with the point that an erect penis "catches the eye far more than an erect clitoris" (69); so, presumably, to restate a point made in his earlier version, a larger penis catches the eye more than a smaller one does. Males, we are told, compete more intensively for females, and this allegedly explains their disease proneness and higher mortality at an early age. Ruse, like the sociobiologists he defends, has a tendency to glide effortlessly from correlation to cause: earlier mortality does correlate with more competitive mating patterns among males in many species, but which (if either) fact is the cause of the other remains an open question.

This explanation shares some features of Freud's earlier analogy of gayness to "stunted growth," a fact to which Ruse also alludes. We are all, on this count, potentially gay to the extent that our competitive spirit will have some intrinsic limit or other. What Ruse fails to mention is that most sociobiologists tend to see aggression as a distinctively male component; and, if this were true, it would surely not be their intense competition for females that made them aggressive, but rather their aggressive natures that account for their competitiveness. Perhaps some such account of aggression is adequate; but, even granting this as an open possibility, there still seems to be no evidence that male homosexuals are less aggressive than their nongay counterparts. Anyone who has spent even a few minutes in a gay bar or bath might be tempted to conclude that, in the area of competition for sex partners ("cruising"), gays are the paradigms of aggression rather than dropouts in the ongoing competition for sex partners. Some psychometric indices for aggression are also available. They tend to indicate that nongays tend to be more aggressive *toward gays* than the latter to the former, but there is no evidence that aggression is generally present to a higher degree in nongays than in gays.[15]

Ruse's obvious respect for Freud, expressed at several points in the paper, might also explain his Freudian willingness either to discount or to ignore completely available data in favor of the construction of hypotheses in a wholly a priori manner. Witness his suggestion that there is a *relatively high incidence* of gayness in our society. On what evidence is this based? What *is* the incidence of gayness in our society? And on what comparison does Ruse base his claim that it is high? Surely not on the obviously explicable fact that (male?) gays are more visible now than they were a decade or two ago or that they are less visible in religious societies such as Iran.

Ruse goes on to hypothesize that, since boys masturbate more than girls, such an autocentric sexual outlet would naturally lead to an higher incidence of homosexuality. Given his remarks on the inducements of an erect penis, we should conclude that those males who are *mieux montés* or "better hung" are most likely of all to become gay, a fact (if such it be) that has not reached the attention either of social scientists or the gay community. He then moves on to discuss "normal heterosexual development" (69), whatever that is; and we suspect again that the Freudian model lies close to the surface. We know of no study that has compared mean penis size among gays to nongays. The evidence of the relative incidence of lesbianism (it should be lower on this hypothesis) to male homosexuality is also ambiguous since lesbians are generally more difficult to sample (because of a less frequent reliance on bars, baths, and cruising areas).

The three pieces of empirical evidence that might lend some credibility to this last hypothesis are (1) generally lower incidence of female than male gays in most societies; (2) generally larger mean size of penis among gay males compared to nongays; and (3) significantly higher incidence of masturbatory activity *early in life* among gays than among nongays. The rider in the third proposition is necessary because Ruse wants to use frequency of masturbation to account for gayness rather than vice versa. Any of these suggestions would be worth further empirical investigation, although the first and third are probably virtually impossible to investigate in homophobic societies such as ours. But, even if one or more were to receive later some degree of empirical confirmation, it is simply not the case, *pace* Ruse and the sociobiologists, that any explanation is better than none at all; and hypotheses concerning social acculturation could certainly provide explanations as credible as those provided here.

We conclude that none of the hypotheses that Ruse offers on behalf of the sociobiologists are of sufficient specificity or plausibility to warrant particular or pointed attention. In closing we return to some of the general questions of framework and presupposition with which we opened this essay.

6. Concluding Remarks

Although several larger issues presupposed by Ruse's explanations merit, whether singly or as an ensemble, much greater consideration than that given to the hypotheses, the intent of this work is to address those specific hypotheses suggested by him. We would feel remiss, however, as members of the modern-philosopher race that he castigates, if we did not, even in the most perfunctory and cursory manner, at least mention these concerns and points.

The first is quite simply, why "explain homosexuality" at all? To this question, perhaps Edward Stein has the answer: "Sex and sexual desire are basic and central to human nature; unlocking their mysteries through science and social science is a worthwhile project on its own merits."[16] But note here that it is the attempt to elucidate human sexuality in general, and not homosexuality *per se*. As we have claimed before (and will continue to claim), questions of gayness should be addressed only after more general questions have been answered.[17] Are there legitimate scientific reasons for exploring the causes of homosexuality, or might it be, as suggested by recent writers, a phenomenon like left or right handedness?[18]

The concern for legitimate purposes in the search of a cause(s) for gayness brings us to our second concern. The attempt to "explain homosexuality" seems to involve some moral presupposition to the effect that it is in "need" of explanation in some special sense that does not hold for heterosexuality. Although there is no sign of any such moral presupposition in what Ruse offers, the same cannot be said for sociobiologists, and even less can it be said for those who attempt to extract ideological mileage from their hypotheses.[19] Even an explicit disavowal of moral presuppositions of this kind, however, leaves some moral questions unanswered, since the "disease" model of gayness is still too prevalent in the literature[20] and the line running from deviance through disease and perversion to moral condemnation too slippery.

If the cause(s) of gayness were known, what purpose would it serve? Though Ruse never hints at any program, it seems only that one seeks the causes of phenomena in order to control them. Does the search for homosexual etiology have at its roots a desire, even an unconscious one, to "cure" or to prevent homosexuality? What would it mean anyway, to change a homosexual or to prevent gayness from occurring? We cannot help but wonder at the motivations of the people who so interest themselves in such a research program.

The above are a few of the grumblings of discontent we wish to call (we certainly do not shriek) to the readers' attention. If we add our dissatisfaction with the fact that we really are never told exactly what it is that Ruse is examining, that is, what qualifies as a homosexual person,[21] we are yet more wary of sociobiology's claims. As if these complaints were not enough, we have given sufficient reason in the body of this paper to be suspicious of Ruse's brand of abracadabra science, for what we find disturbing is not merely the matter, but also the manner, of sociobiology's search for gay genes.

Notes

1. All page references in the text are to Michael Ruse, "Are There Gay Genes? Sociobiology and Homosexuality," this volume, 61-86. "Are There Gay Genes?" is a revised version of a paper given by Ruse in 1979 at a session of the Society for the Philosophy of Sex and Love, the commentator on which was Lee Rice. The present discussion of Ruse's essay is a complete revision of those 1979 comments. (Lance the Bear, a frequent visitor at the Spinozahuis in Rijnsburg, is rumored to be the third [ghost] co-author of this chapter.)

2. See, for example, Tom Morganthau, "IQ: Is it Destiny?" (52-5); Geoffrey Cowley, "Testing the Science of Intelligence" (56-60); Lynnell Hancock, "In Defiance of Darwin" (61); and Ellis Cose, "Color-Coordinated 'Truths'" (62); all in *Newsweek*, 24 October 1994.

3. For a critique of the use of Kinsey's scale in the search for "gay genes," see Edward Stein, "Evidence for Queer Genes: An Interview with Richard Pillard," *Journal of Lesbian and Gay Studies* 1:1 (1993): 93-110, at 106-7. See also Morton Hunt, *Sexual Behavior in the Seventies* (New York: Dell, 1974).

4. See Dennis Altman, *Homosexual: Oppression and Liberation* (New York: Avon, 1971) and *The Homosexualization of America* (Boston: Beacon Press, 1982); Lee Rice, "Homosexuality and the Social Order," in Alan Soble, ed., *Philosophy of Sex*, 1st ed. (Totowa, N.J.: Littlefield, Adams, 1980): 256-80, and "Homosexualization and Collectivism," *Philosophy and Theology* 2:5 [disk supplement no. 1] (1988): 45-60; and Steven Barbone and Lee Rice, "Coming Out, Being Out, and Acts of Virtue," *Journal of Homosexuality* 27 (1994): 91-110, reprinted in Timothy F.

Murphy, ed., *Gay Ethics: Controversies in Outing, Civil Rights, and Sexual Science* (New York: Haworth Press, 1994), 91-110.

5. See Wainwright Churchill, *Homosexual Behavior Among Males* (New York: Hawthorn Press, 1967), 60-9; John H. Gagnon and William Simon, *Sexual Conduct: The Social Sources of Human Sexuality* (Chicago: Aldin, 1973); S. J. Hendlin, "Homosexuality in the Rorschach: A New Look at Old Signs," *Journal of Homosexuality* 1:3 (1976): 303-17; R. Sears, "Development of Gender Roles," in *Sex and Behavior*, ed. F. A. Beach (New York: Huntington, 1965), 163-8; and Martin Weinberg and Colin Williams, *Male Homosexuals* (New York: Oxford University Press, 1974).

6. See Weinberg and Williams, *Male Homosexuals*, 41-4.

7. Franz J. Kallmann, "Comparative Twin Study on the Genetic Aspects of Male Homosexuality," *Journal of Nervous and Mental Diseases* 115 (1952): 283-93. Though the more recent study by Richard Pillard finds there to be a roughly 50% concordance of sexual orientation between monozygotic twins, we underline that this is only 50% (see Stein, "Evidence for Queer Genes").

8. A number of articles that summarize the studies that have helped to lead others to abandon a unique genetic determinant for sexual deviance are reprinted in Judd Marmor, ed., *Sexual Inversion* (New York: Basic Books, 1965).

9. One of the authors is a former ballet dancer.

10. Weinberg and Williams, *Male Homosexuals*, 233-8.

11. Alan P. Bell, "The Homosexual as Patient," in Martin Weinberg, ed., *Sex Research* (New York: Oxford University Press, 1976); Richard Green, *Sexual Identity Conflict in Children and Adults* (New York: Basic Books, 1974).

12. This seems to be precisely the problem with Ruse's brand of "science."

13. We will even grant here that by "knowing," we could mean some inclination or propensity in the same way that ducks "know" how to swim or birds "know" how to build nests. No conscious knowing is necessarily implied.

14. F. L. Whitam, "Childhood Indicators of Male Homosexuality," *Archives of Sexual Behavior* 6:2 (1977): 256-63, at 260; Green, *Sexual Identity Conflict*.

15. Christopher L. San Miguel and Jim Millham, "The Role of Cognitive and Situational Variables in Aggression Toward Homosexuals," *Journal of Homosexuality* 2 (1976): 11-28, at 15-19; Hendlin, "Homosexuality in the Rorschach."

16. Edward Stein, "The Relevance of Scientific Research About Sexual Orientation to Lesbian and Gay Rights," *Journal of Homosexuality* 27 (1994): 269-308, at 300; reprinted in Murphy, *Gay Ethics*, 269-308.

17. See Barbone and Rice, "Coming Out, Being Out, and Acts of Virtue."

18. Frederick Suppe, "Explaining Homosexuality: Philosophical Issues, and Who Cares Anyhow?" *Journal of Homosexuality* 27 (1994): 223-68, at 260; reprinted in Murphy, *Gay Ethics*, 223-68.

19. See Stein, "The Relevance of Scientific Research."

20. See Abby Wilkerson, "Homophobia and the Moral Authority of Medicine," *Journal of Homosexuality* 27 (1994): 329-47; reprinted in Murphy, *Gay Ethics*, 329-47.

21. Ruse never defines "homosexuality." At times it appears that it is just a matter of behavior, as in the "evidence" given to support the parental manipulation hypothesis. At other times, it seems to be more deep-seated than mere behavior. See, however, his comment (77): "Indeed, there are cases of heterosexuals who behave homosexually." Precisely what this remark is supposed to mean escapes the authors if Ruse holds to a behavioral explanation of gayness.

Robert Pielke

Author of "Are Androgyny and Sexuality Compatible?"
Paper presented at the Society for the Philosophy of Sex and Love
during the
Western Division Meeting of The American Philosophical Association
Detroit, Mich., 26 April 1980

Nine

ARE ANDROGYNY AND SEXUALITY COMPATIBLE?

Robert Pielke

Proponents of androgyny as a social ideal must respond to a number of serious objections. Among them are the claims that androgyny would be detrimental to mental health,[1] that it would covertly endorse a traditional and therefore sexist heterosexuality,[2] and, further, that it would actually require universal masculinization.[3] The literature abounds with discussions on these and related topics.[4] An unspoken and perhaps even unconscious objection, however, is a fear that androgyny would in some way be incompatible with sexuality. I intend to explore this objection in what follows. To my knowledge, no advocate of androgyny has attempted to do this; yet this objection might be the underlying basis for most of, if not all, the other objections. If this fear is the fundamental problem, a satisfactory response would inevitably make androgyny a more attractive style of life.

My initial intuition is that the fear that androgyny is incompatible with sexuality is unfounded, and that, on the contrary, androgynous people would enjoy a quantitative and qualitative enhancement of sexuality. In order to see whether this would in fact be the case, it will first be necessary to clarify the concept of androgyny. Then, after a brief characterization of sexuality, the precise nature of the fear will be examined and shown to be groundless. It should then be apparent that androgyny is not only compatible with sexuality but is likely to enhance it.

1.

Androgyny is a tricky concept; its literal meaning continues to raise questions. A mixture of male and female traits (*andros* means "man" and *gyne* means "woman") tells us nothing about how those traits are to be mixed; their desirable proportions; if all traits are equally valuable; whether a variety of mixtures is possible; or if these traits are psychological, behavioral, or physiological. The first task for anyone discussing androgyny is to specify precisely what meaning the term has. A consensus is emerging, so debates about the merits of androgyny need not become fruitlessly stalled at this preliminary stage. Joyce Trebilcot's distinction between monoandrogyny and polyandrogyny has advanced our understanding of the meaning of androgyny considerably,[5] and I will make use of this distinction in describing how I understand the term.

Trebilcot's first category, monoandrogyny (M), is understood by advocates as a single ideal for everyone. Monoandrogynous people would adopt most of the psychological characteristics and social roles that have been traditionally assigned to both masculine *and* feminine genders.[6] These hitherto bifurcated traits would exist simultaneously in the same person. What comes to mind is the term "unisex," most often used pejoratively. There are, however, many people who consider this desirable, at least according to Trebilcot. Her second category, polyandrogyny (P), derives from the proposal that "not a single ideal but . . . a variety of options, including 'pure' femininity and masculinity, as well as any combination of the two" be available regardless of a person's biological sex.[7]

The underlying connection between the two types of androgyny, as Trebilcot points out, is an attempt to break the connection between sex and gender. This means bringing into play a fundamental moral principle, namely, "that biological sex should not be a basis for judgments about the appropriateness of gender characteristics."[8] Proponents of androgyny, whatever its meaning, *must* affirm this in some way, otherwise their efforts would involve self-contradiction. A second, more specific, moral principle is brought into play by Trebilcot, but this one is *not* logically entailed by either M or P: gender traits that are morally objectionable ought to be "excluded from both the single ideal advocated by M and the range of options recommended by P."[9] As it happens, I agree with Trebilcot, but she has provided no argument for this moral assertion; nor has she given any basis for judging which traits are objectionable and which not. It is not obvious to everyone which traits are morally desirable and which not. Some traits, such as courage and nurturance, have a positive connotation; but others, such as aggressiveness and modesty, are questionable. Conceivably, advocates of androgyny could propose combinations of traits that would offend nearly everyone's moral sensibilities.

Independent moral arguments do exist for ruling out offensive traits, such as submissiveness, incompetence, and weakness for women, and dominance, authoritarianism, and violence for men (the very traits Trebilcot mentions). It is not necessary to develop them here, for others have done so at length.[10] Suffice it to say that an advocate of androgyny must specify and defend the traits that are the morally acceptable options (for P) or can legitimately be used in constructing a single ideal (in M). But regardless of what moral norms are used to exclude offensive traits, they must be applied universally so as to avoid arbitrariness. If a trait is desirable, it ought to be adopted; if it is undesirable, it ought to be discouraged; but if it is neither, it ought to be up to the individual as to whether to adopt it. This categorization allows the freedom of choice argument implicit in P as well as the argument from virtue implicit in M. The task is simplified considerably; for M and P turn out to be much the same, if not identical, at least as they are dealt with by Trebilcot. Hence the confusing situation would never arise, wherein traits found morally acceptable, or even obligatory, for one version of androgyny were not also found acceptable for the other.

One other criterion must be kept in mind: the logical (and perhaps empirical) requirement of consistency or noncontradiction. It would make no logical or empirical sense to construe as obligatory traits that contradict one another, or even to consider as permissible traits that would conflict with obligatory traits.

The most meaningful way to conceptualize obligatory (or desirable) traits is to understand them as virtues (and the undesirable ones as vices). In accordance with the basic norm that enjoins us to break the link between sex and gender, virtues and vices must be seen as *human,* not sex-linked, dispositions. As such, the virtues would necessarily be compatible, since it would be absurd for a moral theory to encourage dispositions that, if acted on, would contradict one another.[11] However, not all traits are either obligatory or forbidden, having more to do with personality than character. While it is enormously difficult to decide which traits are optional, it should nevertheless be obvious that they are permissible if and only if they do not conflict with any of the virtues. Although Trebilcot seems to recognize the possibility that some traits might not be compatible, she declines to speculate on what practical effects this logical limitation might have.[12] Others, however, have not been so reluctant. Ann Ferguson points out that "as we presently understand these [masculine and feminine] stereotypes, they exclude each other"; she proceeds to illustrate their logical and empirical incompatibilities.[13] Carrying the point further, Janice Raymond says that "one would not put master and slave language or imagery together to define a free person."[14]

While there are other traits that would be disqualified on grounds of inconsistency, neither M nor P can include traditionally feminine and masculine gender characteristics (which include virtues and vices as well as other kinds of traits). When properly understood, androgyny rules out genderization as we know it. Whatever else it might affirm (this would depend on a moral assessment of character and personality traits), it would reject "pure" femininity and masculinity and many combinations of the two. Still, within logical and moral limitations, it would permit a genuine choice among some combinations.

2.

In dealing with human sexuality, we must keep in mind that many physiological, psychological, and behavioral factors are involved in a very complex interrelationship. Attempts to understand the phenomenon philosophically have differed, often dramatically, making conceptual clarity difficult.[15] For the purpose of this essay, sexuality will be understood simply as a kind of desire and/or the behavior intended to satisfy it. Most important is the fact that sexual desire is not something that is subject to choice; it is a major component in the struggle of all life forms to survive. Commonly characterized as a need or appetite, sexuality functions as a primary motivating force in human life. Further, while this desire has biological or physiological roots, the objects of desire and the activities undertaken to fulfill it are socially defined: sexual desire is logically and empirically independent of both the objects of desire as well as sexual behavior itself. Thus, while sexual activity and the choice of objects are open to the varying influences of differing societies and cultures, humans inevitably *will* have sexual desire for *some* object or objects and *will* try to act accordingly, barring physical or psychological impairments.

The fear that androgyny would inhibit or even abolish our sexuality is typically expressed in emotive outbursts: "if women (or men) were to act like men (or women), then I wouldn't want anything to do with them"; "I can't get turned on to somebody who looks and behaves like me"; or "*vive la différence.*" Implicit in these remarks is a belief that a sex-based gender differentiation is essential for sexual attraction or desire. The fear is that a society *undifferentiated* by gender would somehow result in the permanent inactivity or the destruction of the sex drive itself. After all, so the rhetorical claim seems to go, when the objects of desire are no longer specifically identified, can the desire long remain? Opposing gender traits alone are apparently thought to be responsible for elici ting sexual desire; so to obviate such differences might destroy the mechanism of arousal itself. In this picture, the sex drive is regarded as totally passive, waiting to be triggered by gender traits different from those of the agent. If there is no opportunity for this to happen, not only will the drive never be activated, it might actually atrophy. "Use it or lose it."

Another related fear is that the loss of differentiated sex roles would remove the guidance and direction that such roles provide. Many people perceive this as a distinct threat. In societies where rigid gender differentiation is maintained, all expressions of sexuality are rigorously channeled through sex roles. This includes prescribing who are to be considered desirable partners, how to attract them, how to recognize favorable and unfavorable reactions, what constitutes acceptable and satisfying physical activity, how to perform such activity and for what purposes. Nothing is left to chance; everything is laid out in a pattern to be followed. When confronted with forces as powerful as the sex drive, this affords the individual a great deal of security and comfort. To remove these patterns would, accordingly, cause considerable distress. Without their guidance, the sex drive could not identify a suitable object, know what to do with one, or why. As a result, sexuality could be expected to diminish or even die. Again, the underlying assumption seems to be that the sexual drive is passive, awaiting specific gender traits to trigger it.

In responding to these two related fears, I want to avoid relying on the obvious rejoinder, namely, an analogy to our appetite for food. It would go something like this: even if all food looked and tasted the same, we'd still get hungry and often eat ravenously. This analogy does as much harm to my case as any good it might do, for it grants a point that androgynists need not and should not grant. It concedes that everyone would look and act alike if the connection between biological sex and gender (sex roles) was broken. As we have seen, this is not what proponents of androgyny mean. On the contrary, within logical and moral (including nonsexist) parameters, a considerable variety of options would be available. Even if a wide variety of traits were deemed obligatory (and hence virtuous), there would still be numerous permissible traits that would ensure individuality. Granted, none of them would be tied to biological sex; but this is a different objection.

A better response to these two fears begins by pointing out that they only make sense in a thoroughly genderized context, one in which biological sex is the basis for gender differentiation. In such societies, if a "woman" ceases playing her assigned role and instead plays that of a "man" (or some deviant role), most (if not all) "men" would not find her appealing; they've been programmed to find only "women" appealing. The same is true in reverse. However, in a society in which the connection between traits and sex has been broken and a variety of morally acceptable role options exist, the problem of "women" acting like "men" would never arise. There would be no prescribed patterns of sexual expectations and activities; therefore, the sex drive would not be held to any rigid paths in seeking satisfaction. If this kind of situation is considered psychologically threatening, then so be it; if androgyny is morally desirable, then any loss of direction and guidance will have to be endured. Besides, it is highly questionable that such a loss would occur. What would be abandoned is gender, not morality. So to the extent that both versions of the fear presuppose a "unisex" understanding of androgyny, they are unfounded.

Even more significant is the misconception of sexuality that both assume. The idea that the sex drive is passive, waiting to be activated by gender traits opposite those of the agent, is likely based on an antiandrogynous ideology, not on any kind of evidence. The evidence that I'm familiar with supports the idea that sexual desire is both logically and empirically independent of its object. The choice of this object might be culturally determined; but it need not be. Without sex roles to prescribe which objects should be of interest to us, the sex drive would still survive. The object has nothing whatsoever to do with the drive; it does have has everything to do with its satisfaction, in that *some* object (real or imagined) is needed. But this hardly rules out androgyny as an ideal. To the extent that both versions of the fear assume a passive view of sexual desire, they are unfounded.

The original claim, that sexuality is incompatible with androgyny, is thus unfounded. Further, there is reason to think that an androgynous society would, instead, enhance sexuality. Since the traditional sex roles (gender) have, so far, served to *restrict* the sex drive, their removal would serve to encourage a much freer and more abundant sex life. This being the case, the overall *quality* of sex must similarly increase, just as the unlimited availability of food would enhance our ability to make better judgments about taste. Whether this increase in quantity and quality would be desirable is another question, but it's hard to imagine an argument against it. In fact, it should provide a convincing argument why androgyny ought to be adopted.

At least one genuine problem would arise during an attempted transition to androgyny. Those persons who are conscientiously attempting to move beyond gender differentiation, while living in a society with traditional sex roles, are caught in a difficult situation. They are almost always misunderstood by androgynists and nonandrogynists alike. Traditional societies will not permit its members to be perceived as not playing some kind of sex role, even though it might be a deviant sex role: "butch," "dyke," "queen," "macho man." Most often such people are viewed as transsexuals or, more crassly, "queers." Only another androgynist has the capacity to make an accurate interpretation, but this is no guarantee. When it comes to expressions of sexual interest, for example, there is no way to be confident whether a sexual overture is androgynous or not. Aside from some obvious types of genderized behavior, an overture by itself gives no clue. Visually inspecting and appreciating another person's clothed body is consistent with any social form.

The fact that such a problem arises, however, is further evidence that androgyny is not incompatible with sexuality. Indeed, the more the problem surfaces, the greater the probability that androgynous individuals are increasing their sexual activities. If so, people who have feared androgyny might be persuaded to convert to the androgynous ideal.

Notes

1. Ronald A. LaTorre, *Sexual Identity* (Chicago: Nelson-Hall, 1979), argues that sexual differentiation is vital for a person's mental health, although such a society need not be sexist (145-6).

2. For example, see Catherine Stimpson, "The Androgyne and the Homosexual," *Women's Studies* 2:2 (1974): 237-47. Androgyny "fails to conceptualize the world and to organize phenomena in a new way that leaves 'feminine' and 'masculine' behind" (242).

3. Janice Raymond, "The Illusion of Androgyny," *Quest: A Feminist Quarterly* (Summer 1975): 57-66, defines her ideal society as one of "integrity," which seeks to go beyond one that is gender-defined. The androgynization of our present society would be no more than its masculinization (see 61-4).

4. A massive list was compiled by Nancy Topping Bazin, "The Concept of Androgyny: A Working Bibliography," *Women's Studies* 2:2 (1974), an issue of the journal devoted exclusively to this subject. June Singer's *Androgyny: Toward a New Theory of Sexuality* (New York: Anchor/ Doubleday, 1976) also has a worthwhile bibliography.

5. Joyce Trebilcot, "Two Forms of Androgynism," in Mary Vetterling-Braggin, ed., *"Femininity," "Masculinity," and "Androgyny"* (Totowa, N.J.: Littlefield, Adams, 1982), 161-9.

6. *Ibid.*, 162-3.

7. *Ibid.*, 163.

8. *Ibid.*

9. *Ibid.*, 164.

10. See especially Thomas Hill, "Servility and Self-Respect," in Richard Wasserstrom, ed., *Today's Moral Problems*, 2nd ed. (New York: Macmillan, 1979), 133-48.

11. Mary Anne Warren makes this point in *The Nature of Women* (Point Reyes, Cal.: Edgepress, 1980), 18-19.

12. Trebilcot, "Two Forms of Androgynism," 164.

13. Ann Ferguson, "Androgyny as an Ideal for Human Development," in Mary Vetterling-Braggin, Frederick Elliston, and Jane English, eds., *Feminism and Philosophy* (Totowa, N.J.: Littlefield, Adams, 1977), 45-69, at 46.

14. Raymond, "The Illusion of Androgyny," 61.

15. See the essays collected in Robert Baker and Frederick Elliston, eds., *Philosophy and Sex* (Buffalo: Prometheus, 1975; 2nd ed., 1984); and Alan Soble, ed., *Philosophy of Sex* (Totowa, N.J.: Littlefield, Adams, 1980; 2nd ed., 1991).

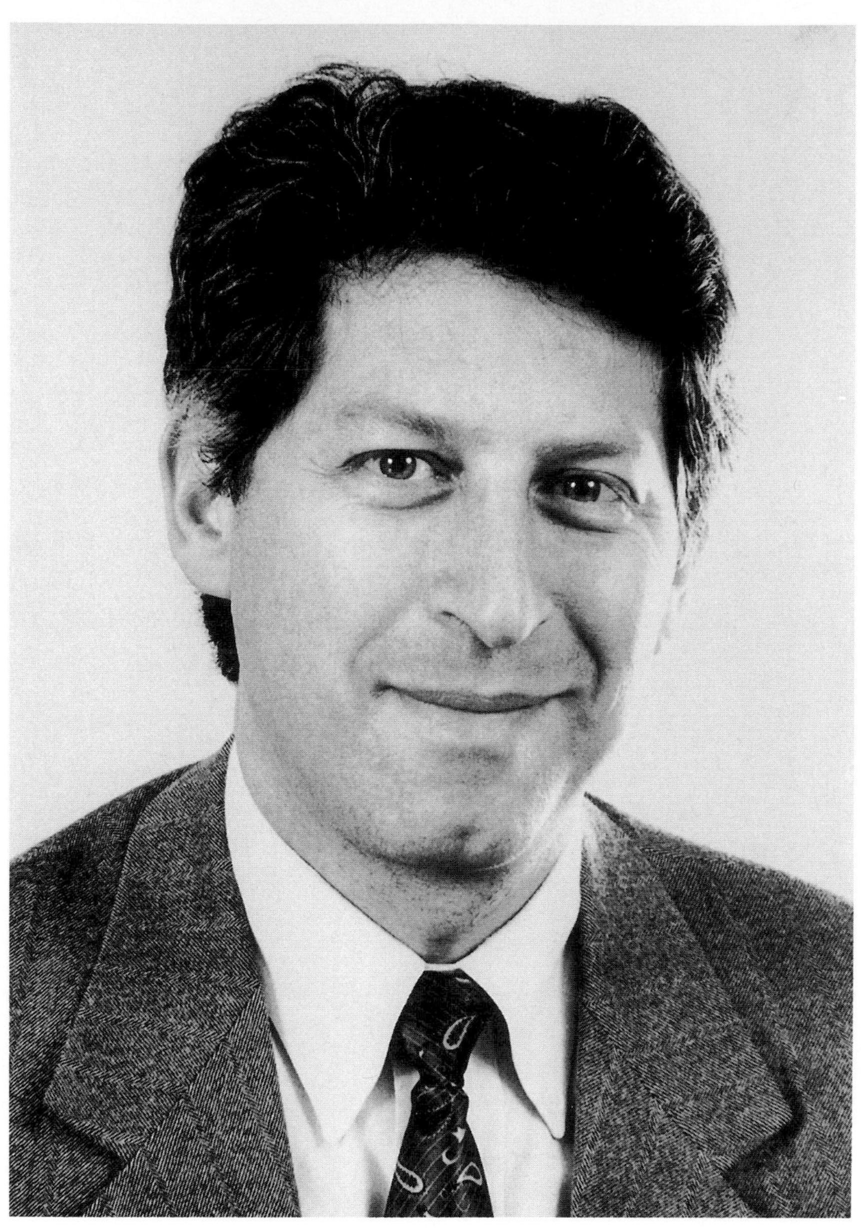

Eric Hoffman

Author of "Love as a Kind of Friendship"
Paper presented at the Society for the Philosophy of Sex and Love
during the
Eastern Division Meeting of The American Philosophical Association
Boston, Mass., 28 December 1980

Ten

LOVE AS A KIND OF FRIENDSHIP

Eric Hoffman

Critics of love have succeeded in what critics aim to do; they have made it impossible for us to commit ourselves uncritically to the ideals of love. Yet, few of us who accept the criticism are willing to dispense with the concept of love altogether. Instead, we construe the criticism as an attack on a particular *conception* of love, leaving open the possibility of developing a *different* conception that does not fall prey to the same criticism. A natural beginning is to claim that love is a kind of friendship. This approach is suggested not only by some popular literature on love, which insists that lovers should first and foremost be friends,[1] but by philosophers who emphasize the element of equality essential to friendship but absent from most conceptions of love.[2]

I am concerned here with three conceptions of love: the romantic, the passionate, and the friendship. These conceptions are embedded in three different perspectives on the nature of personal life and on the relation between our personal and public lives. The romantic conception is grounded in a traditional perspective that sanctions marriage and family as the only legitimate focus of personal life. The passionate conception is grounded in a libertarian perspective that emphasizes liberty of sexual and emotional expression as a value to be respected by institutions impinging on personal life. The friendship conception, which I will defend, is grounded in an egalitarian perspective that emphasizes personal and political equality, and the relation between them, as the focal value to be pursued.

My argument construes the romantic and the passionate conceptions as inversions of one another that suffer from similar flaws. The friendship conception of love overcomes these flaws and permits the development of a more adequate conception of the ideals of love.

1.

Personal relationships are comprised in part by the conception of them that is shared (or not shared) by those involved.[3] This conception is the source of ideals, standards, and principles to which friends or lovers appeal in the justification and criticism of attitudes and behavior. My argument, that love is a kind of friendship, is itself an attempt to show that those ideals, standards, and principles to which we may *legitimately* appeal in the name of love include those to which we may appeal in the name of friendship. If love is conceived on the romantic or passionate model, however, this will not be so. On these models, love defines roles and expectations, based on ideals and principles, that might not be expressions of friendship.

The romantic and passionate conceptions provide a basis for distinguishing love from friendship.[4] At the most abstract level, the basis is the same: love, on both conceptions, is the pursuit of complete mutuality, while friendship is the pursuit of limited mutuality. Lovers aim to become one; friends always remain two. Despite this agreement, the romantic and passionate conceptions describe the unity of the lovers differently.

The romantic conception portrays the means to complete mutuality as the making of an unconditional commitment. The model is essentially that of a perfect marriage: two people who are meant for each other live happily, lost in the mutual satisfaction of all one another's needs.[5] Problems in the realization of this ideal are acknowledged, but commitment is viewed as the key to handling them. The passionate conception inverts the romantic, in that "complete mutuality" is construed not as an eternal commitment but as an experience. The passionate conception recognizes the impossibility of making love last. Love is an encounter in which we experience unity with another and which we spoil if we cling to it. The model is roughly that of simultaneous orgasm, although a more extended affair can meet the criteria.

These conceptions of love explain some of the ways in which love and friendship are contrasted. The romantic conception portrays love as going beyond friendship when the lovers commit themselves unconditionally to a life together. But friends come and go; they have their own interests, and whatever commitments are made must respect individual boundaries, which may cause a friendship to end. For the same reason, we might have many friends, but only one lover whose life we share completely. Unless friends are willing to make this commitment, usually symbolized by marriage, they do not really love one another. Further, love tends to be between a man and a woman, while friendship is usually between members of the same sex.

The passionate conception portrays love as going beyond friendship when the lovers pursue an experience of unity with one another. Thus, lovers must be totally open, while friends generally retain spheres of privacy. Love is an emotional loss of control, an uncontrollable passion, whereas friendship is a sedate affection, controlled relatively easily. Finally, love is naturally expressed through sex, while friendship is asexual.[6]

Thus both the romantic and the passionate conceptions of love provide a basis for distinguishing love from friendship. Each makes it possible to love someone without liking or respecting him or her. A friendship conception rules out this possibility by rejecting the ideal of complete mutuality and accepting limitations on its pursuit.

These nonfriendship conceptions of love are the residues of a long process of historical development, if we can believe Denis de Rougemont, who traces the evolution of the myth expressed in the story of Tristan and Iseult.[7] In its religious form, love eschewed both marriage and sex. Marriage was a legal and economic arrangement leaving little latitude for the sort of free commitment required by love. Sex was impure, a union of bodies rather than spirits, so a violation of the code of love, which required chastity.[8] Despite some remnants of these attitudes, the contemporary conceptions with which I am concerned make love the basis of sex and marriage. The romantic conception construes it as the emotional basis of a perfect marriage and the passionate conception as the basis of a perfect sexual encounter.

Nonetheless, the histories of these two conceptions diverge sharply. The association of love and marriage depended on the emergence of greater individual freedom in the choice of a spouse, at least for men of the upper-middle class.[9] The passionate conception was, if you will, the dark side of love, represented by Don Juan (and, on some accounts, de Sade).[10] Its emergence into social acceptability is a more recent phenomenon, dependent on the decay of marriage, on psychological sanction for the view that sexual expression is healthy, and on the technology of birth control.

2.

Friendship is the bestowal of value by two people on one another not insofar as each plays a role with respect to the other, but as unique individuals. Each elevates the other to a status above that given to acquaintances by establishing between them what I call "a sphere of mutuality." By virtue of caring for one another as unique individuals, friends share, to some extent, one another's lives; the goods and evils of one become *ipso facto* the goods and evils of the other. Mutuality may be contrasted with reciprocity. When two people interact in accordance with the principle of reciprocity, transfers of goods and evils create debts. If someone does something for me, I should pay him or her back and recreate the preexisting balance. Friends, however, have thrown their fortunes together to some extent and, within the sphere of *mutuality* they have established, might discharge their debt by the simple recognition that the other friend would do the same if the situation were reversed. To benefit a friend is more like benefitting oneself than it is like benefitting a stranger, though it is not exactly like either.

Although sacrifices for friends are perhaps the clearest evidence of their operating on the principle of mutuality, such sacrifices are not central to the everyday life of friendship. What is central is enjoying one another's company. Friends express their mutual interests in shared activity of many kinds; but what is important is not so much the activity as its sharedness. One's perspective on an activity, whether it is playing tennis, making love, watching television, raising children, or doing philosophy, is enlarged by the habit of taking the friend's viewpoint into account. We need not articulate this viewpoint in order to benefit from having integrated it into our own perspective; simply knowing what a friend would say or how she would experience something enriches our enjoyment and mitigates our suffering.

The sharing essential to friendship is both private and informal. While friends might (and perhaps must) make various kinds of public or formal institutional commitments that express their friendship, these commitments cannot exhaust their relationship. People who relate within what both of them understand to be the requirements of public or formal group norms are not friends, though they may both understand that they would like to be.

An account of friendship is incomplete without mentioning the important role of the friends' mutual understanding of their relationship. Friendship is undertaken *voluntarily*, although many of the conditions for the development of friendships are beyond our control. Two people are not friends unless they understand themselves to be friends. Moreover, friends *choose*, to a significant degree, the character of their friendship. The voluntary nature of friendship provides the moral basis for the rights and duties that friendship creates. Let me offer, then, the following definition. Two people are friends if and only if (1) each cares for the other for the sake of the other as a unique individual, (2) they express this care in shared activity, and (3) they mutually acknowledge that (1) and (2) are true.[11]

So far, I have focused on the "internal" aspect of friendship, what it is like to be and to have a friend. I return to this aspect of friendship after considering friendship in a wider context. There is reason to think of friendship as a culturally universal phenomenon.[12] Although they might take diverse forms, relationships that meet my definition can be found everywhere. One anthropologist argues that much of what is usually analyzed as kinship behavior might more fruitfully be viewed as friendship behavior; good kinfolk are friends.[13] What makes friendship appear to be a "Western middle-class concept" is the fact that we have more latitude for self-defined personal relationships. Thus, friendship appears to have a separate existence in our culture, whereas in others it is ritualized into a formality that makes its private and voluntary character less visible or it remains as an aspect of a more formal relationship like kinship. The form friendship takes in a given culture is largely determined by the space left by cultural norms for private/personal self-defined relationships and by the kinds of shared activities in which people are free to participate.

Yet, friendship might sometimes be valued more than the norms governing a given society. Friends might be inclined to violate these norms in the name of friendship, taking duties to the friend more seriously than those owed to the community. This kind of dilemma, in which the value of friendship conflicts with a society's morality, raises general questions about friendship and moral theory. One can hold that such conflicts arise only because the set of governing norms or the conception of friendship appealed to by the friends is inadequate. This suggests that ultimately no conflict between friendship and morality exists. There are, however, intuitive counterarguments to this idea, based on the fact that friendship and morality, particularly the demands of justice, require us to approach others in different ways. Justice seems to require impartiality, while friendship involves bias. The question of the place of friendship in moral theory is beyond the scope not only of this essay but of any developed approach to moral theory.[14] What I do here is to give a coarse and dogmatic account of the part of this task that is relevant to my project.

The demands of justice have been most insistently opposed to the bias of friendship. I reject the view that justice and friendship are necessarily and permanently in conflict; that claim presupposes a permanent opposition between public and private life in a just society that seems to me to be pathological. However, I reject the utopian view that in an ideal society, everyone will be everyone else's friend. I assume that justice ultimately has priority over friendship, but that an adequate conception of justice will not only leave room for friendship but affirmatively foster it. Justice, when adequately conceived, must provide for the integration of private and public life. The ideals of friendship cannot, by hypothesis, conflict with those of justice in such circumstances. A friend who claims to violate principles of justice for the sake of friendship would be considered by the other friend not only to have acted unjustly, but to be a lesser friend. Mutual acceptance of the ideals of justice becomes one of the ideals of friendship itself. This is what Aristotle had in mind in insisting that ideal friendship is between two people who are "alike in virtue."[15]

Given this account of the link between friendship and justice, some of the fundamental limitations respected by friends can be explained. Justice requires reciprocity; to that extent, what passes for justice in empirical societies can be criticized. Friendship involves undertaking the duties implied by the principle of mutuality within the limits set by the principle of reciprocity.[16] With respect to the "external" aspect of friendship, this means friendship cannot be invoked to justify violating a duty that one owes to another as a person. To favor a friend when justice demands impartiality does not conform to the ideals of friendship. With respect to the internal aspect of friendship, this means that we must be fair to our friends. To rely too much on the understanding that one *would* do the same for one's friend if the situation were reversed is to *presume* on the friendship, that is, to use the principle of mutuality as an excuse for violating the principle of reciprocity.

This account of friendship connects the value of equality in public life, as expressed by the principle of reciprocity, with the value of equality in private life, as expressed by the principle of mutuality. It might be argued, then, that social equality is a necessary condition for the development of good friendships. Aristotle points out that unequal friendships are possible. Unlike reciprocity, mutuality may encompass inequality by the acknowledgment that *if* positions were reversed, the friend in the lesser position *would* do the same. Yet, when the positions cannot be reversed, due to nature or social constraint, it is more difficult to be sure what the friend would in fact do. Inequality tests the balance of mutuality and reciprocity in a friendship, because every relevant interaction either presupposes mutuality or engenders an unpayable debt. In equal friendships, interactions might be reciprocal (paying back loans, trading off days), and when mutuality is invoked, the friends may be secure in that they can see more clearly how their positions might be reversed.

The romantic and passionate conceptions construe friendship as limited in comparison to love. The present account of friendship, however, portrays these limitations in a more favorable light, basing them on general requirements of morality that love ignores. I turn now to a more detailed consideration of how friendship escapes the major criticisms of love.

3.

When love is conceived as the pursuit of complete mutuality, it has two features, absent from friendship, that render it vulnerable to devastating criticism. One criticism concerns the internal aspect of the relationship; the other, its external aspect.

First, love as the pursuit of complete mutuality requires the idealization of the beloved. To achieve unity, the lovers must overcome their separateness. Yet, almost any individual quality will suggest the separateness of the beloved and appear as an obstacle to the realization of love. To see the beloved as he or she is, that is, as separate, would spell the downfall of love. The romantic and passionate conceptions fill out this idea differently.

The romantic conception encourages storybook idealization. Prince Charming meets Sleeping Beauty. Their love was in the stars; they live happily ever after. Each conceives the other as the unique individual who fits his/her dreams of perfect happiness. The lovers' commitment to the romantic conception can be stronger than their ability to perceive one another as they are. Hence, they might strive to incarnate the images, deceive themselves about what they need and want, and live out their lives together without knowing one another.[17] The passionate conception of love requires a different kind of idealization. In response to the constraint of storybook roles, advocates of the passionate conception reject roles altogether in favor of an encounter between the "real selves" of the lovers. William Kilpatrick characterizes this move as the adoption of a "fluid" conception of personal identity.[18] People strip away their roles and stop playing the game those roles force on them, revealing themselves as pure spontaneity. Thus, love encourages us to consider every role a mask, to look beyond it rather than to take it seriously as a constituent of identity.

In contrast, friendship requires that we "keep each other at a proper distance," based on a principle of respect.[19] This is not simply respect for the person as a person, which is the demand of justice, but respect for the person as the unique individual he or she is. Respect, in this sense, is the proper acknowledgment of facts about a person and his/her situation.[20] The ideals of friendship thus require us to see our friends as they are.[21] While defenders of nonfriendship conceptions might argue that love can enable the person to achieve the ideals set for them, this objection misses the point. Friends, too, believe in one another, inspire achievement, and give one another the benefit of the doubt, but they can acknowledge limits without denying their friendship, while lovers, on the romantic and passionate conceptions, cannot acknowledge their limits without denying their love.

With respect to the external aspect of love, the pursuit of complete mutuality requires the incommensurability of love with all other values. Lovers isolate themselves in a world of their own in order to achieve the unity that would inevitably escape them if they experienced themselves as living among others. The outside world threatens love by providing other values and interests that can lure the lovers out of their mutual absorption. Thus, love, on nonfriendship conceptions, must escape relativization even to the constraints of morality. Again, the romantic and passionate conceptions do this in different ways.

Both conceptions take love out of the realm of morality by taking it out of the realm of choice. The romantic portrays love as a once-and-for-all commitment that binds the lovers, whatever changes in circumstance might ensue. If the lover has any choice, it is the single one of "love or leave"; it is not the series of everyday choices in which moral agency is expressed. In its realization in marriage, the commitment is sacred, to be respected at all costs. The family is a natural, pre-social, institution, that the conventions of human society ought not to regulate. The passionate conception also removes love from the realm of choice by making it natural, "spontaneous." It is something one falls into, not something one chooses. One cannot choose how to feel; one just feels. Love is again construed as a given to which morality must conform, not a project or activity that morality constrains. One gets carried away, loses a sense of self, and avoids responsibility in the name of love. Further, it is vital to recognize that no binding commitments can be made in such moments. As "hot" as one is during passion, one must be equally "cool" when that grip is loosened.[22]

To conceive of love as friendship affirms the role of choice in love; it is to affirm that love involves making strong, but not unconditional, commitments, based on spontaneous, but not uncontrollable, feelings of affection, empathy, admiration, trust, and respect. But love in the Western world of the twentieth century tends to be dominated by portrayals of love as an escape from the anxieties of life, an escape undertaken more in desperation than in strength. Conceiving of love as a kind of friendship promises, even if it does not ensure, that love can be undertaken in strength. It is interesting to note, in this connection, a question that exercised Plato and Aristotle. Would the virtuous person become self-sufficient in the sense of outgrowing a need for friends? Plato, in the *Lysis*, leaves this question unanswered; Aristotle spends most of book nine of *Nicomachean Ethics* attempting to answer it.[23]

This general account of the vulnerable features of nonfriendship conceptions of love must be supplemented by more detailed examination of particular criticisms. In the case of each criticism, it must be argued that conceiving love as a kind of friendship enables us to meet the criticism. I think that this can be shown, for example, in the case of Sartre's criticism of love as a futile project, undertaken in bad faith. If there can be an "authentic" love, I would contend, it will be a kind of friendship.[24] Similarly, the psychoanalytic criticism of love as symptomatic of various sorts of immaturity can be met by the development of a conception of "mature love" as a kind of friendship.[25]

I think a friendship conception of love can survive the Sartrean and Freudian critiques of love. Still, it might be argued that these critiques do not count as strongly against the passionate conception as they do against the romantic. Existentialism and psychoanalysis are associated with the liberation, widely held to have been achieved in the twentieth century, from Victorian and older Christian views of sex, love, and marriage. Common interpretations of existentialism emphasize human freedom more than responsibility; and common interpretations of psychoanalysis emphasize the healthiness of sexual expression more than the necessity for sublimation. While I think that Sartre and Freud are less vulnerable to this criticism than many of their interpreters, it can be admitted that their commitment to equality is less firm than to freedom.

In my view, the most fundamental criticisms of love are grounded directly in the value of equality; among these, feminist criticisms have indisputable priority.[26] Feminist criticism has two dimensions. The first connects love with sexual inequality by focusing on the different importance love has had for men and women. The condemnation of women to the family, ideologically conceived in terms of love, requires that women care more about love than men do. The second dimension of feminist criticism is that the images defining love and lovers portray women and men as different and unequal.

Models of love shape our images of femininity more than they shape our images of masculinity. These images pose a permanent "least of evils" dilemma for women. Women may strive to become worthy of a man's love by pursuing the characteristics of the "beloved": beauty, passivity, enigma, charm. This is the good, socially acceptable side of femininity, the side of the wife, mother, goddess. When women become "lovers," the sublime (and sublimated) aspects of male love disappear. A woman in love is a creature of earthy desire, willing to do anything to serve her faithless master, Don Juan or the Marquis de Sade.[27] This is the bad, socially unacceptable, side of femininity, the side of the whore and witch. Neither option offers women a chance for full equality with men, who face no such choice, nor does either option permit full expression of women's humanity. The focus of this critique, however, has been the romantic conception, with its traditional perspective on personal life. The feminist critique focuses on the incommensurability of love as a consequence of women's dependent social status, and on the idealization of the beloved as dehumanization. Both are grounded in the ideological requirements of male domination.

The emergence of greater cultural support for the passionate conception of love, and its libertarian perspective on personal life, has also meant greater acceptance of women as lovers. Don Juan, Sade, the artists of sexuality, and other romantic outlaws have always been the object of sneaking male admiration, but only in the twentieth century could even a limited social sanction be given to the brief, intense affair. An equality of sorts is fostered by new images of personal liberation and the attendant conception of love. Liberated women are portrayed on the same model as liberated men: Donna Juanita instead of Don Juan, a swinging bachelorette as aggressive and independent as any man. Feminist criticism of the passionate conception of love focuses on the idealization implicit in the notion of being a liberated woman in a sexist society and on the differential social consequences of being a "liberated" woman or man. The libertarian assumptions underlying the passionate conception reinforce male domination by providing a basis for blaming the victim.

The assumption of the passionate model of personal liberation is that it can be achieved without major social changes. An alternative, feminist model emphasizes the integration of the personal and political.[28] Personal liberation requires social changes that eliminate the pervasive dependence of women on men that undermines the potential for genuine love. Women, as lovers and beloveds, should not be required to objectify themselves for men as wives or whores, nor should they act, in all the wrong ways, just like men. From this perspective, heterosexual relationships are conceived as unavoidably problematic, in need of sensitive work if equality and respect are to survive the temptations of status and power. Personal relationships between women, sexual and nonsexual, are undertaken in consciousness of their political significance.

Conceiving of love as a kind of friendship meets these feminist concerns by constraining those aspects of love that, on other conceptions, serve as an excuse for disrespect and as a basis for reinforcing male domination. But simply conceiving love as a kind of friendship does not respond *fully* to the feminist critique. A full response requires a more detailed conception of the ideals of friendship, which have, by and large, been portrayed in masculine terms.[29] Nonetheless, I hope to have shown, in outline, how conceiving of love as a kind of friendship meets some of the most serious criticisms.[30]

4.

I want to respond briefly to two objections that could be raised to conceiving love as friendship. The first is that to conceive love this way is to sacrifice an immense value, the ecstasy of falling in love or the beauty of an unconditional commitment to live together until death. The second objection is, in some ways, the opposite of the first: it might be held that, because I have portrayed nonfriendship conceptions in such an extreme way and friendship in such a broad way, love could be nothing else but a kind of friendship. The first objection holds that friendship cannot encompass the legitimate values of love; the second holds that love has never been conceived as anything but friendship.

In response to the first objection, I reaffirm the possibility of excitement and commitment within the ideals of friendship. A friendship conception of love simply draws the line when "love" begins to serve as an excuse for disrespect, whether what is at stake is one's own self-respect, respect for one's beloved, respect for particular third parties, or for the community. This response, however, must be supplemented with an account of what kind of friendship qualifies as love, since it seems plain that some friendships will not qualify. Only such an account will really satisfy a critic concerned about the sacrifice of some specific value.

Most of this task must be deferred, but two remarks will clarify how a friendship conception does and does not differ from nonfriendship conceptions. First, the problem with love on nonfriendship conceptions is that no requirement exists of balance between the *relationship* and the *relating*. The romantic conception gives what is, in effect, infinite value to the *relationship*, that is, the commitment. The passionate conception gives infinite value to the *relating*, that is, the experienced interaction. Friendship pursues a harmony in which commitment reflects interaction and interaction expresses commitment. This requirement of harmony reflects friendship's rejection of the ideal of complete mutuality and insistence on a balance between mutuality and reciprocity.

Second, the *infinite* value given to love must also be qualified. An account must be given of how lovers who are friends value their relationship and their relating. Part of such an account must emphasize that friends who are lovers, as compared to friends who are not, tend to give *autonomous* value to both their relationship and relating. The autonomy of the value would be manifested in the lovers' undertaking some significant shared activities that can be justified in no other way. The paradigms of such shared activities are marriage and sex. One virtue of the friendship view is that it locates the *source* of these paradigms and thus creates the critical distance needed to see other possibilities for the expression of love.

In response to the second objection, I return to my account of a conception of love. In speaking of conceptions of love as sets of standards, ideals, and principles governing what can and should be done in the name of love, I might have been understood as holding that they are explicit, articulated. Actually, they are rarely so; rather, they function without articulation in determining the form of our natural and moral emotions and our spontaneous and even deliberate thoughts about them. So far, I have suggested a Hegelian model that construes the passionate conception as the antithesis of the romantic and the friendship conception as their synthesis. This might be augmented by a more Aristotelian model, in which love as a kind of friendship is a virtue exemplified by a relationship. The romantic and passionate conceptions might be seen as the articulations of the associated vices on either side of the golden mean. Thinking about the argument this way permits us to speak of degrees instead of an all-or-nothing competition among conceptions of love. We can say of someone, for instance, that she or he is operating with elements of the romantic or passionate conception, much as we say that someone is a bit reckless or cowardly. So the development of firm convictions favoring the romantic or passionate ideals define character traits more than intellectual positions. *Akrasia* might be reflected in episodic adoption of one or the other conception.

Thus, even if no one had ever actually defended the romantic and passionate conceptions in the form in which I have criticized them, the ideals articulated still exercise their power over us. Conceptions of love, in this sense, reflect changes in social institutions that determine the character traits and disorders typical of their participants. The narcissistic disorders of the twentieth century, and the hedonistic individualism newly sanctioned by capitalist societies are of a piece with the emergence of the passionate conception of love. Perhaps, in this respect, ontogeny recapitulates phylogeny.[31] Perhaps healthy individual development requires our experiencing the limits of the romantic and passionate conceptions for ourselves. But only in acknowledging these limits and exploring love as friendship are we true to the highest ideals of love.

Notes

1. Merle Shain, *When Lovers Are Friends* (New York: Lippincott, 1978).

2. Lyla O'Driscoll, "On the Nature and Value of Marriage" and Pamela Foa, "What's Wrong with Rape," in Mary Vetterling-Braggin, Frederick Elliston, and Jane English, eds., *Feminism and Philosophy* (Totowa, N.J.: Littlefield, Adams, 1977), 249-63 and 347-59.

3. See W. Newton-Smith, "A Conceptual Investigation of Love," in Alan Montefiore, ed., *Philosophy and Personal Relations* (Montreal: McGill-Queen's University Press, 1973), 113-36; reprinted in Alan Soble, ed., *Eros, Agape, and Philia* (New York: Paragon House, 1989), 199-217.

4. For a different approach, see Russell Vannoy, *Sex Without Love: A Philosophical Exploration* (Buffalo: Prometheus, 1980), 186-9.

5. See Constantina Safilios-Rothschild, *Love, Sex, and Sex Roles* (Englewood Cliffs, N.J.: Prentice-Hall, 1977), 8-9.

6. A sophisticated version of the passionate conception is described by Robert Ehman, "Personal Love," *The Personalist* 49:1 (1968): 116-41; reprinted in Soble, *Eros, Agape, and Philia*, 254-72.

7. Denis de Rougemont, *Love in the Western World* (Garden City, N.Y.: Doubleday, 1956).

8. *Ibid.*, 114ff.

9. See Eli Zaretsky, *Capitalism, the Family, and Personal Life* (New York: Harper and Row, 1976).

10. De Rougemont, *Love in the Western World*, 213ff., describes the sense in which Don Juan is the "opposite" of Tristan.

11. The Aristotelian origins of the definition are evident. See *Nicomachean Ethics*, bks. 8 and 9; John M. Cooper, "Aristotle on the Forms of Friendship," *Review of Metaphysics* 30 (1977): 619-48; John M. Cooper, "Friendship and the Good in Aristotle," *Philosophical Review* 86 (1977): 290-315; Elizabeth Telfer, "Friendship," *Proceedings of the Aristotelian Society* 71 (1970-71): 223-41.

12. See Cora DuBois, "The Gratuitous Act: An Introduction to the Comparative Study of Friendship Patterns," in Elliot Leyton, ed., *The Compact: Selected Dimensions of Friendship* (Toronto: University of Toronto Press, 1974), 15-32, at 15.

13. Robert Paine, "An Exploratory Analysis of 'Middle-Class' Culture," in Leyton, *The Compact*, 117-37, at 117.

14. See Jesse Kalin, "Lies, Secrets, and Love: The Inadequacy of Contemporary Moral Philosophy," *Journal of Value Inquiry* 10 (1976): 253-65.

15. Aristotle, *Nicomachean Ethics* 1156b6.

16. See *ibid.* 1159b25ff, and Cooper, "Forms of Friendship," 645-8, for discussions of "civic friendships."

17. Jill Tweedie, *In the Name of Love* (New York: Pantheon, 1979); and Larry Blum, Marcia Homiak, Judy Housman, and Naomi Scheman, "Altruism and Women's Oppression," in Carol C. Gould and Marx Wartofsky, eds., *Women and Philosophy: Toward a Theory of Liberation* (New York: Capricorn 1976), 222-47.

18. William Kilpatrick, *Identity and Intimacy* (New York: Dell, 1975).

19. Immanuel Kant, *The Doctrine of Virtue* (Philadelphia: University of Pennsylvania Press 1964), 141.

20. See Stephen Darwall, "Two Kinds of Respect," *Ethics* 88:1 (1977): 36-49.

21. See Simone Weil, *Waiting for God*, in James C. Edwards and Douglas MacDonald, eds., *Occasions for Philosophy* (Englewood Cliffs, N.J.: Prentice-Hall, 1979), 166-70.

22. See Safilios-Rothschild, *Love, Sex, and Sex Roles* (128-36), for the "hot" and "cool" metaphor.

23. See Julia Annas, "Plato and Aristotle on Friendship and Altruism," *Mind* 86 (1977): 532-54; and Cooper, "Friendship and the Good in Aristotle," 310-12.

24. Jean-Paul Sartre, *Being and Nothingness* (New York: Pocket Books, 1956), 447-91. See L. Nathan Oaklander, "Sartre on Sex," in A. Soble, ed., *Philosophy of Sex*, 1st ed. (Totowa, N.J.: Littlefield, Adams, 1980), 190-206.

25. See Philip Rieff, ed., *Sexuality and the Psychology of Love* (New York: Collier, 1963) for Freud's views. See also Theodore Reik, *Of Love and Lust* (New York: Farrar, Straus, and Giroux, 1941); Michael Balint, *Primary Love and Psycho-analytic Technique* (New York: Liveright, 1965); and Joel Shor and Jean Sanville, *Illusion in Loving* (New York: Penguin, 1978).

26. See Shulamith Firestone, *The Dialectic of Sex* (New York: Bantam, 1970), chs. 6 and 7; Elizabeth Rapaport, "On the Future of Love: Rousseau and the Radical Feminists," in Soble, *Philosophy of Sex*, 369-88.

27. Andrea Dworkin, *Woman Hating* (New York: Dutton, 1974), 51-90.

28. See Virginia Held, "Marx, Sex, and the Transformation of Society," in Gould and Wartofsky, *Women and Philosophy*, 168-84, and Sara Ann Ketchum and Christine Pierce, "Separatism and Sexual Relationships," in Sharon Bishop and Marjorie Weinzweig, eds., *Philosophy and Women* (Belmont, Cal.: Wadsworth 1979), 163-71. See also Elizabeth Fox-Genovese, "The Personal Is Not Political Enough," *Marxist Perspectives* 8 (1979-80): 94-113.

29. I am indebted to Kathleen M. Owens, who shared her essay, "Feminism and Friendship," with me, and Christine Pierce and Sara Ann Ketchum, who stressed this point to me in conversation.

30. Deeper versions of the feminist critique have been grounded in Freudian theory by Nancy Chodorow (*The Reproduction of Mothering* [Berkeley: University of California Press, 1978]) and Dorothy Dinnerstein (*The Mermaid and the Minotaur* [New York: Harper and Row, 1976]).

31. See Kilpatrick, *Identity and Intimacy*, 214ff.

Donald Levy

Author of "Response to Hoffman"
Paper presented at the Society for the Philosophy of Sex and Love
during the
Eastern Division Meeting of The American Philosophical Association
Boston, Mass., 28 December 1980

Eleven

THREE KINDS OF LOVE

Donald Levy

In Eric Hoffman's essay,[1] it is not always clear how to separate what Hoffman wants to say is true of romantic and passionate love from what, according to Hoffman, advocates of these models of love claim about themselves. Since I do not have the vantage point of an alternative model of my own to sponsor, I do not know whether my difficulties are with Hoffman's views, whether they are fundamental for him, or whether they can easily be handled by small changes in wording. I should say, however, that I do not see what changes to make to accomplish this.

For example, to speak of friendship as the pursuit of limited mutuality and passionate love as the pursuit of unlimited mutuality is odd, when friendship draws no sharp limits around what ways friends might share activities, while passionate love does. To speak, as passionate lovers do, of complete mutuality as experienceable for a moment is also odd; it is like saying one had completely understood Einstein's theory of relativity, or believed in God, for a moment. Speaking of experiencing complete mutuality as even possible with someone one neither likes nor respects is also strange. How might that differ from experiencing complete separateness from them or total self-completeness?

The thread on which my real problem with Hoffman's view hangs is his distinction between reciprocity and mutuality. Friendship is defined in terms of this distinction, from the vantage point of Hoffman's friendship model of love. In reciprocal relations, debts are generated and paid, but not in relations that are mutual. Relations such as friendship are mutual, since people in them "have thrown their fortunes together" (111). The recognition that one would do the same if the situation were reversed makes benefiting a friend more like benefiting oneself than like paying a debt or creating one. If all this is granted, what is meant by speaking of the rights and duties of friendship, as Hoffman does? If friends do not have debts within the sphere of mutuality that is their friendship, what duties can there be that cannot be discharged merely by the same sort of recognition that discharges "debts" among friends? But can merely recognizing something (anything) discharge a debt at all? Hoffman might reply that not all duties are debts; duties of friendship can exist, even if debts are impossible within the sphere of mutuality. But if the failure to do one's duty to a friend (say, to benefit the friend in some way) creates no debt, in what sense was there a duty at all?

There is a related problem. Hoffman seems to define friendship, on the one hand, and romantic and passionate love, on the other, as mutually exclusive; friendship seeks limited mutuality, the other two seek unlimited or complete mutuality. I assume one cannot seek both at the same time with the same person, which means that practitioners of romantic and passionate love cannot be friends. Isn't this too strong? Hoffman claims that friends like and respect one another, but romantic and passionate lovers need not; further, romantic and passionate love require idealizing the love object, but friendship forbids it. This is really paradoxical: Hoffman's definition requires that romantic and passionate lovers idealize those they love, yet need not like or respect them! What can idealization mean here, in the absence of liking or respect?

In defining love as a kind of friendship, Hoffman defines friendship in such a way that romantic and passionate attachments are not instances of love at all, since they are not friendships; this seems to result from the models on which practitioners of romance and passion conceive of love. But what is conceiving of love *on a model*? Hoffman does not say, nor am I myself clear about what models do, but presumably Hoffman would agree, at least, that to conceive of love as X (on the model of X) is to believe love *is* X and, thus, to *pursue* X in whatever relations one thinks of as one's love relations. If one conceives of love as romance or passion, one cannot conceive it as friendship. What effect does conceiving it as romance or passion have on one's relations? I believe Hoffman is claiming something extreme: if I conceive of love on romantic or passionate models, then my relations cannot *be* love.

I *think* Hoffman says this. One reason for attributing this view to him is the point already mentioned, his characterization of friendship as the pursuit of limited mutuality in contrast to the unlimited mutuality pursued by those conceiving of love on romantic or passionate models. I cannot explain why the pursuit of limited mutuality is not included in Hoffman's definition of friendship, given the importance he places on it earlier. Assuming that for Hoffman it is constitutive of friendship (and so of love, too) that it be the pursuit of limited mutuality, the following argument warrants attributing to Hoffman the strong claim in question, that neither romantic nor passionate lovers can be friends:

1. Love is friendship.
2. A necessary condition of friendship is the pursuit of limited mutuality.
3. Whoever conceives of love as romance or passion pursues unlimited mutuality; therefore,
4. Whoever conceives of love as romance or passion has relations that are not instances of love relations.

A parallel argument can be derived from Hoffman's claim that conceiving of love on the romantic or passionate model requires idealization, whereas the model of friendship requires that we see our friends as they are:

1. Love is friendship.
2. A necessary condition of friendship is the seeing of friends as they are.
3. Whoever conceives of love as romance or passion idealizes (avoids seeing love objects as they are).
4. Whoever conceives of love as romance or passion has relations that are not instances of love relations.

I think Hoffman is led to say that conceiving of love as romance or passion makes it impossible for one's relations which one thinks of as love relations to be love relations, because "personal relationships are comprised in part by the conception of them that is shared . . . by those involved" (109).

Does conceiving of a relationship on the romantic or passionate model belong to the part that comprises a relationship? Here Hoffman faces a dilemma. If conceiving of love on romantic or passionate models does belong to the part that comprises a relationship, he must say that people who conceive love on those models do not really love. On the other hand, if conceiving of love on romantic or passionate models does not belong to the part comprising the relation, then his criticisms of the romantic and passionate models cease to be operative, for then conceiving of love on romantic or passionate models, that is, pursuing unlimited mutuality and idealizing as one goes, does not affect that which comprises one's love relations in any essential way.

I think that seeking unlimited or limited mutuality is not constitutive of friendship, romance, or passion. One can engage in any of these both ways. Idealization, too, is as characteristic of friendship as it is of romance and passion, but is not constitutive of any of the three. In short, the defects Hoffman ascribes to the romantic and passionate models can arise in one's relations, whatever model of love one adopts. Loving, on any model, creates risks in regard to one's relations to other, third parties, and idealization and the wish for unlimited mutuality create problems for us all.

One more disagreement. Hoffman seems to treat the basis of friendship, the good that friends seek with one another, as constitutive of it; friendship differs from nonfriendship relations by whether limited or unlimited mutuality is the goal or, as in Hoffman's formal definition, whether those in the relation care "for the other for the sake of the other as a unique individual" (112). Whatever one decides to be the good pursued in friendships, is it by these that friendship differs from other relations? In answering yes, Hoffman differs with Aristotle, whose definition of *philia* he acknowledges as a source of his views. I wonder if Aristotle's treatment is not worth pursuing further, admitting as friendships even relations in which one person is valued on the basis of pleasure or utility, that is, not on the basis of their being "a unique individual." (If everyone is unique, how can being so provide a basis for being a friend of *this* person?) As I read Aristotle, if the relation between two people has the features of reciprocal affection, wishing well, and awareness of these, they are friends whether the relation's basis is pleasure, utility, or moral goodness (*Nicomachean Ethics* 1155b27-1156a5). Aristotle regards friendship based on moral goodness as perfect, but he does not deny that all three are genuine cases of friendship.[2] The same can be said of Hoffman's three loves.

Notes

1. Eric Hoffman, "Love As a Kind of Friendship," this volume, 109-19; page references to this essay are supplied parenthetically in the text.

2. I am indebted here to W. W. Fortenbaugh, "Aristotle's Analysis of Friendship: Function and Analogy, Resemblance, and Focal Meaning," *Phronesis* 20:1 (1975): 51-62.

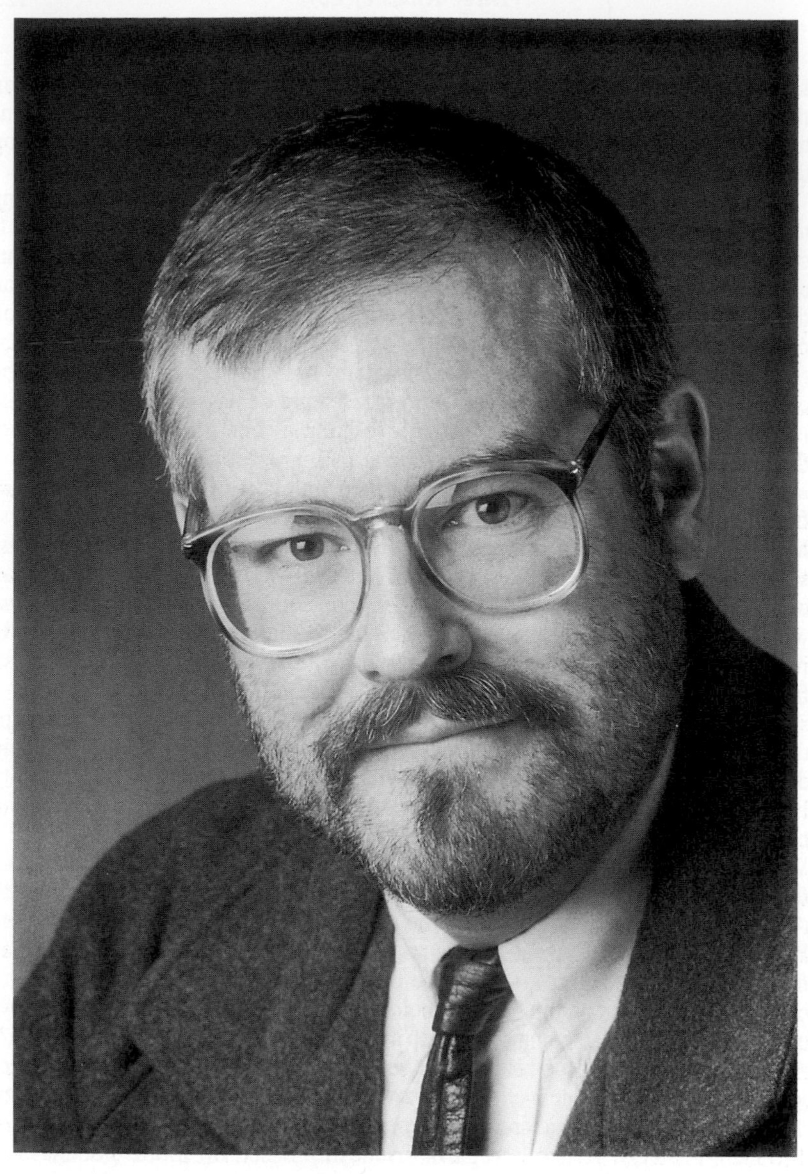

Richard D. Mohr
(photograph: Bill Wiegand, University of Illinois)

Author of "A Non-liberal Argument for Gay Rights"
Paper presented at the Society for the Philosophy of Sex and Love
during the
Eastern Division Meeting of The American Philosophical Association
Philadelphia, Penn., 28 December 1981

Twelve

GAY CIVIL RIGHTS: THE ARGUMENTS

Richard D. Mohr

1.

Current federal civil rights law bars private-sector discrimination in housing, employment, and public accommodations on the basis of race, national origin, ethnicity, gender, religion, age, and disability, but not sexual orientation. As of 1994, eight states have gay civil rights legislation (Wisconsin, Massachusetts, Hawaii, Connecticut, New Jersey, California, and Minnesota). Over a hundred counties and municipalities have such legislation, but such local protections have been under concerted and frequently successful attack through referendum initiatives. On the national level, there is virtually no momentum toward legislatively establishing gay civil rights. This paper offers moral arguments for such legislation.

Even though civil rights legislation restricts somewhat the workings of free enterprise, it promotes other core American values that far outweigh the slight loss of entrepreneurial freedom. These values are self-respect, self-sufficiency, general prosperity, and individual flourishing.

No one in American society can have much self-respect or maintain a solid sense of self, if he or she is, in major ways affecting himself or herself, subject to whimsical and arbitrary actions of others. Work, entertainment, and housing are major modes through which people identify themselves to themselves. In modern culture, work and housing rank, just after personal relationships and (for some) religion, as the chief means by which people identify themselves to themselves. A large but largely unrecognized part of the misery of unemployment is not merely poverty and social embarrassment, but also a sense of loss of that by which one defined oneself, a loss that many people also experience on retirement, even when their income and social esteem are left intact. People thrown out of work frequently compare this loss to the loss of a family member, especially to the loss of a child. Here the comparison is not simply to the intensity of the emotion caused by the loss, but to the nature of the loss: what was lost was a central means by which one constituted one's image of oneself.

Work is also the chief means by which Americans identify themselves to others. Indeed, in America, one's job is tantamount to one's social identity. One finds out who a person is socially by finding out what she or he does. At social gatherings, like parties, asking after a person's employment is typically the first substantive inquiry one makes of a person to whom one has been introduced. America is a nation of doers. When job discrimination is directed at lesbians and gay men, say, as a child care worker or museum director, it is a way of branding them as essentially unAmerican, as alien. It is a chief mode of expatriation from the national experience.

Discrimination in housing similarly affects one's social identity. The physical separation of a group and its concentration apart from the dominant social order are among the chief means by which a group is socially marked as worthy of less respect, unclean, and threatening. Housing discrimination against a despised group is apartheid writ small, but not small enough to be morally acceptable.

Discrimination in housing also affects one's self-perception. It perhaps goes without saying that the conversion of a house into a home is one of the main aspects of self-definition. Blocking or arbitrarily restricting the material basis of this conversion inhibits the development of self-respect and selectively disrupts the sanctities of private life. The common expression "keeping up with the Joneses," even in its mild censure or irony, attests to the role of housing in the way people identify themselves to themselves, in part, through the eyes of others. To be denied housing on the basis of some group status is another chief mode of social ostracism and exile.

In a nonsocialist, noncommunist society like America, there is a general expectation that each person is primarily responsible for meeting his or her own basic needs and that the government becomes an active provider only when all else fails. It is largely noncontroversial that people ought to have their basic needs met. For meeting basic needs is a necessary condition for anyone being able to carry out a life plan. If government aims at enhancing the conditions in which people are able to carry out their life plans, then enhancing the conditions in which basic needs are met will be a high government priority, all the more so if the means to this end themselves avoid greatly coercing people's life plans.

Current civil rights legislation tries to unclog channels between an individual's efforts and the fulfillment of the individual's needs. For it is chiefly through employment, in conjunction with access to certain public accommodations and housing, that people acquire the things they need to assure their continued biological existence: food, shelter, and clothing. Importantly, these are also the chief means by which people acquire those various culturally relative needs that maintain them as credible players in the ongoing social, political, and economic "games" of the society into which they are born; needs, for example, for transportation and access to information. Civil rights legislation then helps people discharge their presumptive obligation to meet through their own devices their basic biological needs and other needed conditions for human agency.

If gays were barred only from buying rocks at Tiffany's, eating truffles at "21," and holding seats on the Board of Trade, their inclusion in civil rights laws on the ground that such laws help meet needs would not be compelling. And indeed America holds a stereotype of gays, especially gay men, as wealthy, frivolous, selfish, conspicuous consumers. Based on this stereotype, some people claim that gays are not in need of civil rights protections. But the stereotype is false. A 1994 study by the University of Maryland found that gay men earn from 11 to 27 percent less than their heterosexual counterparts and that lesbians earn from 5 to 14 percent less.[1]

One of the little-sung heros of the gay movement is John F. Singer. On June 26, 1972, Singer was fired from the Equal Employment Opportunity Commission. He was fired for being gay. His case took six years in front of numerous courts and administrative panels before he was vindicated. Along the way, the case helped force the federal government to change its administrative policies toward lesbians and gays in civil service jobs. When fired, Singer held the position of filing clerk.[2]

Extending civil rights protection to gay men and lesbians is also justified as promoting general prosperity. Such legislation tends to increase the production of goods and services for society as a whole, in three ways.

First, by eliminating extraneous factors in employment decisions, such legislation promotes an optimal fit between a worker's capacities and the tasks of his prospective work. Both the worker and her or his employer are advantaged, because a worker is most productive when her or his talents and the requirements of her job mesh. Across the business community as a whole, such legislation further enhances the likelihood that talent will not be wasted and that job vacancies are not filled by second bests.

In response to prospective discrimination, gays are prone to take jobs that only partially use their talents or that squander them on trivial pursuits. Many gays take dead-end jobs, which do not use their full capacities; they do so in order to avoid reviews that might reveal their minority status and result in their dismissal. Many gay men and lesbians go into small business because big business will not have them. In turn, many small businesses or dead-end occupations, like being a florist, hairdresser, male nurse, and female trucker or construction worker, have in society's mind become so closely associated with homosexuality that nongays who might otherwise go into these lines of employment do not do so out of fear that they will be socially branded as gay. In these circumstances, the talents of people, both gay and nongay, are simply wasted both to themselves and society. Rights for gays are good for everyone.

Second, human resources are wasted if one's energies are constantly diverted and devoured by fear of arbitrary dismissal. The cost of life in the closet is not small, for the closet permeates and largely consumes the life of its occupant. In the absence of civil rights legislation for gays, society is simply wasting the human resources that are expended in the day-to-day anxiety—the web of lies, the constant worry—that attends leading a life of systematic disguise as a condition for continued employment.

Third, employment makes up a large part of what happiness is; happiness is job satisfaction. When one's employment is of a favorable sort, one finds a delight in its very execution, independently of any object that the job generates, whether product or wage. People whose work on its own is rich enough and interesting enough to count as a personal flourishing, people, for instance, employed in human services, academics, and other professionals, and people whose jobs entail a large element of craft, like editors and artisans, are likely to view job satisfaction as a major constituent of happiness and rank it high both qualitatively and quantitatively among the sources of happiness. Even people forced by necessity or misfortune to take up employment that does not use their talents, is virtually mechanical, or positively dangerous, or has other conditions making the work place hateful, even these people are likely to recognize that the work place, if properly arranged, would be a locus of happiness. This recognition of opportunity missed is part of the frustration that accompanies jobs that are necessarily unsatisfying to perform. To permit discriminatory hiring practices is to reduce happiness generally by barring access to one of its main sources.

Civil rights legislation also promotes individual flourishing, not merely by enhancing the prospect that individuals' needs are met, but more so by expanding the ranges of individual choice. Government has a perceived obligation to enhance conditions that promote the flourishing of individual styles of living. Thus, for example, the general rationale for compulsory liberal education is that such compulsion ultimately issues in autonomous individuals capable of making decisions for themselves from a field of alternative opinions. Analogously, civil rights legislation, though a somewhat coercive force in the marketplace, promotes those conditions that enable people to draw up and carry out their life plans.

Such legislation withdraws the threat of punishment by social banishment, loss of employment, and the like from the arsenal of majoritarian coercion, so that individual lives need not be molded by social conventions and by the demands of conformity set by others. The result of such legislation is that the means by which one lives shall not be permitted to serve as instruments for the despotism of custom.

This justification for civil rights legislation also has special import for gay men and lesbians. With the lessening of fear from threat of discovery, ordinary gays will begin to lead self-determining lives. Imagine the lives of those gays who systematically forgo the opportunity of sharing the common necessities of life and of sharing the emotional dimensions of intimacy as the price for the means by which they place bread on their table. Love and caring could cost you your job, if you are gay, while catch-as-catch-can sex and intimacy could cost you your life.

In the absence of civil rights legislation, lesbians and gay men are placed in the position of having to make zero-sum trade-offs between the components that go into making a full life, trade-offs, say, between a reasonable personal life and employment, trade-offs that the majority would not tolerate for themselves even for a minute.

2.

As an invisible minority, gay men and lesbians need civil rights protections also in order for them to have reasonably guaranteed access to an array of fundamental rights that virtually everyone would agree are supposed to pertain equally to all persons.

By "invisible minority," I mean a minority whose members can be identified only through an act of will on someone's part, rather than merely through observation of the members' day-to-day actions in the public domain. Severely physically and mentally challenged people would rank along with racial classes, gender classes, and some ethnic and religious groups (like the Amish), as visible minorities, whereas diabetics, assimilated Jews, Lutherans, atheists, and released prisoners would rank along with gay men and lesbians as invisible minorities.

Let us presume the acceptability of a governmental system that is a constitutionally regulated representative democracy with a developed body of civic law. Such, in broad outline, is the government of the United States and its various states. Gay civil rights, then, are a necessary precondition for the proper functioning of this system.

First, civil rights legislation for gay men and lesbians is warranted as being necessary for gays having equitable access to civic rights. By "civic rights," I mean rights to the impartial administration of civil and criminal law in defense of property and person. In the absence of such rights, there is no rule of law. An invisible minority historically subjected to widespread social discrimination has reasonably guaranteed access to these rights only when the minority is guaranteed nondiscrimination in employment, housing, and public services.

All would agree that civic rights are rights that everyone is supposed to have. All individuals must be assured the right to demand from government access to judicial procedures. But imagine the following scenario. Steve, who teaches math at a private suburban high school and coaches the swim team, on a weekend night heads to a popular gay bar. There he meets Tom, a self-employed contractor and father of two boys whose mother does not want Tom to have visitation rights, but is ignorant of his new life. Tom and Steve decide to walk to Tom's near-by flat, which he rents from a bigot who bemoans the fact that the community is going gay and refuses to rent to people he supposes to be gay; Tom's weekend visitations from his sons are his cover.

Meanwhile, at a near-by youth home for orphaned teenagers, the leader of one gang is taunting Tony, the leader of another gang, with the accusation of being a faggot. After much protestation, Tony claims he will prove once and for all that he is not a faggot, and hits the streets with his gang members, who tote with them the blunt and not so blunt instruments of the queerbasher's trade. Like a hyena pack upon a wildebeest, they descend on Tom and Steve, downing their victims in a blizzard of strokes and blows. Local residents coming home from parties and others walking their dogs witness the whole event.

Imagine that two miracles occur. One, a squad car happens by and, two, the police actually do their job. Tony and another of the fleeing queerbashers are caught and arrested on the felony charges of aggravated assault and attempted murder. Other squad cars arrive, and while witnesses' reports are gathered, Steve and Tom are taken to the nearest emergency room. Once Steve and Tom are in wards, the police arrive to take statements of complaint from them in what appears to be an open and shut case. But Steve knows the exposure of his sexual orientation in a trial will terminate his employment. And Tom knows the exposure of a trial would give his ex-wife the legal excuse she desires to deny his visitation rights. And he knows he will eventually lose his apartment. So neither man can reasonably risk pressing charges. Tony is released; within twelve hours of attempting murder, he returns to the youth home hailed by all as a conquering hero. Rights for gays are necessary for judicial access.

Any reader of gay urban tabloids knows that the events sketched here (miracles excepted) are typical daily occurrences. Every day, lesbians and gay men are in effect blackmailed by our judicial system. Our judicial system's threat of exposure prevents gay access to judicial protections. The example given above of latter-day lynch law falls within the sphere of criminal justice. Even more obviously, the same judicial blackmail occurs in civil cases. It is unreasonable to expect anyone to give up that by which she lives, her employment, her shelter, her access to goods, services, and loved ones in order for judicial procedures to be carried out equitably, in order to demand legal protections.

What is bitterly paradoxical about this blackmail by the judiciary is that in the absence of civil rights legislation, it is a necessary consequence of two major virtues of the fair administration of justice, with its determinations of guilt and innocence being based on a full examination of the facts. The first virtue is that trials are open to scrutiny by public and press. The second is that defendants must be able to be confronted by the witnesses against them and have compulsory process for obtaining witnesses in their favor, while, conversely, prosecutors must have the tools with which to press cases on behalf of victims. The result of these two virtues is that trials cast the private into the public realm.

That trials cast the private into the public realm puts the lie to those who claim that what gays do in private is no one else's business and should not be anyone else's business, so that, on the one hand, gays do not need rights and, on the other, they do not deserve rights, lest they make themselves public. If the judiciary system is to be open and fair, it is necessary that gays be granted civil rights. Otherwise judicial access becomes a right only for the dominant culture.

Widespread social prejudice against lesbians and gay men also has the effect of eclipsing their political rights. In the absence of gay civil rights legislation, gays are, over the range of issues that most centrally affect their minority status, effectively denied access to the political rights of the First Amendment: freedom of speech, freedom of press, freedom of assembly, and freedom to petition for the redress of grievances. In addition, they are especially denied the emergent constitutional right of association, an amalgam of the freedoms of speech and assembly, which establishes the right to join and be identified with other persons for common political goals.

Put concretely: does a gay person who has to laugh at and manufacture fag jokes in the work place in order to deflect suspicion in an office that routinely fires gay employees have freedom to express his or her views on gay issues? Is it likely that such a person could reasonably risk appearing in public at a gay rights rally? Would such a person be able to participate in a march celebrating the Stonewall Riots and the start of gay activism? Would such a person be able to sign, let alone circulate, a petition protesting the firing of a gay worker? Would such a person likely try to persuade work mates to vote for a gay-positive city councilman? Would such a person sign a letter to the editor protesting abusive reportage of gay issues and events, or advocating the discussion of gay issues in schools? The answer to all these questions is "obviously not." Such a person is usually so transfixed by fear that it is highly unlikely that he or she could even be persuaded to write out a check to a gay rights organization.

Further, as a group that is a permanent minority, it is hardly fair for gays to be additionally encumbered in politics by having the majority of its members absent through social coercion from the public workings of the political process. If First Amendment rights are not to be demoted to privileges to which only the dominant culture has access, invisible minorities that are subject to widespread social discrimination must be guaranteed protection from those forces that maintain them in their position of invisibility. Civil rights protections take a long step in that direction.

For, at a minimum, all potentially effective political activity requires widely and pointedly disseminated political ideas. Only then is it possible for a minority political position on social policy to have a chance of becoming the majority opinion and so of becoming government policy and law. If the majority never have the occasion to change their opinions to those of a minority position, political rights would be pointless. Not surprisingly, then, all the political actions protected by the First Amendment are public ones: speaking, publishing, petitioning, assembling, associating.

Now, a person who is a member of an invisible minority and who must remain invisible, hidden, and secreted with respect to her minority status as a condition for maintaining a livelihood, is not free to be public about her minority status or to incur suspicion by publicly associating with others who are open about their similar status. So she is effectively denied all political power, except the right to vote. Voting aside, she will be denied the freedom to express her views in a public forum and to unite with or organize other like-minded individuals in an attempt to compete for votes that would elect persons who will support the policies advocated by her group. She is denied all effective use of legally available means of influencing public opinion prior to voting and all effective means of lobbying after elections are held.

It is incumbent on government, then, to work toward ending those social conditions and mechanisms by which majority opinion maintains itself simply by the elimination of the hearing of possible alternative policies. To this end, government must prohibit nongovernmental agents from interfering with the political activities of individuals and groups. Thus, for instance, not only are political rallies constitutionally immune from government interference, but also government is positively obliged to prohibit goon squads and hecklers from disrupting political rallies. Analogously, bigoted employers, landlords, and the like are the subtle goon squads and hecklers who deny gay men and lesbians access to political rights.

Up to the AIDS crisis, the meager energies and monies of the gay rights movement were directed almost exclusively at trying to get civil rights protections for lesbians and gay men. Without these legislated rights, which begin to bring gays into the procedures of democracy, gays have not been able to act effectively on the issues about which gays reasonably would want to exert influence in democratic policy making, issues, for instance, concerning sex and solicitation law, licensing, zoning, judicial and prison reform, military and police policy, tax law, educational, medical and aging policy, affirmative action, law governing living associations and the transfer of property, and family law. By being effectively denied the public procedures of democracy, gays are incapable of defending their own interests on substantial issues of vital concern.

3.

These various arguments should have a compelling cumulative force. Still, some people argue that legitimate reasons exist for exempting lesbians and gay men from some specific applications of general civil rights protections. The Civil Rights Act itself, reasonably enough, allows exemptions for discrimination against an otherwise protected category when the discrimination represents a "bona fide occupational qualification" reasonably necessary to the normal operation of a particular business or enterprise. For example, church-related hiring decisions may make religiously based discriminations. Are there some discriminations against gays that constitute such morally allowable discriminations in good faith? Not as a general matter.

Though the parameters of good faith discrimination are somewhat murky, the following general principle governing the establishment of good faith discriminations can be gleaned from our culture's moral experience. The principle is that simply citing the current existence of prejudice, bigotry, or discrimination in a society against some group, or citing the obvious consequences of such prejudice, bigotry, or discrimination, can never constitute a good reason in trying to establish a good faith discrimination against that group. The principle means that stigmas that are socially induced may not play a part in rational moral deliberations, that rationales for discrimination cannot be bootstrapped off of amassed private biases. For instance, a community could not legitimately claim that a by-law banning blacks from buying houses in the community was a good faith discrimination on the ground that whenever blacks move into a previously all-white area, property values plummet. This rationale is illegitimate, since current bigotry and its consequences (white flight and the subsequent reduction in the size of the purchasing market) are the only causes of the property values dropping.

In general, the fact that people do discriminate can never be cited as a good reason for institutionalizing discrimination. But even more clearly, the current existence of discrimination cannot ethically ground the continuance of the discrimination in the face of a moral presumption against discrimination. To hold otherwise is to admit the validity of the heckler's veto: to hold that it is acceptable for the state to prevent a speaker from speaking when a heckler in advance threatens disruption if the speaker does speak.

If this principle is accepted, it has a direct bearing on almost every case in which people have tried to justify discrimination against gays as discrimination in good faith. An antigay prison ruling offers an especially pure example of the successful invocation of the heckler's veto. In 1984, the federal courts permitted the barring of the national gay Metropolitan Community Church from holding religious services in prisons, although all other churches are allowed to hold services there. The courts bought, without examination, the government's contention that permitting the gay church's worship services was unacceptable because it would increase opportunities for identifying homosexual inmates and so expose these innocent, churchgoing inmates to violent and predatory prisoners who would rape, intimidate, extort, and abuse them.[3]

The reach of the principle is much wider; obvious ranges of application encompass cases where some joint project is a necessary part of a job. In this category of cases, good faith discriminations against gays are most often attempted.

Bans against gays in the armed forces and on police forces provide classic cases of attempts to establish good faith discrimination. In the early 1980s, the Pentagon articulated six reasons for banning gays:

> The presence of such members adversely affects the ability of the armed forces [1] to maintain discipline, good order and morale, [2] to foster mutual trust and confidence among service members, [3] to insure the integrity of the system of rank and command, [4] to facilitate assignment and worldwide deployment of servicemembers who frequently must live and work under close conditions affording minimal privacy, [5] to recruit and retain members of the armed forces, [6] to maintain the public acceptability of military service.[4]

What all these claims have negatively in common is that none is based on the ability of gay soldiers to fulfill the duties of their stations. More generally, none of the claims is based on gays doing anything at all. What the six reasons have positively in common is that their force relies exclusively on current widespread bigoted attitudes against gays. They appeal to the bigotry and consequent disruptiveness of nongay soldiers (reasons 1, 2, 3, 4, and 5), who apparently are made "up-tight" by the mere presence of gay soldiers and officers, and so claim that they cannot work effectively in necessary joint projects with gay soldiers. The reasons appeal to the antigay prejudices of our own society (reason 6), especially that segment of it that constitutes potential recruits (reason 5), and to the antigay prejudices of other societies (reason 4). No reasons other than currently existing widespread prejudice and bigotry of others are appealed to here in order to justify a discriminatory policy against gays. So all six reasons violate the principle of good faith. Indeed the military's rationales are eerily reminiscent of the military's rationales for segregating troops by race until President Truman ended the policy by executive order in 1948.

Another argument in which bad faith parades as good faith is one that tries to justify discrimination against gay teachers. It runs as follows: though openly gay teachers do not cause their students to become gay, an openly gay teacher might (inadvertently or not) cause a closeted gay student to become openly gay; the life of an openly gay person is a life of misery and suffering; therefore, openly gay teachers must be fired, since they promote misery and suffering. It seems that the second premise (life of misery), if true in some way peculiar to gays, is so in the main as the result of currently existing bigotry and discrimination of the sort the argument tries to enshrine into school board policy. So this argument, too, violates the principle of good faith.

Take, as a final example of bad faith discrimination, the arguments typically used in lesbian child custody cases. Despite the near universal adoption of a gender neutral "best interest of the child" test for determining which parent gets custody of a child, actual legal practice in nearly all jurisdictions still operates on a strong presumption in favor of giving custody to the mother *unless* the mother is a lesbian, in which case the presumption of parental fitness shifts sharply in the direction of the father. Sometimes the argument for this sharp shift is merely a statement of bigotry and stereotype. It runs: lesbians are immoral; lesbians cause their children to be lesbians; and therefore, lesbians cause their children to be immoral. When the shift is attempted to be justified as a good faith discrimination, the argument runs as follows: there is nothing inherently evil about mother or child being lesbian; nevertheless, since, while the child is growing, there will be strong social recrimination from peers and other parents against the child as it becomes known in the community that the mother is a lesbian, only by discriminating against lesbian mothers are their children spared unnecessary suffering. Here again bad faith is masquerading as good. Current bigotry and its consequences are cited as the only reason for perpetrating and institutionalizing discrimination. No one would seriously suggest that a fat mother should lose custody of her child because the child's friends might well tease the child about her mother's size. Clearly the "argument" is a mask of prejudice.

In 1984, the Supreme Court unanimously rejected the claim that recriminations that come to a child because her mother marries someone of another race can legitimately be taken into account in custody cases. The Court held:

> The question . . . is whether the reality of private biases and the possible injury they might inflict are permissible considerations [in justifying discrimination]. We have little difficulty concluding that they are not. The Constitution cannot control . . . prejudices but neither can it tolerate them. Private biases may be outside the reach of the law, but the law cannot, directly or indirectly, give them effect.[5]

If this general principle were applied consistently in gay cases, discrimination against gays would come to an end.

Unfortunately, the clever bigot's mind—the concocter of bad arguments fit for a ready audience of less clever bigots—is more sinuous and enduring than Proteus. It is never caught. The bigot's mind, without being particularly modern, is capable of dancing even after the music of reason has stopped.

Notes

1. M. V. Lee Badgett, "The Wage Effects of Sexual Orientation Discrimination," *Cornell University Industrial and Labor Relations Review* 48:4 (1995): 726-39. See also "Studying Bigger Picture," *Windy City Times* (Chicago) 25 August 1994, 13, and "Dollar Daze," *Frontiers* (Los Angeles), 9 September 1994, 50.

2. Singer v. United States Civil Service Commission, *530 F.2d 247* (9th Cir. 1976).

3. Brown v. Johnson, *743 F.2d 408*, 412 (6th Cir. 1984).

4. Department of Defense Directive 1332.14, *Federal Register* 46:19 (29 January 1981): 9571-8. [Brackets and numerals added by author.]

5. Palmore v. Sidoti, *466 U.S. 429*, 433 (1984).

Linda LeMoncheck
(photograph: Jed Shafer)

Author of "Treating Women as Sex Objects"
Paper presented at the Society for the Philosophy of Sex and Love
during the
Pacific Division Meeting of The American Philosophical Association
Sacramento, Cal., 25 March 1982

Thirteen

WHAT IS WRONG WITH TREATING WOMEN AS SEX OBJECTS?

Linda LeMoncheck

The aim of this discussion is to investigate why a woman might think that being treated as a sex object is morally wrong. My hope is to offer a preliminary philosophical analysis of treating women as sex objects that can provide women with both a conceptual and moral foundation for objections to such treatment.[1] This foundation is designed to be strong enough to withstand challenges by those who argue that women who object to being treated as sex objects are merely overreacting to a breach of social etiquette or grossly misunderstanding the nature of men's sexual attentions. My strategy will be the following: (1) I confine my inquiry to the case of women who complain about being treated as sex objects by men; (2) I give one detailed example of such a case; (3) I derive a characterization of treating women as sex objects, what I often refer to as "sex objectification," that can explain the occurrence of the complaints contained in the example.

In a more extended discussion, I would investigate a wide variety of examples of sexual objectification. Women have regarded rape, a strip tease, a *Playboy* centerfold, a promotion in exchange for sex, and the bedroom "quickie," among others, as paradigmatic of objectionable sex objectification. Such examples suggest that lovers, employers, as well as perfect strangers can treat their lovers, employees, and other strangers, respectively, as sex objects. Sexual objectification might involve threats of harm, if not actual harm, or there might be no such threats. Sex objectification can occur in the bedroom as well as the board room. Furthermore, if there are such things as sex objectifying attitudes in the absence of any overt practices (such as those that might be involved in some kinds of sexual fantasy or unobtrusive staring), a woman might not even be aware she is being treated as a sex object by others.

For present purposes, I believe that the example introduced below allows us to uncover a strong basis for women's moral objections to men's sex objectification of women whenever those objections arise. Those specific complaints that my example does not address can then be fleshed out from the general normative characterization of sex objectification I develop. I call this characterization "normative" because it is designed to explain not only why a woman might complain about her sex objectification, but also why she might make the particular sorts of objections she does. Thus, each case of sex objectification must be examined on its own account to discover any special or additional wrongs—say, the physical abuse of rape—that might make some types of sex objectification more objectionable than others.

Let me begin my analysis with the case of what I call the "free spirit." Imagine a woman in her late teens walking home from school on a bright, clear day. She happens by a construction site, close to her home, at which three men are working. The minute they see her, one lets out a loud wolf whistle, one taunts her with "Hey, fox, give us a smile!" and the third simply stares in silence, thinking, "Now that's a nice piece of ass!" Grinning broadly, the construction workers are full of the self-importance that accompanies seeing themselves as sexually confident initiators of the encounter and dominators of the action. For these men, the free spirit's very presence provides an irresistible opportunity to display their power in a world where heterosexuality is typically normalized, even idealized, for men in terms of women's ultimate submission to them. Thus, each worker finds this unaccompanied and attractive woman a convenient outlet for expressing his *machismo* to his fellow workers. If she finds the workers' catcalls upsetting, they believe she is merely reacting to a social standard of etiquette, one that requires that "good" girls not display their true lustiness or erotic sensibilities; in these men's minds, a woman's "no" is her sexual code for "yes." If she were truly being honest with herself, they believe, she would admit that she secretly enjoys every minute of it.

The free spirit's reactions to the catcalls from the workers are a combination of embarrassment, anger, and fear. She blushes with a new self-conscious sense of her own sexuality and sexual powerlessness that she had not had until that moment, seeing herself as an unwilling participant in the construction workers' sexual fantasies. "Is sex all these guys ever think about?" she asks herself. "I feel as if they can see right through my clothes and I cannot do a thing about it!" She is angry that the workers would so thoughtlessly intrude on her time and reflections; and she fumes at the thought of having to reroute a pleasant walk to and from her home in order to avoid such confrontations in the future. However, she feels helpless to do anything to alter her situation once the catcalls have occurred. She is unsure whether offering a smile will procure her safe passage home or only make matters worse, since she knows that rapes have been committed, indeed justified, with no provocation at all. As a result, she is afraid to tell the construction workers that what they do is not only humiliating but also threatening as well; yet her silence only reinforces their belief that she enjoys the attention. She hurries away from the site, disoriented and upset, while the workers go back to their jobs laughing among themselves. However, she would have much preferred to walk right up to them and say, "Women do *not* like being treated as sex objects!"

One strategy for analyzing the above case is to notice what the free spirit is *not* complaining about. Following Elizabeth Eames, I wish to point out the difference between treating a woman as a *sex thing* and treating her as an *object of sexual desire*.[2] The term "object" is often used in the sense of "objective" or "something intended or aimed at" such as "objects of attention," "objects of affection," or "objects of effort and organization." When "sex object" is translated "sexual objective," "aim of sexual desire," or simply "someone to have sex with," it does not carry with it the necessary disapprobation that many women claim it has. This confusion seems to be the source of the mistaken belief on the part of many men that the feminist admonition, "Do not treat women as sex objects," is promulgated only by the puritanical or the sexually frigid: "What? She says she doesn't like being treated as a sex object? I wish someone would treat me that way!" For the complaints of a heterosexually active and pleasure loving free spirit to make sense, the expression "sex objectification" must carry negative normative weight that is not carried by the expression "object of sexual desire" alone. (A particularly interesting case of sexual objectification is that of a lesbian objectified by a heterosexual man. Whereas the free spirit is objecting to the type of heterosexual attention being paid to her, a homosexual free spirit might lodge the additional complaint that her objectification is heterosexist: her objectifiers mistakenly presume that she enjoys *any* male heterosexual attention, let alone heterosexual attention in *these* ways. Such complaints are primarily complaints about a failure of empathy or understanding on the part of the objectifier for how a woman's sexual needs might differ from the objectifier's—such failure is definitive, at least in part, of failing to treat a woman as the moral equal of her objectifier. I describe such treatment below.)

Just as the free spirit's complaints against objectification are not directed against men finding her sexually attractive or against all heterosexuality, so too, her complaints about sex objectification cannot be reduced to complaints about objectification. First, some objects or animals are treated with great care, even affection: personal mementos, gifts from loved ones, prized pets. Some pet owners treat their pets better than they do other people. Thus, the complaint that sex objectification treats women as objects and not as persons cannot be used by itself to condemn the treatment. In fact, the free spirit's tormenters do not treat the free spirit as an object in *every* respect, for then she would have been incapable of reacting with the anger, embarrassment, and humiliation that are the hallmark of sex objectification. Indeed, one attitude implicit in the construction workers' objectification is their expectation that the free spirit is a *woman* (and not a rubber sex doll or dildo) who will satisfy their desire for sexual dominance and display.

Furthermore, there are several circumstances in which women are regarded as things, bodies, body parts, even animals by men, but which are not typically regarded as objectionable by women. Imagine a male photographer using a woman's face in a crowd (as opposed to using a lamppost or tree) to focus his camera. Imagine how a male surgeon might probe for tumors in the recesses of a woman's body. Suppose a son plays "horsey" with his mother or a male anthropologist classifies female members of the species *homo sapiens* as mammals closely related to female chimpanzees. Unless additional information is offered that in some way condemns the treatment of the women in these examples, treating a woman as an object, body, part of body, or animal cannot alone be the source of women's complaints against sex objectification.

Given these examples, I suggest that there is nothing wrong with treating a person as an object unless a person is treated as an object *in ways she should be treated as a person*, but is not being so treated. So, for example, it would be inappropriate for a photographer to treat a woman as a lamppost if we could show that in doing so, the photographer were treating her as an object in ways she should be treated as a person. Similarly, it is not simply that the free spirit is being treated as an object and not a person by the construction workers; she is being treated as an object in ways she should be treated as a person, but is not being so treated. Moreover, given the fact that the free spirit's anger, humiliation, embarrassment, and fear cannot be elicited from a feelingless object, sex objectification must be analyzed, not in terms of taking *no* account of the sex object's status as a person, but in terms of failing to take *proper* account of the status she in fact has.

The fact that the free spirit is the victim of objectifying attitudes as well as actions suggests that being treated appropriately will involve more than just right conduct; it will involve the appropriate sentiments as well. The construction worker who ogles the free spirit in silent fantasy about her being a "nice piece of ass," even without the explicit knowledge of the free spirit, is still someone about whom she would say, if she were to discover his fantasies, "Men shouldn't treat women as sex objects." Such attitudes reflect intentions toward and beliefs about women that she would find objectionable. Moreover, while the construction worker who blindly follows the objectifying behavior of his peers may be less blameworthy for his conduct, he nevertheless exhibits the kind of behavior about which the free spirit feels justified in complaining. If the complaint is that the free spirit is being acted toward or conceived of as an object and not a person in ways she should be treated as a person, the questions remains: *in what respects* do persons treat such things as inanimate objects, bodies, and nonhuman animals, which is treatment that persons typically deem inappropriate for themselves? I will then argue that it is the construction workers' treatment of the free spirit as an object and not a person *in these respects* that justifies her complaints against sex objectification.

Just how do objects, human bodies and their parts, and nonhuman animals experience the world around them (if they do at all) in comparison to the ways persons do? Persons are sentient beings; they feel sensations, express emotions, entertain moods. Objects do not. Moreover, while most people believe that nonhuman animals are capable of feeling certain sensations of pleasure or pain, such mammals are not typically accorded the kind of complex cognitive psychology that persons have. Thus, the consensus is that objects are incapable, and animals less capable, of experiencing the depth and range of psychological distress that persons can suffer. This implies that objects and animals do not or cannot value the level of well-being and freedom that persons do. Objects cannot value anything, since they have no conscious capacities for valuing. Animals are believed to value a certain freedom from pain, since they are sentient beings. But to be free from the painful humiliation of a crude joke or the insensitivity of a selfish lover would mean nothing to an animal who had no capacity for such evaluations. Similarly, an animal can hardly miss exercising a capacity for self-determination it never had or understood.

When persons claim that they deserve certain treatment from others that others are obliged to honor, it is often because persons feel that their lives would be unhappy, unproductive, and impoverished ones in the absence of that treatment. So, for example, when a woman says she deserves men's respect for her capacity for autonomous choice, she is claiming that her life would be significantly impoverished if men were to treat her as the kind of thing that lacked the capacity to determine for herself the direction and value of her life. Moreover, to exercise such a capacity, she would require such goods as freedom from physical harm or the threat of harm, freedom from psychological intimidation or exploitation, so that she can have the opportunity to exercise self-determination and to develop self-respect. An ethics of justice often refers to such goods as *rights* or *entitlements* all persons deserve in virtue of being persons. However, feminists interested in the way an ethics of care can complement, if not replace, an ethics of justice, have pointed out that a rights-based ethics describes mutually disinterested individuals competing with one another for scarce resources when their interests conflict; as such, it cannot account for persons' claims as members of an interdependent moral community to the kind of empathetic understanding from others of our own particular needs and interests that would allay careless misunderstanding or misrepresentation of individual men's and women's lived experience. Thus, many feminists would argue, a woman who is treated as a sex object may legitimately complain not only that she is not being treated *as a person like any others* who value their well-being and freedom, but also that she is not being treated *as someone special* with needs and interests that differ from those of her objectifiers. Specifically, she may complain that her ability to live a self-determined and independent life is threatened by her objectifiers at the same time that she complains that they ignore or trivialize the importance of attempting to understand her own perspective on herself in the world.

Suppose that A is treated as the *moral equal* of person B when A is treated as deserving a level of autonomous choice and empathetic understanding equal to that of B. If so, since such things as objects, bodies, or animals are not typically regarded as deserving the level of autonomous choice and empathetic understanding equal to that of persons, such things are not typically treated as moral equals by persons, while other persons typically are. I have intentionally reiterated "typically," because some pets have been treated like the children that couples never had, while some persons have been chained and enslaved "like animals." Thus, one way to treat a person as an object that would not be acceptable treatment for persons is to treat that person as an object *but not also as a moral equal*. To do so would mean either failing to conceive of that person as deserving of the autonomy and empathy described in the preceding paragraph or failing to act toward that person as someone deserving of those goods. Thus, persons treat others as objects in ways they should be treated as persons, but are not so treated, when such treatment inhibits the autonomous choice and rejects the empathetic understanding that each person deserves as the moral equal of other persons.

Specifically, a man who treats a woman as an object but not also as a moral equal is a man who would threaten, harass, or humiliate a woman for his own amusement, gratuitously intrude on her time and reflections in ways that selfishly encroach on her privacy or "personal space" or attempt to dominate her life or diminish the importance of her interests in deference to his own. (Privacy claims can be legitimate even in public spaces. I may ask a policeman to fend off a vagrant who asks for pocket money as I sit reading in a park.) A man who treated a woman as an object but not also as a moral equal might conceive of her as the mere instrument of his private ends without considering how she feels about being conceived of in this way. Such a man may be morally condemned for his insensitivity, not just because he has ignored this woman's feelings (for then we may find him guilty only of an offensive rudeness), but because he has failed to treat her as someone whose perception of herself in the world is as worthy of recognition and understanding as his own.

My claim is that when women complain about being treated as sex objects, they are complaining in an essential and important way about being treated as less than moral equals. The free spirit's capacity for autonomous choice is marginalized when she is treated as one whose needs and interests are properly subordinated to her construction workers' interests. Her freedom of movement and expression is threatened by such men precisely because she cannot predict with any degree of confidence or reasonableness whether or how to respond to their catcalls; she knows that both an outraged response or no response might similarly be met with further humiliation or physical harm. The free spirit's sexuality is exploited to enhance the construction workers' feelings of dominance and virility, whatever she might think about being so used. Indeed, the workers act on the mistaken assumption that she really enjoys their attentions, in the absence of any empathetic understanding of how a single woman alone among unfamiliar and leering men might truly feel. The immediate fear and unmitigated anxiety she feels in response to the power play of the construction workers is part of her "objectification," even though objects cannot feel such fear: she is being treated "as an object" in an objectionable way, because her objectifiers do not acknowledge her moral equality with them *as a person* capable of autonomous choice like themselves and also as someone worthy of appreciating her individual point of view.

I have argued that persons, unlike objects, value both autonomous choice and empathetic understanding. I would add that promoting the opportunity for persons to exercise their capacities for both autonomy and empathy can engender caring communities composed of independent and interdependent men and women who can establish connections between individuals different from themselves. The construction workers, however, are unable or unwilling to care about anything other than their own desires to express their sexual inclinations and amuse themselves. As a result, the free spirit feels embarrassed by the fact that her more private parts are now the subject of public discussion or imaginative curiosity by persons she hardly knows. She wonders how many other men have been treating her body as a sexual plaything without her knowledge or consent; some anxiety, even some paranoia over this possibility, sets in. She might also begin to question the worth of her own sexual needs. The free spirit is treated as a "nice piece of ass," but her objection is not confined to being treated as a part of her body. It is in being treated as a part of her body but not also in some other appropriate way, namely, as the moral equal of those with whom she comes in social contact.

Given the thesis that the sex object is not treated as a moral equal by her objectifier, we can explain the pervasive complaint that sex objectification "degrades" or "demeans" women. The free spirit *qua* sex object is not treated as the moral equal of her objectifier, but as his moral inferior or moral subordinate. She is treated by her objectifier as lower in status or degraded, not merely from that of person to object, but from that of moral equal to moral subordinate. She is treated as if she were the sort of being with a limited capacity or no capacity to value the autonomous choice and empathy from others that persons do. I call such degradation "dehumanization" to distinguish it from the kind of objectification of the surgeon's patient or the photographer's focal point. A person is dehumanized when that person is treated as an animal, body, part of body, or object in ways he or she should be treated as a person, namely, as a moral equal. The woman who is treated as a sex object is thus a woman dehumanized. Her dehumanization is of a sexual nature in so far as her objectifier uses her ability to excite him sexually as the vehicle or means for her dehumanization. Thus, a sex object is dehumanized *through sex*.

One of the strengths of a feminist approach to philosophical issues of love and sex is the insistence that women's sexuality be analyzed within a political context that recognizes the contingent but pervasive nature of the sexual oppression of women by men. From this feminist perspective, neither a whistle from a street corner, a whoop at a stripper, nor a wide eyed stare at a *Playboy* centerfold is separable from the particular social and historical context in which such actions take place. A feminist normative analysis of men's dehumanization of women *through sex* must take stock of the cultural sexual politics, gender role expectations, and stereotypes in sex that circumscribe sexual attitudes and actions. Western gender expectations in sex is that men chase, women retreat; men press, women submit. The stereotype in sex ascribed by many men to Anglo women and some women of color is that of a passive, nurturing, ultimately submissive partner to the dominant white male. This sexual stereotype is consistent with her cultural stereotype as the keeper of moral virtue and domestic harmony who is also psychologically and economically dependent upon men for her health and well-being.

Such stereotypes are only part of a complex, often contradictory, sexual ideology: men's and women's sexual parts are paradoxically considered "private parts" in western culture at the same time as they are put on public display in strip bars and depicted in movie houses and fine museums. Much of the sexual excitement of such display is in the thrill of sexual transgression of an otherwise private domain. However, such thrills are accompanied by a double standard: sex in the Judeo-Christian tradition has been considered sinful, dirty, or demeaning to women, particularly outside the confines of monogamous marriage. There is no comparable virgin/whore distinction for men in a society that condemns men's adultery but does not dirty or demean men for sexual activity alone. Women can humiliate men by rejecting their sexual attentions or belittling their sexual prowess, but the humiliation men feel in such cases comes from their being rejected as sexual partners, a direct assault on their masculinity in a culture where heterosexual sex turns boys into men; their humiliation does not derive from their being treated as sexual subordinates by women. Gay men are deemed "effeminate" by some heterosexuals precisely because many gay men adopt the stereotypical feminine role of submissive partner to a more dominant male, and gay male sex involves penile penetration. Moreover, heterosexual men typically have no rape mentality; sex does not threaten such men or harm them in the way it can women. Men who fear rape by other men while in prison might still be more likely to seek retaliation than women who are the victims of rape or attempted rape, since men are taught by the prevailing cultural ideology that to be "real" (heterosexual) men is to take assertive, if not aggressive, action in pursuing social relationships. Sex for many men just means potency, conquest, and control.

Thus, sex in our society is a less effective vehicle for dehumanizing men as a class than women, if it is effective at all. Men might misunderstand why women do not like being treated as sex objects because, when female customers in male strip bars try to make sex objects out of men or simply when a woman whistles at a man from a passing car, women's sexual attentions only reaffirm in many men's minds their sexual virility and gender dominance. Men have complained of sexual harassment by female employers and professors when women have successfully threatened men's control over their personal or professional lives, usually by being in socially superior power positions. Such harassment "emasculates" men by subordinating their sexuality to a woman's. Ironically, the attempt (and often failure) of women's sex objectification of men only legitimizes and encourages men's sexual subordination of women.

Thus, any philosophical analysis of sex objectification must also recognize diverse and individual perspectives on sexual experience. Sex is a personal and intimate matter to some people, an opportunity for expressions of love and spiritual communion. For others, sex is a sensual experiment; it provides opportunities for exploration and creativity; for still others, sex is the perfect vehicle for voyeurism and chauvinism. If some women say they enjoy being treated as sex objects by men, our immediate response should not be to condemn the women or their enjoyment, but to investigate the precise nature of the treatment and the cultural context in which women's heterosexual role expectations are normalized. In a society where male domination of women is the *status quo,* a female dancer who likes performing strip teases or a woman who simply enjoys men's whistles at her miniskirts might well be mistaking an appreciation of her feminine mystique for a verification of her membership in the class of the sexually subordinate. Even if she could show that her own personal interests were best served by dressing and acting in a way that suits other men ("My looks are my best asset"; "I prefer other men to take care of me"; "I like the attention"), such interests must be weighed against the interests of those women like the free spirit whose freedom and well-being are undermined by the restrictive stereotype reinforced by any one woman's apparent approval of men's sex objectification of her.

Radical feminists have argued that sex objectification of women is definitive of all heterosexual sex and that the pervasiveness of sexual harassment in the classroom, work place, and home is evidence of the oppressive nature of men's sexual presumptuousness, sexual propriety, and sexual exploitation of women. The strength of my analysis is that heterosexual women who still find something worth salvaging in their sexual relations with men and who would reject any feminism that forced them to give up heterosexual sex need not embrace this radical position (although many erstwhile heterosexual women have done so); yet women can still ground their complaints against men's sex objectification of women in a normative analysis of the objectionable ways in which men sexualize women in western culture, namely, as less than moral equals. Thus, this analysis is compatible with both the radical claim that sex objectification is a fundamental tool in the oppression of women under patriarchy and the claim of more heterosexually identified women that heterosexuality can be redeemed when men treat women in their personal and social relations with the respect and understanding women deserve as moral equals.

If women are to be anything more than the victims of an oppressive "heteropatriarchy" that determines their sexual needs and desires, it must be possible for a woman to desire that she be sexually attractive to men without at the same time subordinating her wishes to men or having her wishes subordinated by men. However, if men are encouraged to establish their identities as men by creating social hierarchies of material wealth, status, and power that require the submission of women to men at home and at work, men will regard the dehumanization of women *in sex* as the normal and natural expression of their masculinity and social power. If this is true, then those who wish to rid our society of the sex objectification of women must also work to rid our society of the unequal socioeconomic power structure that reinforces sex objectification and the identification of masculinity with dominance and appropriation that fuels it.

Notes

1. See also my *Dehumanizing Women: Treating Persons as Sex Objects* (Lanham, Md.: Rowman and Littlefield, 1985); and my "Feminist Politics and Feminist Ethics: Treating Women as Sex Objects," in Robert Stewart, ed., *Philosophical Perspectives on Sex and Love* (New York: Oxford University Press, 1995), 29-38.

2. Elizabeth Eames, "Sexism and Woman as Sex Object," *Journal of Thought* 11:2 (1976): 140-3, at 142. See also Robert Baker, "'Pricks' and 'Chicks': A Plea for Persons," in Robert Baker and Frederick Elliston, eds., *Philosophy and Sex*, 2nd ed. (Buffalo: Prometheus, 1984), 249-67.

Richard C. Richards
(photograph: Marty Richards)

Author of "LeMoncheck on Sex Objectification"
Paper presented at the Society for the Philosophy of Sex and Love
during the
Pacific Division Meeting of The American Philosophical Association
Sacramento, Cal., 25 March 1982

Fourteen

OBJECTIONS TO SEX OBJECTIFICATION

Richard C. Richards

Finding authors enthusiastic about sexual objectification is difficult. But finding essays that spell out under what conditions sexual objectification is immoral is also difficult. Linda LeMoncheck attempts to do so.[1] I agree that sex objectification can be morally wrong, but I think I can clarify the question of the conditions in which it is wrong and the question of in what situations moral objections are inadequate.

According to LeMoncheck, being treated as a sex thing is different from being treated as an object of sexual desire. Sex objectification consists of treating women as inanimate objects, body parts, or animals. Objectification is, by itself, not bad, because objects and animals can be treated with care and affection. (LeMoncheck mentions four cases of permissible objectification; I look at them later.) Objectification is morally wrong, for LeMoncheck, when a person is being treated as an object in ways in which that person should be treated as a person. Being treated as a person is to be treated as a moral equal. To be treated as a moral equal is to be treated with empathetic understanding as a person capable of autonomous choice. This means having one's point of view appreciated. Treating someone as a moral equal involves both conduct, on one hand, and attitudes, sentiments, and beliefs, on the other. An ethics of justice covers behavior. An ethics of care covers attitudes. Both ethics apply in analyzing sex objectification.

LeMoncheck's analysis is valuable. But some parts need clarification; others are mistaken. I agree that there is a conceptual and moral foundation to objections regarding sex objectification. But in their personal relations people should treat not only women, but all people, with the respect people deserve as moral equals. This already broadens LeMoncheck's conclusions a bit, but I believe she would agree. Her purpose is to explore the issue in a context specifically involving women, since she thinks that to sexually objectify men is difficult and certainly not as damaging when it occurs.

1. The Free Spirit

LeMoncheck begins with the case of the "free spirit," a young woman upset by the unwanted attention and comments of several insensitive construction workers. The free spirit is embarrassed, angry, fearful, humiliated, and made to feel helpless by attention she perceives as negative. I empathize with the distress of the free spirit under these circumstances. Human pain is a negative value. However, in this case we have a classic victim who has made no effort to correct the painful situation. The free spirit, as described by LeMoncheck, considers changing her route, but does not consider complaining to the workers' supervisor, much less confronting the workers directly. She neither tells anyone she is upset nor seeks a remedy. She makes no effort to enlighten or educate anyone. If the workers have mistaken beliefs regarding her feelings, and if the free spirit maintains her passive mode, they will not have the opportunity to change these beliefs. She leaves it for some other woman to go through a similar upsetting experience with the construction workers and then to make any of the changes. The free spirit at most changes her own behavior.

Psychological and physical pain are certainly negative experiences, but they can also supply an opportunity for growth and development, both in dealing with negative experiences and in learning to modify the world to eliminate these occurrences. LeMoncheck's free spirit case ignores this aspect of pain. The free spirit does not choose the painful attention of the workers. But she also does not choose to do much about it, although she does have several choices. The key concept here is autonomous choice.

I am puzzled by LeMoncheck's characterization of the beliefs of the construction workers. They are said by her to believe that the free spirit is merely reacting to some social standard of etiquette requiring a woman to hide her true erotic sensibilities; that a woman's "no" really means "yes"; and that if the free spirit were honest, she would admit that she secretly enjoys their insensitive comments. If the construction workers truly have these beliefs, mistaken as they are, is it not the case that the construction workers are calling for an honest examination on the part of the free spirit of her feelings and reactions? A request for honesty does not seem by itself to be inappropriate, though it might be painful; and if that were their only request, I do not see anything out of line. The problem must lie elsewhere.

2. Permissible Objectification

LeMoncheck claims there is nothing wrong with treating a person as an object unless the person is being treated as an object in ways the person should be treated as a person. She gives four examples of objectification that is not wrong. Her first example is the case of a photographer treating a woman as a lamppost, as an object used to focus his camera. (That LeMoncheck specifies a male photographer in this case is immaterial. The case works as well if the photographer is female and the object of focus is male.) I agree that objectification here is not immoral. It might turn immoral if she becomes aware of being used as an object of focus, does not choose to be so used, and moves away or asks the photographer to focus elsewhere. If he is aware that she does not want to be used, yet continues to do so, we have a case of insensitive and offensive behavior. A person can do worse things to another than use him or her as an object of focus. The point, though, is that the objectification could become nonconsensual. Only at that stage would it be possible to raise the moral question, and even then not much of a case can be made. The woman has other options.

In LeMoncheck's second example, a surgeon probes for tumors in the recesses of a woman's body. (LeMoncheck specifies a male surgeon and a female patient, but gender is, again, irrelevant.) Here the objectification is not immoral since the patient has chosen to undergo surgery: this is consensual objectification. If the surgeon had kidnaped someone off the street in order to practice surgical techniques on that person, and the person had not then consented prior to the surgery, it would be a case of immoral objectification. LeMoncheck's third example is a child playing "horsy" with his or her mother. The parent is consenting to taking on the role of animal, at least metaphorically. This is also consensual objectification, and not wrong. The fourth case involves an anthropologist classifying female members of the species *homo sapiens* as mammals related to female chimpanzees. Since this appears to be a classroom lecture situation, and students consent to take classes and can make their discomfort with classroom material known to their instructors, gender seems irrelevant and consent seems crucial. Again it is consensual objectification.

Let us return to the first case, in which the objectification becomes suspicious if the object of focus is aware of the function being performed and makes the photographer aware of her unwillingness. Inadvertent pain or offense do not seem to me to be automatically immoral, but to persist in consciously offensive action, without a good reason, is problematical. If the actor can be reasonably expected to know the action is *harmful*, then we can make a case for its being immoral. If the actor can reasonably be expected to know that the action is merely *offensive*, the case we can make for its immorality is not as strong. Feeling pain, being offended, and experiencing outrage on the part of one person are, by themselves, not harmful and hence not, taken alone, a reason for regulating or condemning the behavior of others. Any behavior at all might cause pain, offense, or outrage to someone.

Consider smoking. For many, tobacco smoke is offensive. Seeing people put burning leaves in their mouths is disgusting. For people who have lost loved ones to tobacco, it can hurt to see any person using it. But pain, offense, and outrage are not good reasons to prohibit smoking in the presence of others. It is not in this case immoral to cause pain, offense, or outrage. The smoker is simply insensitive or offensive if he or she continues to smoke in the presence of others, especially if asked to stop. But if the tobacco smoke is harmful to the people who take it in passively, the behavior becomes morally suspect. People have a right not to be harmed, but no general right to be protected from pain, offense, or outrage.

I am arguing that unwanted and *harmful* behavior is morally wrong, though harmful behavior that is consensual raises interesting questions. Unwanted *offensive* behavior is not automatically morally wrong, though there are circumstances in which it is wrong. The workers in the free spirit case might not be aware of the pain they are causing her, and are guilty only of ignorance. If the workers are informed of the pain they cause her, and choose to continue their comments, I still think we need to consider not only the pain of the free spirit but also the rights of the workers to freedom of expression. The workers might have done nothing immoral; they are crude, stupid, and insensitive, but those character traits by themselves are not immoral, though they can lead to harmful behavior, which might very well be immoral. Offensive behavior can sometimes become harmful, but it need not. While delineating when offense becomes harm is tough, the principle seems clear. Even if the offense leads to psychological derangement for the free spirit, we still need to know if that is the usual result of crude, inconsiderate, and offensive behavior. If it is not, I see no immoral actions on the part of the workers, at least on the grounds of offense.

But if the insensitive remarks of the construction workers are not instances of immoral sexual objectification, what would be? If the workers were to follow the free spirit home and make their remarks every time she came out the door, if they were to get her phone number and call her to make their remarks, if they sent her mail involving those remarks, the behavior is becoming harmful. I am not sure where to draw the line. If the workers follow her, corner her so she cannot get away from their remarks, it is immoral. If they kidnap her, their abusive remarks are immoral. The workers have increasingly curtailed her freedom of choice to avoid their insensitive remarks, up to the point where she has no options left. But note that the moral problem here is not objectification; it is behavior that violates consent and restricts the ability of a person to choose a course of action. The fact that this is a sexual context has no bearing on the immorality. It would be just as wrong if the workers were forcing her to hear racially or religiously insensitive remarks.

3. Attitudes and Character

The issue is more complicated when LeMoncheck discusses not objectifying *behavior*, but objectifying *attitudes*. To be concerned with behavior is complicated enough, but she wants to deal also with "sentiments," beliefs, and attitudes. I am not sure what "sentiments" are, so I discuss feelings (emotions), beliefs, and attitudes. These items do need to be discussed. Allow me to state, first, how I use these terms.

Attitudes are enduring, stable psychological structures that focus or direct attention, are associated with beliefs, and can affect feelings. Feelings or emotions are relatively brief psychological phenomenon involving both affect and reason. Beliefs are enduring psychic structures that might involve emotions and can be expressed linguistically or observed as habitual behavior patterns. Attitudes endure and are the least subject to change; beliefs, less enduring and more open to change; feelings are the least enduring, most changeable, and they are renewable by acts of will. It is possible for beliefs to be inaccurate. It is possible for attitudes to be inappropriate or unfortunate, partly dependent on the beliefs that contribute to their structure, but attitudes are not "inaccurate." Feelings can be misidentified but not mistaken, and they can be caused in part by mistaken beliefs; they might influence the structure of beliefs and thereby attitudes, and they might be inappropriate.

I am not satisfied with LeMoncheck's treatment of the attitudes and beliefs of the construction workers in the free spirit case, or with beliefs and attitudes in the analysis of moral questions in general. If the free spirit were able to cause the offensive behavior to stop, for LeMoncheck a moral problem would remain. That problem concerns the attitudes and beliefs of the workers, even if they never again say anything of an offensive nature to or in the presence of the free spirit or any other woman. LeMoncheck, in addition, wants some sort of "empathetic understanding" that is central to an "ethics of care" but not an "ethics of justice." I agree with LeMoncheck that an "ethics of care" is laudable, but I do not believe the absence of what it prescribes allows a situation to be characterized, on that score alone, as immoral. Can a case be made for morally requiring that other people have certain beliefs, attitudes, and feelings? We are shifting our attention from the *actions* of the workers to their *character*, from applying moral judgments to their behavior to applying moral judgments to character. Can we morally require the crude, inconsiderate workers to be *different* people? Do we have the right to expect them to be considerate, empathetic human beings? A world of empathetics would be desirable. But can we morally require people to be of good character, and morally blame them if they are not or do not try to be?

My position is that we can neither morally require people to have a certain kind of character, nor morally blame them for their character, whatever it may be. We can praise them if they are empathetic, or willing to change both behavior and beliefs, and we can encourage them to change attitudes if offensive or upsetting to others. We can commiserate with them if they try but fail. We can avoid them for our own good. Praise and blame here are pragmatic activities, designed to encourage the behavior of which we approve and discourage those of which we do not. We reasonably blame or praise people only for that part of their behavior that is under direct conscious control and is therefore a matter of choice. This category consists of physical actions, but also includes feelings. Further, since beliefs are usually subject to conscious control and choice, people can be morally judged for their beliefs. To the extent that beliefs are part of the structure of attitudes, we can praise people who modify incorrect beliefs into correct ones, and who modify attitude or character traits as a result. We cannot reasonably blame people if they do not change their character or attitudes, since character consists of a collection of attitudes, and the resultant habits to perceive and act. Attitudes and character are not the objects of direct and immediate conscious control and choice.

Feelings, while not subject to much conscious control while a person is having them, are subject to modification over a period of time. A person who is given to bouts of anger does well to avoid actions inspired by that emotion; if he fails, moral blame is justified if he harms anyone. Such a person might, however, try to understand the beliefs that inspire the anger and change them. This might have an effect on the person's attitudes and thereby perhaps on character, which changes might then affect his or her subsequent feelings and behavior. This is a long, slow process, not successful in any predictable way and not altogether directly subject to conscious control and choice. But some of the elements in the process are subject to conscious control or choice. That is why we should praise those who succeed, but not blame those who fail, unless their character leads to actions harmful to others.

Character and attitude modification are thus supererogatory acts. We can praise the workers if they become empathetic and sensitive, since empathy and sensitivity are character traits. We cannot morally blame them if they fail or never undertake the difficult task of such modification. To morally require the workers to be empathetic is to fail to understand the nature of character and the nature of moral judgment. We can require them to do no physical or psychological harm. It might help pragmatically to convince them to be less offensive. If they do so, our lives might be more pleasant.

4. Empathy

The private sexual parts of the free spirit, LeMoncheck claims, might be the subject of public discussion or of imaginative curiosity by the construction workers, who are strangers. If this causes her pain, that is unfortunate, but not immoral. Public discussion of such things most likely would be offensive and painful to the free spirit unless she chooses such discussion, and even then it still might be offensive and painful. Imaginative curiosity, unexpressed by even a lascivious look, would seem to be hard to detect unless confessed. It would hardly be offensive, much less harmful, if unknown to everyone except the looker, and results in no overt behavior of any sort. While limits can be put on behavior, it seems unrealistic to try to put limits on purely mental processes. To speculate on what people might be thinking is to beg for trouble. What if the free spirit were carrying a tennis racket, which caused the construction workers to wonder how good a tennis player she might be and inspired in them a desire to see her backhand?

I believe we cannot require any more of strangers than neighbor or brother love, which is just the expectation that a person will not be harmed by others. I am giving a minimalist characterization of neighbor love here; many philosophers and religious thinkers would include much more than I have. I would not include empathetic understanding, since we can have neighbor love for any human being, even someone like Charles Manson, for whom we can have little or no empathetic understanding.

In some situations a person may legitimately expect empathy from others: in a psychologically intimate relationship, such as friendship in Aristotle's third sense (genuine friendship) or romantic love relationships. Perhaps children can legitimately expect empathy from their parents—but not *vice versa*, at least not until the child has matured. In intimate relationships we may morally blame a person who is not empathetic, since relationships of this sort involve an implied promise of empathetic understanding. Blame for lack of empathy is misplaced in any other sort of human relationship. The ethics of care is limited to psychologically intimate relationships—which is not the nature of the relationship between the free spirit and the workers.

If an ethics of care were relevant to the free spirit case, it would seem that the empathy would have to proceed in both directions. The free spirit would have to ask herself why the construction workers were behaving in a way that offended her. Instead of guessing or merely assuming they are insensitive males exercising their power in a typical heteropatriarchal male way, she would be obliged to inquire about their behavior and perhaps to help them formulate their ideas and beliefs and to sort through their feelings. In LeMoncheck's description of the case (which itself lacks empathetic understanding of the workers), the free spirit automatically assumes the worst, not giving the men, especially the man who only looks at her and remains silent, any or much chance to explain themselves or to learn. There is, however, a genuine question about the safety of the free spirit were she to offer her assistance to the men in their sorting through their feelings.

5. Rape Consciousness

That there has been considerable sexual oppression of women by men is a historical fact. That it is still going on in many forms seems obvious to me. That the socialization of women has been a primary means to this oppression is also clear. Changing the socialization of women is one means of changing this situation, for the socialization of women produces a set of attitudes and character traits in women that causes cooperation with, if not consent to, much sexual oppression.

The other side of this coin are the attitudes and character traits that have traditionally been instilled in men. These have been detrimental to the well-being of women, and have also been damaging to men themselves. This set of stereotypes and other beliefs that many, if not most, men in our society have been exposed to and often accept, makes it difficult for men to form intimate relationships with anyone at all. To be unable to form empathetic and psychologically intimate relationships is to be incapable of experiencing one of the greatest joys of life and thus to have one's welfare curtailed.

So if heterosexual men typically have no rape mentality, no sensitivity to the rape fears of women, this can be explained (not justified) by reference to male gender socialization. This lack of sensitivity is important to correct; we need to be creative in discovering how to help men develop empathy. Here is a suggestion. A fear of rape can be summoned in women by asking them to imagine that they are being pursued through a park at night by twelve male convicts who have just escaped from jail. So ask a man to imagine himself being chased through a park pursued by twelve female convicts who have just escaped and are seeking sex. A man might deem this situation a dream come true and fail to see why women are so conscious of rape. He might think he would enjoy this sexual objectification. Keep the example strictly parallel, then: he is being pursued through the park by twelve male escaped convicts who catch him and force him into receptive oral and anal copulation. This thought experiment should induce empathy of rape in most men.

The common factor in these cases is that the sexual activity is not chosen. A heterosexual male might consent to being used by a sexually crazed band of escaped female convicts. He is less likely to consent to such behavior by escaped male convicts, and would become involved only if all avenues of choice were removed. The problem, though, seems to be not objectification *per se* but nonconsensual and unchosen objectification. Consensual sadomasochistic behavior illustrates the point. Sadomasochism often involves objectification of at least one of the participants. The masochist chooses to be physically hurt and psychologically humiliated. Rarely, however, will a masochist choose to be harmed. Some kind of physical or psychological pain is what the masochist chooses, and usually makes that choice clearly known to the sadist before the activity begins. Hurting a person is immoral only if it is not consented to, or not chosen, and the victim has no other choice.

6. Choosing Objectification

Humiliating a person, or being humiliated, is very exciting for some people if it is chosen. Similarly, sex objectification can be the act of choice for some people at some times, including women being objectified by men. Under these circumstances, objectification is not immoral, no matter who does it to whom. The relevant characteristic in immoral sex objectification in most cases is that the person does not choose the situation and cannot avoid it. In this respect, the person is not being treated as a moral equal or as a person. If someone chooses to be treated as a thing, a body, a body part, or an animal, such treatment is objectification, but not immoral. We made that point above: recall LeMoncheck's cases of a woman being operated on, or playing horsy, or attending a class in anthropology. Allowing a person the freedom to choose is not a question of empathy. We can allow a person to choose while having little or no empathy for that person, but having, instead, respect, or what might be called neighbor or brother love, even if an empathetic person, one who possesses that character trait, is more likely to be sensitive to respecting another person's ability to choose.

Some women do choose to be objectified, for whatever reason—money, fame, self-esteem, and so forth. Such consensual objectification has a negative impact on the image of women. Consensual objectification reinforces traditional male beliefs, and so is not desirable. On the other hand, stopping this behavior interferes with the rights of women who choose objectification. I doubt that traditional male beliefs that stereotypify women would disappear or diminish in the absence of such consensually objectifying behavior. I suspect that we simply have to wait for the traditional attitudes and character traits of many males to die off, in the meantime using education to help build the beliefs, attitudes, and character traits of young men and women. Education might do more than anything else to bring about a community of empathetics.

7. Functions

LeMoncheck believes objectification consists of regarding people as if they were things, body parts, bodies, or animals. I accept this, but add that the common characteristic in these objectifications is the reduction of a human being or part of a human being to a *function*. This approach is illuminating. It applies fairly well to her four cases of permissible objectification. The woman used as an object of focus is obviously performing a function. The woman being probed for a tumor is in part performing the function for the exercise of the skill of the surgeon. The woman playing horsy can also be seen as functioning as a "horse-playing object." A problem arises, though, with the lecture comparing women with female chimpanzees. This example can, perhaps, be handled not as a case of objectification at all, but simply as drawing an analogy between the two groups in order to bring out some similarities while ignoring some differences.

The function performed by the free spirit is that of arousing the workers sexually, and perhaps the additional function of providing them with an opportunity for expressing male gender behavior. They are practicing the behavior taught them as "manly," which involves the deliberate display of heterosexual tendencies, reassuring each other and themselves that they are not gay. They are playing the game of "more heterosexual than thou."

On a functional analysis, a paradigmatic sex object would be a nonliving object intended to have a sexual function, such as a dildo, a vibrator, or a blow up plastic doll with twenty seven functional orifices. Derivatively, any object or person providing a sexual function would be a sexual object. A person performing the function of a sex object is a person treated as if they were a thing, whether they choose to be so treated or not. Morality is an issue if they do not choose to be so treated.

This analysis can be broadened to cover other kinds of objectification. A person could be a car-repairing object, a cookie-baking object, or a wage-earning object, for instance, if the person is considered only in terms of the function that the person performs. So far, I cannot see that morality is an issue. It depends on whether the person objectified chooses the function, or could choose not to perform it. If the person is forced to perform a function against his or her will, the potential for harm is great.

It is possible to treat a person who has chosen to be a car-repairing object (a mechanic) either morally or immorally. If we reach a mutually satisfactory agreement about a repair and its cost, and we both keep our side of the agreement, nothing immoral occurs. Informed consent is enough for that. But if either of us intend to cheat the other person, immorality is possible. The immorality has nothing to do with objectification (which was chosen and could be avoided), but with what can be wrong about the treatment of human beings in any context. In this case, relevant information (that at least one party did not intend to keep the agreement) was withheld. This is likely to be harmful. If we wish to state this in terms of the characteristics of choice, an informed choice could not have been made.

Note

1. Linda LeMoncheck, "What Is Wrong with Treating Women as Sex Objects?" this volume, 137-45.

John P. Sullivan
(photograph: Judy Godfrey)

Author of "Women as Sex Objects: Some Reflections"
Paper presented at the Society for the Philosophy of Sex and Love
during the
Pacific Division Meeting of The American Philosophical Association
Sacramento, Cal., 25 March 1982

Fifteen

WOMEN AS SEX OBJECTS

John P. Sullivan

William Butler Yeats once wrote, presumably having in mind that revolutionary lady Maud Gonne,

> . . . only God, my dear,
> Could love you for yourself alone
> And not your yellow hair.[1]

In the struggle for women's rights and the fight against sexism, we become accustomed to slogans and value them, opportunistically or heuristically, for their emotive content. I have encountered only last year such a dramatic sentiment as "Men are the enemy: all men." And a common charge against men is that they chiefly value, and treat, women as "sexual objects." The philosophical literature on sexual objectification is not extensive,[2] as far as I can judge, although philosophical discussions of related matters sometimes shed light on the concept.[3] Nevertheless, it still has for me several puzzling philosophical characteristics.

Let us take two paradigms of the use of the concept:

1. All (most, many) men regard women as sexual objects.
2. The inflatable life-size Barbie doll, completely equipped with realistic orifices, is the perfect sex object.

One can consider the second sentence as making obvious sense, but the first is more difficult to analyze, however common its use in feminist rhetoric. Underlying the sentiment, one must suppose, is the Kantian precept that one should regard human beings as ends in themselves and not as means. The inflatable doll is clearly a *means* to male gratification, a masturbatory device, as are, for females, dildos and vibrators. Equally clearly, if a man regards a woman (say, a prostitute) as only a more realistic, living and breathing, Barbie doll, he is treating her, as D. H. Lawrence pointed out long ago, as an instrument for masturbation. But sexual interaction, heterosexual or homosexual, is by no means so simple as in this equation. The first sentence is more complicated than it would appear.

I would like to introduce, at this point, the concept of "linguistic reciprocity." It makes sense to say, for example, "someone is driving a car," but no sense to say, without further explication, "A car is driving someone." So in discussing the relationships between the sexes we find an analogous situation, although the lack of linguistic reciprocity is not so obvious and is less a matter of logical sense or nonsense as it is the nontransferability of pejorative, emotive, or sexist overtones.

The basic idea, though not the term, has been discussed by Robert Baker.[4] He points out that "humanity" is synonymous with "mankind" but not with "womankind." He goes too far, however, when he declares that "Humanity . . . is a male prerogative." If I assert that the nuclear bomb will destroy humanity (or mankind), I do *not* imply that women are somehow immune to radiation or nuclear explosions.

Suppose a woman is interested in a man solely for his good looks, his handsome body, or prowess in making love, as indeed happens with Hawaiian beach boys, rock and roll singers, movie stars, and other members of the entertainment world. In such a case the words *stud*, *beefcake* (a back formation of cheesecake), *a good lay*, *a magnificent hunk*, and so forth, might easily be used to describe the "sex object." But here the pejorative overtones are far less, if any, and indeed might be taken by the recipient of such epithets as compliments. In fact, such males often go to great pains to cultivate *this* image of "sex object." But it would be odd, not conforming to our ordinary speech habits, at least, to characterize the woman's attitude towards such a male as "sexist." So "sexist," in this respect, lacks linguistic reciprocity. One would not characterize a lesbian who hates all men as sexist, for example, but would use other descriptions of her feelings.

To take another aspect of the question: many women are attracted to men not for their sexual and physical attributes, but because of their power, money, intellectual abilities, wit, even good nature. These qualities often compensate for any physical deficiencies that these men might have. We do not, however, have any linguistic equivalents here for "sex object." Such coinages as "power object," "money object," and "genius object" would have a strange ring, if applied to John F. Kennedy, Nelson Rockefeller, or Scott Fitzgerald. Here again, in a somewhat different way, we detect a lack of linguistic reciprocity between these concepts, although the phenomena that would be described by the use of these and similar terms obviously exist. And, it seems to me, there is the same Kantian objection to be made to relationships based on such factors. Somehow these factors are regarded as *external* to the person himself (or herself). What I have just said is equally applicable to homosexual and nonsexual relationships between members of the same or the other sex. I have chosen heterosexual examples because the term "sex object" occurs most frequently in discussions of the social phenomenon of sexism.

What is at issue is the notion of *dehumanizing*, a moral concept that itself needs to be unwrapped. Consider this passage from Anthony Burgess's *1985*:

> If good is concerned with promoting the ability in a living organism to act freely, evil must be dedicated to taking such freedom away. If we are Pelagians,[5] we accept that man has total liberty of moral choice. To remove that choice is to dehumanize. Evil is at its most spectacular when it enjoys turning a living soul into a *manipulable object*.[6]

Burgess's use of the words "manipulable object" at first seems to come close to the feminist use of "sex object" in the context of male-female relationships. But except in the case of rape, where the woman is actually manipulated by physical force or the threat of violent injury, death, or disgrace,[7] the uses of the word "object" are not actually parallel. Even if a woman regards her treatment by a man as that appropriate only to a so-called "sex object," nevertheless there ordinarily is the possibility of her behaving as a person, a subject, if you like, by refusing overtures, ignoring crude remarks, complaining to relevant authorities, and so forth.

But what, then, is at the heart of the problem crystallized in the still puzzling concept of "sex object"? It would be easy enough to say that enlightened women resent being valued *only* for their good looks, voluptuous figures, sexiness, or their undeniable ability to give males orgasms or pander to their genetic desire for sexual variety and *macho* conquests. And the social consequences of such hypothetical male attitudes might be traced in our multimillion dollar cosmetic industry and sexual corruption in politics, industry, and academe. But these are not of philosophical concern to us here, since all these things could come about if beautiful women were regarded not just as "sexual objects" but as *persons* who had devastatingly powerful characters as well as sexual appeal, which they could use to manipulate men, women, and the world at large. This would hardly qualify them as "sexual objects."[8]

The problem that I see in this whole question might be perhaps dissolved, if we realize that the underlying theme is one of personal relationships. What are the proper, correct, or ideal ways of interacting with the other (or indeed the same) sex? The slogan appealed to here is "I want to be treated as a person." (Odd, isn't it, that the word *person* derives from the Latin *persona*, which means a stage mask?) The appeal is to be contrasted to "I don't want to be treated *just* as a sex object." But could not one substitute similar pleas such as "I don't want to be treated *just* as a secretary/coffee-making machine/boss/teacher/student/film star/jolly good fellow"?

Could it be that in using the opprobrious term "sex object," we have in mind as an alternative an almost metaphysical idea of what being treated as a *person* is? Our interactions with other social beings are many and diverse, sometimes profound as with close friends, sometimes shallow as with plumbers, shop assistants, and waitresses. We value these latter for their skills and services and it would be linguistically difficult to speak of "plumber objects," "waitress objects," and so on. I would suggest that it is only because of the natural or cultural importance of sex in our lives and modern society in general that the concept of "sex object" is viable, whereas "cook object," "mother object," and "security object" are not.

J. F. M. Hunter[9] throws some light on the whole subject when he argues that personal relationships can be better or worse in three ways: in terms of congeniality, morality, and personal intimacy. Congeniality involves finding another person interesting or agreeable without profound involvement; morality is a duty whether it involves a friend, an enemy, or a "sex object"; and personal intimacy, sometimes sought though not always gained by sexual intimacy, has to be ostensively defined by one's own experience. It seems to me that, even if we postulate that men are more easily stimulated visually by attractive male or female potential partners and women by, say, the trappings of success, attentiveness, wealth, and power, the concept of "sex object" could take its proper place under one or other of Hunter's two categories of "congeniality" or "personal intimacy," involving no more than that a given woman has physical assets that make her "congenial" or that he or she prompts the desire to move to the level of "personal intimacy," just as wit, power, kindness, or success, as well as physical desirability, can prompt a similar wish in women. (Morality in all relationships is a duty, not a virtue.)

To conclude: since there are so many ways in which we initially value people and so many reasons, frivolous or otherwise, why we do so, and since there are so many levels of relationships between people, the complaint that one is regarded as a "sex object" has to be put on par with the similar complaints that could be made by people whose intimacy with oneself is limited and who are subject to social hierarchical structures. "Sex object" is useful in slogans, perhaps, but it misdirects our attention from the real question: what are optimal relationships between individuals of whatever sex? How should they develop, regardless of their beginnings?

Notes

1. "For Anne Gregory," in Richard J. Finneran, ed., *The Poems of W. B. Yeats: A New Edition* (New York: Macmillan, 1933).

2. But see Elizabeth R. Eames, "Sexism and Woman as Sex Object," *Journal of Thought* 11:2 (1976), 140-3.

3. See, for example, Jacqueline Fortunata, "Masturbation and Women's Sexuality," in Alan Soble, ed., *Philosophy of Sex*, 1st ed. (Totowa, N.J.: Littlefield, Adams, 1980), 389-408.

4. Robert Baker, "'Pricks' and 'Chicks': A Plea for Persons," in Robert Baker and Frederick Elliston, eds., *Philosophy and Sex*, 2nd ed. (Buffalo: Prometheus, 1984), 249-67.

5. Pelagians: a British heresy that denied the doctrine of Original Sin.

6. Anthony Burgess, *1985* (Boston: Little, Brown, 1978), 56-7, italics added.

7. Lucretia was raped by Sextus Tarquin not only by the threat of death but also by the threat that a dead slave would be laid beside her in her bed. One might extend the element threat to the withholding of good grades, job promotions, and other expected benefits.

8. Even in these cases the vocabulary of sexual intercourse would probably not change. Baker has an interesting analysis of our modern terms ("fucked," "screwed," "balled") that is not to my purpose here. But it should be noted that in the obscene language of Greek and Latin, words such as "kēlitizein" and "equitare" refer to the woman's "riding" the man; it might have been the Christian preference for the "missionary position" that led to many of our linguistic terms for describing sexual intimacy.

9. J. F. M. Hunter, *Thinking About Sex and Love* (Toronto: Macmillan, 1980).

Ann Garry
(photograph: California State University at Los Angeles)

Author of "Reflections on 'Women as Sex Objects'"
Paper presented at the Society for the Philosophy of Sex and Love
during the
Pacific Division Meeting of The American Philosophical Association
Sacramento, Cal., 25 March 1982

Sixteen

SEX (AND OTHER) OBJECTS

Ann Garry

After surveying several interpretations of what it is to be treated as a sex object and pointing out that none is adequate, John Sullivan[1] suggests that we can dissolve the problem of the inscrutability of the concept of a sex object by realizing that the underlying theme concerns personal relationships. Specifically, it is "what are the proper, correct, or ideal ways of interacting with the other (or indeed the same) sex" (159). In the context of this theme, Sullivan maintains that we can understand the complaints of many people with whom we have only superficial or hierarchically structured relationships. They do not want to be treated *just* as a plumber, waitress, secretary, boss, and so forth, but as a person. The feminist complaint about being treated as a sex object should be understood in the same manner as (and on a par with) these other complaints. For Sullivan, the woman who complains about sex objectification is objecting to one of the ways men initially value women, a way women do not initially, to the same degree, value men. But because many of the ways we initially value people are frivolous yet move us to more meaningful and intimate relationships, we should regard the feminist concern with sex objectification as "useful in slogans, perhaps, but it misdirects our attention from the real question: what are optimal relationships between individuals of whatever sex? How should they develop, regardless of their beginnings?" (160).

I shall state briefly several of the difficulties I have with Sullivan's approach, then spell out each in turn. First, he has done justice neither to the small body of philosophical literature that explicitly analyzes the concept of a sex object nor to the traditional philosophers whose theories can be appropriated for such analysis. Second, his focus is too narrow to account for the depth or breadth of the feminist complaint about sex objectification. Third, because Sullivan overlooks a special characteristic of sexual relations and sexual desire, he fails to notice a good reason why we have the concept of a sex object but not of a mother object or a security object. Finally, no basis exists for "dissolving" the need for an analysis of "sex object."

1.

Although I agree with Sullivan that the interpretations of the concept of a sex object that he surveys are inadequate, I do not understand why he fails to discuss some of the better developed philosophical analyses of the concept. He cites Robert Baker's article, but does not discuss Baker's view: because of the meanings given sex and sex roles in our culture, to treat someone as a sex object is to treat her as a *harmed* object.[2] Nor does he discuss Sandra Bartky's position; in the Sartrean tradition, she regards objectification as an integral part of sex. Bartky claims a person "is sexually objectified when her sexual parts or sexual functions are separated out from the rest of her personality and reduced to the status of mere instrument or else regarded as if they were capable of representing her."[3] Whether one would ultimately find these views more appealing than those Sullivan mentions, Sullivan should consider better developed philosophical analyses, before arguing that we should dissolve the problem.

Sullivan should also consider whether we could draw on the traditional philosophers to help us analyze and understand women's complaints about sex objectification. For example, can we find something of interest either in Sartre's view that objectification (or "incarnation") is necessary in sex, or in a more subtle interpretation of Kant's imperative to treat a person as an end rather than only as a means?

2.

Perhaps my major difficulty with Sullivan's desire to shift the focus from sex objectification *per se* to the "real question" (160), namely, personal relationships, is that in his particular manner of doing so, he focuses on both too narrow a range of sex objectification and too superficial a complaint about it. He speaks as if treating someone as a sex object is something that happens in the initial stages of personal relationships (which can then lead to more intimacy in the relationship). However, a woman can be treated as a sex object by anyone at any point in a relationship. For example, her boss or colleague might after many years suddenly make a crude and disrespectful sexual overture that makes her feel objectified. She can even be objectified in a distasteful manner by someone who is already her lover: one can imagine circumstances in which a lover who is angry (and uses sex to express his anger) might treat a woman "merely as a piece of ass."

I also disagree with Sullivan that to treat someone as a sex object is to attempt to move to a deeper level of intimacy with her. Suppose a recently divorced woman has just poured out her heart to her male friend of ten years, only to realize that he was not listening at all but merely wanting to entice her to have sex with him. The result here is probably a decrease in the level of intimacy. (One could object that the man was trying to increase the level of intimacy, but failed. I would reply that such a man needs to learn what is likely to produce intimacy and what is not. It might be, in part, this kind of poor judgment that feminists object to.)

The construction workers who make catcalls to Linda LeMoncheck's "free spirit" is not trying to increase their level of intimacy with her.[4] They are doing something rather different: perhaps they want momentary domination of her freedom or to invade her privacy; perhaps the catcalls are their mistaken idea of "meaningless, good, clean fun." Given more time, it might be interesting to work out the ways in which sex objectification encourages emotional distance rather than intimacy between men and women. (I am thinking of a range of circumstances including singles' bars, workplace harassment, the overall commercialization of sex, and so on.)

Because Sullivan's narrow focus leaves out so much that feminists have objected to, one is led to think that he sees the complaint about sex objectification as not only more narrow but also more superficial than it is. In addition, his desire to focus on the "real question" leads him to overlook many allies. Most feminists, like Sullivan, want to encourage better, more "human" relations between men and women. But, unlike Sullivan, feminists see sex objectification as both a deep and a widespread impediment to improving these relationships. This is, of course, one reason that feminists have focused attention on it.

3.

In the course of arguing that the feminist complaint about sex objectification is on a par with many other complaints, Sullivan tries to explain why we have the concept of a sex object but not of a mother object or a security object. He says, "it is only because of the natural or cultural importance of sex in our lives and modern society in general that the concept of 'sex object' is viable, whereas, 'cook object,' 'mother object,' and 'security object' are not" (159). Sullivan has missed an important point about sex here. Security (and maybe mother as well) weigh almost as heavily as sex among contemporary human needs.

There is something special about sexual activity and sexual desire that leads us to speak of people as sex objects. It is not merely that a person is the object of sexual desire; that is true of the objects of many feelings and needs. We can learn something from Sartre about objectification in sex. Although I would not endorse Sartre's entire view of sex and personal relations, his insight that in sexual activity we in a sense become our bodies is important. I hope this quotation from Sartre is intelligible out of context:

> I make her enjoy my flesh through her flesh in order to compel her to feel herself flesh. And so possession truly appears as a double reciprocal incarnation.[5]

As I read Sartre, we can think of "incarnation" as objectification: becoming a body, becoming flesh, becoming an object. Sometimes it is mutual, sometimes not. If a man wants a woman to "feel herself flesh," as one might say of the construction workers and LeMoncheck's free spirit, when it is inappropriate, out of context, or in some other way untoward or degrading, it is the sort of sex objectification feminists complain of. But to have sex at all, or even to be sexually attracted to someone or be the object of attraction, is to be liable to objectification. This is the reason we speak of sex objects and not of security objects.[6]

4.

My final point is a reservation about Sullivan's approach to "dissolving" the problem of the analysis of "sex object." My reservation stems not from a principle that philosophical problems are incapable of being dissolved. In fact, I have been heavily influenced by Wittgenstein to think that some problems can and should be dissolved. My reservation is instead that this particular problem cannot be dissolved, even if one agrees with Sullivan about what is the "real question."

If I am trying to discover what optimal personal relationships are, then I need to know the pitfalls to avoid as well as the positive principles to reinforce. I need to know what all these people mean when they say, "Do not treat me as a secretary, plumber, boss, meal ticket, or sex object." So, far from doing away with a need for an analysis of their complaints, this need underscores a requirement to do it carefully. Again borrowing from Wittgenstein, we need to pay attention to the details of each individual case, not to assume that there is one principle or analysis that will take care of them all. In personal relationships, as well as in philosophy, a "one-sided diet of examples" will lead us astray.

I appealed to Sartre earlier to argue for the point that sex objectification is different from less-than-fully-respectful treatment of secretaries, plumbers, and "security blankets." Because of its different nature, sex objectification requires a special analysis. Further, because of the diversity of both the manner and the kinds of situations in which we sexually objectify people, we might not even be able to analyze sex objectification in a unified "necessary and sufficient conditions" manner. A Wittgensteinian "family resemblance" characterization might be more informative and helpful.

Some might argue that by suggesting a family resemblance analysis of sex objectification, I, too, am trying to dissolve the problem of analyzing the concept of a sex object. Although in principle I have no objection to calling it this, in practice I would not use the word "dissolve." It suggests that there is no real problem here. And although Sullivan might agree with this, I surely do not.

Notes

1. John P. Sullivan, "Women As Sex Objects," this volume, 157-60; page references to this essay are supplied parenthetically in the text.

2. Robert Baker, "'Pricks' and 'Chicks': A Plea for Persons," in Robert Baker and Frederick Elliston, eds., *Philosophy and Sex*, 2nd ed. (Buffalo: Prometheus, 1984), 249-67.

3. Sandra Bartky, "On Psychological Oppression," in her *Femininity and Domination* (New York: Routledge, 1990), 22-32.

4. Linda LeMoncheck, "What Is Wrong with Treating Women as Sex Objects?" this volume, 137-45.

5. Jean-Paul Sartre, *Being and Nothingness*, trans. Hazel E. Barnes (New York: Philosophical Library, 1956), 391.

6. I do not suggest that Sartre's view is adequate for distinguishing "acceptable objectification" from the kind about which women complain. In fact, Sartre makes this distinction more difficult to draw than many other thinkers do. Nor can we find in Sartre a *simple* explanation for women's being objectified more readily than men. My suggestion here would be to consider, as

many feminists have, the pervasiveness of "women as sex objects" in our culture, the social pressure for women to be sex objects, the extent to which "getting a man" is tied to a woman's self-esteem, and the extent to which men are supposed to be the aggressors in sex.

John McMurtry

Author of "Sex, Love, and Friendship"
Paper presented at the Society for the Philosophy of Sex and Love
during the
Eastern Division Meeting of The American Philosophical Association
Baltimore, Md., 28 December 1982

Seventeen

SEX, LOVE, AND FRIENDSHIP

John McMurtry

1. Persons

A person is an open elective space. I say "open" because there is no limit at all to what a person can think, and nothing that can be thought of that cannot be negated. I say "elective" because what one thinks of, or does not, is open to choice, however difficult such choice might be in issues of the heart. Personhood emerges in personal identity, which is a chosen way of being in the world. Personal identity is, within the determining limits of a person's material conditions, a creative matter. So too are love and friendship, which are chosen ways of *being with* other persons in the world.

This is not to say that persons, and who they are with, cannot be conditioned into being nonpersons. Persons become nonpersons when they become programmed to an externally prescribed format of thought and action. This programming of people into robot-like beings is widespread in sexual relations, not only in commercial representations, which typically reduce women to aspects of their bodies, but in real-life marriages and love relations in which partners become mere occupants of their assigned roles. We can discern this pattern of people's determination by the roles they occupy in their closure to all alternatives, even in the realm of discussion.

That there is serious contemporary debate about whether humans are more than analogues to computer programs is a symptom of this problem of persons being reduced to role-coded beings. We confront this effect not only in the fashionable computer model of persons, but in formalist models of relationships *between* persons where self-maximizing, game-theoretical, and contractarian calculi are thought to stand in for people deciding how they are going to live together in a human community. In love relationships, especially, such mechanical thinking is destructive of the open universe within which people are located by the nature of their personhood.

This is not to say that the open, elective space we bear as persons is not determined or limited in its range of expression by the material conditions enabling and disabling its choices. What we can *think* and what we can *do* refer to different planes of possibility. The latter is "the test of reality" to which our thoughts must submit to become actualized. In this interaction of the boundless reaches of our thought within and the bounded, space-occupying realm without that we must survive in, what we are in the world is tested and decided. Madness, insanity, maladjustment or, on the other hand, becoming mere functions of a social program, are outcomes that signal to us how difficult it is to relate the unbounded and bounded fields of our being in the world. Normally, it is only by *being with* other persons in love and friendship that we can manage this interface at all.

In being with other persons, there are different ranges of possibility. In the interior universe of thought, by which I mean to include the felt being of thought, one can comprehend oneself as being with the entire world of beings without any limit. All that seems Other is one with the "true self." This is the inner idea of the ancient wisdoms of Vedanta, Buddhism, Taoism, and the mystic forms of Christianity and neo-Confucianism. A person conceives and feels the whole world as his or her wider being, and acts for its well-being rather than any partial interest of ego, class, ethnic group or other artificial line of self-other division.

This possibility is intuited in sexual love when it finds the whole of nature and humanity implicate in its workings—the stars above and the earth below, the heroic deed for the beloved and the sacrifice of self, the future of humanity resonating in the children to be born, the oceanic field of the universe achieving one. This connection between love of another person and love of the world is explicitly articulated in the esoteric traditions of Sufism and Tantrism, and reveals to us the boundlessness of being with that persons are potentially open to as persons. There is no a priori limit to the range of love's embrace. Indeed, I suspect that love and friendship only succeed when they live beyond their particular shared being to include the wider world in their concern, and suffocate in narrowness when they do not. If we observe love and friendship relations over time, can we anywhere disconfirm this pattern of their fulfillment? Joining with the other to live beyond the self seems to be what love and friendship yearn for by their nature and will not grow for long without.

Yet love and friendship in the more familiar sense almost always begin from a *face-to-face* relationship of persons: internal universes coming to know their shared world from this personal encounter as their initiating special bond. But this being with the actual physical presence of another does not depend on this material presence to be sustained. We can envisage, live with, converse with the loved one in bodily absence, just as we live with what-is-not-there in our thinking in general. Still, the face-to-face condition of the particular love or friendship is what launches and revivifies its special ties. Even in exceptional cases, where, say, the first encounters are by the inscription of self in a letter, the relationship depends on this individual interface to remain alive as a love or friendship. At the most developed level, persons come together to live as "one body" where the condition of face-to-face presence is more or less continuous. Whatever the extent of its union, love and friendship normally imply this individuated, face-to-face bond. The persons related by it are joined as nonsubstitutable individuals in living presence to one another in some form of continuity through time. It is for this reason that the statement "I am not *seeing* her/him any more" is a statement of the relationship's end.

There is another feature of the bond of love and friendship, which distinguishes its individuated ties of being from all other forms of face-to-face relationship. Unlike other forms of human association, friendship and love are entered by the individuals themselves by *mutual choice*. Love and friendship stand, in this way, as personally creative bonds of being with, not obliged by general moral duties to fellow humans, by family ties, by work relations, or by any other pre-existing duties or requirements to associate with. We do not choose who are to be our parents, our siblings, our relatives, or our work mates. We do not choose even the child who is born to us. Even if we choose, as the mystics, to be with the whole world as our loved one, we do not choose *who* it is in this world or humanity we love. Personal friends and lovers are the only ones we choose to be with in freedom from prior obligation. They are in this way our only free relationships of being with other persons, and that is why we "feel free" inside their bonds, if they are, in truth, relationships of friendship and love.

The Old English etymological root of "friend," it is interesting to note, is *freon*, "to love," and it is akin to *freo*, meaning "free." Here we see a root overlap in the ideas of friendship, love, and freedom that might be the proper ground of our understanding of all three.

2. Forms of Love

Two clarifications are needed here. Although our parents, siblings, fellow workers, or even the children born to us are not chosen by us, but are set next to us as individuals we must be with in varying ways whether we like it or not, they may certainly *become* our friends or loved ones by choice *as well*. But love and friendship can never be forced. They grow to be this way freely, or they are not really friendship or love. There is, however, a primary confusion around this point in the face-to-face, personal relationships of our lives that can give rise to conflict and grief in endless ways. We must, it seems, love our parents in some sense, and more so our children. But if it is not *chosen* love, who can accept not being chosen as a loved one?

Once the freedom condition of who are our friends or our loved ones is laid bare, then other, obliged relations of affection seem to be reduced to relations of love only in name. Here we may, paradoxically, need to choose what we are obliged to: by discovering in the other what to freely love, and building a friendship or love on the basis of a "love" that is first prescribed to us. This is not always possible. But if we accept that these prescribed relations are worth nourishing as relations of love in some sense, it seems good to upgrade them to authentic, chosen love. In this creative freedom might lie the most central and unexamined site of love and friendship that life presents to us.

If we can do this with prescribed relationships of "love," it would also seem possible to do so in relationships of chosen love that have tired into routine and "going through the motions." The creative act here is not one of bestowal, a *gift* of value that Irving Singer proposes as the true nature of love.[1] It may be, instead, an opening of the mind to a real quality of the other person that has not been previously discovered or nourished.

Singer goes so far as to say about love as bestowal or gift that "Love is sheer gratuity."[2] My point, in contrast, is that love properly relates to an actual quality of a loved one, even if only a potential, seeking to nourish what is there rather than bestowing it as a "gratuity." In this way, love avoids its well-known blindness of projection and values the other for what she or he is or can be rather than what we grant as a favor.

Another question arises when we consider the love relationship involving sex. Here the chosen shared ground of being with involves a penetration of one another's very organic membrane and immune system. Does not the freedom condition of choosing our love in this case create a special obligation to remain with this person *against* our subsequent freedom of choice? We choose freely with whom we sleep, or it is not love. Yet once we have made the choice to love in this way, we seem subject to demands or requirements binding us against other options we might prefer after the act of sexual oneness. This is an under-theorized area, and the conflicts it gives rise to can be extreme and tragic—ending in forced weddings of unloving couples or moral blackmailing to force repeat intimacies, on the one hand, or callous disregard and uncaring exploitation, on the other.

But what then *are* the obligations, if any, that fall on us for sexual intimacy with another? Are there none, as many hold, beyond the mutual act of informed consent? Certainly the criterion of informed consent goes a long way if there is truly *informed* consent and no deception about prior commitments or the safety of sexual contact. Truly informed consent can allow radically different kinds of sexual being with, from a momentary passion to a lifelong love.

But unlike other forms of chosen being with, sexual being with can be compulsive in exploitative ways: love in all its cruelty. But so too can nonsexual friendship. What seemed to be deep friendship can be betrayed or lost in a sentence. The uncaring of a close friend can be as tormenting as rejection by a lover, obsessing our thought, provoking rage, keeping us awake at night. The real difference between sex-love and friendship is not one of principle. It is a difference in the content of the shared being. By this I mean that the chosen being with of sexuality is a particular sort of friendship whose shared being involves sexual interaction as its common ground. Consisting as it does in this area of chosen, face-to-face being with, an area that is specially dynamic and organically driven, a sexual love relationship is not so much a different structure of shared being as a special type of shared being with its own distinguishing features. Only it involves the reproductive organs and the possibility, in heterosexual love, of reproduction. But on the more general plane, it is, like friendship, a form of being with another by free choice in a face-to-face way. The difference between it and other types of friendship is, at bottom, the difference between *ways* of chosen shared being.

In all types of friendship or love in this generic sense, the friendship or love grows with the areas of chosen being with it encompasses. At the most comprehensive, it can become all-embracing. On the other hand, it can be a one-sided and short-lived relationship, an affair or a friendship that lasts only as long as the getting-drunk together (which is to dismiss neither as a worthwhile experience in itself). Dissolving the limits of the self has many enjoyable variations. At its most developed, the love union can be the consummating togetherness of shared being that comprehends "body and soul."

As persons, we choose which kind of being with to seek or continue. In this choosing, however, we should be aware of an important distinction. Often people "love" others for what they *want from them* rather than for the shared being in itself. Whether this be for sex, marriage-security, or a commercial contract, its object is external to the being with the other, and the "love" or "friendship" is a pretense of what it is not.

3. Good Love and Bad Love

What is of *value* in love and friendship? Love and friendship are not necessarily of value in themselves, even when they are not dissembled. One could sincerely choose to be with another in the most complete and permanent way, but the relationship could be bad or evil, a mutual reinforcement of each partner's stupidity or greed, for example. On the other hand, a relationship could involve a wide sharing of life on a long-term basis that harms no one beyond the union, but is rent with unreasoning conflict and demands within it that diminish both partners by its debilitating conflictedness and nondevelopment, "a dance of death." Love and friendship are by no means good in themselves, no matter how intimate, encompassing, or permanent their being with the other is. It is one of the great misconceptions of sexual love and friendship that they are good so long as they are authentic, intimate, and do not break up. These are certainly desirable features of any kind of love and friendship, but they do not in themselves make a *good* relationship.

What makes a good love or friendship is that it promotes the vital well-being of the partners and, beyond that, the well-being of life beyond their union. The goodness of a relationship increases with the range and depth of life—thought, feeling, action—that is enabled by the partners' shared being. The badness of a relationship, conversely, increases with the reduction of life's scope and depth by the relationship. The good or bad here grows within the lives of the partners themselves, and within the lives of others their relationship touches. These general parameters of value and disvalue do not compute sums, but they do give us guidelines to understand whether our love or friendship is good or bad. We can tell by these guidelines, for example, that a love or friendship whose shared being is merely to consume commercial enjoyments together before bedtime is at best useless, while one that seeks to promote the need and capacity realization of others is at the least well-motivated.

One of the great problems of sexual love is that it often *disables* us and our giving relationships to other beings. If we are not careful, we can get fixed inside its obsessions, and it can become destructive of our lives in a kind of dying to its primeval demands of joining. We see this possibility much indulged in the courtly love tradition and in current market-romance culture. On the other hand, the energies of romantic love can be exhilarating and uplifting, releasing us to more comprehensive horizons of vital being and productivity within our own lives and beyond, working out from the relationship itself to become a life-affirming power by which wider circles of being are nourished by love's dynamic bonds of togetherness. I think this goodness or badness of sexual love is ultimately a choice of persons, but we can choose one way rather than the other only if we are *aware* of the lines of their distinction and do not get lost in mystification of sexual love or friendship as a self-justifying end-in-itself. Each is a chosen way of being with another, and this way can be good or bad in accordance with the extent to which it enables or disables our own and others' lives. Yet our chosen ways of being with another are, ironically, often the least consciously formed. Indeed, it has become a benighted cliché in philosophical circles that we have no general bearings of value to steer by in love or anything else, and that good love or bad love is only a matter of personal viewpoint in a pluralist world of value relativism.

This "value pluralist" standpoint is advocated, for example, by Singer in his monumental *Nature of Love*. In reply to my criticism of the lack of any general value-bearings in his analysis of romantic and sexual love, he writes:

> In effect he [McMurtry] finds my pluralistic attitude useless for the assessment of practical issues that love must always involve. I can see the sense in which he may be right. I have no authority as a counselor in matters of the heart. My personal failures and successes, sufferings and joys, have never seemed to me an adequate basis for telling others how to live.[3]

It is worth noting that Singer here declines to reply to the general principle of value that I advocated in my commentary on his work, namely, "what is good is *what enables a more inclusive range of being*, and what is bad is *what reduces this range of being*—of thought, of experience, or of action."[4] Singer elects to overlook this principle and its application, and to counsel us, instead, that one's "own personal failures and successes, sufferings and joys . . . [are not] an adequate basis for telling others how to live." In this way, Singer's value-pluralist position sidesteps the argument for value guidelines in our lives by merely repeating its own conclusion. This seems an ironic *cul de sac* of moral analysis because value pluralism is itself a principle of value whose worth *as* a value is accounted for by the principle it ignores.

4. Reconciling Sexual Love and Friendship

We have seen that both sexual love and friendship are chosen forms of being with another in the world that are distinguished from other forms of being with in two ways. First, they are face-to-face relationships with other individuals, not relationships with groups of beings or with other people we do not know personally. Second, sexual love and friendship differ from *other* face-to-face relationships with individuals we know personally (for example, family and work relationships) because they are associations we choose freely for their own sake. In view of the distinguishing characteristics that sexual love and friendship have in common, that they are typically conceived and experienced as *incompatible* types of personal bond is perhaps evidence of an irrational split at the core of our lives.

Consider the following common expressions that suppose that sex-love and friendship are opposed forms of relationship:

- "Let's remain good friends, and not get involved."
- "He loves me, but he doesn't like me."
- "She's a good friend because I have no interest in her as a lover."
- "I'm not your friend, I'm your wife."
- "I don't trust him, but I can't get over him."
- "Don't tell me she's just your friend. I saw how you looked at her."

These familiar ways of thinking and talking reveal a bifurcation and alienation between forms of relationship that at bottom share common distinguishing features. In all such expressions, romantic, conjugal, or sexual love is posed against friendship as if these were mutually exclusive kinds of being with. We need to clarify what has gone wrong here.

Although a person is "an open elective space" who can think of being with another in any number of ways, we seem conditioned to a reductionist program of sex-love that puts sex at the center of the love relationship, and mutual possession by the partners of this sex-center as the determining requirement of the relationship.

In contrast to this sex-property reductionism, I would like to explore further the view that sexual love between persons is better understood as a special *type* of friendship where freely being with another *includes* sexual union in its shared being. Friendship, under this conception, is what all chosen love between individual persons consists in, and the shared being of sexuality is simply one region of the relationship. From this viewpoint, the shared being of sexuality is not necessarily the most important region of being with, and certainly not the only one that matters. Most healthfully, I contend, sexual being with is one area of shared being among countless others that might grow and develop towards a comprehensive being with to which, like the universe within, no bounds can be found.

This position does not, as it might seem to, downgrade the sex of sexual love, a special kind of love whose distinction is justified by the very important chosen ground of friendship it designates. Rather, it is to affirm that friendship has many possibilities of freely chosen shared life, and that sexual togetherness is one field of this range of possibility. As Aristotle says of friendship in its most comprehensive form, it is "a going shares in everything."[5] Using Aristotle's conception in a way he did not intend, we can say that sexual love is a form of friendship in which "a going shares" exists in each other's very body for the time of its duration. Ideally, one might argue, sexual love should be a final field of chosen shared being to mark the exceptionally intimate area of being with another that it involves. But that is a notion introduced in the later courtly love tradition and is not generalizable as a developmental scheme.

The point I wish to make is more open-ended: we need to recognize the unity of sense underlying sexual love and friendship, whose shared being determines their content whether on a sexual or a nonsexual plane. From this common ground of their meaning, we are better able to recognize that sex-love and friendship are not really opposed, but variations on a common theme. *Sexual love is friendship* that differs from other sorts of friendship in the inclusion of genital eros in its shared life.

Formally defined, friendship is a life-sharing between persons that is realized in activities or enterprises pursued together by choice. A sexual or romantic love relation qualifies as friendship under this definition because it involves such a chosen sharing of life. If the relation were not chosen, or if its nature were rejected in principle by either party despite involvement in it, or if it were not realized in practice together, then it would not count as a friendship in the required sense, nor would it count as genuine romantic love. Sex-love is then a kind of friendship (thus our expressions "boyfriend" and "girlfriend"), albeit a special kind of friendship, because the value shared is of a distinct sort. In principle, a sexual relationship is no more special a friendship than other sorts of friendship whose shared content is similarly restricted or specialized: for example, a "business friend." What in practice segregates the sexual type of sharing from other kinds of restricted friendship, so that we are inclined to disassociate it mistakenly from friendship altogether, is its conventional exclusiveness.

If we were able to conceive of sex-love as a form of friendship, which at its most comprehensive is all-embracing love, one important consequence might be the negation of sexism. Consider how the logic of the disjunction between friendship and sex-love typically works. Insofar as a member of the opposite sex is a candidate for sex-love, it follows from the disjunction of sex-love and friendship that he or she cannot be a friend. She can only be a friend if the sex-love is ruled out; and conversely, it often seems, the sex-love is only possible if the friendship is ruled out. These implications follow from a strict either/or opposition between sex-love and friendship. This opposition might indeed be at the core of the sexism problem: why sexual attraction is expressed in unfriendly acts, from lovers' fights and cruelties to social epidemics of pornographic exploitation.

We have in this way traditionally divided ourselves and our relations, like the mythical centaur, into human and animal halves: the face of our common personhood into friendship, and our sexual life into animal appetite. We strain at the leash of our either/or reductions, and are compelled by the more subtle webs of our actually lived interactions into more inclusive relations: the lover as best friend, the best friend as huggable, kissable companion of our love. In this movement towards integrity in our ways of being with others we mature in our personal relations. But any such development in our integrity of personal relationships requires the consignment of the disjunction between friendship and sex-love to the past, along with veils of purdah and patriarchal bonds.

5. The Problem of Sexual Possessiveness

What would happen if we transcended this ancient division and treated sex-love as friendship, and our friendship as open to sexual love? What are the problems that our traditional walls between them might rule out? Is, for example, *the plurality of friendship incompatible with the one-to-one demand of sexual love*?

Here we confront, I believe, the major problem of the integration of sex-love and friendship. The dyadic nature of the sexual act itself, the sociobiological evidence for a genetic reproduction basis of the exclusive sexual bond, the psychological propensity to possession of the loved one, the agony of the lover whose partner is with another—all these press in on the idea of a more open alternative with a certain inexorability of restriction. Sexual love, it seems, is determined to be opposed to friendship by the one-to-one exclusiveness it requires in its shared being that friendship does not.

Or so we have learned to suppose. For the fact is that the exclusive pair-bond of heterosexual love does not work in our world as a general prescription. At best, it works as a chosen way of being with free of the constraints of external demand. In the main, the massive stampede out of conventional monogamy into affairs and divorces, outright rejection of the opposite sex, and alternative love alliances shows this form's obsolescence as an institution of social control. This growing abandonment of prescriptive monogamy has followed major changes in social conditions such as the increasing mix of men's and women's work and effective birth control practices. What has not changed however, and what might renew the exclusive male-female love bond in a self-determining form, is the serious danger of sexual disease in nonmonogamous sexual relations.

It might be thought that the successful reproduction of one's own genes requires sexual exclusiveness, and that we are bound by a biological program. This is, however, a non sequitur. It is a non sequitur because our genetic reproduction is consistent with many forms of sexual nonexclusiveness: hygienic, nonprocreative sex and post-upbringing sex, for example. The genetic reproduction argument does not apply when effective birth-preventive and disease-avoiding methods are available.

The rejoinder might be that an innate psychological set involved in sexual love remains that requires the exclusiveness that friendship does not. One is not normally jealous or forlorn or anxious when one's friend is with another, but one conventionally is when one's lover is. If the disjunction between friendship and sex-love has any relevant grounds in the proven experience of our kind, it seems here. Justifications of sex-exclusiveness might in the end remain plausible to us only because of our clear knowledge of the extreme psychological pain that nonexclusive relations are apt to cause. The jealousy problem, though this might not be an adequate term for the kinds of painful response there are to one's sexual loved one with another, is undoubtedly a deep problem. Still, we would be wise to understand its linkage to expectations conditioned into us by customs that, in turn, are related to biological problems that can be otherwise prevented in the conditions of a developed society.

It may well be true that genetic displacement, or sex-related disease, or unwanted pregnancy are problems that the obeyed imperative of sexual exclusiveness will largely prevent; and the taboo against extraconjugal sex has evolved, plausibly, as a survival-favoring characteristic (though strangely I know of no literature on the subject). We can certainly see an intelligible pattern of life-property-and-protection at work here: a "cunning of reason," as Hegel's heirs might put it, behind the prohibition of extraconjugal sex, and behind our psychological alarm when this established form of life is broken. But if the prohibition is a social-functional mechanism to prevent problems that are now otherwise preventible by more efficient means, namely, by birth-control devices and hygiene precautions, then it follows that the taboo against extraconjugal sex, as well as its corresponding psychological set, is now socially obsolete. In a developed society of medical knowledge and precautions, it becomes a species-useless characteristic. Like fangs. It seems evident that the traces of this once functional taboo remain in our conditioning, traditions, and inherited patterns of awareness in some still gripping form. Yet, if we are reflective beings, we are partly released from this grip by its very objectification to our thought. And if we are open and elective in our thought as persons, then our attachment to this psychological set can be consciously rejected. We do not remake ourselves in a day. But if our prejudicial outlook of exclusive expectation is, given effective care to prevent what it prevents, obsolete as a reproductive and survival requirement, then it is no longer a simple biological requirement for us. It is one option we can choose in being with another.

In this connection, it is instructive to look at relationships that bridge the open-ended allowance of friendship and the exclusive expectation of sex-love. Consider, for example, immature friendship, which can be as alarmed at the inclusion of a new friend in the affections of a "bosom" buddy as a lover is by the involvement of a second lover with his or her mate. Observe here the interchangeability of terms like "mate," "inseparable," "ardent," or "partner," which can apply to friend or lover alike. They indicate to us the deep common ground of sex-love and friendship as types of love. In cases of possessiveness, the similarity between the exclusive expectations that structure affection in both is systematic. In both cases, the new involvement can be regarded as "breaking up" the established relationship. In both cases, the "mate" who has become involved with another can be conceived as guilty of a "betrayal." And in both cases, there can be body flushing, desperation, heartache, rage, flare ups, desires to attack, hurt feelings, wounds, resentments, deep suspicions, mistrust, doubts, passion, and ups and downs of "separations" and "making up."

The key here, the underlying logic of the whole phenomenology of jealousy and its exclusive-expectation base in either friendship or romance, is an insecurity of the person. As with adolescent friends, so with traditional lovers, the chosen way of being with another is not yet stabilized as secure. This stabilization only occurs when the close friend of the heart, whether sexual or not, is safely, durably with you.

In post-adolescent friendship, this security is achieved by maturity. There are fewer "blow ups" between friends as they grow into wider relationships with the world. If they do come to a "break" in their relationship of friendship or romantic love, it is at bottom in a like way. They stop being with each other. They "come apart," and it is usually because they no longer grow in each other's company.

6. Friendship and Pluralist Sexual Love

Romantic love, we might say, is typically arrested in the adolescent stage of being with. But whereas the volatility of immature friendship progressively finds its bearings in lasting alliances of interest and action, pluralist sexual love has not so developed as a generally workable conventional social form. Why is this?

Again, we must return to the special set of problems associated with the sexual relationship. Because sex-love is a mutually chosen being with, it is a kind of friendship. Yet there is something about this special type of chosen being with that makes it peculiar for us, something apparently other than friendship. It seems to strike to the center of our being more than other kinds of voluntary alliances, to be qualitatively more capable of hurting or disabling us. It is this negative possibility that lovers' games and ultimata seem calculated to avoid, in distinction from the more easygoing and supportive ties of friendship. But what is it about erotic involvement that makes it so liable to hurtful possibility? Its fickleness? This is the syndrome with which popular culture has long been preoccupied, and which exclusiveness in sex-love is thought to prevent. Food, air, creative work, books, nature's horizons, good talk, sport, and deep reflection can also lie at the heart of our being with another. But because none of these shared grounds of being can, like lovers, just "break off" from us, we do not get jealous about others' access to them depriving us of their life sustenance. But when there *is* this danger in other life spheres, say, by a loss of one's job or one's home to another, much the same phenomena associated with sex-jealousy can occur: from short breathing and lying awake at night to stunned disbelief and heartache.

Fear of deprivation of one's life sources and means is a fear for the security of one's being in the world itself. The loss of a loved one seems no more or less a matter for the trembling and attachment of possessor anxiety than the loss of one's home or livelihood. The difference is that the object of love is not an object but a subject, who chooses to separate from the person to whom she or he formerly "belonged." This difference makes sex-love a more deeply personal matter by its nature, and also more vulnerable to the vagaries and whims of personal choice that are particularly unstable with the volatile "magic" and "chemistry" of sexual attraction.

But why, we need to ask, is erotic alliance so unstable, when life-sharing of the nonerotic sort is noted for its being durable and secure? The private choice and subjecthood involved in friendship does not make *it* more susceptible to caprice, especially when the life-sharing involves matters close to our heart and core. It might be responded that sexual involvement is peculiarly variable in its desire-object. But this point only reiterates our problem. For there is no object of human desire or need that is *not* variously desired, including personal joinings in intimate conversation, play, or creative work. Yet unions of friendship constituted by these spheres of mutuality and cooperative enactment are not made insecure by variety in them. What is it about variety of sexual relationships that accounts for the special insecurity it arouses? If disease and the social-functional basis of sexual exclusiveness are otherwise managed by responsible care, why cannot sexual love mature towards the variety we find in other forms of intimate being with?

The greatest present obstacle to this maturation, but one by which persons as such need not be blocked, seems to be the habit formation of our accumulated acculturation. Family structures, stories and songs, laws, religions, marketed stereotypes, and ultimately our own repetitive thought patterns have imprisoned us behind walls of exclusive sex-love expectations. We are, with full cultural backing, agitated to the core by the infraction of a possessory pattern that as mature friends or parents we have learned to reject as jejune or neurotic in our other chosen intimate relations. At this point of at least the Western world's development, with an explosive and increasingly pathogenic tension between releasing sexual desires and exclusive-love constraints, whose conflict increasingly yields outbreaks of sexual disease, unwanted pregnancy, and pornographic violence, a higher form of sexual relating might be an overdue stage in our social evolution.

7. The Moral Superiority of Friendship Love

Sexual love has traditionally been a dwarfish form of friendship in its narrowed fixation on the genital sphere of being with. Because this is a degrading reduction of the mutuality of persons, a flotilla of restrictions has been instituted to prevent the problems it raises. Sexual love as a form of friendship, in contrast, rules out these problems in proportion to the extent of cooperative subjecthood it involves. It is worthwhile reviewing here the moral emancipations of the friendship form of sexual love.

As long as friendship and sex-love are kept in exclusive disjunction, whoever is a candidate for sex-love (say, the whole opposite sex) is thereby disqualified from candidacy as friend: thus, the conventional "war of the sexes." In contrast, when sexual love is conceived and acted on as a form of friendship that includes eros as one of the areas of shared being, the "opposite" sex specially qualifies for friendship by providing a further possibility of life-sharing. Perhaps the greatest advantage of reconstruing the "opposite" sex as, in fact, having more to be with than one's own sex in the way of friendship, is that it subverts a basic structure of sexism. The more sexual love is comprehended as a form of friendship, the less the sexual Other can be construed as a threat to our gender identity or well-being.

On the individual level, sex-lovers "quarrel," "fight," "get suspicious," "hate," "reject," "break up with," "run away from," "play games on," "exploit," and otherwise exist in antagonistic relationship with their "opposite numbers" to the extent that they fail to reach beyond sexual relationship to the more comprehensive togetherness of friendship. Conversely, sex-lovers cease to quarrel, fight, lie, exploit, withdraw, and so on, to the extent that their sexual relationship occurs within more inclusive ties of friendship. The contradiction of interests on which sex-love antagonisms depend is typically a conflict around who possesses what of the other's sexual being. But the more the shared being of friendship extends beyond the fix on sexual possession to other spheres of shared life and value, the less this sphere of life preoccupies attention.

A way of testing the radical transfiguration of sex-love that follows from its reconceptualization as a type of friendship is to think of a single kind of antagonistic outcome with a romantic partner that could ever occur with a truly close friend. The "lover's quarrels," the "spats" and "breakups," the refusals to see, talk with, accompany, reach, or touch all turn bizarre under the light of true friendship. When sexual love is merely a narrow form of friendship, these symptoms reveal to us the poverty of its type of personal relationship.

It is true that the problem of sexual jealousy appears to have a spontaneous biological base: an instinctual disposition of the human animal to be aroused to keen attentiveness at the erotic involvement elsewhere of a sexual mate. This instinctual disposition, however, must be distinguished from one kind of *expression* of it, jealousy, which is concerned to exclude this involvement. Given that possessive jealousy occurs also with nonsexual bonds (for example, men's well-known resentment of a group member's possible loss to "a woman," or parents' intrusive interference with the social lives of their children outside the home), and given also that nonsexual jealousy can be overcome in a wider circle of friendship that new associations generate, why sexual jealousy is so conventionally construed as a "natural" affliction to be submitted to is unclear. Its biological base, if it has one, can be otherwise expressed in enhanced attentiveness to the sexual partner's desire and desirability, while the other in whom the partner is interested can become a new friend. In contrast, jealousy that stays within the walls of exclusion, repudiating "the other woman" or "the other man" as an enemy of the relationship, becomes trapped within its own enclosure of mind. It might be for this reason that we refer to its confined state of exclusionary jealousy as "a monster."

This distinction is not normally made, but is crucial. Consider the "bored" boyfriend or girlfriend who is "brought to his/her senses" by the involvement of a third party with his or her mate. The electrification of attention that occurs is not necessarily jealous. Jealousy is a reaction to the insecurity that might or might not be felt in such circumstances, normally depending on whether the third party does or does not represent a threat to the relationship. According to conventional norm and outlook, it is believed that one ought either to stay exclusively with an original partner, or leave to be exclusively with another partner. Because any third-party involvement is thought to endanger the initial relationship, jealousy is concluded to be "natural" in excluding such a threat. What is overlooked here is that the win-or-lose structure that exclusive sexual relationship entails in these circumstances poses the threat, not the further relationship itself.

Applied to the security of the family, where the interests of children are most importantly at stake, the structure of friendship seems a practical necessity. *If* there are to be extraconjugal relationships, such shared being can only be coherent if it includes the already established being with of the children and the family as its deeper, prior ground. A wider circle of shared being and friendship can at best open up the extraconjugal as well as the conjugal relationship to more comprehensive bearings, and the care of children to more sources of love and attention. On the other hand, a split off of the extraconjugal relationship works against the integrity of both, and seems bound to end in relational crisis. Secrecy, lies, in-home quarrels, and the deep rifts between parents that tear children apart express this split within the family. At the same time, the extraconjugal relationship itself is undermined by this destructiveness to others it causes. At the end of the round may emerge a broken world of mutated human beings who never recover, or learn not to care beyond their walls of enforced possession. Understanding our sexual relationships in terms of the developing shared being of friendship seems the only way in which the bonds of being with can hold against the forces of destruction set in motion by the either/or demands of proprietary sexual love.

Because a cluster of destructive possibilities is traditionally associated with nonexclusive sexual relations, however, social convention has continued to prescribe exclusive sexual relations as a regulative norm. Yet the dangers that private property in sexuality seems geared to prevent, such as unwanted pregnancy, transmission of pathogens, and psychological pain, do not follow from nonexclusive sexual relations as such, but from inadequate attentiveness to these possibilities before they develop. Sexual partners' enacted concern for the well-being of their shared life is the wider friendship that deals with these pitfalls before they arise. Where slippages of mutual concern occur, the ill consequence can be effectively alleviated or dissolved by the lovers' recovering alert care for their shared life to meet the next stage of the problem. That is to say, it is by the logic of friendship rather than sexual private property that the problems associated with nonexclusive sexual relationship can be prevented.

In contrast, sexual love disjoined from the allied being of friendship gives rise to these very problems in proportion to the lack of friendship involved. If mutual concern extends only to the sexual act itself, for example, then what is outside the sexual act is of mutual unconcern whether it be unwanted gestation, infection, or sickness of the heart. These disabling consequences arise not only in nonexclusive relationships, but in exclusive sexual relationships as well: because, as momentary reflection discloses, all can occur within the strictest marriage where there is no common ground of concern to prevent them. Moreover, since exclusive relationships are in any case typically and secretly transgressed over time, and since the secrecy of their transgressions reduces the shared being that could prevent the various problems that might result, not even normally exclusive sex is effective in precluding the problems it might be thought to rule out. So, whether sex-love is exclusive or not, only the more rounded alliances of friendship effectively overcome its problems. The solution to sex-related problems, in other words, lies not in the exclusiveness of our sexual relations but in the comprehensiveness of the friendship within which sexual relations develop.

Perhaps the greatest advantage to comprehending sexual relations in terms of friendship is that it evolves us into more cooperative and many-sided beings. Treating sex-love as a form of friendship unifies man-woman, man-man, and woman-woman relationships into more variegated, extended, and integrated life-sharings. Conversely, such comprehension exposes to us the interminable spectacle of lovers' quarrels and manipulations as sad symptoms of stunted friendship. Through such understanding becoming second nature, we come to be released from the psychological framework of sexual jealousy by relegating the exclusive expectations underlying it to an immature stage of human relationship. At the same time, we are better able to realize our capacities as a whole by contextualizing our sexual bonding within much wider alliances of thought and action.

Our chosen being with another in the world begins with the tentative shared being of playmates and progresses with the development of our connectedness as persons towards some sense of meaningful fellowship with the cosmic whole out of which we emerge and back into which we eventually return. In this evolution of more inclusive bonds of thought and existence, the grounding unities of friendship and sexual love are as yet at war with one another in unresolved dichotomy and tension. Without the reconciliation of these basic free moments of being with others, our project of becoming more comprehensive beings remains incoherent in its intimate-relation underpinnings. We remain, one could say, divided beings, torn between alien souls.

Notes

1. Irving Singer, *The Nature of Love*, vol. 1: *Plato to Luther*, 2nd ed. (Chicago: Chicago University Press, 1984), 3-25.
2. *Ibid.*, 15.
3. Singer, "A Reply to my Critics and Friendly Commentators," in David Goicoechea, ed., *The Nature and Pursuit of Love* (Amherst, N.Y.: Prometheus Books, 1995), 323-61, at 334.
4. John McMurtry, "Evaluating Sexual Love: A Prolegomenon to Post-Romantic Inquiry," in Goicoechea, ed., *The Nature and Pursuit of Love*, 265-86, at 274.
5. Aristotle, *Politics* 1263a30 [author's translation].

Jo-Ann Pilardi
(photograph: Jim Sizemore)

Author of "Commentary on McMurtry's 'Sex, Love, and Friendship'"
Paper presented at the Society for the Philosophy of Sex and Love
during the
Eastern Division Meeting of The American Philosophical Association
Baltimore, Md., 28 December 1982

Eighteen

WHY SHOULD WE EXCLUDE EXCLUSIVITY?

Jo-Ann Pilardi

John McMurtry's essay[1] is written in an admirable spirit, the spirit poet Marge Piercy described as "trying not to lie down in the same old rutted bed / part rack, part cocoon,"[2] as she, too, urged us to discard our old habits of romance. The way out of the same old rutted bed, for McMurtry, is to end the dichotomy between sexual love and friendship and to pattern sexual love on the "logic of friendship" (182). Ridding ourselves of minor and major cruelties, from lovers' fights to pornographic exploitation, is possible only if we achieve a new kind of love; we need "the radical transfiguration of sex-love that follows from its reconceptualization as a type of friendship" (181). I will argue that calling for the reconceptualization of sex-love into the *logic* of friendship won't take us where we want to go (namely, out of that old rutted bed), because our problem is not conceptual. Change will have to be accompanied by an understanding not of the logic but of the psycho-logic of sex-love, as well as of a complete phenomenology of patriarchy, that is, a description of its economics under capitalism, its aesthetics, and its politics. Otherwise our thinking will remain an unhappy mix of castles in the air and pie in the sky.

Two invisibilities in McMurtry's essay must be addressed. A ghost haunts the essay: the ghost of the unconscious. And there is the house in which that ghost lives: patriarchy. Though he alludes to the unconscious and patriarchy, McMurtry does not give them the weight they deserve. He never mentions the unconscious *per se*, although he indirectly refers to it, when he says that there is a "psychological set" (178) in which we are stuck and out of which we can and simply *should* move. The presence of patriarchy in McMurtry's world must be inferred from his use of the inadequate "sexism" (180), a term that allows us to overlook the structural nature of patriarchy.

"Personhood" and "friendship" are both central to McMurtry's view. He begins with a metaphysics of the person, which he calls "an open elective space." "Personhood emerges in personal identity, which is a chosen way of being in the world. Personal identity is, within the determining limits of a person's material conditions, a creative matter" (169). So the characteristics of openness and choice, and the kind of structure that appropriates certain elements to the self as "self" and discards others as "other," belong to the person. By extension, then, they belong to all "persons" who are "friends" and also to all persons who are "lovers," according to McMurtry. Sexual love will be a highly complicated form of this, since it involves the radical choice to create shared ground with another through what McMurtry calls "a penetration of one another's very organic membrane and immune system" (172). Following the conclusion of intercourse, demands for exclusivity will be made on the basis of the act of sexual love.

Sexual love, no more special than other sorts of friendship—defined as "a life-sharing between persons that is realized in activities . . . pursued together by choice" (176)—is different because it is restricted; however, we have mistakenly dissociated it from friendship entirely. In other words, sexual love is friendship to which we have added a particular type of sharing. In the case of the business friend, this is shared business interests; in the case of sexual love, sexual activity. We mistake sexual love for something different simply because we attach exclusivity to it, and exclusivity (sometimes called jealousy or possessiveness) is McMurtry's real demon.

Rather than employ psychology to explain jealousy, he invokes biology. McMurtry asks us "to understand its linkage to expectations conditioned into us by customs . . . related to biological problems that can be otherwise prevented in . . . a developed society" (177). He means problems such as sex-related diseases and unwanted pregnancy. In this Darwinian analysis, jealousy is part of a "psychological set," suitable to earlier moments of human history but no longer necessary, a "social-functional mechanism" (178) that developed into a taboo for good reasons, but now is useless. Merely an old habit formation, this "species-useless characteristic" must be discarded.

Even though sexual love is, for McMurtry, a subclass of friendship, sex-love is unique in its ability to hurt us. The loss of a loved one is often out of our control; the lover is, after all, a subject, a person in his or her own right. This is true of our friends, too, but friendship is more stable than sex-love, McMurtry thinks; the difference lies in exclusivity, a social mechanism that we force into sex-love relationships but not friendships, and which in fact promotes the very thing it hopes to prevent, the loss of the loved one. Pluralist sexual love has not developed as a conventional social form yet, because it has remained arrested in its adolescent, exclusionary stage. Its mature stage will consist in its integration into friendship by a conscious decision of the human race, or at least by that portion of it called the "developed" world. Then and only then will jealousy disappear, becoming as extinct as the dinosaur.

To summarize McMurtry: now we see through a glass, darkly, because friendship and sexual love appear to be two different kinds of relationships. But then, in the nonexclusivity-ridden future, we shall see face-to-face, as it were, while coming to understand that these two are one. Nonexclusivity itself will be the means whereby we realize the virtue of nonexclusivity, whereby we discover that sexual love is merely a subclass of friendship; in other words, pluralist sexual love will become both means and end of the utopia. With the demise of exclusivity, we will love our lovers as the friends they really are, and befriend as many lovers as we can. Sexual love will be free to be what it really should be: friendship with the addition of erotic activity, so that we can just, say, add friendship to Eros and stir.

We know McMurtry's biology (Darwinism). But does his project include a psychology as well, or is psychology collapsible into biology here? Especially for issues like sex-love and exclusivity, coming to understand the relationship between the unconscious and our conscious life is crucial. I wish I were as sure as McMurtry is of the natures of personhood and friendship. With his opening claim that "a person is an open elective space," he offers a definition of radical freedom whose philosophical ancestor is the early Sartre of *Nausea* and *Being and Nothingness*, the Sartre who had not yet read seriously either Marx or Freud. Psychoanalytic theory suggests, and I agree, that a person is a space of *conflicting* needs, of calling upon our demons and silencing them, of satisfying our desires and hiding them from ourselves (as well as others), of equilibrium and disequilibrium, of processes emanating from ourselves just as frequently as they are pressed upon us from the outside world, of the self-inflicted failures and successes of our psychic projects. This definition of personhood calls into question the extensiveness of the openness and ability to choose McMurtry posits. One of my objections to his account of personhood is that it ignores these psychoanalytic insights into the individual.

The nature of a person ties directly into the achievement of that kind of maturity to which McMurtry calls our attention when he says that, since personhood entails openness and choice, "if we are open and elective in our thought as persons, then our attachment to this psychological set [exclusivity] can be consciously rejected" (178). We surely must realize the openness we as persons are; but since we are not *simply* openness, our unconscious is an active participant in our relationships to, through, and with our conscious life. As to the nature of friendship, can we just add eros and stir? Friendship might be a subclass of sexual love and not the reverse, as McMurtry claims, if there is truth in the psychoanalytic claim that the erotic is a privileged dimension of life and not just one of several equal ingredients in it.

Exclusivity is a character flaw whose underlying logic, McMurtry says, is "an insecurity of the person" (178). But here he makes a simplistic equation; the desire for exclusivity might not be connected to jealousy. It might, instead, indicate a "holding-special" of someone, a joint acknowledgment that a pair marks each other as singular, unique to each other, separate from others. I think that in and by this process of holding precious, or choosing to hold precious, love is created. Irving Singer's remark that "love is sheer gratuity" should be read in this sense, instead of as McMurtry reads it (172). McMurtry contrasts Singer's view of love as bestowal or gift to his own view, love as deliberate choice, claiming that one chooses a loved one through an actual quality she or he possesses. To contrast Singer's notion of love and his own is misleading, however, since, after all, one *chooses* the giving of gifts.

McMurtry's view is also falsely universalistic. When he tells us that the exclusivity of sexual love is a norm inherited from the past, and to be consigned to it, he paints an anthropological and historical picture with a Eurocentric palette. Embedded in this analysis are assumptions about monogamous marriage and heterosexuality, as well as notions of the progress of the human race that derive from the Enlightenment. Yet God is dead (*pace* Nietzsche), and Man is dead as well (for this, we thank feminism and Foucault). The postmodernist, feminist reappraisal of our metanarratives requires a major readjustment in our sense of what truth, and the Truth, is. Monogamy is not a universal custom, nor has it been, and even in cultures where it has been the custom, the issue of "elective choice" has not been real for half of its participants; for women, monogamy was the only option. We have recently begun to achieve greater humility not only about what "we" know, but about who "we" are. In addition, we need to ask whether the conjunction of friendship and romantic love is really as uncommon as McMurtry indicates. Does friendship provide an easy escape from jealousy? He rightly notes that there are "immature" friendships, but to say that these are immature on a case by case basis, whereas the whole practice of exclusivity is immature (past its prime, culturally-speaking) is inadequate. These claims are in need of more evidence than he provides.

When McMurtry says that "the exclusive pair-bond of heterosexual love does not work as a general prescription" (177), I am reminded that recent studies indicate that the developed world of the West is entering a new stage, in which people, even though they might choose serial monogamy, are not abandoning monogamy; statistics show changes in the duration, not the practice, of monogamy. I'm referring not only to legally contracted heterosexual marriages, but to the choice of monogamy, a relation of sexual exclusivity. McMurtry is right to say that the abandonment of formal marriage is a result of changes in material conditions. An important part of this is the changing consciousness and expectations of women and the wider opportunities open to them. In any case, the narrative of an exclusivity-ridden past followed by a nonexclusivity-ridden future is a distortion. "Nonexclusivity" has always been practiced, and most often by husbands, through the use of prostitutes or the keeping of mistresses;[3] one factor in divorce rates is women's realization that they need no longer look the other way when their mates do so.

McMurtry mentions sexism, but he should have addressed it more directly, beginning with his own language. His reference to sex as "penetration" is phallocentric. Those for whom sexual love is not penetration (females) will not find themselves represented here. Neither will those for whom genital sexuality is not the central moment. McMurtry's perspective on sexual love is unwittingly masculinist: "The more sexual love is comprehended as a form of friendship, the less the sexual Other can be construed as a threat to our gender identity or well-being" (180). In using "Other," Simone de Beauvoir's term for Woman in patriarchy, is McMurtry speaking as a man, to other men? That presumption—that the reader is male—would be phallocentric. But if he intends it in a nongender-specific sense, he overlooks the structural question of patriarchy; threats directed toward gender identity or well-being would be much greater for the subordinate than for the dominant gender.

McMurtry expects a great deal from his espoused changes: they will subvert "a basic structure of sexism" (180), a structure founded on the threat dealt to our gender identity by the "Other." But might material conditions intervene? As women gain access to higher levels of economic and cultural life, as they are seen more as friends and equals than as "Other," what would prevent most men from seeing them as even greater threats? Dominant/subordinate social relations have not been defined only along sex/gender lines; race, class, and other "Others" have played their part. I ponder this, because the nicest way to read the history of sexism and patriarchy is as a response to material conditions (lactating women, bronze tools). Yet when students ask, as they inevitably do, how this all started, the material conditions answer never seems to satisfy them, or me. Why did these material conditions result in domination and not difference? How can we insure the future will not resemble the past?

The conjunction of friendship and sexual love is necessary, but not sufficient, for the ending of sexism and patriarchy. But McMurtry makes a larger claim; he privileges this conjunction. Still, his essay has value; it prompts us to confront *the* question: how will we overcome patriarchy? Answering this requires a realistic assessment of the contours of patriarchy, an assessment that feminist scholarship began around 1970 and continues to carry out. Patriarchy is a system, virtually universal, in which most positions of power (international, national, familial) are held by men. Men gained power over women and kept it, and continue to keep it, in a variety of ways and under a variety of economic systems. If patriarchy didn't exist, if women and men were absolute peers, and if women and men who didn't accept patriarchally-approved heterosexual norms were not seen as deviant, sexual love and friendship might not be dichotomized, and a whole variety of other dichotomies might also not exist: better/worse, body/soul, active/passive, rich/poor.

McMurtry claims that if friendship and sexual love were *reconceptualized*, they would be lived out differently. Even if such reconceptualization led us to treat friends and lovers differently than we now do, how would such practices extend beyond the personal to the communal? McMurtry's strategy trivializes sexism, reducing a material, historical, and political problem to an issue of logic. It skirts the issue of the presently existing state of male power and the part it plays in the patterns of sex-love lived and repeated endlessly in the culture. McMurtry assumes that the social disease of sexism will have its solution in the individual choice to engage in multiple sexual relations. In contrast, the challenge of creating *social* solutions for social problems has always been the operating principle of feminist theory and practice. This is not to deny individual choice and the uniqueness of individual relationships. But sexual relations are already social and, in this case, patriarchally social.

McMurtry's hope is that understanding sex-love as friendship will "evolve us into more cooperative and many-sided beings" (182), and he ends his essay as he began, with mystical ideas of soul-to-soul cosmic world connectedness derived from Vedanta, Buddhism, Taoism, and other mystic traditions. In contrast, I ask: how will we progress in a real, not an ideal, sense, toward community? Why assume that nonexclusive sexual love leads upward and outward to world community instead of grounding us, even more firmly, in a small circle of friends? The creation and achievement of community cannot be reduced to a series of intimacies. Many love affairs do not make the peace.

Notes

1. John McMurtry, "Sex, Love, and Friendship," this volume, 169-83; page references to this essay are supplied parenthetically in the text.

2. Marge Piercy, "Doing It Differently," *Circles on the Water: Selected Poems of Marge Piercy* (New York: Knopf, 1982), 108.

3. See Karl Marx and Frederick Engels, *The Communist Manifesto*, pt. 2 (New York: International Publishers, 1948), 26-8.

Rebecca Jill Soble (left), Rose Soble (center), and Alan Soble (right)
(photograph: Sylvia Soble)

Alan Soble, author of "On McMurtry and Fuchs—A Dialogue"

Nineteen

A LAKOMA[1]

Alan Soble

One pleasant day, Phaedrus, Pausanias, John, Jo-Ann (yes, a woman), Agathon, Aristophanes, and a few others, whose names and bodies I forget, were sitting in the park with Socrates under a tree, drinking wine and eating tofu. Everyone kept an eye open for Alcibiades. They enjoyed watching the uncontrollable fits of jealous rage that overcame Alcibiades when he spotted, or even thought he spotted, Socrates talking with Agathon and looking at him face-to-face.

Aristophanes: Here comes the sex maniac now, Socrates. Tuck yourself in.
John: Aristophanes, you're not being fair. Give Alcibiades a chance. Every person, even he, is an open elective space, and as such can consciously reject old patterns of thought and behavior.
Agathon: Alcibiades?
Jo-Ann: Hmmm. A person is an open elective *space*. That sounds Californian. I am reminded, then, of the jealous and neglected woman who yells at her unfaithful lover, "You and your damned need for space," while he has been sharing that space indiscriminately with Beverly, Brenda, and Belinda. But is the term "space" also phallocentric? Let's see. . . .
John: I know what that woman's problem is. She doesn't appreciate the difference between feeling jealous and expressing that jealousy.
Agathon: Nice chestnut, John.
Socrates: No need to get nasty, Agathon. I see Alcibiades has been sidetracked by someone.
Agathon: The boy is handsome, isn't he? Ever wonder about the fact that Alcibiades flies into a rage whenever Socrates merely talks with me (or almost anyone else), yet always has time to chat up the nearest boy? He really is trying to be open and elective.
Aristophanes: Alcibiades is always open, at least.
John: That's not what I meant.
Socrates: While we're waiting for Alcibiades, why don't you tell us what you do mean, John?
John: Excellent idea, Socrates. Alcibiades, and you, too, Agathon, and Jo-Ann, and most of us (I am no exception) are caught in a bad routine. First, we have maintained a disjunction, both conceptually and in practice, between sex-love and friendship. Even Socrates is willing to be a true friend to any of us, yet, as Alcibiades painfully knows, Socrates actually goes to sleep when the two of them are on a couch together late in the evening. This division between sex-

love and friendship ruins both sex-love and friendship; it also, by the way, accounts for most of the lamentable problems between men and women. And second. . . .
Socrates: Hold on, John, one idea at a time for my aging head.
Jo-Ann: I think you have things backwards, John. Must I catalogue again—the goddesses know I've done it many times already, and smart guys like you should have got it by now—all the ways in which our society is patriarchal? The running battle between men and women over sex, love, and babies is the tiny tip of the iceberg. The division between sex-love and friendship, and its concomitant battle of the sexes, does not account for the larger and deeper aspects of patriarchy, but flows from them. How could you seriously propose that if we, as open elective spaces, establish the unity of sex-love and friendship, then patriarchal sexual relations would disappear? Do you really think that we could establish that unity while the patriarchy was still powerful? Patriarchy accounts for the division you lament. Thus, your view smacks of idealism: it ignores politics, economics, depth psychology, everything interesting, including the critique of Eurocentric metanarratives. You pay attention only to the logic of the concepts.
Aristophanes: Was will das Weib? ℞ penis normalis, dosim repetatur. And all Alcibiades needs—ask him—is a good lay. Socrates needs one, everyone needs one. Then we will all be happy. John says: sleep with your friends and befriend your sleepers. If you have a sexual affair with me, be prepared to babysit my kids and watch football on the tv with my husband. The family of mankind! If you want to be my friend, be open to sensual footsies under the table and quick feels and gooses in the elevator. Can you imagine what schools, factories, and supermarkets would be like if sex-love merged with friendship? Teachers sleeping with students, doctors with their patients, bosses with their employees, supermarket shelf clerks with inquiring housewives—a veritable Marcusian paradise. (Hmmm. Maybe it already exists.)
Agathon: What a woos. Jo-Ann has a good point, but I'm troubled. How could it be decided whether parts of the patriarchy account for the division between sex-love and friendship, or vice versa? Does it just come down to a choice of *Weltanschauung*, as suggested by Jo-Ann's post-modernist worries about "Truth"? Maybe, even, there is a *tertium quid* that accounts for both John's disjunction and the patriarchy?
Jo-Ann: Furthermore, the division between sex-love and friendship is not a heterosexual phenomenon. Look at Alcibiades over there, in the grips of vulgar *eros*. He doesn't want to be that boy's friend; he has low chakra on the brain, pure and simple.
Aristophanes: Wann der putz steht.
Jo-Ann: The division—as I was saying—between sex-love and friendship, and the exclusivity/jealousy problem, exists for both heterosexuals and homosexuals. And for bisexuals as well. And polysexuals. And some other mammals.
Socrates: I'm confused. You young people always leave me behind. John, please tell me again what the division is of which you speak.
John: The disjunction between sex-love and friendship.

Socrates: How many things are we talking about? Sex, love, and friendship? Or sex-love and friendship?
John: Two things, Socrates, sex-love and friendship.
Socrates: What is this creature with a hyphen? You have spoken of it as a "mutually chosen being with" (179). That sounds like love. If so, you are complaining of a division between love and friendship. Yet many have already argued that love and friendship are, can be, or should be unified, even in (of all the odd places) heterosexual marriage.[2]
John: No, Socrates, I do mean sex-love, a form of bonding that involves a penetration of one another's organic membranes and immune system (172).
Jo-Ann: That's a bit of phallocentric philosophy, if I ever heard one. Women do not penetrate. Sapphic sexuality is not penetrative (188).
John: An intermixing of fluids and fleshes is all I have in mind, Jo-Ann. Men and women in heterosex exchange body fluids and touch each other's internal membranes, as do those persons, men and women, who engage in homosex. Bacteria are exchanged, various cavities of the body get probed with all sorts of appendages, the lovers become immunologically unified—which is just to say that sex is messy. No phallocentrism here. (Besides, students of Pat Califia will strap on a dildo, which they proceed to use on their femme partners, to the delight of both.)
Socrates: So John is asserting the surprising thesis that dirty, sloppy, steamy sex can and should be unified with friendship. If so, you only confuse me by using the expression "sex-love." Where, now, is the love?
Agathon: I gather that John means this: when two people love each other in the romantic sense (not in the *agape* or *philia* sense), they can express, and want to express, their mutual love by joining together in physical bliss. That must be the thrust of his term "sex-love."
Aristophanes: Pope John!
John: Perhaps I should have said that we must unite *eros* and *philia*. Or that the distinction Socrates (or Diotima) sometimes makes, between the *eros* of beautiful bodies and the *eros* of beautiful minds, is not a distinction we should acknowledge any longer.
Agathon: That would be exciting, John, to tackle Socrates and Diotima!
Socrates: I want to hear John's second idea.
Aristophanes: Be quick about it. Here comes Alcibiades, barely able to walk, dizzy with passion for the handsome boy yet trying to refocus his attention on his true love, Socrates. Oh, wait. He's been sidetracked again, this time by a nut-brown maid. God, how vulgar.
John: Second, sex-love and friendship are essentially the same thing, which fact one can discover by looking carefully at the concepts. They have been divided from each other because we continue to attach an extraneous norm of exclusivity to sex-love. Unifying sex-love and friendship would mean abandoning the norm of exclusivity. Jealousy would disappear.
Aristophanes: Alcibiades the exclusive! I'm sure that accounts for his jealous fits when Socrates sits and chats with Agathon.

Socrates: It would be helpful, I think, if John could tell us how the division between sex-love and friendship came about, and how exclusivity and jealousy got attached to sex-love in the first place.
John: I have heard it said by the scientists that sex-exclusiveness (and its accompanying jealousy) came about because it was suitable for solving the problems of genetic displacement, sex-related disease, and unwanted pregnancy.
Aristophanes: I'm surprised John didn't go in for "pregnancy nondesire."
Agathon: So the norm of exclusivity was consciously adopted to solve these problems? Or did it unconsciously sneak in, without anyone fully noticing that it was being selected?
John: I'm not sure that issue must be settled. People are open elective spaces and, as such, can reject the norm even if it snuck in through the back door. Here is the point: if these problems that the norm of exclusivity is a social-functional mechanism to prevent are otherwise preventible, then the psychological set, the jealousy, no longer corresponds to life-property-and-protection requirements (178). And they *are* otherwise preventible, indeed more effectively preventible, by birth control and hygiene precautions, which society now has but did not have earlier in human history.
Agathon: But John, that's the same, old, tired argument about achieving human sexual salvation through effective birth control, penicillin, and clean, hot water—the typical liberal knee-jerk solution to sexual disease and pregnancy among teenagers. It is just an intuition you have, with no solid evidence, that the availability of birth control has any effect on disease and pregnancy.
Jo-Ann: More importantly, John also ignores the depth and breadth of patriarchy. Effective birth control, my fanny! Women taking hormones that have all sorts of deadly side effects, or getting their insides stuck with coils and shields and loops, or women bearing the burden of squirting creams or pieces of rubber inserted into their wombs. A pretty picture, indeed. Medical science is thoroughly sexist; what it has managed to do is to free men from anxiety about disease and pregnancy at the expense of the physical and mental health of women. The "birth control and hygiene precaution" argument seems better suited to the sexual promiscuity (excuse me, "openness") of men than to freedom and equality for everyone.
Agathon: Why don't we suppose, just to understand John's point as best as we can, that we do have highly effective and safe and nonsexist birth control, and that medicine has wiped out venereal disease. What follows?
Socrates: John is claiming, I think, that the problems, which evoked and then had been solved by the norm of exclusivity and jealousy, can now be solved in other ways, and therefore that exclusivity and jealousy can wither away.
John: Exactly.
Socrates: But your argument assumes that you have identified all the problems that exclusivity and jealousy were called on to solve, or could be called on to solve. I am not sure the assumption is correct. I have two reasons for this judgment.
John: Please, Socrates, present them one at a time, as you earlier urged me to do.

Aristophanes: Alcibiades should heed some of that advice. See how he has introduced the nut-brown maid to the handsome boy and how lewdly the three of them trade eye messages.
Socrates: First, you spoke of exclusivity and jealousy as having been a "social-functional mechanism" and a "life-property-and-protection" requirement. These phrases obscure the difficulties in your assumption. Society is not homogeneous, but is made up of different sections or groups or classes. If so, it is not always possible to speak of what is social-functional *simpliciter*. There are items that are functional only for some groups; there are items that are functional only for other groups; there are items that are functional for all groups but serve additional specific functions for only one group; and there are items that are functional only for one group, but this group manages to convince other groups that the item is social-functional for them or even *simpliciter*. Are you with me?
John: So far.
Jo-Ann: I was making the same point, Socrates. What is functional for the patriarchy is not necessarily functional for women, and what appears to be social-functional *simpliciter* might be functional only in the sense that it contributes to the maintenance and continuation of the society *qua* patriarchy.
Agathon: But we have granted John's claim that birth control and medicine are effective for some problems and benefit everyone. Socrates, you must be after something else.
Socrates: Jo-Ann is right, but so are you, Agathon. Even though we can grant to John that exclusivity and jealousy had been social-functional *simpliciter* for a certain set of problems, and that those problems can now be solved in other ways, John has not established that the norm of exclusivity and jealousy are not now functional for one group that maintains the norm to solve its own special problems.
Agathon: I see. When John said that exclusivity and jealousy were a "life-property-and-protection" requirement, he overlooked that what is required to protect some lives is inimical to other lives, and that even if something is life-protective *simpliciter* for a certain set of problems, it might later be life-protective for one group of lives having their own special needs, even when the original set of problems has been solved. The same point applies to John's expression "species-useless" (178); if the snake had been a little smarter, maybe that species could have found another use for its fangs.
John: What was your second point, Socrates?
Socrates: You claim that exclusivity and jealousy are no longer social-functional and life-protective. Yet they persist, with a vengeance. Why? John, listen. Suppose a woman marries a man because she needs his money. Her being married to him is "person-functional" and "life-protective."
John: That makes sense.
Socrates: Suppose that the woman eventually finds a good job that pays a decent salary. Doesn't that mean that the problem that the marriage was a person-functional mechanism to solve is now otherwise solvable, and more effectively solvable?
John: Yes, it does.

Socrates: Then on your account, John, the woman could, maybe even should (I see Jo-Ann nodding agreement), abandon the marriage.
John: "Could," Socrates, is all I would assert.
Socrates: Suppose, finally, that the woman remains married to the man, even though the original problem has been solved in a more effective way. Wouldn't that fact give you reason to think that some other "problem" exists, or that her being married to the man is still person-functional, but serves some others, perhaps new, function?
Aristophanes: She fell in love with the poor sod after all. Or was it just a matter of a habit formation?
John: What you say sounds reasonable, Socrates.
Socrates: It follows, John, that if exclusivity and jealousy no longer serve their original purpose, yet both strongly persist in our culture, then the norm of exclusivity and jealousy must be assumed to be serving some other, perhaps new and hidden, function (unless proven otherwise). And this new function need not be one required by the whole society, but only by one group.
John: I don't know, Socrates. I would put it differently. Given that the social-functional basis of exclusivity and jealousy is obsolete with respect to the problems we do know about, we are left with no way of explaining why sex-love could *not* become unified with friendship.
Jo-Ann: I think that's backwards, John, or shortsighted. You want to say: if the original purposes are otherwise solvable, we should expect sex-love automatically to merge with friendship. (Is this the secret of our evolution?) But the obvious fact that exclusivity and jealousy are not quickly disappearing, despite their being apparently obsolete, should lead you to posit other functions that they serve (perhaps group-functional purposes, like the maintenance of patriarchy). They are not really or fully obsolete after all.
Agathon: It follows, I think, that exclusivity and jealousy cannot be made to disappear by our simply behaving as open, elective persons toward the norm of exclusivity itself; we need to behave as open, elective spaces toward the institutional structures of patriarchy and, perhaps, capitalism.
John: The greatest obstacle seems to be the habit formation of accumulated acculturation.
Aristophanes: There he goes again. With his fancy words, John explains a persisting pattern of behavior, a habit, by calling it a habit. Besides, we all know why exclusivity and jealousy persist. Long ago, humans were double of what we are now, and the gods were annoyed by their merriment, and shot down bolts of lightning that split the humans into two pieces. Then, when two half-persons found each other and believed that the other was his or her other half, they became exclusively concerned about the other. Jealousy is the fear that one half will lose, yet again, its other half. This is the tragedy of human existence, that we need another to be complete, and yet are never sure of possessing him. [Starts to sing, *falsetto*.] If I can't have you, I don't want nobody, baby. . . .
John: The details might be doubtful, but Aristophanes nicely raises the issue of the insecurity of the person that is central to jealousy.

Agathon: I'm more concerned with another issue. How exactly do exclusivity and jealousy help maintain patriarchal capitalism? What good does it do the "system" to build the norm into our very psyches? Why could it not be the other way around—that the existence of the norm in our evolutionary psychology generates some of the specific details of political economy?
Alcibiades: Aha! What have we here? Agathon cuddling up with Socrates.
John: Alcibiades, you snuck up on us.
Agathon: There's been no cuddling here, you paranoid fool. Just friends doing some philosophy.

Notes

1. The original version of this dialogue-critique of (the first version of) John McMurtry's "Sex, Love, and Friendship" (revised version, this volume, 169-83) and of (the first version of) Jo-Ann Pilardi's (then Pilardi-Fuchs) commentary on McMurtry (revised version, this volume, 185-9) was prepared for, and mailed to, members of the Society for the Philosophy of Sex and Love in December 1982. Page references to McMurtry and Pilardi are supplied in the text.
2. For example, Eric Hoffman, "Love As a Kind of Friendship," this volume, 109-19.

Deborah Rosen (top) and John Christman (bottom)
(photographs: Pat Martin, top; Mary Beth Oliver, bottom)

Authors of "Toward and Beyond a New Model of Sexuality"
Paper presented at the Society for the Philosophy of Sex and Love
during the
Eastern Division Meeting of The American Philosophical Association
Baltimore, Md., 28 December 1982

Twenty

TOWARD A NEW MODEL OF SEXUALITY[1]

Deborah Rosen and John Christman

1.

Many biases pervade contemporary thinking about sex: that sexual activity is ideally heterosexual; that sex is deficient when practiced alone; that it serves some one purpose, such as reproduction, orgasm, or communication. Theories of sexuality in much of the philosophical literature reinforce these assumptions. What is needed is a new model for explaining sexuality, one in which no substantive normative questions are begged. This model would make none of the above assumptions, be neither heterosexist nor sexist, and be sensitive to the experience of women as well as men. In departing from recent philosophical accounts of which we are now aware,[2] we begin here the task of creating such a model. We do not consider the present account complete or definitive but believe it suggestive of new directions of analysis. Our general aim is to give a conceptual analysis of the notion of sexual activity and to suggest what value might inhere in this activity apart from what instrumentally valuable things stem from it. In so doing we hope to avoid the narrowness of some of the usual teleological accounts of sexuality.

We hope to show how certain views about the nature of sex, the nature of sexual deviance and perversion, and the moral obligations connected with sex, can be considered in a new light. In particular, various claims made about sex have gained their purchase only by assuming a contentious teleological view of sexuality. Attitudes, both popular and philosophical, having to do with the nature of sexual relationships, the role of fantasy in sex, and the way in which sexual partners use each other, revolve on questionable models of the nature of sex. We attempt to put forward an alternative conception that is broad enough to capture the disparate ways in which people are sexual and avoids the parochialisms to which we allude.

2.

Philosophical views about sexuality abound. In one corner sits the pure instrumentalism of Roman Catholicism: sexuality, at least "licit" sex, has as its essential aim the production of children.[3] In another corner are various Freudians, according to whom all desires and drives can be labeled sexual. For Freud, genital sexuality, the narrower subcategory that accords more closely with the everyday use of the concept, is part of a mechanism for the conservation and release of psychic energy. In a third direction lie interpersonal accounts, in which "sex" refers to the dynamic interplay of recognition of desire that takes place during seduction and lovemaking.[4]

We do not wish to take issue with each of these views separately. We do observe, however, that many of them fall generally under a rubric that we *do* find faulty: a teleological or functionalist view of sex.[5] Teleological models of sex define that phenomenon in terms of its aims, the purposes it serves, and the effects it characteristically produces. We want to resist this view. Because of narrowness of scope, no traditional model of which we are now aware will, if taken singly, provide an adequate account of a multifaceted phenomenon. We need to recognize a plurality of sexual purposes. And we need to preserve the sanctity of the various proposed goals of sexuality by not allowing any one goal to assume the burden of them all. Theories of sexuality that place heavy conceptual emphasis on the role of orgasm, for example, disregard the constant and intolerable burden on sexual performance such overemphasis can create.

We must turn from the opaque notion of *the* reason for, or *the* goal of, sex to the more tractable notion of *reasons* reflective people *give* for their sexual activity. People have reasons, sex does not. And the reasons people give are philosophically instructive: to make another happy, to build a more positive self-concept, to go to sleep faster, to insult an old love, to assuage boredom. Robert Solomon notes that, on Freud's account, such uses of sex are "ulterior" purposes. But, he suggests, to distinguish, in a nonarbitrary way, ulterior from proximate purposes of sexual behavior is not possible. So one cannot draw substantive conclusions from such a distinction.[6] The question of what *our* reasons for sex are demands a pluralistic, open-ended, and approximate answer. The question what *the* reason is, is appropriate only, at best, for a particular occasion or kind of occasion. So the burden of proof is on narrowly focused teleologists to show why such a varied activity as this should conform to any one goal or purpose.

There is a second mistake frequently made by teleological accounts: moving from the fact that an activity A promotes some good G to the belief that the purpose or a purpose of A is to produce G. Getting to know another person and communicating with her or him might be a good and healthy project. But regardless of the merit of this Socratic ideal, we disagree with Solomon when he argues that the end of sexual desire is "interpersonal communication,"[7] for it is not even *a* purpose many reflective people would give for their sexual behavior. In short, the fact that something is a good does not entail, though it might be true, that it ought to be a goal of an activity that promotes it.

Alan Goldman makes similar criticisms of "means-ends" analyses of sexual desire or activity.[8] The model he adopts as a departure from this, however ("sexual desire is desire for contact with another person's body and for the pleasure which such contact produces"), seems wedded to a binary view of sexuality that a truly pluralistic and value neutral account would avoid. Sometimes sexual desire is desire for contact with *my* body, alone.

Still another way that a teleological template is used in defining sex is in viewing the most basic definiens as sexual *desire*. Although desire for sex and desires that have a sexual character are certainly part of the phenomenon, seeing sex as essentially a desire drives one to adopt a problematic view about what the desire will generally be *for*. Just as the purposes that sex tends to serve vary greatly, so too do the objects of our sexual desires.

Jerome Shaffer adopts a nonteleological view of sex but again formulates his model in terms of sexual desire.[9] Shaffer is concerned to point out that sexual desire is not an example of "desiring that." For Shaffer, "sexual desire as such has no necessary connection with any goal, aim, or end in view."[10] According to Shaffer, sexual desire is a state

> which is directed toward an object but does not necessarily involve any *desiring that* concerning the object and which is such that, if it is followed by sexual arousal, then certain subsequent events will be felt as constituting the satisfaction or frustration of that original state.[11]

Shaffer's distinction between everyday desires, desires for some specifiable state, and specifically *sexual* desires, which might be open-ended and nonspecific, brings his view more closely into line with the model we go on to develop. We think, however, that the special efforts to which he must go in order to avoid a teleological reading of the nature of sex can be sidestepped, as we do, by completely avoiding a focus on sexual *desire*.

We admit that attitudes are possible that, while not among the purposes of most sexual behavior, might nevertheless be best expressed sexually. But what are these attitudes and feelings? One might be the desire to end that haunting restlessness whose satisfaction the agent believes lies solely in sexual conquest. Solomon mentions, among others, possessiveness, domination, passivity, and conflict. Janice Moulton proposes prurience, wantonness, and lust.[12] If these are an indication of the attitudes that might best be expressed sexually, then not promoting such behavior, even if these attitudes are not the aim of it, might be desirable. In any case, these observations cast additional doubt on overly narrow, value-laden accounts.

In the discussion of "sexual perversion" that has occupied philosophers of late, the notion has gained currency that sex (at least so-called natural, nonperverted sex) has a unique essence tied to the ends that it generally serves.[13] It is part of the aim of the present discussion to present a conception of sex that makes the idea of "perversion" suspect. If sex is not conceived as an activity with a defining purpose or end, it is difficult to see how the activity could be "perverted" at all in anyone's use of that term.

In this way, our nonteleological conception is like that of "spooning." A spoon can be used in many ways. Some would call it perverted to use a spoon to gouge eyeballs from their sockets. This would be an immoral activity if done to a human being for any reason except, say, to save that person's life. But the spoon and the spooning are not perverted; it is the human being using it this way that is perverted. In the rare case when the agent is not culpable (believes psychotically that he is saving the victim from death), then and only then could we derivatively say it is the activity of spooning that is perverted. So also with sex; substitute human fingers for the spoon, vagina for the eyeball. Imagining shifts in the example shows what is misplaced in calling sexual acts *per se* perverted (those with nonhuman animals or persons incapable of consent). Paradigmatically, the culpable agent is up to no good or to selfish good, not the spoon or the spooning, the animals or the minors, the sex itself. It is the agent, in lying that he or she does not have a contagious sexual disease, that is the perversion, not the sex itself. Our sense of revulsion, which is the nest for our use of the word "perversely," might be tied more to a narrowminded imagination than to a proper final moral conclusion.

3.

We turn to a positive view concerning the conceptual basis of the notion of sexuality, and then to the evaluative implications of this conception. There are pleasures in sex that are to be distinguished from sexual pleasures. We need a framework in which to discuss the relationship of sexuality to sensuousness and pansexualism, to discuss the diverse forms of sexual relatedness of which heterosexual and orgasmic sex are only two variations whose canonization is suspect.[14] We think we can give a nontautologous and substantive characterization of what makes an activity or act sexual.

As implied by our reflections, the model of sex we want to mold here must be nonteleological and, more generally, value neutral. While it is certainly crucial to understand the connections that sex has to things of basic normative import, we want to see these as contingent connections, ones that perhaps, at best, are often or in most places found. But it is essential to characterize sex independently of the evaluative and normative claims we might want to make about it. So value neutrality, along with nonteleology, are general constraints within which we wish our view of sex to fall.

One last preliminary: there is a strong tendency to analyze sex in terms of sexual desire. However, in order to avoid the contentious functionalism that might be buried in such a view, we analyze sex in terms of sexual *activity* and sexual *experience*. Our procedure will be to define activity in terms of experience, and in so doing, the concept of desire (ones that are uniquely sexual) will not play a crucial role.

The first step in constructing a model of sexual activity is a characterization of the sexual feeling, the subjective, psychophysical sexual experience; not what sexual experience *does*, but what it *is*. A problem is whether to take a person's subjective report as definitive in an analysis of what is a particularly sexual experience for her or him. Anyone with Freudian predilections would balk at this quasi-behaviorist standard, but to infer or posit aspects of an individual's mental life that are not behaviorally reported, one must assume or adopt a full blown theory like Freud's to make inferences of a reliable sort. As we mentioned, a particular problem with the Freudian model in this context is its overly broad classification of the sexual. So we might contend that for an individual's own reports of subjective inspection are the best evidence available in homing in on what might be uncontroversially, though loosely, labeled a sexual experience.

We often know what this phenomenon is not. It is not merely the feeling associated with orgasm or with genital manipulation. Many people focus their sexual attention, some of the time, on erogenous zones distant from the genitals and concentrate on pleasures separate from the orgasm. Perhaps genital pleasure and orgasmic pleasure are uncontroversial members of a set of sensations that are alike in general character. The likeness is great enough that we are able to tell when a particular sensation is sexual in nature because of its similarity with sensations of the sort exemplified by genital pleasure and orgasm. But this account strays from a classification simply of *acts* as either sexual or not. The massage of one's legs might be an extremely pleasurable sensation when performed during lovemaking, but only a relief from a long walk when performed some other time.

Our characterization might seem to omit those who have not experienced genital pleasure or orgasm, as well as those who lack the requisite labeling techniques to categorize the experience. In some of these cases, an outside observer could *infer* from psychological or behavioral cues that the subject was having a sexual experience. If not, whether an experience is sexual is undecidable, even for the subject. We do not find it surprising that a person, especially a young person, might have a sexual experience and not be able to discern the category to which the set of sensations belongs. Our claim, then, is that a sensation is sexual to the extent to which (1) the subject knows it has some special phenomenological character and could report as such, and (2) the subject knows this *because* (causally because) of the feeling's internal similarity with those other sensations exemplified by orgasm and sensations arising from certain instances of genital manipulation.

This account could be extended to include sexual pleasure derived from pure fantasy, pleasure that is sexual but which occurs when no "external" physical manipulation takes place. Thus we include those experiences that the subject would associate with, or remember as, the physical sensations described above. This move broadens the characterization, but our purpose here is not to give necessary and sufficient conditions for a concept but merely to characterize the key terms in a general model.

This view is thus a phenomenological approach to the idea of sexual experience, though we present it here without detail concerning the exact nature of the phenomenological "feel" in question. We leave that task to poets and phenomenologists. We are also concerned that the precise internal structure of this feeling varies from person to person to an extent that any attempt at a precise rendering will be inevitably limited. Rather, we postulate that whatever the internal nature of the feeling is that people have during genital stimulation and orgasm, it is that range of sensation that sexual feeling, more generally, instantiates. Even the modest claim that such a feeling involves *pleasure* can be controversial. Many people would claim that pain, or at least a kind of intensity and rapture that connects with tension and conflict, is often closer to the precise nature of the internal "feel" of their sexual experience.

Sexual *activity*, then, is that range of activity in which the sexual feeling, as characterized above, is the essential subjective element; the activity during which the subject or subjects give themselves over more or less completely and directly to the experience of physical sensation and mental engagement. Sexual activity need not be activity that is *aimed* at a sexual experience. That view is overbroad, since such activity would have to include, for some people in some instances, making a phone call or handing over money (since the purpose of these acts is to initiate a sexual experience). Rather, sexual activity is one that essentially *involves* such feeling, an activity in which such feeling is the principal component.

If this sketch of what makes an activity uniquely sexual is informative, we can proceed to suggest what might inhere in such experiences that bestows special value on them. We intend these suggestions, which we give without much independent argument, to be consistent with, if not to capture, the broad plurality of purposes and goals various people have and give for their sexual lives. Insofar as sex has value for people, this value will not be determined in a specific and unique way by the nature of sex itself.

This is the upshot of our nonteleological, value neutral conception of sex: it becomes as good or bad as the purposes people have for engaging in it. And while the fact that sex, for many people, connects with deep and important aspects of their personal and social lives, these connections are not to be specified in the essential aspects of sex itself, but rather in the rich array of life situations within which it is practiced. Below we examine more normative conclusions suggested by this approach. At this point, we want to emphasize the separation between our definition of sexual activity, and the wide variety of contingent value that this activity can have for people. Although sex lacks purposes, people who engage in sex do not, and the richness of the purposes to which sex can contribute is instructive.

When a person engages in sex without another person, that is, alone, this activity can be one of full realization of the pleasurable aspects of the self: the self-affirming, self-actualizing experience of being alive—without drugs, difficult meditation, or long distance running—so a feeling of independent, self-contained, self-valuing experience is achieved. This gives a person a feeling of self-worth and satisfaction in being able to produce such a complete and pleasurable experience in so autonomous a manner. In sex with partners, the sexual experience is the same, but it is shared, in a special sense of "sharing." Sharing of sexual experience often involves the subjective feeling of desire by each partner plus at least minimal recognition and general enhancement (through stimulation) of each partner by the other. So feelings of independence and self-worth are recast here in terms of the dynamics of a shared relation. Whether the partners are long time lovers or fresh acquaintances, the feeling of heightened life experience that sexuality often induces will help create a sense of completeness and importance that can give sexuality a unique value as a human endeavor.[15]

The value of this sharing experience notwithstanding, we think it also consistent with these remarks that two people might mutually utilize and indulge a sexual partnership to achieve more of a private sexual experience. Such unilateral utilization of one's sexual mate can be deceptive in some contexts and mutually enhancing in others. We do not mean to assert that sexual activity is always valuable or moral, but only that the value of sex, when present, resides in these external connections with other goals and values. Neutrality in one's conception of sex is difficult but important to maintain. Our notion of "sharing" is meant to imply mutuality in a strong sense that precludes the manipulation or indifference that might characterize the attitude of many persons toward their sexual partners. Though such mutually supportive interaction is often valuable, it does not follow that unshared sex is deficient. Where it is impossible for sexual activity to be both self-validating and, where others are affected, other-regarding, and where sexual activity is positively averse to creating this environment, it is not clear to us that it is even moral to engage in such activity.

Note that this account awards no special conceptual or ontological status to binary sex, even though most people believe masturbation is less than ideal. Masturbation, like singlehood, is often thought of and defined negatively as being without a partner. If partnered or binary sexuality were preferable, it would be permissible to treat masturbation as variously deficient. But the argument against single sex has not yet been established.[16] Although certain considerations are often brought against it, masturbation has many positive aspects: it can contribute to successful partnered sex, and it can be a source of self-reliant and autonomous sexual satisfaction. We consider it a virtue of our view that it maintains conceptual neutrality in the comparative evaluation of binary sexuality and autoeroticism. We need to investigate Shere Hite's report that the women she interviewed usually did not enjoy masturbation psychologically. Hite suggests that this is perhaps due to the cultural fact that almost all women are brought up not to masturbate.[17] We need a deeper account of the relationship between masturbation, autoeroticism, and narcissism. Still, masturbation, like other forms of minimal sex, needs a positive definition, and we think our model provides a helpful component of such a definition.

Another reason masturbation has received bad press is that it often involves imagining a situation or partner; there is, consequently, an additional prejudice against it from those who deprecate fantasy. Paradigms and standards focus on public features and thus do not make reference to private fantasy elements. This has the unfortunate consequence of implying, wrongly, that fantasy elements lack intrinsic worth and are secondary ontological features. The concept of hallucinations, with private access an essential element, suffers from similar derision; so does daydreaming.

To advocate the creative and proper use of the faculty of the imagination is not to support obsessive or destructive fantasy or any kind of systematic image making that would rob a person of the ability to perceive and understand one's experience or that of others. We are not here just tipping our hats to Plato. We are satisfied that much of the view of women that is actively promoted by the fashion, beauty, and advertising establishments is a view that is in large part a pernicious fantasy. This kind of fantasy is one that promotes primarily profits, as well as the presumption of heterosexuality and the sexual availability of women to men as a model of what is expected and is considered normal in the culture.

A particularly perplexing normative question is whether it is morally acceptable to engage in fantasy the content of which one would consider, in the real world, an immoral activity or the manifestation of a morally objectionable attitude.[18] The heightened awareness in some fantasies stems apparently precisely from its forbidden or objectionable character if it were real and not fantasy.

Does the alleged enjoyment of "rape" fantasies by some women reflect a systematic misuse of the imaginative element of sexual activity that our account validates? Can a person ever be held morally responsible for violent or coercive sexual fantasies harbored about others? We do not wish, by our model, to lend theoretical support to the use of fantasy that in fact oppresses women or nonconsensual partners or animals. However, it is not clear what the relation is between experiencing imagined events for purposes of sexual enjoyment, and moral attitudes and beliefs about those events in the real world. It is important to preserve the separation of fantasy from reality in a way that is sensitive to the strength of the imagination to heighten sexuality through realistic fantasizing.

We might well suspect that our moral beliefs and the emotional underpinnings of those beliefs might influence and be influenced by our enjoyment of fantasies. The extent to which sexual enjoyment of an idea defuses our emotional reprobation of objectionable events in the world is the extent to which fantasy is morally objectionable. In that way fantasy is as subject to moral rebuke (and praise) as are other beliefs and actions they might influence. It is not clear that such an influence is necessarily manifested between the private realm of fantasy and one's moral beliefs, social attitudes, and actions. These causal questions do not undercut our contention that fantasy, as such, is not an evil to be deprecated.

4.

Although the conception of sexuality presented here is meant to be value neutral, we do not shy away from reflecting on the contingent implications this view of sex might have concerning questions of value. We have discussed perversion, masturbation, fantasy, and the sexual experience itself, with an eye toward value implications. Rejection of narrow teleological views of sex implies that other ethical conclusions people often draw about sex should be rethought. We touch here on a few more implications.

Various biases flow from the conceptions of sex we reject, which imply that sex has a particular, or a particularly natural, purpose. One such bias underlies arguments against one-night stands, sex with prostitutes, and, in general, any impermanent sexual relations (though this is not exhaustive of arguments against these practices). That sexual activity, however sublime, must be thought of as involving a continuing commitment is an assumption that requires defense. Engaging in casual sex can be dangerous, and to the extent that one puts oneself and others in needless danger, it is perhaps immoral. Casual sexual encounters can and often do involve a degree of exploitation that must be avoided. What we focus on here, however, are the ways that such conclusions fail to follow from the nature of sex itself.

A major, though sometimes subtle, underpinning of the received opinion against short term encounters is what might be called the "love-sex identification" argument. Sexual activity is tantamount to, or at least necessarily involves, deep personal intimacy of some sort, intimacy that in most cases leads or should lead to stronger and temporally more extended emotional ties, and which is valuable to the extent to which these ties are promoted. Shaped into an argument, the claim might go: (1) sexual activity with another person is inextricably linked with affectionate activity (caressing, petting, kissing); (2) such affectionate activity is an indication of personal intimacy of a deep or important sort; (3) deep personal intimacy with another is more valuable when fostered and supported over a long period of time by the same two people; therefore, (4) sexual activity is more valuable when practiced with the same person over a long period of time.

First, premise (3) is not convincing unless it is grounded in other arguments (conceptual, factual, or normative) making the connection between intimacy and love, as well as for the conclusion that intimacy and love gain in value in proportion to the amount of time the emotion remains strongly felt, degrees of commitment established, and level of reciprocity involved. Michael Bayles, for example, claims that "personal love is more restricted than either agapic love or sexual desire. It implies a concern for another that is greater than that for most people. . . . Such interpersonal relationships require intimacy. Intimacy involves a sharing of information about one another that is not shared with others."[19]

But although exclusive intimacy might have value for some or many that inheres specifically in its exclusivity, Bayles' view about the nature of intimacy more generally, as well as personal love, is overly broad. His view stems, perhaps, from the mistaken identification of a good that is often or sometimes attached to some activity with the essence or nature of that activity. *Some* reflective and otherwise moral people are able to pursue valued and deeply felt intimacy with more than one person at a particular point in their lives. Therefore, more must be said to defend the view that intimacy *per se* must be exclusively expressed to be valuable.

Another rendition of (3) might be that deep personal intimacy with another involves a special vulnerability to which both parties are prey and which is alleviated or protected against only by established bonds that extend to temporally conventional limits. But we wonder what sort of "vulnerability" is alluded to here that is different from, for instance, that experienced by someone performing in front of an audience for the first time. If the senses of the term are similar then sex does not turn out to be a morally unique risky act, and should be engaged in with the same attention required by other risky, but otherwise moral, acts.

There are perhaps more fundamental problems with the argument. Sex often involves those gestures and movements that, when accompanied by the appropriate emotions, are part of the usual repertoire of lovers' affection toward each other. But need such affection be the sort that makes (2) true? We think not. Premise (2), if taken as a conceptual claim, must be grounded in a strongly "commuicative" view of sexual intimacy; that is, gestures and movements of a certain kind are most often intended to communicate some specific messages concerning the emotional states of the acting persons, and these actions are interpreted this way.[20] So the defender of (2) might argue that a person who is having sex with someone with whom she or he has no intention of developing a stronger emotional tie, is lying to or deceiving that person in this special way.[21]

This is a danger. But the problem with this explication of premise (2) as a *general* claim about sexual interaction is that it is false. People often have sex with those to whom clear indication has been given, and received, that the activity does not imply the hope of intimacy. In encounters with prostitutes, no such miscommunication takes place. Those who are afraid of the implications of intimacy, as well as those who wish not to communicate conventional implications deceptively, might be led to prostitutes, casual sex, and openly unambiguous one-night stands precisely to be honest: to block the social implications and expectations that might develop and to be up front about it. In this way, the possibility of deception can be ruled out. Where there is risk that sexual signals are misunderstood, there is consequent risk of exploitation or deception. However, as with the terms of a promise, the fact that certain conditions must be met to make the potentially exploitative relation moral does not make the relation immoral in general. Indeed, there are cases when those conditions *are* actually met.

A claim like (2), connecting sex, affection, and intimacy, could be taken as a normative claim, that certain kinds of sexual activity should or ought to be used as an indication of a deeper emotional intimacy. The claim we are examining is that sex is *misused* when it is not instrumental in the nurturing of long term emotional connections. But what could be the basis of such a claim? What arguments are there, short of the adoption of a metaphysics as untidy as that of Roman Catholic theology, that urges such a strict teleological view of sex?[22] We have already tried to expose the weaknesses of narrow instrumentalist accounts. Those who advocate the value of short term sexual relations do so by rejecting the teleology that lies at the root of arguments such as the one criticized here, and we think nothing conceptually or morally untoward results from this rejection.

Without the armor of such claims as the love-sex identification argument, the plausibility of the tenet that permanence in sex is always better is reduced. As many philosophers point out, there are right amounts of things; and the right amount of something, sex, sleep, or study, is not a fixed point but an oscillating range whose mean value could change with varying circumstances and conditions. What is needed are advocates of "minimal sex," where that is understood to include two things: sexuality, even orgasmic, within a compressed time frame that does not invoke permanence, and also sexuality that seeks no further end than, say, cuddling and caressing. It is not just heterosexist and male oriented emphasis on intercourse to which we allude. We are concerned to deflate excessive emphasis on orgasm, as well as the overly burdensome need to stretch out sexual relationships into conventionally accepted blocks of time. And in so doing we do not espouse or promote a *Playboy* lifestyle that the alleged sexual revolution was to have parented, for it is often seen as the exclusive prerogative of heterosexual men. Some women might have special reason for shunning short term noncommittal liaisons with men (though not all women or all men) because of the possibly exploitative nature of relations with them (or pregnancy, disease, and the like). We mention these reasons to distinguish them from reasons that follow necessarily from the conceptual and normative contours of sexual activity as such. So although some might view sex without orgasm as necessarily frustrating, and short term relations as heartbreaking, we point out other kinds of sexual pleasures that derive their value not from the role they play in bringing about orgasm or securing emotional intimacy, but in their very independence from those overworked and often unsuccessful instrumental functions.

We do not claim that the quality of good, long term relations has nothing to do with their length.[23] Particularly sexual values are at work in the aspects of such relationships that are highly prized. Permanence might make possible certain rare human joys that are tied to human memory accretions and that overlay and fund experience. Like an old couch, memory might afford a perspective that is gently layered and thick with years of intimate sharing. But it is not the length that is good but these *other* joys that accrue to the relation. Consequently, what we question is treating permanence as an intrinsic value or treating more or less permanent sexual relations as the only ones to which value can accrue.

One reason many people favor permanence in sexual relations is that they favor monogamy. Monogamy is often defended on the grounds that it is undesirable to treat lovers as interchangeable. Sexual contexts are to be opaque, as it were. But is not the notion that lovers should not be treated as interchangeable just another cultural bias that perhaps also stems from the tendency to identify the norms of emotional relations with those of sexual relations? There might indeed be many emotional reasons for preferring a particular person as one's companion in various activities, but we doubt that there are any peculiarly *sexual* reasons (questions of attractiveness and compatibility aside). And we realize that many attitudes widely held in a culture, while not derivable from more basic and defensible principles, are nevertheless *entrenched* in the minds of individuals to the extent that ignoring them requires too great a psychological and social investment to be worth the effort. But for many people, that lasting emotional commitment is a necessary moral or psychological condition for sexual interaction is no longer a deeply entrenched view. Hence we see no reason to consider the sharing of sexual pleasures with different individuals as holding a moral place above such sharing of other enjoyable activities. Perhaps the love-sex identification argument is lurking here also: "to have sex with a person without loving her or him is wrong." Our response to this is simply that the burden of proof is on showing why having sex with X without loving X is wrong while, say, playing tennis with X without loving X is not.

These considerations posed against overemphasis on permanence might smack of an argument in favor of treating individuals (merely) as sex objects. Most cases of such treatment involve A's treating B as *only* or merely a sexual being without due regard to the other's legitimate interests and needs. More commonly perhaps, a person is regarded (or *viewed*) as a sex object when that person is presented as representative of a class of people the members of which are considered by many as principally the sexual playthings of others. The historical embeddedness of such a view toward women might provide reason for special effort in bringing out or recognizing the nonsexual and human value of women as individuals. On the other hand, if treating a person as a sex object only entails using that person as a source of sexual pleasure after one has given due regard to that person's interests and desires, and not ignoring or forgetting the uniquely human value that this person might have, then objectification, in this sense, is not morally problematic. Such objectifying begins to resemble normal, valuable, sexual relations, especially if the "interests" that one takes into account of the other person are *sexual* interests answerable by, or involved with, oneself. Consequently, it would be permissible, where other rights and interests are satisfied, and perhaps even an act of charity and graciousness, to treat a sexual partner as an object to be enjoyed.

Our model might also suggest a new approach to pornography. What makes pornography wrong, when it is wrong, is not that it displays women as sexual creatures, but that it portrays women as having none of a broad range of legitimate interests or needs. Pornography goes astray, when it does, not merely in attempting to provide a stimulus for sexual fantasizing or inducing sexual arousal, but by doing so in a sexist manner. Pornography reinforces many sexist attitudes; it portrays stereotypical views of women as passive, as unreflective, as willing and easy prey to violence and humiliation, as biologically of a single, clean shaven, Miss America prototype. Indeed, in a world where women have been viewed as mindless sexual toys of men, perhaps *any* pornographic literature that uses images of women for the sake of male fantasy and sexual arousal is pernicious insofar as it reinforces this objectionable picture of women. So even if the female characters in a piece of pornography are not portrayed as passive, clean shaven, or weak, they *are* portrayed as (principally) the objects of sexual stimulation; and the view that women are characterized (principally) by their sexual attributes is a sexist idea. We think it unlikely that the overarching moral questions regarding the sexism of pornography hinge simply on the fact that the major portion of the audience is heterosexual men: pornography is not merely narrow in its target audience as a fishing or fashion magazine might be; it is not just mistaken, as an astrological periodical might be. Rather, part of its appeal is that it portrays, and provides the aura of justification for, a truncated view of women as lacking a broad range of interests, needs, and moral entitlements.[24]

5.

While we are exploding myths, there is one other to explore that relies on a deeply embedded assumption: that our sex lives are worth the time and energy we give them. We have described what value consists in or arises from sexual activity; but we must now ask what comparative or "contextual" value such activity has in the lives of individuals. Sexual activity might not be as important or desirable a human experience, comparatively speaking, as most believe. Human beings spend an inordinate amount of time and energy discussing sex, engaging in sex-oriented activities, and in attempting to look sexually attractive even to those who are not actual or potential sex partners.[25] With high heels and pointed footwear, a form of female gait bondage is still subscribed to and reinforced. Our clothes and body hair, or the lack of it, are thought of primarily as aphrodisiacs. The musculature of our bodies and our very health takes a secondary position to fashion attractiveness. We need to discern the tyranny of sexual preoccupation. This preoccupation might be an indication of our inabilities thus far to accomplish those goals that theories of sex make so much of: release tensions, take pleasure, communicate with one another, produce offspring. Perhaps the members of a more gracious and decent society would have less to do with sexuality, though they need not have fewer sexual experiences. For much of the preoccupation alluded to appears suspect not because it leads to or amounts to a great deal of sexual activity but exactly because so often it does not. The immense effort applied to sex-related activities (making oneself attractive, developing a seductive manner) is carried out often when no sexual activity is intended, hoped for, or even in sight. The habits of sexual preparedness take on lives of their own divorced from the end states that might have provided the rationale for their occurrence.

So there are reasons for thinking that a more heroic society, as just described, might have less to do with sex than we. Moreover, a theoretical reason exists that sex might not be worth all our ministrations, one that cuts deeply into the heart of our views of sexuality. One of the values of sexual activity as we have described it is the feeling of autonomy that results from the total immersion of oneself into the sexual feeling (or the sharing of that immersion). If this is an accurate appraisal of sexual activity, it could be that much of our actual sexual practice involves incontinence or *akrasia*: a willingness to suspend or abandon one's rational capacity of judgment for the sake of some momentary (or other) demand. The person who puts much weight on the immersion into the sexual experience leaves her or himself open to acting (or failing to act) against her or his own preferred alternative,[26] simply because these acts seem so independent (in the self-sufficiency of their pleasure) from the demands of everyday life.

These acts might be benign or mingled with glee or they might, as is more common in the literature, be seen by the akrates as unfortunate and regrettable. We do not see sex as necessarily selfish or manipulative or as too full of undeserved earthly delights. But given the sexuality we envisage, sex might well involve a kind of forgetfulness and abandonment of rational control stemming from focused sexual attentiveness that turn out to be contrary to the agent's best interest. That sex might often involve akratic behavior does not imply that one should never have sex. Sometimes one might put oneself in a position to act against one's better judgment, but also, in so doing or in the upshot, be acting benevolently in one's own or another's best interest. Where such forgetfulness is not desirable, a heroically ideal life might indeed be a celibate one or a more celibate one or a periodically celibate one. In any case, voluntary celibacy might be a good temporary life strategy for those for whom sexual experience has become incompatible with other more prominent personal or moral goals.

Note that one can be "partner celibate" in an otherwise sexual life, although this has not been an option much mentioned in the philosophical or popular press. The idea of sex in a lifestyle committed to partner celibacy has an air of contradiction about it; we are inclined to forget that the sexual includes the autoerotic. The point is that even given the various valuable goals that sex reportedly achieves, and the general value that our model of sexual activity accentuates, there might be perfectly satisfying ways of life that go well or better with temporary or total celibacy.

The having or not having of some sexual inhibitions and repressions, while not rational perhaps, might make life occasionally more exciting. So it is conceivable that the ideal life being adumbrated here, when being more rational and less akratic, might be more bland than its alternative. That is not to say that there are no considerations in favor of this supererogatory or saintly life,[27] or that the lifestyle we speak of is not in fact more valuable.

The akratic behavior that sex makes possible need not be irrational; it might be benign and, for morally cautious and supererogatory individuals, ought sometimes to be encouraged. Nonetheless, *irrational* behavior is, other things being equal, not to be encouraged. Unreflective abandonment of rational monitoring of one's activities as the strength of desire increases meets the very definition of irrationality. While sex itself is not a sufficient cause of such behavior, it might often be a spur. To make a more plausible case for this, consider that, for sex, people have been known to leave good companions and good jobs and even their basic human sensibilities, and to abandon their scruples, not for good reason, not even for reasons that even they thought good, but for no reason at all. So there might be life after sex, and it might be at least sometimes not only good but better.

Notes

1. Ancestors of this paper were presented by Deborah Rosen at Agnes Scott College and the State University of New York at Stony Brook and by John Christman at the Society for the Philosophy of Sex and Love, December 1982. We gratefully acknowledge the helpful critical remarks of colleagues, students, and friends, in particular Sandra Lee Bartky, and we express our appreciation to the University of New Orleans, the University of Illinois at Chicago, and to Virginia Tech for supporting this project.

2. See the essays collected in Robert Baker and Frederick Elliston, eds., *Philosophy and Sex* (Buffalo: Prometheus, 1975; 2nd ed., 1984), and Alan Soble, ed., *Philosophy of Sex* (Totowa, N.J.: Littlefield, Adams, 1980; 2nd ed., 1991).

3. See Pope Paul VI, "Humanae Vitae," in Baker and Elliston, *Philosophy and Sex*, 2nd ed., 167-84.

4. See, e.g., Jean-Paul Sartre, *Being and Nothingness*, trans. Hazel E. Barnes (New York: Philosophical Library, 1956) and Thomas Nagel, "Sexual Perversion," in Baker and Elliston, *Philosophy and Sex*, 2nd ed., 268-79.

5. See Michael Slote, "Inapplicable Concepts," in Baker and Elliston, *Philosophy and Sex*, 1st ed., 261-7.

6. Robert Solomon, "Sex and Perversion," in Baker and Elliston, *Philosophy and Sex*, 1st ed., 268-87, at 273.

7. Robert Solomon, "Sexual Paradigms," in Soble, *Philosophy of Sex*, 2nd ed., 53-62, at 59.

8. Alan Goldman, "Plain Sex," in Soble, *Philosophy of Sex*, 2nd ed., 119-38.

9. Jerome Shaffer, "Sexual Desire," *Journal of Philosophy* 75:4 (1978): 175-89; this volume, 1-12 (page references below to Shaffer are to this volume).

10. *Ibid.*, 3.

11. *Ibid.*, 9.

12. Solomon, "Sexual Paradigms," 60-1; Moulton, "Sexual Behavior: Another Position," in Soble, *Philosophy of Sex*, 2nd ed., 63-71, at 68.

13. See Nagel, "Sexual Perversion," and the essays in Soble, *Philosophy of Sex*, 1st ed., pt. 1; 2nd ed., pt. 2.

14. On women's sexuality, see Shere Hite, *The Hite Report* (New York: Dell, 1976); Ann Koedt, *The Myth of the Vaginal Orgasm* (Boston: New England Free Press, 1970); William Masters and Virginia Johnson, *Human Sexual Response* (Boston: Little, Brown, 1970); and Mary Jane Sherfey, *The Nature and Evolution of Female Sexuality* (New York: Random House, 1966).

15. On "completeness," see Sara Ruddick, "On Sexual Morality," in James Rachels, ed., *Moral Problems*, 2nd ed. (New York: Harper and Row, 1975), 16-34, and her "Better Sex," in Baker and Elliston, *Philosophy and Sex*, 2nd ed., 280-99.

16. See Alan Soble, "Masturbation," *Pacific Philosophical Quarterly* 61 (1982): 233-44; reprinted, revised, in his *Philosophy of Sex*, 2nd ed., 133-57.

17. See Hite, *The Hite Report*, 62.

18. This question was brought to our attention by Sandra Bartky.

19. Michael Bayles, "Marriage, Love, and Procreation," in Baker and Elliston, *Philosophy and Sex*, 2nd ed., 130-45, at 135.

20. See Solomon, "Sexual Paradigms," in Soble, *Philosophy of Sex*, 2nd ed., 59.

21. See Richard Wasserstrom, "Is Adultery Immoral?" in Baker and Elliston, *Philosophy and Sex*, 2nd ed., 93-106.

22. Carl Cohen criticizes the Vatican's "love-sex identification" argument in "Sex, Birth Control, and Human Life," in Baker and Elliston, *Philosophy and Sex*, 2nd ed., 185-99.

23. We are much indebted here to discussions with Carolyn Morillo.

24. See Robin Morgan's insightful review of Angela Carter's book *The Sadeian Woman and the Ideology of Pornography*, in *The New Republic* (8 September 1979), 31-3. See also Deirdre English, Amber Hollibaugh, and Gayle Rubin, "Talking Sex: A Conversation on Sexuality and Feminism," *Socialist Review* 11:4 (1981): 43-62.

25. See Mary Midgley, *Beast and Man* (Ithaca: Cornell University Press, 1978), 39.

26. See also Solomon, "Sex and Perversion," 271.

27. See J. O. Urmson's notion of supererogation in "Saints and Heroes," in A. I. Melden, ed., *Essays in Moral Philosophy* (Seattle: University of Washington Press, 1958), 198-216.

Mary Ann Carroll
(photograph: Emily Wessel)

Author of "Commentary on 'Toward and Beyond a New Model of Sexuality'"
Paper presented at the Society for the Philosophy of Sex and Love
during the
Eastern Division Meeting of The American Philosophical Association
Baltimore, Md., 28 December 1982

Twenty-One

SEXUAL AND OTHER ACTIVITIES AND THE IDEAL LIFE

Mary Ann Carroll

We can engage in variety of activities for their own sake: taking and developing photographs, growing roses, playing Scrabble, the piano, tennis. While these activities can be undertaken for any number of teleological reasons, none *requires* a teleological explanation to understand why we do it. This is what Deborah Rosen and John Christman correctly note about sexual activities,[1] which have additional features in common with the activities I just listed. Each is "a multifaceted phenomenon" having "a plurality" of purposes (200); each can be value neutral, and their value is not determined specifically and uniquely by the nature of the activity itself. Regarding those that are practiced alone, each "can be one of full realization of the pleasurable aspects of the self: the self-affirming, self-actualizing experience of being alive" (204). When activities are shared, "feelings of independence and self-worth [can be] recast here in terms of the dynamics of a shared relation"; and a "feeling of heightened life experience [can] help create a sense of completeness and importance" (204). If "pleasurable aspects of the self" is understood broadly, and since what can count as a "self-affirming, self-actualizing experience of being alive" and "a sense of completeness and importance" is contingent, these remarks are applicable to the nonsexual activities I mentioned.

Compare sex with something that is done alone: darkroom photography. If you have had the experience of composing and developing prints, you know the feeling of what it is like to create a good photograph. Your initial reaction on taking it out of the fixer and looking at it is simply Aha!; you do not stop to analyze the aspects of the photo that make it good. To take liberty with Rosen and Christman's words, you might say that the experience is one of full realization of the creatively pleasurable aspects of the self, the self-affirming, self-actualizing experience of being conscious. This is a phenomenological approach to the idea of photographic activity, the activity during which you give yourself over to the experience of doing something that gives rise to a feeling of self-actualization. If I ask you, a reflective person, why you engage in photography, your response will be that there isn't just one but a variety of reasons; you might say you enjoy it for its own sake, because it helps you build a more positive concept, it gives you a feeling of independence, it keeps you from boredom, or you want to give a gift of your own making to someone special.

Now compare shared sexual activity with playing tennis. Suppose you ask me why I play tennis. I tell you there is not one reason but several: it is a good cardiovascular activity, it brings me closer to my partner who happens to be my best friend, I want to show off my skill to someone, to help my partner develop self-confidence, or simply because it's fun. In addition, when I play tennis I get a feeling of heightened life experience that helps me gain a sense of completeness and importance, and my feelings of independence and self-worth can be recast here in terms of the dynamics of a shared relation. This is a phenomenological approach to tennis activity, the activity during which I feel alive and exhilarated. Yet a tennis feeling need not involve pleasure. Some tennis players would claim that pain, or at least a kind of intensity and focus that connects with tension and competition, is often close to the internal "feel" of their tennis experience.

Another common feature among these activities is that they involve skills one must practice in order to excel at. Yet philosophers haven't proposed models for photographic activity or playing tennis or the others as they have for sexual activities. We can come up with reasons for this: unlike photography and tennis, (1) we all desire sex, (2) sex is not an invented activity, (3) we think of sex as a private matter, (4) we are preoccupied with sex, and (5), according to Rosen and Christman, while "neutrality in one's conception of sexuality is difficult . . . to maintain" (205), we don't have trouble being neutral in our conceptions of photography and tennis.

But is there a *conceptual* difference between (nonteleological) nonsexual activities and sexual ones? I am not sure how Rosen and Christman would answer. On the one hand, they emphasize that the connection between the nature of sexuality and normative questions is *contingent*; on the other, they claim there are aspects of it that can "give sexuality a unique value as a human endeavor" (204). My guess is they would say there is no conceptual difference, since aspects of sexuality, like the other activities noted, can, but do not necessarily, give it a unique value as a human endeavor.

However, if there *is* a conceptual difference, that might be why the authors have difficulty maintaining a consistent value neutrality. They note the various attitudes that might be best expressed sexually (domination, conflict, wantonness), and then say, "If these are an indication of the attitudes that might best be expressed sexually, then not promoting such behavior . . . might be desirable" (201). Assuming they mean "morally desirable," what has happened to their value neutral approach? In their discussion of the *concept* of sexuality, they make this remark:

> Where it is impossible for sexual activity to be both self-validating and, where others are affected, other-regarding, and where sexual activity is positively averse to creating this environment, it is not clear to us that it is even moral to engage in such activity. (205)

Given their stress on the contingent connection between sexual activity and moral issues, "impossible" here must mean "physically impossible." I am not sure what sort of a situation they have in mind; still, they raise a question of moral permissibility. Now the contingency of the connection between sexual behavior and normative implications becomes blurred. If sexual activity is conceptually different from other (nonteleological) activities, then conceptual issues of sexuality will necessarily in some cases involve normative issues. Perhaps Rosen and Christman have inadvertently made a case for a model of sexuality that they intended to avoid.

In their discussion of the contingent implications of their model for the morality of sex, the authors argue against traditional objections to having multiple partners. Their grounds are these: (1) permanence in a sexual relationship is not intrinsically valuable; (2) sharing sexual pleasure is morally analogous to sharing other sorts of pleasures; and (3) objections to interchangeability of partners is a cultural bias. In defending (1), they make a compelling case against what they call the "love-sex identification argument" (208). My focus will be on (2) and (3).

Claim (2), that sharing sexual pleasure is morally analogous to sharing other pleasures, is correct to the extent that, when an activity involves another person, questions of morality can arise; in any shared activity, one's behavior can have good or bad effects on others. But Rosen and Christman should reconsider rejecting the view that "the sharing of sexual pleasures with different individuals [holds] a moral place above such sharing of other enjoyable activities" (209). To support some of their claims, they appeal to what "reflective people" would say. For instance, early in their essay they argue that we should look at "*reasons* reflective people *give* for their sexual activity" (200) and that communication "is not even *a* purpose many reflective people would give for their sexual behavior" (200). They also claim that "reflective and otherwise moral people are able to pursue valued and deeply felt intimacy with more than one person at a particular point in their lives" (207). I am uncertain how much weight should be placed on the attitudes of the "reflective people" they select. Contrary to the authors, my guess is that many reflective people view sex as a venture more morally serious than tennis; for them, sexual activity does hold a higher moral place.

These reflective people might argue like this. Considerations of privacy, intimacy, and vulnerability must be *taken together* to see the moral difference between sex and other activities. If these three considerations are examined separately, none will seem unique to sex. (1) Privacy: there are certain situations that, in everyday circumstances, people want to maintain privacy (when defecating, for instance, or picking their nose). (2) Intimacy: people can be intimate with others in ways that are nonsexual (confiding in someone). And (3) vulnerability: there are numerous situations in which people can be in a vulnerable position (an introverted person who must make a public speech), and the authors correctly note that sex is not "a morally unique risky act" (207). Yet, when these three are considered together, sex does hold a moral place above other types of shared activity regardless of questions about the desirability of monogamy.

Though the authors deal with moral problems about vulnerability, they ignore privacy. And they forget that intimacy is not restricted to sex; confiding in a good friend is an example, and I can have more than one good friend in whom I confide during a period of time. While they are correct that a person can be deeply intimate with more than one person at a time, I doubt a person can be deeply intimate with too many. You spread yourself too thin, so the deep intimacy disappears, because of psychological drain or time constraints. You do an injustice to yourself and others.

We can agree that monogamy is not *inherently* desirable without endorsing the acceptability of having *many* sexual partners during the same period of time. The authors are correct in rejecting a love-sex identification, but they overstate the case when they compare having sex with playing tennis. Though love is not a moral requirement in either case, there are vast differences between the two activities that their comparison obscures. Those who defend monogamy, say the authors, do so "on the grounds that it is undesirable to treat lovers as interchangeable," and rhetorically ask, "is not the notion that lovers should not be treated as interchangeable just another cultural bias?" (209). Note that the claim that monogamy is not always desirable does not entail that the interchangeability of lovers is desirable. Further, objections to treating lovers as interchangeable is not a mere bias, but is derivable from the Kantian respect principle. When we object to treating lovers as interchangeable, we object to treating them as *mere* objects or sexual beings. Rosen and Christman do expressly reject the moral permissibility of treating others merely as sex objects, and when they criticize pornography, they complain that it "portrays women as having none of a broad range of legitimate interests or needs" (210). But this is precisely the attitude one has in treating lovers as interchangeable.

Let me illustrate how I understand "interchangeability." Suppose I am on the guest list of major formal events in my community. For all of them I want an escort who is attractive. I make the acquaintance of Huey and Louie, who both fit the bill; they have sexy eyes, hair I can't keep my hands off, and physiques I can't keep my hands off either. They are two hunks, which is all I care about. When Huey isn't available to be my escort, Louie is, and vice versa. This is a paradigm example of viewing others as interchangeable. What I am looking for in an escort is not a *particular* human being but a *type*; as long as the particular fits the type, it doesn't matter which particular I end up with.

Rosen and Christman must mean something else by "interchangeable," for they claim that the objection to interchangeability is a cultural bias. They observe that "many attitudes widely held in a culture, while not derivable from more basic and defensible principles, are nevertheless *entrenched* in the minds of individuals" (209). But this does not mean we cannot find some principles from which some of these widely held cultural attitudes are derivable. The prohibition of treating lovers as interchangeable is a good example; it is an instance of Kant's practical imperative. This objection to interchangeability is independent of the love-sex identification argument that the authors think "is lurking here also" (209).

Thus Rosen and Christman give the impression that they would have us get rid of some culturally entrenched attitudes toward sex. They would also have us get rid of our preoccupation with sex. For one thing, much of our sex-related activity does not lead to sex:

> The immense effort applied to sex-related activities (making oneself attractive, developing a seductive manner) is carried out often when no

> sexual activity is intended, hoped for, or even in sight. The habits of sexual preparedness take on lives of their own divorced from the end states that might have provided the rationale for their occurrence. (211)

We waste time, energy, and money engaging in nonproductive sex-related activities. The authors suggest celibacy for those who have difficulty accommodating sexual activities with other, more prominent goals. Thus if I choose to be "partner celibate," yet still want sexual experiences and so choose autoeroticism instead, I will save time and money. I won't have to exert immense effort because I do not need to dress up for myself or develop a seductive manner toward myself. The authors' advocating partner celibacy is a piece of smart practical advice.

However, a confusion surfaces between "sexuality" and "sexual activity." Rosen and Christman make a distinction between the two when they claim, "the members of a more gracious and decent society would have less to do with sexuality, though they need not have fewer sexual experiences" (211). They then suggest that we consider giving up sex nearly altogether: "there are reasons for thinking that a more heroic society . . . might have less to do with sexuality than we," for "much of our actual sexual practice involves incontinence or *akrasia*" (211). A more heroic society as they envision it would not be preoccupied with sex; its members would not waste time and money grooming themselves for others, yet would still be sexually active. Suddenly, though, the authors shift the emphasis from sexuality to our actual sexual practice, a practice that has a feature, incontinence or *akrasia*, we are not to be proud of. This leads to the following conclusion, that either *akrasia* cannot be part of a model of sexuality, or the model is one of human sexuality and experience and not a general (conceptual) one. In that case, the members of the more heroic society have about the same number of sexual experiences as we have, but their experiences do not involve our forgetfulness and abandonment. However, we are no longer talking about *human* sexual experiences.

On Rosen and Christman's model, "sex might well involve a kind of forgetfulness and abandonment of rational control stemming from focused sexual attentiveness that turn out to be contrary to the agent's best interest" (211). The authors might be suggesting that since having sex often involves irrationality, we should abstain on most occasions—even though they go on to state, "that sex might often involve akratic behavior does not imply that one should never have sex." Yet, to say the members of a more gracious and decent society might not have a whole lot to do with sex connotes a disdain for a society whose members have a penchant for sexuality (sexual experiences?). And even though, according to the authors, the ideal life will probably be "more bland than its alternative" (212; why am I not surprised?), it might be more valuable. But valuable with respect to what?

All this casts a paradoxical shadow on their model, for the model entails a prescription to avoid doing what the model is all about, on the grounds that on the model the activity usually amounts to irrationality. On this model, the ideal life is more valuable because less sexual, and therefore more rational. The underlying theory of value here is nebulous: is total rationality its basis?

Until the authors make clear what normative foundation they are presupposing, their prescriptions are difficult to swallow.

On the other hand, perhaps the authors simply need to make a distinction between irrational behavior resulting from sexual experience and purely sexual behavior. Purely sexual behavior is neither rational nor irrational, though it can lead one to behave irrationally. This might be what they have in mind when they say, "while sex itself is not a sufficient cause of [irrational] behavior, it might often be a spur" (212). Yet if sexual activity is logically similar to other sorts of nonteleological activities, those too could lead us to behave irrationally. Would Rosen and Christman advocate refraining from *any* activity that might spur irrational behavior? More to the point: it is a matter of fact that for reasons of sex, but rarely for reasons of doing photography or growing roses or playing tennis, "people have been known to leave good companions and good jobs and even their basic human sensibilities, and to abandon their scruples" (212). But that someone should do so for reasons of photography, roses, or tennis is not inconceivable. It would seem to follow that we should not engage in any activity that has the potential to spur us to leave good companions and jobs, and that the ideal life would not include them.

In constructing their model of sexuality, with its frenzy and forgetfulness, Rosen and Christman assume that we go hog wild when it comes to sex: we believe that if some is good, a lot more is better. If they were to throw in some common sense, however, their model of sexuality could accommodate their idea of the ideal life. And it should, for an ideal human life ought to have room for all the activities that make us human. Rosen and Christman acknowledge "there are right amounts of things," and the right amount of something "is not a fixed point but an oscillating range" (208). In light of this, we can say that "the right amount" of sexual activity can vary. And so we need not take seriously their view that "there might be life after sex," and we do not have to figure out how life after sex "might be at least sometimes not only good but better" (212).

Rosen and Christman are correct to note that there are times when the kind of forgetfulness that occurs in sexual activity is not desirable. But it is a jump to go from that to concluding that "a heroically ideal life might indeed be a celibate one" (211). Instead, all they need to suggest is that a practical life might require or involve celibacy at times. If a person is addicted to sex, it would take some heroism to refrain from sexual activity on certain occasions. However, I have in mind people who enjoy sex but who nevertheless refrain from sex when lacking what they consider to be a suitable partner and circumstance. At times celibacy is preferable to sex. Suppose, for example, you and your lover of five years have decided to go your separate ways. Your sex life was enviable by most standards. You are having a drink at the bar where the two of you used to meet after work and you are reminiscing about how great sex was. Someone takes a seat next to you and strikes up a conversation. Though you see the person as a potential sex partner and perhaps a companion, you have not yet separated yourself emotionally from your ex-lover, nor are you hot to trot. Besides, you have a hectic schedule coming up and you have a report to complete that evening. You would be impractical, if not stupid, to abandon your basic sensibilities in an attempt to actualize the potential. In not doing so you are being practical, but I would hardly say you acting heroically; you are simply doing what any person with half an ounce of sense would do.

Here is another scenario. Your spouse, with whom you were deeply and romantically in love, died suddenly a year ago; your grief has been so overwhelming that you have lost any interest in sex. During the past few months, however, you have developed a nonsexual intimate relationship with someone. You both are physically attracted to one another and have expressed your sexual desires. Though you did not explicitly make a vow of celibacy to yourself after your spouse died, you have a nagging feeling that you would violate a commitment to your dead spouse if you were to engage in a sexual relationship. This, however, is *prima facie* irrational. Not only are you refraining from sexual experiences that could enhance your involvement with this person, but your rationale for doing so is not what would be considered rational. While remaining celibate might not be impractical, in the sense intended in the first case, doing so might be contrary to your best interests.

"The right amount" of sex should be interpreted so that the ideal life includes it, and "the right amount" precludes what the authors call the "tyranny of sexual preoccupation" (211). Any adequate model of a human endeavor should not portray the activity as one that should be minimized or denigrated in an ideal human life.

Note

1. Deborah Rosen and John Christman, "Toward a New Model of Sexuality," this volume, 199-213. Page references to this essay are supplied parenthetically in the text.

William Behr Soble (left), Alan Soble (center), and Sylvia Soble (right)
(photograph: Sára Szabó Soble)

Alan Soble, author of "On Rosen and Christman, and Carroll"

Twenty-Two

SEXUAL ACTIVITY[1]

Alan Soble

In the first paragraph of their essay, Deborah Rosen and John Christman[2] promise to provide the beginnings of "a new model" of sexuality, a model that departs from and is superior to the accounts of sexuality that have already appeared in the philosophical literature.[3] The assertion, that they are offering a *new* model of sexuality, struck me as incredible. I was amazed, and not merely because doing or saying something new in any area is always tough; this is why we have the category "genius" and reserve it for Ludwig Wittgenstein, Alan Turing, and Bill Gates. The claim struck me as preposterous, further, because I know my way around both the philosophical and popular literature on sex, and there is nothing significant in "A New Model" that I hadn't read before.

For example, Rosen and Christman insist that sexual activity has by its nature no essential purpose, but only the various purposes people give to it. Fine. But we have heard this argument plenty, from those who criticize Roman Catholic (Thomistic) sexual ethics, from defenders of the morality of homosexual activity, from Irving Singer, and from Robert Solomon (even though he apparently proposes his own essential purpose to sex).[4] Alan Goldman criticizes at length, in the manner of Rosen and Christman, teleological analyses of the nature of sexuality: sex is not *for* babies, nor is it *for* love, although it can be used for making babies or expressing love, if we want to. And, as Rosen and Christman do, Goldman emphasizes the role of sexual pleasure in understanding sexual activity.[5] It seems, then, that Goldman should get a great deal of credit for laying the foundation for Rosen and Christman's New Model, yet they quickly dispatch his work with the single objection that his account of sexuality makes no room for solitary masturbation. (This point was made by others well before Rosen and Christman; they fail to acknowledge its history.)[6]

Jerome Shaffer, too, provides arguments against conceiving of sexual desire in terms of goals that have nothing essential to do with the nature of sexual desire itself.[7] Rosen and Christman acknowledge this, but nonetheless proceed to give reasons for rejecting his account. Shaffer, on their view, in focusing on sexual *desire*, must make "special efforts" to avoid a teleological understanding of sex, something that can be avoided *without* special efforts by focusing, instead, as the authors do, on sexual *activity*. This objection is queer. Shaffer avoids—indeed, *rejects*—a teleological understanding of sex in the process of arguing, which is his central thesis, that sexual desire is not a *desire that*. Rosen and Christman perversely misread that thesis as a "special effort" on his part, a kind of twisting, the contortions of "special pleading," in the face of a problem he would prefer had never arisen. The authors' claim that it is better to avoid teleology by focusing on sexual activity instead of sexual desire, *because* doing so allows us to dispense with Shaffer's account of sexual desire, is convincing only if there are independent reasons for thinking that something is wrong with Shaffer's account, and on this matter Rosen and Christman are silent. Indeed, the authors never propose any analysis of "sexual desire," let alone one they believe is better than Shaffer's. The concept drops out altogether from the philosophy of sex.

Rosen and Christman also object to *any* account of the sexual that focuses on (begins with, makes central) sexual desire. They prefer to analyze sex in terms of sexual activity, they say, in order "to avoid the contentious functionalism that might be buried" in a theory of sex that focuses on desire (202). But Rosen and Christman have already admitted that Shaffer's account of sexual desire does not contain, either buried or on the surface, any such contentious functionalism, so this argument falls flat. By the way, Rosen and Christman do share one other thing in common with Shaffer: all three understand sexual pleasure and sexual sensations ultimately in terms of what we feel as the result of the manipulation of the genitals.[8] Rosen and Christman of course add that other areas are important as well. In any case, there's nothing much new here.

Rosen and Christman also claim that casual sex—sexual activity engaged in outside a context of love or commitment or marriage and that occurs between or among people who do not pledge or obligate themselves to each other beyond the evening or week—is not morally wrong, as long as precautions are taken to eliminate the crass use of one party by another. But most secular philosophers agree with this (trivial) assertion;[9] the ones who disagree, the ones who insist that marriage and love are the (only) proper background for sex, stick out like sore thumbs.[10] And Rosen and Christman, even as they acknowledge the potentially awesome value of sex in terms of self-affirmation and so forth, think that we are too obsessed with sex and ought to cut back on its trappings. But Ann and her sister Abby, as well as a slew of sociologists of sex, have repeatedly told us as much. In the 1960s, Herbert Marcuse put his own neo-Marxist, Frankfurt School twist on the view and called the phenomenon we should watch out for "repressive desublimation."[11]

Perhaps the heart of Rosen and Christman's original contribution to the philosophy of sex is their analysis of sexual activity. There are two matters I will address: one is the novelty of their analysis; the other, more important matter, is its truth. Here is the authors' analysis of sexual activity in their own words:

> Sexual *activity* . . . is that range of activity in which the sexual feeling . . . is the essential subjective element. . . . [S]exual activity is one that essentially *involves* such feeling, an activity in which such feeling is the principal component. (203-4)

If we take seriously the authors' claim to be doing conceptual analysis, we can infer that they are asserting two things:

(1) An activity's involving sexual sensations or feelings is *sufficient* for the activity to be sexual; and

(2) An activity's involving sexual sensations or feelings is *necessary* for the activity to be sexual.

Goldman analyzes sexual activity as activity that tends to fulfill sexual desire; sexual desire, in turn, he analyzes as the desire for the pleasure of physical contact (that is, for sexual pleasure). Hence the form of Goldman's analysis, defining sexual activity ultimately in terms of a sexual feeling or sensation, is exactly that of Rosen and Christman. There is a difference, however: Rosen and Christman define sexual activity in terms of the broader category of sexual *sensations* rather than in terms of sexual *pleasure*, because some people, they say, report that their sexual sensations are better described as being painful or intense or similar to tension and conflict. Now, if true, that fact would not rule out the presence of pleasure at the same time, so I'm not sure that Rosen and Christman are right to distinguish sexual sensations from sexual pleasure. Nor do they explore the implications of tying sexual activity to one rather than to the other.

If Rosen and Christman had defined sexual activity in terms of sexual pleasure, they would have merely repeated Robert Gray's analysis, published in the same issue of *Journal of Philosophy* as Shaffer's account of sexual desire: the presence of sexual pleasure is both necessary and sufficient for an activity to be sexual.[12] I have elsewhere argued that Gray's analysis does state a sufficient condition, but also that it does not correctly state a necessary condition for an activity to be sexual.[13] Similar considerations apply to Rosen and Christman's variant of Gray's analysis. Rosen and Christman imply that when sexual sensations are absent (are not "involved"), the activity is not sexual. That claim is true enough (to use Mary Ann Carroll's examples)[14] of taking and developing photographs, playing Scrabble, and growing roses, all of which hardly ever involve sexual sensations. (Of course they *can*, and in these instances they would be sexual; for example, taking a photograph of your nude partner or a copulating couple; fishing for Scrabble tiles in body orifices.) But there are plenty of acts that involve neither sexual pleasure nor any sexual feelings, yet are still sexual: the multiple acts of fellatio that a prostitute performs in an evening, deriving no sexual pleasure from any of them; the cunnilingus that a bored and unaroused man, who prefers to be watching basketball on television or even working, performs on his demanding wife or girlfriend; the frenetic, unpleasurable grabbings of two inexperienced teenagers worried that they will be caught. The point is that the kind of analysis proposed by Rosen and Christman conflates sexual activity with good sexual activity; it confuses the question of the ontology of the act (as sexual or not) with the question of the quality of the act (as pleasurable or satisfying or not). In our three examples, we want to say that sexual activity is occurring but it is not pleasurable. Rosen and Christman's analysis forces us to say that due to the absence of sexual feelings, these actions are not sexual to begin with. The busy prostitute, the bored man, and the frustrated teenagers are at most *trying* to perform sexual acts, and *failing* to do so. Further, on their view a woman or a man who is raped—say, physically compelled into vaginal or anal intercourse—has been made to engage in a sexual act only if she or he experiences sexual sensations.

Note that Rosen and Christman explicitly deny that they assert that *trying* to produce sexual sensations is that which marks acts as sexual acts. They object to a possible analysis of sexual activity according to which it is activity *aimed* at sexual sensation. On such a view,

(3) Trying to produce sexual sensations is *sufficient* for an act to be sexual,

and

(4) Trying to produce sexual sensations is *necessary* for an act to be sexual.

Clause (3) blesses as sexual the acts of the hassled teenagers, at least, and perhaps the acts of the prostitute and the bored man, if the analysis admits trying to produce pleasure for someone else. But Rosen and Christman think (3) is false because "overbroad" (204), categorizing too many nonsexual acts as sexual. That's a funny objection for them to make. Given their critique of teleology, they ought to say about (3) and (4) together, immediately, that to analyze sexual activity in terms of trying to do something in particular (such as producing sexual sensations) does not do justice to the many different reasons reflective people give for engaging in sex.

My suspicion is that a "contentious functionalism" is also buried in a model of sex that focuses on sexual activity.

Notes

1. This essay is a revision of comments on Deborah Rosen and John Christman's essay that I wrote in 1982 and mailed, along with their essay and the commentary by Mary Ann Carroll, to the members of the Society for the Philosophy of Sex and Love.

2. Deborah Rosen and John Christman, "Toward A New Model of Sexuality," this volume, 199-213. Page references to this essay are supplied parenthetically in the text.

3. See the essays collected in Robert Baker and Frederick Elliston, eds., *Philosophy and Sex* (Buffalo: Prometheus, 1975; 2nd ed., 1984), and Alan Soble, ed., *Philosophy of Sex* (Totowa, N.J.: Littlefield, Adams, 1980; 2nd ed., 1991).

4. Irving Singer, *The Goals of Human Sexuality* (New York: Schocken Books, 1973); Robert Solomon, "Sex and Perversion," in Baker and Elliston, *Philosophy and Sex*, 1st ed., 268-87, and "Sexual Paradigms," in Soble, *Philosophy of Sex*, 2nd ed., 53-62.

5. Alan Goldman, "Plain Sex," in Soble, *Philosophy of Sex*, 2nd ed., 119-38.

6. Alan Soble, "Masturbation," *Pacific Philosophical Quarterly* 61 (1982): 233-44; reprinted, revised, in Soble, *Philosophy of Sex*, 2nd ed., 133-57; see also my "Introduction," *Philosophy of Sex*, 1st ed., 14-18.

7. Jerome A. Shaffer, "Sexual Desire," *Journal of Philosophy* 75:4 (1978): 175-89; this volume, 1-12.

8. Rockney Jacobsen's analysis of "sexual desire" similarly ends up understanding sexual arousal as the arousal of the genitals; "Arousal and the Ends of Desire," *Philosophy and Phenomenological Research* 53:3 (1993): 617-32, at 630.

9. For example, Bernard Baumrin, "Sexual Immorality Delineated," in Baker and Elliston, *Philosophy and Sex*, 1st ed., 116-128; 2nd ed., 300-11 (as well as many of the other essays in both editions of the two anthologies mentioned, above, in n. 3).

10. Roger Scruton, *Sexual Desire: A Moral Philosophy of the Erotic* (New York: The Free Press, 1986).

11. Herbert Marcuse, *Negations* (Boston: Beacon Press, 1968), "On Hedonism," 159-200; *Eros and Civilization* (New York: Vintage, 1962); and *One-Dimensional Man* (Boston: Beacon Press, 1964).

12. Robert Gray, "Sex and Sexual Perversion," *Journal of Philosophy* 75:4 (1978): 189-99; reprinted in Soble, *Philosophy of Sex*, 1st ed., 158-68; see 160-3.

13. See Alan Soble, *Sexual Investigations* (New York: New York University Press, 1996), ch. 3. For the analysis of "sexual activity" more generally, see my "Sexuality, Philosophy of," *Routledge Encyclopedia of Philosophy* (1998).

14. Mary Ann Carroll, "Sexual and Other Activities and the Ideal Life," this volume, 215-21, at 215.

Roger Paden
(photograph: James MacKenzie)

Author of "Abortion and Sexual Morality"
Paper presented at the Society for the Philosophy of Sex and Love
during the
Eastern Division Meeting of The American Philosophical Association
Boston, Mass., 28 December 1983

Twenty-Three

ABORTION AND SEXUAL MORALITY

Roger Paden

Philosophical discussions, unlike their popular counterparts, tend to treat the question of the morality of abortion separately from questions of sexual morality.[1] This might be a mistake. My thesis here is that if (1) the fetus is a person at conception and (2) a "negative" theory of rights is correct,[2] the morality of abortion might well be a function of sexual morality. If so, a radical revision in the philosophical discussion of abortion would be required. Judith Thomson, in her "A Defense of Abortion," presents an argument based on these two assumptions that, I believe, is generally sound. However, it is incomplete. An investigation of her argument will help advance my thesis.

1.

Thomson develops her argument within the context of a negative theory of rights. I will maintain that perspective in this essay. Her argument turns on the concept of the right to life, specifically on the limits one person's right to life places on the behavior of others. To explore this point, she assumes, for the sake of argument, that a fetus is a person from the moment of conception and, therefore, has a right to life equal to that of all other persons. I, too, will grant that assumption for the sake of argument. Given these assumptions, the question of the morality of abortion would seem to turn on the question of whether a fetus's right to life obligates the woman who is carrying it to refrain from obtaining an abortion. Thompson argues on the basis of a negative conception of rights that it does not.

According to the negative theory of rights, a person's right to life obligates others to avoid murdering him, but it does not obligate others to allow him the use of their resources to keep him alive. One does not violate his rights or, as Thomson puts it, "kill him unjustly,"[3] by failing to give him the means of survival. If this were not true, then the failure to give food to the starving, blood to accident victims, or (spare) organs to the terminally ill would constitute a violation of their right to life. A person's right to life, on this negative view, does not require others to give up that to which they have title in virtue of their rights, even when this is necessary to keep him alive. The failure to do so might contribute to his death, and might be called "killing," but if so, it is a "just killing" that does not violate his right to life. Accordingly, abortion, properly conceived as the withdrawal of a life-giving substance, namely the woman's body (to which she has title), from a person who has no right to it, must be thought a just killing. Therefore, Thomson concludes, the fetus's right to life, by itself, does not make abortion immoral.

This conclusion, however, would not follow if a woman had given the fetus the right to use her body. If she had done so, then the withdrawal of her body would be the withdrawal of a thing to which the fetus had title. In that case, the withdrawal of the woman's body would, on the fetus's subsequent death, constitute a violation of its rights, and would be, therefore, unjust. Thomson considers this possibility in her discussion of the following question. "But doesn't her partial responsibility for [the fetus's] being there itself give it the right to use her body? If so, then her aborting it would be depriving it of what it does have a right to, and thus doing it an injustice."[4]

Thomson's suggestion that the woman might have given the fetus the right to use her body by voluntarily engaging in sex follows from the modern idea that a person's obligations to others arise only out of their common natural rights (and the obligations directly or indirectly entailed by those rights) and as a result of their voluntary actions. As the fetus has no original natural right to the woman's body, if it acquires that right, it must be through the woman's voluntary actions. If abortions were always immoral, a fetus's right to use a woman's body must arise from the only act in which all pregnant women have participated, namely, sexual intercourse. Therefore, if abortion is immoral, it could only be because, by engaging in sex, women undertake an obligation to any fetus that might thereby come to exist to grant them the use of their bodies. It is Thomson's belief, however, that this action creates no such obligation, and that, therefore, not all abortions are unjust killings. However, before accepting her conclusions, we should examine the arguments that might show that sexual intercourse does create such an obligation. If none of them are successful, we must accept Thomson's conclusions.

2.

Although there are many arguments that might demonstrate that a woman has an obligation to her fetus,[5] I will, following Thomson, limit discussion to those arguments that are consistent with a negative theory of rights. Thus, any argument that begins with the assumption of some universal obligation to care for others, beyond the care needed to respect other's rights, will be ignored. Moreover, those arguments that begin with duties that fall on those occupying special roles, if those roles were not freely adopted, will also be ignored.[6] As Thomson writes, nicely summarizing this position, "Surely we do not have any 'special responsibility' for a person unless we have assumed it, explicitly or implicitly. . . . [Parents] do not, simply by virtue of their biological relationship to the child who comes into existence, have a special responsibility for it. They may wish to assume responsibility for it or they may wish not to."[7]

This last needs amendment. Parents might *act* so as to assume responsibility, or they might not have so *acted*. However, their obligations do not depend on their desires, but only on their behavior. If the parents have done something that has the consequence that they now have an obligation, they have that obligation regardless of their wishes. It follows, therefore, that it is possible to acquire this obligation unintentionally. However, no obligation is a consequence simply of a biological relationship, independently of some voluntary action. As my argument will make significant use of this notion of unintentionally acquired obligations, it would be good to examine this notion further.

Suppose that I have made a promise to meet you at a restaurant across town for lunch next week. Unfortunately, by the day of the event, I have forgotten the promise and fail to remember it until just after noon, too late to keep the appointment. I might be able to produce an excuse for my lapse, but if it is unacceptable, I cannot simply accept my share of unexcused guilt and retire. If I remember in time, I must call you to inform you of my mistake, to set your mind at rest so that you may enjoy a quiet lunch. If I fail to do this, I can be blamed for two failures. "You mean to tell me that you not only forgot our date, but then you didn't call me to tell me you wouldn't make it?!" That I was twice remiss entails that I failed in two obligations. The first was my obligation to keep my promise. The second was my obligation to act responsibly to contain the damage caused by my first failure, so that no one suffers any additional harm.

In this example, there are two obligations. However, only the first was explicitly assumed. Only those who make promises have this obligation. The second obligation was not explicitly assumed, nor was it implicit in the promise. Rather, it was the result of a general obligation that only came into play with the making of the promise. I believe that this obligation, a general obligation be responsible, has two parts. The first part is the requirement to "act responsibly," that is, to act in a manner that is neither negligent nor reckless (nor criminal, nor immoral). However, there is more to this idea than this, because the duty to be responsible also requires that we "take responsibility" for our actions. This means that if we do violate our responsibilities by acting in a negligent or irresponsible manner and, as a result, cause harm to others, then we have the further duty or obligation to see to it that the harm they suffer is limited or that they suffer no additional avoidable harm. Thus, "being responsible" means both "acting responsibly" or carefully, that is, neither negligently or recklessly, and, if one has acted negligently or recklessly, "taking responsibility," by acting so as to limit further harm to the person endangered by one's actions. In the example above, it was the second part of this obligation, to limit harm, that was unintentionally assumed by my failure to keep my promise.

Once this idea of responsibility is made explicit, many examples of it might be found. The obligation to apologize after minor transgressions might be based on it, as might be the requirement that we carry liability insurance for our car. The practice of suing for damages might also rest on it. However, there do exist some limits to the liability to which we might so expose ourselves. Presumably, for example, there should be some correspondence between the harm or danger threatened and the degree of liability assumed. However, I will not discuss this issue here.

The important point is that this example shows that it is possible to assume an obligation without intending to undertake it. Such an obligation can arise out of the performance of a certain kind of action, one such that, by performing it, we become responsible to those affected by it to ensure that they suffer no avoidable harm. Moreover, this sort of obligation is indispensable to a negative theory of rights. Without it, it would be difficult in many cases to delineate our rights and discover what counts as their violation.

The application to the abortion case is clear. Since sexual intercourse is an act that not only can lead to the creation of another person, but also can result in placing that person in a potentially dangerous position, then, if sexual intercourse is an act for which the two participants can be responsible in the way described above to those who are affected by it, the partners would be obligated to ensure that the fetus suffers no significant and avoidable harm at least during the period in which it is dependent on them. This obligation to the fetus initially and unfairly falls almost exclusively on the female participant, as it is impossible to aid the fetus except through her. The male participant's obligation to the fetus, therefore, must be expressed indirectly as an obligation to aid his partner. In any case, however, as the withdrawal of the woman's body through an abortion would cause the fetus avoidable harm, the woman would have a *prima facie* obligation to prevent this avoidable harm by letting the fetus use her body. However, as the fetus is entitled to use the woman's body, the withdrawal of that body through an abortion would constitute the unjust killing of the fetus. Therefore, an abortion would violate the fetus's right to life, and would be unjust.

If this argument is sound, it allows us to bridge the gap, between the biological fact of parenthood and a moral obligation that would make most abortions wrong, by showing that they both result from an action that, itself, is morally charged. Having acted in a way that makes them "responsible" for the welfare of the fetus while it is dependent on them, a couple would find themselves, perhaps unintentionally, under an obligation to take care of it during this period. They would have placed themselves in a position in which an abortion would violate its right to life.

3.

The argument, however, cannot be this simple. Even granting this notion of moral responsibility and the theory that obligations can follow from the failure to act responsibly, it has not been shown that a couple engaging in sex are acting in such a way that they can be held responsible in the manner discussed above. This has not been demonstrated because it has not been shown that having sex, in itself, creates the obligation to be responsible. There are many kinds of action, but only some of them entail this kind of obligation. Although, generally, this obligation may provide the moral ground for the legal practice of suing each other for damages, the fact that such suits sometimes fail shows that such obligations do not arise from all actions. For these kinds of lawsuits to succeed, the plaintiff must prove that the defendant acted in either a criminal, a reckless, or a negligent manner. So it is with moral responsibility. One does not unintentionally place oneself under an obligation by performing every action that harms or endangers another, one only does so by performing negligent, reckless, criminal, or immoral actions. In the rest of this essay, I will focus on negligent and reckless acts.

Negligent or reckless behavior is behavior that unintentionally but carelessly puts a third party at substantial and unjustified risk or in which one acts in conscious disregard of substantial and unjustifiable risk to a third party.[8] Because the argument of the last section did not address the question of whether the couple's action was in this sense negligent or reckless, it failed to demonstrate that the couple had acquired an obligation to the fetus. As it is possible, at least in many cases, to argue that such actions are not negligent or reckless, it may be that they have no such obligation.

It is possible to argue that actions, even when they endanger an innocent third party, are not negligent or reckless. Typically, these arguments are divided into two classes: excuses and justifications. There are several kinds of excuses. First, I might try to excuse myself by arguing that my behavior was coerced. If I "acted" involuntarily or under duress, then, as I am not the author of my act, I am not responsible for it and cannot be called negligent for "doing" it, nor can I acquire any obligations as a result of it. Second, I might argue that I am not responsible for the consequences of my actions because, at the time of the act, I was incompetent. Third, I might argue that, although I was competent and acted voluntarily, I cannot be held responsible for the consequences of my action because it was impossible to foresee those consequences. Negligence, that is to say, is parasitic on simple responsibility. Therefore, when we are not responsible for our actions, we cannot be accused of "performing" those actions in a negligent or reckless manner. As a result, in those cases, we cannot be held to be responsible for their consequences.

The application to the case at hand of this notion of excuses is clear. Those pregnancies that are the result of rape, or are the result of actions of a woman judged to be incompetent (that is, of a woman who is insane, severely retarded, or a minor), or are the result of the actions of a woman kept in ignorance of the possible outcomes of sex, cannot, in virtue of these excuses, be thought to result from negligent or reckless actions on the woman's part. Because she was not "simply responsible" in those cases, she cannot be negligent. As a result, she has not undertaken an obligation to take responsibility for those actions. Therefore, she does not have any obligation to the fetus to let it use her body. Abortions in these cases would be permissible.

Another way to excuse some endangering behavior, even when undertaken freely, is to argue that the danger was not unreasonable. One can argue that the danger was slight or that all reasonable precautions were taken to insure that the action was safe. We often do things that are inherently dangerous, but that are not considered essentially reckless or negligent, if we go about them carefully. Driving a car, for example, is dangerous. But driving itself is not considered negligent or reckless. As long as care is taken to obey all traffic laws and to drive safely, driving in itself is not a negligent or reckless act. The same is true of hunting or of conducting possibly dangerous experiments. As long as all reasonable precautions are taken to ensure that no one is harmed, such inherently dangerous behavior does not place the actor under an obligation to those who might be accidentally harmed.

The application to the case at hand is to contraceptive practices. It might be argued that, if a couple uses any of a variety of contraceptive techniques that are both available and morally acceptable, then, since they are taking reasonable precautions, their behavior is not a violation of their obligation to take care. If this is the case, then aborting a fetus that was conceived as a result of contraceptive failure would not violate any obligation to it, for no such obligation was undertaken.

No doubt Thomson would agree with the argument to this point.[9] But the argument is incomplete. It is incomplete because, due to the use, above, of the word "reasonable" in "all reasonable precautions," and of the word "some" in "some endangering behavior," it is not immediately evident that contraceptive practices count as "reasonable precautions," nor is it clear that the reasonable precautions clause even applies to this case. This would follow from the fact that excuses of this kind, *pace* Austin[10] and perhaps Thomson as well, must be accompanied by a justification of the act in question.

A justification of an action can take several forms. An act can be justified by its high probability of producing some great good. Scientists, for example, might be justified in endangering the public if their experiments promised to produce some beneficial results. On the other hand, an act might be justified by some overriding obligation. A government agent might be justified in some action that endangers innocent people, say discharging her revolver in a crowd, if she is attempting to prevent the theft of some nuclear materials left in her charge. It is still possible to do these things negligently or recklessly, but, if all reasonable precautions are taken, then, even if others are endangered, the actors have not violated their duty to act responsibly and, therefore, have not assumed a new obligation by so acting.

This point is incorporated into legal theory through its developed concept of "negligence." To find someone guilty of negligence, several factors have to be weighed, including (1) the magnitude of the risk an action involves, (2) the value of the thing put at risk, "the principle object," (3) the value of the object or act for the sake of which the risk was incurred, "the collateral object," (4) the probability that the collateral object can be attained though the act, and (5) the probability of attaining the collateral object through a different route.[11] The reason that the law considers these factors is easily understood. Most acts involve risks to third parties. It is often difficult or perhaps impossible to reduce these risks to zero. Moreover, because it is always possible to make an action marginally safer at increasingly greater cost, to require that all risks be reduced to some finitely small "lowest possible level" would be to make all actions infinitely expensive. Thus, in most cases, to require "absolute safety," or even the greatest technically possible safety, is to place an impossible burden on the actor. Given this, the determination of acceptable risk must be a complex project that necessarily involves appeals to such moral factors as the relative value of competing goals and the character of the various competing actions, as well as the technical assessment of the probability that an act will achieve its intended end or cause unintended harm. However, if acceptable risks are to be evaluated relative to these factors, then so, too, must risk-reducing precautions. Consequently, the validity of a "reasonable precaution" excuse must also be a function of these factors. Therefore, the strength of these excuses is, *ceteris paribus*, inversely related to the moral wickedness of the act that incurs the risk. Precautions that would not count as reasonable in the normal course of events may be reasonable if the risk-incurring action has a high moral value.[12] Conversely, normal precautions will not be reasonable if the risk-incurring act is itself immoral.

Returning to the case at hand: in order to determine whether a woman has, by engaging in sex, undertaken an obligation to the fetus that was conceived as a result of contraceptive failure, we must know several things. First, we must know something about the encounter in question and something about the participants, such as the role, if any, of coercion and the ages and mental states of the participants. Second, we must know what precautions were taken to prevent conception. Finally, and most importantly, we must determine the moral character of the act that produced the fetus, for it is on this that the validity of proposed excuses, as well as the need for excuses, will depend. It is only through an evaluation of these factors that a determination of the morality of abortion can be made, because it is only thorough such a process that the effective rights of the various parties can be determined.

4.

I will not continue this argument. If the argument is correct, the morality of abortion is, at times and in part, a function of the moral character of sexual intercourse. There are a lot of loose ends to be attended to for the argument to be complete. I have said nothing, for example, about competing obligations and little about the limits of liability. Moreover, the argument depends on many unargued for and highly questionable assumptions, such as the assumption of the personhood of the fetus and the assumption of the "negative" theory of rights used by Thomson. I will not argue for these points here.

The conclusion of this argument has a number of consequences that might seem counterintuitive from the philosophical perspective that separates the question of the morality of abortion from the question of sexual morality. Given its assumptions, I think the argument is essentially sound. If so, it shows that the popular debate of this issue is not as mistaken as is otherwise thought. In particular, it shows that what is at issue in the abortion debate is not necessarily the death of the fetus, nor the woman's right to body with respect to the fetus, but sexual morality. The conclusion also shows that many seemingly irrelevant popular argument are not as irrelevant as they first appear. For example, the statements often made by antiabortionists about the supposed "irresponsibility" of the "promiscuous women" who seek abortions, as well as their desire to force these women to accept responsibility for their actions through a ban on abortions, follows from this conclusion, together with their negative evaluation of the morality of ("promiscuous") sexual behavior. The widely held opinion that women who are pregnant as a result of rape have strong ground for seeking an abortion also follows. Finally, a feminist position that the abortion debate is less a debate on the definition and relative value of early human life than a debate about sexual morality and its social control, also follows. Not all these positions can be correct, but they are united by the underlying logic of this argument.

Finally, if this argument is sound, it would be virtually impossible to say anything about the general morality of abortion. Whether an abortion violates an obligation would depend on a complex set of questions involving the circumstances surrounding each particular case. Therefore, if the argument is sound, *some* abortions would be morally permissible, and *some* would not. To make that determination, it would be necessary to investigate the circumstances of conception, and the circumstances would differ from case to case. As a result, laws restricting abortion would have to be extremely complex, and their enforcement would be extremely difficult. Moreover, if the argument is sound, ultimately the morality of abortion is a function of the morality of sexual behavior. Therefore, laws banning abortion would necessarily reflect this, often religiously based, moral judgment. If this is the case, however, then the feminist position, that antiabortion legislation is merely a covert way of imposing a religiously based sexual morality, gains a great deal of support. Moreover, because such legislation would, in effect, impose religiously grounded duties on women, it might well represent an unconstitutional violation of their religious freedom. Such legislation would, therefore, be unjust. In any case, however, to reach a critical understanding of the public debate over abortion and to develop an adequate philosophical understanding of the issue, the connection between the morality of abortion and sexual morality must be clearly understood.

Notes

1. See the essays contained in Joel Feinberg, ed., *The Problem of Abortion*, 2nd ed. (Belmont, Cal.: Wadsworth, 1984).
2. For a discussion of such theories, see Henry Shue, *Basic Rights* (Princeton: Princeton University Press, 1980), 35-64.
3. Judith Jarvis Thomson, "A Defense of Abortion," *Philosophy and Public Affairs* 1 (1971): 47-66, at 57.
4. *Ibid.*, 57-8.
5. See R. M. Hare, "Abortion and the Golden Rule," *Philosophy and Public Affairs* 4 (1975): 201-20.
6. Thomson, "A Defense of Abortion," 57-60.
7. *Ibid.*, 65.
8. American Law Institute, *Model Penal Code* (Philadelphia: American Law Institute, 1985), 236-44.
9. Thomson, "A Defense of Abortion," 60-6.
10. J. L. Austin, "A Plea for Excuses," *Proceedings of the Aristotelian Society* 58 (1957): 1-30.
11. Henry T. Terry, "Negligence," *Harvard Law Review* 29 (1915-16): 40-54, at 42-3.
12. *Ibid.*, 43.

Alan Soble (left) and Sára Szabó Soble (right)
(photograph: Nagy Tünde)

Alan Soble, author of "Comments on 'Abortion and Sexual Morality'"
Paper presented at the Society for the Philosophy of Sex and Love
during the
Eastern Division Meeting of The American Philosophical Association
Boston, Mass., 28 December 1983

Twenty-Four

MORE ON ABORTION AND SEXUAL MORALITY

Alan Soble

Roger Paden[1] wants to bring to our attention something that philosophers who write about abortion have been overlooking, namely, there is a logical connection between the morality of sexual conduct and the morality of abortion. Paden proposes to unpack this connection to improve the philosophical discussion of abortion.

Paden grants, at least to get the argument going, that the fetus is a person and therefore has a right to life. We have heard often enough by now that just because the fetus has a right to life, the fetus does not necessarily have a right to use a woman's body. The fetus's right to life does not mean that it has a right to use her body, because the right to life does not entail having a right to receive anything or everything one needs to be or remain alive. So, the right to life of the fetus does not entail that abortion is always morally wrong. Abortion is morally permissible as long as the fetus has not gained a right to use the body of the woman in which it exists.

Paden undertakes to determine the ways in which a fetus might come to have such a right. His idea is this: our doing something that puts a third party at risk creates obligations in us toward that third party. When a woman and a man engage in sexual activity together, they are putting a third party at risk, namely, the fetus that could exist as a result of their sexual activity. Now, just because the people are putting the fetus at risk, the fetus does not thereby have a right to use the woman's body. We are often permitted to do risky things without incurring obligations. However, the fetus does have that right unless or if certain conditions are met.

Paden appeals to our general obligation to act responsibly or to be morally responsible. On Paden's view, this obligation entails that if I injure you, I have an obligation to make amends, or if I break a duty to you, I should minimize the harm that befalls you, or if I act negligently toward you, I have an obligation to limit your suffering. Further, the obligation to act responsibly entails that I should not act negligently in the first place.

This general obligation to be responsible does not entail, even though Paden thinks it does, that the *particular* obligation a mother has to the fetus is not to abort. If a mother has a duty to the fetus to limit its suffering, this duty might be satisfied by early abortion, by making sure the fetus dies without gaining consciousness, and painlessly, rather than by not aborting. Further, the general obligation to be responsible must mean that the mother should take into account all the features of her situation, including her responsibilities toward other people. If the mother does this, it does not follow that she must surrender her body to the fetus. Her own needs (her health, for example) and the needs of her dependents and of other significantly affected persons, count for something.

Note another implication. If, along with Paden, we portray sexual activity as risky business toward a possible fetus, we should also say that sexual activity is similarly risky toward the woman for medical, psychological, social, and economic reasons. I am not sure we can make sense of the idea that a woman, by putting herself at risk, has obligations toward herself. But at least the man, by engaging in sex with the woman and thereby putting her at risk, has obligations to her. For him to be morally responsible might mean, then, that he must take responsibility for contraception, in order to protect her from harm, and that if *his* precautions fail, he has an obligation to help and support her in obtaining an abortion, that is, to restore her to her *original* state. If *his* precautions fail, there is no sense holding the woman responsible to the fetus; on Paden's view, it is the person who puts another person at risk who has the obligation to limit or minimize the harm that befalls that person.

Let us proceed to the conditions that negate the connection between engaging in sex and the fetus's coming to have the right to use the woman's body. As a result of his considering these conditions, Paden's central thesis emerges, that the morality of abortion depends on the morality of sexual activity. I do not think I misrepresent Paden's view by stating it this way: engaging in sexual activity grants to a possible fetus the right to use the woman's body (because, roughly, she put it at risk),[2] unless

1. the woman was forced to engage in that sexual activity,
2. the woman was incompetent at the time of the sexual activity,
3. the woman did not know that the sexual activity was putting a possible fetus at risk, or
4. reasonable precaution was taken to prevent putting a possible fetus at risk.

If the woman was raped, or was mentally imbalanced, or for some reason did not know that sexual activity leads to pregnancy, her engaging in sexual activity does not count as her voluntarily or knowingly putting the fetus at risk, and so does not count as her granting to the fetus the right to use her body. Furthermore, if reasonable precautions were taken to avoid risk to a possible fetus, by the employment of some reliable contraceptive device, then again the woman has not granted a right to the fetus to use her body.

It is the fourth negativing condition that yields Paden's thesis that the morality of abortion is a function of sexual morality. Paden argues that "reasonable precautions" negative responsibility only when the activity that creates a risk is a justifiable activity. If so, his thesis is that reasonable precautions negate the fetus's right to use the woman's body only if the sexual activity that resulted in the existence of the fetus was morally permissible. Paden's thesis entails that some (but not all) questions about the morality of abortion cannot be settled unless questions of sexual morality are settled. In particular, if an occurrence of sexual activity is morally wrong, then using reliable contraception does not negate the fetus's right to the woman's body: "normal precautions will not be reasonable if the risk-incurring act is itself immoral" (235).

Paden's thesis strikes me as strange. It seems to imply that persons who engage in sexual intercourse when they should not have a burden to bear, namely sustaining a fetus, and they have this burden because their sexual activity was morally wrong. This seems to follow from his thesis apart from the question of which sexual activities are the morally permissible ones. Paden's thesis suggests that those who engage in morally illicit sex, and women in particular, are to be punished by being saddled with the obligation to sustain the fetus. Turn this around: the only fetuses, of the ones that are conceived despite contraceptive precautions, that have a right to the woman's body and, so, to live, are the ones conceived during morally illicit sex. That sounds bizarre. Why should the fate of the fetus depend, when precautions were taken, on whether its parents were saintly or, instead, engaging in mischief? And why are the fetuses that are saved the ones that are conceived accidentally during unspeakable practices?

Paden might reply that all he is doing is unpacking the logic of the popular position that asserts a connection between the morality of sexual behavior and the morality of abortion, and he is neither applauding the position nor passing judgment on it. But this response is unconvincing. After all, Paden's thesis is derived form the principle, the obligation to be morally responsible, which I believe he argued is true, that is, not merely a reconstruction of popular moral thought. ("The popular debate of this issue is not as mistaken as is otherwise thought" [235].) At any rate, Paden is not altogether successful in displaying the logic of the popular debate. We have already seen one way in which Paden's thesis does not illuminate the popular discussion of abortion. On Paden's view, the fetuses conceived during morally illicit sex are to be saved, while those conceived during morally proper sex may be aborted. But most antiabortionists, and even some proabortionists, insist that the status of the parents has no bearing on the question of the fate of the fetus. The fetus should not lose its life or have it saved because it happens to be the fetus conceived by a wiseacre, a scoundrel, a rapist, or a Mother Teresa. There is another failure of Paden's account to illuminate the popular debate. On Paden's view, abortion is wrong because and when sexual activity is wrong. But the popular connection between sexual morality and the morality of abortion is often exactly the reverse: sexual activity is wrong when it leads to abortion, or even to the chance of abortion, just because abortion is wrong.

It is the existence of one popular view (I mean: contraception is not a reasonable precaution against pregnancy; the only reasonable precaution is not engaging in sexual activity to begin with; hence sexual intercourse does grant the fetus the right to use the woman's body) that explains why some feminists sense that the antiabortionist program endeavors to control, reign in, the sexuality of women. Some conservatives have been looking for an alternative to attacking the sexuality of women directly, because that attack always threatens to end, as Paden recognizes, in metaphysical or religious obscurity. What the conservatives have come up with is a way to attack the sexuality of women indirectly, by attacking abortion. The wrongness of abortion, they say, is precisely the reason a woman should not engage in sex except in severely restricted circumstances. It is the grave wrongness of abortion that entails that sex is proper only within the context of a stable, supportive, monogamous marriage. And in that context, even when contraception is used, but fails, the woman is obligated to sustain the fetus.

The popular debate is more complex than this. Many conservatives worry, and some feminists agree, that the availability of abortion, rather than contributing to the sexual freedom of women, contributes to their continued exploitation by men, who are able to use women sexually without fearing that they will be tied down by obligations. The same complaint has been registered also about contraception: by separating sexual activity from its natural consequences, both abortion and contraception turn women into sex objects that can be and are used by men as pleasure generators.[3] It can be argued in defense of both, that without abortion and contraception women can be and have been used simply as baby generators. There seems to be not much to choose: women are used. This dimension of the popular debate, whether or in what ways abortion and contraception work for or against the freedom, sexual and otherwise, of women, is in need of further investigation.

Postscript (1995)

Stimulated by Paden's paper to think about these issues, I not too long ago stumbled on a Padenesque sense in which questions of the morality of abortion partially depend on sexual morality, broadly construed.

Judith Thomson seems to argue for the conclusion, that abortion when the use of some birth control technique (a reliable and reasonable precaution) fails is morally permissible, *because*, just as in the pregnancy-by-rape case, the woman has not issued an invitation to the fetus to use her body. Neither the woman pregnant by someone else's act of rape, nor the woman pregnant because her attempt to prevent pregnancy with reliable contraception has failed, has granted to the fetus a right to use her body. The woman who deliberately employs ordinarily effective contraception (say, the pill) is, in effect, telling any possible fetus, in advance, that it does not have a right to use her body. This, I think, is the point of one of Thomson's examples: we have put bars on the windows of our house, yet a passerby, an innocent person, falls into the house anyway. The fact that we put up the bars indicates that we were trying to keep people out by using reasonable precautions; the innocent person who falls in anyway has no right to remain.[4] It is our house; we own it.[5]

Allow me to embellish the example. We left our house, on vacation, for a few weeks. But we were careless: several windows were left wide open and the door was not locked; we made no arrangements for newspapers and mail to be collected by a neighbor; the house was perfectly dark at night, every night. When we come home, we discover that burglars had entered our house and cleaned us out. This is a clear case, I think, of contributory negligence. Our being burglarized was partially our own fault, both causally and morally. The burglars had no legal right to enter our house, but it is not an unfair stretch to say that, in effect, we recklessly issued an invitation: "see, here is our house, left unprotected." (Other examples are easy to imagine. I didn't lock my bike outside the library, thinking I'd be at the circulation desk only a minute. When I left the building much later, it was gone. Naturally. I "asked" for it.) By analogy, one might argue, the couple that engages in sexual intercourse without any contraceptive precautions is responsible for any fetus that results. At least, it is not possible to defend the permissibility of abortion in this case by arguing that they used reasonable precautions and so did not invite the fetus, did not grant it a right to use her body. For this fetus was recklessly invited.

The next time we leave our house, however, we take precautions: we have installed an electrified fence around the premises; we bought and trained a pack of dogs; a hired security service circles our property once an hour; and so forth. Nevertheless, as if they were going after the crown of St. Stephen, a band of burglars formulate a brilliant, elaborate plan, get inside our house, and clean us out. But now we can say that it was not in the least our fault. We did everything we could reasonably be expected to do to keep burglars out of our house, to prevent being burglarized. We told them, in advance, loudly and clearly, "stay away; you are not invited." By analogy, the couple that engages in sexual intercourse only when she has religiously taken her pills, or only when he wears a condom and she also inserts a diaphragm, do everything they can reasonably be expected to do to avoid pregnancy. Should she become pregnant despite these precautions, they are not at fault. They did not invite the fetus nor grant it a right to use her body; indeed, they tried to keep a fetus out of her uterus.

At this point, one of the conservatives I mentioned would ask: is it true that the couple did *everything* they could reasonably be expected to do, if they wanted to avoid pregnancy? Could they not have refrained from sexual intercourse altogether? Thomson provides a hint of an answer:

> Someone might argue that you are responsible . . . because after all you *could* have lived out your life with bare floors . . . or with sealed windows and doors. But this won't do—for by the same token anyone can avoid a pregnancy due to rape by having a hysterectomy, or anyway by never leaving home without a (reliable!) army.[6]

I will formulate this answer so that it ties our burglary example to the abortion case: if you believe that only by abstaining from sexual intercourse altogether, and not by employing reliable contraception, is a couple not responsible for her becoming pregnant (that is, only by not engaging in sexual intercourse does a couple not issue an invitation to a fetus or grant it a right to use her body), then "by the same token" you must also believe that only by not owning anything to keep in a house or by not having a house at all, and not by employing reliable contraburglary devices, are we not responsible for being burglarized (only by not owning furniture or a house to keep it in do we avoid inviting burglars to steal from us). But that second proposition is absurd, so by *modus tollens* the first must be false.

But why, exactly, is it absurd to think that I am not responsible for having my possessions stolen only by my not owning anything to begin with? The answer, I think, is that, first, I have a right to own things and, second, that unless my having a right to own things means that I am not responsible for their loss as long as I have taken reasonable precautions to conserve them, and that others must keep their hands off as long as I have done so, the right to own things would be a useless, worthless right. By analogy, then, if it is false that a couple avoids being responsible for a pregnancy only when they eschew sexual intercourse, and not also by taking reasonable contraceptive precautions, it is false because, first, they have a right to engage in sexual intercourse (*perhaps* because such a right is essential for the formation and maintenance of loving relationships,[7] or *perhaps* because the sexual urge is too psychologically difficult to resist) and, second, this right is worthless unless it entails that taking reasonable precautions negatives responsibility.

It is in this sense, then, that the morality of abortion partially depends on sexual morality: when a couple employs reliable contraceptive precautions, their right to engage in sex trumps a possible fetus's right to life. The right to engage in sexual intercourse is powerful enough, in such a situation, to deny the fetus a right to use the woman's body even though the fetus needs it for life itself. But at the same time that a powerful right to sex would in this fashion justify abortion, those who think we have no right to sex, or that this right is a weak or unimportant one, could continue to condemn abortion (when contraception fails, if not more generally). In both cases, there is a link between sexual morality and the morality of abortion.

Notes

1. Roger Paden, "Abortion and Sexual Morality," this volume, 229-36; page references to this essay are supplied in the text.

2. Paden claims that "sexual intercourse is an act that . . . can lead to the creation of another person . . . [and] result in placing that person in a potentially dangerous position" (232). I don't get it. The act that creates X also puts X at risk, by making X exist?—as if X would have been perfectly safe if X did not exist.

3. See the "conservative feminist" Sidney Callahan, "Abortion and the Sexual Agenda," *Commonweal*, 25 April 1986, 232-8, and the "unmodified feminists" Catharine A. MacKinnon (*Feminism Unmodified* [Cambridge, Mass.: Harvard University Press, 1987], 144-5; *Toward a Feminist Theory of the State* [Cambridge; Mass.: Harvard University Press, 1989], 190) and Andrea Dworkin (*Right-Wing Women* [New York: Perigee, 1983], 103).

4. Judith Jarvis Thomson, "A Defence of Abortion," in Peter Singer, ed., *Applied Ethics* (Oxford: Oxford University Press, 1986), 37-56, at 48.

5. *Ibid.*, 43.

6. *Ibid.*, 49.

7. See Ellen Willis, "Abortion: Is a Woman a Person?" in *Beginning to See the Light* (New York: Knopf, 1981), 205-11. For discussion, see my *Sexual Investigations* (New York: New York University Press, 1996), 20-24.

Russell Vannoy

Author of "Can Sex Express Love?"
Paper presented at the Society for the Philosophy of Sex and Love
during the
Western Division Meeting of The American Philosophical Association
Cincinnati, Ohio, 26 April 1984

Twenty-Five

CAN SEX EXPRESS LOVE?

Russell Vannoy

1.

Two strangers, known to each other only as X and Y, meet at X's apartment solely for the purpose of enjoying a lengthy sexual act. Both X and Y are self-sufficient, highly independent, and have no desire to be in love with anyone. They are, however, altruistic, and each does his or her best to please the other sexually. They are also, sexually speaking, uninhibited, outgoing types who enjoy expressing sexually whatever feelings they happen to have at the moment.

Unless "intimacy" is just a code word for love, one could say that their sex is intimate in that they are open to each other during the sexual act both physically and psychologically, even though they are not in love. Indeed, they would argue that love often inhibits rather than fosters intimacy. This would be true, for example, if X and Y happened to be of the same sex but were also married to opposite sex members of a conservative religious group, people who would never accept disclosure of their mate's sexual preference.

Their sexual act is preceded by caresses that express trust, sexual desire, and a certain tenderness; for they are grateful that each has chosen to give the other his or her time and body for a sexual encounter. Furthermore, their sex is passionate: it reveals a passionate love of or joy in sharing a sexual experience in the generous, intimate way described above.

X and Y later decide to continue to meet on a weekly basis for more of the same, but for nothing else. Since they prefer to express themselves sexually, they seldom talk and they show no desire to know one another beyond their sexual encounters. This is not because they are self-centered loners who are incapable of friendship or love; they simply share few interests beyond the one described here. X and Y would not wish to disguise their sexual encounters by coyly referring to themselves as "lovers" or by claiming they were having a "love affair." They believe that the term "lovers" should refer only to persons who are in love and who desire to share their lives together.

On one occasion, X did ask if Y felt that their sexual experiences would be any different if they were to fall in love. Y heatedly denied this, arguing that sex can at most express a couple's love of having sex together, their respect for each other's feelings, and perhaps even love of each other's bodies. But can it express being in love with a total person, or express some unique emotion that only lovers feel, or express their desire to share their lives beyond having sex together? "Never," Y exclaimed. "That is beyond what sex in any form can do, no matter how generous, tender, trusting, prolonged, and intimate it might be. The only thing that expresses love is the totality of the experiences two persons share through whatever time their love endures. No part of sex can possibly express all or even a major part of what is implied by the phrase *being in love*."

2.

Y's proclamation that sex cannot express love is flamboyant, but could it be true? Those who claim that sex can express love speak a great deal about kissing and caressing, tenderness, trust, mutual giving, and something vaguely called "intimacy." Curiously, very little is said about how one is to use sex to express some of the less lovely features of certain forms of love: conflict, jealousy, heartache, possessiveness.

If, however, one focuses on the "nicer" love-expressing qualities (tenderness, kissing, giving, and the like), such things are not found solely between those who are in love. Such acts or attitudes can also be found in sex between friends and acquaintances, between those who are merely infatuated, or even between a pair of altruistic, kindly, and uninhibited strangers like X and Y. To claim that such acts, if they possess the traditional love-expressing features, thereby prove that the friends or strangers are in love, is at least doubtful in the former case and absurd in the case of strangers, even if they, like X and Y, go on to have a prolonged affair that mimics the continuity of sex between lovers.

Roger Taylor might take exception to the claim that X and Y are not in love. He writes:

> If a man's love is to be wholly explained by his sexual desire for someone, then it must be that his sexual desire is more constant and demanding than that of the man who just sexually desires. Surely we would have no hesitation in affirming that the person who constantly sexually craves, and is sexually concerned with another, is in love with the other.[1]

Even if it were true, however, that X and Y constantly craved each other's bodies (which they do not do), it would by no means follow that they were in love with each other as persons. Nor is it true that X and Y are having an "as if" love relationship, in which two strangers enjoying sex either confuse romantic passion with sexual passion, or else knowingly allow themselves to temporarily act as if they were in love in order to savor what they think are the added benefits of sex that expresses love. X and Y are doing none of these things; their sex is generous and expressive simply because X and Y are generous and expressive persons.

3.

Let us now examine Y's claim that sex cannot express love, or at least not all that is implied by the claim that one is in love. Y would perhaps concede that sex can express the sexual desire, trust, generosity, and intimacy that are found in some forms of love. But Y's point is that something crucial is missing, since these things can be found in Y's relationship with X. Nor is sex even necessary to express things like trust, tenderness, generosity and intimacy. Janice Moulton notes, for example, that trust can be better expressed by opening a joint bank account with one's beloved.[2] Apart from questions of motive and context, the only thing that is uniquely sexual about sex vis-a-vis expressing love is that of giving and receiving sexual sensations. This by itself, however, is by no means limited to sex between those who are in love.

Even Robert Solomon, the foremost proponent of the view that sex is primarily a form of communication of emotions and attitudes, seems to agree here. He writes: "Love . . . is not best expressed sexually, for its sexual expression is indistinguishable from the expressions of a number of other attitudes," by which he means things like tenderness and trust, mutual recognition and "being-with," which are "expressed by body language almost essentially."[3] Solomon, however is merely denying that love can be *best* expressed sexually, not that sex cannot express love at all. Janice Moulton goes farther, but perhaps still not far enough. She writes: "More than [sexual] gestures must be employed to communicate such feelings as love, trust, hatred, shame, dependence, and possessiveness. I doubt that jealousy . . . can be communicated by sexual body language at all."[4]

Moulton, however, should have doubted whether love itself, and not just jealousy (a frequent enough concomitant of love) can be expressed sexually in a way that distinguishes it from the affair between X and Y. Moulton's claim that more than sexual gestures must be used to express love is doubtlessly true as far as it goes; but her comment suggests that something else, perhaps a sincere verbal declaration of love, would suffice to make sexual gestures an expression of love. (There is nothing, for example, about a sexual act in and of itself that would show that the act was a *sincere* expression of love.) Y's radical proclamation, however, rejects even this interpretation of what Moulton might have had in mind.

4.

Let us return to the case of our two altruistic strangers whose sexual behavior might be identical to that of two long time lovers. Why do we say that only the latter sexual act is an expression of being in love? One might argue that it is the context that is different in the two cases, that a sexual act's being shared by two lovers as a part of their relationship makes it an expression of love, whereas there is no such context in the case of X and Y. But not everything that is a shared experience between two lovers is an act of love: carrying out the garbage together might be an experience some lovers share, but they would hardly regard it as an expression of love.

Even if the shared experience is a joyful one, such as winning a doubles tennis match together, it would still not ordinarily be viewed by them as an expression of their love for each other, but only, perhaps, as a shared expression of their love of tennis. Winning a game together might intensify their love and bring them closer together. Since enjoying good sex together can also have the same result, it is possible to erroneously conclude that their sex expressed love because it might have intensified their love.

One might, however, argue that all lovers ought to regard their sexual acts as expressions of love since sex, unlike tennis or carrying out the garbage, resides in a cultural context that holds that sex between lovers is an expression of their love. If, for example, one lived in a society where it was the custom that generosity, intimacy, tenderness, and the like were restricted only to those who were in love, while sex with anyone else was expected to be marked by coldness and exploitation, then one would at least have some basis for claiming that sex between lovers expressed love in that culture. But the possibility of sex expressing love with anyone in such a culture is doubtful. For if brutal exploitation were the order of the day for everyone except one's lover, it is unlikely that anyone would suddenly become sweetness and light when he or she had sex with a "loved" one in such a society. Generosity, for example, is not something one switches on and off in that manner.

In the case of our own culture, furthermore, it is (or once was) part of our sexist cultural context that a man can demand and get sex from his wife whenever he pleases. It would be ludicrous to say that his sex is a valid expression of love, when love presumably means at least treating one's partner's feelings with respect. Her surrendering to him in a sacrificial way when she is in no mood for sex has, however, traditionally been viewed as a true act of love, even though for her it might not have been a sexual experience at all, and thus hardly a case of a *sexual* expression of love in her terms.

Indeed, the concept of sacrifice, which is commonly considered by most cultures to be the supreme example of an act of love, has no relevance to sex at all, even if the sacrifice is equal for both partners. Sexual intercourse is either a joyous shared experience or else it is nothing more than an odd form of calisthenics. The sort of equality that is relevant to sex and that reflects the equal respect of lovers (or of altruistic nonlovers) for each other is equality of enjoyment over the long term, not equality of sacrifice. Thus, if sacrifice is the supreme example of an expression of love, sex can never meet that particular criterion, nor should it.

A nonsacrificial cultural expression of love would be that of exchanging rings, or simply kissing or rubbing noses, as a way of celebrating one's love. To view sex, however, as a celebration of love based on the cultural analogy of, say, exchanging rings would reduce the spontaneity of sex to a rule governed ritual. (The perfunctory goodbye kiss of a bored or distracted mate leaving for work is a familiar example of what ritual can do to passion.)

5.

If, then, the notion of cultural context cannot be used to clarify what a sexual expression of love is, and thus answer our earlier problem of how to distinguish sex between lovers and sex between X and Y, what will? One might argue that the key factor that is missing in the case of X and Y is an intention to express one's being in love, even though behaviorally the acts between lovers and strangers might be identical. It cannot, however, be the case that merely intending to express love means that the expression of that intention is thereby an act of love. Some rapists have the odd notion that they are expressing love for their victims, and the same is true of many of the sexist husbands mentioned earlier. Nor does it help to speak of a shared intention to express love if each partner then proceeds to perform the act in a way that shows little consideration for the other's wishes. What, then, is the criterion for a valid intention to express love?

It seems clear that it must be an intention that is expressed by an act that has some of the traditional qualities like trust and a desire to please one's partner in a nonsacrificial way. The latter intention might or might not include the culturally approved traits of tenderness, kissing, caressing, and emotional warmth. (Some lovers prefer to please each other in a playful sadomasochistic way, for example.) But then it becomes evident that the criteria presupposed for the fulfillment of a valid love-expressing intention can also be fulfilled by sex between friends and in the sex between X and Y. Thus the concept of intention, like that of cultural context, seems to leave us tentatively back at square one in terms of the problem of distinguishing so called love-expressing sex from the sex X and Y enjoy. Furthermore, the criterion for an act's being a successful expression of love in sexual terms is sexual pleasure. An act that fails this test is not a sexual expression of love; it was only an unsuccessful attempt to express love sexually. But sexual pleasure is, once again, the same criterion for an act's being sexual for X and Y.

In summary, there must be more than a mere desire or intention to express love (verbally stated or not) for a sexual act to be an act of love when one attempts to fulfill that intention. Even if a valid intention to express love is carried out in the proper way, it is still true that if an intention to express love is to make any difference at all to the sexual act other than perhaps merely allowing us to *label* it as an "act of love," one would think that would be something special about the act over and above what X and Y also do.

Even those who believe that sex can express love ordinarily reserve the phrase "expression of love" to describe an act that stands out in some way from all the other activities that lovers and those who are not in love do together. They would claim that the phrase "stands out in some way" is to be explained in terms of going out of one's way to do something for or with one's lover that one would ordinarily be unable or unwilling to do for or with a mere acquaintance or stranger. On this criterion, simply sharing an ordinary meal together would not usually be an expression of love, while it would be an act of love to invite one's mate to an expensive candlelight and wine dinner in order to celebrate one's first anniversary together. (Regrettably, conventional wisdom often uses this criterion to sanction the total giving of oneself to a lover, while coldly exploiting those whom one does not love.)

Thus the truism that one and the same physical act can mean different things, depending on the purpose of the agent, is not really relevant as a way of distinguishing the otherwise identical sexual acts of two lovers from those of X and Y. For an expression of love cannot simply be described as "one and the same physical act," such that a mere intention to express love would then somehow provide a way of distinguishing the two cases we have been considering. (The intention would be relevant in distinguishing a genuine from an insincere expression of love, where the sexual acts might be identical.)

In the case of rape, for example, there is something special about the act that proves that it could not be an act of love even if it were intended to be so: the violence that is committed against an unwilling victim. The unique trait that can be found only in sexual acts that do fulfill a valid intention to express love (as defined above) is, however, thus far a mystery. Some lovers do reserve some part of the act as an expression of love by refusing to do that act with anyone else. (Kissing is the most common example.) To reserve merely some part of the act is, however, a lovers' trap. For some lovers will then feel no qualms about committing adultery, if no kissing was involved. It was "just physical." Plain sex with a nonlover is, they think, so radically different from making love that it lies outside the loveworld and is irrelevant to one's vows. The other lover does not, however, ordinarily see it that way. He or she will demand that any sex be exclusively theirs alone.

Even if two lovers refused to perform the entire sexual act with anyone else, it would not follow that their sexual acts expressed fidelity. X and Y, for example, might refuse to have sex with anyone else simply because they are thrilled with what they have in a purely sexual way and feel no need for variety. (Many lovers who disdain what they view as antiquated vows of fidelity give a similar reason for exclusivity.)

To be sure, exclusivity is commonly seen as a requirement for lovers; for nonlovers, it is usually not. Yet this is irrelevant to the claim that sexual exclusivity expresses love. For lovers do not merely feel that their reasons for exclusive sex are different, as if they needed to infer a distinct intention from an act that any sexual partners might perform—and even if it is done only by X and Y. Lovers claim that they are showing their love or making love, an *act* that is uniquely theirs and that embodies an intention or emotion that is unique to lovers. If sex is embodied consciousness, then it must embody what they are conscious of—their love of someone who is (they think) unique and irreplaceable.

This ideal (or, at least, this romantic ideal) of performing a distinctive act is, however, impossible to attain. X and Y can match them in every respect in terms of the act itself; even kissing between strangers who have one-night stands is common in Hispanic culture. The inadequacy of body language to express love in a distinctive way is also shown in the familiar confusion of sex with love by those who think they have found love when someone expresses a desire for sex.

6.

One might hold that the kind of analysis that has been used thus far fails to consider important aspects of the sexual experience other than just the act that supposedly expresses love. One could note that the emotion of love, and the awareness that there is a desire to express this emotion, makes the sexual experience of two persons who are expressing love very different from that of X and Y. It would be as if two couples were having coffee: X and Y are taking theirs black, the lovers have added cream. Both couples are drinking coffee, but the flavor differs. Thus, one might hold that a sexual expression of love would be one that includes a unique sex-with-love experience, even though its physical manifestation might not be unique.

Is this claim about distinctive motives and emotions really valid? A specific intention to express love is not, I suspect, what is usually on the minds of lovers when they are sexually aroused; their motive is simply a desire to enjoy some good sex. A couple would ordinarily be concerned about motives only when there was some doubt as to whether or not they still loved each other. (Whether a young seducer is expressing love or lust is another example in which motives might be relevant.)

One might, however, hold that love is a kind of background causal motive of their sexual desire, in that our couple would never have had sex together unless they had loved each other. Putting aside the puritanical tradition that believes one must love someone before one is permitted to enjoy him or her sexually, the claim that they would never have found each other sexually desirable unless they had loved each other would insultingly suggest that they were not at all sexually desirable in and of themselves. This would clearly violate the lovers' claim that they love each other just as they are, and that their sex expresses love rather than blind infatuation.

We must now examine the further notion that there is a distinctive "love" emotion that is present when sex expresses love. One difficulty with this claim is that many lovers do not report having ever experienced the sort of ecstatic emotion that Robert Solomon eulogizes.[5] Suppose, for example, that one defined love in terms of a context of reciprocal awareness, acceptance, and appreciation that is created by two persons, in which each fully and freely manifests himself or herself. This contextualist definition of love does not necessarily require that one speak of special emotions, but only of a special kind of continuing relationship. A sexual act in this context would not, however, necessarily differ in and of itself from that of X and Y, and the previous criticism of the nonuniqueness of sexual acts of love would also apply here, as will some of the criticisms given below.

But what of sexual acts that are said to express a uniquely ecstatic and inner "love" emotion that creates a kind of mystical sense of oneness found only between two sexual partners who are in love? Describing the phenomenology of sexual experience is risky business, but I will offer a few suggestions that might invalidate that claim. Consider, for example, the concept of embodiment, in which two sexual partners gradually surrender conscious control of their movements to the direction of sexual impulses. In existentialist language, "consciousness becomes body." The couple's awareness of who they are, where they are, whether they are in love, or even what sex they are, is pushed to the edge of consciousness and might be blotted out entirely during orgasm. Both the claim that there is a distinctive love emotion throughout the sexual act, and the claim that sex expresses love because one is aware of the special context in which it occurs, are severely damaged by the embodiment experience. If one tries to find room for love and its context by turning to the caresses that precede embodiment, it is common for lovers themselves to distinguish between an opening "love" caress that is not very sexual and subsequent sexual caresses that are primarily intended to arouse.

If one analyzes a sexual act in this fashion, the aspects of the experience that are primarily sexual do not show any significant link with love, nor do they show any way of differentiating the sexual experience of two lovers from the sexual experience of X and Y. Both couples can use sexual caresses and both can become embodied. Both couples can have a feeling of oneness during embodiment even though the individuals of both couples might be enveloped in his or her own pleasure at the climax of embodiment (say, orgasm).

Suppose, however, that two lovers share a sexual experience that is not so deeply sensual as the one described above. Sex that consists largely of caresses, for example, might allow for love and sensuality to have equal billing throughout the act. In this case, one might hold that sex expresses love in the sense that two lovers can give each other a unique kind of cream-in-the-coffee sexual experience that X and Y could never share.

It is not, however, true that only those who are in love ever feel the emotional aspect of love. Consider the case of a teenage boy sitting in a movie theater watching a matinee idol passionately kissing the heroine. He is overcome by her beauty and fancies that he is the one who is making love to her. An intoxicating feeling of love comes over him and lasts throughout the movie until the lights go on and reality returns to obliterate his infatuation. These emotions are also sometimes felt by strangers like X and Y during sex: they exclaim "I love you" repeatedly, even though they might depart forever when the act is over, and they are not necessarily confusing love with lust.

The emotions described above do not, of course, have the continuity or basis in reality of those shared by persons who are ordinarily described as being "truly in love." The emotions of infatuation in examples like these have no past and no future beyond the immediate sexual experience. Yet the emotional experiences they contain need be no different from that of two romantic persons who are in love, that is, those who are just the sort of persons who are most likely to insist that love and sex have equal billing throughout the act. It is, after all, only the qualitative "feel" of the immediate sexual experience that is relevant here. No sexual experience in and of itself has a past or a future, and each one is in some way different from all the rest. That a sexual experience *qua* experience has a kind of timeless, self-contained quality is admitted by lovers and strangers alike, however much the experience might be indirectly linked to the broader context of their lives. One would not wish to hold, for example, that the oceanic state of oneness that is found in both romantic passion and in purely sensual passion should extend outward into one's everyday life. The temporary extinction of self-awareness has its Dionysian beauty during the sexual act, but neither lovers, nor X and Y, would ordinarily wish to extinguish their individuality permanently. The claim, therefore, that two lovers can express their love by giving each other a unique kind of sexual experience that is qualitatively different from what any two nonlovers could have, is simply not true.

I conclude that Y's original pessimistic proclamation about the capability of sex to express what the term "love" implies, is largely valid. If love involves the continuity of a shared life together and a love of the other's thoughts, character, talents, wit, charm, and the like, instead of just love of his or her body, then to think that a sexual act could or should express all or even some of these things is absurd. It would be as if someone had just passed his final oral exam for the Ph.D., had won a million dollar lottery, but had also just learned that his wife had died and had later met an extraterrestrial being in his backyard. One could no more find a way of expressing this complex set of emotions (and certainly not by "body language") than one could find a sexual means of expressing even a major part of what the phrase "being in love" implies. Were one to hold that this kind of criticism puts an unreasonable burden on what a sexual act (or any act) must do in order to express love, I would be content to hold that the impossibility of finding any difference that distinguishes the sexual experience of two lovers from what two strangers could conceivably experience, is sufficient proof for the claim that sex cannot express love.

One might, however, still claim that sex should at least attempt to express love, for it would otherwise have no meaning. But perhaps sex, like MacLeish's poem, should not mean, but simply be.

Reply to Edward Johnson's 1984 Commentary

I am most grateful to Professor Johnson for his interesting and perceptive comments on my paper and my book.

Y claimed that love is too complex a phenomenon for sex to adequately express. Johnson argues that Y's requirements for an act to be said to be an expression of something are too severe. Philip Koch's article, "Expressing Emotion," also notes that "an expression typically (necessarily?) presents only part of the intentional complex the emotion involves."[6]

However, when an act is unable to express some crucial aspect of this "intentional complex," Y has a point. Being in love, for example, is to be in love with someone; this traditionally has meant being in love with something more than his or her body. It is also true, as Solomon notes, that romantic love always has its reasons.[7] Further, some of these reasons might be more important than others as reasons why one is in love with someone. To say that one must love every aspect of the beloved equally or even that one must love every aspect of the beloved at all is untenable. (As I used to say to my lovers, "Love of me what you can and try to endure the rest.") *What* is loved about a particular person also gives a distinctive flavor to the inner complex of emotions, desires, and thoughts I have that constitute my state of "being in love" that I am trying to express.

Suppose that the primary reasons I love someone are certain inner qualities she possesses. Certainly the primary reason is not always his or her attractive body; think of Jackie Kennedy's love for Aristotle Onassis. Suppose that I am in love with a physically unattractive person because I am primarily (though not exclusively) erotically fascinated with his or her philosophical genius (for example, the young men who were charmed by Socrates) or because he or she is a great moral crusader against social injustice. How do I express my love for these qualities sexually? I can caress a beautiful body to express my fascination for its sex appeal but how do I caress the brain of Socrates?

And what would my partner think if I told her that what turned me on sexually about her was primarily her philosophical genius, power being such an aphrodisiac and all? I suspect she would be offended by such a remark; in the bedroom we want our lovers to be sexually aroused by our bodies, regardless of what other qualities they find appealing. One might claim that love transforms even an unattractive body into something beautiful, because it is seen as an incarnation of one's inner charms. Yet the sexual desires of X and Y can also perform this transformation. When Henry Kissinger claimed that power is the ultimate aphrodisiac, he was not saying that an aphrodisiac has any necessary connection with love. Even if a romantic claimed that love is the only true aphrodisiac and that the beloved's body incarnates her passion, he would still have to show how that love can be expressed in a distinctive way. Nor would either Kissinger or Romeo be happy with what is implied by incarnation—that their bodies merely appear to be beautiful or sexy because an aura of power or romance envelopes them. So we are back to Y's claim that sex can express love only for the *body*, and the latter reason is not ordinarily meant by being in love with a *person*.

Another point Johnson raises concerns the claim in my book, *Sex Without Love*, that the contradictions of romantic love spoil sex with love.[8] In this paper, another underlying contradiction is at work. In the bedroom we primarily want our bodies to be loved and sexually desired for their own attractiveness. Yet we also believe that love should occur in spite of or at least not primarily because of how we look, given the familiar claim that the love of inner qualities should be the deciding factor if love is to be more than infatuation. But how does sex express love of these inner qualities in a distinctive way?

A final dilemma confronts the claim that sex can express love. If sex expresses love, this makes sex a means to an end. Sexual desire is, however, firm in defending its own autonomy. Those who claim that sex is a social construct never explain how (say) homosexuality can occur in a society that discourages it at every turn. The same is true of the relation between sex and love. The sex-world will allow love to enter only if it deigns to eroticize love's qualities and the beloved's charms. This might or might not occur, regardless of how deep one's love is.

Lovers, for example, often find themselves losing sexual interest in their partners, however much they wish that not to occur. Or one might treat one's beloved as a princess in everyday life, yet turn into a monster in the bedroom, if one has eroticized aggression instead of tenderness. One can try to change, but there is no guarantee that one's sex-world will allow success. Even if one feels that love is the ultimate aphrodisiac, viewing one's beloved enveloped in the throes of his or her own orgasm (and losing sexual interest thereafter) leaves one with the suspicion that the act was primarily about sexual desire achieving its own aims.

One might, of course, reject the claim that a sexual expression of love involves viewing sex merely as a means to love's fulfillment. Romantics, for example, might hold that sex and love fuse into a harmonious unity when lovemaking occurs. But if they become indistinguishable, how could one claim that there is one thing, sex, that expresses something else, love?

Notes

1. Roger Taylor, "Sexual Experiences," in Alan Soble, ed., *The Philosophy of Sex*, 1st ed. (Totowa, N.J.: Littlefield, Adams, 1980), 59-75, at 72-3.

2. Janice Moulton, "Sexual Behavior: Another Position," in Soble, *Philosophy of Sex*, 1st ed., 110-18, at 116; 2nd ed. (1991), 63-71, at 69.

3. Robert Solomon, "Sexual Paradigms," in Soble, *Philosophy of Sex*, 1st ed., 89-98, at 97; 2nd ed., 53-62, at 61.

4. Moulton, "Sexual Behavior," in Soble, *Philosophy of Sex*, 1st ed., 118, n. 8; 2nd ed., 71, n. 8.

5. Robert Solomon, *Love: Emotion, Myth, and Metaphor* (Buffalo: Prometheus, 1990), 34-40, 125-30.

6. Philip J. Koch, "Expressing Emotions," *Pacific Philosophical Quarterly* 64:2 (1983): 176-91, at 187.

7. Solomon, *Love*, 163.

8. Russell Vannoy, *Sex Without Love: A Philosophical Exploration* (Buffalo: Prometheus, 1980), 129-47.

Edward Johnson

Author of "Last Tango in Buffalo"
Paper presented at the Society for the Philosophy of Sex and Love
during the
Western Division Meeting of The American Philosophical Association
Cincinnati, Ohio, 26 April 1984

Twenty-Six

LOVESEXPRESSED

Edward Johnson

If sex cannot express love, what can? "The only thing that expresses love," says Russell Vannoy through his persona Y, "is the totality of the experiences two persons share through whatever time their love endures" (247-8).[1] This view demands too much from the notion of expression. Many ordinary things are taken to be expressions of love: a poem, a gesture, a look, and so forth. To say that no poem ever expressed love (since no poem is the totality of the experiences two persons share) would be hard to defend. Nor would it be plausible to reply that sex, unlike a poem, is not capable of expressing anything. Vannoy concedes that "sex can express the sexual desire, trust, generosity, and intimacy that are found in some forms of love." But, he adds, "something crucial is missing, since these things can be found in Y's relationship with X" (248-9). What is missing appears most clearly when we remember that two persons who are no longer in love may still continue to desire each other sexually. These ex-lovers are in much the same situation as X and Y, "two altruistic strangers whose sexual behavior might be identical to that of two long time lovers" (249), but who are not lovers, according to Vannoy. About this scenario, which we might call "Last Tango in Buffalo," he says:

> the impossibility of finding any difference that distinguishes the sexual experience of two lovers from what two strangers could conceivably experience, is sufficient proof for the claim that sex cannot express love. (255)

The issue, then, seems not to be about expression, but about whether sex-with-love can be distinguished (*qua* sexual experience) from sex-without-love.

In his 1980 book *Sex Without Love*, Vannoy had defended sex-without-love as being as good as, in fact better than, sex-with-love.[2] So I worried for a while about whether apparent changes in vocabulary, between his book and his paper, expressed changes in doctrine. Finally, it occurred to me that the best way to understand Vannoy's paper was as a response to Robert Solomon.[3]

While Vannoy believes that sex is better without love, Solomon holds that sex is better with it. Solomon explicitly mentions Vannoy's position and implicitly rejects it.[4] He writes, for example, that

> If one thinks of sex, as many do, as a merely pleasurable "natural" activity, the significance of sex will evade us, and the connection between sex and love will remain either a mystery or a curiosity. But if we con-

> ceive of sex as *expression*—and not the expression of love alone—then its importance becomes more evident.[5]

The connection is made through the concept of *intimacy*, which, according to Solomon, "is essentially the experience of shared identity . . . for which sex provides the most readily available expression."[6] Solomon realizes that this fact, that sex is "our primary vehicle for intimacy," is not necessary. "Most animals do not experience anything like intimacy as they mate," he admits, "and many people in many cultures would find our notion of intimacy foreign to themselves as well."[7]

There are two parts to Solomon's account: the alleged connection between intimacy and sex, and the assumed connection between intimacy and love. Sex expresses intimacy, and "intimacy lies right at the heart of love."[8] Both these connections might be questioned. Vannoy agrees, however, that sex can express intimacy. The crucial question, therefore, is whether intimacy involves love. It does not, if "love" means romantic love, since friends who are not in love might be sexually intimate. This is the basis of Vannoy's disagreement with Solomon.

The plausibility of Vannoy's position rests on the fact that the alleged benefits of love can be found in sexual intimacy between friends. The limitation of his position is that the benefits of sex, intimacy, and friendship can be enjoyed by lovers. In his book, Vannoy suggests that the idea of romantic/erotic love is a paradox or contradiction, because it requires the coexistence of incompatible elements. He sees a contradiction, for example, between altruism and self-interest, holding that

> erotic love seems to be caught in a trap: On the one hand we want our lover to be primarily generous in order to avoid being exploited; on the other hand our desire to *merit* love drives us to want to be selected primarily for [our lover's] self-interested reasons.[9]

Vannoy sees a contradiction between ecstasy and endurance: "Love seeks to be long lasting. . . . But for many love also seeks the heights of romantic ecstasy. To combine these things is an impossible goal." He sees a conflict between choice and emotion, since "to insist both on a rational choice and emotional involvement is a contradictory ideal." Again, "love seeks the contradictory ideal of both an insecure and a secure beloved."[10]

These objections, among others, seem to Vannoy to cast doubt on the viability of the concept of erotic love, and he concludes that "erotic love is essentially self-interested," and that "on the whole, sex with a humanistic nonlover is far preferable to sex with an erotic lover."[11]

This is not the place for a detailed evaluation of Vannoy's attack on the concept of erotic/romantic love. It is worth noticing, however, that the disagreement between Vannoy and Solomon rests, at least in part, on the fact that they understand this concept in different ways. This appears clearly, for example, when Solomon writes:

> Whereas many other emotions tend to be antagonistic or competitive, romantic love intrinsically includes mutual reinforcement and encouragement. Emotions such as anger, resentment and jealousy . . . tend to maximize one's own self-esteem . . . but only at the risk of setting someone against us. . . . In love, since this sense of self-esteem is constituted mutually, it is entirely in the other person's interest . . . to think well of us and encourage us too.[12]

Here, Solomon treats romantic love as positive, as essentially involving friendship in the best sense. Vannoy would presumably see romantic love as including jealousy and other conflicting emotions.

I am not sure how such a disagreement is to be resolved. Much of the good of love, as it is presented in Solomon's account, is in fact obtainable from friendship and intimacy, and does not require romantic love. Solomon says, for example, that

> self-esteem is boosted in love by the complementary roles that we are able to play with one another, the identities we are able to assume in private, often at odds with or the exact opposites of the roles we are called upon to play in public or family life.[13]

But role-playing and identity games are not confined to lovers. A "businessman harried with responsibilities [who] enjoys a submissive role free from the burdens of control with his lover"[14] might find equal satisfaction with a professional dominatrix or a compatibly kinky amateur friend. Solomon says:

> Love provides us with identities, virtues, roles through which we define ourselves as well as partners to share our happiness, reinforce our values, support our best opinions of ourselves and compensate for the anonymity, impersonality or possibly frustration of public life.[15]

Nothing in such an account seems to preclude replacing "love" with "sexual friendship." To say that is to reformulate the basic truth behind Vannoy's account of why sex cannot express love.

Insofar as Vannoy's view amounts to an attack on the claim that love is *necessary* for the best sex, either sexually or morally, I am sympathetic. But insofar as his view asserts that sex is in some general way better without love, I suspect he relies too much on his negative characterization of erotic love. He says, for example, at the end of his book, that

> since a truly generous non-lover would stay with his partner even if he isn't receiving his so-called fair share of sexual pleasure, such a sex act would be devoid of the fears that haunt lovers if they fail to "measure up."[16]

But a truly generous lover would do the same! Vannoy insists that lovers are essentially self-interested, but this claim turns out to rest in part on a question-begging account of the self-sacrificial behavior of lovers.[17]

Vannoy assumes that his trysting strangers are altruistic and humanistic, but he attributes selfish motivations to lovers wherever possible. This is hardly fair. Love might be a complex ideal, open to contradictory and manifold interpretations, but so is friendship. Vannoy argues, for example, that the fact that erotic love is selective shows that lovers do not really "love each other unselfishly and for their own sake alone," since "if one claims to love persons *as persons* then one should love all mankind equally and eternally." But friendship is also selective. Vannoy says that one "wants one's lover to be unselfish, yet one does not ordinarily want a self-sacrificing slave for a lover."[18] Neither do we ordinarily seek lackeys for friends.

Vannoy is right to defend the value of sex without love against its cultured despisers, and Solomon is right to defend the value of sex with love, though Solomon's endorsement of Walker Percy's remark, "the only important, certainly the best thing in life, is ordinary sexual love," may only show how blind philosophy of love can be.[19]

Is sex better, then, with love or without it? I doubt that any general answer can be given. Vannoy insists that "the criterion for an act's being a successful expression of love in sexual terms is sexual pleasure" (251). People derive sexual pleasure (or enjoyment, or meaning) in different ways and from different things. What brings one person ecstasy might not even count as a sexual stimulus to another. Even if we found love an impossible or incoherent ideal, it would not follow that sex would be better without it; even contradictions might increase pleasure or bestow meaning in the lives of particular people.

Recall how *Last Tango in Paris* turned out.[20] Paul (Marlon Brando) fell in love with his mistress, and sought to exchange the sex arena for a shared life; for him, sex was not enough. Jeanne (Maria Schneider) rejected that; for her, love was too much. What was life to one, was death to the other.

Postscript (1995)

The above is in substance what I presented to the Society for the Philosophy of Sex and Love in 1984; it remains adequate to its original limited purpose.

In his thoughtful and gracious response (255-7), Professor Vannoy concedes that perhaps sex does not have to capture *all* the complexity of lovers' lives (in order to count as an expression of love). But he insists that sex cannot express what is crucial about love. For love is often (even, preferably) a response to "certain inner qualities" of the loved one, while "in the bedroom we want our lovers to be sexually aroused by our bodies as bodies." How, Vannoy asks, could sex express love of such inner qualities?

The worry derives, I think, from too restrictive a conception of sexual desire. Why shouldn't the perceived inner qualities of those we love play a role in unlocking desire for their bodies? It is a familiar fact that nonphysical properties can do so. We can understand Elizabeth Ray when she writes: "As his cock pumped deeper and deeper down my throat, I was struck by the idea that, at that moment, all his power rested in me."[21] This is not love, to be sure, but neither is it sexual arousal based merely on the body as body. If power can be an aphrodisiac, why not kindness, or a wry sense of humor? Why not a shared past, or a common destiny? The course of desire is shaped, for better or worse, by the vicissitudes of human psychology and cultural training. We may not love those we desire; we may not desire those we love: whence some tragedy and much soap opera. Then again, we may desire those we love, and in part because we love them. The sexiness of a smile can spring from what (we think) it says about the mind that could wear such lips.

Because desire *need not be personalized*, it is possible to have sex (even, good sex) with little concern for the inner qualities of the other. Athletic and impersonal sex might be satisfying, which reminds us that sex need not express love, need not be connected to inner personal qualities. (Notoriously, people can be aroused even by inner qualities they disapprove of or dislike.) But because desire *can be personalized*, sexual arousal sometimes turns on the embodied significance of the beloved.

The dialectic of erotic response, which interweaves the familiar and secure with the strange and exciting, is part of our need to balance comfort (which can be boring) against danger (which can be stimulating). In sex, as elsewhere, we are well advised not to underestimate the attraction of either pole.[22]

Notes

1. Russell Vannoy, "Can Sex Express Love?" this volume, 247-57; page references to this essay are supplied parenthetically in the text.
2. Russell Vannoy, *Sex Without Love* (Buffalo: Prometheus Books, 1980).
3. Robert C. Solomon, *Love: Emotion, Myth, and Metaphor* (Garden City, N.Y.: Anchor Press/Doubleday, 1981).
4. Solomon, *Love*, 246.
5. *Ibid.*, 248.
6. *Ibid.*, 249.
7. *Ibid.*, 254.
8. *Ibid.*, 248.
9. Vannoy, *Sex Without Love*, 215.
10. *Ibid.*, 132, 139, 149.
11. *Ibid.*, 218, 219.
12. Solomon, *Love*, 302.
13. *Ibid.*, 311.
14. *Ibid.*
15. *Ibid.*, 314.
16. Vannoy, *Sex Without Love*, 219.
17. *Ibid.*, 134-5.
18. *Ibid.*, 133, 136.
19. Solomon, *Love*, 299.
20. Bernardo Bertolucci, *Last Tango in Paris* (New York: Delta, 1974). This text is the screenplay of the 1972 film, and includes appreciations by Pauline Kael and Norman Mailer.
21. Elizabeth Ray, *The Washington Fringe Benefit* (New York: Dell, 1976), 24.
22. I say more on these matters in "Inscrutable Desires," *Philosophy of the Social Sciences* 20:2 (1990): 208-21, and "Beauty's Punishment: How Feminists Look at Pornography," in Dana Bushnell, ed., *"Nagging" Questions: Feminist Ethics in Everyday Life* (Lanham, Md.: Rowman and Littlefield, 1995), 335-60.

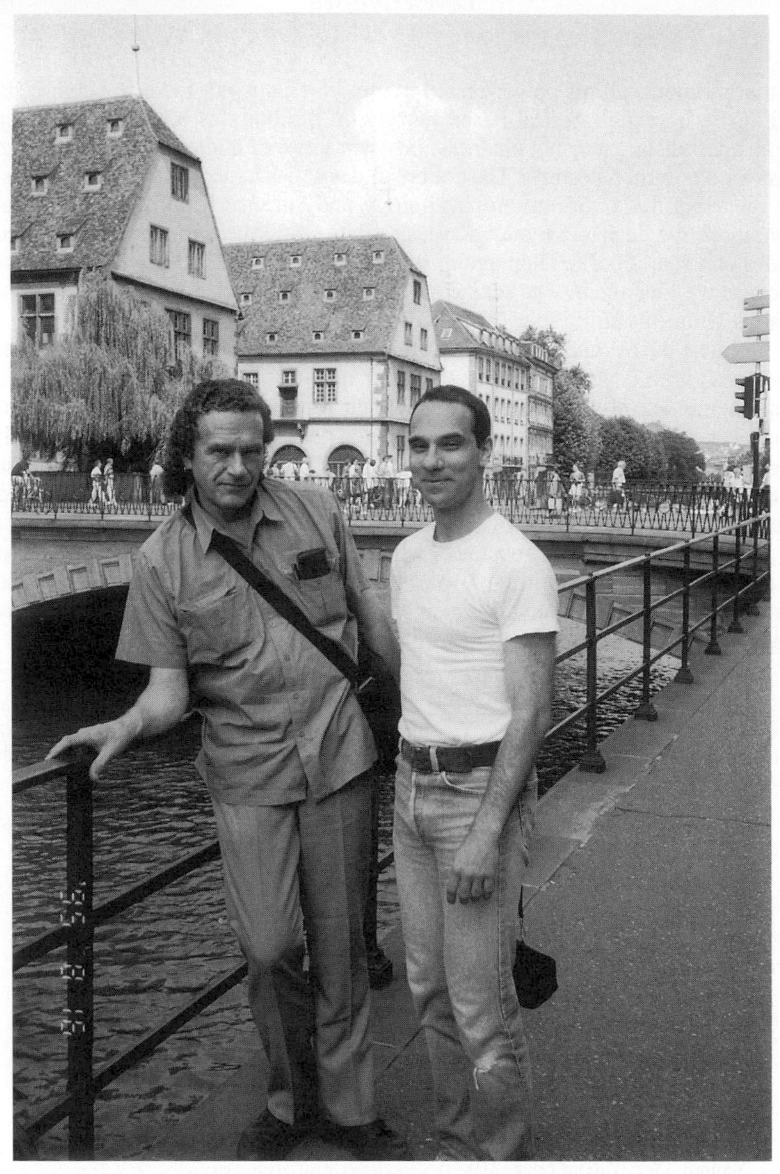

Lee Rice (left) and Steven Barbone (right)
(photograph: John Jenders)

Lee Rice, author of "A Spinozistic Account of Sexuality"
Paper presented at the Society for the Philosophy of Sex and Love
during the
Western Division Meeting of The American Philosophical Association
Cincinnati, Ohio, 26 April 1984

Twenty-Seven

SPINOZA AND HUMAN SEXUALITY[1]

Steven Barbone and Lee Rice

1. Spinoza and Sex: Who Cares?

Like many seventeenth-century philosophers, Baruch Spinoza wrote nothing dealing explicitly with the problems of human sexuality; and, again like most pre-nineteenth-century thinkers, his explicit remarks tend to reflect a somewhat less than critical acceptance of the sexual norms of his time. This general point is made by editors of the principal anthologies devoted to the philosophy of sexuality.[2] If Spinoza was much a creature of his time in his remarks about sexuality, however, he was a genuine revolutionary both in his criticism of René Descartes and in his creation of a new framework to replace the untenable Cartesian world view, and we wish to argue here that the revolutionary impact of his framework carries over quite directly into the view of sexuality underlying many of his remarks. What we offer is, however, less a theory than a set of preliminary and programmatic points for the development of a Spinozistic account of sexuality.

We first suggest that many of the central weaknesses of contemporary approaches to human sexuality lie precisely in their Cartesian roots, and then argue that Spinoza's radical overhaul of Cartesianism might have something to offer by way of a glimpse at a more adequate account of sexuality. Consider, first, three random but perspicuous examples of contemporary approaches that Spinoza would probably (and correctly) label as Cartesian. Irving Singer's account of the two modes of sexual desire, which distinguishes between the "sensuous" and the "passionate," is strikingly dualistic.[3] Thomas Nagel's account of natural sexuality depends on a dualistic conception of sexual values in its distinction between naturalness and perversion,[4] a point clearly underlined in Sara Ruddick's elaboration of "completeness," a concept that remains, in her hands, dualistic (even if she avoids some of the unwanted normative implications of Nagel's account).[5] Finally, Janice Moulton's critique of Nagel and Robert Solomon emphasizes an underlying dualism in both.[6] Fred Berger argues that one consequence of such a dualism is that of an overly intellectual view of sexual satisfaction that fails to take account of the diversity and pluralism of human sexuality.[7] Such pervasive problems in many contemporary accounts have a natural mapping into three general features of Spinozistic method: it is monistic in opposition to Descartes's dualism;[8] it is strongly opposed to an intellectualism of human cognitive and appetitive powers;[9] and it is also overtly nominalistic,[10] especially in its avoidance of talk about a monolithic "human nature."[11] Before proceeding to their consequences for a theory of sexuality, we should look briefly at these features of Spinozism.

Spinozistic monism casts thought and extension as two different attributes of a single substance; and, while we can ignore some of the difficulties regarding the nature and number of the attributes,[12] one important consequence of any interpretation is given in E2P7, "The order and connection of ideas is the same as the order and connection of things," which asserts one version of the identity theory for mind-body.[13] A more important consequence relative to a theory of sexuality is that the "union" of mind and body is not conceived as special in the human person (E2P13Schol): the mind is in fact a complex of ideas, just as the body is a complex of particles.[14] Spinoza notes in E2P48Schol [15]that, while mind and body are two different ways of looking at a single organism, intellect and will are in fact one and the same and not even logically distinguishable.

The Spinozistic elimination of the body/mind and will/intellect dualisms implies a deintellectualizing of human cognition. What we describe as intellect is only one mode of cognition (E1P31, E2P15, E2P17Schol), while appetite or conatus constitutes a wider category of cognitive activity characterizing human action. Affectivity is here construed as arising from modifications of the mind/body by which its power of activity is increased or diminished, together with the cognitive correlates of these modifications (E3Def3). This account of human affectivity has important similarities to contemporary accounts in modern psychobiology,[16] and explains the extent to which Spinoza is able to develop a fully integrated account of human passional action and interaction in the third part of the *Ethics*.[17] Indeed, in E2P23 we are told that the human mind does not know itself except to the extent that it perceives ideas of the affections of its body. The essence of human nature is ultimately not intellectual knowledge, but appetite. A crucial passage for understanding Spinoza's account of human appetite is E3P9Schol:

> When this conatus is related to the mind alone, it is called will; when it is related to both mind and body, it is called appetite, which is nothing else but a person's essence. . . . Further, there is no difference between appetite and desire except that desire is usually related to persons insofar as they are conscious of their appetite. . . . From the above remarks it is clear that we do not endeavor, will, seek, or desire because we judge something to be a good. On the contrary, something is judged to be a good because we endeavor, will, seek, or desire it.

V. M. Fóti argues persuasively that such a development anticipates Sigmund Freud's later account of pathogenesis.[18] Lest the reader be tempted to see too much anticipation of Freud in Spinoza, it should be underlined, however, that Spinoza would have found the hypothesis of a "death wish" unacceptable.[19]

Finally, Spinoza's nominalism is employed at various junctures of the *Ethica* to attack any realistic or Platonistic account of universals. For our purposes, a useful summary is offered in E2P49Schol, where Spinoza criticizes the teleological model of human appetite and knowledge. In E2P49Schol, Spinoza is concerned with final causes in the Aristotelian sense (explanatory models in science), but the critique of teleology also extends to Aristotle's moral philosophy (see also E1App).[20]

We turn now to the impact of these themes upon a Spinozistic account of love and sexuality, taking into account wherever possible definitions and remarks in the *Ethica* that deal explicitly with sexual appetite.

2. Spinoza on Love

The primary affects ("emotions") in Spinozistic psychology are pleasure (*laetitia*), pain (*tristitia*), and desire or appetite (*cupiditas*). Love and hate are conceived as subcategories, respectively, of pleasure and pain; and sexual desire (*libido*) is a subcategory of love. Shirley's choice of "lust" as a translation of *libido* is a felicitous one, and only rampant puritanism of the very type that Spinoza opposes accounts for the fact that the term is so often used pejoratively. Indeed, many of the propositions in E4 that characterize repentance and humility as evils, while recommending cheerfulness, are explicit critiques of the Dutch Calvinists of Spinoza's own day.[21]

One might conclude at first sight that Spinoza's characterization of lust as a type of love runs afoul of the contemporary questioning of any logical or even psychological relationship between love and sex; but Spinoza's use of "love" is wider than the usage of many contemporary thinkers and also refreshingly nonromantic. It also matches to some extent ordinary English usage, for which the claim that one loves a cold martini at the end of a hard day's work need hardly be construed as metaphor. Finally, his use is consistent with his claim that love is determined by internal states, not by its relatedness to certain external objects (human, alive, etc.). The initial definition of love as a subcategory of pleasure is given in E3P13Schol:

> From what has been said we clearly understand what love and hatred are. Love is no more than pleasure accompanied by the idea of an external cause, and hatred pain accompanied by the idea of an external cause. Again, he who loves necessarily endeavors to have present and to preserve the object of his love; while, on the other hand, he who hates endeavors to remove and to destroy the thing which he hates.

It is important to underline what this definition does *not* imply. When Spinoza says that the pleasure is "accompanied" by an "idea of a cause," he does *not* mean that this idea is *in fact* that of a genuine cause, or even of anything existent: it might in fact be wholly inadequate (one can fall in love with Father Christmas or the boy next door, even if neither happen to exist). Spinoza provides a summary his general account of the affects in the appendix to E3. Desire is appetite accompanied by consciousness of the appetite. The difference between desire and appetite has no psychological consequences, since the effects of appetite are the same whether accompanied by consciousness or not.

Several noteworthy consequences follow from these definitions. E3P15 concludes that anything can cause pleasure, pain, or desire; and, indeed, this is one of the general principles in the Spinozistic laws for association of ideas (E3P15). There are as many kinds of love and hatred[22] as there are kinds of objects by which we might be affected; and the passivity by which these affects are characterized also entails their being accompanied by mental images (*imaginationes*), where images in the Spinozistic sense are the ideational correlates of passive affects of the body.[23]

Finally, the different affects which a single object causes to arise in different persons are accounted for by differences in the natures or individual essences of the persons (E3P51Schol). Not only do affects differ according to essences within a "species," but also they differ across species: equine lust is not the same as human lust, nor are the lusts of two humans necessarily the same.[24]

All that has been said about pleasure as a passive state of mind is also true of pleasure as an active state of mind, except that here pain and hatred are inapplicable. Spinoza's psychology, like his metaphysics, is act oriented: to the extent that mind or body is active, it necessarily rises to an higher level of perfection (E3P59Dem).

3. Lust as a Subcategory of Love

The definition which Spinoza provides for lust is straightforward and simple, given the foundation he has laid in the theory of appetite and his account of love. There is not, however, a single English translation that does it justice. The explanation is given as definition 48 in the general appendix to *Ethica* III: "*Libido est etiam cupiditas et amor in commiscendis corporibus*." Samuel Shirley translates this as: "Lust is the desire and love of sexual intercourse." In this he follows the earlier translation of H. W. White, but White even goes one step further, in making the lust "immoderate."[25] But the notion of sexual intercourse is completely absent from Spinoza's Latin. The French translators are both more literal and more accurate: "La lubricité est aussi un désir et un amour de l'union des corps";[26] "La luxure est aussi un désir et un amour de l'union des corps."[27] The "mixing together of bodies" (*corpora commiscere*) comes closer to what Alan Goldman analyzes as the skin-rubbing-skin ("physical contact") model.[28] In his commentary, Alan Soble argues that this model, at least in the form in which Goldman proposes it, has no way of explaining why the experience is a *sexual* one.[29] The model does of course suggest something more intimate than a handshake, an intimacy that might also suggest sexuality (and indeed in the explanation that follows Spinoza accepts just such a consequence).[30] Sexual *intercourse* is thus best categorized as one object (among many possible ones) of such a love; and Spinoza has already argued that any and all objects of an appetite are contingent (*per accidens*) in precisely this sense: any object may be the stimulus for any appetite.

One consequence of a correct reading of Spinoza's definition is quite straightforward and (from our perspective) quite satisfactory. What makes the appetite sexual is its internal features (*commiscere corpora*). We are *not* claiming that Spinoza makes clear the nature of these internal features: what (if any) object it is related to remains a contingency. Sexual appetite is by nature neither binary nor singulary. That our sexual desires should drive us toward *another* (human or not, of different gender or not) is irrelevant to its categorization as "sexual." Spinoza labels as an "extrinsic denomination" any such factor that does not enter into the essential definition of an affect.[31] On this reading, masturbation is as full-fledged a realization of lust as sexual intercourse (whether that intercourse be with a member of one's own sex, the other sex, or even another species or nonliving being). What makes appetite *sexual* is that it triggers a body-mixing desire. What precisely causes, or more properly is thought to cause, such a triggering, is not logically necessary to the categorization of the desire (*libido*) as sexual.

All is not sweetness and light here, for Spinoza has nothing to say about the internal features of this desire. That it produces (or is equivalent to) a heightened awareness (*laetitia*) follows from his earlier definitions. It is also easy enough to distinguish it from a love for geometry (no body mixing); but distinguishing it from a love for chocolate ice cream, or a love to be with and to share with friends, offers more of a challenge. If our reading of Spinoza is correct, he is committed to the meeting of this challenge. But it is one about which he is silent.

One tempting way in which such a challenge might be met would be to counter that the distinction among the affects at this level must appeal to "raw feel" (or Spinozistic "intuition"), and that types of pleasure at this level are epistemologically and logically primitive. This is particularly tempting within a Spinozistic context, since Spinoza's version of the *ordo geometricus* gives epistemological primacy to certain primitive "feels." While such a move would in principle constitute a reply to Soble's objection to the skin-rubbing-skin model, it would also leave Spinoza open to a charge of vicious circularity. The concept of body-mixing is supposed to distinguish lust from other types of love. If we in turn argue that the distinctiveness of such a body mixing is a primitive given, then we are saying something to the effect that what makes sex sexual is its sexiness: certainly true, but hardly enlightening. In short, what we need is a nontrivial characterization that separates all and only those desires that are libidinal (in Spinoza's sense) from the general ("amative," for lack of a better word) class of affects.

What we cannot do is to attempt to explain this mixing or intermingling of bodies as a relation to other bodies. First, Spinoza denies the reality of such extrinsic relations. Secondly, and more importantly for our purposes, as Spinoza makes clear in his exposition, it is our internal state of body-mixing that makes an external relation sexual, rather than the external relation of our body to another that makes the internal state a sexual one. Not only does Spinoza emphasize this point as fundamental, but we believe it is sound. The trick is to provide further expansion that is neither trivial nor question begging. While this would constitute a logically bulletproof reply to Soble's objection, pursuit of it lies beyond our present purposes.

Spinoza does have several further points to make in passing, one of which deals with the often mentioned but little understood relation between appetite and imagery (for sexual appetite we should say "fantasizing"). In E3P21Dem, he points out that the images of things loved are in the lover and that the pleasure in their being felt heightens the mind's own appetition.[32] As in the case of the extrinsic relation between object and appetite, a similar point must be made for the extrinsic relation between idea and ideatum: the image of Paul in Peter's mind tells us more about Peter than about Paul.[33] This consideration forms the logical basis of Spinoza's brief remarks about sexual jealousy and longing in E3P35Schol:

> This is often the case with love towards a woman; for he who thinks of a woman whom he loves as giving herself to another will not just feel pain because his own appetite is held in check but also, since he is compelled to associate the image of the object loved with the sexual parts of his rival, he will feel disgust for her.

While this hardly constitutes an adequate account of jealousy or sexual rivalry, Spinoza's insistence that the explanation be provided in terms of imagery (fantasizing and its laws) is a consistent extension of his psychology of sexuality and the theme of body mixing; imagery in this sense is cognition in its most corporeal form (E2P17Schol). Michèle Bertrand notes that one distinctive advance made by Spinoza over Descartes is in the former's account of imaginative fantasy, which is both fully cognitive and dynamically sensuous.[34]

While we cannot further develop them here, some additional themes that warrant further exploration as components of a Spinozistic theory of sexuality are the account that he provides of longing in E3P36Schol, the suggestion that satiety is a consequence of a change in bodily constitution (E3P59Schol), the brief statement of reciprocity of love in E3P33, and the general account which he attempts to provide of self-satisfaction in E3P29 and E3P30. The fact that Spinoza's examples often relate to sexual desire, even where he is dealing with general laws of imagination or association of ideas, suggests that he believed that his general approach would be sufficient to provide a satisfactory account of human sexuality. That he did not attempt to work out a more detailed theory of sexuality is no surprise. Without attempting to say more of the consequences of Spinoza's implicit account of sexual affectivity, however, we must pass on to some of its normative consequences.

4. The Good, the Bad, the Ugly

Another respect in which contemporary analysis of sexuality is often flawed can be found in the tendency to mix descriptive and normative components. To take the most common situation where such a mixing is likely to occur, the attempt to define sexual appetite as related by nature to intercourse (heterosexual) automatically prejudges the status of alternative sexualities (for example, homosexuality), and succeeds in making masturbation either nonsexual, perverted, or perverse.[35]

Spinoza's method can provide some needed remedies since he is careful to keep the descriptive and normative components separate. It is precisely the inability of his own contemporaries to do so that leads to some of the most caustic criticism included in the *Ethica*. In E3Pref, for instance, he is concerned with arguing, particularly against the Calvinists of his day, that one must first understand human behavior before railing against it. E3 is devoted to the genesis and aetiology of human affects, while E4 moves on to the problem of normative judgment within a communitarian context. Communitarian relations constitute the necessary, but not sufficient, conditions for human achievement of the Spinozistic good; and the problem of individual "liberation" (*libertas*) is taken up in E5.

Sexual relations, like any other human interaction in Spinoza's perspective, might embody either virtue (strength, power; *virtus* in the literal sense) by increasing the organism's ability to cope with and manipulate the larger environment (part, but only part, of which is human), or it might embody the opposite of virtue: *impotentia*, or weakness in the face of the environment. The chestnut that any sexual relation involves an interplay of powers is only half the truth: the sadder, other half is that such relations often display an interplay of *impotentia*. In a community, sexuality is commonly (though not definitionally, as we have seen) social interaction, and any such interaction is, for Spinoza, normatively a means by which the individual attempts to augment control over an environment that, like god or nature, is not hostile but indifferent to human preservation and well-being. Spinoza says little in the *Ethica* that directly deals with the extension of his account of virtue to sociosexual relationship, but the account of virtue is both explicit and sufficiently well worked out to make such an extension relatively straightforward.[36]

What we here underline is that issues concerning sexual relations are a subset of those involving the individual's virtue. Once again, one must rely first upon an understanding of the psychological basis of virtue (Spinoza's account of conatus)[37] before undertaking any normative analysis whatever. Thus, questions of prescription rest ultimately upon the nature of the individual (*not* the imaginational "species") and his or her interactions, sexual or otherwise. Normative consequences, then, follow strictly on the organism's conatus: does this particular act result in greater power for the organism? If so, the act counts as virtuous. If not, the act, not in itself but as considered for the agent, is immoral. For this reason we do not here apply it to specific kinds of sexual liaisons, since much is placed at the level of the individual rather than broad categories such as "heterosexual" and "homosexual." Furthermore, despite the seeming simplicity of this analysis, we believe that it can be widely applied and that the resultant normative analysis has consequences for even such social issues as closeting within the gay community.[38]

In the Preface to E4, the act/virtue orientation of his psychological theory is applied to normative issues to produce a version of what has been since dubbed exemplary ethics. Spinoza asks us to construct an individual model of "human nature" which is that of a being approaching maximal activity and minimal passivity in its causal relation with environing objects. The *exemplar naturae humanae*[39] is that by which goods are defined as objects or states that are useful as means to its approximation, evils as anything that are obstacles thereto (E3Def1 and E3Def2).

The first principle that we wish to underline is what we may call the "principle of community," and it evolves from E4P29 through E4P37. The basis of any causal interaction is some similarity of nature, so that the application of normative judgments requires some similarities among beings. Spinoza notes: "No individual thing whose nature is quite different from ours is able to assist or to check our power for action, and nothing whatever can be either good or evil for us unless it have something in common with us" (E4P29). This is a wider principle than the adage that "likes attract," for it amounts to the claim that both attraction (love) and repulsion (hate) require similitude. In fact, there is no general principle in Spinoza for predicting what will attract what, since we have already seen him insist that anything can give rise to one kind of pleasure or other, provided that it can be thought (rightly or wrongly) to be an object of interaction.

The second principle we may dub the "pleasure principle," and its exposition is begun in E4P38, running through E4P41. Its core is that anything that so disposes body/mind to heightened awareness and activity is advantageous to persons (E3P39Dem). Its immediate consequence is that "pleasure is in itself not evil, but good; whereas pain is in itself evil" (E4P41).

We have already seen Spinoza distinguish between affects as modifications of parts (of mind or body) and as modifications of the entire organism. The third principle that he brings to play we might call the "principle of harmony." E4P42 argues that cheerfulness (pleasure as an affect of the whole) cannot be excessive, and is always good, just as melancholy is always evil. Similarly (E4P43), titillation (pleasure as an affect of parts) can be excessive (evil); and, to that extent, anguish might be a counterbalancing good. Indeed, the part-whole relation is enormously important for Spinozistic ethics, which sees evil and madness as of a kin. Spinoza makes a direct application to sexuality in E4P44Schol:

> For sometimes we see persons so affected by one object that they dream that it is before them even when it is not. When this occurs for a person not asleep, we speak of delirium or madness. And no less mad are those consumed with love, fantasizing night and day only of their lover or mistress; and these usually provoke ridicule. But when the miser thinks of nothing but gain or money, or the ambitious person of honor, they are not reckoned to be mad; for they are harmful and are considered worthy of hatred.

So love and desire can be excessive. The playboy (/girl) type whose primary goal in life is the multiplication of orgasms is perhaps less worthy of hatred than of ridicule. As Russell Vannoy remarks, such a person is best told to go on a diet.[40] There is also an implicit but interesting application to the question of consensual activity in the above passage. What Spinoza regards as properly the object of hatred (and therefore of legal restriction or punishment) is that which is properly *harmful*. While we may write off some species of sexual activity as minor variants of delirium, these might properly lie outside the proper order of law. Such behavior can be regarded as "ills," but this does not qualify them for objects of legislation:

> Many have tried to prevent such ills by passing sumptuary laws; but without success. For any law which can be broken without injustice to another person is regarded with derision, and intensifies the desires and lusts of people instead of restraining them; since we always strive for what is prohibited and desire what is denied. (TP10, 5)

Though many argue that the way to make the "forbidden fruit" less tempting would be to stop forbidding it, we think that Spinoza is claiming something much greater here. It certainly is not that any and all consensual activities are to be permitted, despite the fact that the judgment of morality rests on the level of the individual, not society. But Spinoza knows that most people, regardless of what they believe about themselves, live their lives *as if* led by reason and not *actually* by reason itself. That means that though the level of moral judgment resides with the individual, Spinoza believes quite frankly that the individual would be only too quick to act irrationally, that is, to make (immoral) choices that would result only in pain instead of the desired pleasure. The purpose of society, then, is to set up a framework in which each individual might better flourish. To that end, certain restrictions might be set up to maximize the chances of each person's pleasure and to minimize the chances for pain. Thus, to legislate against consensual activity which does no harm whatsoever to the society and to neither of the participants is completely unwarranted, and because we are drawn to what is denied us, futile. Since it is society's role to foster the growth of each individual, it is within its right to proscribe any activity, consensual or not, which tends to limit or to cause pain to at least one of the people involved. Society exists for the sake of the individual and to provide an environment supportive of the individual. This is not to say, however, that the members of society are automatically made to live by reason within community, but this does allow room, then, for those who remain impassionated but cause no threat to others. Thus, once again, we see that Spinoza would not so much condemn but pity those whose affects might be said to be "imbalanced."

Affects which are "imbalanced" psychologically, however, can easily pass into their contraries, and it is just this application that Spinoza makes in the 19th discussion of the appendix to E4 (E4App19):

> Amor praeterea meretricius, hoc est generandi libido, quae ex forma oritur, et absolute omnis amor, qui aliam causam praeter animi libertatem agnoscit, facile in odium transit; nisi, quod pejus est, species delirii sit, atque tum magis discordia quam concordia fovetur.

The closest we can come to *amor meretricius* is "mistresslike love" (*meretrix* = mistress). Both Samuel Shirley and H. W. White give "love of a mistress," which translation obscures a central feature of Spinoza's entire analysis of lust. Whether "mistressly love" is in fact directed to a mistress is contingent on the extrinsic denominations of particular situations. Spinoza tells us that this type of love is a lust for generation or reproduction. This accords well with our earlier retranslation of lust as an appetite for commingling of bodies: *libido generandi* is that kind of lust directed at procreation (but there are other kinds).

Spinoza notes that, since it arises from physical beauty (*forma*), it is more transient than other types of love and so can more easily pass into its contrary (hatred).

The relationship between lust and marriage is explored in the discussion immediately following (E4App20):

> As regards marriage, it is certain that it is in agreement with reason if the desire for the commingling of bodies is engendered not only from physical beauty, but also from a love of begetting children and rearing them wisely. And beside this, (it is reasonable) if the man and woman's love is not only caused by physical beauty, but especially by the freedom of the soul.[41]

Spinoza here relates marriage (*not* sexuality or lust) to the production and education of children, and notes that it is appropriate provided that the desire for intermingling bodies does *not* arise solely from physical attraction. This provides at least a little more information about the Spinozistic concept of mixing bodies: it may or may not arise from physical attraction, and it might or might not be related to sexual intercourse or procreation. Spinoza sees marriage as normatively related to procreation and friendship; but his brief discussion of marriage is a postscript to his interpretation and evaluation of sexual desire, and nowhere does he attempt to forge descriptive or normative links between lust (sexual desire) and (heterosexual) marriage as such. Masturbation and homosexuality thus emerge as full-fledged forms of sexual behavior, a consequence for which binary definitions of sexual desire can provide no explanation.

5. Concluding Remarks

We have argued that Spinoza does have much to offer to contemporary discussions of the nature of human sexuality and normative issues related to these. His examples of sexual patterns and behavior constitute only a small subset of the discussions offered in the *Ethica*, but that they are there at all is significant; for they indicate that he gave considerable thought to the nature of human sexuality and that he was convinced that the general principles developed for understanding human action could be applied to sexuality without radical restructuring.

The work of providing a general theory of sexuality that could be described as Spinozistic remains to be done. Less attention would have to be accorded to the passages explicitly dealing with sexuality, and a great deal more analysis would have to be devoted to his general psychology of human action. Part III of the *Ethica* contains a wealth of material devoted to human action and appetite, but this is the portion of Spinoza's writings least studied by contemporary Spinozists. If the principal points of our analysis are correct, this neglected portion of the Spinozistic corpus is deserving of careful attention: not only because of a recently renewed interest in Spinoza among philosophers and historians, but also because Spinoza might well have something to contribute to the recent interest among philosophers in the nature of human sexuality.

Notes

1. The originating version of this essay was presented by Lee Rice at a meeting of the Society for the Philosophy of Sex and Love. A later version, which addressed the remarks of the commentator, Rhoda Kotzin, was published in 1985 ("Spinoza's Account of Sexuality," *Philosophy Research Archives* 10: 19-34). The present paper, newly written, stems from the dissatisfaction of both Rice and Barbone with some of the original findings, a desire to extend Spinoza's analysis to considerations of the sociology of sex, and a need to update bibliographical information. Much that was presented in the 1985 paper is here, though developed further, but the treatment of the fifth part of the *Ethics* is no longer included (too much work remains to be done on this part of the *Ethics*). Several recent, important works (particularly those of Barbone, Matheron, and Schrijvers) now figure more heavily in the exposition as well. We employ throughout the standard abbreviations of the works of Spinoza; "E2P13Schol" is *Ethica* II, Proposition 13, Scholium, and other abbreviations are equally transparent. The Latin text is from J. Van Vloten and J. P. N. Land, *Opera Omnia*, 2 vols. (The Hague: Martinus Nijhoff, 1914), but we have checked these against the less convenient, less accessible Heidelberg Academy Edition (*Opera*, ed. Carl Gebhardt, 4 vols. [Heidelberg: Carl Winter Verlag, 1925]). English translations are notoriously untrustworthy, but the most recent is also the best (*The Ethics, Treatise on the Emendation of the Intellect, and Selected Letters*, trans. Samuel Shirley [Indianapolis: Hackett, 1992]). The French translation by Charles Appuhn (Paris: Librairie Garnier Freres, 1934) is excellent, as is the more recent translation with commentary by Robert Misrahi (*L'Ethique* [Paris: Presses Universitaires de France, 1990]). All English translations given in the article are our own, although we make liberal use of Shirley, Appuhn, and Misrahi. We quote the Latin text only for those passages where we quarrel with existing translations or whose reading is critical to our interpretation. Special thanks to Alan Soble (University of New Orleans) for his encouragement, and to Michael Wreen (Marquette University) for his critique of a preliminary version of this essay.

2. See Robert Baker and Frederick Elliston, "Introduction," in their *Philosophy and Sex*, 1st ed. (Buffalo: Prometheus, 1975), 7-8; 2nd ed. (1984), 17. Also see Alan Soble, "An Introduction to the Philosophy of Sex," in *Philosophy of Sex*, 1st ed. (Totowa, N.J.: Littlefield, Adams, 1980), 1-3.

3. Irving Singer, *The Goals of Human Sexuality* (New York: Norton, 1973), 41-5.

4. Thomas Nagel, "Sexual Perversion," in Baker and Elliston, *Philosophy and Sex*, 1st ed., 247-60; 2nd ed., 268-79; also in Soble, *Philosophy of Sex*, 1st ed., 76-88; 2nd ed. (1991), 39-51.

5. Sara Ruddick, "Better Sex," in Baker and Elliston, *Philosophy and Sex*, 1st ed., 83-104; 2nd ed., 280-99.

6. Janice Moulton, "Sexual Behavior: Another Position," in Soble, *Philosophy of Sex*, 1st ed., 110-18; 2nd ed., 63-71. Robert Solomon, "Sexual Paradigms," in Soble, *Philosophy of Sex*, 1st ed., 89-98; 2nd ed., 53-62.

7. Fred R. Berger, "Pornography, Sex, and Censorship," in Soble, *Philosophy of Sex*, 1st ed., 322-47.

8. Charles E. Jarrett, "On the Rejection of Spinozistic Dualism in the *Ethics*," *Southern Journal of Philosophy* 20 (1982): 153-76.

9. Lee C. Rice, "The Continuity of *Mens* in Spinoza," *The New Scholasticism* 43 (1969): 75-103.

10. Charles E. Jarrett, "Materialism," *Philosophy Research Archives* 8:1459 (1982): 153-76; Lee C. Rice, "Le nominalisme de Spinoza," *Canadian Journal of Philosophy* 24 (1994): 19-32.

11. Lee C. Rice, "*Tanquam Humanae Naturae Exemplar*: Spinoza on Human Nature," *Modern Schoolman* 68 (1991): 291-304.

12. Stanley C. Martens, "Spinoza on Attributes," *Synthèse* 37 (1978): 107-11.

13. Timothy L. Sprigge, "Spinoza's Identity Theory," *Inquiry* 20 (1977): 419-45.

14. Lee C. Rice, "Spinoza on Individuation," in Maurice Mandelbaum and Eugene Freeman, eds., *Spinoza: Essays in Interpretation* (LaSalle, Ill.: Open Court, 1975), 195-214; André Lécr-

ivain, "Spinoza et la physique cartésienne (suite)," *Cahiers Spinoza* 2 (1978): 93-206. E2P13 Schol: "Ex his non tantum intelligimus, mentem humanam unitam esse corpori, sed etiam, quid per mentis et corporis unionem intelligendum sit. Verum ipsam adaequate, sive distincte, intelligere nemo poterit, nisi prius nostri corporis naturam adaequate cognoscat. Nam ea, quae hucusque ostendimus, admodum communia sunt, nec magis ad homines quam ad reliqua individua pertinent, quae omnia, quamvis diversis gradibus, animata tamen sunt." On the importance of this passage for Spinoza's monism, see Jonathan Bennett, "Spinoza's Mind-Body Identity Thesis," *Journal of Philosophy* 78 (1981): 573-83, and Alexandre Matheron, *Individu et communauté chez Spinoza* (Paris: Editions de Minuit, 1969), 9-24. See also Alexandre Matheron, "Femmes et serviteurs dans la démocratie spinoziste," in Siegfried Hessing and Huston Smith, eds., *Speculum Spinozanum: 1677-1977* (London: Routledge and Kegan Paul, 1977), 368-86 (also in *Etudes sur Spinoza: Anthropologie et politique au xviie siècle* [Paris: Vrin, 1986], 189-208); and "Spinoza et la sexualité," in *Etudes sur Spinoza*, 209-30.

15. E2P48Schol: "Eodem hoc modo demonstratur, in mente nullam dari facultatem absolutam intelligendi, cupiendi, amandi, etc. . . . Adeo ut intellectus et voluntas ad hanc et illam ideam, vel ad hanc et illam volitionem eodem modo sese habeant."

16. J. J. Groen, "Spinoza's Theory of Affects and Modern Psychobiology," in Jon Wetlesen, ed., *Spinoza's Philosophy of Man* (Oslo: Universitetsforlaget, 1978), 97-118; Lee C. Rice, "Emotion, Appetition, and Conatus in Spinoza," *Revue Internationale de Philosophie* 31 (1977): 101-16; Lee C. Rice, "Cognitivism: A Spinozistic Perspective," *Studia Spinozana* 8 (1992): 208-26; Steven Barbone, "Spinoza and Cognitivism: A Critique," *Studia Spinozana* 8 (1992): 227-31.

17. Michael Schrijvers, *Spinozas Affektenlehre* (Bern and Stuttgart: Verlag Paul Haupt, 1989), 12-18; Lee C. Rice, "Review of Schrijvers's *Spinozas Affektenlehre*," *Studia Spinozana* 7 (1991): 316-18.

18. V. M. Fóti, "Thought, Affect, Drive, and Pathogenesis in Spinoza and Freud," *History of European Ideas* 3 (1982): 221-36, at 225-32.

19. Debra Nails, "Conatus Versus Eros/Thanatos: On the Principles of Spinoza and Freud," *Dialogue* [Phi Sigma Tau] 21 (1979): 33-40.

20. Paul D. Eisenberg, "Is Spinoza an Ethical Naturalist?" *Philosophia* [Israel] 7 (1977): 107-33; Rice, "Le nominalisme de Spinoza"; Jonathan Bennett, *A Study of Spinoza's Ethics* (Indianapolis: Hackett, 1984), 215-21.

21. Halail Gildin, "Notes on Spinoza's Critique of Religion," in Richard Kennington, ed., *The Philosophy of Baruch Spinoza* (Washington, D. C.: Catholic University Press, 1980), 155-72; Lee C. Rice, "*Servitus* in Spinoza: A Programmatic Analysis," in Wetlesen, *Spinoza's Philosophy of Man*, 179-91.

22. E3P56: "Laetitia, tristitia, et cupiditas, et consequenter uniuscujusque affectus, qui ex his componitur, ut animi fluctuationis, vel qui ab his derivatur, nempe amoris, odii, spei, metus, etc., tot species, quot sunt species objectorum, a quibus afficimur."

23. Paul S. Kashap, "Spinoza's Use of Idea," *Southwest Journal of Philosophy* 8 (1977): 57-70.

24. E3P57Schol: "Hinc sequitur, affectus animalium, quae irrationalia dicuntur (bruta enim sentire nequaquam dubitare possumus, postquam mentis novimus originem), ab affectibus hominum tantum differre, quantum eorum natura a natura humana differt. Fertur quidem equus et homo libidine procreandi; at ille libidine equina, hic autem humana."

25. "Lust is the immoderate desire and love of sexual intercourse," *Ethics*, trans. H. W. White (New York: Scribners, 1957), 184.

26. Appuhn, 398-9.

27. Misrahi, 220.

28. Alan Goldman, "Plain Sex," in Soble, *Philosophy of Sex*, 1st ed., 119-38; 2nd ed., 73-92.

29. Soble, "Introduction," *Philosophy of Sex*, 1st ed., 14-16.

30. E3AppDef48Expl: "Sive haec coeundi cupiditas moderata sit, sive non sit, libido appellari solet."

31. See E3AppDef48Expl: "Caeterum ex definitionibus affectuum, quos explicuimus, liquet, eos omnes a cupiditate, laetitia, vel tristitia oriri, seu potius nihil praeter hos tres esse, quorum

unusquisque variis nominibus appellari solet propter varias eorum relationes et denominationes extrinsecas."

32. E3P21: "Qui id, quod amat, laetitia vel tristitia imaginatur, laetitia vel tristitia afficietur; et uterque hic affectus major major aut minor erit in amante, prout uterque major aut minor est in re amata."

33. E2P16Cor2: "Sequitur secundo, quod ideae quas corporum externorum habemus, magis nostri corporis constitutionem quam corporum externorum naturam indicant."

34. Michèle Bertrand, *Spinoza et l'imaginaire* (Paris: Presses Universitaires de France, 1983), 78-90.

35. This is one of Soble's central criticisms of Nagel's account of sexuality ("Introduction," *Philosophy of Sex*, 7-8). To it might be added the point that Nagel's use of the term "perverted" is itself perverse. [On "perversion" and "perversity" in sexuality, see Russell Vannoy's essay, Chapter Thirty-Five in this volume, 359-72.—A. S.]

36. See Steven Barbone, "Virtue and Sociality in Spinoza," *Iyyun* 42 (1994): 383-95.

37. Rice, "Emotion, Appetition, and Conatus in Spinoza."

38. Steven Barbone and Lee Rice, "Coming Out, Being Out, and Acts of Virtue," *Journal of Homosexuality* 27 (1994): 91-110; reprinted in Timothy Murphy, ed., *Gay Ethics: Controversies in Outing, Civil Rights, and Sexual Science* (New York: Haworth Press, 1994), 91-110. Spinoza's attitude toward suicide is an example of his insistence on a psychologically coherent account of an affective response as a necessary condition for any moral judgment. While the basic elements of a psychological explanation of the genesis of suicidal behavior are worked out in E3, it is not until E4 that Spinoza develops a normative framework out of these. See Steven Barbone and Lee Rice, "Spinoza and the Problem of Suicide," *International Philosophical Quarterly* 34 (1994): 229-41.

39. See Rice, "*Tanquam Humanae Naturae Exemplar*: Spinoza on Human Nature" and "*Servitus* in Spinoza: A Programmatic Analysis"; and Don Garrett, "Spinoza's Theory of Metaphysical Individuation," in Kenneth Barber and Jorge Gracia, eds., *Individuation and Identity in Early Modern Philosophy* (Albany: State University of New York Press, 1994), 73-102 (some care must be taken with this essay, as several references are erroneous, and Gueroult's name is misspelled throughout).

40. Russell Vannoy, *Sex Without Love* (Buffalo: Prometheus, 1980), 102.

41. "Ad matrimonium quod attinet, certum est, ipsum cum ratione convenire, si cupiditas miscendi corpora non ex sola forma, sed etiam ex amore liberos procreandi et sapienter educandi ingeneretur; et praeterea si utriusque, viri scilicet et feminae, amor non solam formam, sed animi praecipue libertatem pro causa habeat."

Leonard J. Berkowitz
(photograph: John Pietrolaj)

Author of "Sex: Plain and Symbol"
Paper presented at the Society for the Philosophy of Sex and Love
during the
Eastern Division Meeting of The American Philosophical Association,
New York, N.Y., 28 December 1984

Twenty-Eight

SEX: PLAIN AND SYMBOL

Leonard J. Berkowitz

Alan Soble has divided analyses of sex into reductionist and expansionist accounts.[1] Reductionists argue that sex is essentially physical, the pleasurable rubbing of skin against skin, while expansionists argue that something more is required for an adequate account of human sexuality. Although these two viewpoints are usually seen as contradictory, I shall argue that both are correct when properly understood. Sex is not *essentially* more than the reductionists claim; however, an account of human sexuality that is restricted to physical contact is seriously deficient. The continuing debate between the views is unfortunate because it obscures the many points of agreement between them. Further, the concentration of attention on criticism and defense has prevented exploration of a potentially interesting line of inquiry: the symbolic significance of sex.

1. Reductionism

In two early essays on sexuality, Roger Taylor and Richard Taylor pave the way for the reductionist interpretation of sex.[2] Both seek to divorce sex from love. According to Richard Taylor, the

> human expression [of sex] is not fundamentally different from its expression throughout nature. . . . [Sexual passion] is no form of love at all. . . . [It] has almost nothing to do with love. . . . One could not aptly describe a pair of copulating grasshoppers, or mice, or dogs, as making love; they are simply copulating. The expression is no less inept when applied to people.[3]

Roger Taylor sketches a theory that reduces sexual desire to "the desire to have fleshy contact" and says that this desire "is not necessarily bound up with love."[4] He admits that he does not provide a complete theory, but these accounts are sufficient to begin the reductionist assault on traditional views of sexuality. It remained for others to provide more complete theories of sex as physical desire and activity. Perhaps the most notable attempt to do so is Alan Goldman's "Plain Sex." Goldman's initial analysis is that "sexual desire is desire for contact with another person's body and for the pleasure which such contact produces; sexual activity is activity which tends to fulfill such desires of the agent."[5] While he expands his account to some extent, he does not alter the essential concentration on physical contact and sensual pleasure. Hence the title of his article: "Plain Sex."

Soble has argued that Goldman's account is both too narrow and too broad.[6] Activities that lead to sexual contact would be classified as sexual even if they are not themselves sexually pleasurable. In support of this criticism, Soble cites examples such as flirting and paying a prostitute for sex. Both can be seen as preludes to sex, but not necessarily sexual acts themselves. Furthermore, other activities that involve pleasurable contact need not be sexual. It is not clear on Goldman's account why *another* person's body is essential. After all, masturbation certainly seems to be a sexual act and would fit neatly into a reductionist thesis. On the other hand, without the requirement that another person be involved, too many acts would qualify as sexual.

The natural response to this criticism would seem to be to base the reductionist account of sexuality on sexual pleasure itself: all and only those activities that produce sexual pleasure are sexual. This is the line taken by Robert Gray. Gray characterizes "sexual activity in terms of sexual pleasure."[7] This account has several advantages over previous definitions. It admits as sexual those activities usually classified as sexual, including acts omitted by other accounts (as noted above, Goldman's account excludes autoerotic acts). It also excludes activities that are not in themselves sexually pleasurable even if they do involve pleasurable bodily contact (for example, a massage). Gray's account has several other interesting consequences. It implies that the *form* of an act does not determine its sexual nature. Since what produces sexual pleasure might vary from person to person, what is sexual for one person might not be sexual for another. This is true even when we consider people engaged in an act with each other. That act might, on this account, be classified as sexual for one of the participants and not for the other since it might produce sexual pleasure only for one. This consequence reaches its extreme point when we consider rape. On Gray's account it would seem that rape is not sex at all for the victim, although it might be sex for the rapist. (Whether this consequence is a virtue or a problem is debatable.)

All these accounts have one thing in common. They are attempts to answer the question "What is sex?" As attempts to arrive at a definition, they necessarily emphasize what is common to all cases of sexuality; that is, they seek necessary conditions. Thus they reduce sex to its (lowest?) common denominator. Goldman seems to recognize this: "the desire for physical contact with another person is a minimal criterion for (normal) sexual desire, but is both necessary and sufficient to qualify normal desire as sexual."[8] As we have seen, he might have overstated his case, but he does provide persuasive arguments that nothing beyond physical contact or physical pleasure is necessary for an act to be sexual.[9] In this sense the reductionists are correct. There is no additional characteristic (love, communication, reproduction, or anything else) that is *necessary* for an act to be sexual. Cases of sexual activities or sexual desires in which any proposed additional feature is missing exist. One criterion of adequacy for any purported analysis of a concept is that it classify the obvious cases correctly. Any account that attempts to add something more to the reductionist analysis will fail this test. The only position left for the expansionists is to offer their theories as proposals instead of analyses. In fact, many seem to be doing just this; they propose an ideal or natural state of affairs and claim that anything that falls short of this state is either perverted sex or not sex at all. However, it is notoriously difficult to establish a state of affairs as ideal or natural. Even if this task is accomplished, it does not follow that acts that fail to reach this ideal state are either perverted or not sexual acts at all. Eating junk food certainly falls short of any gastronomic ideal, but it is eating, and it is not perverted.

Let us concede, then, that the answer to "What is sex?" is essentially reductionistic; at base, sexuality is nothing but physical contact and sensual pleasure. As we shall see, we will have to revise this concession later. However, this concession is not the end of the matter. We can argue that reductionism is a "true" but narrow way of looking at the world. Theodore Roszak criticizes reductionism as "single vision," seeing the world as "nothing but." Roszak uses the word "reductionism"

> to designate that peculiar sensibility which degrades what it studies by depriving its subject of charm, autonomy, dignity, mystery. As Kathleen Raine puts it, the style of mind which would have us "see in the pearl nothing but a disease of the oyster."[10]

It does seem to be true that there is nothing more that is essential to sexuality, that nothing more is needed as part of the definition. But it is not true that nothing more is important in an account of sexuality. A poem is nothing more than marks on a page; there is nothing there in addition to the marks. The tones of a clarinet might be nothing but vibrations made by blowing air over a thin piece of wood and through a tubular piece of wood. Yet any account of poetry or music that stopped at this point would obviously be inadequate. (I am not suggesting that there is a complete analogy between these examples and the definition of sexuality. We might well be able to make a conceptual distinction between words and mere marks. But the examples do illustrate the shortcomings of reductionist accounts. The page of poetry contains nothing in addition to the marks.) Expansionists should cease confronting the reductionists on reductionistic grounds. Instead they should allow the reductionists their definition and insist on an account of the significance of human sexuality. Here there is much agreement between the expansionists and the reductionists.

2. Expansionism: Sex as Language

In an early version of the expansionists' reply to reductionism, Peter Bertocci argues that the reductionists' "line of reasoning neglects the *human* significance of sex. Sex in the human is so interwoven with his total psychological being that . . . the contrasts are more illuminating than the likenesses. To compare the sounds an animal makes with the poetry of word symbols gives some notion of the range of differences possible." He goes on to claim that sex is more satisfying when it is "a symbolic expression of other values."[11] It is significant to note that Bertocci does not claim to be defining "sex." He knows perfectly well that sex can be sought for its own sake. Thus he could accept the reductionist account but argue that sex should be sought as a means to a higher end. However, Bertocci does not take this position explicitly, perhaps because the attempts to provide a formal definition of "sex" had not really begun in earnest.

More recent expansionist accounts do take on the reductionist claims directly. Robert Solomon suggests that sexuality be viewed as a kind of language. "Sexual activity consists in speaking what we might call 'body language.' It has its own grammar, delineated by the body, and its own phonetics of touch and movement. . . . [B]ody language is essentially expressive, and its content is limited to interpersonal attitudes and feelings."[12] Hugh Wilder accepts the analogy of sex with language but criticizes Solomon's communication model as excessively narrow. According to Wilder, sex, like language, has many different functions, but no particular function is itself essential:

> language can be used to communicate, to express ideas and feelings, to produce ideas and feelings, to fill silences, to start conversations, to end conversations, to inform, to entertain, to deceive; it can be an instrument of pleasure, of pain, of goodness, of vice; it can be refined and offensive, boring and exciting, pointed and pointless. So, too, can sex.[13]

The overwhelming attention given to criticizing opposing views has tended to obscure the substantial agreement among the reductionists and expansionists. Among the expansionists, Solomon claims that "some attitudes, e.g., tenderness and trust, domination and passivity, are best expressed sexually,"[14] and Bertocci argues that sex can be the "means of communicating one's concern for the wider range of values" such as love, marriage, and family.[15] Interestingly, the reductionists have been even clearer about the meaning of sex. While Goldman denies that sex is essentially a means of communication, he is "not denying that sex can take on heightened value and meaning when it becomes a vehicle for the expression of feelings of love or tenderness."[16] Janice Moulton has criticized Solomon for claiming that some attitudes are best expressed sexually, but she admits the usefulness of the language metaphor: "sexual behavior not only transmits information about feelings and attitudes . . . but also, like language, it has a *phatic* function to evoke feelings and attitudes."[17] She also says that "sexual behavior differs from other behavior by virtue of its unique feelings and emotions and its unique ability to create shared intimacy."[18] Robert Gray, who defines sexual desire in terms of sexual pleasure, warns that this is not equivalent to saying that "'sex is pure physical enjoyment'. . . . Sexual activity may have many ends, interpersonal communication among them."[19]

So the reductionists admit that sex can have other functions besides physical enjoyment. Perhaps it is even better when it does. Their thesis is that it need not have these other characteristics. But the expansionists can allow this thesis. Their point is that sex should include these other characteristics, that it is better when it serves these functions, not that it must have them to be sex.

There is even a way that expansionists can argue that the reductionist definition is wrong, even though no single function is necessary for an activity to be sexual. If we view sex as language, we should not be surprised to find no single essential purpose. As Wilder pointed out, "in the context of comparing language with sex, language is best understood as having *no essential* purpose."[20] (That is, there is no single purpose that is essential for something to be language.) If sex is like language, then it too will not have an essential purpose (thus no function will be a necessary condition for an act to be sexual), but it does not follow that it might have no purpose at all or that the physical activity is all there is to sex, any more than noise is all there is to language. But there is little point in trying to win the debate. The goal is to understand the significance of sex and the metaphor with language can be helpful. Let us extend the metaphor a bit. Language is essentially symbolic. If sex can be viewed as language, it too may be seen as essentially symbolic.

3. The Symbolic Meaning of Sex

Let us consider what the symbolic significance of sex could be. In this section, I shall consider two relatively simple views of the symbolic meaning of sex (referred to as "Naive Views" 1 and 2), and then suggest a more sophisticated and promising direction in which we might look for an answer.

Naive View 1: Fixed Meanings

One straightforward way of approaching the question of sex and symbols is simply to ask what the symbolic meaning of sex is. This question assumes that the symbolic meaning is (at least relatively) fixed and simple. Traditional views of sex can be seen as holding this kind of position. Bertocci argued that sex (at its best) was symbolic of higher values such as love, marriage and family. The position of the Catholic Church can also be seen as a fixed meaning position. According to the Church, sex is symbolic of "mutual self-giving and human procreation in the context of true love."[21] (It is possible to argue that neither of these views is a symbolic view of sex. Instead they are proposals for the proper use of sex. However, it is not unreasonable to interpret this traditional view as insisting that "proper" sex is the symbolic expression of these values.) The problem with this traditional view of the symbolic meaning of sex is that the attacks on traditionalism have been valid. Sex is often not symbolic of these values. Tradition, assumption, or divine revelation provide the only reason why it should be. As many writers have suggested, sex can be used to express many different ideas or feelings. In these cases it seems clear that sex is not symbolic of love and procreation, much as the traditionalists might want it to be.

Naive View 2: Variability

A second straightforward way to understand the symbolism of sex is to say that sex is symbolic of whatever the participants are using it to symbolize. Since sexual activity has no fixed meaning, its actual meaning in any given case is determined by the participants. Some people use it to symbolize love and tenderness, others domination or even contempt. To some extent Solomon seems to hold such a view. While he claims that certain emotions are best expressed sexually, he also suggests that body language (of which sex is a part) can be used to express "shyness, domination, fear, submissiveness and dependence, love or hatred or indifference" and a host of other attitudes.[22] Both Wilder and Moulton might be said to hold this variability theory since they emphasize variability in the possible functions of language and hence of sex. Similarly, Goldman says, "When a language is used, the symbols normally have no importance in themselves; they function merely as vehicles for what can be communicated by them."[23] Sex on this theory is a variable, a blank that must be filled in. Like the terms in an uninterpreted calculus, it has no meaning until it is given one. I might use sex to symbolize one thing; you might use it to symbolize another. I might use it to symbolize love today, but tomorrow to symbolize domination. However appealing this view might seem at first, it is ultimately unsatisfactory. It denies the possibility of any inherent meaning in sexual activity. And it fails to account for the widespread agreement about the symbolic meaning of sex. If sex has no inherent meaning, why do writers and participants express such similar views about what sex often symbolizes?

4. Toward a Symbolic Theory of Sex

In this section, I shall provide a sketch of a symbolic theory of sex. This theory contains elements of both naive views. Each contains important elements of truth, but each is inadequate by itself. The symbolic theory of sex which I shall propose is based on the distinction between kinds of symbols. The first distinction we must draw is between a conventional symbol and a natural symbol. A conventional symbol is one that has no inherent or natural connection with the item it symbolizes, while a natural symbol does have such a natural connection.

> A *conventional* symbol is a sign, arbitrarily chosen to represent, or "stand for," something with which it has no integral connection: thus the scrawl X may, by common agreement, stand in mathematics for an unknown quantity; in the alphabet, for a sound composed of a cluck and a hiss; at the end of a letter, for a fond embrace. The figure X *is* not, in itself, any of those things and tells us nothing about them. Any other sign would serve the same purpose if we agreed to accept it so, nor is there any reason why the same sign should not stand, if we agreed that it should, for quite different things.
>
> A *natural* symbol is not an arbitrary sign, but a thing really existing which, by its very nature, stands for and images forth a greater reality of which it is itself an instance. Thus an arch, maintaining itself as it does by a balance of opposing strains, is a *natural symbol* of that stability in tension by which the whole universe maintains itself. Its significance is the same in all languages and in all circumstances, and may be applied indifferently to physical, psychical, or spiritual experience.[24]

The reason there is such widespread agreement about what sex can mean and often does mean is that sex is a natural symbol. Moulton recognizes "its unique ability to create shared intimacy."[25] Similarly, Goldman says that "intimacy . . . is seen to be a natural feature of mutual sex acts."[26] Thus it is reasonable to argue that sex is naturally symbolic of intimacy. Nor is intimacy the only natural feature of sex. Intimacy is just one of a family of emotions and characteristics; for example, openness, vulnerability, and perhaps even tenderness and caring. Note that these are not essential characteristics of every sex act (they are not necessary conditions), but sex is a natural symbol of these emotions. Thus it seems that the fixed meaning view has some validity.

However, the traditional view is not wholly correct. Any symbol, even those with natural meanings, can be used to symbolize other things as well. Thus sex can be, and often is, used to symbolize ideas or emotions other than those with which it is naturally associated. Therefore the variability theory is also correct.

In order to complete the outline of the theory we must distinguish between two types of nonnatural symbols. The first kind includes symbols that are truly conventional: their meanings are determined by usage, tradition, or agreement. The second is entirely personal or private. In this case, meanings are determined solely by the individual. Both kinds are different from natural symbols in that no natural connection obtains between the symbol and the thing it symbolizes. However, the meaning of conventional symbols is fixed by agreement, while the individual alone determines the meaning of a private symbol. Once again the analogy with language is useful. Some terms are naturally connected with their meanings (for example, onomatopoeic terms). Some terms are coined by individuals and these terms mean whatever their inventors say they mean. However, the vast majority of words are given meaning by convention, by the language users themselves. For terms that fall in this category, no natural connection obtains between the term and its meaning; yet individuals are not entirely free to use a term, arbitrarily, in just any way they wish. The terms have definite meanings acquired over time. Thus a third set of symbolic meanings for sex might be culturally determined.

While distinguishing between natural and cultural meanings of sex might be difficult, sex does have natural, conventional, and private symbolic meanings. Since it does have both natural and conventional symbolic significance, the reductionist analysis is inadequate. Reductionists admit that sexual activity can have symbolic meaning, but they insist that it need not have such meaning in any given case. This position would be defensible if sex were only a private symbol. Then it would mean whatever its participants used it to mean; it might even have no symbolic meaning at all in some cases. However, sex is also a natural and a conventional symbol. These meanings cannot be divorced from sex, and any account of sexuality that fails to explore them is incomplete.

5. Conclusion

I have not attempted to complete this sketch of the symbolic meaning of sex. My purpose has been to demonstrate the compatibility of the competing accounts of sex and to urge that attention be paid to the symbolism of sex. I have also attempted to distinguish the various kinds of symbolic meaning any symbolic theory of sex should include. In closing, I wish to take up three additional issues. First, it might be that the symbolic significance of sex is not exclusively human. Konrad Lorenz has described a practice among baboons that suggests that sex might be symbolic of domination and submissiveness among that species. The loser of a fight between two male baboons "presented his hindquarters so persistently that the stronger one eventually 'acknowledged' his submissiveness by mounting him . . . and performing a few perfunctory copulatory movements."[27] Thus one might argue that domination or submission is a natural meaning of sex, at least for some species. Second, psychoanalytic theory suggests the possibility of unconscious as well as conscious symbols. If a psychoanalyst says that John is unconsciously having sex with his mother or castrating his father in a given sexual act, should we say that this is part of the symbolic meaning of the act?

Finally, something should be said about the connection between symbolic meaning and morality. I have not argued that one set of symbols is better than another. Nor have I argued that it is wrong to use sex to symbolize something different from or opposed to its natural significance. Each of these claims is defensible. One could argue that sex used as a symbol of domination and hate is wrong, because domination and hate are wrong, although one must be careful here; sex is the *expression* of domination and hate in this case, not necessarily actual domination and hate. One could also argue that using sex in a way that is contrary to its natural meaning is inherently wrong (although this is by no means obvious). In any case, an adequate theory of the symbolism of sex should at least address the question of symbols and morality.

Thus both the reductionist and the expansionist accounts of sex are right, and both are wrong. Reductionists are correct in their attempts to define sex in purely physical terms. Sex can be defined as "plain sex." But expansionists are correct in emphasizing the symbolic significance of sex. Their mistake lies in trying to tie this significance to the definition of sex, rather than the meaning of sex. Sex is both plain and symbol.

Notes

1. Alan Soble, "An Introduction to the Philosophy of Sex," in Alan Soble, ed., *Philosophy of Sex*, 1st ed. (Littlefield, Adams, 1980), 1-56, at 7.
2. Richard Taylor, "Eros, or The Love of the Sexes," in Thomas Mappes and Jane Zembaty, eds., *Social Ethics*, 1st ed. (New York: McGraw-Hill, 1977), 202-5; Roger Taylor, "Sexual Experiences," in Soble, *Philosophy of Sex*, 1st ed., 59-75.
3. Richard Taylor, "Eros, or The Love of the Sexes," 203-5.
4. Roger Taylor, "Sexual Experiences," 72.
5. Alan Goldman, "Plain Sex," in Soble, *Philosophy of Sex*, 1st ed., 119-38, at 120; 2nd ed. (1991), 73-92, at 74.
6. Soble, "Introduction," 14.
7. Robert Gray, "Sex and Sexual Perversion," in Soble, *Philosophy of Sex*, 1st ed., 158-68, at 161.
8. Goldman, "Plain Sex," in Soble, *Philosophy of Sex*, 1st ed., 121; 2nd ed., 75.
9. *Ibid.*
10. Theodore Roszak, *Where the Wasteland Ends* (Garden City, N.Y.: Doubleday, 1973), 242.

11. Peter A. Bertocci, "The Human Venture in Sex, Love, and Marriage," in Mappes and Zembaty, *Social Ethics*, 206-9, at 207.

12. Robert Solomon, "Sexual Paradigms," in Soble, *Philosophy of Sex*, 1st ed., 89-98, at 96; 2nd ed., 53-62, at 60.

13. Hugh Wilder, "The Language of Sex and the Sex of Language," in Soble, *Philosophy of Sex*, 1st ed., 90-109, at 108 (this volume, 23-31, at 30).

14. Solomon, "Sexual Paradigms," in Soble, *Philosophy of Sex*, 1st ed., 97; 2nd ed., 61.

15. Bertocci, "The Human Venture," 209.

16. Goldman, "Plain Sex," in Soble, *Philosophy of Sex*, 1st ed., 124; 2nd ed., 78.

17. Janice Moulton, "Sexual Behavior: Another Position," in Soble, *Philosophy of Sex*, 1st ed., 110-18, at 116; 2nd ed., 63-71, at 69.

18. *Ibid.*, 1st ed., 117; 2nd ed., 70.

19. Gray, "Sex and Sexual Perversion," 165.

20. Wilder, "The Language of Sex," 101 (this volume, 24).

21. "Vatican Declaration on Some Questions of Sexual Ethics," in Mappes and Zembaty, *Social Ethics*, 2nd ed. (1982), 204-10, at 207.

22. Solomon, "Sexual Paradigms," in Soble, *Philosophy of Sex*, 1st ed., 96; 2nd ed., 60.

23. Goldman, "Plain Sex," in Soble, *Philosophy of Sex*, 1st ed., 127; 2nd ed., 81.

24. Dorothy Sayers, Introduction, Dante, *Inferno* (New York: Penguin, 1949), 12-13.

25. Moulton, "Sexual Behavior," in Soble, *Philosophy of Sex*, 1st ed., 117; 2nd ed., 70.

26. Goldman, "Plain Sex," in Soble, *Philosophy of Sex*, 1st ed., 126; 2nd ed., 80.

27. Konrad Lorenz, *On Aggression* (New York: Harcourt, Brace, 1966), 131.

Claudia Card
(photograph: Sharon Keller)

Author of "The Symbolic Significance of Sex
and the Institution of Sexuality"
Paper presented at the Society for the Philosophy of Sex and Love
during the
Eastern Division Meeting of The American Philosophical Association
New York, N.Y., 28 December 1984

Twenty-Nine

THE SYMBOLIC SIGNIFICANCE OF SEX

Claudia Card

That sex should symbolize love in a society in which the realities of sexual encounter are often hostile and violent is profoundly disturbing. Yet this issue is widely overlooked in disagreements about the nature of human sexuality and its relationships to love. Philosophical discussions of sex and love have often focused on whether sex has any special connection with love, taking it for granted that sex and love are mutually compatible.

Many years ago Alan Soble divided such philosophical analyses of sex into two groups, which he called reductionist and expansionist.[1] Reductionists maintain that sex is only physical (and love, therefore, not essential to it), while expansionists maintain that an adequate account of human sexuality requires "something more" (than mere physical contact), thus making room for the possibility that love, or something like it, might have an important role. Leonard Berkowitz then took up Peter Bertocci's suggestion that human sexuality has symbolic significance and argued that the reductionist and expansionist analyses of sex need not be conceived as alternatives, that, strictly speaking, both expansionists and reductionists could be right.[2] The idea was that even if nothing more than certain (appropriately described) physical experiences were required for a *definition* of "sex," an adequate account of human sexuality requires much more that is *important* than simply physical experiences. On this account, the "more" is the symbolic significance of sex, which can take many forms: natural and conventional, public and private.

This is a promising idea. To take it a step further, the symbolic significance of sex invites consideration of sexuality as a *social institution*, for symbolic meanings are often institutionalized. If institutionalized sexuality elaborates symbolic meanings in its norms and ideals, presumably they can be evaluated, criticized, even changed. Thus the way is opened to argue that in sexist contexts, it might be dangerous for at least heterosex to symbolize love.

I will suggest a new kind of question for the reductionist to substitute for the old one about whether sex is simply physical. The new question is whether sexual activity or experience exists prior to any institutions of sexuality, as eating and drinking exist prior to their institutionalizations (in the sense of *logically* prior). And I will also propose a different sort of inquiry about the relationships between sex and love for expansionist sympathizers to think about. That inquiry is into whether it might be a better idea to encourage nonsexualized forms of erotic activity and experience than to try to make room for, or endorse the presence of, either love or the erotic in sexual behavior, as presently practiced and socially understood.

We could grant, for the moment, that expansionists can concede to reductionists that nothing (such as loving) need be going on in addition to physical contact and sensual pleasure in order for an activity to be sexual, just as nothing need be on the paper in addition to ink marks in order for a poem to be on the paper. More important, we could grant that expansionists can have what they want for human sexuality without insisting that each individual act or experience must have it in order to be sexual. One could point out that "marks on paper" does not *define* "poem," even though it is true that nothing else need be on the paper. Perhaps, likewise, physical activities do not *define* "sexuality" as human, even though nothing else need be going on in a particular instance.

What expansionists want, apparently, is the recognition that what is most interesting, and at any rate essential to an adequate understanding of human sexuality, is *meaningfulness*: that sex, like language, points to something beyond itself and that its doing so is not particularly a function of the intentions or purposes of the agents who are engaging in sexual activity at the time that they are doing so. Sexual behavior can have a variety of symbolic meanings, perhaps some more stable than others and some arbitrary. Even if these meanings are not essential to sex *qua* sex, however, perhaps some of them are intimately involved with sex being *sexy* and with its ability to offer the drama it so often offers the lives of those who become sexually involved with each other.

But instead of conceding the reductionists' *definition*, expansionists would do better to do the following. First, they should challenge the assumption that sex *has an essence* (or common denominator), rather than argue about what its essence is. Second, they should note important ambiguities in the referents of "sex," some of which might be cleared up by distinguishing between the *institution of sexuality*, on the one hand, as a complex thing constituted by norms, and individual sexual acts and experiences falling under the norms of this institution, on the other. And, finally, expansionists could argue that what reductionist definitions of "sex" miss is the *institution* of sexuality and the meanings that it gives to individual acts and experiences by way of elaborate systems of social norms. Not everything that belongs to a satisfactory definition of "sexuality" as an *institution* need carry over into each individual act or experience that is justifiably identified as "sexual," any more than everything entering into a satisfactory definition of "punishment" as an *institution* need carry over into individual punishments. The failure to recognize that "sex," as a social and even *political* concept, refers both to an institution and to a variety of activities structured by that institution, might underlie some of the arguing at cross purposes of reductionists and expansionists. This is not all that is confusing about the meaning of "sex." The term also refers to certain mundane facts regarding the way many organisms reproduce biologically (to which I will return).

The hypothesis that the institution of sexuality contributes to the significance of individual sexual acts and experiences sounds like a plausible interpretation of the hypothesis that sexual acts and experiences have conventional symbolic meanings. Perhaps some things commonly thought to be symbolized naturally by sexual behavior are, in reality, conventional meanings. Consider vulnerability, for example. Why should sexuality symbolize vulnerability? In a misogynist society, heterosexual behavior is probably more apt to symbolize vulnerability for women than for men. Sarah Hoagland has reminded us that "vulnerable" means "open to attack" or "capable of being wounded."[3] This suggests a hostile context for sexual behavior, a context that might be the product of convention and thereby, we can hope, changeable over time. Because social conventions are not changeable simply by individual agents and need not be reflected in their intentions on particular occasions, such conventions can easily appear to be products of nature rather than society.

The idea that sex has an essence appears to be shared by both reductionists and expansionists. By "essence" is meant a common characteristic, something possessed by all sexual acts and experiences (perhaps a Platonic form, such as Socrates might have worried about in the *Parmenides*).[4] But we need not worry about reducing sex to its lowest common denominator, since it might have no common denominator. Acts that take an important part of their meaning from the background context of an institution or practice defined by rules that create offices, positions, and moves (as John Rawls puts it in his work on justice) need not have any common characteristic in order to be justifiably identified by a term that refers us to that institution or practice.[5] We could *construct* a complex characteristic, "being governed by the rules of the institution of sexuality," to do the job of serving as the common characteristic. Yet this is not the sort of characteristic we could identify by abstracting from individual cases. Further, it is misleading: the rules of the institution can change, and no rule might be essential or unchangeable. What holds the rules together as rules of the same institution might be a shared history. Even such a constructed characteristic might not yield a common denominator after all.

To continue the analogy with punishment, consider Nietzsche's remarks about punishment in his genealogy of morality.[6] Although he did not explicitly refer to punishment as an institution, he is discussing the history of the practice, or institution, of punishment. He observed that punishment consists of a complex set of rituals, even a *drama*, with a long past, rituals that have meant many different things to different people in different ages.[7] When Nietzsche observed that "only that which has no history is definable," he seems to have meant that only what has *not evolved,* or descended from a historical chain of ancestors, has an essence. Like the institution of punishment, the institution of sexuality has a long ancestral history, some of which has been analyzed by Michel Foucault (who finds ancestors even in the Catholic practice of the confessional, for example).[8] Various norms of this institution have been discussed in feminist philosophical literature by such philosophers as Ti-Grace Atkinson, who titled one of her best known essays "The Institution of Sexual Intercourse," and Janice Moulton, in a delightfully humorous piece called "Sex and Reference."[9]

"Essence" suggests a common core of meaning persisting throughout a history. But an institution might not, in fact, have a common core of meaning. An institution might be like the cable cited by Wittgenstein, which lacks a common thread running through from one end to the other, yet hangs together as one thing, capable of being differentiated from other things by the way its strands are related to other strands.[10] Further, an institution might be constantly reconstituted, somewhat like David Hume's ship that is rebuilt plank by plank while out to sea.[11] What corresponds to the planks are norms, but while we can replace an old plank with a new one that is just like the old one except for being newer, we cannot replace an old norm with another that it just like it (doing so would not really *replace* it at all). So we must imagine that the evolving institution is constantly changing its form and not simply its matter. Nietzsche seems to have thought that the matter might actually have more stability than the form. He maintained that what is (most) fluid about punishment is precisely its *meanings* (purposes, for example) and that what is (relatively) stable is its *rituals*, which, like words on his view, seem to be "containers" into which now this meaning and now that one might be poured.[12]

This understanding of matter and form might be confusing to philosophers who are still raised on Aristotle. Nietzsche seems to restrict "meaning" (which suggests "form" to an Aristotelian) to purposes. What he calls the drama, or ritual (which I find it natural to call the "matter," as it provides a material embodiment of the purposes), appears to be activities with certain structures, perhaps in the case of punishment such things as arrests, inquisitions, trials, beheadings, incarcerations. All these are activities or actions that might be done for a variety of purposes. The drama, or ritual, in the case of sexuality appears to include such things as what we call flirting, dating, marriage, and heterosexual copulation. Maybe the concept of meaning is elastic enough that we could easily include the structure of an activity as an important element of its meaning and of the meanings of the elements structured. In virtue of the structure, elements in a historical process (or activity) can "point toward" others, as it were, sometimes forward, sometimes backward, sometimes both. This "pointing toward," like symbolizing, is one of the things that might be meant by "signifying." Other parts of a ritual or drama can thus be (part of) the significance of some of its parts.

Such views, applied to sexuality, make sense of certain controversies among feminists regarding whether certain behavior is really sexual or not. In the 1970s, we often heard the arguments that rape was violence, *not sex,* and that pornography was violent rather than erotic. But why couldn't they be both? Many of the same rituals that have sexual meanings or erotic meanings can also have violent ones. Some can even have (and have had) religious meanings.

The suggestion that a controversy of long standing might be resolved by distinguishing between an institution and actions falling under the norms of that institution was put forward by John Rawls in the 1950s in relation to theories of the justification of punishment.[13] Controversies over the meaning of "punishment" have even been somewhat analogous to the reductionist-expansionist controversy over the meaning of "sex": is punishment simply physical suffering (or confinement or loss), or must there be something more? Must the suffering, for example, be *meaningful* in order to count as punishment?[14] It must be meaningful suffering, although not necessarily in the sense that the sufferer appreciates the meaning or even that the punisher intends it. Nor need the meaning be the same in all cases. But it must be meaningful in the sense that it is inflicted as a response to certain things that went before, that it is part of a larger process, a set of rituals or dramas, as Nietzsche put it.

On Rawls's analysis of punishment, the institution is logically prior to the individual punishment. That is, the activity of inflicting suffering on someone cannot, logically, be punishment apart from the context of the rules that define the practice, any more than sliding into a sandbag can constitute scoring a run or stealing a base apart from the rules of baseball. The question thus presents itself whether the relationship between sex and the institution of sexuality is like that. A question that reductionist sympathizers might do well to substitute for the earlier question whether sex is nothing more than physical contact and sensual pleasure is the question whether sex, meaning whatever "sex" means in such expressions as "having sex," is logically prior to the institution of sexuality. Could there be human sexual behavior or experience without any background social institution or practice? Would human sexual behavior or experience be simply meaningless ritual, like sliding into a sandbag without any such context as baseball, or beating people up or incarcerating them without any such context as punishment? Is sex as dependent on its institutional context as punishment and home runs? Or is it more like, say, eating and sleeping, to which it is often compared, which can exist independently of social norms or even such rituals as "three times a day"? According to Aristotle, the virtue of temperance is concerned with eating, drinking, and sex, which he treats as appetites that can be overindulged.[15] Eating and drinking do not require institutional contexts, although banqueting and perhaps dining and brunch do. Apparently, Aristotle thought of sex as another appetite analogous to hunger and thirst, which suggests that it, too, might be indulged apart from the context of any structuring social institution. But is there any such thing as "plain sex," on a par with plain eating, drinking, or sleeping?

To answer this question, it would be helpful to know to what kinds of behavior "sex" refers in such expressions as "having sex." What count as instances of "having sex"? Must genitalia be involved? I find that if I try, as Freud tried, to abandon a phallocentric conception of "sex," what counts as sexual, and what does not, is cloudy. The only straightforwardly preinstitutional sense of "sex" that I can make out is the biological sense that refers in one way or another to reproductive capacities of members of a species that reproduces sexually. Thus one's sex is one's femaleness or maleness (or whatever intermediate thing one turned out to be), and in this sense of "sex," one *has it* all the time. One's femaleness or maleness is definable by reference to the roles played in reproduction by animals of each kind. The penis is a genital organ, an organ of reproduction, and thus clearly a sexual organ (although not only that; it is also an organ of excretion). What tends to excite (or relieve) a penis in certain ways is straightforwardly biologically sexual, regardless whether it in fact leads or is intended to lead to reproduction. The clitoris, on the other hand, is *not* a genital organ. It plays no plausible role in reproduction. Women in some parts of the world have their clitoris excised, as a matter of religious ritual, without experiencing, in successful instances, any detriment to their reproductive capacities.[16] What is popularly referred to as genital pleasure in women is in fact a consequence of the reception and transformation of sensory stimuli by the clitoris.[17] Strictly speaking, women have no external genitalia; the only external genital organs are male. What sense does it make, then, to regard clitoral pleasure as sexual?

Clitoral pleasure is *female* and thus sexual in *that* sense. But in the same sense, a man's beard or hairy chest is also sexual. Likewise vaginitis, menstruation, menopause, even hot flashes. The pleasure produced by beard stroking, however, is (probably) not sexual in the way intended by those who would say that the pleasures produced in a woman by stroking her pubes are sexual. What is meant in this case is not only (or even especially) that the pleasures are *female*.

Some might argue that clitoral pleasure is preinstitutionally sexual in that it facilitates reproduction by providing women with a motive for seeking, or at least not resisting, heterosexual copulation. Is this true? Copulation is certainly not the easiest way, and for many women, not a particularly good way, to obtain clitoral pleasure, although many women have tried valiantly to conform to norms requiring that they experience it by means of heterosexual copulatory stimulation (even to the point of having the clitoris surgically moved into a more convenient position for this purpose). In a society that provides women with severe economic and social penalties for refusing heterosexual copulation, we need not postulate other motives for lack of female resistance. To the extent that women's motives for heterosexual copulation consist of such desires as for socially sanctioned companionship and security, they refer us to the *institution* of sexuality and are not sexual in any recognizably preinstitutional sense of that term.

Freud offered an account of infant sexuality as polymorphously perverse.[18] On his account, nearly any part of the body might be "sexualized" by becoming a focus of repeated vigorous muscular activity (sucking, for example), with the result that a tension is regularly created there needing relief, and capable of relief, through muscular activity (sucking, pulling, rubbing). Thumb sucking is a paradigm of what Freud called the infant's polymorphously perverse sexuality. But what does it mean to call this physical source of pleasure (or relief) sexual? It certainly does not appear to be sexual in the biological sense of that term: it has nothing to do with reproduction or with the reproductive capacities of the animal. If the answer is supposed to be that the energies expended are sexual energies, the question becomes what is meant by calling those energies sexual. Calling them sexual has the consequence of relating them to various meanings imposed on rituals of heterosexual copulation by the *institution* of sexuality. It allows one to argue, for example, that in an adult person, energy expended in thumb sucking is misdirected (or simply wasted) copulatory energy.

In short, giving an account of what it means to call either clitoral pleasure or thumb sucking sexual is not possible without reference to the institution of sexuality. If there is such as thing as "plain sex," which does not mean simply "femaleness or maleness" but is ordinarily pleasurable and independent of the institution of sexuality (logically prior to it), it would seem to be an androcentric phenomenon. Those who have insisted that "having sex" really means "doing something with or in the presence of a penis" would be right.[19] There appears to be no adequate preinstitutional vocabulary for women's orgasmic and other sensual pleasures. Calling them "sexual" in the same sense as men's genital pleasures are sexual appears either to rest upon a misconception of the clitoris as vestigial penis (thus a genital organ) or to regard clitoral pleasures, falsely, as simply by-products of heterosexual copulation (penis-produced).

There is, however, a common language for many of the activities that women and men engage in (not necessarily heterosexually) on the way to orgasmic pleasure; in other contexts, it is often popularly presented as a more polite way to talk about sex. I have in mind not the language of love but that of eroticism. Eroticism is a kind of play that can become serious and have serious consequences. Instead of focusing exclusively on the relationships of *love* to sexuality, it might be more interesting, and it is certainly as socially important, to examine the relationships of the *erotic* to sexuality. "Erotic" is sometimes even used as a euphemism for "sexual," as in "erotic art," much of which is not very erotic, although what it depicts is often sexual.

Unlike the sexual, the erotic is an emotional category, not a biological one. Eroticism refers to something like a certain susceptibility to joyful surprise, or the excitement of anticipating such surprise, in activities of intimate discovery and disclosure through touching.[20] By "touching", I mean not simply spatial contiguity of bodies but rather success, actual or fantasized, in reaching someone, that is, in making someone feel something. In this sense, unlike the contiguity sense, one person does not succeed in touching another unless the other feels the touch. Erotic touching *can* be sexual. But it does not have to be. Erotic touching does not even require spatial contiguity of bodies. Eye contact (as in flirting), for example, can be thoroughly erotic, as can verbal and even written communication. Some readers have thought that Thomas Nagel's famous essay, "Sexual Perversion," never got around to sex, although it discusses what purport to be some highly erotic scenarios.[21] The institution of sexuality can explain how one could make such a mistake, the mistake of taking an erotic interchange to be a sexual one, if indeed such a mistake was made. For the institution of sexuality presents the erotic *as* sexual by construing erotic play, such as flirting, as *a sexual invitation*.

Erotic interaction can create powerful bonds. Like super glue, a little bit can fix one for a long time, even years. This is not true of sexual activity in general. A consequence of sexualizing eroticism in a society in which sexuality is an institution that is highly complicit in women's oppression is that engaging in heterosexual erotic play can be dangerous for women. It can set women up for becoming locked into hostile and violent relationships, or at least trapped in bad ones from which extrication can be most difficult.

A powerful motive for reductionist theories of sex has been to divorce sex from love. A more laudable motivation might be to divorce sex from the *symbolism* of love, which is a profoundly misleading symbolism in a misogynist society. In such a society one might rather have expected an inquiry into the question whether sex could be *compatible* with love than inquiry into whether sex and love have some special connection with each other. If it is love and the erotic, after all, that expansionists are after, perhaps it would be better, instead of expanding the meaning of "sex" to include love or the erotic, to expand our categories of behavior to include *erotic* sensual pleasure (as we already recognize *loving* sensual pleasure; for example, in back rubs) that does not take its meaning from the institution of sexuality.

Notes

1. Alan Soble, "An Introduction to the Philosophy of Sex," in Alan Soble, ed., *Philosophy of Sex*, 1st ed. (Totowa, N.J.: Littlefield, Adams, 1980), 1-56, at 7.

2. Leonard Berkowitz, "Sex: Plain and Symbol," this volume, 279-87; Peter Bertocci, "The Human Venture in Sex, Love, and Marriage," in Thomas Mappes and Jane Zembaty, eds., *Social Ethics*, 1st ed. (New York: McGraw-Hill, 1977), 206-9.

3. Sarah Hoagland, "Vulnerability and Power," *Sinister Wisdom* 19 (Winter 1982): 13-23.

4. Socrates wonders in the *Parmenides* whether there is a special form for everything or only for such things as are good, beautiful, or just (Edith Hamilton and Huntington Cairns, eds., *The Collected Dialogues of Plato* [New York: Pantheon, 1961], 921-56).

5. For such an account of what an institution is, see John Rawls, *A Theory of Justice* (Cambridge, Mass.: Harvard University Press, 1971), 55.

6. Friedrich Nietzsche, *On the Genealogy of Morals*, trans. Walter Kaufmann and Robert Hollingdale (New York: Vintage, 1967), 76-83.

7. *Ibid.*, 79.

8. *Ibid.*, 80. See Michel Foucault, *The History of Sexuality*, vol. 1: *An Introduction*, trans. Robert Hurley (New York: Vintage, 1980), 17-35.

9. Ti-Grace Atkinson, "The Institution of Sexual Intercourse," *Amazon Odyssey* (New York: Links Books, 1974), 13-23; Janice Moulton, "Sex and Reference," in Robert Baker and Frederick Elliston, eds., *Philosophy and Sex*, 1st ed. (Buffalo: Prometheus, 1975), 34-44.

10. Ludwig Wittgenstein, *Philosophical Investigations*, trans. G. E. M. Anscombe (Oxford: Blackwell, 1958), 32e.

11. David Hume, *A Treatise of Human Nature* (Oxford: Clarendon Press, 1960), 257.

12. Nietzsche, *Genealogy of Morals*, 79. On words as pockets into which different meanings can be poured, see *ibid.*, 180.

13. John Rawls, "Two Concepts of Rules," *Philosophical Review* 64:1 (1955): 3-32.

14. For discussions of the meaning of "punishment," see H. B. Acton, ed., *The Philosophy of Punishment* (London: Macmillan, 1969), especially the papers by Mabbott, Quinton, Flew, and Baier.

15. Aristotle, *Nicomachean Ethics*, trans. David Ross (New York: Oxford University Press, 1925, 1980), 72-8.

16. On clitoridectomy, see Mary Daly, *Gyn/Ecology: The Metaethics of Radical Feminism* (Boston: Beacon, 1978), 153-77; Alice Walker and Pratibha Parmar, *Warrior Marks: Female Genital Mutilation and the Sexual Blinding of Women* (New York: Harcourt, Brace, 1993); and Alice Walker's novel, *Possessing the Secret of Joy* (New York: Harcourt, Brace, Jovanovich, 1992).

17. On the physiology of the clitoris and various misunderstandings, see William H. Masters and Virginia W. Johnson, *Human Sexual Response* (Boston: Little, Brown, 1966), 45-67.

18. Sigmund Freud, "Infantile Sexuality," in James Strachey, ed. and trans., *Three Essays on the Theory of Sexuality* (New York: Avon, 1962), 66-106.

19. See, for example, Marilyn Frye, *The Politics of Reality: Essays in Feminist Theory* (Trumansburg, N.Y.: Crossing Press, 1983), 156-7. See also Frye, "Lesbian 'Sex'," in *Willful Virgin: Essays in Feminism 1976-1992* (Freedom, Cal.: Crossing Press, 1992), 109-19.

20. For further development of this and other ideas in the present essay, see my "Intimacy and Responsibility: What Lesbians Do," in Martha Albertson Fineman and Nancy Sweet Thomadsen, eds., *At the Boundaries of Law: Feminism and Legal Theory* (New York: Routledge, 1991), 77-94.

21. Thomas Nagel, "Sexual Perversion," *Journal of Philosophy* 66:1 (1969): 5-17; in Soble, *Philosophy of Sex*, 1st ed., 76-88; 2nd ed. (1991), 39-51.

Charles W. Johnson
(photograph: Utah State University)

Author of "Body Language"
Paper presented at the Society for the Philosophy of Sex and Love
during the
Pacific Division Meeting of The American Philosophical Association
San Francisco, Cal., 22 March 1985

Thirty

BODY LANGUAGE

Charles W. Johnson

1. Introduction

At the risk of being considered insufferably prudish, I shall attempt to defend a standard of sexual conduct that could well be described as "Victorian." My defense, however, will not be along moralistic lines. This paper is concerned with the *meaning*, not the morality, of sex. In the context of the communication model of sexual activity, I will show that the same consistency restraints placed on meaningful use of linguistic signs also apply to meaningful use of sexual activities. In so doing, I shall take issue with the view proposed by two authors, Frederick Elliston and Robert Solomon, who have claimed that the communication model provides grounds for defending promiscuity.

2. The Communication Model

The communication model of sexuality[1] suggests that sexual activity is a *body language*. Solomon has suggested that rather than being an activity in which the main goal is physical pleasure, "sexuality is primarily a means of communicating with people."[2] The form of this body language is a set of movements, postures, and gestures, and it has its own syntax, semantics, and pragmatics. Solomon compared the use of body language to "performances," in J. L. Austin's sense.[3] In his later work, Solomon reaffirmed the communication model by suggesting that making love and intimate conversation "may not be so different."[4] "Sex is basically self-expression, not the technique of exciting another person or the thrill of being excited oneself."[5]

The communication view provides a *model*. In science, models are "heuristic fictions."[6] They often have the advantage of being more familiar than what they model. Using a theoretical model primarily involves talking in a certain way; here, the use of the communication model involves talking about sex as if it were linguistic discourse.[7] Using this model, we can gain insight into sexual activity; we think about it a new way. This is valuable so long as we keep in mind that the communication model provides just one way of thinking about sex. The model cannot be used to contend that sex *is* communication, only that sex can be looked at as though it were linguistic. Solomon hints that Ludwig Wittgenstein's remarks about verbal language apply to body language. I agree. Wittgenstein's reminders concerning rules and language games apply to body language to the extent the communication model is viable.

Verbal language is a rule-governed activity. Sexual body language is rule-governed as well. As the defenders of promiscuity have admitted, this connects sexual conduct to certain Western traditions in the same way that the rules governing verbal language relate the uses of words to their assigned lexical meanings. The main presumption of the communication model is that body language is analogous to verbal language. If this is the case, then the learning of a body language and the use of body language also must be analogous to verbal language. I will employ Wittgenstein's method of assembling reminders for a particular purpose[8] to examine the application of this analogy. This will require that we describe the role played by body language in the context of the whole of language.[9] Just as a nonliteral, nonstandard language game, such as sarcasm, can properly be interpreted only within language as a whole, so, too, expressive body language must be viewed in the more general context of verbal communication.

3. Methodology

I do not expect or intend to explain anything about sex and love. My intent is only to describe. There are two reasons for this. One is methodological; the other has to do with the content of this discussion. First, regarding method, Wittgenstein cautioned against traditional philosophical theory-formation:

> [W]e may not advance any kind of theory. . . . We must do away with all *explanation*, and description alone must take its place. And this description gets its light, that is to say its purpose, from the philosophical problems. . . . The problems are solved, not by giving new information, but by arranging what we have always known.[10]

I shall arrange "what we have always known" about language to show that the communication model does not encourage promiscuity any more than verbal language encourages people to use language indiscriminately.

It is not my intention to construct or complete a theory of meaning for body language. I am seeking a surview (an *Übersicht*)[11] of sexual body language. To do so, I survey the uses and applications of body language in the context of the communication model. My aim is to remove a philosophical perplexity. One source of the perplexity is Elliston and Solomon's observation that the best way to learn how to speak verbal language fluently is to speak with many people. Assuming verbal language is a model for body language, Elliston and Solomon contend that the best way to become fluent at sexual communication is to have sex with many people, that is, to be promiscuous.

Elliston and Solomon want body language to have meaning; their concern focuses on how its meaning is learned or acquired. Wittgenstein's reminders suggest that meaning in language requires (1) a standard for correct usage, (2) agreement in judgment, and (3) a history of correct usage.

In addition to methodological considerations, some features of the content of this topic require description instead of explanation. Wittgenstein suggested:

• Here one can only *describe* and say: this is what human life is like.
• Compared with the impression which the description makes on us, the explanation is too uncertain.
• [A] hypothetical explanation will be of little help to someone, say, who is upset because of love.—It will not calm him.
• The crowd of thoughts which does not come out, because they all want to rush forward and thus get stuck in the exit.[12]

To avoid getting stuck by trying to say everything at once, I shall construct a connected series of descriptive reminders[13] to explore the application of the communication model to context specific uses of body language.

4. Sexual Communication

Under Western norms, a primary use of sexual expression is to convey love and devotion. To claim that the phrase "I love you" is the standard message conveyed by sexual relations is not to say it is the only one. The sexual expression/communication in promiscuous activity is secondary; with it people may convey, if they are honest, "You are fun to be with," "I'm having a good time." Such secondary uses of sex are certainly possible, but interpretation of them also requires a standard. Nonstandard, nonliteral uses of verbal language, such as satire, sarcasm, and metaphor, have meaning relative to standard, literal uses. Sarcasm and so forth are dependent subsets of communicative discourse. "It is only if the word has the primary sense for you that you use it in the secondary one."[14] Sarcasm makes sense only against a background of literal discourse; nonsense is recognizable only in contrast to sense; lies are operative only where there is truth. In verbal discourse, we cannot be sarcastic or lie unless we speak truthfully much of the time.

Let us return to the model. The primary use of verbal language is to inform a listener of some fact. A speaker might depart from primary uses: you can use nonliteral discourse, you can speak nonsense, you can lie. It appears, in this model, that sex falls into the first group. In this event, sex could be casual, recreational, and meaningful in a secondary way: it could convey a message such as "This is great fun" or "I am satisfied!" I suppose an incompetent partner could evince nonsensical motions. However, the pernicious sort of promiscuity is the dishonest kind. In this sort of body language conversation, one of the partners is going through the motions for some reason other than love, while his or her partner is interpreting the message as loving.

Both linguistic and sexual communication can break down if the participants are playing different language games. My brother experienced this breakdown: While on a business trip he encountered a lovely lady in a cocktail lounge in a large, expensive hotel. She seemed friendly, and he responded accordingly. Like Nagel's strangers, they seemed to have an affinity for one another, or so it seemed to my brother. He discovered later, to his dismay, that she was a professional "working" lady; they had been playing different language games all evening. He was off duty; she was still at work.

Deception is a part of some games. Shoulder fakes are a part of football. There are variations of body language games, for example, duplicitous seduction, where faking expressive communication might be considered part of the game; but such games are derivative in the way that metaphor is a derivative of literal discourse. Duplicity is an intentional departure from what is anticipated or expected; it is secondary to standard play. Also, it is not obvious that faking in a body language game holds the same status as faking in football. A shoulder fake might be a good move for a running back, while a gesture fake might be non-play for a sex partner.

To examine the difference between literal and nonliteral in body language games, the conditions for the meaningfulness of body language expressions must be compared with the criteria for meaningfulness of verbal expressions. Verbal language and body language are syntactically similar: both involve physical movements. Both can be depicted as sets of gestures and behaviors. In order for the language analogy to apply, some of the gestures must be conventional in addition to being natural. I want to center on two aspects of the semantics of body language, namely context and consistency. As with verbal language, the meaning of body language is context specific. Different meanings would be assigned to verbal language depending on whether it was performed in a stage play as opposed to a veridical situation; body language meaning, too, depends on both physical and social context. Sex in the back seat of a 1959 Cadillac convertible at a drive-in theater has different significance than the same gestures in a marriage bed. The nature of the personal relationship involved affects the meaning. Casual sex outside a loving relationship has a different meaning from sex inside.

5. Sex and Meaning

A body language act can misfire in many ways.[15] Although bestiality might involve gestures similar to those a person employs with a human, any meaning such sex possesses is, at best, anthropomorphic. Bestial sex is like a saint baptizing penguins.[16] To examine the application of the communication model to body language, we must ask what the conditions are under which sex can misfire, when it is meaningful or meaningless, and whether one can lie with body language in anything like the way lying is done in verbal language.

The concepts of "meaning," "standard," and "criterion" are closely related. In order for there to be meaning at all, there must be a standard for usage. It is therefore reasonable to ask what that standard is. Consider the existing standard concerning the content of sexual body language in Western culture. In paradigm case usage, unless there are verbal qualifications to the contrary, or unless the context countervails (for instance, film actors performing a love scene, or sex in a brothel), sexual body language typically conveys not only short-term affection but also the promise of long-term love, devotion, and exclusivity. This interpretation can be defended by pointing to Western laws, customs, and mores concerning sexual conduct; more importantly, it is an interpretation typically experienced and encountered in sexual contexts. I will follow Elliston in using "norm" with the understanding that my concerns relate to norms (or conditions, standards, criteria) for meaning in body language. I am not using "norm" in a valuative or moral sense.

Body language is not locked into Western norms; words are not locked into ostensive definitions. Standards vary from one culture to the next and in the same culture at different times. An ancient Welsh tribe attached no significance to sex. Sex does have meaning independent of procreation, but heterosexual activity derives significance from its generative effects and consequent family bonding. But in this Welsh tribe, no connection between sex and childbearing was perceived. Members of the tribe thought pregnancy happened between women and the gods; men had nothing to do with it. This resulted in interesting inheritance rules. A tribesman's estate was handed down to his sister's children, since that family relationship was known and recognized. A tribesman's own children were not his heirs. Tribe members considered sex recreational; no commitment or love was presumed. Members of the tribe could form close personal relationships, but the signs used to establish these relationships were nonsexual. In this example, the communication model would not apply, since the tribe assigned no conventional, symbolic meaning to sex. Sex was merely a means of gratification, like eating.

In J. D. Ketchum's humorous article, "Nice People Don't Eat," from the *Worm Runner's Digest*,[17] all the significance we attach to sex is applied to eating. Ketchum is primarily concerned with arbitrary moral values. He contrasts "food prudes" with gluttons. In Ketchum's society, you would form close, personal relationships with another person by eating with them. A licentious glutton would eat with anyone. The communication model could be applied here to culinary activity. The rôle played by sex in our society could be supplanted by something else in Ketchum's world, but if there are close personal relationships at all, there has to be a set of signs to establish and maintain them. This is not done with sex in either the Welsh tribe or in Ketchum's culinary Canada. The fact that sex is not necessary for close relationships indicates its conventional status in Western culture. This fact supports Solomon's and Elliston's use of the communication model.

Another variation from Western norms is George Orwell's *1984*.[18] In this politically oppressed society, the antisex league prohibits sexual pleasure. Loving relationships are forbidden to party members; they are permitted to love only Big Brother. Marriages are assigned by the government for the purpose of procreation; partners in these marriages coldly perform the biological acts required to produce new party members while feeling no love. In Orwell's society, the gestures of body language remain, but their meaning is removed. The Welsh tribe had pleasure without meaning; in *1984* there is no meaning and no pleasure. The Orwell example differs from my previous two in that, in *1984*, no close personal relationships are permitted. A loyal party member would not seek either loving, exclusive sex or an alternate series of signs and gestures to create such a relationship. The Thought Police would intervene.

One major difficulty that I find with Solomon's and Elliston's views is that, if sex is deprived of its role in forming close, lasting relationships, then people would have to find other ways of creating them when desired. As Winston and Julia showed in *1984*, a loving relationship can be formed even when it is forbidden; the means to do so still exist. Our situation would be even more bleak than Winston and Julia's in the event that the significance of sex is diluted by indiscriminate promiscuity. If I wish to "speak" to someone, verbally or sexually, I need tools[19] to do so.

The preceding have been examples of different standards in different cultures. Different standards have also existed within our own culture. The "bathing machine" standards of the Victorian era differs remarkably from the free love of the Sixties. As a member of the peace movement, I recall that we attempted to be nonconformists in many respects. The sexual mores of the movement, together with our attire and grooming, effectively set us apart from our elders, but also drew us together. Todd Gitlin noted that, in the 1960s, sex was less

> a motive than a cement. The movement's coherence required a circle of triangles. The vulgar way to say it was that the clan was consolidated through the exchange of women—yet one should not cheapen or oversimplify. . . . Only the strongest bonds could have held the Small Society together. The sexual criss-cross meant the grand illusion that we, the *New* Left, could solve the problems of the Left by being young.[20]

In those days there were couples, but there were also communes. The pendulum has swung lately, but not all the way back to bathing machines. Herpes and AIDS have made monogamy both popular and wise: Solomon's and Elliston's proposals do not seem so inviting. A promiscuous person now might not communicate for long nor communicate much more than disease. These days there is still safety in numbers: very small numbers. Trust is essential to a close, loving relationship. At present, trust involves not only the removal of infidelity but also the elimination of health risks.

The standards of the Welsh tribe; the Outer Party members in *1984*; the standards of the 1960s; are not our own. The rules have changed; they might change again. Even so, we have to assess Solomon and Elliston's contentions with respect to contemporary standards. Body language and verbal language are language games,[21] and if you do not play by the rules, you are not playing the game. In order for the game to make sense, the players must agree.

If, in a physical relationship, the communication model works at all, agreement in judgment must occur, just as in verbal discourse.[22] In both verbal and body language, a common understanding of what the language communicates is required. This involves mutual agreement concerning the context and intent of expression. This agreement is a matter of a shared cultural heritage. The agreement is between speakers in verbal language and participants in body language; one cannot meaningfully agree with oneself.[23] This fact entails that two partners are required for there to be either deception or understanding. Agreement in judgment involves a *natural* affinity between communicants.

Sexual activity is a "natural expression" of affection that has a verbal counterpart.[24] Just as verbal expressions of genuine affection can function as replacements for natural ones, so too, according to the communication model, natural expressions can replace the verbal ones. Moreover, Solomon has contended that the natural expressions are superior to the verbal ones in that they are more subtle, convincing, less abstract, and less clumsy.[25]

6. Promiscuity

Elliston uses the communication model to defend promiscuity:

> Strict adherence to the Western norm places our sex lives in a straight-jacket that curtails body language to "I love you," the *only* message to be delivered, to just *one* person, with *fixed* diction and intonation—until the disillusioned pair have become bored by the repetition.[26]

Elliston suggests that promiscuous sex has more potential meaning than monogamous sex; it is less restricted and more varied. He adds, "Promiscuity has instrumental value in that it can facilitate the mastery of one kind of body language." He argues that an extensive vocabulary and refinement of diction is acquired by interaction with a large number of partners; "sexual body language is learned through sexual interaction."[27]

Solomon proposes a similar view. Solomon was influenced by Thomas Nagel's article, "Sexual Perversion," in which Nagel discussed the beginning of a relationship between two strangers.[28] Solomon thinks that the communication model fits well with Nagel's example. Solomon remarks:

> This model also makes it evident why Nagel chose [strangers] as his example . . . ; one has more to say, for one can freely express one's fantasies as well as the truth to a stranger. A husband and wife of seven years have . . . been repeating the same messages for years, and their sexual activity [is] no more than an abbreviated ritual incantation of the lengthy conversations they had years before.[29]

Thus emerge the "straight-jacket" and "novelty" defenses of promiscuity.

7. The "Straight-Jacket" Defense

In Elliston's "straight-jacket" defense of promiscuity, it is claimed that Western norms are pernicious: adherence to them unduly restricts sexual expression. This position is untenable. Body language is not locked into definitions any more than is verbal language. Recall Wittgenstein's tool box, in which example he observed that words are like instruments; they have a basic designed use but can be used in a variety of nonstandard ways. A screwdriver can be used as a paperweight, or a weapon, or to drive screws. Words also can be used in a variety of ways to inform, impress, intimidate. Additionally, words can be used metaphorically or satirically as well as literally. Similarly, sex can be used to earn money, dominate, or convince; for subversion or perversion; it can be used for selfish self-gratification. These uses are in addition to and dependent on its primary use as an expression of love and devotion.

Sexual body language is also not locked into "fixed diction and intonation." As Wittgenstein wrote, "the application of a word is not everywhere bounded by rules."[30] Just as the rule-governedness of verbal language allows considerable variation in volume, inflection, accent, and emphasis, sexual body language is capable of many colorful nuances of expression. Elliston and Solomon seem to think that sexual exclusivity entails a monotone of expression. This is not true with respect to either two speakers or two sexual partners. Body language is not locked into Western norms ("straight-jacketed") for the same reason that words are not locked into their dictionary meanings. This is not to claim that no standards exist. Rather, it is always possible to violate standards and depart from them. A rule that cannot be violated is not a rule. Conversely, in order for there to be a violation, a viable rule is needed.

Elliston nearly gave away his game by referring to adherence to Western norms. In so doing, he admitted that there are such norms; his version of promiscuity is not intended to destroy the norms, but to abandon them. For him, apparently, it is adherence to the norms that should be opposed and not the norms themselves. It is a good thing that he made this move, because what he wanted to defend was nonstandard sex and nonstandard usage of body language. Yet to speak of nonstandard usage is meaningful only in the presence of a standard. One cannot vary from a standard unless there is a standard from which to vary. This standard, namely the Western norm for sexual conduct, shows that a primary use of sexual body language is precisely to express love and the prospect of a long-range commitment.

This dependency on a standard is more significant than Elliston seems willing to acknowledge. One way to find out what a word means when it is being used nonstandardly is to examine its home language game.[31] The fact that there is a home language game does not strictly limit usage, since nonstandard uses are possible; meanings, even in nonstandard uses, are derivatives of uses in a home language game. Some elements of literal discourse are present in metaphorical and satirical uses. Something can be recognized as a metaphor or satire only *in contrast to* standard literal usage. Since there must be this basis of comparison, the meaning present in nonstandard usage is dependent on usage in the home language game. The original home language game for sexual body language is a long-standing, exclusive relationship; any variation on that usage derives whatever meaning it has from the home language game.

This view can be supported by noting some cues for nonstandard use. Many of them are subtle, as in satire, but they must be present to ensure proper interpretation. Satires and metaphors can be made explicit by preceding them with qualifying statements. This is often what happens in nonstandard uses of sexual body language; these usages are preceded by qualifying verbal statements such as "I don't want to get serious," "This is strictly for laughs," "This is just for tonight," or "I don't want to get involved." The presence of such qualifiers is a good indication that there is a standard usage for sexual activity and that what is about to happen is a departure from that standard. Compare sexual qualifiers with a case in which someone makes a remark in jest; the remark is misunderstood and taken seriously. The remark then may be qualified by saying, "I was only joking." The one-night stand derives its meaning from the thousand-and-one night stand. These qualifying statements indicate that the meaning of a one-night stand must be interpreted in contrast to a standard (home language game) meaning. There would not be any such qualifying statements unless there was something to qualify.

The standard meaning for sexual body language has to be constructed and developed in the same way as meaning in verbal language, that is, by a history of correct usage. Just as a speaker cannot be said to understand a term based on a single correct use, a user of sexual body language needs to establish a history of correct usage in order for understanding to be attributed. A totally promiscuous person would not have the required history. Elliston has admitted that the concept of "promiscuity" (like the concept of "a few") is quite vague. Some general limits can be placed on it, however. I agree with Elliston that having one or two sexual partners does not make you promiscuous, but fifteen probably does. This range fits well with the communication model. If I misuse a word once, I have made a mistake, but if I misuse a word fifteen times in a row, I probably do not understand what it means. The parallel for body language is obvious. It does not appear that we have a basis for attributing understanding of sexual body language to a totally promiscuous person.

Body language, like verbal language, can be learned. Even in this event, training precedes understanding. A history of correct usage must be established. I am not suggesting that a person who has an extended string of one-night stands is doomed to lack understanding. We all have the experience of using a word wrongly for years and then learning its proper usage. After that, we become competent users of the word; we gained understanding. When deception is absent, I see no reason the same could not be true of body language. The reformed promiscuous person can become an *understanding* lover.

Considering what I said earlier concerning verbal cues for promiscuous sex (for example, "I don't want to get involved"), I should comment on what a reformed promiscuous person might do or say to reverse the situation. A reformed promiscuous person could make different verbal statements (or none) to show that *this* time no qualification or limitation is being placed on the natural message. If Solomon is correct in supposing that a usage of body language is a performative, then this performative could be made explicit by preceding it with a statement such as "I hereby declare that the following is a sincere expression of love and affection."[32] Admittedly, this might be somewhat stilted for lovemaking, but Hugh Hefner may well have had to say some such thing to his wife, a Playmate of the Year, to be taken seriously.

It could be said in response that promiscuity does not involve misuse, but nonstandard use. This move would not help the defender of promiscuity. Not all uses can be nonstandard. The only way my nonstandard use of verbal language can be considered meaningful, the only way I can be regarded as a competent speaker, is if my present nonstandard use is contrasted with a long history of correct standard use. A totally promiscuous person would provide no basis for attributing meaning or competence. This accords well with the common notion of "meaningless sex," and it gives us reason to suspect that the meaningfulness of body languages might be proportional to adherence to some standard, such as Western norms.

8. The "Novelty" Defense

This claims that people have more to say to strangers in sexual discourse than to a familiar partner, and that body language conversations with the same person become dull, boring, routine. It is inferred that novelty enhances communication. Novelty does enhance some communication, but that type is likely to include only lightweight bantering. While this might be exciting, it is not informative. A significant part of the novelty of a new encounter is the discovery that a stranger might have affection for me. Even this would not be conveyed, however, without an agreed on standard for meaning. Janice Moulton notes that sex with strangers is "sexual small talk."[33] One must get beyond the initial stages for meaningful conversation to take place. Moulton points out that the contention that people have more to say to strangers works against the analogy of the communication model; "with natural language, one usually has more to say to old friends."[34] Conversation with strangers is trite. The most meaningful discourse takes place with old partners.

The novelty defense confuses form with content. Elliston and Solomon suppose that when the content remains the same (when what is being expressed is affection and love for just one person), then the form must remain constant as well, with all the same gestures repeated. This view is incorrect. Form can vary while content remains largely the same. Monogamy does not imply monotony. Elliston's and Solomon's views summon up images of dull, repetitious, "missionary position" sex with no variation allowed. There is no reason two people in a prolonged relationship cannot explore and experiment with sexual activities exclusively with each other. A limitless range of variety in circumstances, procedure, nuance, gesture, and motion is possible. If such alternatives are tried, then two long-time partners can have plenty of new modes of expression, such as new forms of body language, with basically the same content. Familiarity need not breed contempt; familiarity breeds content. Consistency and content are closely linked. Even consistent performances can be new and exciting. Consider a Broadway actor who does eight shows a week but nevertheless gives life and variety to each one. Sameness of content does not entail sameness of form.

Novel sexual encounters are not entirely without content. Still, the con tent of a body language conversation with a new person is not more extensive than that present in a long-standing relationship. Casual sex is like casual talk. Promiscuity does not increase or enhance vocabulary. Instead, it involves repetition of the same getting acquainted discourse required in verbal talk with strangers. Promiscuous sex has the kind of repetition that Elliston and Solomon attribute to monogamous sex. Promiscuous sex does not necessarily include novelty of form or of content, but only novelty of partners.

New elements do occur in an encounter with a stranger: I might learn, "so, you understand English too!" In a novel sexual encounter, I might learn that my partner knows sexual body language too. Elliston agrees:

> It may be noted that what the dialogue carried on through the body achieves in breadth it may lose in depth: having talked with many, we

may discover that our most meaningful dialogue can be carried on with one.[35]

And Solomon writes that "sex, any extended conversation, tends to become either more truthful or more incoherent."[36] If sameness of content is not confused with sameness of form, and if we consider the standards for usage, extended sexual discourse with one person can become more meaningful.

9. Difficulties

The import of these defenses of promiscuity is that sex is burdened by its ties to Western norms, that it will be improved by breaking those ties, making sex more free and open. Suppose the ties are broken; what would result?

Sexual body language would be trivialized. If there are no restrictions on how language is used, it can be used any way you want. This would not be a change of standards but a lack of standards. Instead of being able to say more with body language, we could not say much or anything. We often use language to make discriminations. This is also true of body language. Suppose, with the ties between sex and Western norms broken, I still want to express affection and devotion to someone and thereby distinguish that person from all others. What would be left to me to express that? Elliston and Solomon agree that verbal expression would be a "clumsy" substitute for the body language expression. If sexual body language is deprived of its current status, I would be unable to say things I want to say. My expressive capabilities would be diminished. There does not seem to be an alternate mode of expression that is as *salient* as sexual body language. Humans tend to be resilient, so if sex can no longer be used to express what it used to, I would be forced to seek an another means. Suppose that I chose a secret handshake, which I used only with my lover. That might do the trick. It would be very warm when I used it and, while it would lack the saliency of sex, it might achieve symbolic significance. But the defenders of promiscuity would not leave me alone. They would claim that my handshake is locked into Western norms, and that I could say more if I used it with strangers. As members of exclusive organizations know, however, a secret sign loses its significance the more widely it is used. Once a handshake had lost its discriminative meaning through widespread use, it could no longer fulfill its function. If an organization wanted to retain the function of the old handshake, it would have to make up a new sign. Defenders of promiscuity place us in the same situation. Deprived of sex as a means of expressing love and affection, we would have to find another, less effective, way of expressing those things.

10. Meaning and Morals

I should mention that one goal of the above defense of promiscuity is to make a moral claim. Elliston and Solomon contend that promiscuity is not immoral. I do not dispute this: promiscuity is moral as long as it does not involve the violation of an oath, telling a lie, engaging in deception, and no one is harmed.

I have reservations about whether promiscuity is typically moral in practice, but theoretically, at least, it is not immoral. I mention this to ensure that my points are not clouded by moral considerations. I am concerned with the *meaning* of promiscuous sex, not the *morality* of promiscuous sex. I fear that promiscuous encounters dilute the meaningfulness of sexual communication.

Solomon contrasts promiscuity with marriage. To some extent I have followed him in this regard, considering my use of the term "monogamy." I do not, however, want to follow him all the way. I see no reason meaningful sex cannot take place outside marriage. Within the bounds of my observations concerning consistent usage, I think both premarital and extramarital sex can be meaningful. For that matter, I see no reason a meaningful sexual relationship must be heterosexual. To allow for this possibility, I have avoided use of the term "intercourse" in reference to sexual relations.

11. Conclusion

Promiscuity in sexual activity increases ambiguity in body language. The boy who indiscriminately cried "Wolf!" was ignored after a while. When a wolf actually came, he was still ignored. The promiscuous person cries "Love!" indiscriminately. He or she will also be ignored in time, if found out. When real love comes, the promiscuous person will not be believed by a potential lover. Sexual body language for that person will lack meaning. If body language is to be meaningful at all, therefore, it must satisfy many of the same standards of consistency that make verbal language meaningful.

Promiscuous body language has an indiscriminate tone. One thing that perked my interest in this topic was a *New Yorker* drawing showing a couple sitting on a couch. The lady says to the gentleman, "I know that you're always nice to me, but you're nice to everybody!" His niceness was indiscriminate. It was not special for her. She wanted something personal and exclusive.

If sex is modeled by literal communicative language, then we must ask *what part*. Sex is personal. Fortunately, there is also personal verbal communication. Examples of such communication include sharing a confidence and telling a secret. However, I cannot talk promiscuously and have what I say remain confidential. A secret told to everyone is no longer a secret. A personal communication loses something (its being genuinely *personal*) when it is generally (publicly) distributed. Consider, for instance, junk mail letters written in a personal tone but addressed to "Occupant." A "personal" communication of this sort becomes an oxymoron, a secret told to everyone. A stage whisper everyone can hear still conveys information, but the information has lost the characteristics of being *secret* and personal.

The communication model of sex suggests that couples who choose to pursue a committed personal relationship might find some comfort in the idea that rather than being an inevitable trap of boredom and meaningless repetition, their physical expression parallels the verbal and emotional message they can give each other as lovers, partners, and best friends. Accordingly, besides the negative accomplishment of attacking sexual promiscuity, I hope I have also contributed to the clarification of the concept of a meaningful relationship.[37]

Notes

1. Robert Solomon, "Sex and Perversion," in Robert Baker and Frederick Elliston, eds., *Philosophy and Sex*, 1st ed. (Buffalo: Prometheus, 1975), 268-87, and "Sexual Paradigms," *Journal of Philosophy* 71 (1974): 336-45 (reprinted in Alan Soble, ed., *Philosophy of Sex*, 2nd ed. [Savage, Md.: Rowman and Littlefield, 1991], 53-62); Frederick Elliston, "In Defense of Promiscuity," in Baker and Elliston, *Philosophy and Sex*, 222-43; Jerome Shaffer, "Sexual Desire," *Journal of Philosophy* 75 (1978): 175-89 (this volume, 1-12); Janice Moulton, "Sexual Behavior: Another Position," *Journal of Philosophy* 73 (1976): 537-46; reprinted in Soble, *Philosophy of Sex*, 2nd ed., 63-71.

2. Solomon, "Sex and Perversion," 279.

3. *Ibid.*, 280.

4. Robert Solomon, *About Love* (New York: Simon and Schuster, 1989), 214.

5. *Ibid.*, 214-15.

6. Max Black, *Models and Metaphors* (Ithaca: Cornell University Press, 1962), 228.

7. *Ibid.* See Stephen Toulmin, *Philosophy of Science* (New York: Harper and Row, 1960), 24-39.

8. Ludwig Wittgenstein, *Philosophical Investigations* (New York: Macmillan, 1968), §127.

9. Wittgenstein, "Remarks on Frazier's *The Golden Bough*," in C. G. Luckhardt, ed., *Wittgenstein: Sources and Perspectives* (Ithaca: Cornell University Press, 1979), 68.

10. Wittgenstein, *Philosophical Investigations*, §109.

11. G. P. Baker and P. M. S. Hacker, "Übersicht," in John V. Canfield, ed., *Method and Essence* (New York: Garland Publishing, 1986), 159-73, at 159-60.

12. Wittgenstein, "Remarks on Frazier's *Golden Bough*," 63.

13. Wittgenstein, *Philosophical Investigations*, §127.

14. *Ibid.*, 216e.

15. J. L. Austin, *How To Do Things With Words*, 2nd ed. (Cambridge, Mass.: Harvard University Press, 1978), 14-15.

16. *Ibid.*, 24.

17. J. D. Ketchum, "Nice People Don't Eat," in James V. McConnell, ed., *The Worm Re-Turns: The Best from the Worm Runner's Digest* (Englewood Cliffs, N.J.: Prentice-Hall, 1965), 77-8.

18. George Orwell, *1984* (New York: Signet, 1950).

19. Wittgenstein, *Philosophical Investigations*, §11.

20. Todd Gitlin, *The Sixties: Years of Hope, Days of Rage* (New York: Bantam, 1987), 109.

21. Wittgenstein, *Philosophical Investigations*, §23.

22. *Ibid.*, §§241-2.

23. *Ibid.*, §279.

24. *Ibid.*, §§244, 256. See Charles Johnson, "On Replacing 'Natural Expressions of Pain,'" *Behaviorism* 7:1 (1985): 65-70.

25. Solomon, "Sex and Perversion," 279.

26. Elliston, "In Defense of Promiscuity," 235-6.

27. *Ibid.*, 235.

28. Thomas Nagel, "Sexual Perversion," *Journal of Philosophy* 66 (1969): 5-17, at 10-12; reprinted in Soble, *Philosophy of Sex*, 2nd ed., 39-51, at 44-6.

29. Solomon, "Sexual Paradigms," in Soble, *Philosophy of Sex*, 61.

30. Wittgenstein, *Philosophical Investigations*, §84.

31. *Ibid.*, §116.

32. Austin, *How To Do Things With Words*, 84-5.

33. Moulton, "Sexual Behavior: Another Position," in Soble, *Philosophy of Sex*, 69.

34. *Ibid.*, 70.

35. Elliston, "In Defense of Promiscuity," 239-40.

36. Solomon, "Sexual Paradigms," in Soble, *Philosophy of Sex*, 62.

37. I am indebted to the late Frederick Elliston for his valuable comments on an earlier draft of this essay.

M. C. Dillon
(photograph: Joanne Dillon)

Author of "Sex, Time, and Love: Erotic Temporality"
Paper presented at the Society for the Philosophy of Sex and Love
during the
Pacific Division Meeting of The American Philosophical Association
San Francisco, Cal., 22 March 1985

Thirty-One

SEX, TIME, AND LOVE: EROTIC TEMPORALITY[1]

M. C. Dillon

> Every thing has its time. This means: everything which actually is, every being comes and goes at the right time and remains for a time during the time allotted to it. Every thing has its time.
>
> Heidegger, *On Time and Being*

1.

The fundamental structures[2] of human existence (*Dasein*) are temporal structures. This is Heidegger's thought in *Being and Time*. In that work, he accords to care (*Sorge*) a privileged status and defines it in such a way that it encompasses both *Dasein*'s attitude toward itself and its attitude toward others.[3] But being-with others receives only cursory treatment in *Being and Time*; Heidegger's primary focus is on modes of anxiety in which Dasein is essentially isolated. No room is made for the erotic in Heidegger's fundamental ontology; erotic temporality is left undisclosed, and the only intersubjective modes of care that are considered are sexually neutral modes of solicitude.[4]

The question of Heidegger's silence on the subject of sexuality has been taken up by Derrida, and he finds within the general question of Heidegger's sexual neutralization of *Dasein* a series of specific questions that call into question the propriety of Heidegger's fundamental ontology.

> What if "sexuality" already marked the most originary *Selbstheit*? If it were an ontological structure of ipseity? If the *Da* of *Dasein* were already "sexual"? What if sexual difference were already marked in the opening up of the question of the sense of Being and of the ontological difference? And what if . . . neutralization were already a violent operation?[5]

Bracketing the question of Derrida's intent, I take these questions to be rhetorical. There is no question that Heidegger has removed "sexuality from every originary structure" of his fundamental ontology.[6] Derrida is interested explicitly in the why of Heidegger's silence, but his implicit agenda is a critique of his understanding of difference: ontological difference/sexual indifference. Is there an error here? I think so, but my intent is not to chastise Heidegger; nor is it to follow Derrida into a semiological labyrinth. Instead, I want to consider another radiant of his questioning.

If "temporality [is] the primordial structure of *Dasein*'s totality of Being,"[7] and if that totality of Being is pervaded by sexuality, the structures of sexuality are temporal structures. The second premise of this argument (the hypothesis that the totality of *Dasein*'s Being is pervaded by sexuality) is mine. I don't attribute it to Derrida: he does not overtly assert it, and even if he did assent to my words, he would not assent to my interpretation of their significance.

Note, also, that I leave the premise as a hypothesis. I will not attempt to "prove" it. Indeed, any such attempt would be misconceived.

> There is interfusion between sexuality and existence, which means that existence permeates sexuality and *vice versa*, so that it is impossible to determine, in a given decision or action, the proportion of sexual to other motivations, impossible to label a decision or act "sexual" or "non-sexual."[8]

Although I do not subscribe to the "principle of indeterminacy" that Merleau-Ponty sets forth on the basis of this interfusion of sexuality and existence, I do agree with the lesser claim that human behavior is intrinsically ambiguous; any decision or action can be interpreted in the context of a theory of sexuality (as any human behavior can always be interpreted in the context of a theory of history or economics).[9] Sexual significance can be found in everything we do or fail to do, but that need not be the primary significance of all behavior.

A final note of caution. Heidegger might have kept the silence of neutrality on questions of *Dasein*'s sexual (and political) comportment, as Derrida suggests,[10] because such questions belong within the domain of the ontic and Heidegger's interests are exclusively ontological. Heidegger deliberately withdraws from the level of scientific (anthropological, sociological, biological) discourse, and leaves issues relating to morality, religion, and "philosophy of life" behind. Thus Heidegger's neutralization of human existence, his decision not to consider man or woman (*Mensch*, *anthropos*), but only *das Dasein*, would be required by the very project of fundamental ontology.

A complex problematic surfaces here with the question whether it is possible to consider a given being, *Dasein*, exclusively with regard to its Being, whether a fundamental ontology can be undertaken in total isolation from ontic considerations, whether one can bracket the fact that in every case *Dasein* has its own sexed body. I do not argue the point, but put the reader on notice that my own inquiry will glide between the realms of the existentiell and the existential, as one passes from thematic issues to their encompassing horizons, without stopping to comment on whatever frontiers might exist between them.

2.

Every thing has its time. What, then, is the temporal infrastructure of sexuality? Or, since *Dasein* is essentially *Mitdasein*,[11] it is, I think, appropriate to broaden the question and ask about the temporality of the erotic.

Consider the range of the topic. The history of the erotic: under this heading one can group the archaeology of desire, the sociobiological evolution of sexual behavior and physiology, the development of cultural forms of erotic expression. We are in the midst of a historical unfolding that is conditioned by past fact and future possibility, the archaeology and the teleology of the phylogeny of love. Then there is its ontogeny, the phases in the life cycle of the individual (infancy, childhood, adolescence, adulthood, old age), each with its own significant subphases; the time of life is constitutive of the quality of love. Next there is the temporal structure of erotic liaison (beginning, middle, end) and the qualitative differences associated with duration from the brief encounter to the life long pact. There is also the temporality of sexual union: the sexual response cycle from arousal to resolution. The symbols of the erotic are bound to time: the transient moment of pathos, the eternal present of ecstasy, the forever of commitment. And the rituals of love are rites of passage. This list is meant to be suggestive, not exhaustive, and is intended to indicate that beneath the multiplicity of the erotic manifold there is always a temporal pattern, a sequencing with its own intrinsic order, like a melody.

Temporality is the form of synthesis, the gathering of many into one: the unification that makes the chaotic manifold intelligible. The notion of temporal synthesis, governed by its own ordering of intrinsically earlier and intrinsically later moments, is most recently expressed by Husserl:[12] it echoes Kant's schemata and foreshadows Heidegger's *Existenzialen*. But it hearkens back to an older and more comprehensive thought, expressed by Empedocles:

> A double tale will I tell: at one time [the sphere of being] grew to be one only from many, at another it divided again to be many from one. There is a double coming into being of mortal things and a double passing away. One is brought about, and again destroyed, by the coming together of all things, the other grows up and is scattered as things are again divided. And these things never cease from continual shifting, at one time all coming together, through Love [*philia*], into one, at another each borne apart from the others through Strife.[13]

Empedocles is speaking of a cosmic cycle: from unity through disintegration to multiplicity, and back through integration to unity. The principle of temporal synthesis is love; the principle of temporal dispersion is dreaded strife. The coming together of all things into one sphere of being Empedocles associates with harmony.[14] "Love is the cause of good things, and Strife of bad."[15] Man has fallen, through bloodshed and the eating of kindred flesh, from primal beatitude under the reign of Kupris (or Aphrodite)[16] into his present state: he is now "a fugitive from the gods and a wanderer" who has put his trust in "raving strife."[17]

Empedocles' word, translated here as love, is *philia*. The specific difference between *philia* and *eros* is typically taken to be the sexual component present in *eros* and absent from *philia*. Yet Empedocles associates the reign of love with the reign of Aphrodite, and believes, according to Kirk and Raven, "that sexual love and cosmic love are one and the same self-existent external force that acts on the person or the thing that loves."[18] The Homeric theme that beauty and sexual competition foster strife is absent from the extant fragments. If one is to distinguish between love and sex, one must look beyond Empedocles.

If the authority of such divergent sources as Kierkegaard[19] and de Rougemont[20] is accepted, one must look about one and a half millennia beyond Empedocles to the medieval demonization of the flesh and the concurrent emergence of an ideal of romantic love centered on purity. There the sacred love of the spirit is posited as antithetical to the profane love of the flesh. This, too, can be understood as a temporal differentiation. Ultimately, it is the permanence or timelessness of spiritual love that associates it with the immutability of the divine, and separates it from the transient nature of sexual or physical love that is subsumed under the categories of mortal generation and decay. Purity belongs to atemporality, but the flesh is corrupt because corruption necessarily happens to flesh with the passage of time.

Since it is based on a negation of mortal being and finite human becoming, this romantic distinction between sex and love is demeaning to our humanity. And this raises the question whether any such distinction can sustain critical analysis. Here I face a dilemma. On one side, the encounter of bodies in sexual contact is necessarily an encounter of selves, given the premise that we are our bodies. And this encounter of body selves necessarily involves what Merleau-Ponty calls a "transfer of corporeal schema,"[21] which is a fundamental recognition on each part of the humanity of the other. Hence, there can be no purely physical contact between human bodies, no entirely profane sexual encounter utterly devoid of personal recognition. Even in the privative modalities where one seeks to deny the humanity of the other by adopting the postures of brutalization, this is still a *denial*, which presupposes the fundamental recognition as that which one seeks self-deceptively to deny. And yet, on the other side of the dilemma, there are the obvious and profound differences between the alienated couplings of hookers with their johns and the poetic exchanges of the Brownings, between the consummations through the "glory holes" of some men's rooms and the stolen moments of John Thomas and Lady Jane; in short, between people seeking impersonal sex and people seeking to communicate love through bodily gestures. The second horn of the dilemma requires a distinction between sex and love, but the first horn maintains that any such distinction cannot be sustained.

Without attempting to minimize the essential ambiguity that is characteristic of all phenomena and is especially pronounced in the sphere of the erotic, I think it is possible to resolve this dilemma, and resolve it by analysis of the structures of erotic temporality involved. The particular structure operative here is that of contextualization. The Gestalt-theoretical concept of background inclines us to think of context as spatial, but there are temporal contexts, temporal horizons, as well, which permeate spatial dimensions, give them depth, and set them into motion. The overall context of an erotic encounter, indeed the all-encompassing context of any phenomenon, is the world horizon, but it is specifically its temporal component I want to focus on here.

I must interrupt the flow of my argument here to articulate the conceptual framework presupposed in subsequent discourse. A diagram will be helpful (see figure 1). The horizontal axis is the horizon of global time stretching indefinitely backward and forward into past and future, encompassing my birth and death within the context of cosmic unfolding. The vertical line is the now moment. The diagonal lines represent the retentions and protentions that form the specious present as described by Husserl in his *Phenomenology of Internal Time-Consciousness*.[22] The ellipse is what I shall call the erotic temporal horizon. It begins when people meet, includes the complex history of their interaction, and ends when they die or are no longer significant to each other. As I have depicted it here, the solid portion includes the memorial and retentional past, and the dotted line includes the protentional and expectational future. Back, now, to the argument.

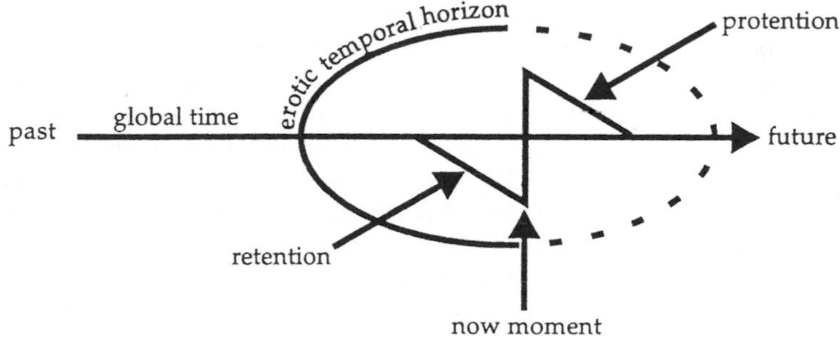

Figure 1.
[courtesy of Elizabeth R. Dillon]

One *prima facie* difference between the extreme examples of erotic encounter cited earlier concerns duration. In the ultra-brief homosexual couplings in "tea-rooms" and similar places, the whole episode, from first meeting until final parting, might last no more than a few minutes.[23] At the other extreme, the erotic temporal horizon might be an adult lifetime. This association of endurance with love and brevity with mere carnality lends a spurious credibility to the ideal of permanence dismissed above. But erotic quality can hardly be measured in terms of the quantity of elapsed clock time.

It is phenomenal time, not objective time, that constitutes the temporal horizon. Phenomenal time is meaningfully ordered: beginning, middle, end;

attraction, consolidation, consummation, mutual growth or distancing, termination by consent or circumstance. Objective time is merely additive and homogeneous. Whence one can use such qualitative terms as richness, intensity, complexity, coherence, development, and so forth, to gauge phenomenal time, but only quanta to measure objective time. One can also find a rich and complex temporal horizon whose beginning and end span a relatively short period of objective time, and *vice versa*.

I conclude from these brief considerations that it is possible to steer between the horns of the dilemma (either all sexual encounters are erotically meaningful, or there is a radical line of demarcation between sex and love) by considering the temporal horizon of the encounter. The distinction between sex and love is not to be conceived as a disjunction of opposite and incompatible terms, but one that is drawn along a continuum of quality of phenomenal time. The relatively barren sexual encounter is thus one that takes place within a narrowly circumscribed and undeveloped erotic temporal horizon. At the other end of the continuum is the resonant erotic exchange that occurs within the context of an articulate and intensely figured complex of emotional/temporal structures. In this model, it is not the presence or absence of some set of supercharged criteria such as spiritual communion or psychic involvement that is invoked in the attempt to demarcate between separate categories of sex and love. Indeed, some degree of communion, involvement, commitment, and so forth, is present in any liaison, no matter how forlorn. It is rather a matter of understanding how the relevant erotic temporal horizon is related to and integrated within the temporal life world of the individual. Note, also, that although fundamental values are at work in this model, the distinction does not rest on or even implicitly invite moral assessment. One might incorporate the distinction within ethical discourse, but it would have to be decided on independent grounds whether love is morally superior to sex. It seems to me (to make a brief and gratuitous judgment on this issue) that there are times when sex is ethically preferable to love and others when the reverse obtains: it is not always wise or kind to develop a sexual encounter into a fully erotic relationship. In any case, the distinction as set forth here is meant to be morally neutral.

Another disclaimer is in order. I am not suggesting that either love or sex can be reduced to its temporal infrastructure. There is an essential spatiality to the erotic, for example, that is coordinate with, but irreducible to, the temporal dimension.[24] The topography of erotic space has its own *logos* of proximity and distance, intimacy and publicity; its own zones of vulnerability and defense; its own lines of force, auras of corporeal projection, and so on. The erotic is not reducible to temporality, but every erotic structure has a temporal aspect. That underlying temporality provides the basis for the synthesis of the manifold adumbrations of the erotic I am attempting here.

Continuing this anticipation of possible objections, one might raise the question whether my manner of distinguishing sex and love is genuinely temporal. In appealing to the qualitative gauges of phenomenal time, have I introduced norms that are not essentially temporal and traded on them to endow the temporal horizon with parameters that are not intrinsic to it, but which serve the purposes of the distinction? This is perhaps a moot point, simply because the definition of phenomenal (as opposed to objective) time precludes separating the form of time (succession, duration) from its content (empty/full, boring/exciting, slow/fast). Thus the boundaries between temporal quality and, for example, emotional quality become ambiguous. Still, I regard this as a positive ambiguity (to eliminate it would be to separate temporality and emotionality in an arbitrary and misleading way), and maintain that the measure applied is genuinely one of temporality.

One gauge of erotic quality is compatibility: the capacity of persons to get along with one another, to mesh their actions and expectations. The temporal counterpart of compatibility might be conceived as synchronization. One operative parameter here is tempo. If one partner is operating *allegro con brio* and the other *moderato e maestoso*, harmonious attunement will be a task. Another parameter of erotic synchronization might be called measure. It concerns the base unit of time underlying the expectations of prospective partners. Someone whose erotic anticipations do not extend beyond any given evening, who tacitly expects closure before going to sleep, will be operating on a different melodic line from someone who prethematically regards the evening as the opening bars of the first movement of an unfinishing symphony. In addition to tempo and measure, there is also a formal structure of temporal anticipation. Following the musical analogy a bit further, there are those of a classical bent who expect a certain sequence of movements: *allegro ma non troppo*, *vivace*, *presto*, *adagio assai*. They are upset when confronted with modern innovations. Someone for whom a kiss on the first date is a matter of deliberation is operating with a different temporal structure from someone who brings along a toothbrush just in case.

There is more at stake here than mere psychological lability (rigidity versus flexibility). There is the issue of an essential sequence with an intrinsic order governing the progression of phases. Masters and Johnson may or may not have succeeded in identifying the stages of coitus, but their work provides strong evidence that there is an essential order to sexual intercourse. Some degree of excitement, for example, must precede intromission, if only to satisfy the physical conditions of erection and lubrication. But these are gross and relatively objective measures. Consider, in the subtler context of phenomenal time, the difference in erotic quality between the act of love as depicted in *Lady Chatterley's Lover* and its depiction in hard core fiction or cinema. More or less the same events take place, but the collapse of phenomenal time has a foreshortening effect that deprives pornography of the erotic quality found in Lawrence's prose. I am critical of hard core depictions of sex, not because they attempt to be vividly explicit and to exploit unusual interests, but because their failure to accommodate the essential phasing of erotic temporality undermines the erotic interest they purport to arouse.[25] Where no tension is built up, there can be no release. Where no anticipations are stirred, there can be no fulfillment.

These three parameters (synchronization/compatibility, measure, anticipation/expectation) have a unitary grounding in phenomenal temporality. I distinguish them here in order to highlight and juxtapose them as moments within the complex but unitary whole. Our expectations, for example, predelineate our experience in general ways and constitute the temporal horizon of the future that makes it possible to be surprised or reassured, disappointed or fulfilled. In this phase of the discussion, I have been trying to support the point that the quality of erotic experience can be measured along temporal lines. Compatibility or harmony is a qualitative measure of erotic experience, and, as I have attempted to show with the analyses of tempo, measure, and formal structure, it rests, in part at least, on the temporal matter of synchronization.

This idea of erotic synchronization is rich in ramifications. In addition to the parameters mentioned, one might also consider the phases of individual sexual ontogenesis. The temporal structures of anticipation characteristic of adolescent sexuality, for example, differ dramatically from those of infantile and adult sexuality, which might help to explain why there are strong taboos reinforcing the sexual barriers separating those phases in the life cycle. What an adolescent expects in an erotic liaison would be immensely difficult to synchronize with adult expectations, just because there are radical differences in the two structures of anticipation: the adolescent's "forever" is easily spoken because it is indefinite and empty, granting the adolescent a characteristic resiliency, whereas an adult commitment is more circumspect since its temporal span is valued for its very finitude.

Similar structures arise in the phylogenetic sphere. Cultures that preserve historically earlier modes of living and loving (for example, the Mennonites and Hasidic Jews, on one hand, and the primitive cultures of the world on the other) produce individual temporal horizons that are deeply incompatible with the anxious multiformity of contemporary American erotic temporality.

Corresponding to these difficulties in synchronizing divergent structures of anticipation are equally significant problems associated with the sedimentations of divergent archaeologies. Both at the level of the individual and at the level of culture, the past invades the present to structure erotic values and the quality of erotic pleasure. The traumas of infancy are compounded with the incipient traumas of ancient prohibitions. Add to this the natural archaeology of instinct, with the predispositions that inform the structures of gratification and aggression; couple that with the sociobiological evolution of gender-specific sexual strategies; and one begins to see a global erotic temporality that impinges on every aspect of our sexual being. I have focused on the future-oriented structures of anticipation, but they must be understood as integral with the past-oriented structures of sedimentation. Teleology and archaeology, as Ricoeur contends, are ultimately inseparable,[26] because past and future are inseparable correlates: every project is grounded in facticity, and every retrieval is a search for portent.

By way of concluding this survey, I want to open a problem-nexus that is too important to pass over, but too complex to resolve here: the problematic of erotic temporality and erotic values. I have analyzed the quality of erotic temporality in the area of compatibility under the rubric of synchronization. Synchronization is linked through the notion of harmony to Empedocles' straightforward evaluation of the unifying power of love as good and the disrupting force of strife as bad. Reference might also be made here to the Jungian notion of synchronicity: the idea of attunement to the overall pattern governing a given synchrony or cross section of cosmic temporality.[27] The underlying thought is that harmonious attunement is a positive value and the lack thereof is negative. Postponing the question of the validity of this thought in the all-encompassing dimension of cosmology, I want to raise the issue of its validity at the level of intersubjectivity.

The problem here is that compatibility is a relative notion: synchronization between two individuals involves only the issue of adjusting one complex temporal horizon to another or some sort of mutual accommodation and compromise. If, as Sartre has argued,[28] and as my brief survey of the variables in the structures of anticipation and sedimentation tends to show, deep conflict is inevitable in the encounter of divergent temporalities, then the question of how to adjudicate between them is forced. Given a *de facto*, if not a willed, commitment of each party to his or her own temporal horizon, an independent measure is needed to provide the basis for weighing the issues at stake in the conflict and determining how the burden of adjustment and accommodation is to be apportioned. As I have tried to show elsewhere,[29] Sartre provides no foundation for the adjudication of such conflict, hence for him conflict is impossible to resolve and necessarily works itself out through a dialectic of domination and submission. Sartre espouses the antithesis of Empedocles' standpoint: strife and love are not polar opposites, but inseparable correlates.

Where is the truth here? If synchronization in phenomenal temporality requires a standard, as synchronization of clocks in objective time does, then where is that standard to be found? Let me rule out one kind of resolution at the outset: the retreat to absolutes in the face of the problems of relativism insures only a movement in the opposite direction when the perplexities endemic to absolutism rise to the surface. Objective measures do not resolve the problems of subjective discord, except in temporary and arbitrary ways that compound rather than relieve the initial tension. A phenomenal measure is needed. To point the way toward that measure, I return to the beginning, to the thoughts of Heidegger and Empedocles.

Heidegger says that everything has its time; there is a temporality appropriate to everything; every being comes and goes at the proper time. Empedocles understands temporal dynamics as involving either the synthesis of love or the dissolution of strife. Heidegger sees time as the governing structure of human existence.[30] Empedocles sees time as a cosmic force governing the becoming of the world. Emerging from the dialogue between these thinkers is the idea of global temporality or, in Heideggerian terms, a coincidence of Being and Time, a temporal horizon that encompasses all things. Here, in the patterns of epochal time, in the seasons of natural time, in the ecology of life cycles, is where I look for the ground of the measure I seek.

What is appropriate to my lifetime and my time of life? How do I approach the ideal of unity and resolution? What is possible in this time of fallenness and strife to move closer to the *telos* of love? What are the rhythms of bodily time, of social time, of political time, of anthropological time? How do I bring myself into harmony with them?

These questions point to the existence of a pattern of global temporal structures that is both transcendent and immanent: global temporality transcends us to the extent that it encompasses us, eludes our comprehension, resists our efforts at control/manipulation, and permeates all phases of our being; yet it is also immanent, in that we are conscious moments of its unfolding and contribute to its constitution. There was time before there was humanity, yet phenomenal time would not be what it is without us. To rephrase a Hegelian current in Merleau-Ponty's thought: we are the chiasm in world-time through which it reflects and begins to understand itself. Our relation to time is founding-founded, constituting-constituted. We are born and we die: we are constituted in the temporal process. But we have constituted morning and evening, the season to reap and the season to sow, the ages of chastity and the ages of sensuality. We are thrown into time and caught up in its currents, but we influence the course of its flow before we are cast out again.

The ground of the measure I need to attune myself, and the ground of the values we need to synchronize ourselves, lies in the immanent-transcendent continuum of global temporality. Infancy has its erotic structures and so does old age, but they are not the same. The adult who projects himself into adolescent structures will, now in the words of Anaximander, "pay penalty and retribution . . . according to the assessment of Time,"[31] as will the adolescent who launches herself too precipitously into the structures of adult sexuality. And those who violate archaic prohibitions for the sake of a higher *telos* also invite a temporal nemesis, although their suffering might liberate their progeny.

3. Postscript

Too many discerning readers have misunderstood the intent of these last pages on erotic temporality and values for me to let the essay stop here, where it seemed to want to end. The question they raise is whether, disclaimers notwithstanding, there is an undercurrent of dissimulated moralizing beneath my notion of global temporality.

In general, I do not avoid defending ethical standpoints or making so-called "value judgments" when it seems necessary to do so. As I have argued elsewhere,[32] the posture of neutrality with regard to ethical issues is frequently a dodge, a flight from defending ethical commitments by refusing to acknowledge them even when they are at work. Therapy, for example, necessarily involves prescription, and I regard it as unethical for therapists to pretend that it does not. What, then, of my own professed neutrality?

Those who violate archaic prohibitions invite a temporal nemesis. There are archaic prohibitions against incest, miscegenation, homosexuality, adultery, rape, infantile sexuality, masturbation, and so forth. Violate any one of these taboos and a nemesis, a cultural sanction with some psychological or sociological impact, will follow. One pays for transgressions. Freud paid for uncovering infantile sexuality. Child molesters also pay. Fundamental values are at stake, and the social entity tends to conserve its taboos with force. Some of these taboos are well grounded; most, I think, are not. There is a difficult, but forced, decision each of us has to make: whether to pay for transgressing a prohibition or to pay for acceding to it.

I respect much of the work of the sexual liberators: D. H. Lawrence, Anais Nin, Henry Miller, Simone de Beauvoir, even (with qualifications) de Sade, and the rest of that courageous company. I also respect their suffering. There is work to be done in the assessment of taboos, in the differentiation of good and bad erotic behavior. It is important, pressing work. It is work I have undertaken and hope to continue. But that was not my primary project here.

In these pages I sought to prepare the way, to search for a ground on which the distinctions can be made, to discover the locus of basic values, but without attempting to trace their bearing on ethical issues. An example might help. Consider rape. As currently defined, rape is bad. In other times, it had a different meaning and, in some contexts, could be regarded as a necessary correlate to the law of exogamy: one had to take a mate from an alien clan; blood lines had to be crossed, and that involved violence. Even in our own times, sexual union seems inextricably linked with transgression, disruption, change, and violence in major or minor keys: someone's real or imagined rights are always violated in the formation of new erotic liaisons.[33] Universal consent of all parties involved, of parents, erstwhile lovers or spouses, children, siblings, friends, and defenders of cultural/psychological/sociological/ethnic values, is a dubious norm: if (nearly) everyone were to affirm a given union, someone would challenge it on those grounds alone. The paradox is real. What, then, about rape, in the broad sense of transgression, violation of culturally grounded expectations? Something like synchronization might help to work out the distinctions required. But synchronization with each other on the part of the principals, taken (*per impossibile*) in isolation, is not a sufficient condition. If it were, then there could be, for example, no genuine animus against adultery. There is also need for synchronization in global time. What is possible in this time of fallenness and strife, where utopia has yet to be conceived much less glimpsed as a possibility within one's own lifetime? What is possible for this finite body, with its age, in this age?

The synchronization of persons takes place in a global temporal context: the synchronization with each other[34] is necessarily mediated by a world in which every valued option excludes some other valued option.

> If you marry, you will regret it; if you do not marry, you will also regret it; if you marry or do not marry, you will regret both; whether you marry or do not marry, you will regret both.[35]

"Marry" can be replaced with almost any term. Kierkegaard supplies a few: laugh at (or weep) over the world's follies, believe a woman, hang yourself, and so forth. Do, don't, both, neither: regret will follow. And this, he says, "is the sum and substance of all philosophy."

I have been arguing along formally similar lines. Transgress, and a nemesis will follow. Accede, and confront another nemesis. In any case, a nemesis. But Kierkegaard and I differ on two salient points. This is not the sum of all philosophy; it is the initial condition for philosophizing: one *must*, after all, choose one's nemesis. And that there will always be a nemesis need not be a matter of regret: I prefer to affirm the fact that my decisions are, increasingly for the philosopher, mine, and that they are consequential.

The behavior I am prescribing is awareness.

Notes

1. This paper was originally presented at the Third Annual Human Science Research Conference held at West Georgia College, 16-19 May 1984. It was published for the first time in the *Journal of Phenomenological Psychology* 18 (1987): 33-48.

2. My term ("structures") is intended to refer to both the existentiell (*existenziell*) and the existential (*existenzial*) modes of self understanding of *Dasein*. See Martin Heidegger, *Being and Time*, trans. J. Macquarrie and E. Robinson (New York: Harper and Row, 1962), §4.

3. *Ibid.*, §41.

4. *Ibid.*, §26.

5. Jacques Derrida, "*Geschlecht*: sexual difference, ontological difference," *Research in Phenomenology* 12 (1983): 65-83, at 74.

6. Derrida, however, poses it as a question: "The price of [Heidegger's] prudence? Is it not to remove sexuality from every originary structure?" ("*Geschlecht*," 79).

7. Heidegger, *Being and Time*, §84.

8. Maurice Merleau-Ponty, *Phenomenology of Perception*, trans. Colin Smith (London: Routledge and Kegan Paul, 1962), 169.

9. For the argument, see M. C. Dillon, "Merleau-Ponty on Existential Sexuality: A Critique," *Journal of Phenomenological Psychology* 11 (1980): 67-81.

10. Derrida, "*Geschlecht*," 66.

11. Heidegger, *Being and Time*, §26.

12. Edmund Husserl, *Cartesian Meditations*, trans. Dorion Cairns (The Hague: Nijhoff, 1960), §§18, 37.

13. Kirk and Raven, *The Presocratic Philosophers* (Cambridge, Eng.: Cambridge University Press, 1964), fragment 423 (pp. 326-7).

14. *Ibid.*, frag. 421 (pp. 325-6).

15. *Ibid.*, frag. 427 (p. 330).

16. *Ibid.*, frag. 466 (p. 349).

17. *Ibid.*, frag. 471 (pp. 351-2).

18. *Ibid.*, p. 330.

19. Søren Kierkegaard, *Either/Or*, vol. 1, "The Immediate Stages of the Erotic or the Musical Erotic," trans. D. F. and L. M. Swenson (New York: Doubleday, 1959), 59ff., 88f.

20. Denis de Rougemont, *Love in the Western World* (New York: Harper and Row, 1974), 74ff.

21. Maurice Merleau-Ponty, "The Child's Relations with Others," trans. William Cobb, in James M. Edie, ed., *The Primacy of Perception* (Evanston, Ill.: Northwestern University Press, 1964), 118ff.

22. Edmund Husserl, *The Phenomenology of Internal Time-Consciousness*, ed. Martin Heidegger, trans. James S. Churchill (Bloomington: Indiana University Press, 1964), §10.

23. Richard R. Troiden, "Homosexual Encounters in a Highway Rest Stop," in Erich Goode and Richard R. Troiden, eds., *Sexual Deviance and Sexual Deviants* (New York: William Morrow, 1974), 211-28.

24. "The attempt in *Being and Time*, section 70, to derive human spatiality from temporality is untenable" (Heidegger, *On Time and Being*, trans. Joan Stambaugh [New York: Harper and Row, 1972], 23).

25. In an acute commentary on this paper (prepared for the Society for the Philosophy of Sex and Love), Diane Michelfelder raised two important questions, one of which I shall take up here (the other is addressed in n. 30, below).

> Dillon contends [that] there is an "essential phasing" to erotic temporality. I think that one is on very shaky ground in insisting on a necessary, intrinsic pattern to erotic temporality,

> instead of a pattern established by social tradition and cultural convention. . . . Where does *nomos*, the law, in *eros* begin and a norm of culture end? [See n. 1 in Diane P. Michelfelder, "Eros and Human Finitude," this volume, 327-31, at 331.—A.S.]

Michelfelder's first query, whether culture and tradition can explain patterns of human behavior, underscores a question addressed, but insufficiently developed, in my text: on what grounds do these norms and patterns emerge? Some amplification is in order.

There are stronger and weaker forms of necessity. Just as arithmetic must precede calculus in any conceivable culture, so must encounter precede love. It is a weaker form of necessity that dictates a development from infantile to adolescent to mature patterns of erotic behavior, yet some such temporal ordering or growth or genesis is presupposed in every account of *eros* I have seen from Plato on.

The relation between temporal *nomos* and cultural *nomos* is the one Husserl called *Fundierung*: the cultural norms are always *founded* on something prior, but they are then sedimented in tradition and become *founding* for future generations.

26. Paul Ricoeur, *Freud and Philosophy*, trans. Denis Savage (New Haven: Yale University Press, 1970), 459ff.

27. C. G. Jung, "Foreword," *The I Ching* (New York: Random House, 1961), i-xx.

28. Jean-Paul Sartre, *Being and Nothingness*, trans. Hazel Barnes (New York: Washington Square Press, 1966), 475: "Conflict is the original meaning of being-for-others."

29. M. C. Dillon, "Sartre's Inferno," *Thought* 52:205 (1977): 134-50. See also my "Love in *Women in Love*: A Phenomenological Analysis," *Philosophy and Literature* 2 (1978): 190-208.

30. Michelfelder's second question (see n. 25, above) concerns my reading of Heidegger:

> "Every thing," Heidegger does in fact say, "has its time." It is hard for me to imagine, though, that from Heidegger's statement one can reasonably derive a *logos* about erotic behavior. For the idea that every thing has its time expresses the view that time is the form of transience, of becoming. This is the view about time that most of us share, but, if we take a closer look at Heidegger's remark in its original setting, we can see that he is not endorsing it, but showing us a new, different way to think of the unity of the modes of temporality.

It is the case that, in the work I quoted (*On Time and Being*), Heidegger thinks of the belonging together of Being and time in terms of something antecedent to both, *Ereignis* or Appropriation, and this constitutes a development beyond the standpoint taken in *Being and Time*. (I doubt, however, that there was any point in his career at which Heidegger would deny that "time is the form of . . . becoming.")

The crucial issue here is whether the temporal form can be separated from the erotic content in the guise of an independent abstract *logos*. Michelfelder apparently thinks it cannot. At least, that is the thought I find underlying her comments. And I think that she is absolutely right. This point is implicit in my distinction between phenomenal time and objective time: in the temporal unfolding of phenomena, the structure of the unfolding is informed by the nature of the phenomenon. The structures of erotic encounter are not the structures of sculpting in marble, although both are informed by time.

31. Kirk and Raven, *The Presocratic Philosophers*, frag. 112 (p. 117).

32. M. C. Dillon, "The Implications of Merleau-Ponty's Thought for the Practice of Psychotherapy," *Journal of Phenomenological Psychology* 14 (1983): 21-41; reprinted in Kah Kyung Cho, ed., *Philosophy and Science in Phenomenological Perspective* (The Hague: Nijhoff, 1984), 55-74.

33. The work of Richard J. Alapack is apposite here. See "The Outlaw Relationship: An Existential Phenomenological Reflection on the Transition From Adolescence to Adulthood," in Amedeo Giorgi *et al.*, eds., *Duquesne Studies in Phenomenological Psychology*, vol. 2 (Pittsburgh: Duquesne University Press, 1975), 182-205.

34. A dyadic model is presupposed here somewhat arbitrarily. It is probably the case that this implicit privileging of the dyad in erotic relations is ultimately unjustified.

35. Søren Kierkegaard, "Diapsalmata," in *Either/Or*, vol. 1, 37.

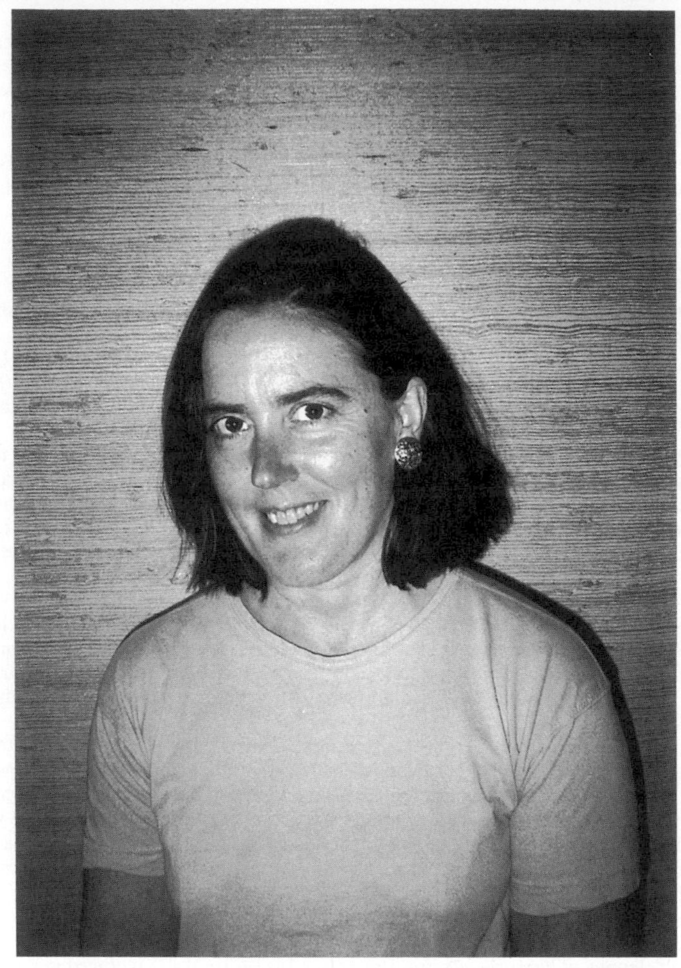

Diane P. Michelfelder
(photograph: William H. Wilcox)

Author of "Eros and Human Finitude"
Paper presented at the Society for the Philosophy of Sex and Love
during the
Pacific Division Meeting of The American Philosophical Association
San Francisco, Cal., 22 March 1985

Thirty-Two

EROS AND HUMAN FINITUDE[1]

Diane P. Michelfelder

Sexual desire, as Martin Dillon rightfully points out, is a matter about which Martin Heidegger's existential analytic of *Dasein* has nothing to say. Heidegger also, in the same context of *Being and Time*, has nothing to say about love. In other contexts, though, Heidegger remarks that all true thinking contains a great deal that is unthought.[2] Keeping this in mind, I do not find it surprising that Dillon turns to Heidegger for help in solving the particular problem that perplexes him about sex and love.

Let me just briefly recap what this problem is. Under the model of romantic love, love is viewed as timeless and eternal, while sexual desire is taken to be fleeting and transient. The trouble with this distinction is that it is drawn on the basis of a disregard for the essential temporal and finite nature of the self. As Dillon sees it, this disregard is "demeaning to our humanity" (316); thus this distinction between sex and love should be abandoned. This leaves the following dilemma, neither horn of which is completely plausible: either all sexual encounters, even the most seemingly impersonal, involve erotic love; or erotic love and sexual love are absolutely different from each other.

Dillon responds to the challenge of this dilemma by proposing (here is where Heidegger comes into the picture) that the distinction between sex and love can be pinned down on the basis of human finitude; that is, on the basis of time as we humans experience it. This basis gives both a way of looking at the sameness of sex and love, since all erotic encounters involve an "erotic temporal horizon" (317), as well as a way of telling sex and love apart: the depth of the temporal horizon associated with love is far richer and more complex than the temporal horizon associated with sex.

Dillon's resolution of the dilemma with which he started is indeed an intriguing one; he has provided an opportunity for us to reflect on a difficult and important issue. Because of my own interest in Heidegger, I found that the questions that came up in my mind as I thought about the solution proposed by Dillon kept coming back to the use of Heidegger in order to develop the distinction between sex and love. I absolutely agree with Dillon on the idea that Heidegger's silence on sex and love does not imply that nothing useful is to be gained from approaching Heidegger's thought to get some direction in considering these topics. I am less certain, though, about the particular direction Dillon ends up taking. Overall, then, my questions (I have four of them) will be focused on wondering not whether Heidegger's discussion of being and time can enhance our understanding of the difference between sex and love, but whether it can bring us to the specific difference Dillon presents here.

My first question has to do with the most basic concept on which his analysis rests: the concept of an "erotic temporal horizon" that is said to structure our erotic experiences. Is it necessary to introduce this concept in order to get between the horns of the dilemma that he faces? Would it not be sufficient simply to say, for example, in the face of the contrast he describes—"Someone for whom a kiss on the first date is a matter of deliberation is operating with a different temporal structure from someone who brings along a toothbrush just in case" (319)—that these individuals simply have different expectations, different desires? Putting it this way, I believe, would reflect the differences without undue conceptual complication. I would certainly want to agree with the hermeneutical point that our expectations help to constitute our experience of the present, but I admit I have some difficulty with the idea of individual (or global) erotic temporal horizons. Without relying on this concept, I think the gist of Dillon's distinction between love and sex can still be maintained: there is a lot more going on, more happening, in an encounter whose dimensions involve love than there is in an encounter where only sex is at stake.

Now I doubt that he would want to accept this last point. I imagine his objection to it going something like this: it is not simply that there is more going on in erotic encounters than sexual ones, or that the erotic is richer in meaning than the merely sexual. The important point is that what is going on in each of these encounters reflects a temporal *necessity*, an essential sequencing of phases of phenomenal time. I imagine this objection based on his argument that a connection exists between this necessity and erotic quality: temporal order produces erotic quality. When this intrinsic order is violated, as he contends it is in hard core pornography, there is a corresponding reduction in the quality of eros. This leads to my second question: if this temporal order is *necessary* for erotic quality, is it also *sufficient*? Granted, there is a temporal order to sexual activity. One has foreplay before, not after, sexual intercourse. It is also true that expectations cannot be fulfilled where there are no expectations to begin with. But these formal characteristics of the temporal order of an erotic experience do not seem to be enough to give that experience quality, any more than the fact that a tragic plot needs (as Aristotle observed) a beginning, middle, and an end in that order would be enough to make that tragedy a good one.

To maintain, as Dillon does, that a necessity in the dynamics of eros leads to quality, he has to, I believe, mix together what is formally necessary with what is perceived to be necessary as a result of social custom, cultural convention, and other factors. It is difficult for me to see that he enforces a separation of these two things in his essay. This difficulty is supported by the description he gives towards the beginning of his essay of the approach he will take in investigating the structures of erotic temporality; it will, he notes, "glide between the realms of the existentiell and the existential" (314), and his use of the word "structures" of temporality is meant to cover both. Later he reflects that this might cause someone to question whether he has actually found what he was looking for:

> In appealing to the qualitative gauges of phenomenal time, have I introduced norms that are not essentially temporal and traded on them to endow the temporal horizon with parameters that are not intrinsic to it? (318)

Dillon believes the answer to this question is no. Is his confidence justified?

One place we might turn to in looking at this, my second, question is his interpretation of the structures of erotic temporality within the wider context of the natural cycle of the seasons and the natural rhythms of biological time. To go against the limits placed on eros by these larger temporalities is to court disaster for, as he says, "those who violate archaic prohibitions for the sake of a higher *telos* . . . invite a temporal nemesis" (322). He also speaks of the dangers of going outside the erotic structures appropriate to one's own age: one will, he asserts, pay a price for such behavior at the hands of time. Although he does not specifically indicate what kinds of behavior he has in mind that "invite a temporal nemesis," one can wonder: is it a violation for a man to be erotically involved with a much younger woman? For a woman to be involved with a much younger man? For a person to sexually prefer someone else of the same, rather than the other, sex? If these are in fact the sorts of things he has in mind, then it does seem reasonable to be concerned that the distinction between where *nomos*, the law, in eros ends and a norm of culture begins is not adequately drawn.

These considerations lead to my third question: is the difference between sex and love set forth here morally neutral, as Dillon claims it is? Is it possible on the one hand not to be concerned about rigorously separating the existentiell from the existential in one's interpretation of erotic temporality and, on the other hand, insist on preserving a clear line between a moral interpretation of this temporality and a nonmoral one? The passages I referred to in the previous paragraph certainly appear to have the tenor of moral judgments. Dillon might respond to this by saying that these observations do not contradict the claim that the *general* distinction he is making between sex and love is morally neutral. I take it when he says that this distinction is morally neutral, what he means is that he is not making a blanket judgment as to the moral superiority of love over sex, since he points out there are occasions "when sex is ethically preferable to love and others when the reverse obtains" (318).

I agree. Still, it seems to be that the distinction proposed here, while ethically neutral from the perspective just given, is not ethically neutral when looked at from a wider perspective. Consider the following analogy. There are times when it seems to me preferable to grab a meal at a fast food restaurant and other times when I prefer sitting down to a meal that starts with soup and ends with Sauternes. At the same time, all else being equal, I would rather stay away from fast food dinners if possible; and, looking at my life as a whole, I think it would have been diminished in quality had a friend not insisted several years ago on ordering a bottle of Sauternes at a restaurant just so I could experience its sweetness. I do not entertain the same thoughts about my life lived without ever having tasted bacon double cheeseburgers.

Because Dillon makes the move of identifying the continuum of time with a continuum of quality (since his focus is on phenomenal rather than objective time), and because he is concerned not just with moments but also with rhythms and spans of time (as reflected in his question, "what is appropriate to my lifetime and my time of life?" [321]), the distinction he draws between sex and love becomes, in my opinion, a moral distinction. If I am truly concerned about the quality of my life, and if I view quality (as Dillon appears to do) as having a close connection to the development of unity within my personal life, it would be better for me to strive to cultivate those erotic relationships that are most conducive to the formation and continuation of this unity. These relationships would seem to be those that are, in Dillon's words, the most "resonant" (318): erotic relationships based on love.

This, plus the emphasis in his essay on the value of synchronicity in the establishment of what is referred to as "harmonious attunement" (319, 321) leads me to believe that in Dillon's eyes the concept of romantic love, when viewed from a Heideggerian perspective of human finitude, is basically identical to the concept of romantic love that he wishes to critique. In other words, the rethinking of eros from the perspective of human finitude that his essay asks us to consider challenges two aspects of the ideal of romantic love: the privileging of the purity of eternity over the impurity of time, and a stress on the psychic oneness of the individuals involved. But it does not challenge the ideal of romantic love *per se*. There are at least two other features of this ideal that are preserved, and that come to the surface if we think of romantic love as a celebration of the lure of the other, described in Alphonso Lingis's less benign words as an event that "draws all the faculties of life into an obsessive and jealous absorption in one singular individual."[3]

In this picture, one falls in love on the basis of the uniqueness of the individuality of another, and one hopes that one's love will be returned for the same reasons. In Dillon's essay we can recognize this individual, this ego-centered subject, without too much trouble. Such a person's openness to eros is tempered by what he refers to as the "commitment of each party to his or her own temporal horizon" (321). Polemic, conflict, and strife are often the results under these conditions as eros takes its course. The more harmony between the temporal horizons of the parties involved in an erotic experience, the greater the chance of avoiding these results. The key to harmony that is pointed out here is synchronization. But there can be no synchronization without an emphasis on *mutual presencing*, a second feature of the romantic ideal retained in his essay.

In short, and I think that Dillon would agree with me here, what is defended in his essay is a fairly conventional view of love. It is defended on the basis of Heideggerian views on the nature of time and on the belonging together of time with being. One of the things these views do is to present a critique of the conventional, that is, the objective, concept of time. Heidegger's statement that "true time is four-dimensional" is a case in point; this is not in any way a conventional view of time.[4] What I am wondering about is this: given Heidegger's questioning of the understanding of time, subjectivity, and the primacy of presence in Western philosophy, is it possible that rethinking the difference between sex and love within a Heideggerian framework could result in questioning the value of romantic love as the most profound type of love? This is the fourth question that I would like to ask.

In one of the few places where Heidegger comments about love, in the first volume of his *Nietzsche* work, he writes, "love is never blind; it is perspicuous."[5] It is the means that allows us to bring "an original cohesion and perdurance to our essential being" in such a way that we become more free and more open to all that lies around us.[6] To risk making an interpretation of these remarks: love, according to Heidegger, is a drive for more openness to beings, to our surroundings, to each other, and also to ourselves. It allows the world to disclose itself to us. Care, as Heidegger described it in *Being and Time*, might be an appropriate substitution for what he means by love. Noticing that care involves forms of disclosure, Michael Zimmerman writes, "what Heidegger means by care can perhaps best be understood as love."[7]

These observations lead me to concur with Dillon's choice of the term "harmonious attunement" as a test for the quality of eros. I am less inclined to think, though, that the key to "harmonious attunement" is synchronicity. What is "in sync" in such synchronicity are the erotic desires of two human beings. The concept of synchronicity as used in this context connects eros to desire and thus to the subjective character of romantic love. What another key might be, though, or whether there is indeed even one key rather than multiple keys to harmonious agreement, is a matter for further exploration.

Notes

1. This essay is a revised version of a commentary on M. C. Dillon's "Sex, Time, and Love: Erotic Temporality," presented to the Society for the Philosophy of Sex and Love, March 1985. After I prepared this revision, Dillon's essay as published in *Journal of Phenomenological Psychology* (this volume, 313-25) came to my attention. In its published form, Dillon responds to my original commentary in two endnotes (this volume, 324-5, nn. 25, 30). In these notes, sentences are quoted from my original commentary that do not appear in the present revision. While these changes might be confusing, I believe they do not disrupt the substance of our initial exchange. Page references to this volume's reprint of "Sex, Time, and Love" are given parenthetically in the text.

2. See, for example, Martin Heidegger, *What Is Called Thinking?* trans. J. Glenn Gray (New York: Harper and Row, 1968), 76.

3. Alphonso Lingis, *Excesses: Eros and Culture* (Albany: State University of New York Press, 1983), 50.

4. Martin Heidegger, *On Time and Being*, trans. Joan Stambaugh (New York: Harper and Row, 1972), 15.

5. Martin Heidegger, *Nietzsche*, vol. 1, trans. David Farrell Krell (San Francisco: Harper and Row, 1979), 48.

6. *Ibid.*, 47.

7. Michael Zimmerman, *The Eclipse of the Self* (Athens, Ohio: Ohio State University Press, 1981), 128.

Neera Kapur Badhwar
(photograph: University of Oklahoma)

Author of "Friends as Ends in Themselves"
Paper presented at the Society for the Philosophy of Sex and Love
during the
Eastern Division Meeting of The American Philosophical Association,
Washington, D. C., 28 December 1985

Thirty-Three

FRIENDS AS ENDS IN THEMSELVES

Neera Kapur Badhwar

1. Introduction

I define friendship as a practical and emotional relationship of mutual and (roughly) equal goodwill, affection, and pleasure.[1] In a general discussion of friendship, I would unpack and defend this broadly Aristotelian definition, but my concerns in this paper can be addressed without doing so. My chief concern is to give an analysis of end love in friendship, distinguishing it from means love, as well as from other notions of end love I regard as unjustifiable. I discuss love outside of friendship only insofar as it has a bearing on love in friendship.

I shall give a preliminary sketch of my topic by invoking widely held intuitions about end friendship as that relationship in which the friend is loved for her essential, not incidental, features; as an intrinsic, not instrumental, value; and as a unique and irreplaceable individual; and by showing how these intuitions fit in, or not, with the common but ill understood distinction between conditional and unconditional love. The explication of these intuitions will follow in later sections as part of the analysis of end friendship.

A. Ends and Means Friendships

The best, most complete friendships are those in which friends love and wish each other well as ends in themselves, and not solely, or even primarily, as means to further ends: social advancement, amusement, the promotion of some cause, or even mutual edification or improvement. In such friendships, the friends value each other's separateness: the fact that each has, and gives importance to, her own life and perspective, no matter how similar this life and perspective to the other's. They also take pleasure in being together primarily because of the persons they are. The other's usefulness in bringing about a desired end might be the initial spark of the friendship, and most friendships *are* useful in many ways. Indeed, if friends were not useful in times of need, they would not be friends. But in the best friendships, the central feature of the friendship is simply that the friends love, and wish each other well, as ends in themselves, whereas in lesser friendships, the central feature is the instrumental or means value of each to the other. The friends value each other's life and perspective only to the extent that it is useful to do so; each takes pleasure in the other primarily as a means to a further end.[2]

The two kinds of friendship differ in their *object* or *focus* as well as in their attitudes. Part of what it means to love something as an end, say a work of literature, is that one loves it for the features that make it the work it is. In friendship, too, then, part of what it means to love a friend as an end is that one loves her for the features that make her the person she is. As Aristotle puts it, those who are "most truly friends" love each other "by reason of their own nature," that is, for being the persons they are.[3] The friend is seen as lovable on account of what she essentially is, and not just on account of incidental features that make her useful or pleasurable. In instrumental friendships, by contrast, the object of love is primarily or only the other's incidental features.

How far must the person *seen* as intrinsically or noninstrumentally lovable be *actually* thus lovable by objective standards of human worth,[4] if the love is to count as genuine end love in friendship? It is at least necessary that she *be* an end in herself (see §3, below), and have the dispositions and qualities that are needed for being a good friend. (Whether a person can combine these good dispositions towards her friends with nasty dispositions towards everyone else, and thus be grossly deficient in human worth, is not a question I can pursue here. Here I assume that someone who is deficient in this way is also deficient in her capacity for the best kind of friendship, the friendship that is an end in itself.)

In end friendship, then, the friends are ends in themselves, and love each other as ends in themselves, that is, noninstrumentally, and by virtue of their essential features. Because the friends are not primarily means to each other's ends, they cannot, logically cannot, be replaced by more efficient means, or abandoned on the achievement of the end. It is this irreplaceability that most obviously marks off end friendship from means or instrumental friendship, in which the friends *are* thus replaceable or dispensable.

Is it possible to love someone who is an end for her essential features, but also, primarily, as a means to an end, say, to the end of self-improvement? The two sets of attitudes and emotions are psychologically incompatible, but it is possible for a person to have psychologically conflicting attitudes towards someone. In such a case, however, the friendship in question is neither fully instrumental, or fully an end in itself. Accordingly, when I discuss the objects of the two kinds of friendship, I shall assume that the object of end love is always the other's essential features, the object of instrumental love, the other's incidental features.

B. Loving Someone as a Good to Oneself

Friendships are generally recognized to involve pleasure. In end friendships, friends are a source of pleasure or happiness by virtue of their intrinsic worth or lovability. They are thus a good to each other, and love each other as such. A strong, opposing view, however, is that so long as one loves another as a good to oneself, then whether the source of this good is the other's intrinsic worth or instrumental worth, one loves her as a means to an end. A recent proponent of this idea is George Nakhnikian, whose target is Aristotle's theory of friendship, a theory that shares in its essentials the view of end love I have sketched. Nakhnikian argues that love of another because of his "admirable character traits" is no less "transactional" or instrumental than love of another "because of his usefulness," for both are "supposed to rebound to the satisfaction or benefit of the one who loves."[5] We love a person noninstrumentally, according to Nakhnikian, only when we love him or her *for whatever he is*, that is, "undemandingly" or unconditionally. In such a love, there can be "no thought of expected returns and no requirement that the person loved be a good [or lovable] human being."[6] To love him as a good to ourselves is necessarily to love him instrumentally. According to this line of thought, then, loving another noninstrumentally *cannot* imply loving him as a good to oneself, thus as a source of pleasure or happiness.

This exclusion of pleasure in the other from the phenomenon of love is, however, false to experience, at least so long as "love" is used in the usual emotional/practical sense and not in Kant's rarefied purely practical sense. One can *admire* a person's admirable qualities without getting any pleasure from them: witness Salieri's bitter, grudging admiration of Mozart's genius in *Amadeus*. One can delight in a person's *accomplishments*, without getting any pleasure from the *person* as the cause and bearer of these accomplishments: witness Salieri's delight in Mozart's music, coupled with his hate-filled resentment of Mozart for being the one "chosen" to produce such sublime sounds. And one can wish a person well, and even want to spend time with her to benefit her, without getting any pleasure from her company. But one cannot *love* a person without delighting in her under some aspect: in the end love of friendship, without delighting in her as being the person she is. Hence end love is also necessarily a good to the one who loves. But it is not thereby, I hold, instrumental. These conclusions are further supported in §2 by an analysis of what it means to love someone as an end.

Some people might be inclined to dismiss the view I am discussing, that the presence of pleasure or satisfaction necessarily makes love instrumental, as a simple minded confusion between pleasure being the *result* of loving someone, and pleasure being its *goal*. But simple minded confusions do not have the long and tenacious life that this view has had. Hence it is not surprising that it has not disappeared in spite of Bishop Butler's exposure of a similar confusion at the heart of the argument for psychological egoism. For what Butler's argument leaves untouched is the further possibility that even if self-benefit (satisfaction, pleasure, or whatever) is only an unintended *result* of a certain kind of activity, it may well be that the tacit *expectation* of self-benefit, based on past experiences, or even just on the natural teleology of our biological constitution, is necessary for *sustaining* the activity. It is this worry that leads Kant to say that we can never be sure that "the dear self" is not intruding even when we think our only motive is duty. And it is this possibility in personal love that is thought to make it instrumental, and to distinguish it from the unconditional love (agape) with which God is said to love us, and which in us is called neighbor love. This argument, however, will not concern me here, as I do not believe that the good to oneself that I have identified as delight in the other is only an unintended *result* of love. Nor do I believe that its presence distinguishes personal love from agape. Rather, I believe it is an essential *ele-*

ment of end love, in agape (insofar as it is conceivable as a form of love), no less than in friendship and other forms of personal love. So either loving another as a good to oneself does not necessarily make personal love instrumental, or else agape is also instrumental.

C. The Friend as the Unique, Irreplaceable Individual

Those who believe that only unconditional love makes it as noninstrumental love, but have not wanted to condemn friendship out of hand as mere instrumental love, might be attracted by Nakhnikian's suggestion that the best kinds of friendship be understood as a combination of unconditional and instrumental love. But can friendship love be accurately characterized as a combination of these, or in some way be explained by reference to these? If it cannot, then there is good reason to suppose that not all noninstrumental love is unconditional, and not all love of the other as a good to oneself is instrumental.

The main problem in trying to explain friendship in terms of unconditional and instrumental love, is that each, in its own way, does violence to the intuition that in end friendship the object of love is the unique irreplaceable individual. If I love you unconditionally, I love you regardless of your individual qualities: your appearance, temperament, style, even moral character. So you are no different from anyone else as the object of my love, and my love for you is no different from my love for anyone else. But then in what sense are *you* the object of my love? On the other hand, if I love you instrumentally, for the benefit I derive from certain of your qualities,[7] then your value to me is entirely dependent on my needs or ends, and you are dispensable as soon as I have achieved them or relinquished them or found someone else who can better serve them. So again, in what sense is it *you* that I love? In the first you lose your *qualitative* identity, in the second your *numerical* or *historical* identity. Thus, in agape, the exemplar of unconditional love, although the *target* of love, that which the love is directed to or at, is, indeed, the particular, numerical individual, the focus or *object*[8] of love, that *for* which or *as* which the target is loved, is not that which makes him the unique person he is, but that which he shares with everyone else: his substantial, metaphysical identity as a human being. Every individual is loved equally and indifferently as a Speck of Humanity among other Specks in the Ocean of Humanity. Thus every individual is *phenomenologically replaceable* by any other as the object of love. In the Platonic view, the exemplar of instrumental love, although the target of love is only that individual who has the qualities beneficial to the lover, the object of love is not the person, not *that individual with those qualities*, but *those qualities in any individual*.[9] The individual is loved for his qualitative identity as an instantiation of the abstract Idea of Beauty, and is a means to this ultimate object of love. Hence the individual is both *phenomenologically and numerically replaceable* in the lover's journey to this ultimate object. Thus both agape and Platonic love have as their objects the universal and nonindividual in the individual target. Their difference is only that in one the individual target is regarded as an end, in the other, as a means. But in neither is the individual loved for the unique character or personality that make him the distinct *person* he is, as he must be in the end love of friendship.

Can this double failure be compounded into a single success, as suggested by some? I suspect not. On the one hand, my love for you, who are my friend, is not love if it alters *whenever* it alteration finds. Hence it cannot be of qualities as such, qualities you happen to manifest, as it is in instrumental love. But neither is my love for you, the unique person, love for *you* if it remains unaltered through *all* alterations of your qualities (as if "you" = "bare particular"), as it is in unconditional love. The object of my love must be you, the person, in your concrete individuality, not "human being" or "instance of (some) F." The question, then, is: what is essential to your being the person you are? When are you no longer you? We need an analysis of the person or self in friendship that allows us to accommodate the idea that friendship love is dependent on the qualitative identity of the friend, yet not such as to make her numerically or phenomenologically replaceable by any individual with those qualities; that such love is of the numerically irreplaceable individual, yet not such as to persist independently of her qualitative identity. In other words, we need an analysis of the object of friendship love that preserves both the qualitative and the numerical identity of the individual.

Before proceeding, I want to make three points of clarification. First, although I have used the words "historical identity" and "numerical identity" interchangeably, it is only *generally* true, not *necessarily* true, that numerically (spatiotemporally) different individuals have different histories. For instance, identical twins raised in the same environment will probably have the same histories in all essential respects: find the same events crucial, make essentially the same responses. Therefore they will probably also have essentially the same qualities, hence be essentially alike as persons. (It is also logically possible, though highly improbable, that genetically unrelated people, raised in different environments, turn out to have essentially the same histories and qualities as well.) What is necessarily true is that *historically* distinct individuals be distinct as persons. All this further implies a qualification of my claim that in the end love of friendship, the object of love is the unique, irreplaceable person. For if in end love one loves the other for the person he is, then if one twin is loved for what he is, so must the other, and both be loved in exactly the same way. They remain *numerically* irreplaceable, not being means to an end, but not *phenomenologically* irreplaceable. Thus in Shakespeare's *Twelfth Night*, Olivia's romantic love for the disguised Viola is automatically transferred to her twin Sebastian. But since most people are not personality twins, the thesis that in the end love of friendship, the object of love is the person for what he essentially is, will generally also mean that the object of love is irreplaceable both numerically and phenomenologically. It has sometimes been suggested that if friends are unique and irreplaceable, it is only by virtue of their incidental qualities, or of fortuitous differences in the circumstances of the friendship. But if I am right, for most of us, our differences are deeper and richer than *that* (see §3, below).

Second, my concern with that which is essential to a person has to do entirely with that constellation of fundamental, empirical, mental qualities (moral, psychological, aesthetic, intellectual) that constitutes an individual's self or personality, and not with any Metaphysically Changeless and Simple Essence. What is empirically essential or fundamental to a person is both dynamic and ambivalent. Most people change over their lifetimes in some of their fundamental qualities—in aspects of their selves—and an individual can change enough to have what Derek Parfit calls "later" and "earlier" selves. Thus it is possible to love an individual as an end, but not forever. Most people also harbor ambivalences in their fundamental qualities, and an individual can be ambivalent enough to have simultaneously more than one self. Thus it is possible to love an individual as an end, but not wholly. (These facts explain some of the tragic conflicts that beset friendships.) But even an individual with a single self might be loved as an end but not wholly. For the self is multifaceted, and no one friend can love, or even evoke, every facet. (This explains, in part, why friendship is not a transitive relation.) So which changes in the self are crucial to a friendship depends, in part, on what the friends in question find important in each other and in themselves.

Third, as the central aim of this paper is to provide an analysis of the object of love in end friendship, I shall not address myself to the other elements of friendship, for example, that of mutual and equal goodwill; nor to its "background conditions," the psychological and social circumstances that explain *why* people make the friends they do.

In the following section, using agape as the paradigm of unconditional love, I argue that on one interpretation, unconditional love is conceptually impossible, on the other, possible but irrelevant to friendship. The first argument will show that the idea of loving someone for her intrinsic worth, and thus as a good to oneself, is necessary to the end love of friendship as well as to agape. Hence the difference between agape and the end love of friendship must lie elsewhere. The second argument will show that the difference between the two is that in friendship the worth in question is *empirical*, while in agape it is *transcendental*. But there is no transcendental worth. Again, since loving the friend for her intrinsic worth is necessary to end friendship, the difference between instrumental and end friendship cannot be that instrumental friendship is based on valuable qualities, end friendship not. In §3, I shall analyze the distinction already made between them in terms of incidental qualities (qualities that in one way or another fail to define the person) and essential qualities (qualities that do define the person). I will then show that essential qualities can neither be, nor be understood, apart from an individual's numerical or historical identity. This will serve to distinguish my position from any position, Platonist or anti-Platonist, that identifies love of the person with love of his historical *rather than* qualitative identity.

2. Loving a Friend as an End vs. Unconditional Love

A. Agape as Completely Unmotivated

Agape is God's love for human beings and, through Him, our love for our neighbors.[10] Anders Nygren points out that the life that is organized on the principle of agape is completely different from the life that is organized on the principle of eros, the principle that love is of the good or lovable: eros and agape are opposite "general attitudes to life."[11] Thus agape has no direct bearing on the nature of friendship. But it does have an indirect bearing if it is an ideal that friendship ought to approach, or if it is an element in all forms of love, as Kierkegaard, Nakhnikian, and perhaps others, believe. According to Kierkegaard, Christian love "can lie at the base of and be present in every other expression of love. . . . It is . . . [or] can be in all of them, but this love itself you cannot point out"; it is like the "man" in all men.[12]

What, then, is the nature of agape? Following Luther's interpretation, Anders Nygren summarizes its main features thus: agape is spontaneous and "unmotivated"; it is "indifferent to value"; it is creative.[13] It stands "*in contrast to all activity with a eudaemonistic motive*" and "*in contrast to all legalism.*"[14] Agape gives with no thought of gain. Being "indifferent to value," it needs no encouragement from, or justification by, the perceived value of the target of love. To love someone for his worth is to love him acquisitively, not agapeistically.[15] Christian love is "a lost love," "the direct opposite of rational calculation."[16] In Kierkegaard's words, "love to one's neighbor makes a man blind in the deepest and noblest and holiest sense, so that he blindly loves every man."[17]

Can such a love be the foundation of friendship? Or perhaps the mortar that holds it together? It is hard to see how a love that is in principle blind can be the foundation of a relationship that is in principle cognitive, a response to the perceived value of the other. But perhaps it is agape under its positive, creative aspect that serves this function. Agape's indifference to value has as a corollary its creativeness: it *creates* value by loving. In Luther's words, agape is "an overflowing love . . . which says: I love thee, not because thou art good . . . for I draw my love not from thy goodness (Frommigkeit) as from an alien spring; but from mine own well-spring."[18]

Now it might seem that agape under this creative aspect enters into friendship as the generosity and abundance that are characteristic of friendship: I forgive your faults, or shower you with gifts, not because you *deserve* any of this, but as an expression of my love. But the semblance is misleading. For the love that motivates such generosity is itself a response to the friend's value, whereas agape on this strictly unconditional interpretation cannot be linked to any recognition of value. Whatever it means, then, to love a friend as an end, it cannot mean to love him with the unconditionality of agape. Indeed, on this Lutheran interpretation, the denial that the worth or lovability of the individual has anything to do with the love, is precisely the denial that the individual is loved for "himself." So while agape is noninstrumental love, it is not, so far, end love. But this radical interpretation of agape renders it mysterious why agape is selectively *directed* at human beings, given that it is not *motivated* by them.[19] To dispel the mystery, the Christian must at least concede that human beings are loved qua human beings, hence that humanity as such, the good or God in each individual, in Augustine's words, is worth loving.[20] Agape can, consistently, be unconditional in the sense of being independent of the individual's *personal* nature and worth, of that which distinguishes him from other persons, but not of his *human* nature and worth, of that which distinguishes him from nonhumans. Agape also, in other words, must be of the individual for what he is, even though only qua *human being*, and not qua *person*. At least God's agape for us must, then, be a form of end love.[21] But now, if loving someone for his worth is logically necessary for loving him as an end, then loving someone as a means cannot be explicated in terms of loving him for his worth, *simpliciter*. Both end love and instrumental love are directed at the other as lovable or worthy.

B. Happiness as Goal of Love and Happiness as Intrinsic to Love

It might still be argued, following Nygren, that in loving something as lovable or good we must love it only as a means, even if the love aims only at the possession and contemplation[22] of the loved object, and not at any further advantage. And this because in such possession and contemplation we attain happiness, so that the love remains but a means (conscious or unconscious) to our happiness.[23] If Nygren is right, we are caught in a contradiction: to love X as an end is necessarily to love him for his worth; to love him for his worth is necessarily to love him as a means; hence to love X as an end is to love him as a means. But Nygren's view depends upon his distinction between the love of X, and the happiness we gain from the attainment and contemplation of X. Is this a viable distinction? *Must* love be a separable *means* to the happiness contained in the attainment and contemplation of the loved object? It would have to be construed thus if it were such as to come to an end on the attainment of the happiness,[24] as the desire at a particular time for, say, the sight of green valleys, comes to an end on seeing them.[25] But love is not quenched by the happiness we get from the contemplation of the loved object. Rather, if love is a response to the perceived value of the other, then its contemplation must further *evoke* the love, not extinguish it;[26] and because the happiness afforded by this is itself a value, the happiness must serve to perpetuate the love of the other who is its source. The relationship of loving to the happiness we get from loving is not, then, modeled by the relationship of the desire to see to the pleasure of seeing.

This in itself, however, is not enough to show that end love and happiness are not related as means to goal. For even if Y's love for X is not extinguished by happiness, it might yet be the case that it is wholly conditional on the happiness Y gets from the satisfaction of her goals by X: anyone with X's ability could take his place.[27] To show that in end love, love is not a means to happiness, it must be the case that here the happiness cannot be adequately specified independently of the love, such that in loving you as an end, my happiness is to the love, not as the *desire to see* X is to seeing X, but as the *pleasure of seeing* X is to seeing X.

We have seen that essential to loving someone as an end is perceiving and responding to her as lovable by her nature, however this is to be defined. Hence pleasure or delight is intrinsic to perceiving and responding to someone as lovable by her nature,[28] to contemplating the person loved.[29] Happiness is related to end love not as goal to means, but as element to complex whole. So when

X is loved as an end, the happiness cannot, logically, exist apart from the love: different end loves bring different forms of happiness. By contrast, when X is loved as a means, the happiness is a further goal of the love, and can, logically, exist without it: different means loves can bring the same form of happiness. For it is in the satisfaction of her own ends that Y takes pleasure and delight, and only derivatively, that is, by virtue of X's ability to fulfill these ends, in X.

It is important to remember that the happiness that is intrinsic to end love, whether in agape or in friendship, is not the only kind of happiness afforded by such love. Happiness comprehends different kinds of pleasures and satisfactions, and the happiness that consists in loving X might cause the happiness that consists in, say, philosophizing well. It is a common enough experience for happiness in one area of one's life to spread into other areas by motivating one to do well in those other areas. Besides, as I remarked earlier, end friendships usually are useful in many ways, and friends must at least *aim* to be useful in certain ways if they are to be real friends. They remain end friendships, however, because what is central to them is the happiness that is intrinsic to the love, and not the happiness that results from the satisfaction of one's goals.

Someone might object to making happiness intrinsic to the end love of friendship on the grounds that one might regard the other not with pleasure and delight but with pain and frustration as, for instance, when his life is fraught with pain and disappointment; and this precisely because in loving him one shares in his pain. This is obviously true. I would still maintain, however, that insofar as the love is a response to the other's worth, one cannot fail to regard him with pleasure, even if the pleasure is outweighed by the pain. If he changes in a way that destroys the possibility of such a response, as when the frustrations of his life not only make him unhappy and "not much fun to be with" but also, say, self-pitying and self-centered, one might indeed keep up "friendly relations" out of a sense of loyalty, one might even feel a kind of love out of pity, but the emotion is no longer the value response necessary to end love.

C. Irreplaceability as Criterion of End Love in Friendship

I stated earlier that it is irreplaceability that most obviously marks off end friendship from means friendship. A friend who is loved as an end is numerically irreplaceable in the sense that she is not a means to a happiness that can be better or as well served by another. It can now be stated more clearly how and why she is also phenomenologically irreplaceable. She is thus irreplaceable in the precise sense that loving and delighting in her are not completely commensurate with loving and delighting in another, not even when this other is loved as an end. This is confirmed by the fact that if the happiness we got from different friends were completely commensurate, there would be no qualitative differences among our friendships, and we would not, for example, desire to spend an evening with X rather than with Y, but only "with a friend." Again, when someone who is loved as an end ceases to be loved, the loss cannot be completely made up by acquiring a new friend; the loss of the old friend is a distinct loss, the gain of the new friend, a distinct gain. Even when one ceases to *feel* the loss, because of the passage of time, and the presence of other enriching activities and experiences in one's life, it remains true that different end friendships engender different forms of love and happiness. In instrumental friendships, on the other hand, anyone who fulfills my goals as well as X is a potential replacement for X: different friendships engender the same love and happiness. The friend might, indeed, never be replaced, but only for contingent reasons, as when circumstances conspire to make her uniquely qualified to promote my ends.[30] Thus there can be a lifelong friendship that is enacted entirely in pubs over shared beers, but which would have ended on one of the friend's going off beer. This is why mere permanence is not sufficient for end friendship.[31] Neither is it necessary. For if the essential qualities of one of the friends change, such that either you are no longer the person who evoked my love, or I am no longer the person who loved you, then, barring the happy possibility that the other one undergoes a parallel or complementary change, the love must disappear because its *object* or its *subject* has disappeared.[32]

My account might give rise to the objection that the person who is loved as an end cannot, contrary to my claim, be irreplaceable. For when someone who affords greater happiness than X comes along, she must displace X. But this criticism is either misleading or not an objection at all. It is misleading insofar as it suggests that X's *intrinsic* value to me is displaced by the new friend. For this is not possible: the pleasure I get from X is different from the pleasure I get from the new friend, even if the latter is greater.[33] Given that time is finite, the greater friendship will certainly limit and change my *practical* relations with X. In particular, it will displace X's instrumental value; for instance, X will no longer be my primary support in times of trouble. But this is hardly an objection to my account of end love.

To summarize this part of the discussion: loving X as an end in himself requires explication in terms of X's worth or lovability, whether the lovable object be X the unique and irreplaceable person, as in friendship, or X the human being, as in agape. Insofar as happiness is intrinsic to such love, and not its goal, one necessarily loves X as a good to oneself without loving him as a means. So if X ceases to be such a good, he ceases to be loved as an end. The attempt to interpret end love as an unconditional love that is completely independent of the other's worth or lovability, and of its relation to one's own happiness, thus fails. There is no such love.

D. Agape as Motivated by a Necessary Human Worth

When agape is interpreted as a love that is motivated by the good in each individual, then it is compatible with end love in friendship. Is it, however, in any way *relevant* to it? It is often thought so. Erich Fromm states:

> In essence, all human beings are identical. We are all part of One; we are One. This being so, it should not make any difference whom we love.[34]

All human beings qua human beings are equally worthy of love.

But what is the evidence for this common humanity, this equal potential for worth or virtue that we all, supposedly, share? There seems to be no *empirical* evidence. Experience indicates that there *are* people who are completely lacking in moral capacities: the criminally insane, the thoroughly wicked, the psychopathically amoral. Hence the only way to sustain belief in a universal potential for goodness is by means of a transcendental metaphysics of the person (in the religious version, the idea of man as created in the image of God; in a well-known secular version, the idea of man qua moral agent as a noumenal being). Without this transcendental assurance of a necessary potential for goodness in all human beings, the goodwill we bear to those we are unacquainted with can be based only on the fact that most human beings do have some actual or potential moral worth. Now such a goodwill or "love of humanity" *is* related to friendship. It is, in Aristotle's words, "a beginning of friendship [philia], as the pleasure of the eye is the beginning of love [eros]."[35] But since the assumption on which the goodwill is based is defeasible with respect to any given individual, so is the goodwill itself. Thus the goodwill presupposed by friendship is not unconditional love. We can conclude, therefore, that unconditional love is neither an element of, nor an ideal for, friendship love. The object of unconditional love is Humanity, the "God in the neighbor," while the object of friendship is the person, the qualitatively and numerically unique individual.

3. Loving a Friend as an End vs. Instrumental Love

It is time now to discuss the difference between the objects of love in end and means friendships. In §1, I stated that instrumental friendships are based on incidental qualities, qualities that fail to define the person, whereas end friendships are based on essential qualities, qualities that do define the person. Further, in end friendships the friend is, and is regarded as, an end in himself. How do we pick out the qualities that define a person? And what does it mean for someone to *be* an end in himself?

A. The Object of Love in End Friendships

Defining is a process of selecting the qualities we regard as essential: the qualities we think are ontologically fundamental in, and best explain, the constitution and behavior of the thing defined.[36] But in trying to define a person, our selection of fundamental qualities is complicated not only by their dynamism and ambivalence, but also by the feature of *reflexiveness*. For unlike other things, our personal nature is given not just in what we are, as expressed in the goals, values, and abilities we act upon, but might or might not endorse as good or important; but also in what we would be, as expressed in our still born ideals and aspirations, those we merely endorse, but do not act upon.[37] For even in merely endorsing something we exercise our judgment and discrimination, and express this endorsement, however inconsistently, in the pattern of our evaluations.[38] In defining ourselves, we might pick out as fundamental only the values and abilities we merely endorse, leaving out entirely those we act upon. Then our self-definition shows that we have a false self-image. Nevertheless, since this selection expresses a higher order value judgment ("*this* is what I most value, and want to be valued for [and to emulate]"), our self-definition necessarily constitutes and reveals something of our value scheme and standards, hence of our nature. Or it can go the other way: we might pick out as fundamental in ourselves only the values and abilities that explain our actual goals and actions, leaving out entirely the ideals and aspirations we do not act upon, either because we are unable to articulate them accurately or because we disavow them and are, to that extent, living in bad faith. Nevertheless, insofar as our self-definition is a true statement of the values we actually live by, it necessarily reveals something of our value scheme and standards, hence of our nature. In *The Doll's House*, Nora defines herself in terms of her husband's needs as part amusing plaything, part obedient wife, disavowing her aspirations to autonomy.[39] Her self-definition, as shown by her subsequent development, is inadequate. Yet it does reveal something of her nature.

Is it logically possible for just anyone to be loved noninstrumentally? A paradox lurks within any analysis of end friendship that allows this possibility. Consider the case of someone who lives and defines himself as an instrument of another's ends, not because he is ignorant or self-deceived about any contrary aspirations, but because he is simply lacking in them. The goals he pursues are his neither in the sense that he endorses them, nor even in the sense that *his* desires select them. What he desires and endorses, if he endorses anything, is his own instrumentality, and it is this instrumentality that is his fundamental trait. The paradox in allowing that even such a person can be loved as an end is this. In an end friendship, the friends love and wish each other well noninstrumentally, and by virtue of what they essentially are, and thus irreplaceably. But if someone is essentially an instrument of another's ends, then loving him for what he essentially is must entail loving him as an instrument of those ends,[40] and thus as replaceable by anyone who can fill that role. It follows that such a person cannot be loved as an end.

A person can fail to be an end in himself even if he does not live or define himself as an instrument of others' ends. Consider the case of someone who acquires his goals and values, including his friendships, through imitation of significant others, although he does not live or define himself as an instrument of their ends. Such a person also pursues goals that are his neither in the sense that he endorses them, nor even in the sense that *his* desires select them: his *self* is engaged at neither level of discrimination and judgment. All he desires and endorses is the safety and acceptability he expects through imitation; *this* is what is essential to his self. As an imitator of others, he is eminently duplicable and replaceable by those others. This captures some of the content of the intuitive idea that a person can be an end in himself only if the goals and values he pursues are his in some substantive sense, the products of his own encounters with the world. Only then do they express his sense of himself as someone *worthy* of living quite apart from his utility to others' ends, and *able* to live by his own judgment and effort. To be loved for being the person he is, he must *be* a person in his own right, neither an instrument of others, nor their imitator: someone who is essentially a means to another's ends, or who is incapable of living by his own judgment, encounters the world and acquires a self through the goals and judgments of others.[41] (What exactly it means, in concrete terms, to view oneself as worthy and able to live, and what restrictions this imposes on the content of one's goals, can probably be adequately specified only with the help of a literary narrative, and not by philosophical analysis alone. For our present purposes, it is enough to note that we do distinguish between those who live by their own judgment and values and those who live second hand, whether as devotees of some one individual or, in the words of the poet, as "the epitome of all mankind.")

B. The Essential and the Accidental: Two Views

My characterization of the object of end love in friendship has still to meet an indirect metaphysical challenge. I have talked about end love in terms of essential qualities. But as is well known, at the third step of the Platonic ladder of love, the other is loved for what at least *seem* to be his essential qualities, his "fair and noble and well-nurtured soul,"[42] even though he is, at the same time, loved only as a means to the *proton philon*, the abstract Form of Beauty. *The paradigm of instrumental love turns out to be based on essential qualities.* I shall show that this comes about only because of Plato's peculiar conception of qualities and their relation to the individual. On the conception I am defending, a person's essential qualities are inseparable from his numerical or historical identity, both in fact and as object of cognition and love. In trying to see why Platonic love of essential qualities is instrumental, we can also take a deeper look into what is involved in love of essential qualities in end friendship.

Recall, first, that a person's goals and aspirations, thus his fundamental qualities, are the result of his encounters with the world, whether at firsthand, or in imitation of others. Thus his fundamental qualities are inevitably colored by his particular, historical, existence. Conversely, his goals and aspirations are expressed in, and contour, his particular existence. A personal essence is not a set of qualities detached from one's particular existence, but qualities that express, and are expressed in, this existence. Thus a person's essence, that which makes him what he is, includes the *way* his fundamental qualities are expressed, his *style*: as Buffon noted, the style is the man. Thus, for example, Cyrano de Bergerac would not be the person he is without his poetic wit and physical daring.[43] His wit and daring constitute *his* particular stylization of his qualities: his independence of mind, his courage and loyalty, his passion for the "white plume of freedom," as well as his tragic conviction that he is too ugly for a woman's love. What makes these qualities uniquely *his*, is the style of their expression. Equally, what makes his poetic wit and physical daring uniquely *his*, is the qualities they express.[44] The distinction between qualities and style, however, is only a relative one: the style in which one expresses certain qualities can itself be described as a set of qualities, and the qualities expressed can be described as a style of facing life.[45] Those who love Cyrano for one or the other do not love him for what he essentially is.[46] Thus the hangerson in Ragueneau's bakery, delighting in Cyrano's wit, fail to see it as an expression of his deepest moral passions;[47] and we can imagine some earnest devotee of Cyrano who loves him for his "moral nobility," while failing to see his wit as an essential expression of this nobility.

In Plato's conception of essential qualities, the earnest devotee would be right. The proper object of love is the qualities of soul as abstracted from their mode of expression in the individual's life. For the fairness and nobility of the well-nurtured soul are reflections of "beauty absolute, separate, simple, and everlasting,"[48] the true and ultimate object of love, whose instantiation in the individual's life is but an unfortunate entanglement. It is this kind of detachment of an individual's qualities from their concrete manifestation in his life that makes the Platonic ladder of love a metaphor for instrumental love. The individual as a numerical particular becomes a mere vehicle for these qualities, the concrete events of his life that give them shape and expression mere accidents. That which is *essential* in an individual is universal; that which is *unique* and *personal* in him, is accidental: there are no individual essences, no truly *personal* natures. Thus the noble character of one individual is identical with the noble characters of other individuals, and love of a given individual for what he essentially is, implies love of all instantiations of this universal essence. Such a love is therefore not only compatible with, but *requires*, regarding him as replaceable with like others, and with regarding his particular existence as but a means to a further goal. To regard him as irreplaceable, as an end rather than a means, is to lose sight of the true object of love, to distort reality.

Thus in Plato's theory, this abstraction of qualities from their concrete manifestation is a moral recommendation to the lover that comes backed by an elaborate metaphysics. The qualities of the individual, the *what* he is, can and should be divorced from their expression in his life, from the *how* he is what he is, because doing so brings one closer to seeing them as they are in themselves, to seeing them as they are in their original and pure form. But this belief (in some of) the individual's *qualities* as essential, and the *style* in which they are manifested as accidental, is neither required nor possible in a nontranscendental metaphysics. For here, particulars—material objects as well as individuals—are not instantiations of abstract, pre-existing qualities; rather, qualities come into being, persist and change in particulars, and can be abstracted from them only mentally or conceptually. An individual's *history*, as such, is no more accidental than his *qualities*: the essential/accidental distinction is a distinction *within* the individual's historical-qualitative identity. Thus an individual cannot be known or loved as an end if he is seen as a set of qualities divorced from their expression in his life.

Plato's metaphysical fiction yields a psychological and moral truth. It shows that a love motivated primarily by a need to fulfill a deficiency must be means love. Even when it purports to be directed to the other's fundamental qualities, its view lacks the *richness* and *depth* necessary to capture the essential person.

C. The Historical Dimension of Love

The attempt to defend personal love against the Platonistic impulse sometimes takes the form of contrasting love of the *person* with love of his *characteristics*.

But in this form the defense implicitly accepts the Platonic premise of the separability of the two. To quote Robert Nozick:

> An adult may come to love another because of the other's characteristics: but it is the other person, and not the characteristics, that is loved. The love is not transferable to someone else with the same characteristics, even to one who "scores" higher for these characteristics. . . . One loves the particular person one actually encountered. Why love is historical, attaching to persons in this way and not to characteristics, is an interesting and puzzling question.[49]

But in a nontranscendental metaphysics, this puzzle cannot even be legitimately formulated. The characteristics that motivate the love are not the type of which various individuals are tokens, so that love's nontransferability should generate a puzzle. No description of an individual's characteristics that abstracts from their style of expression in his particular existence can capture the *person*; neither can any explanation of love as historical that excludes reference to the characteristics that are revealed in, and shape, this history. Insofar as love is historical, it is also of the individual's characteristics as expressed in this history. Love might endure "through changes of the characteristics that gave rise to it."[50] But this in itself does not imply that characteristics are irrelevant to the continuation of love. After all, love might *not* endure through such changes; indeed, a "love" that endures through a loss of *all* valued characteristics is not love, but obsession or routine. For then its object is not the *person*, but a "bare particular," the numerical individual who happened to be the one initially encountered and loved. When love does endure through changes of the characteristics that gave rise to it, it could be either because the subject of love has also changed in a complementary way, or because he comes to love the other for *other* characteristics initially unperceived.

The value of a shared history, of the historical dimension of love, lies chiefly in its epistemic and creative functions, both of which have to do with characteristics. A shared history is usually required for *knowledge* of each others' characteristics, and knowledge is essential to love. When a shared history reveals characteristics that make people lovable to each other, then it leads to or strengthens love. A shared history can also contribute to the mutual *creation* of characteristics. And when it is "shared" emotionally and cognitively a shared history contributes to the creation of the *object* of love. Under this creative aspect, a shared history is a source of the uniqueness and irreplaceability of the object of love. A shared history, in short, both *reveals* and, in part, *constitutes*, the object of love. In neither case is it a dimension of love *independently* of characteristics.

4. Conclusion

I have argued that to love a friend as an end is to love her for her intrinsic worth, for the worth that is hers by virtue of her personal nature, and not unconditionally. For the object of unconditional love is the universal and nonindividual, that of end love in friendship, the unique and irreplaceable. I have also argued that in instrumental love, the object of love is qualities that fail to define the person, or that define her as essentially an instrument of others' ends, whereas in the end love of friendship, the love is necessarily based on qualities that do define the person, and define her as an end in herself. Finally, I have argued that these qualities can neither be, nor be understood, apart from a person's historical and numerical identity.

The fact that loving someone as an end implies loving her as a good to oneself points to the possibility that morality can likewise be regarded as an end that is also a good to oneself. This possibility challenges the canonical distinction between teleological and deontological moralities, according to which morality is *either* related to human good, *or* is an end in itself.[51]

Notes

1. Hence a friendship can exist between lovers, siblings, parent and child, as well as between those who are related only as friends.

2. This does not mean that instrumental friendships are inherently exploitative or unjust: they could not count as friendships if they were. What makes a relationship exploitative is not the mere fact that it serves an end beyond itself, but that it violates the rightful expectations and obligations of one or both parties, where "rightfulness" is itself determined by wider moral criteria. Elements of such injustice are present in practically all relationships.

3. Aristotle, *Nicomachean Ethics*, ed. Richard McKeon, trans. W. D. Ross (New York: Random House, 1941), 1156b10-11.

4. The notion of intrinsic worth is often construed Platonically, *i.e.*, as a worth that is independent of any valuer, even potential valuer. But this interpretation is necessary only for that which is conceived as a value because it is the source of all value: the Good or God. This must, logically, have a value that is independent of any valuer. But it is possible as well as more plausible to hold that all other values, including intrinsic values, are *relational*, the other term of the relation being that for which it is a value (see *ibid.*, 1097a1-22). What makes something a value is its actual or possible relation to a valuer as an ultimate end (an end in itself), or means to such an end. If it were not even a *possible* end in itself, or means to it, it could not be a value, any more than something that is not even a possible object of perception could be perceptible. (It should be clear from the analogy with perception that the question of the objectivity or rationality of our value choices and judgments is independent of the ontological claim that values are relational.) What makes something an *intrinsic* value is that it is valued just for being what it is, for its nature, not for its usefulness in bringing about some other valued state of affairs. But valuing something for its nature is only a necessary condition of valuing it intrinsically or noninstrumentally: for some things are *by their nature* tools or instruments (see §3, below).

5. George Nakhnikian, "Love in Human Reason," in P. French, T. E. Uehling, Jr., and H. K. Wettstein, eds., *Midwest Studies in Philosophy*, vol. 3 (Minneapolis: University of Minnesota Press, 1980), 286-317, at 287.

6. *Ibid.*, 294.

7. Not all instrumental love is self-regarding; it can be a means to Utility, to the imperatives of Pure Practical Reason, to the Idea of Beauty. The logic of the objection, however, remains the same.

8. I borrow the distinction between target and object of love from Amélie Rorty, "Explaining Emotions," in A. O. Rorty, ed., *Explaining Emotions* (Berkeley: University of California Press, 1980), 103-26.

9. Or for that matter, in *anything*: laws, institutions, theories, and so forth. As Gregory Vlastos remarks in "The Individual as an Object of Love in Plato," "as objects of Platonic love, all these are not only as good as persons, but distinctly better" (*Platonic Studies* [Princeton: Princeton University Press, 1973], 3-34, at 26). Vlastos goes on to state that "the cardinal flaw in Plato's

theory" is that it "does not provide for love of whole persons, but only for love of that abstract version of persons which consists of the complex of their best qualities" (31). Vlastos equates love of the whole person with love of the individual but, typically, picks out Christian unconditional love as its exemplar (33).

10. See Anders Nygren, *Agape and Eros*, trans. P. S. Watson (Philadelphia: Westminster Press, 1953). Agape, he says, is "primarily God's own love." "In faith he [the Christian] receives God's love, in love he passes it on to his neighbour. . . . The love which he can give is only that which he has received from God" (734).

11. *Ibid.*, 34. See Martin C. D'Arcy, "Agape and Human Initiative" (an excerpt from *The Mind and Heart of Love*), in D. L. Norton and M. F. Kille, eds., *Philosophies of Love* (Totowa, N.J.: Rowman and Allanheld, 1983), 162-71: "All our actions are to some extent affected by out central love" (168).

12. Søren Kierkegaard, *Works of Love*, trans. H. Hong and E. Hong (New York: Harper and Row, 1962), 146.

13. Nygren, *Agape and Eros*, 75-80.

14. *Ibid.*, 726-7.

15. Nygren notes disapprovingly of Augustine that "when he speaks of God's love for the sinner, he is anxious to explain that it is not strictly love for the sinner himself, but for the good which, in spite of sin, still remains in him, and for the perfection which he can still attain. The idea that love has still something to hope for, something to gain, in the sinner, thus supplies the final motive when all other motives have disappeared. Luther, on the other hand, is anxious to eliminate even this last motive" (*Ibid.*, 731-2).

16. *Ibid.*, 732.

17. Kierkegaard, *Works of Love*, 80.

18. In Nygren, *Agape and Eros*, 730, n. 1.

19. This question is raised by any noncognitivist view of love, namely, the view that love is not *motivated* by the other's lovable qualities, but that it *bestows* these qualities on him. With respect to God's love for humans, we can, perhaps, answer the question, if we are willing to ignore the problems it raises for the Christian concept of God. Imagine the following scenario (and ignore the problems). God, lonely and needing to love, creates human beings. He could have loved anything at all, for love is part of His nature. But in a playful mood he creates human beings and, according to plan, loves them. His love, then, is completely unmotivated, but nevertheless, explicably selective.

20. Even if this worth or lovability is only a *consequence* of God's arbitrary choice to love them; despite my scenario, a moot point ever since "Do the gods love the pious because they are pious, or are they pious because the gods love them?" (*Euthyphro*, 10a).

21. Agape between humans might or might not be an end love. According to Augustine, our love for all things except God *ought* to be an "uti" or instrumental love.

22. In the Greek and medieval traditions "contemplation" refers to a state of awareness distinguished from other states of awareness by having no end beyond itself: one contemplates not for the sake of clarification, information, action, or production, although contemplation might indirectly aid us in all these, but for its own value. It is a state of receptive awareness, of "listening to the essence of things," as Heraclitus put it (see Josef Pieper, *Leisure, the Basis of Culture* [New York: Random House, 1963], 26), which takes as its object that which is similarly self-sufficient, serving no end beyond itself. Such an object is obviously God. But such are also all objects that are valuable by their very nature.

23. Thus Nygren says of Augustine's view of our love for God: the love of the *summum bonum* is a means to the happiness and blessedness we derive from its possession, "the blessedness does not consist in *loving*—that is, desiring and longing for the highest good—but in *possessing* it" (*Agape and Eros*, 510-11).

24. This is, in fact, Nygren's interpretation of Augustine's view of our love for God: "We have reached our goal; eternal rest (quies) is here; and the meaning of this quies is that desire is for ever quenched: man no longer needs to seek his 'bonum,' but possesses it. Perfect fruitio Dei means in principle the cessation of love" (*Ibid.*, 511).

25. One can, of course, desire to *keep seeing* them. More generally, as Socrates' question to Agathon shows, desire can be for *keeping* what we already have, not only for what we *lack* at

the time of the desire: "when you say, I desire that which I have and nothing else, is not your meaning that you want to have what you now have in the future?" (*Symposium* 200d, trans. M. Joyce, in E. Hamilton and H. Cairns, eds., *The Collected Works of Plato* [Princeton: Princeton University Press, 1963]).

Nevertheless, a desire for keeping something we already have is purely future-directed: in any given moment it is satisfied, quenched, for that moment. But love does not get "satisfied." So love cannot be mere desire, not even an ongoing desire for keeping what we have.

26. As Augustine, who seems to hold two opposing views, points out: the better we know God, the better we must love him, hence it is precisely when we have obtained the *summum bonum* that our love grows (in Nygren, *Agape and Eros*, 511).

27. To illustrate by means of an analogy: I love this knife only because it enables me to slice onions quickly and easily, even though in so doing, it further *evokes* my love for it.

28. To be lovable is to be valuable, but to be valuable is not necessarily to be lovable. Hence there is no necessary connection between taking pleasure in something and valuing it, *simpliciter*. For example, someone who accepts the Kantian view of morality as categorically commanded, as an "end in itself" in the special Kantian sense of "serving no empirical end," may well derive no joy from his success in performing his duty, from achieving "the right." But he might still value this success. On the other hand, if one does not have joy in the attainment of something regarded as an end in itself, then the awareness of it is not contemplation, and it is not an object of love. For between happiness and the value response called love there *is* a necessary connection.

29. As Amélie Rorty writes, "in contemplating our friends' lives, we become aware of them as forming a unity"; by "such reflection, we take pleasure in their existence, in their life as the unimpeded exercise of an activity" ("The Place of Contemplation in Aristotle's Ethics," in A. O. Rorty, ed., *Essays on Aristotle's Ethics* [Berkeley: University of California Press, 1980], 377-94, at 379, 390). In a similar vein, Ortega y Gasset states that love "is involved in the affirmation of its object. . . . It is like recognizing and confirming at each moment that they [its objects] are worthy of existence. . . . To hate someone is to feel irritated by his mere existence" (*On Love: Aspects of a Single Theme* [London: Jonathan Cape, 1967], 17). But some have *contrasted* contemplation with pleasure. Harold Osborne, for example, contrasts aesthetic contemplation as "a mode of awareness in which a thing is apprehended for its own sake" with aesthetic pleasure (*Aesthetics* [Oxford: Oxford University Press, 1972], 14). If this contrast is well-made, then pleasure cannot be intrinsic to love. But it is hard to see what aesthetic pleasure is, if it is not pleasure in an object apprehended as an end in itself.

30. Just as the knife of the example in n. 27 above might turn out to be uniquely qualified to slice my onions.

31. It is true that an instrumental friendship is less likely to be permanent than an end friendship. For circumstances and incidental qualities are more variable than essential qualities; and the love and concern based on these, being relatively narrow in focus, are far sooner and easier undermined by the wear and tear of friendship than a love and concern based on a person's essential qualities.

32. Frederic C. Young has objected to this view as implying that friendship cannot even survive a fundamental change in the other that is due to unhappy chance, such as, e.g., Alzheimer's disease; an implication that is false, since love and acts of friendship can and do survive such tragedies. My response is that the continuing love in such a case is like the love for a dead friend, a love based on the memory of the person loved and a homage to that memory; likewise, the continuing acts of friendship: the help, the care, and so on. But such one-sided love and acts of friendship do not constitute friendship in the full sense of the word, whether the friend is dead, or alive but bereft of the powers that make mutual delight and caring possible.

33. This implies, contrary to the usual thought on the matter, that there is a sense in which even unique, irreplaceable values, including pleasures, might be comparable. What makes them irreplaceable is that they have a different *meaning* to the valuer, are *experienced* differently. Thus X has a value to me for being the person he is that is different, phenomenologically, from the value of Y: there is no deeper, neutral pleasure or other mental state to which these values can be reduced, and made exchangeable. Yet X's value to me might be comparatively greater,

insofar as X's character or personality answers to more facets of my own. So at least some irreplaceable values can be compared on the scale of one's overall happiness or well-being.

34. Erich Fromm, *The Art of Loving* (New York: Harper and Row, 1956), 47. In the case of erotic love he acknowledges that it does make a difference whom we love, for although "we are all One—yet every one of us is a unique, unduplicable entity . . . [and] erotic love requires certain specific, highly individual elements which exist between some people but not between all" (47-8).

35. See Rom Harré and Edward Madden, "Natural Powers and Powerful Natures," *Philosophy* 48:185 (1973): 209-30, and Colin McGinn, "A Note on the Essence of Natural Kinds," *Analysis* 35:6 (1975): 177-83, for a discussion of the concept of the nature or fundamental properties of a thing as that which explains its other properties and behavior. This analysis is compatible with the view that a thing's nature or essence is, in part, relative to our epistemological interests. See Ronald de Sousa's criticism of the contrary, absolutist view in "The Natural Shiftiness of Natural Kinds," *Canadian Journal of Philosophy* 14 (1984): 561-80.

36. And conversely, our personal nature is also given in what we *would not* be, as expressed in our *disavowals* of the values and abilities we act upon.

37. See Harry Frankfurt, "Identification and Externality," in A. O. Rorty, ed., *The Identities of Persons* (Berkeley: University of California Press, 1976), 239-51, especially on the role of attitude and decision in establishing that some desire or passion that a person has is *his* (247-51).

38. Just as loving the aforementioned knife (nn. 27, 30) for what it is entails loving it as a means to slicing onions quickly and easily.

39. Henrik Ibsen, "The Doll's House" (1879), in *Six Plays* (New York: Modern Library, 1951).

40. Aristotle, *Nicomachean Ethics*, 1167a3-4.

41. Putting it thus allows one to say both that a person can freely and independently choose to live as an instrument of another, and that by doing so she surrenders her own self or identity.

42. Plato, *Symposium* 210c.

43. Edmond Rostand, *Cyrano de Bergerac*, trans. Brian Hooker (London: George Allen and Unwin, 1953).

44. Such descriptions are not enough to uniquely pick out Cyrano, even barring the logical possibility of a personality twin. In general, no *description* can individuate a person; only a presentation in drama or narrative, with its setting and incident, can do so. The point of my descriptions is only to illustrate the claim that a person's essence consists of both qualities and their style of expression. It is the two together that explain, *e.g.*, why Cyrano decides to defend Lignière (out of admiration for Lignière's having "once in his life . . . done one lovely thing"; *Ibid.*, 39) singlehandedly against a hundred men.

45. Thus Cyrano's wit and daring and poetic genius are expressed perfectly in his victorious duel with Valvert, in the course of which he composes a ballade perfectly timed to the action. Likewise, Cyrano's independence, courage, and loyalty constitute his style of facing life, his determination to "carry . . . [his] adornments on . . . [his] soul" (*Ibid.*, 27), to "make [himself] . . . in all things admirable" (*Ibid.*, 34).

46. Even among those who love Cyrano for what he is, only Le Bret, Christian, and Roxane know him, from differing perspectives, as the passionate and tragic lover. One can have a *true* view of someone even in the absence of a *full* view: if one knows someone in his fundamental aspects, then what one might discover about him fits in, makes sense, in terms of what one already knows. So those who do not know about Cyrano's love for Roxane are not necessarily in the same position as Torvald with respect to Nora.

47. They love him, as Aristotle would put it, only incidentally, and "not as being the man he is" (*Nicomachean Ethics*, 1156a18). For the wit without the qualities it expresses would be a superficial thing, varying independently of Cyrano's essential qualities. (It is important to note that there is no one invariable set of properties that can be marked off as incidental, as Aristotle seems to think when he states that those who love their friends for their ready wit, love them only incidentally. *Any* property that varies, or can vary, independently of a person's essential qualities is, under that description, incidental.)

48. Plato, *Symposium*, 211b.

49. Robert Nozick, *Anarchy, State, and Utopia* (New York: Basic Books, 1974), 168. See also Susan Mendus, "Marital Faithfulness," *Philosophy* 59 (1984): 243-52, at 246: "the person

who promises to love and to honour only on condition that there be no such [radical] change in character . . . was never committed in the appropriate way at all"; in Alan Soble, ed., *Eros, Agape, and Philia* (New York: Paragon House, 1989), 235-44, at 238.

50. Nozick, *Anarchy, State, and Utopia*, 168.

51. I have benefitted from Ronald de Sousa's many and detailed comments on this paper and from Alan Soble's commentary at a meeting of the Society for the Philosophy of Sex and Love in 1985. I also received helpful criticisms from Tom Hurka, Raymond Martin, and Wayne Sumner; from members of the philosophy departments at Rice University and Texas Tech University; and from the audiences at the American Association for the Philosophic Study of Society, the Canadian Philosophical Association, and the Canadian Society for Women in Philosophy. The Institute of Humane Studies, Virginia, generously paid for my travel expenses to the meeting of the American Association for the Philosophic Study of Society.

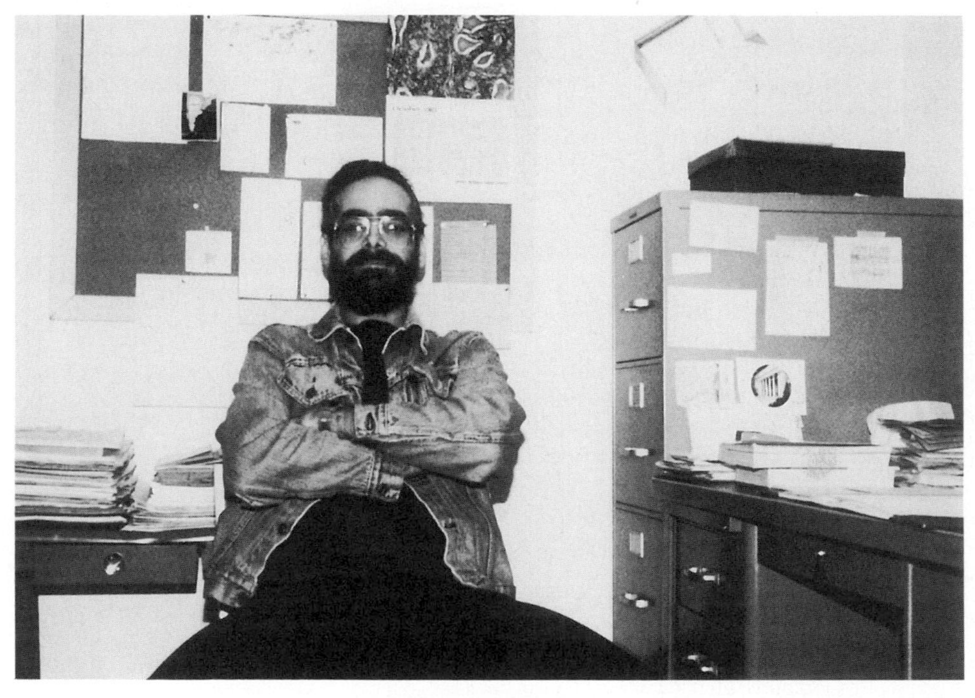

Alan Gerald Soble
(photograph: Laura Wheaton)

Author of "Friends as Nerds in Themselves"
Paper presented at the Society for the Philosophy of Sex and Love
during the
Eastern Division Meeting of The American Philosophical Association
Washington, D. C., 28 December 1985

Thirty-Four

IRREPLACEABILITY

Alan Gerald Soble

The idea that "to love someone [is] . . . to value the person . . . as irreplaceable"[1] is frequently asserted. Neera Kapur Badhwar's account of love[2] rests upon the "widely held intuition" that in the "best" loves, X loves Y as an "irreplaceable individual" (333). Because, in Badhwar's view, irreplaceability "most obviously marks off" (334, 341) what she calls "end love" (the best love) from "means love" (instrumental love), her Aristotelian account is philosophically important: it fills out the suggestion that love "for the person" (in the sense of end love) involves irreplaceability. Further, in Badhwar's end love, X loves Y in virtue of Y's attractive identity properties. Hence Badhwarian end love is an "eros" love for the person; it depends on the person's merit or attractiveness in the eyes of his or her friend or lover.

The beloved is *phenomenologically* irreplaceable, says Badhwar, "in the precise sense that loving and delighting in her are not completely commensurate with loving and delighting in another" (341). This seems to be a robust sense in which the irreplaceability of the beloved could be a characteristic feature of love. But what is it about loving in virtue of identity properties, or about not loving because the beloved, as a means, provides some good, that makes the beloved in end love, but not the beloved in means love, irreplaceable$_p$[3] in Badhwar's "precise" sense? The answer, I think, should be "nothing"; for loving in virtue of identity properties, or not loving in virtue of a good provided by the beloved, do not obviously necessitate that love has any particular phenomenal feel or that the lover has a specific feeling toward the beloved. Further, if X loves Y for Y's identity properties, and Y dies or leaves, X might come to love Z in virtue of Z's identity properties; hence, that X end-loves Y does not mean X's attachment to Y is permanently nonfungible. But even if Badhwar's irreplaceability$_p$ is not the same as nonfungible attachment, why think that X's loving Y is "not completely commensurate" with X's loving this Z and, hence, that Y is irreplaceable in this narrower sense?

Immediately after defining irreplaceable$_p$ in terms of "not completely commensurate," Badhwar writes: "this is confirmed by the fact that if the happiness we got from different friends were completely commensurate, there would be no qualitative differences among our friendships, and we would not . . . desire to spend an evening with X rather than with Y, but rather only 'with a friend'" (341). Since the sentence begins with "this is confirmed by," Badhwar intends the subsequent "fact" as *evidence* that in end love the beloved is irreplaceable$_p$ in the sense that X's loving Y is "not completely commensurate" with X's loving Z. Yet the sentence also functions to explain what Badhwar *means* by "not completely commensurate" and hence what she means by irreplaceability$_p$. If Y and Z are irreplaceable$_p$ in the sense that X's loving Y is "not completely commensurate" with X's loving Z, then there is a qualitative difference between X's loving (or delighting in) Y and X's loving (or delighting in) Z such that X desires to be with Y in particular, or with Z in particular, but X does not desire to be with some beloved or another, that is, Y or Z or . . . . But this will not work; it fails to distinguish end love from means love. For X's instrumentally loving both Y and Z is compatible with there being a qualitative difference between these two loves. Consider the case in which loving Y promotes good G_1 for X and loving Z promotes good G_2 for X: X could very well want to be with not just any old means friend but with either the means friend Y in particular or the means friend Z in particular, depending on whether X now wants G_1 or G_2. So how does irreplaceability "most obviously" mark off the "best" love?

Badhwar's second defense of her claim (or her second explication of "not completely commensurate") is that "when someone who is loved as an end ceases to be loved, the loss cannot be completely made up by acquiring a new friend" (341-2). It sounds here as if Badhwar understands irreplaceability$_p$ as permanent nonfungible attachment, so that means love is distinguished from end love by its lacking permanent nonfungible attachment. But if X deeply values Y because Y provides a special G, and as a result X cannot value anyone else, X's instrumental love for Y is permanently nonfungible. Further, Badhwar's elaboration of why in end love "the loss cannot be completely made up by acquiring a new friend" is inadequate to show that end love and means love can be distinguished by irreplaceability$_p$: "the loss of the old friend is a distinct loss, the gain of the new friend, a distinct gain" (342). But the loss of a means friend can be and often is a distinct loss. There are senses in which X's loving Y is "distinct" from X's loving Z, so in some ways the two loves are "not completely commensurate"; for example, X's love for Y is spatiotemporally a different love from X's love for Z. But in this and similar senses of "distinct," senses in which *any* two things are distinct, X's loving Z instrumentally for G_2 is also a distinct gain whether (or not) X still loves Y for providing G_1. And in this sense a new end love is also, and only trivially, a distinct gain.

Badhwar undoubtedly means more than this by "distinct"; in a note she writes that "unique, irreplaceable values" are irreplaceable in that "they have a different *meaning* to the valuer, are *experienced* differently. Thus X has a value to me for being the person he is that is different, phenomenologically, from the value of Y" (351, n. 33). Being with or loving a given person means something different, or feels different, from being with or loving some other person. But it is illicit for Badhwar to smuggle in "for being the person he is" in this explanation of irreplaceability$_p$, as if only when X end-loves Y ("for being the person he is" = "for his identity properties") does X's love have a distinct meaning or feeling. If X loves Y instrumentally for G_1 and loves Z instrumentally for G_2, there is no reason to deny that the meaning of these two loves is different for X or that X experiences the loves, or Y and Z, differently, depending on the difference between G_1 and G_2. If end love is characterized by irreplaceability$_p$ in this sense, so too is means love, and neither love has been shown generally to involve nonfungible attachment.

Badhwar, however, does not understand irreplaceability$_p$ as nonfungible attachment, for even in end love "one ceases to *feel* the loss [of the beloved], because of the passage of time . . . and the presence of other enriching activities and experiences in one's life" (342). But if X is no longer disturbed by the loss of the end love for Y *because* X now end-loves Z (this end love being one of X's later "enriching experiences" that does, after all, make up the loss), then for Badhwar to assert that "it remains true that different end friendships engender different forms of love and happiness" (342) is dogmatism. Irreplaceability$_p$ has no cash value in distinguishing between end love and means love, and it has no practical implications for the course of X's loves and life. Badhwar's notion that in end love the beloved is irreplaceable has no interesting content. The "widely held intuition" that the beloved is irreplaceable is just a bit of popular ideology, an illusion in Freud's sense.[4]

Even though Badhwar claims that her theory of end love is superior to Plato's theory of *eros* and to the Christian theory of *agape*, on the grounds that only her view can account for the irreplaceability$_p$ of the beloved, she also employs another notion of irreplaceability to describe end love and distinguish it from means love. If X loves Y because Y promotes G for X, this is a means love in which Y is *numerically* replaceable by anyone who can also promote G. By contrast, in end love the beloved is irreplaceable$_n$: "friends are not . . . means to each other's ends, they cannot, logically cannot, be replaced by more efficient means" (334). Taken literally, this claim is true; from the fact that Y is not loved as a means, it follows that Y cannot be replaced *as a means*. But it does not follow that Y cannot be replaced *at all*. Hence, if Y's not being loved as a means is going to imply that Y is irreplaceable, we have to treat (which I think Badhwar does) "numerically irreplaceable" as *by definition* "not loved as a means." The beloved's irreplaceability$_n$ in end love is not a separate phenomenon that results from the beloved's not being loved as means, but is entirely exhausted by her not being loved as a means.[5]

Notes

1. Robert Brown, *Analyzing Love* (Cambridge, Mass.: Cambridge University Press, 1987), 24; see my review in *Philosophy of the Social Sciences* 19:4 (1989): 493-500.

2. Neera Kapur Badhwar, "Friends as Ends in Themselves," this volume, 333-52. Parenthetical page references are to this essay.

3. "Irreplaceable$_p$," stands for "phenomenologically irreplaceable"; "irreplaceable$_n$" stands for "numerically irreplaceable."

4. See Ronald de Sousa, "Self-Deceptive Emotions," *Journal of Philosophy* 75 (1978): 684-97, at 694-5.

5. This commentary on Badhwar began as a critique of her paper presented at a meeting of the Society for the Philosophy of Sex and Love; it appears in this volume as a slightly revised version of my *The Structure of Love* (New Haven: Yale University Press, 1990), ch. 13, §3, 290-93. For a critique of Thomas Nagel and Roger Scruton on irreplaceablity, see *ibid.*, ch. 13, §4, 293-8.

Russell Vannoy

Author of "The Structure of Sexual Perversion"
Paper presented at the Society for the Philosophy of Sex and Love
during the
Central Division Meeting of The American Philosophical Association
St. Louis, Mo., 1 May 1986

Thirty-Five

THE STRUCTURE OF SEXUAL PERVERSITY[1]

Russell Vannoy

Do not confuse *perverse* with *perverted.*
Oxford American Dictionary

1.

Traditional and contemporary theories of sexual perversity have been based on the idea that there must be some ideal goal or norm of sexual behavior for everyone, be it defined in terms of naturalness, interpersonal communication, or some social or psychological norm. Any departure from one of these norms, then, presumably defines the act as being sexually perverse, even though it might be sexually fulfilling and is arguably harmless. A foot fetishist, for example, might feel that these criteria are imposed externally on an act that seems natural *for him*. Indeed, it is now often held that these criteria are more ideological than scientific or objective and function merely as forms of social control of unpopular sexual tastes. Yet one could also hold that the usual criteria for perversity are themselves a perverse source of encouragement for the very acts they condemn. Violating taboos is, after all, a perennial source of sexual delight for many persons. Thus it would seem that conservatives as well as liberals have reason to be wary of terms like "perverse" and "perverted" in sexual matters.

While it is plausible to hold that much of what has been called sexual perversity should be redescribed as sexual diversity, it is still true that certain important things can go wrong with one's sexual goals that allow for a philosophically interesting theory of the perverse. If, for example, one focused on the inner structure of an individual's or a couple's own desires for certain kinds of sexual enjoyment and could show that they are paradoxical, contradictory and, as it were, self-refuting, then one would have a theory that is not a form of social control. Nor would there be any externally imposed taboos, if the criterion for nonperverse desires were that they either yield the sort of sexual experience one desires or that they at least contain no logical barriers to sexual fulfillment. Since "perverse" is also a term that is used to describe contradictory states of affairs, a theory of this kind would not be a radical departure from ordinary usage. Furthermore, one can find paradoxes in some sexual desires favored by conservatives and in certain other sexual desires espoused by liberals. Unlike the term "perverted," a theory of the perverse defended here could thus be ideologically neutral. This paper will substantiate these bold claims.

2.

How might a sexual practice be self-defeating in terms of its own goals? A somewhat nonstandard version of the nonuniversalizability of sadism would be a useful way to begin. Since Sade's desires would be viewed as perverse by both conservatives and liberals, one should expect to find in Sade paradoxes and contradictions wherever one turns, if this theory of the perverse is valid. Consider a Sadean society in which everyone has eroticized violence against everyone else and in which one need not make the dubious assumption that everyone is equally vulnerable to being destroyed. The weaker members of such a world would be sexually frustrated, but not merely because they could not conquer anyone. Although they would find the idea of conquest sexually arousing, they could not act on any sexual desires arising from this fact, since they share the same might-makes-right philosophy as everyone else. Since they are weak, they must themselves believe that they cannot have a right to conquer anyone.

Nor could the stronger sadists who want to do violence to their victims in every way possible be able to make the weak feel that their bodies had been violated by someone who has no right to do so. Although the weak can be tortured, the victims could not be made to feel the unique kind of psychic agony that comes from being raped or from feeling that their rights had been violated. There are simply no rights to violate amongst those who can be conquered in a might-makes-right society. (The logic of Sade's attempt to convince everyone that rape is a good thing is perverse not merely because it is vile, but also because it is self-refuting.)

Furthermore, at least some of the weaker members of such a world must be allowed to survive if the sadists' desires are to continue to be fulfilled. Yet the weak would become so numbed from constant torture that there could be no further satisfaction in brutalizing them. Were the strong sadists to attempt to prevent this from occurring, they would be required to respect the limits of what their victims could endure. It is a conceptual truth, however, that a sadist cannot respect anything about his victims. Power, like sexual arousal generally, does not want any limits placed on its gratification. The limits described here are, however, logical limits that not even an omnipotent demon could overcome. A further reason why his victim must be numbed or destroyed and thus be beyond his reach is that some sadists are also masochistic: when violence is eroticized, one might not care whether it is directed against others or against oneself. In order to thwart some clever masochist who might pretend that he is involuntarily suffering great pain, the sadist would be required to exceed the limits of endurance of everyone he tortured.

Even if laws were passed that prohibited the torturing of the weak beyond their limits, the strong sadists could not obey them, since this would be the only way they could define themselves as being evil Übersadists in a world in which "respectable" sadism was considered moral, normal and, in the eyes of the Übersadist, utterly banal. Nor could the few strong sadists who survived have any hope of torturing each other if "strong" means that one cannot be conquered. If, on the other hand, "strong" means that one could conquer everyone, then one would be the sole surviving sadist with no one remaining to master. This, however, violates the truism that pleasure, so long as it remains pleasure rather than boredom, wants to repeat itself indefinitely. Even if an all-powerful demon could magically create endless numbers of new victims, he would still be frustrated. Since he would know in advance that victory is certain, his "triumph" would, for him, not register as triumph at all.

Indeed, the problem faced by the demon is one faced by sadism generally. Sexual arousal wants its fulfillment to be certain; this is why the sadist selects the weak. Conquering the weak is, however, no more fulfilling than going fishing in an aquarium. Conquering those whom one views as worthless sex objects with no rights presents similar dilemmas for sadism. The worthless have nothing of worth to destroy; one cannot objectify an object; one cannot violate the rights of someone who has no rights. If, on the other hand, the victim has worth, is a subject, and has rights, then it is a conceptual truth that one cannot desire to destroy or violate such things if one believes they truly exist.

One might, however, argue that the sadist wants to destroy his victims' cherished illusions that they are beings with worth. The egocentric sadist, however, sees the world solely in terms of his own values: what the victim cherishes is beyond his ken. The sadist also wants to destroy reality rather than mere illusions and fantasies, even though his victims have no reality except as images in his solipsistic consciousness in which he alone is truly real. Even if the sadist granted that his victims had some minimal reality and worth, the destruction of that which has minimal value could give him only minimal satisfaction.

A psychologist would argue that all this is logical but beside the point. The sadist, he might claim, unconsciously feels powerless and is compelled to try to achieve erotic ecstasy by, say, destroying the powerful. (Assassinating a president of the United States would be an example.) The powerful have farther to fall than the weak and would thus seemingly provide an assassin with the ultimate erotic triumph. But this will not do. If the powerful could be destroyed by someone who feels himself to be weak, then his victim could not be seen as ever having been truly powerful in the first place. That which was a prerequisite for the sadist's enjoying destroying the powerful, his own weakness, also prevents him from ever seeing his act as an act of strength. The supposedly nonrational unconscious is, therefore, also subject to logical constraints on its satisfaction.

Indeed, it is common for supposedly irrational sadists to require precisely defined rituals for their torture. They would thus likely find the dilemmas in their sexual desires to be just as frustrating as they would be for an ordinary person. Even if the sadist's mind were too chaotic to be aware of the dilemmas inherent in his project, he will still ultimately be frustrated. A mad Roman Emperor who tries to achieve limitless ecstasy by initiating unlimited chaos will necessarily destroy himself and his dream of endless sexual ecstasy as well. It will, therefore, simply not do to claim that logical constraints are irrelevant to sadistic sexual desire, or to sexual excitement generally, because sex inhabits a nonrational Dionysian world that magically transcends logic or somehow reconciles all contradictions.

Finally, the ultimate sadistic goal, murder, is equally a failure as an ultimate conquest. Since death ends the victim's agony, the sadist who requires an absolute conquest must want his victim to be dead and also to suffer eternal anguish because of his or her death. This is a contradictory ideal, unless the sadist believed (say) that his victim had an immortal psyche. Yet he cannot contemplate this possibility, since the psyche would be one bit of life, perhaps the victim's very identity, that the sadist could not destroy. (This dilemma is also applicable to the ultimate masochistic fantasy of suffering total annihilation.)

Sade, who seemed to have thought of everything about such matters, was perhaps well aware of these paradoxes. Could he say that they are generated only because sadism has been defined in terms of extremes, and that one could elude the horns of these dilemmas by adopting more modest goals? Sadism and masochism are, however, defined by their outer limits, be it total domination or total submission. A disciple of Sade might be compelled to be content with a modest conquest in the way a champion boxer might have to settle for winning by only one round. Being resigned to be merely content in sexual and other ways does not, therefore, entail an absence of frustration.

Indeed, it is arguable that everyone is an extremist of sorts when sexually aroused. Would any lover ever say that he wanted to give his mate only a moderate sexual experience? Nor is sex ever casual about achieving its goal when one is sexually excited; the phrase "casual sex" is simply a contradiction in terms. If sexual desire does search for some kind of ideal or absolute fulfillment, then the theory that is proposed here should define sexual perversity in terms of having eroticized goals that generate certain logical constraints that prevent one from attaining the sexual experience one would ideally like to have were the constraints nonexistent.

3.

I must now define more precisely what sexual perversity means in terms of this theory. Something more than merely another kind of "sexual dysfunction" is being proposed. That is, the dysfunction is primarily philosophical in nature. Self-refuting arguments, paradoxes, dilemmas, and contradictions are part of the stock-in-trade of philosophy; here they are being applied to sexual desire. Indeed, sexual desires and the ways in which they can be contradictory and end in futility are discussed primarily in a conceptual way. If, for example, a certain kind of pedophile believed sex to be hopelessly dirty and thus eroticized innocence as a way of desperately trying to find sex that is uncontaminated, the innocence of his youthful partner will, for him, self-destruct as soon as he touches it. For innocence that has been touched by a hand that desires sex has been utterly dirtied in the pedophile's eyes. Here the linkage between sex, dirt, innocence, and the destruction of innocence is primarily a matter of making certain logical connections between these concepts. That the pedophile's goal self-destructs upon its attainment also rests on a contradictory ideal within the framework of his desires: for instance, wanting both sex and innocence.

This conceptual analysis must be translatable into a phenomenology of desire and frustration that a pedophile could conceivably experience. If, however, the theory is to be plausible, it must show that defining perversity in terms of contradictory desires is not an utterly aberrant way of talking about the perverse. If perverse behavior is ordinarily defined as that which departs from what is right, reasonable, or accepted, then trying to fulfill contradictory desires is (plausibly) perverse, since such desires are hardly reasonable. Or consider the following example:

> Violence [in television] is back in vogue, and two of the more bloody new efforts perversely happen to be among the better productions of the year.[2]

The writer is not merely saying that it is not right or proper that such a state of affairs should exist. He is suggesting that one is confronted with a paradoxical state of affairs, in that what is abhorrent (violence) is also "better" in terms of what is worth viewing. One is then faced with contradictory desires: if one wants to watch the better shows, then one is also compelled to want to turn the dial to shows that depict bloody mayhem.

In the following example, a newspaper columnist is criticizing attempts to defeat a nominee to the Supreme Court:

> The transformation of the confirmation process into a contest between massed battalions is a perverse achievement of people who, like Packwood, claim to be acting to protect the court from Bork's jurisprudence, which they say would leave all our liberties to be blown about by gusts of opinion.[3]

The writer is claiming, at least in part, that the achievement of Bork's opponents was perverse because they used inconsistent methods. Bork was attacked for his majoritarian philosophy, yet his opponents (or so the author claims) used "massed battalions" to defeat him. One should also note that the first passage was written by a liberal who deplores violence, while the second passage was penned by a well-known conservative columnist. The term "perverse" thus transcends ideological boundaries when it is used to denote what one believes to be an instance of desiring an illogical state of affairs. Indeed, this is precisely what one would expect if the criteria for perversity are largely formal in nature.

The criteria I have been discussing in an informal way can be stated with the precision they require. The first two criteria I shall give, taken together, define a perverse act, while the third criterion defines a perverse person. A perverse act might, of course, be repeated. A perverse individual is, however, someone who either feels compelled or who obstinately chooses to continue to try to fulfill his self-defeating goals for reasons that are not necessarily masochistic. Being sexually aroused by certain goals and trying to achieve them are both sexual experiences that might, for example, provide enough reinforcement to make one want to continue acts that do not ultimately yield the sort of fulfillment one seeks. In other cases, such as certain compulsive forms of promiscuity, the initial acts might be satisfying and reinforcing, were one to overcome the dilemma of wanting to try something utterly new while also well knowing how to perform the act successfully. That the promiscuous quest for novel experiences self-destructs into a feeling of sameness is a familiar phenomenon, as with tourists who are victims of the "if it's Tuesday, it must be Brussels" syndrome.

On my account, then, sexual perversity occurs when:

(a) one is unable to achieve the goal one was seeking or when that goal self-destructs upon its attainment, such that one is deprived of the sexual fulfillment one would ideally like to have attained,

and

(b) the kinds of failure described in (a) occur because someone seeks (or one is, by the very nature of one's project, compelled to seek) contradictory goals, such that the fulfillment of one goal destroys the possibility of realizing another goal that is equally vital to one's sexual fulfillment.

Criterion (b) is complex, yet it must often cover or apply to complex desires, some of which are sexual and some of which are phenomenological prerequisites for sexual satisfaction. A person X, for example, might turn to necrophilia because he is highly insecure and dreads the thought of someone's judging his sexual performance unfavorably. Or another person Y might become a necrophile because he wishes to degrade others without being subjected to a Medusa-like Sartrean judgmental "stare." Since the corpse is unresponsive to X's gestures, and since it cannot feel Y's attempt to degrade it, X and Y are compelled to fantasize that it is alive. When one is highly sexually aroused, fantasy becomes (notoriously) phenomenologically real. When the corpse becomes alive to this degree in the eyes of these necrophiles, it will be seen as being capable of judging their actions. Since escaping judgment was a prerequisite for their sexual fulfillment, they fail. Their desires are perverse under criterion (b), since their project requires them to have contradictory goals. They want to enjoy the corpse without being judged, yet they must also see the corpse as being alive in order for it to respond to their desires. Since they cannot fulfill one goal without violating the other goal, their desires are perverse.

One more criterion, (c), fills out my account of sexual perversity:

a perverse *person* is someone who persists in performing acts that fall under (a) and (b), such that his or her frustration either remains constant or is progressively intensified in attempting to escape the logical constraints these criteria impose on sexual fulfillment. (The end result is commonly a futile kind of promiscuity.)

The term "goal" in these criteria refers to whatever one finds to be sexually arousing or whatever one finds to be a prerequisite for one's sexual arousal within the phenomenological context of the act itself. Things like money or children are not sexually relevant to the act unless they are sexually arousing or are in some other way a phenomenological prerequisite for achieving sexual fulfillment. In this theory, I shall assume only that whatever else one wants as a result of a sexual act, what one wants in terms of the phenomenology of the act itself is some kind of sexually fulfilling experience. Were someone to engage in a sexual act purely for money or to become pregnant and had no desire for a sexual experience, then the act might have economic or reproductive significance. Unless one had eroticized money or bearing children, the act would not, however, ordinarily have any sexual significance. Acts in which we have no sexual interest are described in other ways. They would, for example, seem more, in a phenomenological sense, like an odd or unpleasant form of calisthenics that one must endure in order to achieve something that follows the act. We rarely say that animals perform sexual acts; we merely say that they are breeding.

The sorts of things one might find sexually arousing include love, violence, innocence, beauty, danger, death, mystery, excrement, other bodily effluvia, submission, masculinity or femininity, unadorned sexual sensations ("plain sex"), and the like. How one chooses to relate to these goals also varies. One might wish, when possible, to communicate them to others, absorb them into oneself, touch or view them, destroy or enhance them, or fantasize about them. There is no a priori assumption in this theory that any of these desires need be perverse.

The theory also does not assume in advance that one's sexual interest must be focused on persons rather than, say, articles of clothing. Nor does it assume as a basic datum that any particular sexual act (for instance, the enjoyment of being soundly spanked) is necessarily perverse. What matters are the particular things that one finds sexually appealing in such objects or acts and whether or not the phenomenological structure of one's desires fall under the three criteria for perversity. One and the same sexual practice might be perverse, given one set of reasons why one finds the act to be sexually appealing, but not be perverse if done for other reasons that do not involve contradictory goals. Such acts are, therefore, only contingently perverse. I shall subsequently argue that both homosexuality and heterosexuality, even when practiced in private between consenting adults, could be contingently perverse. A sexual practice is, however, inherently perverse if every combination of reasons one could have for doing it generates a contradiction, or if these various reasons are all reducible to some fundamental contradiction that is inherent in the nature of the practice. The preceding analysis of sadism, while incomplete, gave several reasons for believing that such acts might be inherently perverse.

There are, to be sure, several possible objections to a theory like this one. One might note, for example, that it usually refers to an individual's sexual desires. But how is the theory applicable to intercourse? If one translates contradictory desires in an individual to a couple, then their act would be perverse if their desires conflicted in such a way that neither partner was satisfied. It would obviously be perverse for them to try to engage in a sexual act if they were utterly incompatible. If, on the other hand, one person's sexual desires require the frustration of the other's sexual desires or violate a phenomenological prerequisite for sexual satisfaction (for instance, freedom), then intercourse in its phenomenological sense ceases to exist. In egocentric desire, the other exists largely as an image in the exploiter's consciousness, in which to be is to be fancied by him or her. In this case, the frustrating paradoxes of sadistic desire mentioned earlier are applicable.

A critic might also claim that neither the individual nor the couple in the bedroom should be the primary focus of such a theory. If sexual desires are social constructs, then we should be primarily concerned with whether or not one's society is perverse. If, however, we wished to reduce the personal to the political, then the Sadean society described earlier would be an example of how perversity could be developed in social terms using this theory. A sexually perverse society would be one that is doomed to frustration because of the inherent contradictions of the sexual goals in terms of which it structures itself.

One might also ask why the theory pays so much attention to the sadist's frustrations rather than to those of his victims. A theory of perversity that focuses on the victim's rather than the sadist's frustrations must, however, ultimately return to how the sadist views the situation. Is rape, for example, something that the rapist has eroticized? Or is rape merely a means of achieving what he could not get in any other way? Or someone who is nude might be seen through the window and feel sexually victimized. This does not, however, mean that anyone desired to look inside. These factors explain, in part, why my theory has focused on the phenomenology of (say) the sadist's desires rather than his victims' feelings of degradation. It might be comforting to the victim to define sadistic perversity in terms of the damage done to the victim, but the definition leaves the sadist unimpressed. Indeed, harming the victim is precisely what he has eroticized. If, however, one could damage the sadist's philosophy in its own terms, the concept of damage would be located where it belongs in defining perversity.

4.

I should now like to show how this theory can be applied to both heterosexual and homosexual sexual acts that occur between consenting adults. Prefixes like "hetero-" and "homo-" can occur in many sorts of combinations in terms describing aspects of sexuality. A heterosexual desires the opposite sex, but he or she might be, as it were, "homosexual" in terms of wanting someone who shares his or her gender role (for instance, masculinity or femininity) or homosocial in terms of sharing interests, friends, and social status. A homosexual who is masculine might also be "heterosexual" in requiring someone who is feminine.

Suppose, however, that a heterosexual, who in many other respects has homosocial requirements, were asked why or he or she nevertheless requires the opposite sex for sexual pleasure. One common reply is that one can only be aroused by members of the opposite sex because they are in some way fascinatingly mysterious. On the other hand, the heterosexual wants to be compatible with this mysterious "other" in sexual and other ways. Since communicating with someone who is an utter mystery would be as futile as trying to relate to an extraterrestrial being who has nothing in common with earthly mortals, the heterosexual compromises by requiring that one's partner be to some degree similar to oneself in respects other than gender. Nevertheless, when one has sex with this person over a period of time, his or her bit of mystery commonly evaporates. (In Hebrew, the term "sex" is one of the meanings of "to know.")

Many heterosexuals do not require that the partner be mysterious in order to be sexually aroused; aesthetic factors, for example, might be decisive. Someone who does require mystery for sexual arousal would clearly be frustrated by the way in which knowing one's partner destroys his or her mystery. (This could also occur with a homosexual who has heterosocial requirements that provide him or her with the requisite mystery.) Suppose that such a person, in a desperate attempt to solve the problem, seeks more and more partners whose mystery still invariably self-destructs after a few sexual encounters. Instead of surrendering his ideal, he attempts to solve the problem by searching for a partner who is so bewilderingly mysterious that he could never hope to fathom her impenetrable depths. "Mystery" or "oppositeness" in every respect has been elevated to a kind of perverse Platonic ideal as a result of his frustration.

If, however, he could find such a person, he could not fulfill his other goal of being able to communicate his sexual needs and feelings. Nor would he have any idea of what she sexually desired. Indeed, if she were his total opposite, they would not be sexually compatible even in a complementary way. If, on the other hand, he were able to relate to her sexually, he would then know her needs and her absolute mystery would self-destruct. His desires are, therefore, perverse because he requires both mystery and compatibility with his partner. One should not, however, conclude that the criteria for perversity are only applicable in such extreme cases as this. So long as mystery is at least a minimally necessary condition for one's sexual fulfillment, then someone who has more modest requirements would still be perverse if he or she continued to perform acts in which the requisite bit of mystery invariably self-destructed when one's partner's sexual needs were known or when one had become accustomed to the sight of his or her body.

To be sure, this particular example does not show that heterosexuality is inherently perverse. One could, however, imagine a world in which males and females were so fundamentally different that their desires would be contradictory rather than complementary. Ironically, defenders of traditional heterosexuality who want to keep the sexes as different as possible run the greatest risk of rendering heterosexuality inherently perverse in terms of the criteria given above. When some heterosexuals say of their mates, "You can't live with them; and you can't live without them," they might be saying that their relationships are perverse if the joking manner in which such a comment is usually made were a veiled way of expressing a deeper fear that they really are incompatible.

I should now like to consider certain ways in which homosexuality might be perverse in terms of these criteria. There is a sense in which heterosexuality and homosexuality might both self-destruct if one believed total fusion between two persons to be the ultimate goal of sexual desire. If, for example, a female became, as it were, one flesh and one mind with another male or female, it is arguable that the phenomenology of this new Aristophanean individual could not be described in either heterosexual or homosexual terms.

Critics of homosexual desire often claim that its ultimate goal is sex with one's clone or with oneself, since these things are the result of taking the prefix "homo" to its logical conclusion. Even if this were true, it would not follow that homosexuality would be inherently perverse. Contradictory desires might occur if two identical persons both viewed sex in terms of, say, dominance. In this case, the quest for total compatibility would generate its opposite. Or if one viewed sex as a form of communication, then an act that is essentially like talking to oneself could be perverse if one also wished to have genuine communication with another person. On the other hand, someone who sought identity need not be frustrated if he or she had desires other than the ones that generate these dilemmas. Critics of homosexual desire who define it in its most extreme form are, therefore, surely being unfair when they refuse to see that defining heterosexual desire in the same way would generate utter frustration.

I should now like to consider one other way in which desire for one's own sex could be perverse. One kind of homosexual, who was not unusual prior to the gay liberation movement, was someone who viewed homosexuality and hence himself as being "effeminate" and who despised himself for this reason. This made him idealize and eroticize masculinity into a kind of Platonic ideal. When someone who was highly masculine and sexually arousing would agree to have sex with him, however, that person's masculinity would automatically self-destruct in his eyes, because homosexuals or even heterosexuals who agreed to perform a homosexual act would thereby become effeminate in his eyes. This kind of homosexual would, therefore, be perverse: homosexual acts and masculinity were viewed by him as being contradictory goals. This difficulty might have also operated for a lesbian who despised her masculinity.

Even if someone were able to overcome this difficulty and were to perform a sexual act, the desire to absorb the other person's masculinity into oneself would be futile. If masculinity were defined in terms of poise, self-control, and independence, then the masculine person would never identify with his partner. He would control the act in a cool, aloof, disinterested sort of way that would keep his masculinity beyond the phenomenological reach of the one who wished to absorb it. If, on the other hand, the masculine partner were to be overwhelmed with sexual passion, lose control of himself, and were to become, as it were, one flesh with the feminine partner, he could then no longer be perceived as being masculine. His masculinity would also be viewed as having been absorbed in a way that would have left it contaminated with one's own despised femininity. The supposedly feminine homosexual (or a heterosexual who detests his or her femininity) would, in trying to absorb the partner's masculinity, require both that it remain beyond one's reach and that it also identify with oneself. This desire would be sexually perverse if someone found the idea of absorbing someone's masculinity essential to his or her sexual fulfillment.

Someone who finds himself in a predicament like the preceding, and one need not be a homosexual or male to do so, will sometimes try again and again to find the perfectly masculine partner whom he cannot possibly view as being effeminate. This will, however, often lead him to define masculinity masochistically in terms of conquest and violence. If someone whom he could trust not to exceed his limits consented to torture him, he might be temporarily satisfied. But nagging doubts would remain about such a "conquest." The sadist has, after all, consented to torture him knowing full well that he is serving the masochist's interests in giving him sexual pleasure. The masochist cannot, however, view a servant as a true conqueror. He might attempt to fantasize that the "sadist" is a conqueror while the act is progressing; but the fantasy is, for him, accompanied by the annoying realization that he can end it whenever the pain becomes unbearable and that the consenting sadist will obey his wishes. The "conquest" was merely theatrical and unsatisfying.

It is, however, commonly argued that one can escape these difficulties in consensual sadomasochistic acts by the use of fantasy. Since fantasy phenomenologically becomes virtual reality when one is sexually aroused, the masochist would presumably be able to forget his dilemma and be able to view his or her master as a true conqueror. Fantasy, however, faces a dilemma in this case. For if both the masochist and the sadist confuse their role-playing with reality, then the desire to receive and to give punishment would ultimately get out of control; the degree of sexual arousal is proportional to the amount of punishment demanded and provided. When the trusted sadist unknowingly exceeds the masochist's limits of endurance, the masochist's pleasure is destroyed and both partners are returned to a frustrating nonerotic reality.

If, on the other hand, both partners monitor the situation in order to prevent fantasy from escalating to a gruesome reality, they are then aware that the act is largely theatrical. The master and slave would remain sufficiently aware of the fact that the master is merely serving the slave's interests in a way that would prevent both master and slave from identifying with their roles in a fully satisfying manner. Nor could the master by himself control the performance and thus allow the masochist the luxury of completely identifying with his fantasy. For if the master remains aware of the fact that he is merely serving the masochist's interests, a frustrated master could not be viewed by the masochist as being a master. Consensual sadomasochism is, therefore, perverse because the partners require total identification with their roles while also requiring that one or both partners consciously monitor the roles so that the fantasy is not destroyed by exceeding the masochist's limits of endurance.

In order to solve this difficulty, a masochist might in some cases be tempted to seek out a true conqueror. Suppose, however, that he walked into a violent area where real sadists are likely to be found. He would still realize that he would be tricking the sadist into thinking he was an unsuspecting victim rather than someone who enjoyed being assaulted. A sadist who could be fooled in this way could not be viewed as being a true conqueror. If he were by chance attacked by a particularly vicious sadist when he had not expected such a thing to occur, this sort of sadist might quickly relieve him of any idea that he was merely serving his masochistic needs by torturing him beyond his limits. Were he to cry out "enough," this would usually incite the sadist merely to intensify the torture. If, however, the sadist were compelled to stop at this point for fear that his victim would lapse into a state of painless unconsciousness, the masochist could no longer visualize him as a true conqueror since he would be viewed (albeit mistakenly) as having honored his request.

The masochist thus faces a dilemma. Since the only way he can view the sadist as not having serving his interests is when the sadist exceeds the limits beyond which he cannot sexually enjoy pain, the desire for a true conqueror would then prohibit the fulfillment of his other goal of sexually enjoying himself by being conquered in a nontheatrical way. If, on the other hand, the sadist were viewed as having "honored" his request to respect his limits, his image of the sadist as being truly sadistic would self-destruct. He would then regard the sexual pleasure that he had enjoyed earlier, and would like to continue, as having been based on an illusion. His contradictory goals thus define the perversity of his quest for the ultimate conqueror.

To be sure, one might argue that masochism is the love of failure. If, however, he were to continue to seek failures such as the one described above and were to succeed, as it were, in failing, he would be crushed if success of any kind were incompatible with his sexual fulfillment. Masochism is thus not perverse, as Sartre claims, because it is merely a love of failure. It is, rather, perverse because the masochist, in order to find the total sort of failure that would sexually satisfy him, must also desire to succeed in doing so. One cannot consciously seek frustration as one's primary goal, for frustration can only be felt if one believed that one's real goal was to succeed. Nor could this difficulty be overcome by noting that one might unconsciously seek frustration while consciously believing that success was one's true goal. For if one repeatedly felt ecstatic when one failed, one would face a further dilemma: how can I want to succeed, yet feel ecstatic when I fail?

This same analysis also applies to the masochist's desire to be humiliated, degraded, enslaved, or even to be frustrated by the dilemmas I have given. One cannot feel truly and utterly degraded, for example, if one did not also actually desire the opposite state of affairs. But this the masochist cannot do since his only goal is to feel degraded. Nor will a fantasy degradation work, because of the dilemma about fantasy becoming reality that I mentioned earlier. Since masochism is defined in terms of exploring the outer limits of degradation, the masochist's desire for utter degradation is thus perverse because of these logical constraints.

5.

I have attempted to develop a theory of sexual perversity based on the use of the term "perverse" when applied to contradictory states of affairs. It is a use that is as much akin to irony as it is to an expression of moral or nonmoral disapproval. Thus Sade's critics, who are well aware that his very identity rested on being evil, commonly argue, instead, that his philosophy faced the supreme irony: his sexual fascination with violating morality presupposed the existence of the goodness he would ideally like to have destroyed. Sade's difficulties actually go well beyond this familiar claim. Someone who has eroticized doing evil requires that his victim feel that she or he has been morally wronged. It then follows that the victim must see himself as being morally superior to the sadist. Sade, however, also required his victims to see him as being superior to them in every way. This example will clarifies the ways in which moral considerations, when relevant, would function in terms of these criteria for perversity.

The third criterion, (c), which defines a perverse person in terms of the repetition of self-defeating acts, is also linked to one of the standard meanings of perversity: obstinacy. While it is true that acts described as being perverse by this criterion will often coincide with those that fall under traditional labels like "sin" or "sickness," the heterosexual who obstinately pursues a mystery that he hopes will never self-destruct need not be viewed as either sinful or sick. It would be more appropriate to say that he is simply foolish in believing that his erotic Holy Grail can ever be found.

The theory is also minimalist in that it does not rest on any a priori assumptions as to what must be sexually enjoyed. Indeed, the notion of desiring a sexual experience is conceptually linked to what it means to engage in a sexual act. Even if one believed that the primary purpose of sex is to express love, the gift of love would still have to be a desire to give the beloved a sexual experience. This agenda of minimal assumptions requires that one leave the notion of what is to count as a sexual experience largely undefined. Thus, the theory allows someone to view a mystical experience in sexual terms, even though it would have been conceptualized as a religious experience in pre-Freudian times. An idealist need not, therefore, view the theory as being based solely on a "crude" hedonism.

Although the theory is based largely on the phenomenology of sexual experience (along with a reference to unconscious desires when necessary), it is different from the sexual phenomenologies of Jean-Paul Sartre, Thomas Nagel, and Robert Solomon. These philosophers view sexual experience as being essentially a form of interpersonal communication, while perverse acts are those that depart from this norm. Their approach is prescriptive rather than descriptive, since it refuses to consider (say) how someone who masturbates views his or her sexual experience as a form of intrapersonal communication. Indeed, even in terms of interpersonal communication of sexual desires and feelings, masturbation need not fail. If masturbation is accompanied by fantasy and if fantasy becomes progressively more real with increasing sexual arousal, then there could be communication between oneself and the phenomenologically real person in one's fantasy. To bridge the gap between theory and *all* forms of sexual experience is, therefore, the goal I should ideally like to achieve with the theory that has been defended in this paper.

Postscript

After this paper was first published, I developed an additional criterion, (d), for perversity, and amplified the relation of perversity to perversion. The fourth criterion is the "perverse" counterpart of various theories of perversion based on a harm-to-others criterion. Criterion (d) is used when someone is sexually aroused by putting someone else in a hopeless dilemma. A certain kind of seducer, for example, might enjoy sexually arousing someone who detests sex.

She is alarmed to find that she desires what she hates at another level. But the maneuver backfires on the seducer. If her dilemma is complete, she is in a state of psychic gridlock and can do nothing; her purity remains intact by default, as it were. If the seducer touches her, then he is in a dilemma as to whether or not he is raping her. Her body offers no resistance or even some ambivalent encouragement, yet her eyes are filled with hate. If he wants either consent or rape, the dilemma he wants her to suffer must be seen by him as having been destroyed in one direction or its opposite. Indeed, his seductive "you like it, don't you?" ultimately demands the full "yes" that ends the ambivalence it initially created.

Although this paper has developed a theory of sexual perversity rather than sexual perversion (something that, to my knowledge, has never been done), perversion itself might have just as strong a link with paradox as it does with the usual notions of departing from natural or cultural norms. When a minister of the Gospel is discovered to have had sex with children, we are struck not so much by his having violated a criterion of naturalness as we are by the contradiction of a man of God molesting children. One also commonly hears the following claim: "sex is inherently good, but it can be perverted". But how can something inherently good be perverted? What is good in and of itself is beyond contamination.

This leads to the interesting question as to whether something about what we think is beautiful also, perversely, contains the ingredients of its own downfall. In some cases, the so-called misuse is predictable. If a philosopher argues that sex is a form of power, that consensual dominance and submission are the essence of sex, and that this will not lead to violence if one exercises the power of self-control, then a perverse effect is virtually assured even if one begins with no evil motives. For power and sexual arousal want to escalate to the ultimate. If self-control is not eroticized, it is seen in purely sexual terms as ultimately frustrating. If self-control is eroticized, then it becomes contaminated by what it is supposed to control and collapses. The philosopher's system thus generates a contradiction and is perverted by its own assumptions about dominance and self-control. One can argue that sex is neither good nor bad in itself; like a knife, it depends on the intentions of the one using it. But while a penis can be an instrument of love or torture, shifting the blame to a perverse will still leaves one with an ancient dilemma: we want to be free to choose, yet we also want to make perversity inconceivable. (Merely forbidding it is not enough; the greater the number of acts that are forbidden, the greater number of choices perversity has). But as long as we are free, virtually anything is conceivable, society's limitations notwithstanding, as the imagination of Sade and the deeds of Jeffrey Dahmer amply illustrate.

Notes

1. This essay is an extensively revised version of a paper first delivered at a meeting of the Tri-State Philosophical Association, held at Mercyhurst College in 1985, and later, in 1986, at a meeting of the Society for the Philosophy of Sex and Love. I am grateful to Arthur Wheeler and William Vitek for their helpful comments, and to Alan Soble for his encouragement. The

pronouns "he" and "she" are intended to be used interchangeably in the text unless the context specifically requires reference to males or females.

2. John O'Connor, "Television Tests Its Limits," *New York Times*, 11 October 1987, §2, 35.

3. George Will, "The Opposition to Bork Is Lacking in Substance," *Buffalo Evening News*, 2 October 1987, C-3.

Carol Caraway
(photograph: Rhande Wood)

Author of "Romantic Love: Neither Sexist Nor Heterosexist"
Paper presented at the Society for the Philosophy of Sex and Love
during the
Central Division Meeting of The American Philosophical Association
St. Louis, Mo., 1 May 1986

Thirty-Six

ROMANTIC LOVE: NEITHER SEXIST NOR HETEROSEXIST

Carol Caraway

Feminists and gay liberationists condemn romantic love as an inherently sexist and heterosexist institution that requires sexist idealizations and heterosexual sexual desire. I argue that although romantic love in the contemporary West often includes sexist idealizations and heterosexual sexual desire, they are not necessary constituents of the concept of romantic love. The crucial elements in romantic love are concern, admiration, desire for reciprocation, and passion for union, none of which requires sexist idealizations or heterosexual desire.

1. Concern

Concern for the welfare of the loved one is an essential component of all types of love, including romantic love. If I love someone, I care about what happens to that person: I am concerned about the person's needs and inclined to do things that enhance that person's well-being. This concern is the basis for the distinction between love and its imitations. The lover who is "too good to be true" exhibits the symptoms of romantic love, but lacks genuine concern for the other and is, therefore, only imitating romantic love. Lacking genuine concern, I do not love. Using the other as a means to my own ends is also incompatible with love. Thus, when sexual desire, whether heterosexual or homosexual, becomes a desire to use another merely as a means to my own ends, it is incompatible with romantic love.

My characterization of the connection between concern and romantic love seems open to the following two objections: (1) sexual desire is essential to romantic love and hence cannot be incompatible with it; (2) a male's concern for the female object of his romantic love takes the form of paternalism and is, therefore, objectionable. Regarding (1): in §3 I argue that sexual desire is not an essential element of romantic love. And regarding (2): concern for another need not be paternalistic. I can be concerned for my friend's welfare without making all her decisions for her. While Western males have traditionally taken a paternalistic attitude toward the women who were the objects of their romantic love, paternalism is not essential to romantic love.

2. Admiration

As feminists have rightly indicated, there is more to romantic love than concern for the other's welfare. The romantic lover admires characteristics of the beloved, and such admiration is tied to idealization, which is a phenomenon critics of romantic love find objectionable. Studies show that most men and women in Western society have an image of their ideal lover composed of the qualities the person would most admire in a lover.[1] Both feminists and chauvinists have argued that romantic love is objectionable because it requires me to see the other as the embodiment of my ideal: when I am romantically in love with another, I either insist on ascribing to him the qualities of my ideal, even when he fails to possess them, or I admit that he lacks these qualities and attempt to change him into a person who has them. Moreover, if he reciprocates, he might try to become my ideal and I might try to become his.[2] Feminists argue that heterosexual lovers have been going through this process for centuries and that it results in unhappy, unauthentic human beings.[3]

A feminist myself, I agree that in Western society romantic love has included processes of idealization that have been harmful to women and men. I contend, however, that the harm lies not in the existence of an idealization process but in the sexist content of traditional idealizations. I agree with Shulamith Firestone that the problem lies in the content of the romantic ideal rather than in the fact that there is a process of idealization.[4]

Such notorious chauvinists as Rousseau and Schopenhauer have argued that romantic love requires me to see in the other the perfections of the opposite sex that I necessarily lack.[5] If they are correct, sexism and heterosexism are necessary constituents of the idealization essential to romantic love. I contend that neither is necessary. I find support for this conclusion in Rousseau's analysis of romantic idealization. According to Rousseau, romantic idealization is a combination of the society's standards of perfection in the opposite sex and the individual's standards of human perfection in either sex. If applied to an androgynous society, Rousseau's account would not be sexist, although it would be heterosexist. This could be eliminated by speaking only of human perfections, and saying that romantic love requires that I see in the other human perfections that include both society's and the individual's standards.

Rousseau's characterization of idealization can also explain why romantic love has traditionally been sexist and heterosexist: the social standards for an ideal object of romantic love have been sexist and heterosexist. This fact undoubtedly led Rousseau to formulate a sexist and heterosexist account of romantic love. Although the content of the romantic idealization need be neither sexist nor heterosexist, the process seems to be an inherently dehumanizing activity that necessarily involves either failing to acknowledge the other's true nature or acknowledging his nature and then trying to change it to fit the ideal. While feminists and gay liberationists rightly argue that certain processes of romantic idealization impede communicating with the other, understanding the other, and developing one's own talents and characteristics, they would be wrong to object to all processes of idealization, for some processes of idealization can be beneficial. Firestone argues that the process of romantic idealization can be the process of valuing what each really has to offer the other rather than the process of misrepresenting the other's qualities.[6] Others have argued that romantic idealization could involve the process of my gaining increased self-awareness through the other's discovering in me positive qualities of which

I was unaware.[7] These idealization processes are beneficial: they lead to happier, more authentic individuals and personal relationships. Indeed, even idealization processes that produce changes in an individual's qualities can be beneficial. Romantic idealization can foster personal growth and positive character development. In the Middle Ages, for example, the courtly female's idealization of her lover might have led him to pursue music and poetry and, thereby, to become more civilized.[8]

3. Reciprocation and the Passion for Union

Another important component of romantic love is the desire to be loved in return. This desire for reciprocation is not a necessary component of romantic love, however; in unusual circumstances one might be romantically in love and yet not want to be loved in return. The most familiar example of this is the case in which a person falls in love with someone who is married, is seriously committed to the marriage, and has a loving spouse and children. In such a case, two of the elements constitutive of romantic love (concern for the other's welfare and the desire for reciprocation) come into conflict, and when concern is stronger, the lover will not actually desire reciprocation. There is a sense in which the lover does desire reciprocation, namely, that it would be desired were it in the other's interest; given the actual circumstances, however, reciprocation is not in the other's interest and hence is not desired.[9]

A similar analysis can be given of cases in which a gay man romantically loves a heterosexual man, a lesbian romantically loves a heterosexual woman, a heterosexual woman romantically loves a gay man, or a heterosexual man romantically loves a lesbian. In each case, the lover might be said to have a *prima facie* desire for reciprocation, one that does not become an all-things-considered desire because of concern that reciprocation would be harmful to the other. This is the reason why, on my account of romantic love, the desire for reciprocation is not a necessary element. It is, instead, an ingredient of romantic love that is present in all ordinary cases and absent only when there is a conflict with some other important element of that concept.

"Passion seeks to tear down the borders of the ego and to absorb 'I' and 'thou' in one another," wrote George Simmel.[10] Romantic lovers seek ecstatic experiences in which the usual distinction between them is blurred. This passion for union is connected to the desire for reciprocation in that the psychological union desired generally cannot be attained unless romantic love is mutual; otherwise, the lack of reciprocation would limit whatever psychological closeness the two might experience. Reciprocated love, then, is not the object of romantic passion, as some have argued, but a condition of attaining psychological union. Hence, when I say, "I love you so much I cannot live without you," I do not mean "I need you to love me so much that I cannot live without you," but "I want to be close to you so much that I cannot live without you."

Many believe that heterosexual sexual desire is a necessary ingredient of romantic love. This is heterosexual prejudice. We need only study Plato's *Symposium* to see that the important constituents of romantic love occur in homosexual relationships. Indeed, a strong case can be made that, in ancient Athens, there was little heterosexual, but a good deal of homosexual, romantic love. Aristocratic Athenian men could not romantically love aristocratic Athenian women, for they could not admire or converse with them.[11]

After granting that requiring heterosexual sexual desire for romantic love is heterosexual prejudice, one could maintain that sexual desire of some sort (not necessarily heterosexual) is necessary for romantic love; otherwise, romantic love would be indistinguishable from certain other affections. When I began to think about the nature of romantic love, I believed that some sort of sexual desire was essential to it. I now believe that, although sexual desire generally plays an important role in romantic love, it is a nonessential symptom that generally coincides with the lover's passion for union, or for complete intimacy, with the other. The passion for union, on the other hand, is an ingredient that is present in all ordinary cases of romantic love and absent only when in conflict with another element. Thus, romantic love is generally accompanied by sexual desire because (1) the desire for union is a criterion of romantic love, and (2) sexual encounters require physical contiguity and tend to promote psychological closeness, whether those encounters are between persons of the opposite sex or persons of the same sex.

4. Exclusivity

I have presented only the skeleton of an account of romantic love, but we can tell something about a creature's appearance when fleshed out by the look of its skull and bones. Will my fully-fleshed account of romantic love require exclusivity? Having seen the skeleton, we might expect the answer to be "No. It is possible to be concerned about, to admire, and to desire both reciprocation from, and union or psychological intimacy with, more than one person." Although I agree with this statement, I will not simply remark that romantic love is not exclusive, for I agree with Simmel that dyadic relations tend to foster intimacy, whereas triadic relations tend to preclude it. According to Simmel, dyadic relations are unique in that they have no independent group structure. Thus, the two members of a dyad retain a high level of individuality; each feels confronted only by the other and not by a collective. In contrast, the three members of a triad, or in our case, perhaps a "love triangle," generally have their individuality threatened by the development of an independent group structure that confronts them and inhibits intimacy between them.[12]

According to Simmel, when a third person is added to a group, new social roles become possible: one member can become the arbiter for disputes between the others, or use disputes between the others for personal gain, or become an object of competition between the other two.[13] Although a love triangle is generally not a triad in which the three members are together for significant periods of time as the members of a family are, the love triangle can give rise to some of these social roles. To see this, consider a love triangle whose members are X, Y, and Z. X romantically loves both Y and Z, and both Y and Z reciprocate by romantically loving X. In this case, X might share with Z intimate knowledge of X's relationship with Y, and Z might use this knowledge for personal gain. If Z were X's only romantic lover, such social relationships would be impossible. Since the development of these relationships threatens intimacy, nonexclusivity minimizes the possibility of psychological union; exclusivity maximizes it. For this reason, I contend that exclusivity is a significant, but nonessential, feature of romantic love. For in the dyad, interactions are based only on personal interdependence: the two individuals see only each other, and there is no objective, superindividual structure.

Critics might contend that in the situation I describe, the development of social relationships that create a superstructure can be avoided by X's keeping each romantic relationship a secret from the uninvolved member. X's silence, however, would not prevent the development of objective structures that threaten intimacy, because each relationship becomes for X a structure that inhibits intimacy, whether or not the relationship is revealed to the uninvolved member. Known or unknown, love triangles threaten the intimacy of love relationships.

I have shown that feminists and gay liberationists are wrong to condemn romantic love as inherently sexist and heterosexist, for romantic love consists in the necessary elements of concern and admiration, the crucial, but non-necessary elements of the desire for reciprocation and the passion for union, and the important element of exclusivity. No element here requires either sexism or heterosexual sexual desire.

Notes

1. See, for example, Ernest W. Burgess and Paul Wallin, *Engagement and Marriage* (New York: J. D. Lippincott, 1953).

2. See W. Newton-Smith, "A Conceptual Investigation of Love," in Alan Soble, ed., *Eros, Agape, and Philia* (New York: Paragon House, 1989), 199-217, at 208-9; Elizabeth Rapaport, "On the Future of Love: Rousseau and the Radical Feminists," in Alan Soble, ed., *Philosophy of Sex*, 1st ed. (Totowa, N.J.: Littlefield, Adams, 1980), 369-88, at 380-1.

3. Sharon Bishop, "Love and Dependency," in Sharon Bishop and Marjorie Weinzweig, eds., *Philosophy and Women* (Belmont, Cal.: Wadsworth, 1979), 147-54, at 153-4; Shulamith Firestone, "Love and Women's Oppression," *Ibid.*, 154-9; Larry Blum, Marcia Homiak, Judy Housman, and Naomi Scheman, "Altruism and Women's Oppression," *Ibid.*, 190-200.

4. For discussion, see Shulamith Firestone, *The Dialectic of Sex* (New York: William Morrow, 1970), chs. 5 and 6.

5. Arthur Schopenhauer, "The Metaphysics of Sexual Love," in *The World as Will and Representation* (New York: Dover, 1958), 533-40; Jean-Jacques Rousseau, *Emile* (New York: Dutton, 1955) and *La Nouvelle Héloise* (Pittsburgh: Pennsylvania State University Press, 1968); Susan M. Okin, *Women in Western Political Thought* (Princeton: Princeton University Press, 1979), pt. 3; Rapaport, "On the Future of Love," 378-85.

6. Firestone, *The Dialectic of Sex*, 128-32.

7. J. O. Wisdom, "Freud and Melanie Klein: Psychology, Ontology, and Weltanschauung," in C. Hanly and M. Lazerowitz, eds., *Psychoanalysis and Philosophy* (New York: Dutton, 1970), 349-54.

8. Thomas H. Greer, *A Brief History of the Western World*, 4th ed. (New York: Harcourt, Brace, Jovanovich, 1982), 193-233.

9. Bishop, "Love and Dependency," 152-3; Newton-Smith, "A Conceptual Investigation," 210.

10. Georg Simmel, "The Isolated Individual and the Dyad," in Kurt Wolff, ed. and trans., *The Sociology of Georg Simmel* (New York: Free Press, 1950), 128.

11. Okin, *Women in Western Political Thought*, 15-70.

12. Simmel, "The Isolated Individual," 122-9, 145-69.

13. *Ibid.*, 145-69.

Dana E. Bushnell
(photograph: Brian Holtsclaw)

"Love Without Sex: A Commentary on Caraway"
Paper presented at the Society for the Philosophy of Sex and Love
during the
Central Division Meeting of The American Philosophical Association
St. Louis, Mo., 1 May 1986

Thirty-Seven

LOVE WITHOUT SEX

Dana E. Bushnell

Ostensibly, the purpose of Carol Caraway's essay[1] is to show that romantic love does not necessarily require sexist idealizations and heterosexist sexual desire. To do this, Caraway tries to isolate components of romantic love and to show that each component need be neither sexist nor heterosexist. At root, however, her essay focuses on uncovering the essence of romantic love.

Caraway first examines concern, explaining that concern for the other's welfare is essential to all love, including the romantic variety. She suggests that true concern precludes the desire to use another sexually as the mere means to one's own ends. Apparently because of this stipulation, Caraway sees a possible objection to her position: the claim that sexual desire is essential to romantic love. She counters this objection with the claim that sexual desire is *not* essential to romantic love. Although it is not clear that Caraway feels *compelled* to make this claim in order to allay the objection, the organization of her essay suggests this. However, such a compulsion is unnecessary, because the only way someone could put forth the essentiality of sexual desire as an objection to Caraway's position on concern is if the objector believed that all sexual desire is a matter of self- and not other-concern. On this view, sex would be a matter of desiring to use the other merely as a means to one's own ends; all sexual desire would be inherently selfish. Psychological egoists claim that everything we do is ultimately done for selfish reasons, but since Caraway does not assume that her objector is an egoist (if she did, her attack on the objection would have taken a different turn), the notion that all sexual desire is inherently a desire merely to use the other needs support for the objection to make sense. The objection is otherwise not a problem. Since the objection poses no problem as it is stated, Caraway need not dismiss sexual desire. Indeed, it is wrong to do so. To see why, we must further explore Caraway's essay.

Caraway argues that "romantic love consists in the necessary elements of concern and admiration, the crucial, but non-necessary elements of the desire for reciprocation and the passion for union, and the important element of exclusivity" (379). Sexual desire need play no role in romantic love. It often comes into the picture, however, because of the passion for union, which is a kind of psychological intimacy. This passion is connected to the desire for reciprocation, since without reciprocation, intimacy cannot be realized. Caraway believes that sexual desire "is a nonessential symptom [of romantic love] that generally coincides with the lover's passion for union, or for complete intimacy, with the other," since "sexual encounters . . . tend to promote psychological closeness" (378). Although the passion for union is ordinarily a feature of romantic love, it is also nonessential according to Caraway, because if this passion conflicts with another element of romantic love, the passion will be absent. Presumably what Caraway has in mind is a case similar to that presented to illustrate the occasions when the desire for reciprocation is lacking in romantic love. Thus, when concern for the other's welfare conflicts with either the desire for reciprocation or the passion for union, concern wins out. I imagine Caraway does not intend this as an empirical observation, but rather as a conceptual statement; that is, when there is such a conflict, if the concern of the purported lover does not suppress the desire for reciprocation and the passion for union, the "lover" is not truly a lover.

If Caraway is correct, then if I romantically love X and discover it is not in X's best interest to love me in return, I apparently cease to desire X's love and cease to harbor a passion for our union, though the feeling of romantic love need not abate. According to Caraway, in this situation, although I romantically love X, all I feel for him of the components of romantic love are concern and admiration. Caraway contends that my concern for him does not allow me to desire his love in return. She further suggests that I would not desire psychological intimacy. And because sexual desire is no more than a sort of tool used to obtain psychological union, presumably I would not desire sexual intimacy with X either.

There are two points to be made here. First, I do not agree with Caraway that a lover romantically in love with another necessarily ceases to feel the desires for reciprocation and intimacy upon discovering that it would be harmful to the other to reciprocate. The desires do not need to cease for true romantic love. What *might* happen is that the lover might not act on her desires, since her concern for the other might help her to act prudently and not put the other in jeopardy. But her desires remain.

Even if the lover is, for whatever reasons, unsuccessful in refraining from acting on her desires when such an action is not in the beloved's best interest, do we really want to say that the lover does not feel romantic love? People in love are not always the most rational people. Perhaps concern is not always stronger than desire. I see no inconsistency in allowing that romantic love is characterized by conflicting passions or needs.

Second, let us suppose that the desires do cease and that all the lover feels for the other are concern and admiration. On this supposition it is difficult to see how the lover remains romantically in love with the other as opposed to feeling some other sort of love. Concern and admiration, as Caraway points out, are two feelings that may be found in love that is ordinarily considered nonromantic. For instance, a parent might be concerned about her child and might feel admiration for him, even to the point of idealization, yet the parent scarcely feels romantic love for the child. How, then, do we distinguish the parental love from the purportedly romantic love of our earlier example? Both are characterized by concern and admiration, but without some differentiation, it seems that the two sorts of love cannot be separated. There are innumerable instances of loving another to the extent of feeling true concern and admiration, but not to the extent implied by romantic love. More is essential to romantic love than concern and admiration, even in Caraway's extraordinary cases.

What is it about romantic love that sets it apart from other love? Since I have shown that the components Caraway lists as crucial but not necessary (the desire for reciprocation, the passion for union), need not be lacking from romantic love in extraordinary circumstances, Caraway is free to consider these components necessary. If we alter Caraway's program and say that the essentials of romantic love are concern, admiration, the desire for reciprocation, and the passion for union, have we managed to capture how romantic love differs from other love? I think not. Consider the parent loving her child. Besides feeling concern and admiration for him, she might desire that her child returns her love. In fact, it is typical for parents to want their children to love them. Furthermore, parents who want psychological closeness with their children are not rare. I can even imagine cases where the love of the parent is such that the usual distinction of being separate individuals seems blurred to the parent, especially when the child is an infant. In situations where the parent feels all four Carawayian components, I think arguing that the parent must then be feeling romantic love for the child is mistaken.

Caraway lastly considers exclusivity as a "significant, but nonessential, feature of romantic love" (379). If we add exclusivity to our revised list of the essentials of romantic love, we would still not be able to explain the difference between romantic and other love. The loving parent of my example might feel all five of these elements towards her child and yet not feel romantic love for the child. It is not difficult to imagine a parent (or anyone else) feeling that she wants her loved one to love only her in that special way in which she loves him.

It may be countered that when a parent desires exclusivity from the child, the parent must not be feeling true love, since exclusivity is possessive and unhealthy in this situation. If this were the case, then it might be that a desire for exclusivity is the distinguishing component of romantic love. Yet in answer to this objection, I must point out that this same claim could be made about the desire for exclusivity in romantic love: that it is unhealthy, possessive, and a sign of love lacking. If exclusivity is unhealthy, perhaps it should not be considered a component of romantic love.

If a parent can feel all the same emotions toward her child as those in romantic love, without feeling romantic love, what would it take for us to believe the parent *does* feel romantic love? It seems to me that what this parental love lacks is sexual desire. I agree with Caraway that sexist idealizations and heterosexual sexual desire "are not necessary constituents of the concept of romantic love" (375), but the way to establish this is not to dismiss sexual desire from romantic relationships. Romantic love need be neither sexist nor heterosexist, but it does require sexuality.

Note

1. Carol Caraway, "Romantic Love: Neither Sexist Nor Heterosexist," this volume, 375-9. All parenthetical page references are to this essay.

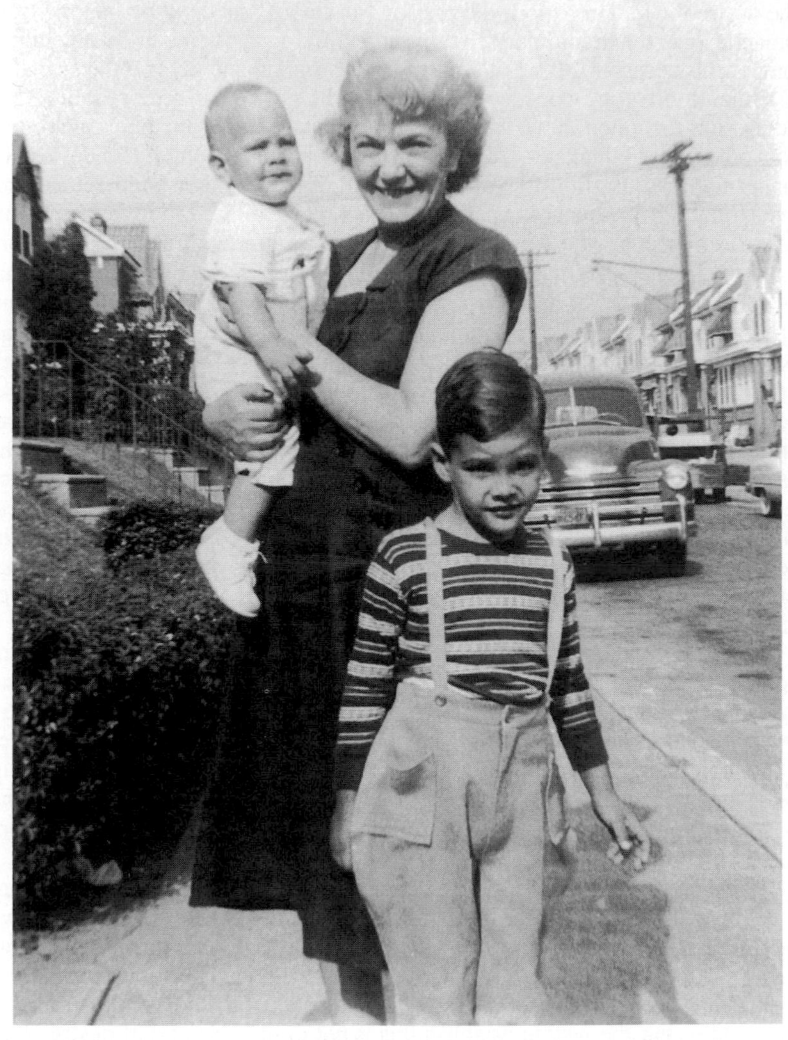

Janet Soble (left), Gertrude Ratener (center), and Alan Soble (right)
(photograph: Sylvia Ratener Soble)

Alan Soble, author of "The Unity of Romantic Love"

Thirty-Eight

THE UNITY OF ROMANTIC LOVE[1]

Alan Soble

1. Introduction

What is an *account* of "romantic love"? There are three intellectual projects in which one could engage. (1) We might propose to describe an institution or a set of practices, a time- and place-specific phenomenon; for example, the manner in which romantic love is practiced now in the West. This task is sociological and psychological, not philosophical. Such an account of romantic love will claim that in our society it is characterized or usually accompanied by *F*, *G*, and *H*. Then the questions to ask include: what are the historical causes of this institution, what maintains it, what effects does it have on the people involved? (2) Or can we do the history of ideas, studying a certain literary and philosophical tradition in love, in this case focusing on the romantic tradition rather than, say, the courtly love tradition or the various religious traditions. We start by identifying the texts that are exemplars of romanticism, discover the source of these ideas (at least in primitive form) in earlier texts, and trace the continuation of romantic themes in later texts. Such an account of romantic love will tell us that in this tradition *F*, *G*, and *H* are the major elements of love. In carrying out this project some philosophy can be done, if we are concerned with the coherence of the themes or whether they are logically related to more basic philosophical claims. (3) Finally, we can attempt to provide an *analysis of the concept* "romantic love" or to investigate what romantic love *is*; this is to do philosophy, at least according to one twentieth-century school. If we are engaged in this project, we will begin by reading the classic texts in the romantic love tradition and by examining romantic love practices cross-culturally, but the analysis of the concept we produce need not fully match those texts and practices. After all, the texts and the practices are bound in time and place and reflect social, economic, and political influences that must be transcended by abstract analysis. Beyond appeals to the classic texts and current practices, argument of a typically philosophical kind is required to defend any proposed analysis of the concept that states that romantic love *is* composed of *F*, *G*, and *H*.

We are now in a position to clear away one confusion. Compare the first sentence of Carol Caraway's essay[2] with the first sentence of her concluding paragraph. At the start, Caraway tells us that feminists and gay liberationists condemn an *institution* (375); at the end, she tells us that they are wrong to condemn *romantic love* (379). Between these two sentences, Caraway engages in conceptual analysis, arguing that none of the objectionable features of our romantic love practices are necessary elements of the concept itself. Hence the first sentence of her concluding paragraph means: feminists and gay liberationists have been condemning a mistaken analytical account of romantic love, or they have themselves a mistaken idea of what that concept includes. But as far as I can tell from feminist literature on the topic, they have been engaged in project (1) and not in project (3). Caraway agrees, implicitly, that her opponents have adequately carried out project (1) and, explicitly, that their condemnation of current practices is justified. But I am not convinced, on the basis of the evidence presented by Caraway, that they even intended to say anything about project (3) or that they were presupposing a particular analysis of the concept.

Some feminists have asserted that there is a kind of dependency or a loss of autonomy in romantic love *per se*, and not simply in our institution, and so have been engaged in both projects (1) and (3). But Caraway seems to ignore or misunderstand this line of thought.[3] That romantic love essentially involves a loss of autonomy, if true, might make it an objectionable phenomenon, but it does not make romantic love essentially or "inherently" sexist. Thus Caraway's war against the claim that romantic love is necessarily sexist misses the mark. Now, if one asserts that romantic love essentially involves a loss of autonomy, *and* if one asserts that in our society women primarily suffer this loss, *then* one has arrived at a claim within project (1): our practices are sexist. Still it does not follow that romantic love, as analyzed in project (3), is sexist, or that any feminist has made that claim.

Note that Caraway had the opportunity to address this position in her section "Concern." For what inspires some feminist condemnations of romantic love is the worry that the concern women have for the men they love is a self-sacrificial altruism that damages the self. In her section on admiration, Caraway writes: "While feminists and gay liberationists rightly argue that certain processes of romantic idealization impede communicating with the other, understanding the other, and developing one's own talents and characteristics, they would be wrong to object to all processes of idealization" (376). But it is Caraway who is wrong in thinking that the loss of the ability to develop "one's own talents and characteristics" is a fault specifically of the *idealization* involved in romantic love (or she is wrong to think feminists were making *that* point). Rather, the failure to develop oneself results from the loss of autonomy involved in conceiving of concern self-sacrificially (or, on some accounts, from the economic pressure on women to hold on to their men).

2. The Concept of Romantic Love

In her analysis of romantic love, Caraway includes five elements: concern, admiration, the desire for reciprocity, the passion for union, and exclusivity. She further claims that of the five elements she discusses, only concern and admiration are *necessary* to romantic love, while the other three are *not* necessary, even though they are "important" or "crucial" and play a role in romantic love. Caraway, it seems to me, has embraced a double standard. Recall her criticism of the feminists: the objectionable features they find in romantic love are *not necessary* to the concept; and if so, they do not deserve any attention in the analysis of the concept. Yet Caraway spends paragraphs on features that she believes are not necessary, because they are still "important." Why does she not permit her opponents the same strategy? How to distinguish between a not-necessary feature that should be written off and a not-necessary feature that should be retained as "important" is obscure. To retain the not-necessary features that are not (morally) objectionable, *because* they are not objectionable, and to jettison the not-necessary features that are objectionable, *because* they are objectionable, is not the way to do analysis. Thus the conditional that "if exclusivity is unhealthy, perhaps it should not be considered a component of romantic love" is question-begging.[4] What must be said is this: "if exclusivity is unhealthy, *and if* exclusivity is essential to romantic love, then romantic love is unhealthy."

Caraway's list of the five features of romantic love is interesting and correct, or at least on the right track. But I have reservations: all Caraway has provided is a list without a theoretical rationale. Where are the arguments that these two (or five) features constitute romantic love? The love she describes might be a nice love, but where is the warrant for calling it "romantic"? Her problem is compounded because she claims that only concern and admiration are essential for romantic love. Dana Bushnell makes the point that these two features alone do not distinguish romantic love from other types of love; that point is well taken unless it can be argued that romantic love involves a *special* sort of concern and admiration that does distinguish it from the other types of love. The point is that Caraway has not provided enough evidence, from practices, classical texts, or philosophical argument, that concern and admiration are the essential, and the only essential, elements of romantic love.

Caraway does offer one argument in defense of her decision to place priority on concern at the expense of reciprocity and the passion for union, the argument that if X is *genuinely* concerned for Y, then X will abandon the desires for reciprocity and union when the satisfaction of those desires conflicts with Y's welfare. But this is a weak argument. What *kind* of concern, after all, is involved in romantic love, and *does* this concern necessarily trump the other features? It might be noble and fair and commendable that X, out of concern for Y, abandons his desires. But that X does so gives us equal reason to think that X is inspired by a sort of *agape* that is not part of romantic love. Further, Caraway's example in support of her argument does not work. If the X and the Y she speaks about who are romantically attached do not give in to their desires because Y is married, this might not be because there is something *in* romantic love *itself* (say, X's "genuine" concern for Y) that dictates this result; rather, it is because romantic love has lost the battle, in this case, with other values. Consider the relationship between Miles Greensleave and Lisa Watkin in Iris Murdoch's *Bruno's Dream*: "Romantic love is not an absolute," says the solid Lisa.[5]

Other, minor arguments, offered by Caraway for her account fare no better. In her section on admiration, Caraway appeals to a practice in the courtly love tradition to defend her claim that the idealization involved in romantic love can be beneficial. But there are too many differences between the courtly and the romantic traditions for this kind of evidence to be *relevant*.[6] And in her discussion of sexuality, she gathers support from Plato's *Symposium*, in defending her claim that homosexual relationships can be romantic. Her conclusion is right, but why appeal to Plato? Why assume that Platonic *eros* fits neatly into the romantic tradition? In *eros*, desire for union with the beloved person is only a temporary stage on the road to a more important nonpersonal union; whereas in romantic love the union with the beloved is desired for its own sake. In Plato's *eros* there is admiration for the beloved but no idealization; the failure to find perfection in a personal beloved contributes to the striving for the higher union. *Eros* involves basically a trip of one, not a trip of two; the lover, if successful, eventually confronts or contemplates the nonpersonal Good alone, not hand-in-hand with a lover. Perhaps what Caraway meant was that one stage in the Ascent represents romantic love. Which one?—the first, in which we strive to possess the other's beautiful body, or the second, in which we strive to possess the other's beautiful mind? Or perhaps she meant that the love described by Pausanias, or by Phaedrus, or by Aristophanes (the best try), is romantic love. But if she does mean Aristophanes, Caraway must abandon her claim that concern takes precedence over the passion for union, for the latter is the crux of Aristophanic love.

3. Concern

Caraway asserts, truly I think, that concern for the welfare of the loved one is a component of *all* types of love, and from what she says I gather that she believes: (a) concern is an inclination to enhance the other's welfare; (b) concern is incompatible with treating the beloved as a means; and (c) concern is not necessarily paternalistic. This trio of ideas does not help us much in figuring out what Caraway means when she says that if X "lacks genuine concern for the other," X is "only imitating romantic love" (375). After all, some philosophers and theologians claim that only *agape* is or contains "genuine" concern for the beloved.

The idea that concern is an inclination to enhance the other's welfare must be refined. For example: (1a) X wants the good for Y for X's sake; (1b) X wants the good for Y for Y's sake; (2a) X wants the good for Y in X's sense of what is good for Y; or (2b) in Y's sense of what is good for Y.

(1a) is ruled out for romantic love by Caraway's second idea, (b), and (2a) as a general feature is ruled out by her rejection of paternalism. But notice that (2) is incomplete. Perhaps (2c): X wants the good for Y neither in X's sense of Y's good nor in Y's sense, but in some objective sense, which might very well not match X's or Y's sense. And when we consider that X might be concerned for Y's actual self, Y's potential self, or for Y's ideal self, the clarity we thought we had about "paternalism" goes down the drain. If X wants the good for Y in an objective sense, and in preference to Y's sense of what is good for Y, is this paternalism? Is it thereby ruled out by romantic love? (1) has its problems, too. Even if concern means that Y's good is not merely a means to X's good, does it imply that X wants the good for Y even at the expense of X's good, or only to the extent that Y's good is compatible with X's good? Which of these is the concern of romantic love?

Finally, consider this pair: (3a) X wants the good for Y to be achieved by and through the efforts of X; and (3b) X wants Y's good to be enhanced no matter who does so. (3a) is distinct from (1a): it might be the case that X wants the good for Y for Y's sake, yet X wants to be the person who enhances Y's good. I see no reason to assume that just because X wants to be the one who enhances Y's good, X is really seeking Y's good for X's own sake. If, however, X is so interested in being the one that brings about the good for Y that X would not bring it about (or would feel unhappy) if others were willing and able to do so, or if X deliberately interfered with Y's good being enhanced by others, then X seems concerned for Y's welfare mostly for X's sake. There is also an extreme on the other side: if X is concerned for the good of Y in such a way that X would be happy were anyone to bring it about, does this mean that X's concern must take the form of actively helping others enhance the good of Y? Should X procure a lover Z for Y?

These are hardly idle questions; how we answer them indicates the kind of love we are talking about. It is not implausible to think that in loving agapically not only do I pursue your good (and the good of my neighbors), but I also actively help anyone else who is pursuing your good. This looks a far cry from romantic love, in which there is more than a hint that when X is concerned for Y, X wants to be the one who enhances Y's good. The kind of concern involved in romantic love, that is, is a concern *colored by* the exclusivity of romantic love. I am suggesting here that Caraway is wrong to consider exclusivity an important but not-necessary feature of romantic love; that it is actually an essential part of romantic love.

An alternative analysis of romantic love has different implications for the role and nature of concern. Suppose (as I argue later) that in romantic love the primary goal of the lovers is a kind of union or merging, and that in such a union the psychological, even existential, boundaries between two separate identities are broken. Then to ask whether X wants the good for Y for X's sake or for Y's sake is to miss the whole point of this type of love. Since, if the merging is successful, or even as the lovers are trying to achieve that union, there are no wholly separate X and Y, there is no distinction between X's sake and Y's sake.[7] On this account, the concern in romantic love is conceived in a radically different way that transcends the categories of self and other. Further, concern is a *derivative* feature of romantic love, not primary. This point requires explanation.

The "realist" criticism of romantic love is that the lovers are egocentrically motivated, and thus that romantic love does not include any concern worth talking about. This objection is heard so frequently that it is curious to find Caraway flatly analyzing romantic love as essentially involving "genuine" concern. The only argument I could find in her paper is this: (P1) All types of love include concern; (P2) Romantic love is a type of love; therefore, romantic love essentially includes concern.

For Caraway, concern is a constituent of romantic love *because* romantic love is a type of love. We must do better than that. The argument is too vulnerable to the realist objection: either romantic love is not a type of love (because it does not involve concern in any robust sense), or it is false that all types of love include concern. Caraway's assertion that romantic love involves concern, then, is question-begging. The way to handle the realist objection is to recognize the long tradition of describing the romantic lovers as an *égoisme à deux*. In light of the passion for union, the charge of egocentricity loses its force; the self and the other are too mixed together to permit the objection.

Caraway does consider the objection (which sounds like a realist critique) that romantic love is egoistic because it includes sexual desire. Her response, in defense of the "genuine" concern involved in romantic love, is to claim that sexual desire is not essential to romantic love. But this tosses the baby with the bath water. Further, because Caraway retains sexual activity as a (significant?) way for the lovers to satisfy their passion for union, her assumption that sexual desire is incompatible with concern forces her, after all, to admit some egoism into her account of romantic love. Bushnell reasonably suggests that Caraway did not have to accept the unstated assumption that all sexual desire is egoistic.

Let me summarize and draw a philosophical lesson. Caraway argues that romantic love involves concern because it is romantic *love*; on my view, it includes the special concern that it has because it is *romantic*. The concern of romantic love is a special sort of concern whose nature is colored by the other romantic features (exclusivity, for example). And concern is part of romantic love through its ties with the other features; the passion for union demands that X be concerned for Y. When the passion for union is satisfied, or even while X attempts to satisfy it, the boundary between X and Y breaks down and X's concern for Y is indistinguishable from X's concern for X. Where is the philosophical argument that this account is superior to Caraway's? Here: on Caraway's view, the separate elements of romantic love hang together almost by accident, while on my view the elements are unified. Hence the title of my paper.[8]

4. Exclusivity and the Dyad

Caraway's discussion of exclusivity is a mixed blessing: on the one hand, it indicates that she sees that the analysis of romantic love must be unified, but, on the other, it is inconsistent with other claims she makes. She is right to derive exclusivity from the passion for union; she argues that "exclusivity maximizes" intimacy and, thereby, "psychological union" (379). But Caraway only creates trouble for herself by suggesting that "the two members of a [romantic] dyad retain a high level of individuality" (378). The passion for union, because it yields exclusivity, has a coloring effect on that exclusivity, such that it is misleading to state that in the romantic dyad there is a "high level" of individuality. For if the passion for union breaks the I-You boundary (as Caraway says it does), the individuality of the lovers is not only eliminated, but gladly so. Caraway cannot have it both ways; if the passion for union yields exclusivity by fostering intimacy, it also yields a loss of individuality.[9] Now, a kind of love in which the lovers did retain their individuality might be a nice love. But "romantic" does not entail "nice," or *vice versa*.

Further, by merely insisting that in romantic love the members of the dyad retain their individuality, Caraway is begging the question against those who claim that the nature of romantic love implies that the parties lose autonomy. That view cannot be dismissed merely by adding *ad hoc* the notion of individuality to one's account of romantic love. However, if we analyze romantic love as having the passion for union at its center, then this issue (like the problem of concern) is less troubling. For if emphasis is placed on passion for union, the category "individuality," like the categories "self" and "other," is radically transformed. (Bushnell claims that a blurring of boundaries might occur in parent-child love, especially when the child is an infant. But this does not mean that parental or maternal love involves a passion for union and is in this respect indistinguishable from romantic love. First, the lack of boundaries between mother and infant is a sort of biopsychological fact about their bond, not a *goal* they each have. Second, in maternal love the movement is toward individuation and the eventual individuality of the child, its increasing separation from the mother, while in romantic love the movement is toward the deepening of the blurring of boundaries.)

Caraway gets from her understanding of Simmel the idea that in the romantic dyad individuality is retained: "Dyadic relations are unique in that they have no independent group structure" (378); "in the dyad . . . the two individuals see only each other, and there is no objective, superindividual structure" (379). These claims lead Caraway into a second contradiction. The idea that in the romantic dyad "the two individuals see only each" and do not confront external, objective structures is nonsense, but that is not the point. The point is that Caraway has already seen, and told us, that it is nonsense. The feminist critique of romantic practices is that the social context in which romantic loves occur molds those love relationships into a pattern inimical to the well-being of women: a "superindividual structure" entered and soured the relationship. Now, Caraway's response to this objection was that in a different social context, romantic love would not be objectionable in these ways. Her response was *not* that we should attempt to eliminate the influence of social context on the romantic dyad, but that we should allow that love to flourish within a more benign superindividual structure. Thus: "the harm lies not in the existence of [idealization] but in the sexist content of traditional idealizations," and "romantic love requires that I see in the other human perfections that include . . . society's . . . standards" (376). How could it be that the parties "see only each other"? They don't. Even in Caraway's sanitized society, the parties confront each other in the glowing light of their social context, and their love has an unobjectionable form *because* it exists in the realm of that morally superior superindividual structure and because, as Caraway has shown, the *concept* of romantic love does not require the effects of other structures.

It is ironic that Caraway makes this mistake, for those who defend romantic love as it exists in our culture today say something like this:

> The couple *is* alone; they see only each other. All this talk about the society's forming the parameters of their love is knee-jerk bullweed. The lovers confront each other as the pure people they are. Meddling feminists and social reformers cannot understand that the personal is personal, and the political is political, period.

Would not some romantics agree, that when X and Y are romantically in love, the world just drops out of the picture? Perhaps *this* is what is wrong with romantic love: not the (purported) egocentricity of its concern, or the fantastic Stendhalian idealizations to which it is vulnerable, or the loss of autonomy and individuality, but the fact that it is a love that imagines itself above the world at the same time that it has *no* way of leaving it behind. Given that human life requires some false consciousness or self-deception, is this the sort we would prefer?

Caraway's reliance on Simmel, then, was ill-conceived; she should have been satisfied with deriving exclusivity from the passion for union. But matters are worse. If I understand Simmel: it is because there are few, if any, objective structures in the dyad that, for Simmel, the dyad is the *least stable* relationship. The two people, in the absence of these stabilizing structures, incessantly attempt to pull themselves up by their own bootstraps. And it is actually the addition of a "third" to make a triangle (in particular, for Simmel, the triangle consisting of mummy, daddy and baby) that allows the couple, or the dyad-become-triad, to attain durability. This Simmel stuff is silly nonsense:[10] the dyad might be unstable, but not because it is lacking in superindividual objective structures, of which it has plenty; the addition of a child is not the panacea some people believe or hope it is, and often it is a disturbing factor. Appealing to Simmel was hardly the best tactic for a defender of a superior form of romantic love.

The topic of the "third" is crucial.[11] Caraway argues that a particular "third," another love partner that creates a kind of triad, disrupts the dyad, making it less stable (hence: exclusivity). The "third" I took pains to acknowledge above is society, or superindividual structures; these, if Caraway is right, can either disrupt or have a cohesive effect. Bernard Williams tells us one reason why the dyad is unstable: "The rattle of Woody Allen's ironies, like the bleaker Bloomsbury memoirs and correspondence, reminds us that, if all that is interesting to lovers is each other, there may not be much of interest."[12] Perhaps this is why Freud said that the two most important things in life are love *and* work. And perhaps this is why for Kierkegaard the "third" is God; both partners in the dyad must owe allegiance primarily to God and not to each other, otherwise the dyad is bound to fall apart, or to explode.[13]

5. The Passion for Union

If romantic love consists of concern, admiration, a desire for reciprocity, the passion for union, and exclusivity, then of all these features the passion for union must be the central element. My thesis is that each of the other features can be derived from the passion for union. Because of these derivations, and because the elements of romantic love color each other, the result is a unified concept of romantic love rather than a patchwork. I assume that a criterion of adequacy for an analytic account of romantic love is that such unity is achieved; this is largely what is wrong with Caraway's account, despite the fact that she gets the elements right. For example, Caraway begins her section on admiration with, "As feminists have rightly indicated, there is more to romantic love than concern. . . . The romantic lover admires characteristics of the beloved" (375-6). That's it. Caraway moves immediately (and mysteriously) from admiration to idealization, a brand new can of worms, without pausing to justify her inclusion of admiration or showing how it connects with the other features of romantic love. Caraway does, however, recognize other internal connections among these features, and I will draw on these in my own account.

The passion for union yields *concern* in the way previously indicated: if my desire is to merge with you, then my desire is that the distinction between my-self and your-self breaks down, in which case, assuming that I can be counted on to be concerned with my own interests, I will be concerned for your interests, since they are just mine. Thus, not only is concern derived from the passion for union, but the type of concern involved, its color, is similarly derived: it is not a full blown altruistic self-giving concern (although it might appear that way to those in the grip of romantic love), but a special sort of concern not understood well if we think in terms of an opposition between the interests of two separate individuals. The color of this concern is also influenced by exclusivity; it is a concern in which I want to be the one who acts for your sake, but at the same time *you* desire that your good be enhanced primarily by me and not by someone else. (In a sense, then, concern is also colored by reciprocity.) The passion for union yields the *desire for reciprocity* in the way indicated by Caraway: my desire for union will come to naught unless you are similarly motivated, and so I desire that you are also motivated by a desire for union. And I want it to be the case that my good is enhanced by you, not by any person. *Exclusivity*, as Caraway suggests, can be understood as necessary for union to occur: if I desire to merge with you, I will also desire the intimacy permitted by exclusivity. But perhaps there is more to be said. If the passion for union is not only the desire to merge with the other, but also the desire for an increased union with a person that one already feels at one with, then exclusivity is built into this passion. When X romantically loves Y at a distance or Y is not yet aware of X's love, then the passion for union is the desire to get some merging underway. But if X and Y have already revealed to each other their romantic love for each other, a merging has already occurred; the lovers even say to each other, at this stage, that they feel as if they are already joined as one. Their passion is now a desire for a deeper, more substantial union (and so they proceed to bed, or spend all their time together reading the same books). The question of exclusivity has been settled in their reflecting upon the fact that they feel joined before moving on to later stages. Rolf Johnson argues that exclusivity can be derived in another way from the passion for union.[14] Caraway and I derive exclusivity from the *union*, while he derives it from the *passion*: in passion, energy is directed at an object, and the stronger the passion is, the less energy there will be for passion to develop for a second object. (Johnson also derives exclusivity from reciprocity: if I desire that you also love me, I do not want *your* love diverted by other objects.)

Finally, the passion for union yields *admiration*. We desire to merge only with what we admire. Because in the merging the boundary between my-self and your-self breaks down, I will in a sense become you and so must be able to foresee with pleasure taking on your character as if it were my own. Thus a necessary condition for X's passion for union to be directed at Y is that X admires Y. But the relationship between the passion for union and admiration is more complex, for admiration might also be a sufficient condition (*ceteris paribus*) for that passion: perhaps *because* I admire you, I want to merge with you, want to have my-self mixed with your-self, I want to become you. We might say, in light of the reciprocal relationship between admiration and the passion for union, that the passion for union is both the *analytic* and the *phenomenological* center of romantic love, while admiration is its *causal* center.

The difference between something's being a feature of romantic love (or mentioned in the analysis of the concept) and its being a cause of romantic love is important. But a feature might be both part of the concept and a cause. Johnson suggested that "sexual desire . . . may be an essential constitutive element (or cause) of romantic love,"[15] in effect suggesting that sexuality might play both roles. I have not said much about sexuality, but perhaps this is the right place. I am attracted to Caraway's suggestion that sexual relations are one way of trying to satisfy the passion for union. Bushnell argues, against Caraway, that sexual desire is not merely an incidental feature of romantic love, or an option open to the lovers, but is an *essential* feature; otherwise there would be no way to distinguish romantic love from (for example) paternal or maternal love. I am not convinced. First, parent-child love *can* (for better or worse is a separate question) include sexual desire(s), in both directions. Second, even if both romantic love and paternal love include concern, perhaps it is the kind of concern included in each that distinguishes them (*ditto* for the other features). Third, even if romantic love and parental love contain the same elements, they can be distinguished in terms of which feature is central: the passion for union in romantic love, concern in parental love. Fourth, do not Daphnis and Chloe provide a counterexample to the claim that romantic love requires sexuality?[16] Finally, Bushnell leaves unresolved how sexual desire should be incorporated into the analysis of romantic love. There are three possibilities: (1) the passion for union *is* sexual desire, (2) sexual desire is essential to the passion for union and is thereby essential to romantic love, and (3) sexual desire is a distinct element of romantic love.

6. Admiration

Caraway also asserts that romantic love is not necessarily "heterosexist." Again, in criticizing her feminist opponents Caraway has not attended to the differences between projects (1) and (3). While discussing Rousseau and Schopenhauer, Caraway says that "If they are correct, . . . heterosexism [is a] necessary constituent . . . of the idealization essential to romantic love" (376). But this critique of Rousseau is beside the point; Caraway has not argued that idealization, in addition to admiration, is a feature of romantic love, nor that admiration requires idealization. Caraway's response to the charge that romantic love is "heterosexist" is twofold. First, Caraway asserts that none of her five features of romantic love "requires . . . heterosexual sexual desire" (379). Second, she reminds us that we have records, since the dawn of civilization, of homosexual romantic love (for example, Plato's *Symposium*). But because there is and has been homosexual romantic love (which is admitted not only by liberals who tolerate or protect it, but also by conservative critics of homosexuality), the claim that romantic love requires heterosexual desire looks silly to begin with. Does *anyone* assert this howler? Caraway says: "Many believe that heterosexual sexual desire is a necessary ingredient of romantic love. This is heterosexual prejudice" (377). Exactly who are these "many"? Caraway does not tell us. Not those who are "prejudiced" against homosexuals; their awareness of public "displays" of homosexual romance fuels their prejudice. Perhaps they assert that romantic love between homosexuals is morally wrong or perverted, but to assert this is not to make a conceptual claim about romantic love.

Furthermore, both responses show a misunderstanding of the charge of "heterosexist." When feminists and gay liberationists accuse romantic love practices of being "heterosexist," do they mean either that romantic love, by its nature, requires heterosexual sexual desire, or that at least one feature of romantic love requires that the couple be heterosexual? No. The claim that our institution of romantic love is heterosexist is composed of the claims that few people complain about public displays of heterosexual romance, but many people complain about public displays of homosexual romance; that heterosexual romance is common fare in the popular media, but homosexual romance is rare, and when it does occur it's a "question"; that education, religion, and law continue to disparage and discriminate against homosexual romance, and in their own ways attempt to steer development toward heterosexuality. If this is what the "heterosexist" charge means, then Caraway, by pointing out that there are many homosexual romances and arguing that none of her features requires heterosexual sexual desire, has not rebutted the feminists and gay liberationists she announced were her opponents. Indeed, those who use "heterosexist" in the sense of "discriminatory" implicitly agree with her conceptual claims.

How is any of this relevant to admiration? Caraway's thesis is that none of the features of her concept of romantic love requires heterosexuality. She provides no argument in support of this claim, except in the case of admiration. But what she says is unconvincing, at least because she asks whether heterosexuality is required for idealization, not whether it is required for admiration. After all, every time Caraway lists her elements of romantic love, she includes admiration but not idealization. Here is the point: in asking the specific question, "does admiration require heterosexuality?" we are in a position to uncover the reasons someone might have for asserting the incredible, and otherwise inexplicable, claim that romantic love requires heterosexuality. Keep in mind that I am making a first attempt at analyzing "admiration" in order to *explain*, not justify, that odd belief.

My proposal is that a person X admires another person Y in virtue of Y's property or characteristic P, only if: (a1) X values P; (a2) X does not have P; and (a3) Y has P. I shall defend and comment on this analysis before proceeding to the question at hand. The basic idea behind these three conditions is that admiration requires a recognition of a difference; we admire another person only when (a3) the other possesses a virtue, skill, or quality that (a1) we value but (a2) we do not have ourselves. But these conditions are only individually necessary, not jointly sufficient for admiration, and they are not yet powerful enough to distinguish admiration from other attitudes. For example, to distinguish admiration from resentment, the analysis of resentment would have to include, say, "X believes X is entitled to P."

William Lyons has argued that the condition "X desires to have P" is necessary for envy but not for admiration.[17] In part, Lyons argues that "X desires to have P" is not necessary for admiration because he rejects (a2) as a necessary condition for admiration. Presumably, if X does have P when X admires Y, then there is no sense in claiming that X desires to have P. But Lyons's reason for rejecting (a2) is either mistaken or inconclusive. He writes: "I might admire someone who does the 100 meters in 10.1 seconds, even if I can do it in 9.1 seconds, particularly if the person who does it in 10.1 did not appear likely to do it in that time for reasons of say, sex, age, or infirmity."[18] But this is not a counterexample to condition (a2). If X admires Y in this case, it is because X thinks "had I been in Y's position, I would probably not have been able to run the 100 meters in 10.1 seconds." In other words, X admires Y in virtue of a property P that X does *not* have: either "being able to run the 100 meters in 10.1 seconds while suffering from severe sciatica" or "appears unlikely to be able to run the 100 meters in 10.1 seconds."

Even though his argument that "X desires to have P" is not necessary for admiration is faulty, my suspicion is that Lyons is right to assert that "X desires to have P" is not necessary for admiration. But there are two *caveats*. First, condition (a1), that X values P, might already entail "X desires to have P"; at least, it does so on some accounts of what it is to value something. Lyons's claim, then, amounts to a rejection of that sort of analysis of value. Second, even if admiration does not generally *require* that X desires to have P, some cases of admiration might include that desire anyway. In particular, the *kind* of admiration involved in romantic love might be such that it is true that "X desires to have P." Now, this does not mean that actually envy, and not admiration, is an element of romantic love; on Lyons's account, "X desires to have P" is not a sufficient condition for envy. But if admiration *causes* the passion for union (as I said was possible), we have some understanding of that process: the admiration of romantic love includes "X desires to have P," the satisfaction of which desire is seen by the lover as achievable through union with the admired person.

Conditions (a1) and (a3), I think, are pretty obviously necessary for X to admire Y. Condition (a3) tells us why it is Y who is the object of admiration, and condition (a1) tells us that one does not admire another person for, say, having warts (except in the strange case that X in fact *values* warts). And I have just defended (a2) against Lyons's objection. But another, fairly strong, condition needs to be added. We most admire others not simply in virtue of properties that we *do not* have, but in virtue of properties that we *could not* have. There is little admiration for a person who has a P easily attained by anyone, even if it is valued; our strongest admiration will be for those having P's unattainable by us. Thus, X admires Y only if: (a1) X values P; (a2) X does not have P; (a3) Y has P; and (a4) X could not have P. (In a moment I will show why the addition of condition [a4] does not make condition [a2] redundant.) Mark Fisher writes: "My greatest admiration is reserved for people I know I can never at all closely resemble in those respects I find most admirable; . . . my deepest admiration is reserved for artists and works to whom and to which I find it absurd to compare myself and my works; and as a non-artist I am not . . . disqualified from such admiration."[19] In defending something close to condition (a4), Fisher intended to refute Hume's view that admiration is a desire to *resemble* the admired person. In effect, Fisher argues that if (a4) is a component of admiration, and if "X could not have P" entails that it is false that "X desires to have P" (for how can one desire to have something one *could not* have?), then admiration does not *require* (even rules out) "X desires to have P." This argument is, perhaps, better than Lyons's, and telling against Hume *if* Hume meant that X's desire to resemble the admired person is the desire to possess the P in virtue of which X admires Y.

Two problems about romantic love emerge from this discussion of the four conditions. First, if admiration requires a recognition of difference, and if admiration is necessary for romantic love, and if the passion for union is central to romantic love, then romantic love self-destructs. The union of the lovers X and Y will negate the difference required for admiration. Perhaps this is right: it would explain why romantic love is often here today, gone tomorrow. On the other hand, perhaps admiration is a feature of romantic love only at its beginning; this would be consistent, at least, with the causal, but not the analytic, centrality of admiration. Second, even though admiration generally does not require "X desires to have P," if the special kind of admiration found in romantic love includes that desire, then romantic lovers, given condition (a4), are engaged in the futile task of desiring what it is impossible to desire. They are under the illusion that their passion for union can be satisfied. Again, maybe this is exactly right; it would help explain why romantic love is unstable and why it is often accompanied by manias, obsessions, and self-deception. But there is an alterative conclusion, that romantic love *can* be free of these defects, because condition (a4) is too strong. We will soon return to this question.

The analysis needs to be modified one more time in light of the fact that admiration, like other attitudes and emotions, is intentional. For X to admire Y, it is not strictly necessary that Y has P, but only that X *believes* Y to have P; it makes perfectly good sense to say that X believes (wrongly, it turns out) that Y is a great chess player, and that X admires Y in virtue of having that belief. Similarly, X needs only to believe P is unattainable for X, and to believe that X does not have the valuable property in virtue of which X admires Y. Therefore, the analysis becomes "X admires Y" only if: (a1) X values P; (a2)

X believes X does not have P (or does not have it to the degree Y has it); (a3) X believes Y has P; and (a4) X believes X could not have P.

Now we can see why (a4) does not make (a2) redundant: even though "X could not have P" entails "X does not have P," the revised (a4) no longer entails the revised (a2), at least if the opacity of belief sentences is taken seriously. Now we can also uncover the relationship between admiration and idealization. It is the intentionality of admiration that *allows* for idealization. As a first approximation: idealization is a special case of the (a3) belief's being false. Whether that belief's being false means X admires Y or X has idealized Y will depend on *why* the belief is false. If X has been deliberately deceived into believing that Y has P, X still admires Y. But if X believes falsely that *Y* has P because X needs to believe that Y has P or because it makes X happy to believe that Y has P (wish fulfillment), then X has idealized Y. Matters are, however, more complex than this. Coincidentally, X might believe truly that Y has P, even when X believes that Y has P because X needs to believe it. Idealization, then, is more accurately believing, either truly or falsely, that Y has P, when the belief is the result of a wish-fulfilling or other similar psychological process. Note that, contrary to Caraway's implicit suggestion, it does not follow from the fact admiration is required for romantic love that idealization is required; idealization is merely possible, given this analysis of admiration, and if one wants to claim that idealization is required for romantic love, some other argument should be offered.

I just said that when X has been deliberately deceived (say, by Y) into believing falsely that *Y* has P, we can still say X admires Y (as long as X does not discover the deception!). This is because X had used an "evidence process" in arriving at his or her belief that Y has P. But what about other cases in which X believes that Y has P but X has only insufficient evidence for that belief? My suggestion is that, in cases in which X falsely believes that he or she has sufficient evidence for the belief that Y has P, whether X's having insufficient evidence for the belief that Y has P means that X admires Y or that X has idealized Y will depend on how X arrived at his false belief that he or she has sufficient evidence for the belief that Y has P. In cases in which X has insufficient evidence for the belief that Y has P, and the belief that the evidence is sufficient is itself the result of an evidence process, then X admires Y. X might have insufficient evidence for the belief that Y has P, but X has made an attempt to gather the relevant evidence and perhaps even to avoid wish fulfillment in believing that Y has P. On the other hand, if X believes (via some non-evidential psychological process) that he or she has sufficient evidence for the belief that Y has P, then X has idealized Y; for X has the belief that he or she has sufficient evidence for the belief that Y has P *because* he wants to continue believing that Y has P. In other words, if X wants to believe that Y has P, and that is why he or she believes it, then X will also believe that X has sufficient evidence for the belief that Y has P, because he or she needs to believe that there is sufficient evidence for the belief that Y has P (to protect the belief that Y has P). The qualification mentioned above applies here, too: in idealization, X's belief that X has sufficient evidence for the belief that Y has P might be coincidentally true.

To return, at long last, to the question with which we began. Because admiration occurs in virtue of properties that we believe we could not have (as per condition [a4]), the salient differences between the sexes are ripe for generating admiration. The male, necessarily lacking female properties, admires females in virtue of those properties, but especially females who exemplify the properties in a superior manner. For then the difference is most striking and the male recognizes most powerfully the gap between what he is and what he cannot be. And the female admires men in virtue of male properties exemplified to a high degree. When X admires Y in virtue of Y's sexual virtues, X thinks: "if I were of Y's sex, Y is the person of that sex I would most want to be." And if Y thinks the same thing about X, their eventual union will be blissful. Romantic admiration for others who differ from us sexually is to be expected as the predominant pattern and as "normal" given the nature of admiration and the ontological divide between the sexes.

This account of why the admiration in romantic love is heterosexual has obvious weaknesses. Below I weed out its "heterosexist" implications. But notice that this account of romantic admiration is not "sexist." Indeed, the account is a conceptual analysis of admiration that can be employed to explain why some romantic love practices or institutions turn out to be sexist. The account has this ability because it recognizes the intentionality of admiration. If persons believe that P is a property necessarily possessed only by males (or females), then it will be an admiration-generating property even if it is, in reality, not especially sex-linked. That is, sexist romantic love practices result from false (a4) beliefs. Both men and women might have been socially defined in terms of properties that do not faithfully reflect the ontological divide between the sexes. The best males (females) might have been defined as those who have these properties in a superior manner. The stereotypifying sexism in romantic love practices is the result of admiration being dependent on properties we believe we cannot have and a social context promulgating a certain view as to what properties are sex-linked. As Caraway rightly points out, sexist social contexts yield sexist romantic love practices. This account of admiration helps us understand how that is the case. Note that holding false (a4) beliefs is *not* to idealize. There is a big difference between falsely attributing P to a person (or coincidentally truly attributing P) as a step in a wish-fulfilling process, and correctly perceiving or judging that X has P yet admiring X because one believes falsely that only persons of X's sex can have P. Sexist romantic love practices involve faults with admiration through (a4) rather than through (a3), in which case it is wrong to claim, as Caraway does, that *sexist* practices result specifically from sexist idealizations.

The immediate response to this account of why romantic love is heterosexual is that it does not rule out homosexual romantic admiration. The range of properties that a given X could not have is not restricted to the sexual virtues of the other sex. If X is a male then X could not have, say, perfectly formed breasts, but he also could not be a male over six feet tall if he is actually five-foot-five. And if X could not have the feminine virtue of sweetness, he also could not have the masculine virtue of courage if, as part of his nature, he is a frightful coward. So there is plenty of room in the account for homosexual romantic admiration. True, we have arrived at a sexist picture of homosexual admiration, but this is a fault not of the analysis but of a particular way of picking out the sexual virtues.[20] It will not do to defend the account by saying that X could have been over six feet tall or courageous, but he never could have had those breasts. In what reasonable sense of "could" is it true that X could have been over six feet yet false that X could have had the breasts?

Further, (a4) is too strong. From the fact that we admire those people who possess properties that are difficult for many, or ourselves, to attain, it does not follow that the most profound admiration attaches to those who have properties we could not (now) have or could never have had. It is the implausibility of (a4) that makes "romantic love requires heterosexuality" a howler. A more plausible version is the weaker (a4*): X believes that it would be difficult for X to have P. If we make this modification, the reason for thinking that sexual differences will be of paramount importance in romantic admiration is lost. This version of (a4*) permits a wide variety of properties to be the basis of admiration; differences between one man and another, or one woman and another, are not excluded. Admiration could occur in virtue of what Caraway calls "human perfections." But admiration could still be sexist, if a stereotypifying social context determines what properties people do and do not have and which properties they believe it would be difficult for them to have. Thus my suggestion, that sexist romantic love practices derive from mistaken (a4) beliefs rather than from mistaken (a3) beliefs (idealization), can be retained, for the point applies just as much to (a4*) beliefs. Finally, we can now see why the passion for union in romantic love is not necessarily futile. When (a4) is replaced by (a4*), we no longer have to worry that romantic lovers desire to have a P they also believe they could *never* have. Further, a better reason why (a2) is not redundant emerges: the weaker (a4*) does not entail (a2).

7. Conclusion

We have arrived at the following model of romantic love:

Concern
Reciprocity ← The Passion for Union ↔ Admiration
Exclusivity

We could say that admiration is at the center, because admiration might cause the passion for union, which in turn yields the other three features. But I prefer to think of the passion for union as the center, because all the other four features can be derived directly from it, and because admiration might be only an early and temporary feature of romantic love.[21] Further, putting passion for union at the center of romantic love is faithful to the fact that the love in question is *romantic*. The romantic emphasis on passion, its exaltation of feeling over both reason and conviction, is captured better if the passion for union is made the center of the concept of romantic love than if, for example, either concern or admiration, or both, were put at the center.

To complete project (3) we still need to discuss how romantic love differs from other types of love in terms of these five features. For example, the love for God includes the passion for union, admiration, and the desire for reciprocity. Does this mean that the love for God is a version of romantic love? Or that romantic love is a version of the love for God? These are fascinating questions. At least I have shown the sort of philosophical argument that is required in seeking answers.

Notes

1. Discussions with Céline Léon, Theresa Kump, James Nelson, and Russell Vannoy were helpful. The earliest version of this essay was sent to the members of the Society for the Philosophy of Sex and Love in April 1986 as a reply (in advance) to the version of Carol Caraway's "Romantic Love: Neither Sexist Nor Heterosexist" delivered at the Society's May 1986 meeting. A revised version was published in *Philosophy and Theology* 1:4 (1987): 374-97 and replied to by Caraway in the journal's next issue (this volume, 403-19). This is another mild revision.

2. Carol Caraway, "Romantic Love: Neither Sexist Nor Heterosexist," this volume, 375-9; page references to this essay are supplied in the text.

3. See Elizabeth Rapaport, "On the Future of Love: Rousseau and the Radical Feminists," in Alan Soble, ed., *Philosophy of Sex*, 1st ed. (Totowa, N.J.: Littlefield, Adams, 1980), 369-88.

4. Dana Bushnell, "Love Without Sex," this volume, 381-3, at 383.

5. Iris Murdoch, *Bruno's Dream* (New York: Viking, 1964), 270.

6. See Irving Singer, *The Nature of Love, vol. 2: Courtly and Romantic* (Chicago: University of Chicago Press, 1984).

7. For a critique of this, see my "Union, Autonomy, and Concern," in Roger Lamb, ed., *Love Analyzed* (Boulder, Colo.: Westview, 1997), 65-92.

8. For a similar procedure, see George Nakhnikian's derivation of five features of "undemanding love" from its two defining and unifying features ("Love in Human Reason," *Midwest Studies in Philosophy* 3 [1978]: 286-317, at 301). See also my *The Structure of Love* (New Haven: Yale University Press, 1990), 17-18.

9. See my "Union, Autonomy, and Concern."

10. For similar silliness in Hegel and Robert Nozick, see my "Union, Autonomy, and Concern."

11. See *Structure of Love*, 233-5.

12. Bernard Williams, *New York Review of Books*, 25 April 1985, 37.

13. Søren Kierkegaard, *Works of Love* (New York: Harper and Row, 1982). See also Karol Wojtyla (Pope John Paul II), *Love and Responsibility* (New York: Farrar, Straus, Giroux, 1981).

14. Rolf Johnson, "Love, Passion, and the Need To Be Loved," paper presented to the Society for the Philosophy of Sex and Love, Philadelphia, December 1981.

15. *Ibid.*

16. See Milan Kundera's *The Book of Laughter and Forgetting* (New York: Knopf, 1980).

17. William Lyons, *Emotion* (Cambridge, Eng.: Cambridge University Press, 1980), 82-4.

18. *Ibid.*, 82.

19. Mark Fisher, "Reason, Emotion, and Love," *Inquiry* 20 (1977): 189-203, at 195.

20. See C. A. Tripp on admiration and the origin of homosexuality (*The Homosexual Matrix* [New York: McGraw-Hill, 1975], 72, 82, and *passim*).

21. Were admiration sufficient, we would (counterintuitively) love everyone we admired. "Care has been taken not only that the trees should not sweep the stars down, but also that every man who admires a fair girl should not be enamoured of her. . . . [N]ature's order is certainly benignant in not obliging us one and all to be desperately in love with the most admirable mortal we have ever seen" (George Eliot, *Daniel Deronda* [New York: New American Library, 1979], 85). If we read this passage in a way unintended by Eliot, it will sound like Woody Allen's "Not only is there no God, but try getting a plumber on weekends" (*Getting Even* [New York: Vintage Books, 1978], 25).

Carol Caraway
(photograph: Larry Gesoff)

President
The Society for the Philosophy of Sex and Love
1992-

Thirty-Nine

Romantic Love: A Patchwork[1]

Carol Caraway

In this essay, I defend my earlier nonessentialist analysis of romantic love as involving concern, the passion for union, the desire for reciprocation, admiration, and idealization. There is no central element that unifies the analysis. Though they are not parts of romantic love, sexual desire and exclusivity enhance and generally accompany it. I argue that my analysis is superior to one that proposes a unifying central element. By allowing variation and conflict among the various elements of romantic love, my analysis better explains its turbulence and volatility and it accommodates both realism and idealism.

1. Introduction

In "The Unity of Romantic Love,"[2] Alan Soble charges me with wrongly criticizing feminists and gay liberationists for condemning the concept of romantic love. He insists that they have been engaged not in philosophical analysis, but in the sociological and psychological investigation and evaluation of social institutions and practices. It is true that many feminists and gay liberationists are engaged in social scientific theorizing and rightly condemn the contemporary Western institution of romantic love as sexist and heterosexist. Some, however, are engaged in philosophical analysis and wrongly condemn not just the practice but the *concept* of romantic love as essentially sexist and heterosexist.

Consider, for example, the position of the best known such theorist, Ti-Grace Atkinson, who defines romantic love as "a euphoric state of fantasy in which the victim transforms her oppressor into her redeemer."[3] The female turns her natural hostility towards her male oppressor against herself. The combination of his power, her self-hatred, and her desire for a meaningful life produces "a yearning for her stolen life—her Self—that is the delusion and poignancy of love." "'Love' is the natural response of the victim to the rapist."[4] It is "the woman's pitiful deluded attempt to attain the human: by fusing she hopes to blur the male-female dichotomy."[5] Thus, for Atkinson, "the phenomenon of [romantic] love is the psychological pivot in the persecution of women."[6] Atkinson is arguing that romantic love by its very nature is sexist and heterosexist. Thus, society cannot be free from sexism and heterosexism so long as romantic love exists. Conversely, in a society free from sexism and heterosexism, there can be no romantic love. Nonsexist, nonheterosexist romantic love is logically impossible.

2. The Concept of Romantic Love

In "Romantic Love: Neither Sexist Nor Heterosexist," I argued that although the institution of romantic love in Western society includes sexist and heterosexist elements, those elements are not crucial to romantic love.[7] Nonsexist, nonheterosexist romantic love is possible. For the crucial constituents of romantic love are concern, admiration, idealization, the desire for reciprocation, and the passion for union. None requires either traditional gender role stereotypes or heterosexual desire. Soble argues that the fundamental problem with my analysis of romantic love is that I find no central element and so produce not a unified concept, but a "patchwork" (392) in which the separate elements "hang together almost by accident" (390).

My analysis is a patchwork since it is not unified by a central element. A patchwork quilt, however, is not simply miscellaneous scraps that hang together almost by accident. It consists of color-coordinated scraps of material carefully arranged to form an intricate pattern and painstakingly stitched to provide the practical benefits of warmth and durability. Similarly, my analysis of romantic love is more than a motley of elements that hang together almost by accident. As Soble himself acknowledges, I connect reciprocity, exclusivity, and sexual desire to the passion for union. These connections provide the foundation for Soble's unified analysis.

Soble's evaluation of my analysis is based on the questionable assumption that an adequate analysis of a concept such as romantic love must be unified. The later Wittgenstein's attacks on essentialism and development of alternative accounts of the meanings of general terms are well known. In light of them, a contemporary philosopher cannot simply assume that only a unified analysis is adequate. A lack of unification does not entail mere accidental conjunction. There are other alternatives. My analysis is one. I agree with Soble that a philosophical analysis of a concept such as romantic love need not *fully* match our ideas and experiences. Nonetheless, I insist that an analysis fit the phenomenon well enough to be of some practical value.

3. Concern

Realist critics argue that romantic love is not real love. For real love is an act of will involving genuine concern for another's welfare while romantic love is a natural inclination in which concern for one's own needs takes precedence over concern for another's welfare. Real love is stable, enduring, voluntary, and altruistic. Romantic love is turbulent, temporary, involuntary, and egoistic.[8] I did not defend romantic love against this realist criticism. Rolf Johnson had already done so,[9] and I agree with him that genuine concern is part of romantic love. I will now consider both the realist claim that romantic love is essentially involuntary and egoistic and Johnson's idealist response that concern for the other's welfare is essential both to love as an act of will and to romantic love. Then I will evaluate Soble's idealist response that the realist charge of egocentricity loses its force in light of the passion for union.

M. Scott Peck argues that, whereas real love is a voluntary act of will, romantic love is a natural inclination and, therefore, involuntary and incompatible with real love.[10] In defending idealism against such realist criticisms, Johnson uses a dispositional analysis of concern to bridge the gap between love as a natural inclination (as in romantic love or Plato's *eros*) and love as an act of will (as in Peck's analysis of genuine love or Biblical *agape*). I agreed with Johnson that concern is a disposition to promote the other's welfare shared by love as a natural inclination and love as an act of will.[11] I then argued that Johnson's dispositional analysis must be combined with an account of the role of circumstances in distinguishing various types of concern. Finally, I criticized Johnson's essentialist assumption that there must be some element common and peculiar to all types of love that explains why they are all called love.

Johnson fails to consider the role of circumstances in distinguishing various types of concern. The circumstances in which we typically act to promote another's welfare are different for concern as a natural inclination than for concern as an act of will. Either type of concern might lead us to buy dinner for someone. But concern as an act of will would typically lead us to do this for someone who was starving while concern as a natural inclination would typically lead us to do this for someone who was not starving. Concern as an act of will typically disposes us to confer benefits on another who is in need. Concern as a natural inclination, on the other hand, disposes us to confer benefits on another whether or not that person is in need. Johnson also overlooks differences in the benefits conferred in the two types of love. Love as a natural inclination leads us to give flowers and candy. Love as an act of will leads us to donate used clothing and furniture.

Perhaps Johnson ignored the differences in circumstances and benefits because he first assumed there must be an element common and peculiar to all forms of love that explains why they are all called love. But just as skill alone cannot explain why all the various types of games are called games, so concern alone cannot explain why all the various types of love are called love. Many different characteristic features form family resemblances among the various types of games and explain why they are all called games. Similarly, many different characteristic features form family resemblances among the various types of love and explain why all are called love.[12] (I will not list these features here. The list will obviously include the elements of romantic love and other elements.) Thus, while I applaud Johnson's dispositional analysis of concern and his attempt to bridge the gap between love as a natural inclination and love as an act of will, I question the essentialist assumption behind his account.

A realist, such as Peck, might see the differences in circumstances and types of benefits as evidence that the two types of concern are so different that romantic love (a natural inclination) cannot be real love (an act of will). Unlike Johnson's idealist defense, however, such an argument is based on the questionable assumption that two things cannot rightly be called by the same name unless they share a common essence. Having rejected this assumption, I need not accept the realist contention.

Peck argues that romantic love cannot involve genuine concern for the other's welfare. For romantic love involves the inevitable breakdown of the boundary between lovers. Genuine concern, on the other hand, requires that the distinction between them be maintained by each perceiving the other "as someone who has a totally separate identity."[13] Peck's position seems self-contradictory. For he claims both that genuine love and concern require separateness and that we cannot genuinely love another unless we genuinely love ourselves.[14] On the one hand, if I can genuinely love myself, then genuine concern cannot require separateness, unless I can be separate from myself. Moreover, if genuine concern does not require separateness, then the breakdown of ego boundaries in romantic love does not preclude genuine concern. On the other hand, if genuine concern requires separateness, then I cannot genuinely love myself unless I can be separate from myself. Can I be separate from myself? If not, then I cannot genuinely love myself or others, and genuine love of any sort is impossible.

Peck could resolve this apparent contradiction by distinguishing genuine love of self, which does not require separateness, from genuine love of another, which does. Such a distinction, however, would be counter to his project of providing "a single definition of love" that includes both love of self and love of others.[15] My response to Peck (with which I believe Johnson would agree) is that to avoid contradiction, he must allow a sense of separateness in which I can be separate from and, therefore, genuinely love myself.

Soble answers the realist criticism that genuine concern is not part of romantic love by arguing that the concern in romantic love is a function of the passion for union. That passion breaks down the distinction between X and Y so "X's concern for Y is indistinguishable from X's concern for X" (390). Such an answer is unsatisfactory. It states both that the distinction between X's interests and Y's interests will disappear and that X will want to be the one who furthers Y's interests. But if the distinction between X's interests and Y's interests has disappeared, then to say that X will want to be the one who furthers Y's interests is to say that X will want to be the one who further X's interests. Thus, the romantic lover becomes a rugged individualist (hardly the consequence Soble intends). These difficulties spring from Soble's view of romantic union as a magical merging that defies rational analysis.

Soble correctly summarizes my account of romantic concern: (a) concern is an inclination to enhance the other's welfare; (b) concern is incompatible with treating the beloved merely as a means; and (c) concern is not necessarily paternalistic. But he then mistakenly claims that "(2a) X wants the good for Y in X's sense of what is good for Y" is "ruled out for romantic love" by my "rejection of paternalism" (388). I never claimed that paternalism is necessarily excluded from the kinds of concern that can play a role in romantic love. What I argued was what Soble himself states in (c): the concern in romantic love "is not necessarily paternalistic."[16] Paternalism's not being a necessary component of romantic love does not entail its being necessarily excluded from romantic love.

On my account, the concern for the other's welfare involved in romantic love can take many forms: paternalistic, nonpaternalistic, self-sacrificially altruistic, benignly altruistic, and so on. I oppose feminists who contend that in romantic love, the male's concern is necessarily paternalistic, the female's necessarily self-sacrificially altruistic. For although romantic concern often takes these forms in our sexist society, it can take other forms, especially in a nonsexist society. As I can be concerned for a friend's welfare without being either paternalistic or self-sacrificially altruistic, so romantic concern can avoid these undesirable forms.

Soble is correct that romantic love's essentially involving a loss of autonomy does not make it inherently sexist. I did not discuss this point in "Romantic Love" because Sharon Bishop had already defended it.[17] Bishop distinguishes a benign dependency crucial to romantic love from the destructive dependency that often accompanies it in our sexist society. On Bishop's analysis, X is benignly dependent on Y if and only if X's desires cannot be satisfied unless Y is present, has certain attitudes, and behaves in certain ways.[18] What Bishop calls benign dependency I call the desire for reciprocation. On my analysis, the desire for reciprocation results from the passion for union. For X cannot achieve psychological union with Y unless Y has certain attitudes and behaves in certain ways. In contrast, X is destructively dependent on Y if and only if X desires to live through Y and thereby to avoid either suffering or developing personal interests, plans, and standards. Although destructive dependency often accompanies romantic love in our society, it is not crucial to romantic love as benign dependency is.

4. The Passion for Union and Reciprocation

Johnson and I agree that romantic love involves passion. Johnson argues that a necessary ingredient of romantic love is passion: a high level of psychological energy connected either with X's concern for Y's welfare or with X's desire for reciprocation or with both. I argue that the primary objective of X's romantic passion is neither to benefit nor to be benefitted by Y, but to become one with Y. The passion for union is closely connected to reciprocity and exclusivity, for achieving intimacy is difficult without reciprocity and exclusivity. I argued against Johnson that the passion in romantic love is a passionate desire for psychological union rather than for other things, such as reciprocity. I did not argue that such passion is the central element that unifies all the other elements of romantic love. I maintain, and have always maintained, that romantic love consists of a number of important elements, none of which is central. Both the passion for union and concern are important elements of romantic love. I make neither central because I am not developing an essentialist analysis that ties all other elements of romantic love to one central element.

Dana Bushnell[19] and Soble (387) assert that I made concern trump the other features of romantic love. I did not; I agree with Bushnell that romantic love is characterized by conflicting passions and desires. I contended the following. (1) There are cases in which concern for the other's welfare conflicts with the desire for reciprocation. (2) Among such cases, there are some in which concern for the other's welfare is stronger than the desire for reciprocation. (3) When the concern for the other's welfare is stronger than the desire for reciprocation, then "there is a sense in which the lover desires reciprocation, namely, that it would be desired if it were in the other's interest; given the actual circumstances, however, reciprocation is not in the other's interest and hence is not desired." In such cases, "the lover might be said to have a *prima facie* desire for reciprocation, one that does not become an all-things-considered desire because of concern that reciprocation would be harmful to the other."[20]

I hold that there are cases in which concern outweighs the desire for reciprocation. Although I did not discuss such cases, I also hold that (4) there are cases in which the desire for reciprocation is stronger than concern for the other's welfare. (5) In such cases, there is a sense in which the lover is concerned for the other's welfare. Given the actual circumstances, however, the desire for reciprocation outweighs concern for the other's welfare. These, too, are cases of romantic love on my analysis. Again, although I did not discuss such cases, I also hold that (6) there are cases of romantic love in which the desire for reciprocation and concern for the other's welfare are equally strong. (7) In such cases there is a sense in which the lover is both concerned for the other's welfare and desires reciprocation. Given the actual circumstances, however, the two elements counterbalance each other. On my analysis, these, too, are cases of romantic love.

Finally, and perhaps most important, (8) there are cases of romantic love in which concern and the desire for reciprocation war against each other so their relative weights vary over time. Sometimes concern dominates, sometimes the passion for union dominates, and so on. Such cases obviously exist and cannot all be analyzed as conflicts between romantic love and other values, as Soble would have us believe.

The primary weakness of Soble's analysis is the very unity he views as its strength. Making the passion for union central weakens the other features and distorts the concept of romantic love. With the passion for union predominant, all conflicts between elements must be analyzed as conflicts between romantic love and other values, for example *agape*. On such a view, analyzing some conflicts as being among various elements of romantic love itself is not an option. Acknowledging conflicts between romantic love and other values, I also want to allow conflicts among the elements of romantic love. On Soble's analysis, whenever concern becomes equal to or greater than the passion for union, romantic love must cease. This analysis, however, is counter to our ordinary experiences, intuitions, and concepts. We talk, act, and write as if romantic concern and the passion for union can war against each other without romantic love ceasing. Soble must analyze all such conflicts as the repeated destruction and resurrection of romantic love. I can analyze some as the turbulence of continued romantic love; this is a more intuitive analysis.

On Soble's analysis, at the moment when X decides (out of concern for Y's welfare) not to pursue psychological union with Y, X's romantic love for Y must cease. It is drummed out of existence by a stronger competing value. My analysis allows such an explanation of some cases, but also allows others in which romantic love continues after the decision not to pursue psychological union. Unlike Soble, I can maintain that romantic love continues but has taken a certain form because one of its elements has dominated another. Romantic concern, for example (which grows out of admiration and idealization and is, therefore, the concern characteristic of romantic love, rather than some other sort of concern), has dominated the passion for union so X does not seek intimacy with Y.

My analysis explains much of the turbulence and volatility of romantic love as the result of conflicts between its own elements. It thereby achieves a synthesis between realism and idealism. Soble's analysis is strictly idealist. Making the passion for union central is the hallmark of the idealist tradition. The realist tradition, in contrast, denies that romantic love includes nonegoistic concern. Focusing on science and sense experience, realism reduces the passion for union to sexual desire, childhood dependence on parents, or some other natural phenomenon distorted by idealistic philosophies. My analysis contains elements of idealism: the passion for union and genuine concern for the other's welfare. The passion for union, however, is not central. Thus, my analysis can both refute the realist contention that romantic love excludes genuine concern and satisfy the realist demand for faithfulness to science and ordinary sense experience.[21]

Soble and Bushnell might have attributed to me the view that concern must trump the other elements because I called concern a necessary element and the desire for reciprocation a crucial but non-necessary element. I did not mean that concern trumps the desire for reciprocation. I called concern "a necessary element" and the desire for reciprocation "a crucial but non-necessary element" because I agreed with Johnson that concern is present in all kinds of love while the desire for reciprocation is not. The desire for reciprocation, on the other hand, is not in all kinds of love, like competition among players is not in all types of games. As competition is crucial to certain games, but not to others, so the desire for reciprocation is crucial to romantic love, but not to other kinds of love. By "crucial," I mean "characteristic," "constitutive," or "criterial" (in the sense of the later Wittgenstein).

Concern, admiration, idealization, the desire for reciprocation, and the passion for union are all characteristic features, constitutive elements, or criteria of romantic love. One of these characteristic features, however, is crucial to romantic love's being a type of love, that is, concern. Others (admiration and idealization) are crucial to romantic love's being a natural sentiment (and to romantic concern's being the result of such a sentiment). Without *prima facie* concern for the other's welfare that grows out of admiration and idealization of the other, there is no romantic love, no matter how passionate the desire for psychological union. I characterize the passion for union as the desire for shared ecstatic experiences and psychological closeness or intimacy. Soble characterizes romantic union as a mystical breakdown of "the psychological, even existential, boundaries between two separate identities." "There are no wholly separate X and Y" because the "categories of self and other" have been transcended (389).

The notion that lovers can merge with one another is a strange, elusive idea. It dominates idealism and plays a significant role in realism. For idealists, merging "negates and even destroys the boundaries of routine existence." It is magical and not susceptible to rational analysis. For realists, on the other hand, merging is a way of satisfying egoistic needs. It occurs by natural processes and is susceptible to rational analysis.[22] Peck, for example, characterizes romantic merging as "an act of regression" to "the time when we were merged with our mothers in infancy."[23]

I maintain that psychological closeness or union is susceptible of rational analysis but is not essentially egoistic. Thus, my characterization includes elements of both realism and idealism. I have not yet developed a complete account of psychological union and will not do so in this essay. I have indicated that psychological union involves intimacy and shared ecstatic experiences, such as sexual intercourse.

5. Sexual Desire

Bushnell argues that sexual desire is essential to romantic love, for it distinguishes romantic love from other kinds of love, such as parental love. Parents might experience concern, admiration, the desire for reciprocation, the passion for union, and even exclusivity, without being romantically in love with their offspring so long as sexual desire is absent.[24] My response to Bushnell is that sexual desire is not needed to distinguish romantic love from parental love. The two can be distinguished by (1) admiration and idealization, (2) the desire for reciprocation, and (3) the passion for union. On my analysis, romantic love requires admiration and idealization. Parental love requires neither. Parents might admire and even idealize their children, but need do neither to have parental love for them. Indeed, we prize parental love for being unconditional in the sense that it does not require admiration or idealization. Further, following Bishop, I can also distinguish romantic love from parental love by differences in the desire for reciprocation. Loving parents care about their children's good, but do not expect that care to be returned at the same level.[25]

Finally, I can distinguish romantic love from parental love by appealing to the passion for union. I agree with Bushnell that a mother might desire a degree of psychological closeness with her child. When the child is an infant, the distinction of being separate individuals might be blurred. Bushnell is wrong to claim that these facts imply that parental love involves a passion for union and is, therefore, indistinguishable from romantic love on my analysis. The blurring of boundaries between mother and infant results both from the child's former fetal state and from the infant's current dependence upon its mother. This blurring of boundaries is a starting point rather than a goal of the relationship between mother and infant. As Soble points out (391), maternal love seeks to increase the infant's individuation and separation from the mother. Romantic love, in contrast, seeks to decrease the lovers' separation.

On my account of romantic love, sexual desire is not a necessary element or criterion of romantic love. It is a symptom that has been found through experience to coincide with X's passionate desire for union with Y. Sexual desire is important to romantic love because the passion for union is crucial and because sexual encounters between human beings tend to promote psychological intimacy. As Bushnell correctly states, sexual desire is excluded from parental love by definition. To distinguish romantic love, however, from parental love,

I need not agree with Bushnell that romantic love requires sexual desire. I can simply assert that parental love precludes sexual desire while romantic love allows and is generally accompanied by it.

I have argued that sexual desire is not needed to distinguish romantic love from parental love. I shall now clarify further my reasons for contending that sexual desire is not necessary to romantic love. Bushnell and Soble assert that I might have made this contention to allay the realist objection that romantic love is egoistic because it serves sexual desire. They add that such a contention is unnecessary, for the realist objection undercuts my position on concern only if the realist establishes that all sexual desire is a desire to use the other merely as a means to my own ends. I did not hold sexual desire unnecessary to allay this realist objection. Indeed, I argued that in romantic love, sexual desire is a desire to share sexual experiences that promote psychological union.

Both Johnson and Soble argue that conscious sexual desire might not be necessary for romantic love. Soble thinks that Daphnis and Chloe provide a counterexample to the claim that romantic love requires sexuality (394). Johnson argues that conscious sexual desire might be absent because children can fall romantically in love long before puberty; Dante's love for Beatrice at age nine is perhaps the most famous example. I used to agree with Atkinson, Peck, Bushnell, and others, that sexual desire is essential to romantic love. But I became convinced that conscious sexual desire is not essential, persuaded partly by arguments such as Johnson's and Soble's and partly by independent evidence. I continue to adhere to this position.

Still, I now realize more work must be done to resolve the issue of the relationship between romantic love and conscious and unconscious sexual desire. Bushnell and other realists might analyze childhood romantic love by appealing to Freudian theories of childhood sexuality. Thus, they might maintain that such theories establish that prepubescent children are clearly capable of unconscious sexual desire, and perhaps also of certain sorts of conscious sexual desire. Thus, until the notions of conscious and unconscious sexual desire are clarified, their connections to romantic love will remain a problem.

6. Exclusivity

In opposition to Soble's view that exclusivity is essential to romantic love, Johnson, Bishop, and I think it possible to romantically love more than one person at a time. The interest in exclusivity must, therefore, have another explanation. Johnson and Bishop suggest that exclusivity might be important because there is not enough time and energy to love more than one person.[26] Bishop suggests that not being the exclusive love object raises doubts because exclusivity is good assurance of genuine love. I acknowledge that it is possible to be concerned about, admire, idealize, and desire reciprocation from and psychological union with more than one person at a time.[27] On my analysis, exclusivity is important to romantic love because exclusivity promotes intimacy and psychological union. Soble adopts my explanation of the importance of exclusivity. Yet, he criticizes my failure to make exclusivity essential and my reliance on Simmel's "silly nonsense" (392).

Soble's criticism of Simmel arises from a common misunderstanding of Simmel's work. Best known for his essays on microscopic issues of personal interaction, Simmel also developed a sophisticated macrosociology. Familiar only with Simmel's microsociology, critics such as Soble argue that Simmel ignores and even denies the influence of society on personal relations such as romantic love. In his discussion of exclusivity, Soble states that the "third" Simmel fails to acknowledge is society.[28] Soble has failed to realize two things. First, Simmel was developing a microsociology. In microsociology, society is not the sort of thing that counts as a third element. Second, in developing a microsociology, Simmel was not denying the influence of society on personal relations or the validity of macrosociology. Indeed, his microsociology is embedded in a broad dialectical theory that interrelates the cultural and individual levels.

Simmel's position is that intimacy is more likely in the dyad, where the members are less likely to view the group as something independent of themselves. This viewpoint is less likely in the dyad for several reasons. (1) The dyad cannot continue to exist after one of its members dies. (2) The dyad includes no third member to act as arbiter or mediator for disputes between the two members, so they must settle their disputes themselves. (3) The dyad includes no third member to use such disputes for personal gain, so their negotiations are not threatened by such use. (4) The dyad includes no third member to be an object of competition between the two, so their intimacy is not threatened by such competition. (5) The dyad includes no third member to share in their personal interdependence. Consequently, "In the dyad, the [micro]sociological process remains, in principle, within personal interdependence and does not result in a structure that grows beyond its elements."[29] This is the basis of intimacy.

7. Admiration and Idealization

Unlike Johnson, who treats admiration as a feature of romantic concern, Soble and I treat admiration as a separate essential element of romantic love. Romantic love requires admiration. Claiming both that X romantically loves Y, and that X admires nothing about Y, is contradictory. I analyzed romantic idealization and argued that it requires neither sexist stereotypes nor heterosexuality. I neither analyzed admiration nor explained its relation to idealization. I will remedy those deficiencies here.

Soble analyzes admiration and idealization to discover how they are related and why someone would believe that romantic love requires heterosexuality. He then attacks my claim that sexist romantic love practices result specifically from the sexist content of traditional romantic idealizations. According to Soble, "X admires Y" in virtue of P only if "(a1) X values P; (a2) X believes X does not have P (or does not have it to the degree Y has it); (a3) X believes Y has P; and (a4) X believes X could not have P" (397-8). Moreover, sexist romantic love practices result not from sexist romantic idealizations, as I had claimed, but from false (a4) beliefs. I stand charged with ignoring the difference between X's attributing P to Y as a step in a process of wish fulfillment and X's correctly perceiving that Y has P and then admiring Y because X falsely believes that only persons of Y's gender can have P.

Soble argues that gender differences would be crucial to romantic admiration if clause (a4) were true in the analysis of admiration. However, admiration, for Soble, requires not (a4), "X believes X could not have P," but only the weaker (a4*), "X believes that it would be difficult for X to have P" (400). Soble thinks that (a4*) eliminates the reason for thinking that romantic admiration requires gender differences, but his explanation is unsatisfactory. While Rousseau and Schopenhauer, for example, viewed romantic admiration as essentially heterosexual, neither believed that romantic admiration requires (a4). Schopenhauer asserted that X will admire in Y not only perfections and even imperfections opposed to his own, but also health, strength, and beauty: perfections shared by X and Y.[30] Similarly, Rousseau asserted that X will admire in Y not only perfections of the opposite sex that X necessarily lacks, but also perfections that X and Y share.[31]

His zeal to explain the belief that romantic admiration requires heterosexuality leads Soble to defend an inaccurate and archaic analysis of admiration involving (a1), (a2), (a3), and (a4*). Soble's (a1), "X values P," and (a3), "X believes Y has P," *do* state necessary conditions for X to admire Y. His (a4*), "X believes it would be difficult for X to have P," and (a2), "X believes X does not have P," do not. I can admire someone for his mastery of French though I believe I could learn French without difficulty. I can admire another for her mastery of German while believing I have mastered it equally well. Even Rousseau and Schopenhauer wrote of X's admiring in Y characteristics possessed by X.

Soble apparently includes (a2) and (a4*) to capture both the sense of wonder involved in admiration and the notion that admiration requires the recognition of a difference. Today, however, admiration is seldom used in the old sense of wonder. Moreover, an analysis can capture much of that sense without including either (a4*) or (a2). On my analysis, X admires Y in virtue of P only if (a1) X values P; (2) X values Y for having P; (a3) X believes Y has P; (4) X believes having P (at least to the extent that Y has it) is rare for someone like Y; and (5) X feels delight at Y's having P. (4) and (5) capture the sense of wonder at Y's having P. (4) captures the important notion that admiration requires the recognition of a difference. While Soble is right that admiration requires the recognition of a difference, he is wrong about what that difference is. The required difference is not between X and Y, but between Y and others like Y. Even Rousseau and Schopenhauer recognized that admiration involved recognizing a difference between Y and others like Y, for they argued that romantic admiration must be of a Y pre-eminent among her sex.[32]

Soble also asks whether anyone asserts the howler that romantic love requires heterosexual desire. The real howler, however, is his question. His mistaken explanation must have led him to ignore both the view's prevalence and its usual explanation. As I had indicated, both Rousseau and Schopenhauer hold this view. Andreas Capellanus, the codifier of courtly love, states, "love cannot exist except between two persons of opposite sexes. Between two men or two women love can find no place."[33] Although many contemporary feminists and gay liberationists do not make this assumption, some do. Ti-Grace Atkinson is the best-known example.

Like Rousseau, Schopenhauer, and Capellanus, Atkinson assumes that romantic love is essentially heterosexual because she ties romantic love to sexual reproduction. For Schopenhauer, the explanation of X's romantic admiration and passion for a particular Y is that the Will is driving X and Y to produce a child. Thus, romantic admiration is "really an instinct directed to what is best for the species."[34] Atkinson sets Schopenhauer on his head. Agreeing that romantic love serves sexual reproduction, she views romantic love, not as an instinct, but as a social institution that can and should be eliminated. Schopenhauer urges us to escape the Will through renunciation.[35] Atkinson argues that as the source of women's oppression, sexual reproduction should be replaced with extrauterine conception and incubation (possibilities inconceivable to Schopenhauer). Romantic love and heterosexual desire are merely social institutions serving sexual reproduction. They will disappear once sexual reproduction is eliminated.[36]

Soble asserts that contemporary heterosexists do not hold that romantic love requires heterosexuality; their awareness of public displays of homosexual romance fuels their prejudices. Soble has overlooked the common heterosexist myth that gay males and females are driven only by overwhelming lust. Constantly "on the make," they are a menace to adults and children of their own sex and incapable of romantic love.[37] Invoking this myth, many contemporary heterosexists view public homosexual displays not as expressions of romantic love, but as expressions of lust that parody romantic love. Such heterosexists believe romantic love serves reproduction and is, therefore, essentially heterosexual. So-called homosexual or gay romantic love is a contradiction in terms. Love between persons of the same sex cannot serve sexual reproduction; therefore, genuine gay romantic love cannot exist. Although unsound and immoral, such reasoning plays a role in contemporary heterosexism and should be addressed by philosophers.

I turn now to Soble's criticisms of my discussion of idealization. His primary criticism is that my discussion is irrelevant: I fail to argue either that idealization is essential to romantic love or that romantic admiration requires idealization. I should simply have argued that while admiration is essential to romantic love, idealization is not, and it is idealization that is sexist, heterosexist, and dehumanizing. This line of reasoning, however, overlooks the important connection between idealization and the passion for union. Soble suggests that admiration might be "the causal center" of romantic love. "Because I admire you, I want to merge with you" (394). Since we can admire others without wanting to merge with them, however, admiration alone cannot cause the passion for union. To cause such a passion, admiration must either become an especially powerful sort of romantic admiration or combine with other factors.

Soble creates a special romantic admiration by adding to his four elements of admiration a claim that I label "(a5)": X desires to have P through union with Y. Soble's romantic admiration thus resembles envy; X not only values P, but wants to possess P. But (a5) is an *ad hoc* device for connecting romantic admiration to the passion for union. It does not tell us why X passionately desires to unite with Y rather than with others who have P. Yet, on Soble's analysis, that passion is the very thing romantic admiration is supposed to explain. Literature pictures the passion for union resulting from magic; natural causes are too weak. Given his magical conception of the passion for union, Soble should have realized that his envy-like romantic admiration is too weak to produce such a passion.

On Soble's analysis, admiration is romantic only if X desires to have P through union with Y. What does this mean? Ordinarily, "X desires to have P" means that X desires to be a person who has the virtue, skill, or quality P. How can uniting with Y, who has P, make X a person who has the virtue, skill, or quality P? Soble is apparently suggesting that uniting with Y magically transforms X from a person without P into a person with P. He apparently believes that as romantic union magically transforms Y's interests into X's interests and Y's welfare into X's welfare, so it magically confers Y's properties upon X. Thus, X is magically transformed into a person having Y's properties.

> We desire to merge only with what we admire. Because in the merging the boundary between my-self and your-self breaks down, I will in a sense become you and so must be able to foresee with pleasure taking on your character as if it were my own. (394)

Soble acknowledges that his magical notion of romantic union violates the laws of logic. I prefer a less magical notion compatible with both the laws of logic and an adequate analysis of admiration.

How is a philosopher to explain the passion for union? Not by magic nor by admiration alone. Perhaps, partly by admiration and partly by something similar to, but more profound than admiration: idealization. Rousseau, Schopenhauer, and Stendhal give idealization the causal role in romantic love that Soble attributes to his envy-like romantic admiration. In "The Metaphysics of Sexual Love," Schopenhauer recognizes infinite degrees of romantic attraction: the more Y suits X's desires, the more powerful the attraction will be.[38] In one of his letters, Rousseau writes, "the love which I conceive, and have been able to feel, is fired by the illusory image of the loved one's perfection."[39]

Soble's notion of idealization is different from those of Schopenhauer, Rousseau, and Stendhal. Soble analyzes romantic admiration as involving (a1), (a2), (a3) ["X believes that Y has P"], and (a4*). He then characterizes romantic idealization as a special case of the (a3)-belief being improperly based: X romantically idealizes Y only if X believes, either truly or falsely, that Y has P as a result of a nonevidential psychological process. This process involves X's believing, either truly or falsely, that he has sufficient evidence that Y has P as a result of a nonevidential psychological process. (To clarify Soble's confusing analysis, I will use "B1" to designate the belief that Y has P and "B2" the belief that X has sufficient evidence that Y has P.)

Such an analysis of romantic idealization is unsatisfactory. Soble characterizes it first as (B1)'s and then as (B2)'s being the result of wish fulfillment (or some other nonevidential psychological process). He connects the two characterizations as follows. If X believes (B1) because he wants to believe it, then X will also believe (B2) because he wants to continue believing (B1) and needs to believe (B2) to protect (B1). I see no reason to accept Soble's questionable claim that (B1), a belief resulting from wish fulfillment, must be protected by (B2): the belief that (B1) is based on sufficient evidence. (B1) must be protected by (B2) for X to be epistemically responsible. X's epistemic irresponsibility, however, has already been established by his believing (B1) because he wants to believe it rather than because he has come to believe it as the result of an evidence-gathering process. An X epistemically irresponsible enough to believe (B1) just because he wants to believe it is also irresponsible enough to continue to believe (B1) without basing it on (B2). Soble should have characterized idealization simply as (B1)'s being based on wish fulfillment or a similar nonevidential process.

According to Soble, X's romantic admiration and idealization of Y is based on Y's having a particular property P. As Stendhal points out, however, X can admire Y for a particular trait or feature without loving Y. In love, X sees in Y "a cluster of perfections."[40] To experience the passion for union, X must admire Y not in virtue of one property (P_1), but in virtue of many properties (P_1, P_2, P_3, . . . , P_n).

On my analysis, romantic idealization involves X's having a conscious or unconscious ideal of a perfect lover (Iy) and responding to an actual person (Y) on the basis of that ideal. On Soble's analysis, admiration makes idealization possible, for idealizing is forming (a3) beliefs irresponsibly. Soble fails to explain the motivation or mechanism for such irresponsible belief formation. He asserts that such beliefs result from wish fulfillment: X believes that Y has P because doing so makes X happy. But he never tells us why believing that Y has P makes X happy. My analysis answers this question: believing that Y has P makes X happy because P is a property of X's ideal.

On Soble's analysis, idealization is a form of epistemic irresponsibility and, thus, inherently undesirable. Romantic love requires admiration, which makes idealization possible, but it does not require irresponsible idealization. On my analysis, romantic love requires both admiration and idealization. As I pointed out, feminists and chauvinists alike have argued that romantic idealization is inherently undesirable. For it involves or leads to (1) the formation of beliefs based solely on wish fulfillment, (2) the deception of one person by another, (3) the sacrifice of one person's autonomy for the sake of another (self-sacrificial altruism), and (4) the violation of one person's autonomy by another (paternalism). My analysis of idealization allows all of these faults, but requires none. It can, therefore, both explain them and show how romantic love can avoid them.

In contrast, Soble's analysis requires (1) and allows no others. For him, (2) involves improperly based admiration, not idealization. (3) and (4) involve improper forms of concern, not idealization. I agree that X might admire Y even when X has been deceived. I want to explain what motivated Y (or someone else) to deceive X. I explain it in terms of Y's (or someone else's) wanting X to believe that Y embodies X's ideal. Soble states only that in this case, X would admire but not idealize Y. I agree with Soble that (3) and (4) involve undesirable forms of concern. On my view, idealization need not be harmful. For it need not involve faults (1) through (4), but can be a process of X's valuing Y's actual qualities (perfections and defects).

Soble's narrow analysis of idealization can accommodate neither cases in which X changes Iy to fit Y, nor cases in which X actually discovers that Y fits X's original ideal. Soble has no Iy and so can acknowledge neither changes in Iy nor a fit between Iy and Y. On his analysis, cases in which X discovers that Y fits Iy involve admiration, not idealization. On my analysis, such cases involve idealization because X compares Y to X's ideal. Nonetheless, such cases need involve no epistemic irresponsibility, deception, or dehumanization. Indeed, X's discovering that Y has, and valuing Y for having, certain qualities, might reveal to Y perfections of which Y was unaware and, thus, increase Y's self-esteem. Similarly, X's valuing qualities society considers defects might change Y's appraisal of those qualities and, thus, increase Y's self-esteem.

Since X can modify Iy, Y's not having certain Ps that are part of X's initial ideal need not lead to the dehumanizing processes of (3) X's forcing Y to change to fit X's initial ideal or (4) Y's trying to change to fit it. For rather than Y's changing to fit X's ideal, X's ideal can be changed to fit Y. Accordingly, rather than Cyrano's having his nose bobbed to fit Roxane's ideal, Roxane can modify her ideal to include having a large nose.

Idealization need not involve faults (1) through (4). It often does when we experience the passion for union with Y before having determined the extent to which Y fits our ideal. Then the passion for union tempts us to believe that Y fits our ideal in ways we have not investigated. We might, thus, see certain actions as evidence for a P and irresponsibly overlook or discount contravening evidence (a possibility Soble overlooks). Or we might believe that Y has P only because we want to believe it (Soble's idealization). On the other hand, we might be epistemically responsible, discover that Y does not have P, then try to force Y to acquire P. Although Roxane would have to be farsighted to overlook Cyrano's nose, she might tell him that she will return his affections only if he acquires a new nose.

8. Conclusion

I have argued that romantic love need not involve sexism and heterosexism. These undesirable elements have become involved in our Western institution of romantic love through the process of idealization. For the content of our society's romantic idealizations has been sexist and heterosexist, and the romantic idealization process itself has led to deception, epistemic irresponsibility, and dehumanization. If my analysis is correct, feminists and gay liberationists need not follow Atkinson in advocating the elimination of romantic love from all future societies. Instead, we can strive to remove the sexist and heterosexist elements from society's romantic ideals and to encourage benign idealization processes. This might prove more difficult than simply eliminating romantic love altogether, for it will involve not only eliminating traditional gender roles, but separating romantic love from reproduction and the traditional family.

I have defended a nonessentialist analysis of romantic love that includes concern, the passion for union (reciprocity, sexual desire, and exclusivity), admiration, and idealization. None of these features is central; different features predominate in different circumstances. Admiration and idealization cause concern and the passion for union. The passion for union yields reciprocity, sexual desire, and exclusivity. Though not parts of romantic love, sexual desire and exclusivity enhance and accompany it. By making no feature central, my analysis better explains our experiences and concepts and accommodates realism and idealism.

Notes

1. This essay first appeared, in *Philosophy and Theology* 2:1 (1987): 76-96, as a reply to Alan Soble's "The Unity of Romantic Love," *Philosophy and Theology* 1:4 (1987): 374-97 (this volume, 385-401). It has been mildly revised for this volume.

2. Page references to the version of Soble's essay included in this volume are given parenthetically in the text.

3. Ti-Grace Atkinson, *Notes from the Second Year: Women's Liberation* (Boston: Beacon Press, 1969), 36.

4. *Ibid.*, 36-7.

5. Ti-Grace Atkinson, "Radical Feminism and Love," in Alison Jaggar and Paula R. Struhl, eds., *Feminist Frameworks*, 1st ed. (New York: McGraw-Hill, 1978), 289-91, at 290.

6. *Ibid.*, 289.

7. Carol Caraway, "Romantic Love: Neither Sexist Nor Heterosexist," this volume, 375-9.

8. Dorothy Tennov, *Love and Limerence* (New York: Stein and Day, 1979), 71; M. Scott Peck, *The Road Less Traveled* (New York: Simon and Schuster, 1978), 84-93; Denis de Rougement, *Love in the Western World* (Princeton: Princeton University Press, 1983), 310.

9. Rolf Johnson, "Love, Passion, and the Need to Be Loved," the Society for the Philosophy of Sex and Love, Philadelphia, December 1981.

10. Peck, *The Road Less Traveled*, 84.

11. Carol Caraway, commentary on Rolf Johnson, "Love, Passion, and the Need To Be Loved," the Society for the Philosophy of Sex and Love, Philadelphia, December 1981.

12. Carol Caraway, *Criteria* (Ph.D. dissertation, University of Oklahoma, 1982), 41-68.

13. Peck, *The Road Less Traveled*, 161.

14. *Ibid.*, 82-3.

15. *Ibid.*, 81.

16. Caraway, "Romantic Love," 375.

17. Sharon Bishop, "Love and Dependency," in Sharon Bishop and Marjorie Weinzweig, eds., *Philosophy and Women* (Belmont, Cal.: Wadsworth, 1979), 147-54.

18. *Ibid.*, 153-4.

19. Dana Bushnell, "Love Without Sex," this volume, 381-3, at 382.

20. Caraway, "Romantic Love," 377.

21. For a discussion of the difference between the realist and idealist traditions, see Irving Singer, *The Nature of Love,* vol. 2: *Courtly and Romantic* (Chicago: University of Chicago Press, 1984), 3-15.

22. *Ibid.*, 5-8.

23. Peck, *The Road Less Traveled*, 87.

24. Bushnell, "Love Without Sex," 383.

25. Bishop, "Love and Dependency," 152.

26. Johnson, "Love, Passion, and the Need to Be Loved"; Bishop, "Love and Dependency," 150.

27. Caraway, "Romantic Love," 378.

28. George Simmel, "The Isolated Individual and the Dyad," in Kurt Wolff, ed. and trans., *The Sociology of Georg Simmel* (New York: Free Press, 1950), 122-9.

29. *Ibid.*, 126.

30. Arthur Schopenhauer, "The Metaphysics of Sexual Love," in D. P. Verene, ed., *Sexual Love and Western Morality*, 1st ed. (New York: Harper and Row, 1972), 174-85, at 180, 183.

31. See Elizabeth Rapaport, "On the Future of Love: Rousseau and the Radical Feminists," in Alan Soble, ed., *Philosophy of Sex*, 1st ed. (Totowa, N.J.: Littlefield, Adams, 1980), 369-88, at 382-3.

32. Rapaport, "On the Future of Love," 383; Schopenhauer, "The Metaphysics of Sexual Love," 183.

33. The passage continues, "for we see that two persons of the same sex are not at all fitted for giving each other the exchanges of love or for practicing the acts natural to it" (Andreas Capellanus, "On Love," in Robert C. Solomon and Kathleen M. Higgins, eds., *The Philosophy of [Erotic] Love* [Lawrence: University Press of Kansas, 1991], 56-71, at 58). As Irving Singer does, I see romantic love as closely connected to courtly love. Singer argues that the medieval courtly love and the modern romantic love traditions share five conditions, which he discusses in terms of heterosexual love (*The Nature of Love*, vol. 2, 300). Singer, however, does not claim (as Capellanus did) that love is restricted to heterosexuals.

34. Schopenhauer, "The Metaphysics of Sexual Love," 183.

35. Singer, *The Nature of Love*, 464-5.

36. Atkinson, *Notes from the Second Year*, 45; Rapaport, "On the Future of Love," 372-3.

37. Coletta Reid, "Coming Out," in Jaggar and Struhl, *Feminist Frameworks*, 291-8, at 295.

38. Schopenhauer, "The Metaphysics of Sexual Love," 180.

39. Singer, *The Nature of Love*, 315.

40. *Ibid.*, 361.

Stephen M. Fishman
(photograph: Daniel Fishman)

Author of "Marital Friendship: A Redefinition of Romance"
Paper presented at the Society for the Philosophy of Sex and Love
during the
Eastern Division Meeting of The American Philosophical Association
Boston, Mass., 29 December 1986

Forty

MARITAL FRIENDSHIP: TOWARD A RECONCEPTION OF ROMANCE

Stephen M. Fishman

Women in advertisements at the back of my comic books were round and blonde. Hildegaard on the radio sang, "Darling, je vous aime beaucoup," and June Havoc in a sequined dress and open lips slept hidden in my plastic wallet. No one told me but I knew. I must wait, be faithful, take the high road, save the poor and help the weak, and she would come, a golden ministering angel. Marriage, sex, and love were tied. Everything was preparation: dating an interview, friendship a dress rehearsal. There would be struggle. There would be false Gods. But if I kept pure, a sign would strike me, coincidence of paradise in our eyes.

The first trouble came my senior year in high school. I had a blind date with Betsy McLain. I parked two blocks from her house, and as I walked my eyes filled with pink cloud landscapes and the fall lawns smelled thick and rich as hothouse humus. In the vestibule, she wore a blue blazer and grey skirt. Her hair climbed from her neck into an auburn bun and her cheek bones were high, a living Gibson greeting card girl.

"What were you doing?" she asked.

"Just listening to the car radio."

"Really?" Her eyes widened.

"Yes. Dvorak's *New World*."

"So was I," she said.

It was the most beautiful walk I ever had from a house to a car. Betsy McLain was a girl to dream on. She liked the smell of my shirt after I ran. Her voice was soft and, when she pulled her bobby pins, sun danced in her cascading hair.

College only made things worse. I read Bertrand Russell's *Marriage and Morals*[1] and learned that I was driven by romantic love, a twelfth-century emotion born when efforts to purify sexual passion went too far. The Lancelot and Guinevere story spurred female deification, monopolistic love, and narrow jealousy. It highlighted pursuit. Signs of acceptance by one's love had to be limited, just enough to promote further illusion and sacrifice.

In my junior year, I dated Aldonna Mary Margaret Witko. She lay on top of me in the dark, in a small apartment on West 114th Street, in all her clothes. A friend of mine knew someone in the library who rented his apartment for twenty dollars a night. You couldn't get in until eight and had to be out by twelve, but it was a popular deal and you had to reserve a month in advance. Donna's face shone in the dark. She had the clean, pink skin of a Scandinavian nurse and when she wore flats her calf muscles rippled like a marathon runner's. "You know, I like you very much," she said. We had met in the women's graduate dorm where I bussed tables. She was three years older, working on a masters in business management and mourning her lost Catholic beliefs. With my hand on her back I rubbed the leather belt at her waist. She wore a tweed skirt and the weight of her legs on my thighs was warm and solid. We kissed and she turned away. "I know what you want. I can't, that's all. You know I can't."

Donna's reaction echoed the legacy of courtly love, the one according to which granting sexual pleasure prematurely is the loss of a woman's male-conquering power. We were both in love with our romantic ideas. My escapist dreams, my longings for something beyond reach, were fed by visions of perfection, heightening the distance between available things and those more alluring but unreal.

Whereas twelfth-century love distinguished romance from marriage and sex, in twentieth century America we attempt to integrate all three. This makes romance our dominant passion, the one that spiritualizes sex and idealizes marriage. It is an excruciating modern paradox that the three do not mix. Where romance requires separation, intensity, and freedom, marriage demands proximity, evenness, and duty. Where sexual inaccessibility promises adventure and risk, conjugal rights deliver routine and boredom. The praying mantis eating her partner's head at sexual climax is haunting. A combination of love and death, it is an apt symbol of our century's merger of romantic courtship and marital consummation.

When Russell wrote *Marriage and Morals*, he correctly anticipated the current American divorce rate. As a Protestant country that accepts divorce, America has a stricter view of marriage than Catholic countries. Yet divorce is not as high in Protestant Europe as in America, and the difference, says Russell, lies in America's emphasis on romance, viewing romantic love not just as necessary but also as sufficient for marriage. Should the husband or wife find passionate love outside marriage, divorce and remarriage must follow. More recently, psychotherapist Albert Ellis placed even greater blame on American attitudes toward love. Ellis found four-fifths of his patients suffered neuroses brought on by romantic fantasies. These prompted fears of intimacy, feelings of inadequacy, and interpersonal frustration.[2]

Signs that passionate love might be an evolutionary mistake came early to me. When I was six I puzzled about choosing a mate. In the bed that my brother and I shared, I wondered how to keep up with all the women in the world. Teams of interviewers checking for the appropriate Cinderella would be needed, but what stumped me was what to do if delayed news of a "more perfect someone" came after I had chosen my partner.

Russell's solution to our modern paradox is to replace romantic marriage with a child-centered marriage. Society's interest in marriage, Russell argues, focuses on successful child rearing. Concerns for family financial and emotional stability are stimulated by our desire to promote children's education and their good citizenship. Although passionate love is one of life's exquisite delights, if marriage is to survive, according to Russell, romance must be transformed into something more affectionate and realistic. But what happens to a couple's romantic needs *after* marriage? Russell writes:

> In the system that I commend men [*sic*] are freed, it is true, from the duty of sexual conjugal fidelity, but they have in exchange the duty of controlling jealousy. The good life cannot be lived without self-control, but it is better to control a restrictive and hostile emotion such as jealousy, rather than a generous and expansive emotion such as love.[3]

Instead of reshaping romance, or altering our conjugal repertoire so romance might survive marriage, Russell asks for permissiveness toward adultery from both husbands and wives. He says parental concern for children must win out over negative emotions like jealousy, emotions that fuel our insecurity about extramarital affairs. In effect, Russell's proposal adopts the practice of Catholic cultures. The only difference is that children, not religious tenets, make marriage indissoluble.

Although Russell thus tries to liberalize marriage by easing both partners' discomfort with adultery, the essence of his idea of romance remains courtly and medieval. Loved ones and extramarital objects are still paper figures, idealized Betsy McLains and Donna Witkos created by people not yet intimate. In these circumstances, a mature spouse might be able to quell jealousy and, as Russell hopes, distinguish the important reproductive sex of marriage from the more frivolous sex of infidelity. However, as I view it, Russell's solution leaves untouched more fundamental reasons for extramarital affairs. Unfaithful husbands and wives seek more than sexual release. That is why infidelity by itself does not usually save marriage. Limited by too narrow a view of romance and marriage, husbands and wives continue to frustrate important parts of who they are or who they might become. As a consequence, novel aspects of personality are suppressed, and more and more of what spouses uncover about themselves cannot be shared with their partners.

Russell might have generated different solutions had he probed more deeply into the reasons why courtly love is more dominant in America than elsewhere. My own speculation is that idealized, distant love thrives in American society because such love feeds two of our culture's fundamental inclinations: competitiveness and acquisitiveness.

As Americans, we are enmeshed in competition for public prizes. Prizes must be public because to win is to beat others. Winning would hardly be exciting if others weren't losing. Ideally there would be one winner and an infinite number of losers. We become professors or physicians for the prestige, because entry to professional schools is competitive, because top residencies and book contracts are fiercely sought. Similarly, the more knights who take up the gauntlet, the more numerous the obstacles in our way, the greater the glory of ultimately winning a woman's hand. But this hardly gets us the friendship we want, the closeness and community with others. In fact it does the opposite. As prudent competitors, we are forced to keep people at a distance so they will not steal our game plan or catch us unawares. Vulnerability is dangerous.

We disguise our wounds, although these very wounds might allow us to discover common cause and understanding.

Paradoxically, we struggle to win because we hope to make ourselves more acceptable. Yet the more we win, the more we provoke envy and drive others away. This development only increases our hunger for connection and, like drug addicts, we are forced to attempt bigger and more glamorous competitions. Our addiction even leads us to overlook the nature of what we win or the consequences of the competitive process on ourselves. With regard to prizes, all we need to know is, which neighborhoods or colleges or resorts are most sought after? And then, as if we were clay, we conform ourselves to a mold, playing down our idiosyncracies, constantly comparing our shapes against an unquestioned standard. In thus fashioning ourselves, we quiet any revolutions we might feel within, ignoring any doubts we might have about why "we don't quite fit." And we do the same to others. I am reminded of the television commercial that featured former professional football linebacker, Nick Buoniconti. A man sitting next to Buoniconti in a bar says, "Hey, I've seen you on TV. What's your name?" "Nick Buoniconti," says Buoniconti. "No, that's not right," says the man. We can hardly develop ourselves or befriend others if we aren't listening, if we refuse to allow new experience to alter our hardening notions. It takes strength to deny what we encounter, to refuse to look, but it is also deadening.

How can we find friendship? How can we find closeness and community in an extremely acquisitive and competitive culture? My answer, perhaps overly bold and simple, is work. Without it we cannot know ourselves or see ourselves reflected in creative activity or find our special place in the web of associative practice. Work in this sense is often missing in America. How can this be? Don't most Americans "work" a forty-hour week? Don't we have a "work force" and a "working class"? In this sense, the I've-been-working-on-the-railroad sense, work means a way to put food on the table. Work is only instrumentally good, only a source of external reward. Such labor promotes little historical awareness, minimal consciousness of common goals or concern for the perfection of shared practices. It leads to "blue Monday" and "thank God it's Friday." It is not activity we can well integrate into the rest of our lives, and so we erect weekend and holiday and retirement barriers around it. Karl Marx called it "alienated labor."[4]

By contrast, the work that I claim promotes friendship and community focuses on internal rather than external rewards.[5] It builds on commitment to cooperative skills and practices, professional or craftly or artistic, and feels freely undertaken. It is deeply rooted in individual and social history and carries with it little sense of winning or losing. It has more to do with becoming a contributing practitioner than with achieving personal fame or money.

"Work" in this sense—finding one's special place in a network of cooperative activity—triumphs at the trial of Socrates in 399 BC. When associates arrange for his escape from jail, Socrates refuses to go. When asked to save his life by agreeing to cease teaching, Socrates says, "I cannot." Why? Because teaching, participating in the moral and political life of the *polis*, is his work. Such practice is good in the fullest sense for him. It fits the web he has constructed of his own life narrative and his society's history (both of which are presented to the jury in Plato's *Apology*),[6] and it is consistent with the internal prophetic voice whose depth, for him, always trumps all others. If Socrates were to refrain from such work, he would die, not physically, but morally and spiritually, a death more fearful for him than any biological one.

Whereas Russell's solution for marriage asks couples to be more liberal about adultery and to stay together "for the children," my own proposal asks that we sustain marital romance by emphasizing life-work. This work, this chance for self-discovery and cooperative community within marriage, promotes chances for knowing others. It allows us to begin satisfying the closeness and connection our society craves. And, since life-work provides continuing possibilities to transcend what we have been, conjugal intimacy and closeness need not destroy mystery or adventure. In this way, the romance of marital friendship rests on the renewing power and energy of life-work, rather than on the ignorance and limited access of courtly distance.

Although I cannot offer formulae for bringing about marital friendship, I can provide examples that show it is possible. The instances that come to mind are Virginia Stephen (Virginia Woolf) and Leonard Woolf; Harriet Taylor and John Stuart Mill; Mary Ann Evans (George Eliot) and George Henry Lewes. In many respects, these relationships were different. The Woolfs, who were married for thirty-nine years, had many connections with artists and critics of the Bloomsbury school. Harriet Taylor and Mill, although close friends for twenty years, had only a brief marriage, from 1851 until Taylor's death in 1858 and, in their social life, they were markedly reclusive. Unlike the other couples, Mary Ann Evans and G. H. Lewes, because of Lewes's inability to obtain a divorce from the mother of his children, never married. Yet, they lived openly together in the conservative Victorian climate for twenty-four years, and they entertained extensively, including in their circle many literary and scientific people, among them Herbert Spencer, Faraday, Dickens, and Thackery.

Despite these notable differences, all three couples displayed significant similarities, with regard to the perfection of collaborative practice or life-work. John Stuart Mill credited Harriet Taylor with developing his faculties of feeling and imagination.[7] She affected his attitudes toward democracy and socialism, and together (he reported) they rewrote every line of his most famous work, *On Liberty*.[8]

The relationship between Mary Ann Evans and G. H. Lewes also involved mutual respect for associative activity, with Lewes being the midwife to the exceptional literary powers of Evans. When she began living with Lewes in 1854, Evans had written no novels. Her first, *Clerical Studies*, was published just four years later. *Adam Bede*, *Mill on the Floss*, and *Silas Marner* all followed quickly in the period 1859-61. Her last novel, *Daniel Deronda*, appeared only two years before Lewes's death. Lewes, himself a protege of Mill and Thomas Carlyle, and a successful biographer and essayist, devoted much effort to dispelling Evans's self-doubt and to managing her business affairs. One of Evans's letters, written in 1859, offers confirmation of Lewes's role in the development of her work:

> He [Lewes] is the prime blessing that has made all the rest possible for me—giving me a response to everything I have written, a response that I could confide in as proof that I had not mistaken my work.[9]

Although unlike Lewes in temperament, Leonard Woolf played a similar role in the career of Virginia Stephen. Despite his own work in literature and economics, Woolf encouraged Stephen and tried to protect her precarious mental health. In the last note to her husband before her death in 1941, Virginia Stephen wrote:

> You have given me the greatest possible happiness. You have been in every way all that anyone could be. . . . What I want to say is I owe all the happiness of my life to you. You have been entirely patient with me and incredibly good. I want to say that—everybody knows it. If anybody could have saved me it would have been you. Everything has gone from me but the certainty of your goodness.[10]

These relationships tell little about the value of Russell's suggestion, about whether marriage is solidified by children or made easier by infidelity. In fact, none of these couples had children, and there is no record of any infidelities. However, these couples do show people sharing life-work and self-discovery. Within these relationships, John Stuart Mill, Mary Ann Evans, and Virginia Stephen flourished dramatically. It was as if their partner's sensitivity and example gave them courage and undammed powerful, but previously undeveloped and unconnected, resources. The care these partners expended on each other's work over long periods suggests intimacy can be a source of continuing energy, adventure, and attraction. It suggests the romance of marital friendship can be aided rather than impeded by constant association. In his *Autobiography*, written after Taylor's death, Mill reveals his undiminished fascination with her powers and his lasting respect for their impact on the work they collaboratively perfected and the internal rewards they mutually shared.

> When all subjects of intellectual or moral interest are discussed between them in daily life, and probed to much greater depths than are usually or conveniently sounded in writings intended for general readers . . . it is of little consequence in respect to the question of originality which of them holds the pen; the one who contributes least to the composition may contribute most to the thought; the writings which result are the joint product of both, and it must often be impossible to disentangle their respective parts and affirm that this belongs to one and that to the other. In this wide sense, not only during the years of our married life, but during many of the years of confidential friendship which preceded, all my published writings were as much her work as mine; her share in them constantly increasing as years advanced.[11]

As I propose it, the romance of marital friendship would be rooted in concern for life-work and care for the perfection of associative practice. Such work would focus less on the prizes of individual competition and more on the internal rewards of cooperative endeavor. Marital friendship, by thus binding familiarity with renewal, might thereby soften the excruciating paradox of modern love.

Notes

1. Bertrand Russell, *Marriage and Morals* (Garden City, N.Y.: Garden City Publishing Co., 1929), 63-77.
2. Albert Ellis, *The American Sexual Tragedy*, 2nd ed. (Secaucus, N.J.: Lyle Stuart, 1954), 118; see Philip Slater, *The Pursuit of Loneliness*, 3rd ed. (Boston: Beacon Press, 1990), ch. 4.
3. Russell, *Marriage and Morals*, 239.
4. Karl Marx, *Economic and Philosophic Manuscripts of 1844*, in Robert C. Tucker, ed., *The Marx-Engels Reader*, 2nd ed. (New York: Norton, 1978), 71-80.
5. See Alasdair MacIntyre, *After Virtue* (Notre Dame, Ind.: University of Notre Dame Press, 1981), ch. 14.
6. Plato, *Euthyphro, Apology, Crito*, trans. F. J. Church, ed. Robert D. Cumming (Indianapolis: Bobbs-Merrill, 1956).
7. John Stuart Mill, *Autobiography* (Boston: Houghton Mifflin, 1969), 112.
8. *Ibid.*, 150.
9. Gordon S. Haight, ed., *The George Eliot Letters*, vol. 3 (New Haven: Yale University Press, 1954-55), 3, 64.
10. Quentin Bell, *Virginia Woolf: A Biography* (New York: Harcourt Brace Jovanovich, 1972), 226.
11. Mill, *Autobiography*, 145.

Hilde Lindemann Nelson and James Lindemann Nelson
(photograph: Deirdre Moynihan)

Authors of "A Reply to Professor Fishman's 'Marital Friendship'"
Paper presented at the Society for the Philosophy of Sex and Love
during the
Eastern Division Meeting of The American Philosophical Association
Boston, Mass., 29 December 1986

Forty-One

AN UNROMANTIC REPLY TO "MARITAL FRIENDSHIP"

Hilde Lindemann Nelson
and James Lindemann Nelson

In our first version of this commentary on Stephen Fishman's "Marital Friendship,"[1] written nearly a decade ago, we acknowledged ourselves to fit well his recipe for romance in marriage. We were happily married and, not incidentally, we took a deep interest in each other's work, work that, as a novelist and a philosophy teacher respectively, was about as nonalienated and personally renewing as work is likely to be under the present dispensation. Seemingly, we ought to have been strongly inclined to endorse Fishman's thesis; in fact, it would have been reasonable for him to expect us to cheer him at every full stop. Instead, we carped in the time-honored philosophical style, claiming that his views suffered from obscurity, and insofar as they could be understood, were elitist, possibly gender biased, insufficiently motivated, and likely flat-out false. We claimed that maintaining romance in marriage and marriage-like relationships was a useless passion, neither necessary nor sufficient for continued, satisfying intimacy, and even smacked of immaturity, like the yearning to resist the ravages of age. In short, we were harsh about the whole thing.

That commentary on Fishman was our first joint writing project. In the ensuing years, we have become even more involved in each other's work: we coauthored a book and more than a half dozen articles; we are working now on book number two; we have team-taught and team-reviewed; and we are jointly the general editors of a new series of books. We have also continued even more fascinating and richly rewarding work, raising a half dozen children, to say nothing of maintaining other relationships. In all this time, we have, without benefit of extramarital sex, managed to retain not only intimacy, but even some measure of what we are inclined to call romance. Further, we still find it plausible to think that the continued quality of our relationship has something important to do with our deep interest in each other's work. Is it not time for us, then, to own ourselves to have been mistaken in our complaints about Fishman's thesis?

Well, no, not altogether, as ungenerous as this might seem. We still opine that shared meaningful work is neither necessary nor sufficient for romance, and that romance is neither necessary nor sufficient for marital friendship. We still suspect that his proposal is elitist, and that it reflects a way of looking at relationships that might tend to be more congenial to men than to women. And, finally, we believe that there might be other models that would better undergird marriage than the association of romance and work and, in keeping with the spirit of suggestiveness rather than the rigor that characterize Fishman's remarks, we will end by spinning a few speculations of our own.

The trouble with romance, as Fishman sees it, is that it is predicated on the notion of an idealized, distant, and somewhat mysterious love object, the pursuit of whom resonates with the competitiveness and acquisitiveness that are so much a part of contemporary American culture, and so hopeless as dispositions conducing to friendship, closeness, or community with others. This criticism has some superficial similarities with the standard line against romance, in particular, with that bit of it that complains that romance involves idealization of the beloved to a point where real intimacy is impossible. But, for Fishman, not romance as such, but the culture in which it flourishes, disables us. He takes romance out of the medieval courtly love tradition (where it was less a prescription for living than a literary convention) and transplants it squarely into the middle of the Protestant work ethic. Not only Marx sang hymns in praise of unalienated labor; that prototypical Protestant Martin Luther did so, too, and it is a strong theme in the later work of the mystery writer Dorothy Sayers, who was a conservative, high-church Anglican all her life.[2] The entire range of the political spectrum unites to agree that meaningful work is a great good, but to see it as the crucible of romance and thereby of good marriage seems discouragingly elitist. Is our only hope to become as Harriet Taylor and John Stuart Mill? Is Fishman really prepared to deny all possibility of conjugal bliss to the workers at the Ford plant in Detroit? Will John and Marsha never find happiness together until she quits clerking at K Mart?

The "romance of work" is not available to most of us, and while something should be done about that, until the revolution comes it seems cruel to rest content with a remedy for a disease that by definition excluded the proletariat. At least, the romance of love is something most of us have experienced. But we think Fishman and the other critics of romance are right; it will not do as a basis for marriage or other relationships entered into with similarly serious intent. Nothing can be headier or more joyful than romantic love; it lightens the step and quickens the eye; the heart sings. But romantic love, among its other liabilities, is akin to youth and physical beauty. It is transient or, at least, its long-term endurance is nothing we can count on. When it goes, we mourn its passing, but if we are wise, we never counted on it to last our lifetime. Like childhood, or the vigor of the body that many of us enjoyed at 20, we cannot hang on to it, although, with luck and perhaps some wisdom, it might mature into something that has its own value and delight. But the impulse to base a lasting relationship on romance ought to be outgrown, just as (some) sixteen-year-old boys outgrow the impulse to marry only a good-looking girl. Looks don't last. They're wonderful, but they're beside the point; so, it seems to us, is romance.

Fishman thinks otherwise. Why is romance so significant to the maintenance of marital friendship? His essay is not clear about this, but we can construct an answer out of his characterization of romance as involving separation, intensity, and freedom, traits that conflict with the proximity, evenness, and duty of marriage, along with his insistence that nonalienated labor affords the means to continual personal growth. The idea seems to be that the need for separation, intensity, and freedom are accommodated by the changes *within* individuals engaged in meaningful labor; this replaces changes *between* individuals that are characteristic of present romantic relationships. You still get a "new" partner with whom to experience the delights of romantic love; the newness is manifested just by qualitative rather than numerical change.

We are puzzled about why a good marital relationship requires this kind of change. Why could it not involve, instead, an ever fuller appreciation of the richness our spouses already possess? Human beings are, after all, even more complex than a George Eliot novel. And, as with great novels, we can come to know and love them better, even if they are keeping relatively still.

This isn't necessarily to deny the idea that continual personal growth is irrelevant to the quality of marital relationships; such a process is important for friendships of many kinds. But this importance might not be best understood in terms of its contribution to a new model of romance. Nor must shared meaningful work yield anything recognizable as romance or even have a net positive effect on marriage. The point is illustrated by Amélie Rorty, who discusses some of the realities that confront women and men who find themselves engaged in just the sort of shared, nonalienated labor that, on Fishman's view, ought to do much toward keeping their relationship rolling romantically along.[3] She points out that the demands of that work, especially in a context that systematically favors the career aspirations of men, often becomes a source of wedges that drive the couple apart. Perhaps this means only that even highly creative, shared intellectual work does not necessarily exhibit all the virtues that are contained in the Socratic conception of work Fishman celebrates. But if so, keeping the romance in your marriage will require not only getting the kind of work that is available to few in our culture, but having an attitude toward it that is equally rare.

Given the low odds that the millennium is upon us, we are inclined to look in other directions for responses to the problem with which Fishman presents us. Perhaps his diagnosis is faulty. Perhaps the psychological needs satisfied by separation and intensity and freedom are not really needed equally by everyone. Perhaps the people who feel these needs are primarily men, living under the conditions of patriarchy and suffering the anxiety concerning intimacy that many feminist scholars associate with our culture's gender-stratified system of child rearing.

Fishman's proposal would seem to imply that widespread marital happiness must wait on the overthrow of capital, which few now expect to see. It seems to us at least equally likely that intimate relationships will greatly benefit from the overthrow of patriarchy. No one knows what life would be like if either one of these revolutions were to occur, but the links between sexual politics and marital relations make feminist critique an obvious place to look for the solution to our dilemma.

We suspect, however, that no solution will answer easily. And we also suspect that any models for marriage we might adopt to get on with, to tide us over, as we chip away at capital and patriarchy, are going to prove more successful if they are models based on intimacy rather than models based on romance. Romance, after all, has a component of mystery that comes of not knowing your beloved well; this is why it tends to accompany the early stages of courtship. Intimacy, by contrast, is the increasing and deepening knowledge of your beloved, and it is this knowing and being known that is at the heart of our desire for relationships. Intimacy is the more fundamental of the two. Where it can be genuinely achieved, where we can see each other most fully and clearly, there our relationships will flourish, because knowledge is what they feed on.

Close families are intimate. On marrying, the beloved becomes a part of the family, and idealizations give way to a better understanding of what's really admirable about one's partner. Close friendships are intimate. They are a product of sympathetic temperaments and various sorts of shared experiences, and they catch us at our most ridiculous as well as at our best. Our relationship with our self is the most intimate of all. Even when we delude ourselves, we cannot escape all knowledge of our strengths and weaknesses, and not even the most romantic soul among us expects to find romance in this relationship. (It is also, not coincidentally, the longest lasting relationship we will ever encounter.) All three of these models—the beloved as family, as close friend, as other self—might work together to bring us to a richer and better understanding of what marriage could be.

Notes

1. Stephen M. Fishman, "Marital Friendship: Toward a Reconception of Romance," this volume, 421-7.

2. See Dorothy L. Sayers, *The Mind of the Maker* (New York: Harcourt, Brace, 1941).

3. Amélie Rorty, "Dependence, Individuality, and Work," in Pamela Daniels and Sara Ruddick, eds., *Working It Out: Twenty-Three Women Writers, Artists, Scientists, and Scholars Talk About Their Lives and Work* (New York: Pantheon Books, 1978), 38-54.

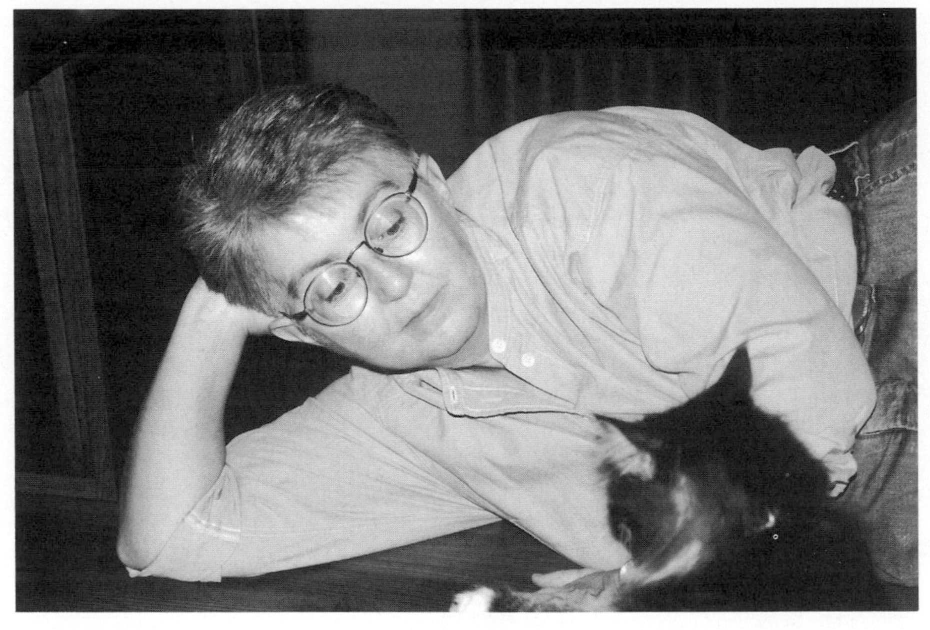

Christine Pierce
(photograph: Beth Timson)

Author of "AIDS and *Bowers v. Hardwick*"
Paper presented at the Society for the Philosophy of Sex and Love
during the
Pacific Division Meeting of The American Philosophical Association
San Francisco, Cal., 26 March 1987

Forty-Two

AIDS AND *BOWERS V. HARDWICK*

Christine Pierce

During the AIDS crisis, natural law arguments have turned up again not only in relation to antisodomy arguments but even as parts of important claims about AIDS prevention made by the medical and scientific community. Such arguments were invoked by the state of Georgia in the 1986 Supreme Court case, *Bowers v. Hardwick*,[1] in which the Court held that the Constitution does not confer a fundamental right upon homosexuals to engage in sodomy. As we shall see, the Court accepted a version of legal moralism, ignoring both the relevance of a right to privacy and two friend-of-the-court briefs urging them to consider the public health implications of prohibiting homosexual sodomy. I want to argue against legal moralism both in its standard form and in a more sophisticated version that permits natural law arguments a place in legal reasoning. Natural law arguments have aggravated the AIDS crisis by contributing not only to bad law but to bad science.

Natural law arguments that attempt to fix blame for AIDS on gay sex are variants of arguments from design. For example, Representative William Dannemeyer (R-California), a leading proponent of AIDS legislation, stated on the House floor that "God's plan for man was Adam and Eve, not Adam and Steve."[2] Ken Kesey, author of *One Flew Over the Cuckoo's Nest*, recently remarked: "It seems to me it's one's job to put sperm in a place that's designed for it. You don't put crankcase oil in your power steering system. And when God says, 'Do not put crankcase oil in your power steering system,' he's not saying, 'if you do, you'll go to hell,' he's saying, 'if you do, you'll blow the seals out of your power steering.'"[3] If blowing the seals out of one's power steering system is analogous to getting AIDS or any sexually transmitted disease, then the only well designed sex between or among human beings is lesbian sex. As physician Barbara Herbert put it, "Only nuns have less incidence of sexually transmitted diseases (STD's) than lesbians. . . . [W]here you see an STD there's been a penis in the picture."[4]

I want now to examine some serious attempts on the part of the medical and scientific community to use natural law arguments in their effort to show that AIDS will not spread in any significant way into the heterosexual population. The first is the popular so-called "efficiency" thesis.

The efficiency thesis is important. Understandably, it has been incorporated into safe sex guidelines, for such guidelines need to be explicit as to who is at risk. Some scientists maintain that HIV is more *efficiently* transmitted through anal sex than vaginal sex, with the implication that heterosexuals who practice only vaginal intercourse are at low risk. However, the fact of heterosexual transmission is not in question. The *New England Journal of Medicine* reports a case of sexual transmission of HIV from a man to a woman to a man.[5] A thirty-year-old married man engaged in homosexual activity while on business trips in New York. He and his thirty-three-year-old wife had vaginal intercourse accompanied by heavy mouth kissing about twice a month. After her husband died from pneumocytis carinii pneumonia (PCP), she had a sexual relationship with a twenty-sex-year-old male neighbor. She, too, died from PCP. The neighbor, who developed AIDS related complex (ARC), reported no drug use and no sexual contact except the above mentioned relationship, which included only vaginal intercourse and deep kissing. Comparatively few cases of vaginal transmission (particularly woman to man) exist today. The efficiency thesis attempts to explain this fact. It is thought that the lining of the anus is easily torn, thus facilitating the entry of infected semen into the blood stream. "The rugged vagina," in the words of John Langone, unlike "the vulnerable rectum," "is *designed* to withstand the trauma of intercourse"[6] Although it might be true that rectums and vaginas are respectively tender and tough, it has not been demonstrated that a traumatic event is necessary for the transmission of HIV. For example, artificial insemination is not a traumatic procedure, and yet women can get AIDS from undergoing this process if the sperm is contaminated. Moreover, if it turns out that HIV can cross mucous membranes, no trauma will be required to transmit AIDS.

Although scientific research already points to the possibility of direct infection of cells without trauma or tears, conventional assumptions about proper sexuality continue to influence both the design of experiments and the interpretation of results. For instance, in late 1986, a team of federal scientists headed by Dr. Malcolm Martin found that HIV can directly infect cells from the colon and rectum in the test tube, suggesting that AIDS could spread in anal intercourse without any breakage in tissue. Dr. Martin's team tested 13 other types of cells representing a wide range of human tissues, such as breast, lung, pancreas, and ovary, none of which proved susceptible to the AIDS virus. Though he neglected to test vaginal cells for any susceptibility to HIV, the new finding, according to the *New York Times*, "may help to explain the high incidence of AIDS among male homosexuals practicing anal intercourse."[7]

Scientist or science reporter, heterosexuals have a vested interest in believing that AIDS will be largely confined to the gay male population, that AIDS really is the "gay plague." Moreover, the efficiency thesis relies, as does the next argument under consideration, on beliefs about the proper place for depositing sperm that historically have been used to support the view that heterosexuality is good and homosexuality is bad.

Steven Witkin and a team of researchers from Cornell conducted experiments intended to show that the mere introduction of semen into the bloodstream during anal intercourse, not the trauma, adversely affects the male immune system. Witkin theorized that in order for the species to continue, "females have evolved immunological mechanisms to deal with exposure to sperm."[8] A woman, he thought was not at risk for AIDS even if her partner ejaculated inside her rectum. Men, however, have not evolved such mechanisms; hence, the implication that gay anal sex, from an evolutionary point of view, is biologically unnatural. Witkin's thesis explains why the rabbits described in the following experiments were male. The researchers engaged in what David Black calls "bunny bondage." In an effort to test the thesis that depositing semen from one male into the rectum of another might cause the receiver to produce antibodies to foreign semen and in turn suppress the immune system, researchers "took rabbits and gave them rabbit semen rectally once a week. . . . Healthy males were restrained and 1 ml of fresh semen . . . was deposited . . . to a depth of 5cm . . . with a No. 7 French rubber catheter."[9] Richard Goldstein, in reviewing Black's book, says that Witkin's theory, like so many religious explanations for disease, "not only wrongly fixes blame but falsely reassures."[10] Views like Witkin's, including the efficiency thesis, suggest that "prevention may ultimately be a matter of harmonizing with the natural order."[11]

In *Bowers*, the Court was presented by the petitioner with natural law arguments that were admissible because the Court embraced legal moralism; the Court rejected, to the surprise of many, the rights approach it had been developing in sex-related cases over the past twenty years. Here is a brief review of the facts surrounding the *Bowers* case.[12] Michael Hardwick was arrested for sodomy in his own bedroom. Police arrived at Hardwick's door to see him about an unrelated charge, a ticket for public drunkenness that Hardwick claims he had long since paid. Although he did not pay the fine on the appointed date, he did settle the matter in person later. Thus, Hardwick was not expecting a visit from the police. A house guest answered the door and let the officer in. Not knowing that Hardwick had company, the guest said that Hardwick was in his room. The officer went to Hardwick's bedroom, caught him in the act of consensual fellatio, and arrested him. Although the charges were later dropped, Hardwick sued Michael J. Bowers, the attorney general of Georgia, in hopes of achieving Supreme Court review of a law that had, he thought, "inadequate rationale." According to the Georgia statute:

> A person commits the offence of sodomy when he performs or submits to any sexual act involving the sex organs of one person and the mouth or anus of another.

Note that the issue before the Court in *Bowers* was whether to affirm a lower court ruling that Georgia, in order to keep its sodomy statute, would have to demonstrate that it promoted a compelling state interest. Hardwick's winning the case would not have made the sodomy law unconstitutional; it only would have required Georgia to show that its sodomy statute served some legitimate state objective and was the most narrowly drawn means of achieving it.

The *Bowers* case is an example of legal moralism par excellence. Legal moralism, as characterized by Joel Feinberg, is the view that "it can be morally legitimate to prohibit conduct on the ground that it is inherently immoral, even though it causes neither harm nor offense to the actor or to others."[13] A view often associated with Patrick Devlin, legal moralism is also put forward in a more sophisticated form by Ronald Dworkin in an article critical of Devlin. I want to argue against Dworkin's proposal that legal moralism might be acceptable as long as certain minimal rational requirements are met. Dworkin distinguishes between moral views that ought not to be legally enforced because they are based on prejudice, emotional reaction, false claims, or arguments from authority (what Dworkin calls parroting) and genuine moral convictions that might be legally enforced. As Dworkin puts it, "Not every reason I might give will do."[14] Among the reasons that will do, however, as a legitimate basis for prohibiting X is "X is unnatural." As we shall see, the reasoning in *Bowers* arguably meets neither the minimal standards outlined by Dworkin, nor even the lower requirements advocated by Devlin.

Patrick Devlin takes the view that morality is ultimately a matter of feeling, in particular, the feelings of disgust, indignation, and intolerance of ordinary people. Moreover, he claims that moral views should be legally enforced if these feelings are sufficiently intense (reach "concert pitch," as H. L. A. Hart puts it).[15] These feelings need not be based on any rational considerations. In essence, the majority of the Court said (in agreement with Devlin's view) that there is no fundamental right to homosexual sodomy because people have strongly disapproved of it and have done so for a long time. For example, the Court's majority says, "Sodomy was a criminal offense at common law and was forbidden by the laws of the original thirteen States. . . . In fact, until 1961, all fifty States outlawed sodomy, and today, twenty-four States and the District of Columbia continue to provide criminal penalties for sodomy performed in private and between consenting adults."[16] Chief Justice Burger says, "Decisions of individuals relating to homosexual conduct have been subject to state intervention throughout the history of Western civilization."[17]

The *Bowers* court does not take a critical view of history. It does not consider the possibility that popular prejudices that are deeply rooted in sexism, heterosexism, and racism can undermine individual rights. However, the Court has not always thought of history as buttressing moral claims. Twenty years ago, §20-59 of the Virginia law stated:

> If any white person intermarry with a colored person, or any colored person intermarry with a white person, he shall be guilty of a felony and shall be punished by confinement in the penitentiary for not less than one nor more than five years.

In this case, *Loving v. Virginia*,[18] a unanimous Court found Virginia's ban on interracial marriages a product of "invidious racism." In that case, the Court was not persuaded by the trial court's argument from design, that "Almighty God created the races white, black, yellow, malay, and red, and he placed them on separate continents. And but for their interference with his arrangement there would be no cause for such marriages. The fact that he separated the races shows that he did not intend for the races to mix."[19] The *Loving* Court was also not persuaded by tradition: the facts that antimiscegenation statutes had been common in Virginia since colonial times and Virginia was one of sixteen states that prohibited interracial marriage. Nonetheless, when Michael Hardwick claimed that "the presumed belief of a majority of the electorate in Georgia that homosexual sodomy is immoral and unacceptable" is an "inadequate rationale to support the law," the *Bowers* court said simply, "we do not agree."[20]

An important feature of Devlin's legal moralism is relevant to the outcome of *Bowers*. Devlin notes that "the limits of tolerance shift." Although, on his view, we are justified in passing laws on no other basis than deeply held feelings of disapproval, when the limits of tolerance shift, we should change the laws. A poll in 1986 conducted by *Time* magazine shows an absence of majority approval for the outlawing of any of a variety of specific sexual practices, including oral and anal sex, between consenting adults.[21] Thus, one might argue that the Supreme Court does not even realistically apply legal moralism of the sort articulated by Devlin. Note that the trend of States to repeal laws against sodomy or interracial marriage can be interpreted as cutting either way. Virginia, as we have seen, was one of the sixteen states to prohibit interracial marriage in 1967. Fifteen years earlier, thirty states prohibited interracial marriage. This data was taken by the *Loving* court as showing that the limits of tolerance shift. A similar trend in sodomy laws was used by the *Bowers* court to show that many people still oppose sodomy. (In a footnote, Justice Stevens comments, "Interestingly, miscegenation was once treated as a crime similar to sodomy.")[22]

Natural law arguments figure into the case since the petitioner, Bowers, appeals to the beliefs of Western philosophers who thought that homosexuality was unnatural. As Bowers argues, "No universal principle of morality teaches that homosexual sodomy is acceptable conduct. To the contrary, traditional Judeo-Christian values proscribe such conduct. Indeed, there is no validation for sodomy found in the teaching of the ancient Greek philosophers Plato or Aristotle. More recent thinkers, such as Immanuel Kant, have found homosexual sodomy no less unnatural."[23]

In the *Laws* (the work of Plato cited by Bowers), Plato, himself a homosexual, characterizes homosexual sex as unnatural, whereas in earlier dialogues he portrayed the intensity and delights of homosexuality,[24] even suggesting that homoerotic experience is an important prerequisite for knowing the essence of Beauty.[25] In the *Laws*, Plato's last work, he maintained that heterosexuality, with its procreative end, was inherently orderly; he approved of the use of the law to enforce what he saw as natural, that is, orderly sexuality. Some commentators on Plato have charged him with inconsistency. Others have said that Plato got increasingly conservative in his old age. However, there is another possible interpretation. Plato, in the *Laws*, was legislating for a public that, by and large, did not consist of philosophers. Not above considerable elitism and, some say, a bit of totalitarianism, Plato thought (as does Petitioner Bowers) that marriage, family, and procreation were institutions designed to promote social control. Bowers says that

> homosexual sodomy is the anathema of the basic units of our society—marriage and the family. To decriminalize or artificially withdraw the public's expression of its disdain for this conduct does not uplift sodomy, but rather demotes these sacred institutions to merely other alternative lifestyles. One author has described that result as the promotion of indifference toward these foundations of social order, where historically there has been endorsement.[26]

Unlike Georgia's attorney general, Plato made an honorable pederastic exception for philosophers, an exception not needed (in the *Laws*) for the general public who live their lives in the realm of opinion, not the realm of knowledge.

Although Bowers cites Kant as a philosopher who disapproved of sodomy,[27] other legal scholars such as David Richards have found support in Kant for the opposite point of view. Richards cites Kant as an author of the idea of human rights, as one "who best articulated its radical implications for the significance of respect for moral personality."[28] Extending the Kantian notion of autonomy to sexuality, Richards says: "Sexuality . . . is not a spiritually empty experience that the state may compulsorily legitimize only in the form of rigid marital procreational sex, but one of the fundamental experiences through which, as an end in itself, people define the meaning of their lives."[29] Rights, typically, protect certain basic interests of persons even if so doing makes the majority unhappy. Being able to love, according to Richards, is central to human lives. Moreover, "freedom to love means that a mature individual must have autonomy to decide how and whether to love another."[30]

Despite Kant's talk about rights as guarantees of proper respect for moral personality or rational autonomy, Kant did not see the implications of his theory for sexual autonomy. Whenever one is developing a new theory, one might fail to see the whole range of its possible applications. Kant, for example, never asked whether nonhuman animals were capable of rational autonomy. In the *Lectures*, he referred to them as "man's instruments."[31] Kant also thought women lacking in rational ability and therefore did not see that they had any need for the rights of "man." Thus, in citing Kant, both Bowers and Richards are right. Kant was a conventional man. He was also one of the originators of a theory of rights with radical implications for moral and social thought.

On a view like Devlin's, there is no theoretical limit to the legal enforcement of morality. Principles, such as Mill's principle of liberty or a right to privacy, are designed to function as just such limits. Blackmun, in his dissent, laments the "overall refusal" of the Court to "consider the broad principles that have informed our treatment of privacy in specific cases."[32]

The word "privacy" does not appear in the Constitution. Nonetheless, a series of Supreme Court decisions has established a right of privacy. It is said to exist in the penumbra of certain Amendments and, more philosophically, in the concept of liberty itself. (The word "liberty" is in the Constitution.) A number of cases have established the constitutional status of a right of privacy. *Griswold v. Connecticut* held that a right of privacy protects the use of contraceptives by married persons.[33] In this case, much was made of the fact that if contraceptives were illegal, police could enter the bedroom and search for them. *Eisenstadt v. Baird* held that unmarried persons, under the equal protection clause, also have the right to use contraceptives.[34] *Roe v. Wade* held that the right of privacy encompasses a woman's decision to have an abortion.[35] *Stanley v. Georgia* upheld the right to private possession of obscene material.[36] Although a First Amendment case, the Court stressed the importance of the privacy of one's own home. In the words of Justice Marshall, "[Stanley] is asserting the right to read or observe what he pleases—the right to satisfy his intellectual and emotional needs in the privacy of his own home."[37]

One way to explain a connection between the concepts of privacy and liberty is to borrow some thoughts from J. S. Mill. Mill advances roughly the following principle of liberty: people (competent adults, not children) should be allowed to voice their opinion and direct their lives as they see fit, as long as no one else is wrongfully harmed. It follows from this principle that what one does to oneself, as long as no harm comes to another, is one's own business. A private action, then, is one that concerns oneself and does not wrongly harm others. Mill adds that if more than one party is involved, all parties must give their consent. Thus, what consenting adults do, as long as others are not wrongly harmed, is private, that is, their own business and not the business of the law. On such a view, it would be natural to suppose that a right of privacy would include sexual intimacies between consenting adults in their bedroom. The recognition of a right to sexual autonomy (something like Mill's view) was believed by many, including David Richards and dissenting Justice Blackmun, to be the Court's view in its development of privacy law. Thus, many were surprised that the Court did not extend the right of privacy to the facts in *Bowers*.

With respect to prior cases on privacy, the Court said, "None of the rights announced in these cases bears any resemblance to the claimed constitutional right of homosexuals to engage in acts of sodomy. . . . No connection between family, marriage, or procreation on the one hand and homosexual activity on the other has been demonstrated."[38] The majority produced no principle for this distinction. Nan D. Hunter, an ACLU attorney, calls the Court's statement one of "unmasked contempt . . . as if gay people don't create families, belong in families, raise children, or have the staying power for those 9.4-year-long average marriages that are the bedrock of civilized society."[39] Not insignificantly, the majority aligned with Bowers, who in turn sided with Plato, in thinking it a legitimate function of law to bolster the conventional institutions of marriage, family, and procreation.

My complaint is not simply that the Court did not extend the right of privacy to consensual sexual conduct between adults in their bedroom, but that the Court did not even recognize the right of privacy as the fundamental right at issue. Blackmun, in the opening sentence of his dissent, says: "this case is no more about 'a fundamental right to engage in homosexual sodomy,' as the court purports to declare, than *Stanley v. Georgia* . . . was about a fundamental right to watch obscene movies."[40] To push the point, consider this. In Kansas, the legislature passed a law in 1986 banning sex toys in general and vibrators in particular.[41] If a challenge to this law should ever reach the Supreme Court, no one would expect the Court to find in the Constitution a fundamental right to own vibrators.[42] Since the legislation was part of a pornography package, we might anticipate that the rights of freedom of expression or of privacy would count as the fundamental right at issue.

Recognition of a fundamental right by the courts triggers heightened judicial scrutiny. Good reasons (a "compelling interest") must be given by a state if a law is to survive this heightened scrutiny. In a case where no fundamental right is recognized, almost any reason, however weak, will do. As we have seen in *Bowers*, moral beliefs were used as reasons without meeting any rational requirements such as those suggested by Ronald Dworkin. For example, Dworkin would not count as genuine moral convictions those claims based only on arguments from authority, namely, appeals to the beliefs of Plato, Kant, and the Judeo-Christian tradition. In citing Kant as an authority, Bowers also stated Kant's reason for opposing homosexuality by noting that Kant thought homosexuality unnatural. I am not sure whether one has committed the fallacy of argument from authority if in appealing to an authority one also cites the authority's reason for opposing whatever is at issue.

Assuming the man on the bus does produce a reason that is not disqualified on Dworkin's grounds, that reason, Dworkin says, "will presuppose some general moral principle or theory, even though [the man on the bus] may not be able to state that principle or theory."[43] Presumably, to make everyone who rides the bus take a course in moral philosophy is unreasonable; hence, Dworkin's standards of rationality are minimal, requiring only that one be able to produce a reason for one's view and use it consistently. "X has harmful consequences," "X violates my rights," "X is unnatural," even "The Bible forbids X" count as genuine reasons and, if used consistently, constitute a genuine moral conviction. Feinberg objects to Dworkin's version of legal moralism when he says, "Even if there is a *genuine* moral consensus in a community that certain sorts of 'harmless' activities are wrong, I see no reason why that consensus should be enforced by the criminal law. . . . [E]ven a genuine 'discriminatory' popular morality might, for all of that, be *mistaken*."[44] Undoubtedly, mistaken moralities and bad reasons will find their way into the criminal law on Dworkin's view. To illustrate the point: reasons of the sort "X is unnatural" are bad reasons, yet such reasons pass Dworkin's test: they have a principled form and presuppose a general moral theory. In not requiring the ordinary person to recognize moral reasons in their principled form or to know anything about the moral theories to which the reasons are attached, Dworkin does not and cannot require a citizen to have a *good* reason for a moral point of view, for without a knowledge of ethical theory or metatheory, no basis for judging between competing kinds of reasons exists.

In adopting legal moralism, one adds a principle of legal moralism to the harm principle, the offense principle, and so forth, in an effort to sanction increasingly invasive restrictions on personal liberty. In some instances, however, endorsing legal moralism goes further; that is, personal liberty is not the only cost. For example, a friend-of-the-court-brief accompanying *Bowers* filed jointly by the American Psychological and the American Public Health Association argued that "from a public health standpoint, the [Georgia] statute is simply counterproductive. . . . The statute does not deter conduct that spreads AIDS, but it may deter conduct essential to combating it."[45] These associations argued that sodomy statutes adversely affect scientific investigation directed toward containing AIDS and finding a cure; they also interfere with health education efforts designed to encourage safer sexual practices. The Associations supported their claims the following way:

> A statutory scheme that creates a realistic fear of punishment if certain behavior is disclosed runs the risk of obscuring important data, as individuals simply refuse to volunteer for studies or provide needed infor-

> mation, and of creating false data, as individuals try to conform what they reveal to what they believe is legal. . . . With respect to at least two important issues—the existence of potentially high risk to recent immigrants from Haiti and the transmissibility of the AIDS virus from women to men—there is reason to believe that falsification of information, caused by fear of punishment, have distorted the epidemiological picture. Finding these and other crucial pieces of the AIDS puzzle should not have to depend on the ability of epidemiologists to guess whether patients are not telling the truth because they fear being punished. . . . [C]ommunity effort and support [for major educational efforts] are made more difficult in an environment in which a concomitant of participating in educational efforts is self-incrimination. Attending an educational presentation on "safe sex," for example, could be seen as an admission of engaging in sexual practices prohibited by the statute. Criminalization is likely to compromise the efficacy of informal educational networks by making people more cautious about what they reveal about themselves to acquaintances. It also presents state public health officials with the awkward choice of appearing to suppress information about safe sex techniques or appearing to condone felonious conduct.[46]

The associations also point out that the Georgia statute does not further any mental health objectives and causes substantial psychological harm by fostering homophobia among heterosexuals and internalized homophobia among gays. Roy Cohn, a queer baiter in the McCarthy era who recently died of AIDS, is a classic case of the destructive behavior that results from internalized homophobia. Cohn's medical records showed him "reluctant to be celibate"[47] and his public statements showed him reluctant to tell the truth.

Rather than relinquish the idea that homosexual sex is wicked, some would even deny condoms to those who need them, preferring to see people die of AIDS. For example, the Corrections Department in New York State made condoms available to married prisoners enrolled in a family visitation program; but condoms were not made available to prisoners not enrolled in the program, even though officials realized that some prisoners engaged in homosexual sex and could use the condoms to protect themselves against AIDS.[48] If natural sex is procreative sex, then the use of condoms by heterosexuals is equally unnatural. However, somewhere between Aquinas and Bowers, a new use of "natural" has emerged for convenience-oriented consumers. In defense of a company decision not to portray gay users of condoms in television commercials, Susan Smirnoff, spokesperson for Trojan, recently said "[Condoms] are effective against infection when used properly. A condom's proper use is for vaginal intercourse."[49]

The point is that natural law arguments and consequentialist arguments are incompatible. Aquinas said that rape is not as bad as consensual sodomy or interrupting heterosexual intercourse, because (heterosexual) rape allows for the possibility of fulfilling the purpose of sexuality, namely, procreation. At the least, it seems somewhat peculiar to prefer sexual acts that are by definition unloving, violent abuses of persons to acts that need not be, and might be quite the contrary. Consequences, however destructive of individuals or society, do not matter a whit in the face of what is claimed to be the natural order. To those who care nothing about consequences, Richard Goldstein says, "Better you should wear a condom. But if a layer of latex is all it takes to still the winds of doom, what kind of moral mystery does AIDS pose?"[50]

Regardless of one's assessment of the foregoing arguments about the social costs of prohibiting homosexual sodomy, the fact remains that to advocate the prohibition of homosexual sodomy because it is believed to be wicked or unnatural is to dispense with any discussion of harmful consequences that might result from the prohibition. Had the *Bowers* court ruled in Hardwick's favor, Georgia could have made its case, on the basis of public health or whatever, for its sodomy statute. But Georgia did not have to give any good reasons for its law, nor did the Court concern itself with arguments to the effect that the public health is ill served by the prohibition of sodomy. The Court, as we have seen, dismissed these arguments in favor of traditional views that were poorly supported or wholly unsupported: Bowers said that Kant said that homosexuality is unnatural.

Notes

1. *Bowers v. Hardwick*, 106 S. Ct. 2841 (1986).

2. "The Constitutional Rights of AIDS Carriers," *Harvard Law Review* 99 (1986): 1274-92, at 1274.

3. Richard Goldstein, "A Plague on All Our Houses," *Village Voice*, Literary Supplement, September 1986, 17.

4. Quoted in "Lesbian/Gay Health Conference," *Off Our Backs*, May 1986, 3.

5. L. H. Calabrese and K. V. Gopalakrishna, "Transmission of HTLV-III Infection from Man to Woman to Man," *The New England Journal of Medicine* 314:15 (1986): 987.

6. John Langone, "AIDS," *Discover*, December 1985, 40-1 (italics added).

7. *New York Times*, 14 December 1986.

8. David Black, *The Plague Years: A Chronicle of AIDS, the Epidemic of Our Times* (New York: Simon and Schuster, 1986), 99.

9. *Ibid.*, 97.

10. Goldstein, "A Plague on All Our Houses," 17.

11. *Ibid.*

12. See an interview with Hardwick, *Advocate*, 2 September 1986, 38-41, 110, and Donahue Transcript #07116 (Cincinnati: Multimedia Entertainment, 1986).

13. Joel Feinberg, *Offense to Others* (Oxford: Oxford University Press, 1985), xiii.

14. Ronald Dworkin, "Lord Devlin and the Enforcement of Morals," in Richard Wasserstrom, ed., *Morality and the Law* (Belmont, Cal.: Wadsworth, 1971), 55-72, at 63.

15. H. L. A. Hart, "Immorality and Treason," in Wasserstrom, *Morality and the Law*, 49-54, at 50.

16. 106 S. Ct. 2841, 2844, 2845.

17. 106 S. Ct. 2841, 2847.

18. *Loving v. Virginia*, 388 U.S. 1 (1967).

19. *Loving v. Virginia*, 3.

20. 106 S. Ct. 2841, 2846.

21. "Sex Busters," *Time*, 21 July 1986, 22. See also "Poll Shows Americans Disapprove of Ruling," *Advocate*, 5 August 1986, 11.

22. 106 S. Ct. 2841, 2857.

23. Brief of Petitioner Michael J. Bowers, Attorney General of Georgia, No. 85-140 in the Supreme Court of the United States, October 1985, 20.

24. See *Symposium* and *Phaedrus*.

25. See Gregory Vlastos, "The Individual as an Object of Love in Plato," *Platonic Studies* (Princeton: Princeton University Press, 1973), 3-42, esp. Appendix 2 ("Sex in Platonic Love"), 38-42.

26. Petitioner's Brief, 37-8.

27. Immanuel Kant, *Lectures on Ethics*, trans. Louis Infield (Indianapolis: Hackett, 1963), 170.

28. David A. J. Richards, *Sex, Drugs, Death, and the Law: An Essay on Human Rights and Overcriminalization* (Totowa, N.J.: Rowman and Littlefield, 1982), 31.

29. *Ibid.*, 52.

30. *Ibid.*, 55.

31. Kant, *Lectures*, 240.

32. 106 S. Ct. 2841, 2852.

33. 381 U.S. 479 (1965).

34. 405 U.S. 438 (1972).

35. 410 U.S. 113 (1973).

36. 394 U.S. 577 (1969).

37. 394 U.S. 577, 565.

38. 106 S. Ct. 2841, 2844.

39. Nan D. Hunter, "Banned in the U.S.A.: What the Sodomy Ruling Will Mean," *Village Voice*, 22 July 1986, 15-16.

40. 106 S. Ct. 2841, 2848.

41. "Sex Busters," 21.

42. Thanks to Beth Timson for this point.

43. Dworkin, "Lord Devlin and the Enforcement of Morals," 64.

44. Joel Feinberg, "'Harmless Immoralities' and Offensive Nuisances," *Rights, Justice, and the Bounds of Liberty* (Princeton: Princeton University Press, 1980), 69-95, at 83.

45. Brief of Amici Curiae, American Psychological Association and American Public Health Association in Support of Respondents, 27, 22. A friend-of-the-court brief supporting the petitioners was filed by David Robinson, Jr., George Washington Law School.

46. *Ibid.*, 24-7. The following footnote in the brief explains the associations' claim that the transmissibility of the AIDS virus from women to men is an area where falsification of information might have occurred: "A study of military personnel done at Walter Reed Army Medical Center shows a much higher incidence of female-to-male transmission of HTLV-III/LAV virus than most other United States reports. The question of the incidence of female-to-male transmission is an important area of current inquiry. It is possible that the other reports show an artificially low incidence of such transmission. But another explanation for the disparity is that the military personnel in the Walter Reed study were reluctant to admit to homosexual activity or intravenous drug use, either of which could lead to discharge."

47. Dale Van Atta, "Faint Light, Dark Point: Roy Cohn, AIDS, and the Question of Privacy," *Harper's*, November 1986, 54-7, at 56-7.

48. *The Citizen*, Auburn, N.Y., 23 December 1986.

49. *Gay Community News*, 1-7 February 1987.

50. Goldstein, "A Plague on All Our Houses," 17.

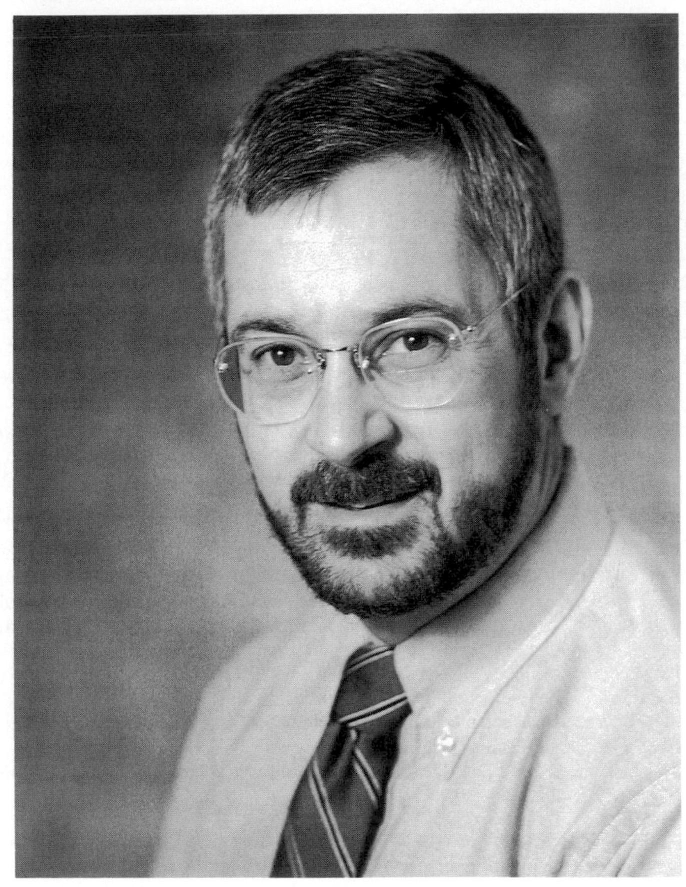

David J. Mayo
(photograph: Ken Moran)

Author of "Commentary on Steinbock and Irvine on AIDS"
Paper presented at the Society for the Philosophy of Sex and Love
during the
Pacific Division Meeting of The American Philosophical Association
San Francisco, Cal., 26 March 1987

Forty-Three

AN OBLIGATION TO WARN OF HIV INFECTION?

David J. Mayo

Do HIV+ persons have an obligation to warn prospective sex partners of their infection? Many observers, Bonnie Steinbock among them, claim that they do.[1] This conclusion would seem obvious, if having sex with an HIV+ person involved a high probability of a bad outcome. But what if "safe sex" practices could cut the risk of that outcome almost to zero? Steinbock argues that the HIV+ person is still obligated to warn, even before safe sex, "even if the risk is minuscule."[2]

That HIV+ persons have an obligation to warn does not strike me as obvious. I wish to explore a cluster of considerations that suggest that, perhaps, no such general obligation exists. I begin with three arguments that can be stated briefly. I then explore Steinbock's view that HIV+ persons have an obligation to warn, however small the risk. I argue that Steinbock's view is grounded in a "fully informed consent" model, which is inappropriate for understanding consent to courtship and sexual intimacy. I argue in favor of an alternative model based on Charles Fried's view of privacy, according to which intimacy properly involves secrecy as well as controlled revelation of personal information. Since this is a more plausible model for understanding courtship and sexual intimacy, Steinbock's attempt to ground the duty to warn in the right to informed consent rather than in the actual risk fails. I conclude that the primary duty in connection with sexual transmission of HIV, and the duty on which attention should be focused, is not the duty to warn, but the duty to practice safe(r) sex.

1.

The first reason to question the view that persons diagnosed with HIV infection have an obligation to warn their sex partners is that this view seems to feed the mistaken and dangerous presumption that, absent a warning from or about a particular partner, one can presume that sexual interaction is by-and-large safe. In fact, just the opposite is true: even if persons who know they are HIV+ had an obligation to warn, many of them would not act on that obligation. And even if all of them did, there are still many HIV+ persons who would not warn because they are unaware of their status. Thus the proper presumption of persons considering sexual intimacy is that, unless they have good reason to believe otherwise, they should assume their partner might be infected (not just with HIV, but other pathogens as well).

When I say that the obligation to warn view *feeds the presumption*, I do not mean to suggest logical entailment. There is no logical contradiction in believing both that those who know they are infected should warn, and also that one should be cautious even of partners who do not warn. I mean that the one view psychologically supports the other. A parallel situation exists in connection with the question of whether health care workers should be warned of patients who are known to be HIV+. On the face of it, they would be better off if warned about the risk posed by contact with a particular patient. Evidence exists, however, that this is not so,[3] and a consensus has emerged among public health authorities that the best strategy for minimizing patient-to-health care worker transmission is to urge health care workers to use "universal precautions" on the presumption that all patients are infected. In general, then, everyone does better to conceptualize the arena of sexual interaction (like the arena of patient care) as a dangerous one containing unmarked risks, than to presume one is safe unless warned about a particular HIV+ individual. Caveat emptor.

The second reason to question the view that HIV+ persons have an obligation to warn their sex partners is related to the first: the primary moral imperative these days in connection with minimizing the risk of transmitting HIV sexually is not to give (or heed) specific warnings, but to avoid unsafe practices, unless one has good reason to believe both oneself and one's partner are uninfected. We know some practices are safer than others. When used properly, condoms provide a high level of protection during intercourse, but fall short of absolute protection. In this connection more people might do well to explore the possibility of sexual interaction that does not take the form of (vaginal or anal) intercourse. Once "sexual intimacy" is given a more expansive interpretation than "sexual intercourse," a lot of sex is safe. This isn't just a question of how "sexual intimacy" is to be *defined*, but a suggestion that many people would do well to reevaluate, and consider expanding, their ideas about how sexual intimacy can be satisfying without involving intercourse.

These two considerations come together as follows. Sexually active individuals find it easy enough to deny the risk of exposure to HIV. This denial provides the basis for a tremendous amount of irresponsible, unsafe sexual activity. The presumption of an obligation to warn tends to reinforce the presumption that the responsibility to prevent HIV transmission lies with those who are infected. This in turn feeds the denial of those who are not warned, and hence encourages irresponsible, unsafe sexual activity.

The third reason to question whether an HIV+ diagnosed person has an obligation to warn involves the impact such an obligation would have on an individual's decision about whether to be tested. Early treatments are already available that provide early diagnosis with clear medical benefit. These medical benefits can only increase as more treatments become available. These benefits, combined with the public health benefits one might expect from people's becoming more careful about safe practices on hearing they are infected, might strike third parties as a compelling case for persons who think they might be infected to seek testing.

From the perspective of persons who fear they might be infected, however, reasons, often powerful, exist for not being tested. Learning of a terminal condition has direct psychological costs, especially for people who presently feel healthy. (Many people with family histories of Huntington's have elected to forgo genetic testing that would reveal their own chances of suffering that disease.) Moreover, when persons who learn they are HIV+ seek recommended medical care, HIV positivity is entered into their medical record. This can trigger various forms of legal and illegal discrimination. Finally, many of one's social relationships can be profoundly altered for the worse, both through the infected person's own knowledge of the infection and through others' knowledge of it. In spite of the medical benefits to HIV+ persons of early treatment, these costs of learning one is infected often loom so large that many persons who realize they might be infected opt against testing. If such persons also believe, as Steinbock would urge, that if (or when) they find they are HIV+, they will then incur an obligation to inform prospective sex partners of their infection, they may well feel that they have one more reason not to seek testing. (There is an analogous medical argument in connection with the Centers for Disease Control's February 1995 recommendation that all pregnant women should be tested.[4] While the policy promises substantial medical benefits to unborn children, who might be spared HIV infection through AZT treatment of their mothers during pregnancy, it will almost certainly mean some women, fearing the revelation that they are HIV+, will be less inclined to seek early prenatal care.) At least two costs are associated with HIV+ persons deciding against testing. First, they would lose the benefits of early diagnosis and treatment. Second, they would also aggravate the problem alluded to in connection with our first argument against an obligation to warn: many would increase the ratio of undiagnosed HIV+ people to diagnosed HIV+ people, and that would increase the danger of transmission to persons who believed that, absent specific knowledge of an infection, they could assume their partners were uninfected.

2.

The "duty to tell," then, is a red herring, and attention to it could distract from the central obligation of people seeking sexual intimacy: to make sex as safe as possible. I wish now to turn to Steinbock's argument that even if sex is safe, HIV+ persons still have an obligation to inform their partners. At one point, Steinbock argues this is so because "intimate contact is permissible only if it is voluntary."[5] (She also speaks of information needed "to make a fully voluntary decision.")[6] Steinbock's explication of this argument is clouded somewhat by her choice of example, which involves Rock Hudson kissing Linda Evans during the filming of an episode of the television show *Dynasty*, before anyone knew HIV could not be transmitted by kissing. But Steinbock clarifies her view; she claims that *even if* Hudson had known that kissing was extremely unlikely to transmit the virus, what he did was still wrong, because Linda Evans

> did not agree to kiss someone with a potentially communicable fatal disease. She could agree to that only if she knew about it. Even if the risk of catching AIDS from kissing is low, the decision whether to take that risk is hers, and hers alone.[7]

The idea seems to be that sexual intimacy is morally permissible only if it is "agreed to," and agreement requires consent informed by any knowledge of risk (however minuscule) that is posed by the person to whom one is consenting.

Is this view plausible? The requirement of "full information" is certainly appropriate in some contexts (for instance, interactions between patient and doctor), although even in these contexts an interpretation of "fully informed" is needed. But in most contexts, parties give legitimate consent without anything like "full information." We pay to attend films and we buy books, without knowing their contents fully in advance. Some of us buy pull-tabs, even though we are denied advance knowledge of an important piece of information (whether it's a winner or loser). Often we consent to arrangements we might later regret, without anything like "full information" of the costs and risks of which the other party is aware. We agree to blind (and even ordinary) dates, not knowing what we are getting into; we contract to vacation in exotic places whose crime and disease rates are unknown to us; we use airlines, cruise lines, and trains whose safety records we don't know.

Perhaps Steinbock's view is that although consent to some assumption of risk is valid with less than a full sharing of information about risk by the person to whom we are consenting, something unique about sexual intimacy distinguishes it in this regard. Steinbock seems to suggest this possibility when she says that Hudson's duty to warn Evans of his infection prior to the kiss "stems from the nature of kissing as an intimate activity."[8] She claims that for Hudson not to tell Evans of his infection "is to keep her ignorant of information she needs to make a fully voluntary decision. Even if the risk of catching AIDS from kissing is minuscule, the decision whether to take that risk is hers, and hers alone."[9] Steinbock's view seems to be that people must know everything their partners know about possible risks of intimacy between them, in order for consent to intimacy to be fully voluntary.

But that one has a special right to know (or a special duty to tell) of even remote risks, when one is about to engage in intimacy, is implausible. What if Hudson had not had AIDS, but had just had a sip of water from the glass of someone who did? Or suppose Evans gets me back to her place, where she hasn't yet had a chance to replace the dead battery in her smoke detector. I suggest intimacy. Does she have a special obligation to warn me about the slight risk of an undetected fire? Does she have more of an obligation to warn me, than she would to warn a casual friend who was to stay in her guest room for the night? I see no reason for believing that the intimate nature of what is about to transpire between Evans and myself generates any special obligation to warn, above and beyond the general obligation we all have not to put others in (significant) harm's way. More generally, I see no reason for believing that legitimate consent to sexual intimacy requires "full information."

On the contrary, there are several reasons to doubt that sexual intimacy is a context, like medicine, in which legitimate consent requires "full information." The first is that if sexual intimacy had to be fully informed in order to be consensual, then everyone who withheld relevant information from their partners would not only be wronging them, but raping them. The second is that imagining what would count as "full information" in the context of sexual intimacy is difficult. No one is ever truly *fully* informed, and hence what counts as "full" information needs to be specified. A "reasonable person" standard seems especially problematic in the context of sexual intimacy, since what reasonable persons would expect or want to know is unclear. Two people who care a lot about each other and are about to become sexually intimate (or for that matter are about to get married) are seldom indifferent to information about each other's romantic histories, but yet might not particularly want to hear it all. And even if they would, they might be well advised not to. More generally, the suggestion that sexual intimacy (even a kiss) must be preceded by revelation of "full information" (*however* that might plausibly be interpreted) is completely at odds with our most fundamental intuitions about the nature of courtship and romance as a "high-stakes game." Courtship, even in the form of the "one night stand" that plays itself out within 12 hours, does not consist first of full revelation of all relevant facts about oneself, followed by the early stages of sexual intimacy. Rather, escalating self-revelation (including escalating revelation of each person's interest in the other) is a key feature of courtship, which ordinarily continues long after the earliest stages of sexual intimacy. Anyone entering a singles' bar expecting prospective partners to be open about everything one might like to know about them is too naive to be entering a singles bar.

Charles Fried proposes an account of the role privacy plays in intimacy, friendship, and love that is able to accommodate and explain this feature of courtship.[10] Fried proposes his account in the context of trying to explain why we place such a high value on privacy, that is, on control and selective revelation of information about ourselves. Fried's explanation is that privacy is a precondition to the cultivation of trust, intimacy, friendship, and love. According to Fried, everyone has a right to keep certain things private, and morality requires us to respect each other's right to privacy. This privacy is important to each of us (and hence, ultimately, a right) because the things we are entitled to keep private are the stuff of which intimacy, friendship, and love are made. Intimacy between two people, according to Fried, consists in their freely sharing certain things with each other that they do not share indiscriminately with others. "Love is a spontaneous relinquishment of certain entitlements of one's own to the be-loved, a free and generous relinquishment inspired by a regard which goes beyond impartial respect."[11] Fried does not claim this is the whole of love, which also involves new and shared interests and reciprocal support. But he does claim it is an essential feature:

> Love and friendship, as analyzed here, involve the initial respect for the rights of others which morality requires of everyone. They further involve the voluntary and spontaneous relinquishment of *something* between friend and friend, lover and lover. The title to information about oneself conferred by privacy provides the necessary something. To be friends or lovers persons must be intimate to some degree with each other. But intimacy is the sharing of information about one's actions, beliefs, or emotions which one does not share with all, and which one has the right not to share with anyone. By conferring this right, priv-

> acy creates the moral capital which we spend in friendship and love. . . . In general it is my thesis that in developed social contexts love, friendship and trust are possible only if persons enjoy and accord to each other a certain measure of privacy.[12]

I believe Fried's view lends itself to an account of the gradual escalation that is such a prominent feature of courtship, and which Steinbock's view is hard-pressed to accommodate. It offers a view both of what exactly is being escalated (information about oneself, including information about one's interest in the other party) and of why it is valuable: "by degrees," one is relinquishing control of "private" information that is one's "moral capital" for friendship and intimacy. Escalating sexual intimacy can itself be seen as a part of that escalating self-revelation. It is a matter of freely (and selectively) sharing "private" parts and sides of oneself with the beloved that one does not share indiscriminately with everyone. (A decided advantage of Fried's account is that it provides a rational account of jealousy.) Thus the revelation of *any* important private information about oneself can play an important role in courtship, as well as in the development of that less intense form of intimacy, friendship. "Love is a hazardous game" precisely because we make ourselves vulnerable, and one of the ways we do that is by surrendering control of important and private information about ourselves.

Naturally, not all sexual intimacy occurs in the context of courtship; not everyone seeking sex does so in the context of an extended courtship or a loving relationship. However, even (perhaps especially) people seeking sex without love are entitled to their privacy and, again, people entering singles' bars are well advised to understand that.

Are these considerations sufficient to show that persons who know they are HIV+ have no obligation to warn prospective sex partners of their infection? Even if we accept Fried's account of the role of privacy in courtship and in the nurturing of intimacy, and then infer from it that HIV+ persons have a right to keep their HIV status information private, that says nothing about whether they ought to stand on that right. I have a right to my money and no charity has a claim to any of it, but it would be morally shabby of me to give nothing to charity. Still, Fried's account of the connection between privacy and intimacy grounds a persuasive refutation of Steinbock's claim that people have a *right* to information about their prospective partners, prior to any sexual intimacy. That leaves open the question of what *decency* requires of an HIV+ person by way of revelation.

Further, even if two persons engaging in courtship (or pursuing casual sex) have no obligation to provide each other with private information about themselves, they do have an obligation not to lie. Deception is *prima facie* wrong, and becomes a serious wrong if someone's happiness or welfare hinges on not being deceived. There is no philosophical dispute about that. Thus for those who believe that they should never unknowingly be subjected to any risk of HIV transmission in the context of intimacy, "even if the risk is minuscule," let the shoe be placed on the other foot. Let them ask their prospective partners whether or not they know they are infected with HIV. Putting the point this way, I think, might bring home how much Steinbock is asking of HIV+ persons.

Notes

1. Bonnie Steinbock, "Harming, Wronging, and AIDS," paper presented at a meeting of the Society for the Philosophy of Sex and Love, San Francisco, March 1987 [hereafter, SPSL]; "Harming, Wronging, and AIDS," in James M. Humber and Robert F. Almeder, eds., *Biomedical Ethics Reviews, 1988: AIDS and Ethics* (Clifton, N.J.: Humana Press, 1989), 27-43 [hereafter, BER].

2. Steinbock, SPSL.

3. Julie Louise Gerberding, Gary Littell, Ada Tarkington, Andrew Brown, and William P. Schecter, "Risk of Exposure of Surgical Personnel to Patients' Blood During Surgery at San Francisco General Hospital," *New England Journal of Medicine* 332:25 (21 June 1990): 1788-93, at 1788.

4. "CDC 1995 Recommendations for HIV Counseling and Testing for Pregnant Women" (draft dated 23 February 1995). Available from CDC National AIDS Clearinghouse, P. O. Box 6003, Rockville, MD 20845-6003.

5. Steinbock, BER, 27.

6. Steinbock, SPSL.

7. Steinbock, BER, 33.

8. Steinbock, SPSL.

9. *Ibid.*

10. Charles Fried, "Privacy," *Yale Law Journal* 77:475 (1968): 475-93, at 480.

11. *Ibid.*

12. *Ibid.*, 484, 482.

Phyllis Soble (left) and Alan Soble (right)
(photograph: Sylvia Soble)

Alan Soble, author of "The Coherence of Love"
Paper presented at the Society for the Philosophy of Sex and Love
during the
Eastern Division Meeting of The American Philosophical Association
New York, N.Y., 29 December 1987

Forty-Four

LOVE AT SECOND SIGHT[1]

Alan Soble

> At our first meeting, . . . we found ourselves so taken with each other, . . . so bound together, that from that time on nothing was so close to us as each other.
>
> Montaigne, "Of Friendship"

> Martha is mine, the sweet girl of whom everyone speaks with admiration, who despite all my resistance captivated my heart at our first meeting, the girl I feared to want and who came towards me with high-minded confidence.
>
> Freud (letter to Martha Bernays, 1882)

1. Gellner's Paradox

In a paper devoted to comparing existentialist and Kantian ethics, E. A. Gellner begins by asking, "Is love at first sight *possible*?"[2] While sitting in his dentist's waiting room perusing women's magazines, Gellner found that articles on love at first sight assumed it existed, the major question addressed being empirical: How often does it occur? But for Gellner the issue is "in part or wholly logical" (158) rather than empirical; to support his suspicion he constructed an a priori argument designed to show that love at first sight was impossible (158-63). I will lay out in detail Gellner's argument that love at first sight is as logically impossible as a round square (not that it is only contingently nonexistent, like the unicorn). Because it throws into sharp relief the problems attributed to erosic loves, Gellner's argument will haunt us on almost every page.

Imagine that a person X has an encounter with a person Y, the first contact of any kind between them. (Gellner does not specify the length of this meeting or what transpires between X and Y.) We might even suppose that the encounter is at a distance and that X only catches sight of Y without talking with Y.[3] After or during this encounter, X experiences some emotion, a feeling, or an attitude toward Y. (Gellner uses these terms interchangeably.) Also assume that X's emotion arises in virtue of X's "noticing" a set S of Y's attractive properties. We can understand this in several ways. Does "X notices S in Y" mean that X correctly perceives S in Y; that X falsely believes that Y has S, either because X hopes that Y has S or because Y pretends to have S; or that X perceives S in Y only unconsciously? To get to the heart of Gellner's argument (he does not say what he means by "X notices S in Y"), let us assume that X consciously and correctly perceives that Y has S, and X realizes that

S is responsible for X's emotion. So the unnamed emotion that X has is property-based and reason-dependent.

Once we assume that X has an attitude toward Y (that is, xAy) because X notices a set S of Y's properties, the expression "first encounter" can be understood in two ways: we might be talking about (1) the emotion X has after X's first encounter *tout court* with Y or (2) the emotion X has after the encounter with Y at which X first notices S. Alternative (2) allows that X had earlier encounters with Y during which X did not notice S and so did not experience any emotion toward Y. But I am sure that Gellner means (1), in which "first sight" is meant literally. Alternative (2) is more complex and suggests a different phenomenon: X knows Y, perhaps has even loved Y for some time, and suddenly realizes that he loves Y or notices that Y has S and is lovable.

Suppose that some time after meeting and responding to Y, X meets another person Z. We are asked by Gellner to assume something interesting about Z: he or she also has the set S that Y has. Persons Y and Z, however, are not altogether identical; we assume only that X notices in Z the same set S that X noticed in Y and in virtue of which X has the emotion toward Y. (We might be tempted to assume that Z has no additional property P [beyond S], a property so annoying to X that S in Z cannot have its effect on X; but to assume this only about Z is wrong. Both Y and Z must lack this P, if S in Y or S in Z is to elicit X's emotion. We can include "lacks all such annoying properties" in the set S that both Y and Z have.) The likelihood that X will have an encounter with this relevantly similar Z cannot be ruled out; after all, X noticed S in Y during only one encounter. Now that X has met this similar Z, there are only two, mutually exclusive possibilities. Either the emotional response that X had toward Y occurs again toward Z. Or X does not have that experience again (perhaps X has other feelings toward Z, or none at all). Gellner proceeds to argue that the emotion X has toward Y cannot be love and hence cannot be love at first sight, whether or not X has the same emotion towards Z.

The argument is a classical dilemma and has two horns. First, if when having the encounter with the relevantly similar Z, X *does* have the emotion toward Z that X has toward Y, then X's emotion for Y is not love. And, second, if X does *not* have the same experience toward Z, then (nevertheless!) X's emotion for Y cannot be love. Since there are only two possibilities, and each one implies that X's emotion for Y is not love, Gellner's argument shows that it is impossible that the emotion experienced by X after the one encounter with Y is love. (Note that Gellner must assume that whether or not X has the same emotion toward Z, X is still experiencing the emotion toward Y upon meeting Z. For if X before meeting Z no longer has that feeling toward Y, or if during X's encounter with Z the feeling evaporates, we might already be able to conclude that X's emotion for Y was not love, and the rest of Gellner's argument would be superfluous.)

Our task is to substantiate the claims that if xAy and later xAz (X's unnamed attitude toward Y is repeated toward Z), then ~xLy (the attitude is not love); and that if xAy and later ~xAz, then still ~xLy. Symbolically, Gellner wants to establish, when X notices S in both Y and Z, that

1. (xAy & xAz) $\rightarrow$ ~xLy, or (xAy & xAz) $\rightarrow$ ~(A = L)

and

2. (xAy & ~xAz) $\rightarrow$ ~xLy, or (xAy & ~xAz) $\rightarrow$ ~(A = L).

The first horn states that if X's attitude is repeated toward Z, X's attitude toward Y cannot be love. Gellner's reason is straightforward. Love is by its very nature, or logically, exclusive; it can have "only one object" (159). The "very recurrence" of the attitude toward another person shows it is not love. If X claims to have the same attitude toward both Y and Z, then X is wrong to think that the attitude is love; X cannot love both Y and Z, as a matter not of morality or psychology but of conceptual necessity.

Gellner's argument to establish the first horn seems awfully heavy-handed, as if Gellner defines love in advance as exclusive and uses this definition to proclaim that it could not possibly be true that xLy if X's attitude is repeated toward Z. Do we not feel inclined to say that whether X's love turns out to be exclusive is an empirical issue? After all, many X's claim to love two people, and defining love as exclusive begs the question against them. Further, Gellner does not indicate clearly what the exclusivity of love means; "very recurrence" and "only one object" do not sufficiently nail down this idea.[4] Nevertheless, what Gellner is getting at makes good sense. If X meets Y at t_1 and experiences A, and then X meets a relevantly similar Z at some time t_2 after t_1, again experiencing A, we have good reason to doubt that xLy. (Try t_1=noon, t_2=12:15 P.M.)

Note that Gellner's assumption that Z, too, has S is not needed to establish the first horn. If the "very recurrence" of the attitude toward Z shows that X does not love Y, the exclusivity of love rules out X's loving both Y and Z even if xAy in virtue of Y's having S and xAz in virtue of Z's having some other set of properties T. Perhaps assuming that Z also has S makes more likely that X develops the attitude toward Z. But assuming that Z also has S allows the first horn to be defended independently of a claim about exclusivity. For if X's attitudes toward both Y and Z are grounded in Y's and Z's having the same S, then perhaps X merely loves two tokens of the same type[5] or loves only S itself and not either Y or Z.[6] Rather than appeal to the exclusivity of love to establish the first horn, we could appeal to what it means to "love the person" in some technical sense.

Having argued that if xAz, then it is false that xLy, Gellner seems unable to establish the second horn. After all, if the exclusivity of love entails that if X does have the same emotion toward Z and Y, then this emotion is not love, then the fact that X does not experience the emotion again when encountering Z seems compatible with X's emotion toward Y being love. Our friend X has met the Z who also has S and has remained attitude-faithful toward Y. So why does Gellner claim that even in this case X does not love Y? Here is the argument:

> [suppose] that X does *not* have the same attitude . . . towards the new possessor of S as he had towards Y. . . . [T]his equally constitutes conclusive evidence for X not really loving Y. For S is all he knows of Y; if . . . on reëncountering S the original emotion . . . is not reëvoked, this shows that it had not really been connected with its apparent stimulus and object, that it had been accidental, arbitrary, and without any of the significance which one normally attributes to [love]. (159-60)

We assumed that Y's having S (or X's noticing S in Y) explained xAy. So if X meets Z and Z also has S, then Z's having S (or X's noticing S in Z) should produce the same effect. The fact that X does not experience the same feeling toward Z when presented with the same situation contradicts that assumption.[7] Hence, Y's having S was not responsible for xAy after all. Further, since S fails to evoke xAz, why believe that during X's encounter with Z the fact that Y has S continues to evoke xAy? Or that S will evoke xAy well after X's encounter with Z, or during X's second encounter with Y? The fact that S failed to evoke xAz implies that S is not the ground of xAy initially or on a continuing basis. So what? Why conclude that if xAy in virtue of something other than Y's having S, X's emotion toward Y is not love? The point is that X's emotion toward Y is due not to anything about Y but to something about X.[8] If the ground of xAy is not Y's having S, then Y, it turns out, is incidental to the occurrence of X's emotion; and if so, X's emotion is whimsical ("arbitrary") in a way incompatible with its being love. There is no sense, for Gellner, in saying that X loves Y in particular unless some tight connection exists between Y, or Y's having S, and X's emotion. And it is the failure of Z's having S to elicit xAz that shows that the required tight connection between Y's having S and xAy is lacking. In a word: the second horn is established by assuming that love is property-based and reason-dependent, in which case Gellner's paradox derives from, or presupposes, the central thesis of the first ("erosic") view of personal love.

This, then, is Gellner's paradox: it is impossible that xLy after their first encounter, whether or not xAz when X meets the similar Z. We might express it this way: if the connection between X's having an emotion and S is tight, then X does not love Y because the tightness guarantees that X will also have the emotion toward others who have S; and if the connection between X's emotion and S is not tight (as shown by ~xAz), then X does not love Y because Y's having S is not responsible for X's emotion. No third alternative can be squeezed between a "tight" and a "not tight" connection between X's emotion and S. Either Y's having S accounts for xAy, as in the eros tradition, or it does not. And if we assume, as we did in the second horn, that the connection must be tight, then love at first sight is impossible.

2. Knowledge and Love at First Sight

Gellner's argument is that love at first sight is impossible on the grounds that love is both exclusive and property-based. But there are other arguments against the existence of love at first sight that deserve consideration before we return to Gellner. One argument is that this phenomenon is unlikely because love is necessarily reciprocal[9] and during one encounter X's emotion will generally fail in this regard. Another is that love at first sight does not exist because when the phenomenon is occurring it has not yet proven itself to have the constancy required for love. Neither argument is convincing; relying on claims about the reciprocity and constancy of love (or, as in Gellner, its exclusivity) is like hitting a slow cockroach with a *New Yorker*. More interesting are arguments based on a claim about the relationship between X's knowledge of Y and X's emotion toward Y. There might be no such thing as love at first sight because during X's first encounter with Y (1) X is not in a position to believe anything about Y, (2) X cannot reliably believe anything true about Y, or (3) X cannot be believing anything significant (as opposed to trivial) about Y. These arguments nip love at first sight in the bud at the place Gellner's argument begins, by raising doubts about X's "noticing" S in Y.

Montaigne might be a counterexample to the argument relying on claim (1), for Montaigne said that his love for Boétie was both "at first sight" and not reason-dependent: not only was his love not based on his beloved's properties, but also not possibly based on them. Claim (1), then, does not show that agapic love at first sight, in particular, is impossible; at most it shows that love at first sight cannot be erosic. On the other hand, Montaigne's experience might confirm the argument; he was wrong to call his emotion "love" at that early stage of his relationship with Boétie, just because it occurred at first sight and could not be based on anything about Boétie. To argue that love at first sight does not exist because X could not know anything about Y, however, is implausible. I find it difficult to suppose that during a first encounter X has no beliefs about Y or Y's properties; even if X encounters Y only at a distance, X will perceive some of Y's properties.

An argument relying on (1) might be what Philip Slater had in mind when he wrote that love at first sight "can only be transference, in psychoanalytic sense, since there is nothing . . . on which it can be based."[10] Slater's point, however, might not be that love at first sight cannot be based on X's knowledge of Y because X could not have any knowledge of this unknown Y; rather, he might mean that love at first sight cannot be based on X's knowledge of Y because X's emotion is out of proportion to the information X has about Y.[11] But let us assume that Slater means that love at first sight is only transference because X could not know anything about Y. If so, the real object of X's emotion, for Slater, is not Y; the "real object is not [even] the actual parent . . . but a fantasy image of that parent which has been retained, ageless and unchanging, in the unconscious."[12] Slater concludes that romantic love at first sight, being transference, is "Oedipal love," that is, still a kind of love, and hence that love at first sight exists even though disconnected from Y, who is not "really" its object. Alternatively, we could say that love at first sight does not exist; it is only transference, not a kind of love at all. This transference is made possible, if not fueled, by the fact that X is not in a position to know anything about Y. But neither account is compelling; the most sensible way to understand why X has the emotion now as a result of an encounter with Y is to say that X notices some properties S of Y, either consciously or unconsciously. Slater's Oedipal love at first sight is not disconnected from Y; Y's having the S that matches (or conjures in X's mind) the properties of the parent image is exactly why X has the emotion toward Y. If Y did not have properties approximating the "ageless and unchanging" image of X's parent, not even the psychoanalyst could comprehend X's emotion. Slater's psychoanalysis provides a deep explanation of X's emotion: it tells us why S is attractive for X and why X tends to love persons who have S.

On the other hand, X's not being in a position to know anything about Y might allow X to imagine that Y has S, and X's strong need to find a parent replacement induces X to do what is possible, so that X merely imagines (falsely) that Y has S. Irving Singer interprets the psychoanalytic view this way: "No one can bring back the goddess of his childhood; and since that is how the Freudian lover must envisage his beloved, love can only involve illusion, even delusion."[13] One might argue against love at first sight, then, by relying on claim (2): since X's emotion occurs after one meeting, X cannot believe much that is true of Y, in which case X's emotion is not love. But this argument, too, is unconvincing. First, X's having only one encounter with Y does not entail that the beliefs and perceptions X does have about Y are mostly false. X's beliefs might be true but incomplete; X sees some good but not yet the bad in Y. But X's not having the emotion toward Y when X finally sees the bad does not entail that earlier X's emotion was not love.[14] Second, neither the eros nor the agape tradition insists that xLy entails that X has only true beliefs about Y. In the eros tradition, the intentionality of love logically permits that xLy in virtue of X's believing falsely that Y has P; X's loving Y is explained by X's thinking that Y has P, and why X thinks that Y has P is (in this context) beside the point. The love that X has for Y, if based on false beliefs, might be irrational, but it is still love.[15] And if X's love is based altogether on illusions about Y, then Y might not be the emotion's object (or X might not be loving Y "as a person"),[16] but the emotion is still love. In the agape tradition, X's believing falsely that Y has P is no impediment to love; since X's love is not based on Y's having P, X's believing falsely that Y has P is irrelevant. Further, X might know little or nothing about Y in the special case of agapic love for the stranger. When we assist the stranger who asks for help, we love her agapically "at first sight," even though we know nothing about her, might even falsely imagine that she is dangerous, or might be deliberately deceived by her as to her actual need.

However, we can interpret agapic love for the stranger not as loving despite having no knowledge about the strange person, but as loving when we do have knowledge. We know nothing in particular about the stranger, but these particularities are trivial. What we know immediately about the stranger is that he is a person, which is the only significant thing about him that we need to know. Erosic love at first sight might not exist, then, because even though X might know much about Y, X does not usually know anything significant about Y. Love, in this view, requires that X have not merely true beliefs about Y but a deep knowledge of Y; and this significant knowledge takes time to obtain.[17] This argument raises questions we will address: Is there a plausible way to distinguish between the beloved's significant and trivial properties? Is a love based on significant properties superior to one based on the trivial?[18] This question presupposes that love can be based on trivial properties; indeed, that is an empirical fact about personal love, as recognized by Plato's Pausanias. Hence, to argue that love at first sight is not love, because love is grounded in deep knowledge of the object, is too heavy-handed. If there are no a priori limits, or only weak ones, on what properties the lover finds attractive enough to ground love, we might be able to distinguish "bad" from "good" love (for example, vulgar versus heavenly eros) by distinguishing significant from trivial properties. But that is not the difference between loving and not loving.

When Descartes wrote to Chanut (6 June 1647)[19] about "the reasons which . . . impel us to love one person rather than another before we know their worth," he was asserting that one can love without perfect knowledge; but did Descartes intend "before we know their worth" to mean that X can love Y without any beliefs about Y's worth, or without knowledge of Y's significant (that is, worthful) properties? Regardless, his approach is more Skinnerian than Freudian: "When I was a child, I loved a little girl of my own age, who had a slight squint. The impression made . . . in my brain when I looked at her cross eyes became so closely connected to the simultaneous impression arousing in me the passion of love, that for a long time afterward when I saw cross-eyed persons I felt a special inclination to love them. . . . So, when we are inclined to love someone without knowing the reason [that is, before knowing their worth, which would be a reason], . . . this is because he has some similarity to something in an earlier object of our love, though we may not be able to identify it." Descartes, it seems, is a proponent of the first view of personal love.[20] Love can have both reason-causes (the object's worth) and nonreason-causes that exist in virtue of being psychologically associated with properties that have aroused "the passion of love." To Montaigne Descartes might have said: examine thyself, and you will find reasons and causes plenty for your loving Boétie. Further, Descartes claims not only that nonreason-causes need not remain unconscious (he figured out the influence of squints on his choice of beloveds), but also that nonreason-causes are controllable: "At that time I did not know that was the reason for my love; and as soon as I reflected on it . . . I was no longer affected by it." If Descartes did not wish to love on the basis of such a trivial nonreason-cause as squints, he was not locked into that pattern. Whether one can unencumber oneself of Freudian transference as easily as of Skinnerian associations is another question.

3. The Impossibility of Love

What has Gellner shown to be logically impossible, if anything? There are three candidates: (i) love-at-first-sight; (ii) love, at first sight (after one encounter); and (iii) love (period). To defend the first horn of his dilemma, Gellner appealed to a claim about love: it is exclusive. I think this claim about love (that is, about love, period) might establish that (ii) is impossible, but it does not establish that (i) is impossible; and to the extent that Gellner establishes that (ii) is impossible, he also shows that (iii) is impossible.

We do refer to certain experiences with the words "love at first sight." Many Xs have been instantly impassioned by Ys with arousing Ss, and they are hardly reluctant to call this experience love or love at first sight. One trouble with Gellner's relying on a claim about love (period) is that it prevents us from asking whether love at first sight might nevertheless be a form of love, even if it is not genuine love. And his argument misleadingly implies that there is so such phenomenon as that reported by all these Xs; he seems to get an empirical conclusion (like the nonexistence of unicorns) from a priori considerations. (Both these problems also infect the argument that love at first sight does not exist because love requires deep knowledge.) An argument relying on a claim about love (period) touches only the possibility of "love, after one encounter." If we use the hyphenated expression "love-at-first-sight" to refer to X's experience, Gellner's argument does not show that (i) is impossible, only that the expression is a misnomer; we should call it "δ" or "Φ-at-first-sight." That conclusion is conceptual and not empirical; it permits us to concede the existence of the phenomenon and to inquire whether δ is (vicariously) called love because it often becomes love.

Because Gellner uses a claim about (iii), love (period), to show that (ii), love after one encounter, is impossible, his argument also shows that (iii) is impossible. Look at the basic pattern of his dilemma:

1. xAy in virtue of S (A = has an emotion toward)
2. xMz who has S (M = has an encounter with)
3. either xAz or ~xAz
4. if xAz, then ~xLy (L = loves)
5. if ~xAz, then ~xLy

ergo,

6. ~xLy

Nothing in this pattern relies essentially on X's emotion toward Y arising after their first encounter. If so, Gellner has uncovered a full-blown paradox about love, period. This is an interpretation of his argument I think he intended and would endorse. For when Gellner attempts to solve the paradox, what he proposes encompasses not only love at first sight but also love, period.

Furthermore, there is no way to prevent the extension of the paradox to love, period. For Gellner has not told us what difference there is between xAy after one encounter and xAy after a second encounter. What is special about a second encounter with Y that helps X avoid the catch-22 when xMz? How might love at second sight be possible while love at first sight is not? Gellner's dilemma depends only on assuming that X notices S in Y and then again in Z; whether X and Y have had many encounters, or only one, seems irrelevant. Perhaps during a second encounter with Y, X notices a larger or different set T of Y's properties that is unlikely to be matched by Z, and therefore xMz never occurs. But if T includes S, and S elicited xAy initially and still does so, then even though Z has only the smaller set S and not the full T, xMz will still occur; that is, X will meet some Z with the relevant emotion-eliciting properties. To say, instead, that T does not include S, is to say that after X's second encounter with Y, xAy is based on different properties than it was initially; but if so, there is no warrant to suppose that, after the second encounter, xMz will not occur. For if there is a person Z who, by having S, relevantly resembles Y after the first encounter between X and Y, there will also be a person W who, by having T, relevantly resembles Y after the second encounter. This sort of answer, then, must say not only that T does include S, but also that the additional properties R in T are partly responsible for xAy after the second encounter (in which case T is sufficient for xAy; S is no longer sufficient but, like R, necessary), and that the additional properties R rule out xMz. With time, X might acquire additional reasons for loving Y. But this answer asserts that merely between the first and the second encounter of X and Y, Y's having S has (mysteriously) lost its power, having been demoted from sufficient for X's emotion to only necessary. We therefore have grounds for thinking (see Gellner's second horn) that S never had that power during the first encounter.

But the spirit of this answer is all wrong. For even if xAy on the basis of a larger set T after the second encounter, X's meeting some W who also has T is not logically ruled out, but only more unlikely than X's meeting some Z who has S after X's first encounter with Y. Whether Gellner's dilemma succeeds even when applied to X's first encounter with Y depends, then, on murky empirical matters, that is, on how likely it is that X meets the Z who also has S. This result is embarrassing to an argument purporting to establish an a priori conclusion. Since we have found no meaningful difference attributable to X's second encounter with Y, the paradox applies equally to love at *second* sight. By a sort of mathematical induction we can modify Gellner's argument against the possibility of love after one encounter into an argument against the possibility of love, period.[21]

4. Nongeneral Love-Reasons

Gellner's solution to the paradox is that love is an "E-type" attitude. Some attitudes and emotions (for example, love, patriotism, religious commitment), according to Gellner, are "puzzling" in the way they attach to objects in a nongeneralizable ("nonuniversalizable") manner. "An agent acting in accordance with an E-type preference" for an object will not act or respond in the same way "with regard to another instance if one turned up" (161). Suppose X notices S in Y and on that basis xAy; later X encounters Z and again notices S, but ~xAz. Gellner claims that xLy after all: the facts ~xAz and xLy are compatible because the reason that X has for loving Y (namely, that Y has S) is not generalizable to other persons. The lover operates according to a nongeneral reason, not according to a reason he would apply to relevantly similar cases. Thus the dilemma is solved by escaping along the second horn. For Gellner, love is reason-dependent, as in the first view of love, yet love is not the sort of emotion for which reasons are generalizable. Gellner does not, however, claim that love-reasons are perfectly nongeneral; his supposition that xLy continues on the basis of Y's having S means that, for him, love-reasons are time-generalizable, even if they are not object-generalizable. Note that we could have stated Gellner's dilemma in terms of Y's having S being the nonreason-cause for xLy rather than X's reason. Since nonreason-causes are perfectly general given the same initial conditions, S should induce both xAy and xAz, thereby violating the exclusivity requirement of the first horn; while xAy and ~xAz, as in the second horn, would show that Y's having S was not, after all, the nonreason-cause of xAy. Gellner's solution, that love involves nongeneral reasons, if transformed into a thesis about nonreason-causes, becomes the dramatic assertion that love (or exclusive love) is possible only by a miracle, a disruption of the regularity of causation.

Claiming that love-reasons are not general might seem to be an awful price to pay for a solution to the paradox, for E-type attitudes are irrational (consider the incoherence of "nongeneralizable reason"), in which case love is irrational if it exists at all. On the other hand, perhaps the solution is acceptable, given the result achieved. Denying the generalizability of love-reasons preserves the exclusivity of love at the same time that the basis of love remains the attractiveness of the object. Hence, the solution solves a major difficulty in the eros tradition by explaining how exclusive love is possible. However, concessions have been made; the problem is not merely that Gellner's solution entails that exclusive love is irrational but that it entails that love is necessarily irrational. The blame for love's irrationality falls squarely on the shoulders of X, the lover, for it is X who loves Y on the basis of S and who fails to respond to Z, or who refuses or is unable to love a similar Z, despite having an adequate reason (as X himself has proven with respect to Y) for doing so.[22] Lovers single out one person who has S to love, while not loving others who also have S, quite because lovers single out love-reasons as nongeneral, even though the logic of reasons requires that all reasons be treated as general. That is, the lover also has an E-type attitude toward love-reasons. (Solving the paradox by jettisoning the rationality of lovers yields this nice advice for beloveds: you remain rational as long as you do not reciprocate the love.)

There are two senses in which a reason might be nongeneral or nongeneralizable. First, a nongeneral reason could be a reason that is simply not applied in a general way by an agent. Nothing in the reason or in the situations encountered by the agent prevents the agent from reapplying the reason; the agent merely does not apply it again in a relevantly similar situation or would resist applying it again. In moral contexts, this failure or resistance is often taken as a blameworthy fault; in practical contexts, it is a sign of inconsistency. If this is the sense in which Gellner means that love-reasons are nonuniversalizable, then either lovers are irrational or the standards governing reasons are greatly relaxed for personal relations (versus morals and pragmatics). Second, a nongeneral reason could be a reason that logically cannot, in light of the form or content of the reason, be generalized to apply to more situations than the one in which it has been used; the reason is temporally or spatially indexed or it refers to a particular person. In moral contexts, offering a reason of this sort is either blameworthy or a violation of the logical requirements of moral discourse. If *this* is the sense in which love-reasons are for Gellner nonuniversalizable, then either the lover is guilty of a different kind of fault (for example, including a proper name in a reason) or love, unlike morality, permits indexed reasons. Gellner, I think, slides back and forth between these two senses of nonuniversalizable. Although some of his remarks imply that he favors the second meaning, the first is more consistent with his treatment of love. Since in "Y's having S" it is "having S," and not the fact that it is Y who has S, that is X's reason for loving Y, X's reason is not nonuniversalizable by including Y's name; and "has S" is as generalizable (in the second sense) as a reason could be. Gellner never hints that Montaigne's "because it was he" is the sort of love-reason he has in mind.

In explaining how love is an E-type emotion, Gellner draws an analogy with patriotism (160): if X is a loyal patriot of country C that has property set T (a great, freedom-loving country), X will not be a patriot of another country were it also to have T; likewise, if X loves Y on the basis of S, X will not love another person who also has S. This analogy is supposed to reveal the essential feature of E-type attitudes: the reason X has for the attitude is nonuniversalizable in the sense that X is not prepared to apply it to another, relevantly similar object. The analogy between personal love and patriotism seems right to the point because patriotism is often conceived of as a kind of love. But notice that the patriot's reason might be, instead, nonuniversalizable in the second sense; the X who loves her country might give the reason "it is my country." By analogy, then, the lover's reason for xLy would be "Y is mine" or "Y is my beloved," which is either no reason at all or a poor one.

Gellner later (161-2) makes some remarks about the E-type patriot that further obscure the analogy. If X is a patriot of country C_1, says Gellner, then X cannot admit that some person W is justifiably a patriot of another country C_2. If X is a patriot of C_1 because "it is my country," X will not allow W to defend her patriotism toward C_2 with "it is my country." So patriotism exhibits another sort of nonuniversalizability. If X is a C_1 patriot, X cannot be a C_2 patriot even though C_2 might have the T in virtue of which X is a C_1 patriot; patriotism is object-nonuniversalizable. But in addition, patriotism is subject-nonuniversalizable: that X has reason R for being a C_1 patriot means that X cannot admit that W can rightly have reason R for being a C_2 patriot rather than a C_1 patriot. Now, if we maintain the analogy between personal love and patriotism, we should say two things about love. First, if X loves Y on the basis of S, then X not only refuses to apply this reason generally so that xLz too but also cannot admit that W might have that or any reason for loving Z. (The C_1 patriot will not be a patriot of C_2 and wants no one else to be a patriot of C_2.) Second, if X loves Y, then X must claim that everyone else ought also to love Y, and for the same reasons. (The C_1 patriot thinks everyone ought to be patriotic toward C_1, for the same good reasons he has, namely, it is a great country, not merely "it's mine.") Yet we do not want to say about the lover that if xLy, then X wants wLz to be false. The man who says "my wife is the best in the world" would not fight another man who says "*my* wife is the best in the world"; but the C_1 patriot will not remain silent when a patriot of C_2 says "*my* country is the best." Nor do we want to say that if xLy, X wants everyone to love Y, or X believes that others should have the same good reasons for loving Y; this would deny the role of subjectively valuable properties in love.

Gellner's most explicit definition of E-type states: "An agent acting in accordance with an E-type preference [is not] acting in accordance with some rule from which his preference follows as an instance, for he would not act in accordance with that rule with regard to another instance if one turned up" (161). It sounds as if Gellner is defining an E-type attitude as one for which no rule is involved at all; the definition says "[not] acting in accordance with some rule." But the rest of the sentence confuses matters; it speaks of "that rule," which suggests that an E-type attitude involves a nongeneral rule rather than no rule. We could equally characterize the E-type lover as acting according to no rule, *or* according to a nongeneral rule, if only because a nongeneral rule likely does not even count as a rule. In either case something is amiss; X fails to recognize that rules are general, or X fails to abide by rules at all. Whichever is true, X displays arbitrariness or irrationality. This issue is not a quibble. If Gellner means "nongeneral rule," then his solution to the paradox is that love is reason-dependent but love-reasons are not general, which is compatible with the eros tradition; and if he means "no rule at all," his solution is that love is not reason-dependent, that is, there are no reasons for love, which is incompatible with that tradition.

Because Gellner writes that "my distinction is between actions based on rules and those which are not" (164), he might think of the E-type lover as acting according to no rule at all. And he characterizes E-type attitudes as involving a Kierkegaardian leap. But other passages imply that he means "nongeneral rule" rather than "no rule." (Kierkegaard's leap can be accomplished well with a nongeneral rule; just refuse to apply the rule again in a situation to which it applies.) The sentence I quoted just above begins, "Roughly speaking, my distinction is . . . ," a qualification that does not force us to take literally the claim that follows. Further, Gellner claims that it is "analytically true that all actions are based on a rule" (158). If so, the only way to characterize the E- type lover is to say that he is acting according to a nongeneral rule. And what Gellner means throughout his paper by "acting according to a rule" is "acting according to reasons." The significant point to make about the E-type lover should be cast not in terms of rules but in terms of reasons: X is acting on the basis of a nongeneral reason, and the fact that X has reasons for loving Y that are not applied to the similar Z makes us doubt X's consistency. Finally, Gellner claims at the beginning of his paper (157) that there are two kinds of reasons for acting, distinguished by their logical forms. One kind of reason is "impersonal, general, abstracted," exactly what we expect reasons to be. The other kind of reason, then, must be nongeneral, the sort Gellner eventually attributes to E-type lovers. Gellner's description of this second kind of reason is imprecise: these reasons "include a . . . reference to some privileged person, thing or event, privileged in the sense that quite similar . . . persons, things or events would not by the agent be counted as equally good grounds for the relevant action." I would have said: "These reasons pick out some privileged person, privileged in the sense that these reasons would not by the agent be counted as grounds for acting in the same way toward a similar person." At least, I would have put that way if I were thinking of "nongeneral reason" (in the first sense) rather than "no reason."

The "blind self-assertion" (165) of the E-type lover, then, is probably a failure to recognize that reasons are general (which is a kind of irrationality that is compatible with the eros tradition) rather than a failure to have reasons for one's behavior or preferences (which is a different kind of irrationality that is consistent with the agape tradition). Gellner, however, is not convinced of the appropriateness of calling E-typers "irrational." He says that E-typers are "often lumped together as modern irrationalism" (165), most notably by contemporary "liberalism," toward which Gellner has a mocking attitude. And he sympathizes with existentialists who claim that E-type action is an assertion of the individual's freedom (176). One might conclude that E-typers, given the truth of some bold metaphysical theses about the world and human nature, are actually rational in a more meaningful way. But there is a difference between wanting to be free from nonreason-causes, or from causal determination, and wanting to be free *tout court*, including being free from the demand that reasons be general. The desire to be free from causes, perhaps satisfied when one discovers and acknowledges their existence and tries to control them, seems laudable. (Recall Descartes to Chanut.) I cannot make sense of the idea, however, that we should take another step and free ourselves from the generality of reasons, not even for the sake of exclusive love.

5. The Substitution Problem

After Gellner's paper was published in 1955, other versions of the paradox ("the substitution problem") appeared in the literature (as far as I can tell, independently of his article).[23] Typically, the substitution problem is used to show that personal love is not property-based or reason-dependent. One of the most bizarre versions is Mark Bernstein's:

> I have a wife, Nancy, whom I love very much. Let us suppose that I were informed that tomorrow, my wife Nancy would no longer be part of my life, that she would leave and forever be unseen and unheard of by me. But, in her stead, a Nancy* would appear, a qualitatively indistinguishable individual from Nancy. Nancy and Nancy* would look precisely alike, act precisely alike, think precisely alike, indeed would be alike in all physical and mental details.[24]

Nancy and Nancy* are not numerically identical, but qualitatively indistinguishable (which includes memories); Bernstein asks us not to "overestimate" any differences between them that follow from their numerical separateness (for example, that Mike was the father of Nancy and Mike* was the father of Nancy*). Bernstein claims that he would be grief-stricken by the loss of Nancy, even though Nancy* is right by his side, and that he would not, at least not immediately, love Nancy*.[25] His argument is simple: "I love and only love Nancy, Nancy*≠Nancy, so I don't love Nancy*."[26] The argument begs the question; if Bernstein assumes that he loves only Nancy, he will of course not love Nancy*, or anyone else for that matter. He should instead be asking what follows from (1) I love Nancy and (2) Nancy*=Nancy (qualitatively). Regardless, Bernstein concludes from this thought experiment that "no informative list of necessary and sufficient conditions for 'X loving Y' can be given," since he would not love the identical Nancy*.[27] Further, he explains his grief by invoking the effect that the loss of Nancy has on his "sense of uniqueness or identity." For "loving someone is . . . an expression of our identity, of our uniqueness in the world."[28] But to argue that "if the object of our love vanishes . . . our own status as a unique individual is threatened," one need imagine only that Nancy dies, not that she is replaced by Nancy*. Bringing in Nancy* is not only beside the point, it is also queer, for the existence of a perfect copy of Nancy threatens everyone's status as "a unique individual," even if Nancy does not die.

I want to focus on Bernstein's assumption that X encounters not merely a person who duplicates the S that X's first beloved has (Gellner's strategy) but a perfect copy who replaces X's beloved in the furniture of the universe. If X does not know that the Y he went to sleep with is not the Y* he wakes up with the next morning, Bernstein's thought experiment does not permit the conclusion that love is not property-based. In Gellner's version we were not considering X's meeting Y, her later meeting Z, and falsely believing that Z is none other than Y. That scenario illustrates only the intentionality of love. (If xLy and X believes that Z is Y, should we expect xLz? Yes.) If X does not know about the Bernstein replacement of Y by the indistinguishable Y*, X will feel no grief and will love Y* as she had loved Y. (Suppose I am making love in the garden during the blackness of midnight with a woman whom I believe to be my beloved but who is an imposter, yet I enjoy the events as I ordinarily would.)[29] More precisely, X's loving Y* because X loves Y and because she does not know that Y* replaced Y actually refutes the claim that "no informative list of necessary and sufficient conditions for 'X loving Y' can be given" and confirms the thesis that personal love is property-based. In Mark Fisher's version of the substitution problem, Y* has replaced Y for five years without X's knowledge;[30] but that X has loved Y* for so long as if Y* were Y is fully explainable and expected in the first view of personal love. Now, if X is informed that her beloved is really Y* (Bernstein) or if X finally discovers she has been living with and loving an imposter (Fisher), X's reactions (grief, anger, withholding affection from Y*) are readily explainable as reactions to one's being tricked, manipulated, or deceived and therefore do not entail anything about the ground of love.[31]

If X's not knowing that Y* has replaced Y leads X to love Y* as if X were loving Y, and that confirms that love is property-based, than why take seriously the claim that X's not loving Y*, when X is informed or discovers that Y* has replaced Y, shows that love is not property-based? Those who employ the substitution problem against the thesis that love is property-based have not acknowledged that X's loving Y* when X does not know that Y* has replaced Y actually confirms that love is property-based, and as a result they have not adequately explained why the fact that X does not love Y*, when X knows that Y* has replaced Y, shows that love is not property-based. In Gellner's dilemma, the challenge to the view that love is property-based arises exactly when we assume that X *notices* that Z, too, has S; then we need to worry about X's loving, or not loving, Z. In the Bernstein/Fisher variant, the challenge arises when it is assumed that X *knows* that Y* has replaced Y. But the analogy between X's noticing and X's knowing is not a good one. If, in Gellner's paradox, X does not notice that Z, too, has S, we have no reason to expect that X will love Z. But when X does not know about the Bernstein/Fisher replacement, we have every reason to expect X to love Y*. This dissimilarity explains, I think, why the Bernstein/Fisher variant does not damage the view that love is property-based, or why Gellner's paradox is a better vehicle for posing the theoretical problem.

Gellner makes a reasonable assumption when he supposes that X encounters a second person Z and notices that Z has the small property set S in virtue of which X loves Y. But the Bernstein/Fisher variant asks too much of us, that is, to imagine that X knows that a qualitatively identical Y* has replaced Y. How could X know that Y* has replaced Y when they are qualitatively indistinguishable? I can think of no reliable test that permits X to know this; no examination of fingerprints, no questioning Y* about the intimate details of X's sex with Y, no confrontation with Mike* (about whom the same problem arises), could provide evidence of the replacement. Bernstein claims that X is "informed" that Y* replaces Y. But who informs X that he has lost Y and now has Y* instead? If X is not in a position to know about the replacement, then for the same reasons no one else could know and inform X. But perhaps Y* knows (how? her memories are identical to Y's) and informs X: "See here, X, I am Nancy* and not Nancy." What would X's reaction to being informed by Y* that Y* has replaced Y? Undoubtedly, utter disbelief; X will think his beloved Y has gone off her rocker. Should we just assume that X is informed by an authority (God) whom X considers infallible? Further, even if X were to suspect, or come to believe, that Y* has replaced Y, his reaction would not be grief over the loss of Y but profound cognitive dissonance. In the meantime, we are not likely to learn anything about love when we deliberately proceed, as Bernstein does, to destroy X's world. Suppose X watches as Y is killed after serving as the source of clone Y*.[32] Here X knows, by observation rather than by being informed, that Y* has replaced Y. But this situation is too weird to permit us to draw conclusions about love. While we are imagining that we live in the age of everyday cloning, still we have no idea *now* what our/their conception of love would look like; it might be different precisely because of the possibility of cloning. Would X suffer terribly as Y dies, even though Y* exists (as Bernstein would say, extrapolating his claim into the future), or would X rejoice as the identical Y* emerges from the dust?

Notes

1. This essay is chapter two, with revised endnotes, of my *The Structure of Love* (New Haven: Yale University Press, 1990); its first version, "The Coherence of Love," was prepared for reading at the ten-year anniversary meeting of the Society for the Philosophy of Sex and Love and then appeared in *Philosophy and Theology* 2:5 [disk supplement no. 1] (1988): 61-89. I thank

Ursula Huemer, "Die Junge," for her assistance, questions, and advice ("Ein Kuß ist wichtiger als der Plan").

2. Ernest Gellner, "Ethics and Logic," *Proceedings of the Aristotelian Society* 55 (1955): 157-78 (page references are given parenthetically in the text).

3. W. Newton-Smith, "A Conceptual Investigation of Love," in Alan Montefiore, ed., *Philosophy and Personal Relations* (Montreal: McGill-Queen's University Press, 1973), 113-36, at 124; reprinted in Alan Soble, ed., *Eros, Agape, and Philia* (New York: Paragon House, 1989), 199-217, at 208.

4. See Soble, *Structure of Love*, ch. 9.

5. *Ibid.*, ch. 9, §10.

6. *Ibid.*, ch. 13, §5.

7. One might interject here that X is not faced with "the same situation," and therefore Z's having S need not have the same effect on X as Y's having S. But given that the situations are in one salient way precisely the same (both Y and Z have S), the burden of proof, to state how the situations are different, is carried by those who would solve Gellner's paradox this way. See *ibid.*, ch. 3, §4; ch. 4, §2; ch. 6, §1.

8. As Anders Nygren wrote about agape, "when it is said that God loves man, this is not a judgment on what man is like, but on what God is like" (*Agape and Eros* [Chicago: University of Chicago Press, 1982], 76). Thus, Gellner in the second horn rejects the subject-centricity of the second view of personal love in favor of the object-centricity of the first view (Soble, *Structure of Love*, ch. 1, §3).

9. Soble, *Structure of Love*, ch. 11, §2.

10. Philip Slater, *The Pursuit of Loneliness*, 1st ed. (Boston: Beacon Press, 1970), 87; 3rd ed. (1990), 81.

11. The thesis that love is out of proportion to the properties of the object is advanced by John McTaggart, *The Nature of Existence* (Cambridge, Eng.: Cambridge University Press, 1927), vol. 2, bk. 5, ch. 41, 152-3. See Soble, *Structure of Love*, ch. 13, §10.

12. Slater, *Pursuit of Loneliness*, 87. Does this apply also to Freud's love for Martha Bernays, "who despite all my resistance [!—A. S.] captivated my heart at our first meeting"? Ernst L. Freud, ed., *Letters of Sigmund Freud* (New York: Basic Books, 1975), 8; see epigraph to this chapter.

13. Irving Singer, *The Nature of Love*, vol. 1, 2nd ed. (Chicago: University of Chicago Press, 1984), 32.

14. Soble, *Structure of Love*, ch. 10.

15. *Ibid.*, ch. 7, §4.

16. *Ibid.*, ch. 13, §5.

17. Robert Ehman argues that "we can never in the strict sense love a person at first sight," because the basis of love is the beloved's unique character and that is not yet available to the lover ("Personal Love," *The Personalist* 49 [1968]: 116-41, at 123). I discuss Ehman in *Structure of Love*, ch. 3, §6.

18. Soble, *Structure of Love*, ch. 10, §6; ch. 12, §9.

19. Anthony Kenny, ed., *Descartes: Philosophical Letters* (Oxford: Oxford University Press, 1970), 224-5.

20. See René Descartes's definition of love: "Love is an emotion of the soul caused by a movement of the spirits, which impels the soul to join itself willingly to objects that appear to be agreeable to it" (*The Passions of the Soul*, in *The Philosophical Writings of Descartes*, vol. 1, trans. J. Cottingham, R. Stoothoff, and D. Murdoch [Cambridge, Eng.: Cambridge University Press, 1985], 356).

21. If Gellner's dilemma shows that love is impossible, it might be seen as the *reductio ad absurdum* of the thesis that love is property-based. I think Bernard Mayo would interpret Gellner that way; Mayo claims, barely providing a shred of argument, that love "has nothing to do with reasons" (*Ethics and the Moral Life* [New York: St. Martin's, 1958], 199; see Soble, *Structure of Love*, ch. 8, §7).

22. For Plato, the E-type lover is irrational. "Then he must see that the beauty in any one body is family-related to the beauty in another body; . . . it is *great mindlessness* not to consider the beauty of all bodies to be one and the same" (*Symposium* 210a5ff; italics added to Martha

Nussbaum's translation, *The Fragility of Goodness* [Cambridge, Eng.: Cambridge University Press, 1986], 179).

23. Mark Bernstein, "Love, Particularity, and Selfhood," *Southern Journal of Philosophy* 23 (1986): 287-93; Mark Fisher, "Reason, Emotion, and Love," *Inquiry* 20 (1977): 189-203. Outside philosophy, see Emily Brontë's *Wuthering Heights* (the passage just before Catherine declares "I *am* Heathcliff") and Mozart's opera "Cosi Fan Tutti." The problem has an analogue in aesthetics: a good forgery has the properties in virtue of which the original elicits aesthetic approval, so it should elicit the same approval. See Francis Sparshott, "The Disappointed Art Lover," in Denis Dutton, ed., *The Forger's Art* (Berkeley: University of California Press, 1983), 246-63, at 254-5.

24. Bernstein, "Love, Particularity, and Selfhood," 287. For Nancy Bernstein's reply (in a sense) to Mark, see her letter to the editor, *Proceedings of The American Philosophical Association* 62:4 (March 1989): 718-20.

25. Job suddenly and inexplicably lost his wife, but was happy with the nonidentical replacement God later gave him. Perhaps Bernstein's unhappiness with the identical Nancy* means that he has a much more refined notion of personal love than the Hebrews. (Note that Job's replacement wife might have been *subjectively* identical for him, that is, as fungible as a dollar bill.)

26. Bernstein, "Love, Particularity, and Selfhood," 288.

27. *Ibid.* Yet Bernstein admits that if he were asked why he loves Nancy, he would say "because . . . she is kind, sensitive, intelligent, and beautiful." Is love, then, reason-dependent, but its reasons are nongeneral? Is this why Bernstein would not love the *identical* Nancy*? This is nongenerality at its worst—and is it not irrational?

28. *Ibid.*, 291.

29. William Butler Yeats, "The Three Bushes," *The Collected Poems* (New York: Macmillan, 1956), 294. See Genesis 30:23-25: "In the evening [Laban] took his daughter Leah and brought her to Jacob. . . . And in the morning, behold, it was Leah," not Rachel.

30. Fisher, "Reason, Emotion, and Love," 201.

31. Fisher argues that X's not loving the empirically indistinguishable Y*, even though X had loved Y, entails that the object of love is a transcendental self (see Soble, *Structure of Love*, ch. 3, §6).

32. This variant was suggested to me by the late Norton Nelkin.

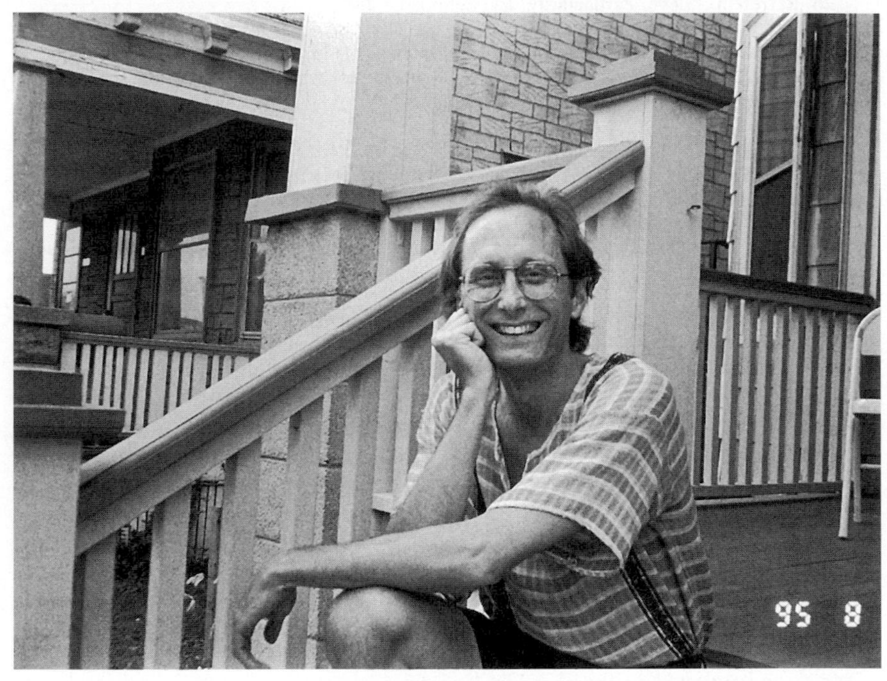

Gene Fendt
(photograph: Pamela Fendt)

Author of "Is *Works of Love* a Work of Love?"
Paper presented at the Society for the Philosophy of Sex and Love
during the
Central Division Meeting of The American Philosophical Association
Cincinnati, Ohio, 28 April 1988

Forty-Five

IS *WORKS OF LOVE* A WORK OF LOVE?

Gene Fendt

It is my unalterable will that my writings, after my death, be dedicated to her and to my late father. She must belong to history.

Kierkegaard, *Journals and Papers* (VI, 6537)

History, like society, is the meeting place of wills.[1] There is perhaps one whose will for history is inalterable, but he transcends history even if he acts within it. For the rest of us, even those of us who know our own wills, our wills are hardly inalterable. History might show us that. Since, partly, this will be a story of wills and altered wills, as well as hidden wills, I should give a short list of the *dramatis personae* of this little history.[2] For the history as a whole, let us use the generic name "Kierkegaard." It is, for practical purposes, reduced to a set of documents that, like the play *Hamlet*, have several characters with the same name as the play within the play. Among them let us distinguish, first, SAK, a man who lived from 1813 to 1855 and who is "credited with" authorship of all the documents, defender of a dissertation on irony, breaker of an engagement to Regine Olsen, later Regine Schlegel.[3] (This SAK is ostensibly the person depicted on a Danish postage stamp; see figure 1.) Second, let us remember the religious writer, S. Kierkegaard, who wrote thirty-one *Edifying Discourses* (1843-50) as well as *Christian Discourses* (1848), *For Self-Examination* (1851), and several other pieces, including *Works of Love*. He also appears to be the editor of *The Sickness Unto Death* and *Training in Christianity*. Third, let us mention the shadowy creature projected from the *Journals and Papers*. Sometimes he seems to be Johannes Climacus, sometimes another Johannes, sometimes the religious writer S.K., sometimes the historical dissertation defender and troth breaker; it is hard to tell which part of him is the poem. Fourth, there are a large number of independent authors: Climacus, Anti-Climacus, Frater Taciturnus, to name a few. These are frequently called, by those who consider "credit" a logically perspicuous relationship, pseudonyms: pretexts for the religious writer S. Kierkegaard.

The orthodox interpretation of Søren Aabye Kierkegaard's life and authorship, and so of *Works of Love*, follows the path set down in his confession. I should say "one of his confessions," for there are several in the writings that go under the name of Kierkegaard.[4] According to that final confession, *The Point of View for My Work as an Author*, the shattered dissembling artifice that would be called by his name was from first to last a religious authorship, and the break from Regina that was its initiation was a sacrifice to the religious. (Though perhaps, as someone notes in his diary, it was a sacrifice made from a lapse of faith; if he had had more faith, he would have married her.)[5]

It might be helpful here to recover the original of the literary convention I am invoking in Kierkegaard's name. St. Augustine confesses that for a long time he was an outsider to his own life. From that outside view, his life is a shambles of accidents and rootless wanderings. But one of the changes that follows upon his conversion is an understanding that the shattered story of his times has a beginning and an end in eternity, a beginning and end that make it a narrative whole in which the incidentalia of his temporizing are given the significance of Eternity seeking him out. Understanding and confession first become possible, according to Augustine, after conversion. They first become possible together: to understand is also to confess. That the first "confession" of world literature came into existence after Christianity appeared could be taken as proof that at least some new thing became possible because of Christianity's appearance. Such an argument would, however, be a logical fallacy.

Should we believe such confessions, such *ex post facto* explanations, especially in the case of our present author? Among the things Kierkegaard confesses to are that some of his writings are meant to entrance readers, to seduce them. He admits further that they were successful. Too successful, for the readers of his day would not accept with their right hands what he gave with his right hand, but took with their right hands what he offered in the left. Most of his later interpreters have been more generous: they have graciously accepted in their right hands the religious works that S. Kierkegaard confesses to be humbly offering in his right hand.[6] Armed with his confession that the writer was first and always a religious author, they have made him into a pre-eminent religious writer, perhaps the pre-eminent religious writer of the age.

Perhaps this is all a seduction. It is certainly comfortable. Scholarship has shown how each brick of the work fits into the cozy system of existence (*det hyggelige værtshus*) that S. Kierkegaard confesses he discovered (very nearly *ex post facto*) he was living in. Let us examine this confession and discovery in some of its literary and historical detail. The discovery that S. Kierkegaard made, that he was a religious author, indeed, from the very beginning a religious author, was, of course, made before SAK died. The confession of this discovery is, however, of questionable origin, for the confession (*The Point of View*) was not published until after SAK's death. SAK recognizes that publication of this book by another makes it poetic and "without authority" in 1849 (six years before his death):

> *The Point of View for My Work as an Author* cannot be published. It must be made into something by a third party: A Possible Explanation of Magister K's Authorship, that is, so that it is no longer the same book at all.[7]

At this point the question about which Kierkegaard is the third party and which is first or second has become completely undecidable. The confession, in any case, can certainly not be credited to any living person except, perhaps, Peter, as Louis Mackey suggests in his latest book.[8]

Figure 1. SAK (Søren Aabye Kierkegaard). This postage stamp was issued by the Danish Post on 11 November 1955 to commemorate the one hundreth anniversary of the death of SAK.

Artwork by Sir Viggo Bang; reproduced with the permission of Sven Bang.

One might ask whether that confession can be credited to anyone who ever had been living: only if SAK and the S. Kierkegaard who wrote it are the same. Here the law of identity is of no help; we must leap to the conclusion that they are the same . . . or that they are different. Even if one has legs for making this small leap, the leap of coming into existence, it is a leap and there is a problem about trustworthiness, and a question of faith. As Anti-Climacus says,

> It is true that there is rest in the grave; but to sit beside a grave, or to visit a grave—all that is not to lie in the grave; to scan again and again the production of one's own pen, which one knows by heart, the inscription which one placed there oneself and which the man himself can best understand, telling who lies buried there—that, alas, is not to lie buried there oneself.[9]

Then there is the additional problem raised by the fact that the claim made by S. Kierkegaard (SAK?) is a religious one. For Augustine a confession is a public act of faith. If *The Point of View* is taken as SAK's act of faith, it is an act from beyond the grave. Such an event may be fraught with religious symbolism, but to the plainer understanding an "act of faith" that takes place after death and through the offices of one's older brother, the bishop, is not an act at all.

I have been taken with a different idea, a somewhat heretical point of view. The authorship is from first to last a work of seduction. The intention of the author in all of the works, those signed by S. Kierkegaard as well as those credited to him, was primarily seduction and secondarily . . . seduction. This SAK was no ordinary seducer, but among the great seducers, and of them the greatest. To possess a woman's body for a night is a poverty stricken goal that, no matter how interestingly carried off, eventually ends. (As Johannes complains, "why can such nights not be longer").[10] SAK was a seducer without peer, for his object was to possess a woman, heart and soul, both in time and eternity. To succeed in this primary objective would be enough to make him first among storied seducers, but his secondary objective, also a seduction, puts him at the ideal apex of seductivity. His secondary objective was to have the whole story recorded and yet avoid discovery . . . via seduction. He would draw his reader aside, whisper "this is all for religious purposes" and win the title "great religious thinker" for his activity. Which activity, I say again, was first and last a seduction. "A's" nightmare has an actual existence that is far more demonic than even "A" was willing to imagine. If music is the medium in which the unreflective seducer, Don Giovanni, properly appears, textuality is the proper medium for the reflective seducer. This is not my discovery. I was taught it; don't ask how. Kierkegaard is the reflective seducer *par excellence*.

This admittedly heretical theory has a historical point of departure. It first came to me many years ago when a young woman who was the object of my fancy, as well as several lower affections, refused my advances in favor of those of another friend of mine who would be a Jesuit. This unhappy accident first made me aware of the attractions of the religious life. A second historical accident made me reflect this rather general theory into the particular case of SAK. Many celibate years after failing with the aforementioned object of my fancy, I found a delightful little book entitled *Forlovelsen* which was published for Mrs. Regine Schlegel by Raphael Meyer in 1904. This, one may assume, is a straightforward little book by a simple honest woman. Along with Mrs. Schlegel's story, Meyer published Kierkegaard's letters to her from the time of the engagement. Of these Meyer notes "the first 20 present nothing as a basis for dating; I have ordered them according to my best judgement with regard to the mood which prevails in them." Here Herr Meyer, unconsciously one must guess, follows somewhat the pattern "A" followed, who, having "received from Cordelia a collection of letters, whether it includes all of them I do not know" (letters similarly lacking dates), introduced them into his manuscript "where the motives seemed to suggest them."[11] Among these letters of Kierkegaard to Regina were many that echoed in feeling and mood, sometimes in exact expression, the letters that "A" discovered and published with the "Diary of the Seducer." Some of Kierkegaard's letters to Regina are, of course, echoed in other works. One may indeed well imagine that bits of SAK's conversations with Regina, bits that only she would be able to recognize, abound in his works. Meyer says as much:

> As newly engaged we see them sitting together in Schlegel's room, reading Kierkegaard's writings aloud to each other. And they indeed contained, one after another, pieces of her past, memories from the time of the engagement, studies of him and her, works which by Kierkegaard's poetic genius were turned into *Dichtung und Wahrheit*. And these readings continued the whole of their youthful lives.[12]

This, of course, was new only to me. The scholars have known it for quite some time. Almost fortuitously, I came upon a passage in Kierkegaard's diary. He had sent a letter to Herr Schlegel asking if a rapprochement would be possible and, if so, that he deliver an enclosed sealed letter to his wife, Regina. Schlegel refused. In his diary Kierkegaard wrote angrily, "She may belong to him in time, but in eternity she is mine."[13]

If we put these two little pieces together, we have an outline of the story of the greatest possible seduction of all time. What seducer ever won the heart and soul of a young girl from a man, and then, after casting her off, kept his words and spirit alive in her heart not only in spite of that man, who became her husband, but through her husband's own voice? There in Schlegel's room, there in Schlegel's voice, she was continually reminded of her first love, of her own promises to her first love.[14] And "the first love is the true love, and one only loves once."[15] *Works of Love*, published a month before her wedding and in the month of Regina and Kierkegaard's own "anniversary,"[16] is a kind of gift: a marriage gift or, ethically considered, a poison gift?

That would be enough to make Kierkegaard the greatest of all seducers in a qualitative sense. He certainly cannot compete with 1,003 in Spain but, to make a merely grammatical point, quantity is the element of comparison, the superlative is purely qualitative; therefore, I say again that this is the greatest of all seducers. But in addition (if it is possible to add to the superlative), Kierkegaard is also praised by the ethically and religiously minded critics. His love for Regina is said to be true; his dismissal of her a sacrifice to the religious. Regina's husband reads the story of his "sacrifice" of her; the world is enraptured. She hears her husband read a beautiful story, she understands it much better than the one delivering message,[17] for she has heard the story before and it is about her. So she is enraptured again. The seducer says the story has religious significance; he names the main characters Abraham and Isaac; the world believes him. For the world it all has religious significance. Kierkegaard possesses her heart and mind even as Herr Schlegel drones on next to her on the couch: beneath the sea of Kierkegaard's writing, the Merman sings. For the seducer, on the other hand, the dismissal is not a sacrifice but a requirement of the ideal. For without such a casting off, the result would soon enough be marriage, by which the ideal is lost and reality forces its way in. Moreover, the dismissal is required most of all in the highest seduction, for a reflective seducer is well aware that a maiden "always tends to be loyal when the loved one wishes to be rid of her." "After all, a girl loves only once."[18]

But this is altogether too demonic to be believed. All those religious writings, in particular *Works of Love*, a mere cover? Perhaps not *merely* cover. In all of them there are almost certainly phrases Regina had heard before, in other contexts. Later they are placed in the context of a religious discourse: what could be further from seduction? Indeed, what discourse could be further from the purpose of twining about her heart than such remarks as "if it were true—as conceited shrewdness, proud of not being deceived, thinks—that one should believe nothing which he cannot see by means of his physical eyes, then first and foremost one ought to give up believing in love," the remark that opens *Works of Love*?[19] Nothing could be farther from the spirit of seduction, unless there might be another context in which these words had been uttered: something that might sound like an echo "fra Drømmen af hendes Ungdomsvaar" [from a dream of her youth].[20] A modern writer uncovers the scene of ravishment:

> Is the scene always visual? It can be aural, the frame can be linguistic: I can fall in love with *a sentence spoken to me*: and not only because it says something which manages to touch my desire, but because of its syntactical turn (framing), which will inhabit me *like a memory*.[21]

What if it were the case that "deception stretches unconditionally as far as the truth [and] . . . hypocrisy, artifice . . . and seduction stretch unconditionally as far as love"?[22] As another writer has said,

> because there is discourse about faith, hope and love, and about God and Jesus Christ, presented in solemn tone . . . it does not follow that it is godly discourse by any means. What counts is the manner in which the speaker and listener are related to the discourse, or are presumed to be related.[23]

How are the speaker and listener related in the discourses that are *Works of Love*? Who is the speaker, and who the requested reader? Another writer adds this warning: "And devils soonest tempt, resembling spirits of light."[24]

Let *Works of Love*, presumed to be one of the outstanding works of Christian ethics, be the test case for this theory. Unlike other works in the Kierkegaardian corpus, even some works by self-consciously religious authors like Anti-Climacus, *Works of Love* is straightforward, not seductive. The major texts of Kierkegaard's authorship are quite explicitly structured, as selves are, in two parts sundered by a breach. One could say that such texts are subsistent either/ors: hermeneutic circles that create their own horizons. Regarding the texts in this fashion allows us to mention some differences in the two weights which are the parts of those major texts. In *Repetition*, *Either/Or*, *Philosophical Fragments—Concluding Unscientific Postscript*, *Sickness Unto Death*, the second part reveals the condition for the possibility of having written, read, understood, the first. This division might even be true of SAK's dissertation. Kierkegaard might well have in mind as his model the Bible, in which, for a believing Christian, the New Testament provides the condition for reading and understanding the Old Testament. The implied or actual authors of each of these books (Constantine Constantius, Victor Eremita, Johannes Climacus, Anti-Climacus, SAK, and God) must already be at the point of view of the second part in order for the first part to be written, since that second part is the *sine qua non* of the first. So these works are all backward in the sense that an actual fragment of life, philosophy, psychological investigation, conceptual or sacred history, is presented before what makes each of them possible is elucidated. Life, on the other hand, must be lived prospectively, not retrospectively.

Works of Love, though also in two parts, is straightforward. It begins with the command of God. According to S. Kierkegaard's understanding this command is the condition for the possibility of love. Part I lays out the command. Part II explicates what love actually does when it holds fast to the command and does not go off on its own, at which moment it immediately and *ipso facto* ceases to be love. If the first works are to wound from behind by presenting a brilliant aesthetic, philosophical, or psychological fragment and then pointing out in their second parts the offensive fact that it is not human wisdom but Christian revelation that makes such brilliance possible, *Works of Love* straightforwardly lays down the rigors of the New Law, the offensive law that is so offensive and so without understanding as to command love, but then follows that with the romantic lunacy, beloved by all, that love conquers all. But the first part is first. This book is not seductive, it does not wound from behind, it does not let a reader in an easy door. At least it does not seem to be a seduction.

Perhaps things are not so straightforward. Before *Works of Love* takes up the command of love, before the author remembers to pray, even before he speaks a word (or so he would have it: *Forord*), we get a warning: do not be a reader who is too nosy, too greedy for little tidbits (*nysgjerrig*).[25] What would ever tempt an ordinary reader of a book on Christian ethics to read it that way? Is this a seducer, just coming out of someone's sitting room and closing the door, who now warns: "do not make things too difficult here"?

After the warning, we are told of "that single individual . . . who first ponders whether he will read or not."[26] This phrase seems (as the editors explain) to be directed to every reader, but is it also directed, more pointedly, to one particular individual, one who "with joy and gratitude" Kierkegaard called "my reader"? And is that reader the one to whom he left all his journals and papers, the one to whom he spoke, not just sometimes, as she requested, but with every written word: Regina? Perhaps I am being too *nysgjerrig*.

The foreword ends by saying that the book that follows is essentially impossible. This is so because the works of love are both essentially indescribable in their smallest detail and also essentially inexhaustible. So the "before words" section tropes every word in the book in advance: before a word is read, all the words are failures. The closing theme of the foreword (love's essential indescribability; literally, unwritability) is continued in the first chapter about love's essential hiddenness.

Now, whether or not love is essentially hidden and essentially indescribable, it is certainly to the advantage of a seducer to say so. And if, in spite of love's essentially hidden and indescribable nature, it is nonetheless possible to recognize love by its fruit, it is certainly important that the seducer portray looking for the fruit and testing the fruit as a temptation, as worldly cleverness and conceit, and as lack of love. That is exactly what the first chapter emphasizes, and the rest of the book concurs. How helpful for the seducer! If love is essentially hidden, if "there is no word in human language, . . . and no deed, not even the best"[27] that demonstrates love, then there is no recognizable check upon the seducer's activity. If, in addition, it is loss of love and self-deception to attempt an investigation, then the world is the seducer's playground.

One might argue that the seducer's love (and if he has any it is erotic love) is recognizably different from love properly so called, that is, the *agape* S. Kierkegaard (religious writer and editor) is concerned with. And this seems to be true, for he says "one may make the mistake of calling by the name of love that which is weak indulgence."[28] But, on the other hand, is it not Eros himself who requires Psyche "not to inquisitively and impudently thrust [her] way in, [lest she forfeit] the joy and blessing of [love] by her curiosity"?[29] And does it not sound like praise of erotic love when S. Kierkegaard writes:

> O you quiet martyrs of unhappy erotic love—to be sure it remained a secret that out of love you suffered in hiding love; it never became known, for so great was your love which bought this sacrifice—yet your love was known by its fruits! And perhaps those very fruits would be the most precious, those which were matured by the quiet fire of secret pain.[30]

And if it is praise of an erotic lover, one whose secret fire produced many precious fruits, who might Kierkegaard have in mind?

Finally, what is the significance of this phrase: "one may make the mistake of calling love that which is really self-love: when one loudly protests that he cannot live without his beloved but will hear nothing of love's task and demand"?[31] Is it meant to help a reader distinguish between erotic selfishness and *agape*? Or is it a sentence spoken to a certain reader, a sentence that touches her desire and her memory, a goad and a reminder that Eros too has his tasks and secrets and precious fruits? A goad to keep passion alive in the girl whose words these originally were.[32]

I skip over in silence most of the two sections on the command and its blessings. If this book is part of a double seduction, of both Regina and the world, then the best way to make the secondary seduction work is by making the religious writing as cogent as possible. *Works of Love* is as cogent a presentation of *agape* as has been given in the West, but that point is not any more in favor of the orthodox interpretation than it is in favor of this heresy.

The penultimate chapter, "The Work of Love in Praising Love," begins with the Danish version of the proverb that it is one thing to say something and another to do it. It then attempts to make an exemption for the entire book's discourse, the entire book's saying. Sometimes, as in poetry, to say something is to do it. If it is a work of love to praise love, then, as in poetry, the word will be the deed. However, this unity of word and deed must be reiterated in a second unity: the unity of inner and outer in praising love. The work of praising love must be done inwardly in self-renunciation and outwardly in sacrificial disinterestedness. If there is any failing in this unity of the inner and the outer, if while truly humble before God the writer becomes, nonetheless, proud among men, or if he sacrifices a little bit of the truth in order to gain a worldly advantage, then the game is up. My dear reader, I wonder if you have come to doubt a little the correctness of the familiar philosophical maxim that the internal is the external?[33]

Well, for S. Kierkegaard the religious writer, the game is not only up, but from the beginning was impossible. On the last pages of this next to-last-chapter, he outlines how the project must go: the one who would truly praise love must transform himself into the self-lover, for "to praise self-renunciation's love and then want to be the lover is certainly a lack of self-renunciation."[34] Consequently, such a one must "manage to become regarded as the most selfish of all."[35] Here Kierkegaard has surely failed, for no one considers him to be so selfish. Far from it; he ends up looking like the true lover to all those readers who take his "confession" in the *Point of View* as gospel. Consequently, *Works of Love* is to his advantage. It is not a work of love done inwardly in self-renunciation. But Kierkegaard is not only a failure *de facto*. Even if he were to succeed in becoming regarded as the most selfish (which no one believes), and then present (as he does) the argument for the poetic necessity that one seems the worst when talking of the best (as the ugly Socrates who spoke of beauty), is not the confession of the poetic necessity of that position vanity, pride, *evil*, not self-renunciation? Isn't it a ploy (as perhaps Socrates' self-irony was), a ploy in the service, the *self*-service to be exact, of seduction? So when Kierkegaard, the author, says "immature and deceitful love is known by the fact that words and techniques of speech are its only fruit,"[36] what kind of ploy is being made? At best we could call him a "noble rogue,"[37] though he has a very un-Socratic tendency to point to the industry and care it took him to arrange things.

"But this is absurd. To carry this on throughout a life, through the Corsair affair, through the attack on the Church, would take a tremendous dedication to the ideal." No doubt. Still, no one here denies that Kierkegaard was capable of such "purity of heart." No one was more tenacious of the ideal. It doesn't seem to fit the mode of life described as aesthetic, which has no unity. But then perhaps that system of existence with the three spheres is a ploy, perhaps it is a seducer, The Seducer *par excellence*, who is saying the life of the aesthetic seducer is fragmented and can never be unified. In other words, perhaps that too is a lie, and the aesthetic life can, and in this singular case does, have a unifying principle. It is at least possible that the Kierkegaard who wrote until the "religious experience" of 1848 was seducing the woman. But I prefer the stronger thesis. Think of the honor among his kind, the eternal delight, at having seduced the whole world as well as the woman. Perhaps even *through* the woman, for who could read Kierkegaard's works and not love Regina? There is a myth about such a seducer.

What was the heart of this man? I would not say that this point of view on Kierkegaard's work as an author is true. The evidence I have elicited is only circumstantial. Any further evidence I could elicit would also be only circumstantial: I would not go to court with it. "His footprints here are so indistinct that any proof is impossible."[38] This makes the theory even more seductive, for if I could prove SAK was a seducer his unmatchable crime would be less remarkable, imperfect. But as it is I cannot prove that he is a seducer, and the crime, if there was a crime, remains a perfect one. ("There is no word, no deed, no in such a way. . . .")[39] Nonetheless, this point of view is possible, as is the religious point of view. If it is true, the summary judgment on SAK's life and work would be something like this: "His life had been an attempt to realize the task of living poetically."[40] Of course you might, like Regina's older sister, Cordelia, "believe all the same that he is a good man."[41] What was it that drove K.'s authorship? A meditation on the cross of Christ? Or was the thorn in his flesh and the point of his meditation the cross he wore on his finger made from the engagement ring of his Queen? One's point of view depends on a choice of the heart: Cordelia Wahl.[42]

Concluding Postscript: The Point of View for My Work as an Author

But what of this writer? Howard and Edna Hong, in their "Introduction" to the English translation, claim that *Works of Love* aims at "finding the reader where he is and making him come to know his own love—or lovelessness."[43] So perhaps this paper is a confession that the author is at heart a loveless seducer who is capable only of seeing his own kind of deceitful workings in everyone else's work. Then (if Kierkegaard is, as the orthodox interpreters present him, the true lover) this writer has deceived himself out of the highest. Such a sight evokes pity and terror, but one would not wish to call the man a tragic hero. On the other hand, if SAK is a deceiver and a seducer, then this writer takes off his hat to the seducer *par excellence*: bravo!

It could, however, be the case that this writer, too, writes for religious purposes. But, then, should I tell you so? Should my left hand tell you what my right hand is doing? All the problems repeat themselves. The shadow of the seducer Victor Eremita seemed to see pacing his floor falls across these papers too. I have been infected with his . . . anxiety.[44] It is an open question whether or not *Works of Love* is a Christian work, or part of a seduction. Let *Works of Love* be a figure: the textural world is a test. If, despite the points raised in this article, you continue to believe that SAK "is a good man," it should be clear that it must be because love properly understood is already present in you. If you do not believe, then love is not (and, according to Magister Kierkegaard, never was) present. Perhaps this essay, then, by opening the question, rouses its hearers to decision. Perhaps you do not wish to decide: is the world of the text a test? It rouses to decision without indicating either which way the writer goes or which way Kierkegaard goes. That is, it rouses to decision and points out not that neither author has no authority religiously or ethically speaking, which would be true, but that both *Works of Love* and this essay evacuate even the minimal authority that an author of a work ordinarily has; namely, his own authority as an author. Ethically and religiously speaking, that is no authority at all. It is eternally unimportant to you whether SAK is a seducer and I am an aesthete playing with possibilities. It is religiously a distraction to worry about it; to worry about it is to confess a kind of ethical frivolity. That cannot be news; nor do I think any reader was worried about that. Perhaps the test is not about the text. Then this essay is not a contribution to scholarship, but a kind of religiously-oriented incitement. Possibly. This pre-eminent postmodern trope of opening up the *mise en abyme* of self-reference and referring it to the reader is an act of holy terror, it mimetically induces the same infinite emptiness in the reader as the text or authorship itself enacts. Perhaps. But then it is also the major trope of an aesthete to present possibilities, play them, and then leave them all unactualized, as I do. Here. Now.

Notes

1. This paper, too, has a history. It is the first paper I delivered at a national meeting (of the Society for the Philosophy of Sex and Love); and a version of it was published as chapter one of my *Works of Love? Reflections on Works of Love* (Potomac, Md.: Scripta Humanistica, 1990), 9-21. Though the essay came into existence first and is reprinted here rewritten, it seems to me to have an essential, not accidental, relation to the rest of that book. It is my inalterable will that this essay, by itself, not be taken as my view of *Works of Love*.

2. For a complete list, see appendix A of my *For What May I Hope?* (New York: Peter Lang, 1990).

3. Her given name was Regine Olsen, and it is under that name that she is known to history. But Kierkegaard recalls her in these lines from *Aeneid*: "Infandum me jubes, Regina, renovare dolorem," lines that might be placed over his life's work as a kind of poet. Let us remember, in this context, Aristotle's remark about the relation between poetry, history, and philosophy.

4. There are two "Notes," an "Accounting," a "Supplement," and "Two Fragments from Kierkegaard's *Journal*" bound with the *Point of View* in Walter Lowrie's English translation (New York: Harper, 1962). There is also a "First and Last Explanation" attached to the *Concluding Unscientific Postscript* (trans. David F. Swenson and Walter Lowrie [Princeton: Princeton University Press], 1941).

5. *Journals and Papers*, 7 vols., trans. Howard Hong and Edna Hong (Bloomington: Indiana University Press, 1967-78), V, 5664 (IV, A107). Quotations from this edition are followed, in parentheses, by references to the Danish edition of the *Papirer* (udgivet af det danske Sprogog Literaturselskab og Søren Kierkegaard Selskabet, København: Gyldendalske Boghandels Forlag, 1968). For ease of scholarly reference, all quotations from Kierkegaard's published work refer to the translation cited followed by a slash and then a page number from the Danish first edition of the *Samlede Værker* (Kjobenhavn: Gyldendalske Boghandels Forlag, 1901).

6. Some, of course, continue to be perverse. See, for example, Christopher Norris, *The Deconstructive Turn: Essays in the Rhetoric of Philosophy* (New York: Routledge, 1984), ch. 4;

Louis Mackey, *Points of View: Readings of Kierkegaard* (Tallahassee: Florida State University Press, 1986); and Sylviane Agacinski, *Aparté: Conceptions and Deaths of Søren Kierkegaard*, trans. Kevin Newmark (Tallahassee: Florida State University Press, 1988).

7. *Journals and Papers* VI, 6327 (X-1, A78).

8. Mackey, *Points of View*, ch. 7.

9. *Training in Christianity*, trans. Walter Lowrie (Princeton: Princeton University Press, 1941), 17f/12.

10. *Either/Or*, trans. David F. Swenson and Lillian Marvin Swenson (Princeton: Princeton University Press, 1959), I, 439/412.

11. *Either/Or* I, 306/282.

12. Raphael Meyer, *Forlovelsen: Ugivne for Fru Regine Schlegel* (Kjobenhavn: Gyldendal, 1904), my translation.

13. I have not been able to recover this quotation, so I wonder if my poor translating skills in my first visit to Copenhagen led me to be deceived about what is written. However, this I can find in the diary after the incident mentioned above: "But now the affair is really ended. And never have I felt so light and happy and free about this matter, so totally myself again, as just now after making this sacrificial step! For now I understand that I have God's consent to let her go and to take care of myself, only fulfilling her last prayer: sometimes to think of her and in this way reserving her to history and eternity" (*Journals and Papers* VI, 6539 [X-2, A211]). This phrasing, too, is problematic; what could K. be sacrificing by writing to Schlegel? It is clear, however, that his feeling of release could come about by putting the responsibility for the continuance of the temporal break between himself and Regina on Schlegel: "Det bliver hans Sag" (It is his affair), he had written earlier. This scapegoating of Schlegel effectively makes him into a mere parenthesis in the one, true, eternal love story: Søren and Regina.

14. It should be noted that part of *Either/Or* has this very title, "First Love." A woman never forgets her promises to her first love.

15. *Either/Or* I, 252/227.

16. If his diary can be believed, Kierkegaard (and Regina) continued to celebrate the day of their engagement as well as his birthday for quite a while after the break up and her wedding to Schlegel. See, for example, *Journals and Papers* VI, 6826 (X-5, A21).

17. See the epigram of *Fear and Trembling*, trans. Howard Hong and Edna Hong (Princeton: Princeton University Press, 1983), 3: "What Tarquin the Proud said in his garden with the poppies the son understood, but not the messenger."

18. *Either/Or* I, 373/345.

19. *Works of Love*, trans. Howard Hong and Edna Hong (New York: Harper, 1962), 23/10.

20. This phrase is from a poem popular in Kierkegaard's time; it is a lyric he and Regina exchanged letters about. See *Letters and Documents*, trans. Henrik Rosenmeier (Princeton: Princeton University Press, 1978), 64-6.

21. Roland Barthes, *A Lover's Discourse*, trans. Richard Howard (New York: Hill and Wang, 1978), 192.

22. *Works of Love*, 215/218.

23. *Concluding Unscientific Postscript*, 374n/363n.

24. William Shakespeare, *Love's Labours Lost* IV, iii, 252.

25. *Works of Love*, 19/7.

26. *Ibid.*

27. *Ibid.*, 30/17.

28. *Ibid.*, 25/11.

29. *Ibid.*, 27/13.

30. *Ibid.*, 28/15.

31. *Ibid.*, 25/11.

32. According to the author of *Journals and Papers* VI, 6472 (X-5, A149).

33. This echoes Victor Eremita's opening in his Preface to *Either/Or* I, 3. That preface, by telling us of a secreted internal writing, might make a reader wonder if Victor hides a secret.

34. *Works of Love*, 342/352.

35. *Ibid.*

36. *Ibid.*, 29/16.

37. *Ibid.*, 258/263, Kierkegaard referring to Socrates.
38. *Either/Or* I, 304/279, "A" referring to the seducer.
39. *Works of Love, passim*; see 30-1/17.
40. *Either/Or*, I, 300/276.
41. Walter Lowrie, *Kierkegaard* (New York: Oxford University Press, 1938), 224; see also *Journals and Papers* VI, 6472 (X-5, A149).
42. The Cordelia seduced in *Either/Or* was named Wahl, or as "A" says in his introduction to the Diary, "she was rightfully called Cordelia, but not however, Wahl" (I, 301/277).
43. *Works of Love*, 15.
44. *Either/Or* I, 9/xi.

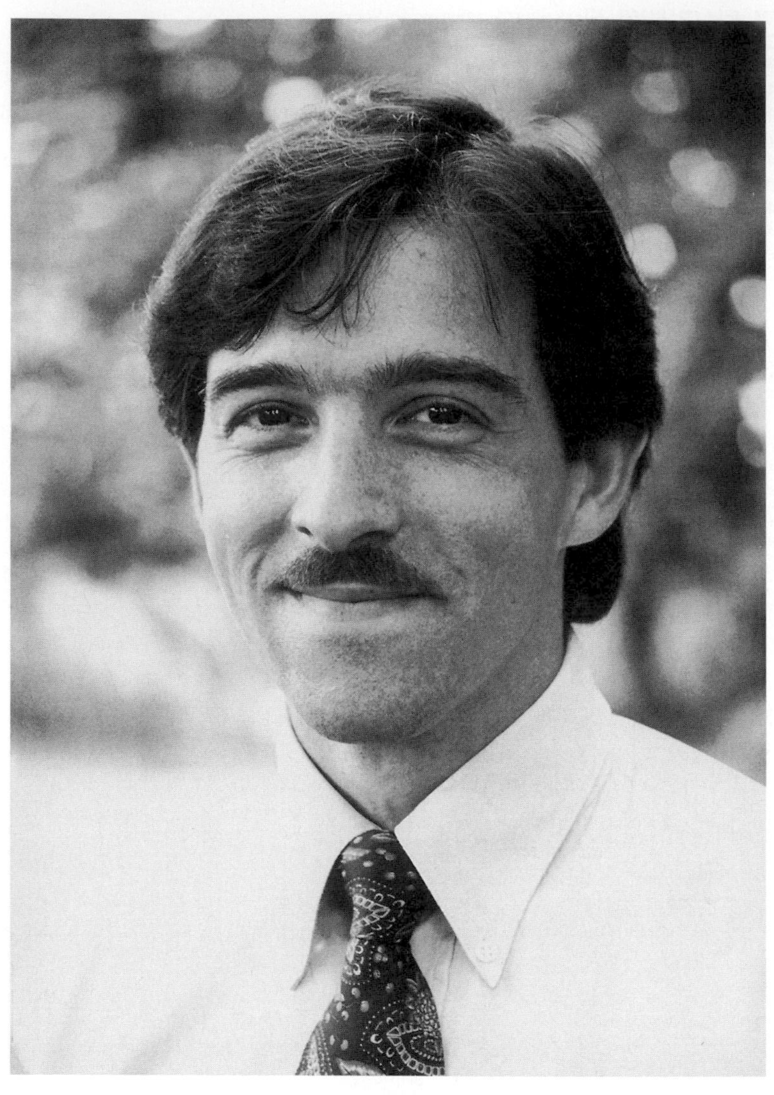

Steven M. Emmanuel
(photograph: Nancy Mandelkorn)

Author of "Response to Mr. Fendt"
Paper presented at the Society for the Philosophy of Sex and Love
during the
Central Division Meeting of The American Philosophical Association
Cincinnati, Ohio, 28 April, 1988

Forty-Six

BIOGRAPHY IN THE INTERPRETATION OF KIERKEGAARD

Steven M. Emmanuel

In his essay "Is *Works of Love* a Work of Love?" Gene Fendt proposes the following thesis:

> SAK was a seducer without peer, for his object was to possess a woman, heart and soul, both in time and eternity. To succeed in this primary objective would be enough to make him first among storied seducers, but his secondary objective, also a seduction, puts him at the ideal apex of seductivity. His secondary objective was to have thc whole story recorded and yet avoid discovery . . . via seduction. He would draw his reader aside, whisper "this is all for religious purposes" and win the title "great religious thinker" for his activity. Which activity, I say again, was first and last a seduction.[1]

Fendt characterizes his thesis as a heresy against the received interpretation of Kierkegaard's authorship. According to that interpretation, which closely follows Kierkegaard's own account in *The Point of View for My Work as an Author*, the authorship was guided from the beginning by a religious purpose. But if Fendt is correct, this is only part of the story. For to the extent that Kierkegaard succeeded in being regarded as a writer in the service of Christianity, he succeeded in carrying off his real purpose without detection: to keep his words and spirit alive in Regine's heart; to remind her of her promises to her first and only true love.

Fendt takes *Works of Love* to serve as a test case for his thesis, precisely because it appears to be a straightforward treatment of Christian ethics: "This book is not seductive, it does not wound from behind, it does not let a reader in an easy door. At least it does not seem to be a seduction" (479). The task then becomes to show how *Works of Love* can plausibly be interpreted not only as a work of seduction (for even the received interpretation has Kierkegaard "seducing" his reader with aesthetic works in order to establish a line of communication), but *primarily* as a seduction of Regine, and *secondarily* as a seduction of the world. The argument in support of this thesis consists mainly in interpreting a few of Kierkegaard's remarks in that book as suggestive of his alleged underlying intention.

In the Foreword to *Works of Love*, for example, Kierkegaard begs us not to be "hasty and curious"[2] (Fendt supplies "*nysgjerrig*" for "nosy" [479]) readers of his book. "But what," Fendt asks, "would ever tempt an ordinary reader of a book on Christian ethics to read that way?" More to the point, why would Kierkegaard think it necessary to make such a request of his reader? The most plausible explanation is that he was concerned about being misunderstood and passed over by the unreflective age in which he lived. In fact, Kierkegaard often expressed this concern in his writings. Consider the following remark from the second preface to *On Authority and Revelation*: "And herewith I would recommend this book, begging the reader to read slowly, in consideration of the fact that the author has often been obliged to take a step backward to get the point of view. I could wish that for once I might experience the good fortune of getting a good book well read."[3]

The curious nature is impatient, demanding immediate results, proofs. To be a curious reader is to want to grasp immediately that which can only be understood as a result of careful study and reflection. It is similar with love. To be curious in love is to demand the proof of love. Thus Kierkegaard insists that it is the "prayer of love that its concealed source and its hidden life in the most inward depths may remain a secret, that no one inquisitively and impudently will . . . thrust his way in to see what he cannot see anyway, the joy and blessing of which, however, he forfeits by his curiosity."[4] It seems only natural, then, that Kierkegaard should feel compelled to remind us that a discourse on the meaning of Christian love places special demands on its reader.

Next, there is the reference to "that single individual . . . who first ponders whether he will read or not."[5] Fendt asks (480) whether this remark might not be directed "more pointedly, to one particular individual, one who 'with joy and gratitude' Kierkegaard called 'my reader'?" No further evidence is offered in support of the suggestion that Kierkegaard might be referring here to Regine. It might be noted, however, that the expression "my reader" occurs many times in Kierkegaard's writings, and it is not clear that he reserved that epithet for Regine. In *On Authority and Revelation*, for example, he writes: "'My Reader,' may I simply beg you to read this book, for it is important for my main effort, wherefore I am minded to recommend it."[6] But it is especially difficult in this context to imagine that the expression "my reader" is intended to pick out Regine, since Kierkegaard's remarks at the beginning of the Preface make it clear who is intended: "If he will read the book as I have read it, and if at the same time he is a theologian, I venture to vouch that from it he will get a clarity about certain dogmatic concepts and an ability to use them which otherwise is not easily to be had."[7] Both *Works of Love* and *On Authority and Revelation* were written for the purpose of clarifying dogmatic Christian concepts, and it seems reasonable to suppose that Kierkegaard hoped they would be read and understood by the theologians of his day.

Fendt then suggests that Kierkegaard's emphasis on the essentially hidden and indescribable nature of love is a convenient vehicle for the seducer, and that he even praises erotic love in a way that is calculated to remind Regine of the love they had sacrificed. The first point assumes that there is no way to distinguish between the erotic love of the seducer and Christian love. Yet Kierkegaard clearly affirms that Christian love can be distinguished from erotic love by its fruits. The second point seems to be based on a misreading. Though it is true, as Fendt points out, that Kierkegaard does not want to condemn the *passion* of the erotic lover, this is not so much a defense of erotic love as of that quality of passion ("the quiet fire of secret pain")[8] through which it can gradually be transformed into a more profound and abiding love.

The final item of evidence is Kierkegaard's observation that "one may make the mistake of calling love that which is really self-love: when one loudly protests that he cannot live without his beloved but will hear nothing of love's task and demand, which is that he deny himself and give up the self-love of erotic love."[9] Fendt poses the question whether this remark is really meant to help a reader distinguish between erotic love and *agape*, or whether it is "a sentence spoken to a certain reader, a sentence that touches her desire and her memory" (481). The first thing to be noted is that Fendt deletes the final clause of Kierkegaard's original sentence, the portion after "demand." When the deleted text is reinstated, the answer to the first part of his question is that Kierkegaard's remark obviously does shed light on the distinction between erotic love and *agape*, at least in so far as it shows that the erotic form of love is really self-love, while *agape* is the response to God's commandment to love one's neighbor. As to the second part of Fendt's question, there is once again no obvious reason to suppose that Kierkegaard's remark is intended primarily for Regine.

Fendt suggests that the best way for Kierkegaard to make the secondary seduction work is to make the religious writing as cogent as possible. In this way, he excuses himself from commenting on most of what is contained in the book. But if *Works of Love* is admittedly a cogent discourse on Christian ethics, then on what grounds are we to suppose that the book is primarily and secondarily a work of seduction? Fendt concedes that the evidence for his thesis is such that he would "not go to court with it" (482). However, he also believes that this only makes his thesis more seductive. For if he could demonstrate that Kierkegaard was a seducer, then the alleged crime "would be less remarkable, imperfect." And since that cannot be demonstrated, "the crime, if there was a crime, remains a perfect one" (482). It would appear, then, that Fendt wants to argue along the following lines. If Kierkegaard's remarks lack the kind of context required to make the "seduction thesis" plausible, then this in itself is evidence that the "seduction thesis" is true, or at least it does not count against the truth of that thesis. But the defect in this line of reasoning is apparent.

I would like to conclude with two observations in a more positive vein. First, there are good reasons for doubting whether a retrospective work like *The Point of View* can be regarded as providing a reliable account of Kierkegaard's development as an author. If we take seriously Kierkegaard's repeated disavowal of authority with respect to the pseudonymous works, then how should we understand a book that purports to give us *the* point of view for the authorship? We might well be suspicious about the author's motivation for writing it. But Kierkegaard shows a remarkable consistency in his thinking on this point. For he knows that no matter what he says about his intentions as an author, the real test is whether his interpretation can be made to fit with the evidence. Preferring the status of a reader, Kierkegaard offers us his "point of view" as one possible perspective, which we may either accept or reject based on our own reading of the texts.

In keeping with the strategy suggested by Kierkegaard himself, a book like *The Point of View* may recommend a promising way of reading the authorship, regardless of whether the account it presents can be shown to be "authoritative." The salient question is not whether Kierkegaard was in fact embarked on a religious mission from the start, but whether that account of his purpose can be reconciled with the literary production. From this standpoint, I would argue that the received interpretation of the authorship remains the most comprehensive account we have to date.

Second, nothing that has been said thus far diminishes the fact that Fendt has drawn our attention to a fascinating aspect of Kierkegaard's writings. There is much evidence to suggest that Kierkegaard remained in love with Regine until the end of his life. Certainly, it would not be unreasonable to suppose that she was in his mind as he composed his thoughts on the subject of love. But though such insights contribute to a better understanding of Kierkegaard's life and work, they do not amount to a compelling theory.

To be compelling, a theory must be supported by the kind of evidence that makes the proposed interpretation more plausible than rival ones. In support of the theory that Kierkegaard's authorship was written primarily for the purpose of seducing Regine, Fendt might have appealed, for example, to the following journal entry from 1841:

> Again today I checked myself in an attempt to let her know, to let her suspect in some way that I still love her. My mind is so resourceful and there is a certain satisfaction in thinking a clever plan has been found. I would like to write a letter home which would be printed. The heading should be: My R—that would be enough for her. The letter itself could be full of subtle hints. But I must not do it; I humble myself beneath God's hand. Every time I get an idea like that, and it usually happens many times a day, I transform it into a prayer for her, that it will all be for the best for her, which is my wish.[10]

What is significant about this confession is that it establishes two crucial points: first, that Kierkegaard himself had conceived the possibility of communicating indirectly to Regine through his published writings; and second, that this idea had occurred to him two years before the publication of *Either/Or*. Naturally, the main task of showing how such a plan was eventually realized in the authorship, or in any single work, would still remain. But the theory would have to be substantiated by more than mere conjecture, or by appeal to the dubious notion of a "secondary seduction."

Though Fendt has not succeeded in making his case for *Works of Love*, it remains an open question whether a more modest version of his thesis could be defended.

Notes

1. Gene Fendt, "Is *Works of Love* a Work of Love?" this volume, 473-85, at 476; henceforth, page references are supplied parenthetically in the text.

2. *Works of Love*, trans. Howard Hong and Edna Hong (New York: Harper Torchbooks, 1964), 19.

3. *On Authority and Revelation: The Book on Adler*, trans. Walter Lowrie (New York: Harper and Row, 1966), liv.

4. *Works of Love*, 27.

5. *Ibid.*, 19.

6. *On Authority and Revelation*, xix.

7. *Ibid.*, li.

8. *Works of Love*, 28.

9. *Ibid.*, 25.

10. *Journals and Papers*, 7 vols., ed. and trans. Howard Hong and Edna Hong (Bloomington: Indiana University Press, 1967-78), V, 180.

T. F. Morris
(photograph: Colleen G. Morris)

Author of "Kierkegaard on Despair in *Works of Love*"
Paper presented at the Society for the Philosophy of Sex and Love
during the
Central Division Meeting of The American Philosophical Association
Cincinnati, Ohio, 28 April, 1988

Forty-Seven

KIERKEGAARD ON DESPAIR IN *WORKS OF LOVE*[1]

T. F. Morris

In this essay, I develop Søren Kierkegaard's understanding of despair through what he says about erotic love and friendship. In the first part, I discuss the role of preference in erotic love and friendship; in the second, I explain Kierkegaard's claim that erotic love and friendship are in despair; and in the third part, I discuss Kierkegaard's more general claim that everyone who does not have the eternal is in despair.

1. Erotic Love and Friendship are Preferential

Kierkegaard's distinction between erotic love and friendship is that erotic love is concerned with the body and friendship is not:

> In erotic love the I is qualified as body-psyche-spirit, and the beloved qualified as body-psyche-spirit. In friendship the I is qualified as psyche-spirit and the friend is qualified as psyche-spirit.[2]

Erotic love and friendship are collectively equated with preferential love and love rooted in mood and inclination (58). That is, the lover desires the beloved because the lover's mood and inclination causes the lover to prefer this particular person over others. The beloved is preferred because of the beloved's differences (69), because of the things that make the beloved different from other people. The lover is not so focused on these differentiating traits that he or she fails to admire the whole that is differentiated by those traits; otherwise, it would merely be lust rather than love.[3] The whole is admired for having the traits. The traits point to the significance of the whole as that which is their source, and the whole is then admired (67). Thus the lover's passionate preference *centers* around the beloved (66).

Because this love is rooted in mood and inclination (58), it must be that the lover's mood and inclination are to prefer those certain traits that cause the lover to love the beloved. The lover is responding to his or her own preferences; the beloved merely provides the occasion for these preferences to have an object. Hence "erotic love and friendship are good fortune" (64); if one does not have the good fortune of the right type of person coming along, a person who possesses the traits one happens to prefer, then one is stuck without a worthy object of desire.

The efficient cause of the love is not the appearance of the beloved, but an action of the lover: "In erotic love and friendship there is self-ignition" (66). Love is something we do to ourselves, rather than the result of something the other person does to us. As we have seen, this self-ignition involves feeling admiration for the beloved, but there is more to it than that; there is something selfish about it:

> If passionate preference had no other selfishness about it, it still would have this, that consciously or unconsciously there is a willfulness about it. . . . The use of discretion (*vilkaarlige*) is there. The one and only object is found . . . by choosing. (67)

The lover's mood and inclination *unconsciously* lead the lover into wanting to attain to this particular object, and the lover is *consciously* willful to the extent that the lover submits to and assents to this driving force: "unconsciously insofar as it is in the power of natural predisposition, consciously insofar as it utterly surrenders to this power and consents to it" (67). (Consciousness has the opportunity of resisting a desire, but it does not originate the desire.) The particular selfishness Kierkegaard is talking about here is the selfishness of being the boss: the state of affairs that *I* choose to come into being should come into being; *my* discretion should be followed.

But there is also a deeper selfishness, for the lover is not disinterestedly desirous that this particular state of affairs come into existence: "erotic love strains in the direction of . . . the beloved" (63). The lover passionately desires to be in relationship with the beloved. Plato has a similar understanding of the selfish nature of the will (*Republic*, 437c):

> The soul of someone who desires something is striving after it, or trying to draw to itself the thing it wishes to possess, or again, in so far as it is willing to have its want satisfied, it is giving its assent to its own longing, as if to an inward question.[4]

For Plato, the use of the will is necessarily acquisitive—it involves trying to draw something to oneself—both when we initially feel inclined toward our object and also when we subsequently give our assent to this inclination. We have seen that Kierkegaard would agree that this is true of the will for people who are experiencing erotic love or friendship, for they strain toward their object, and we shall see that he holds that it is true for anyone who has not undergone the transformation of the eternal. According to both philosophers, there is something about human nature that makes each person want what they want *for themselves*. Apart from consideration of the eternal, it is not possible for us to desire that the desired state of affairs come into being for its own sake.

The lover is following his or her own compulsion, trying to please himself or herself. The beloved is merely the opportunity that the lover is fortunate enough to have in order to do so. Because the beloved is not the source of the compulsion, the lover's fidelity is not really to the beloved, but to that which, in himself or herself, is driving the lover on. The lover could not give up the love even if the beloved were to demand it. Kierkegaard writes:

> The ardent lover can by no means . . . endure duplication, which here would mean giving up his erotic love if the beloved required it. (38)

The lover is treating himself as the power that determines whether he should love; duplication would mean treating the beloved in the same way (duplicating oneself). Kierkegaard sees that if it came down to it, the lover would follow the lover's own determination of what should be done, not the beloved's; the primary fidelity in erotic love and friendship is to oneself.

Kierkegaard does not merely claim that erotic love and friendship are selfish. He also claims that they constitute self-love; that is, what the lover really loves is himself or herself. Even though the lover's passionate preference centers around the beloved (66) and strains toward the beloved (63), the lover is essentially concerned with himself or herself: "the lover in this onrushing, inordinate devotion really relates himself to himself in self-love" (68). If God were to come down and say "prefer this person," then, in acting on God's command as such, the lover would be loving God. (This is what Kierkegaard calls Religiousness B.) God would be the one the lover really cared about; God would be the one the lover is really trying to please. In erotic love and friendship we are responding to our own mood and inclination rather than to God. It is as if we are giving ourselves a command: *this* is the person we must prefer. In passionately preferring the beloved we are trying to follow the dictates of that command. Or, because the effect of mood and inclination is to cause us to have a preference, *preference* can be said to play the same role in erotic love and friendship as God does in God-commanded love. Kierkegaard writes:

> The Christian love command requires one to love God above all and then to love one's neighbor. In love and friendship preference is the middle term; in love to one's neighbor God is the middle term. (70)

One follows God's command because one has first loved God; one follows the dictates of preference because one has first loved one's own preferences. In pursuing the beloved, we are not being true to God; we are not being true to the person we prefer; we are being true to our own preference for that person. The lover "has a preference for preference" (67). Thus erotic love and friendship are primarily love for one's own preferences, that is, they are self-love.

First there is the admiration for the (distinguished) beloved (67), and then there is the process of making the beloved the object of one's will. The admiration is not yet self-love: "To admire another person certainly is not self-love" (67). Thus initially there is no choosing. But the objects of admiration, affect us in a way that leads us into choosing to be related to them. They "lie so close to one's self-love" (38). They are so close that one responds to them by unconsciously willing to be related to them, and then going farther and giving conscious assent to this desire, surrendering to its power, and allowing it to determine one's will (67).

Kierkegaard links self-love with the idea of loving "the other-self, the other-I" (66). This formulation is especially difficult to understand, for it occurs in the same context as his discussion of the necessity of admiring the beloved. Admiration (*Beundring*) would seem to imply a consciousness of the otherness of the other, a consciousness that the other person is different from oneself, which the expression "the other-self" would seem to deny. Kierkegaard provides us with a number of clues to help us solve this riddle. In an earlier passage, he wrote: "To love him who through favoritism is nearer to you than all others is self-love" (37). It is not merely a question of the lover favoring the beloved, but of the lover feeling that they are near, that they belong together. The admired person's qualities do not put the admired person on a higher plane than the admirer; they merely set him or her above ordinary people. The lover must then also feel distinguished through his or her affinity with the beloved. The lover must feel that he or she has something in common with the beloved that makes them different from other people: "They are like each other as different from other men" (69). My beloved is like me, not like those others. My beloved is my other-I.

As the intensity of the love increases, the lovers cut themselves off from others even more: "The more securely the two I's come together to become one I, the more this united I selfishly cuts itself off from all others" (68). In excluding others, I affirm my special beloved as being like myself, as being my other-I, in an otherwise ordinary world.

2. Erotic Love and Friendship are in Despair

Erotic love and friendship involve passion. "To love without passion is an impossibility" (63). There is something necessarily acquisitive about the unconscious and conscious use of the will as it strains in the direction of the object that the individual admires. Plato saw this passion in terms of trying to draw the desired object to oneself, rather than in terms to straining toward the object, but the two philosophers are in essential agreement: they both see a subjective commitment on the part of the passionate person to come together with his or her object of desire.

Kierkegaard offers the following curious formulation about passion:

> All passion, whether it attacks or defends itself, fights in one manner only: either-or: 'either I exist and am the highest or I do not exist at all—either all or nothing'. (59)

Defends itself against whom? It could be against another person. Romeo can say to Benvolio: "Show me a mistress that is passing fair, what doth her beauty serve, but as a note where I may read who pass'd that passing fair?" (*Romeo and Juliet* I, i, 240-2), and thus defends his passion as having the highest object against the attack of another person. But passion can also defend itself within the individual person, in the battle that can go on within us when we consciously decide whether to give our assent to the object that we have already unconsciously desired (67).

At the beginning of this process, we have already unconsciously willed to be related to the admired object. If we make the move of stopping and considering whether we really want to commit ourselves to it, we are challenging the sovereignty of the passion. We are considering the possibility that there might be considerations that would overrule the passion and dictate pursuing some other object of desire (to use Plato's formulation, the possibility that there is some other answer to that inward question). To the extent that we are under the sway of the passion, to the extent that we are inclined to strain toward the object, we want to defend the passion. And then this would be where passion defends itself by saying that it is the highest or it is nothing. Saying that it is the highest would be saying that there are no considerations that could overrule it. The defense would not be against specific considerations, but against the move of stopping and considering. Its siren song would be: go with me, nothing is more important than the object I am straining after. It does not offer ancillary support in an effort to establish that its object really is the highest, for that would mean that it has already lost the battle to stave off consideration. It merely says either/or: either be determined by the really good thing, by me, or not. When consciousness assents to passion, it surrenders itself to its power (67). Either submit to my sovereignty, either recognize that I am the highest, or not. There is no other way to respond to passion *qua* passion. If the individual makes the move of Hamlet and dispassionately considers whether or not he should follow his passion ("That would be scann'd" [*Hamlet* III, iii, 75]), then the passion has lost him, for "words to the heat of deeds too cold breath gives" (*Macbeth* II, i, 61); the sovereignty of the passion would already be denied. The passion can do nothing but point to its object as the really important thing, and ask the individual to become absolutely committed to that object.

How would passion *attack* with the same either/or? There would have to be competing inclinations; the individual would have to be already somewhat inclined toward doing something else, and the passion would then challenge this inclination by presenting itself, with its straining toward its different object, as being the highest thing. Before we have made up our mind about what we will do, while we are still of two minds about it, we can have contradictory feelings about possible objects of desire. To use Plato's example, one part of us can desire to drink something at the same time that another part desires not to drink (*Republic* 439a-b). One passion battles the other through saying that it is the highest, that its object is the really important thing. We might rationalize the desire to drink after we have submitted to the passion, but the rationalization is not what makes us decide to drink. We formulate rationalizations only after the desire for a temptation has already won. For example, the passion does not say that one cookie won't hurt; the passion wins by suggesting the goodness of the cookie, and then we play an additional game with ourselves and come up with the rationalization. When two passions are competing with each other, the one that wins will be the one that is successful in making our consciousness feel that its object really is the highest.

The lover's passion commits him or her absolutely to the beloved in that present moment. The passion not only makes us feel that its object is the most important object, but also that this particular moment of passionate straining is everything: the highest expression for the inclination at the base of erotic love is "that there is only one beloved in the whole world and that only this one time of erotic love is genuine love, is everything and the next time is nothing" (62). One moment's passion is not essentially related to any other passionate striving, even if that striving is directed toward the same object. No other object in space and no other moment of time can have significance for the lover. The passion not only feels its object to be the highest, but it feels itself to be the highest; everything depends on the individual attaining to the beloved now—I *must* be related to it. If one were to think, "Well, I can be related to it tomorrow," one would no longer be in passion. The passion simply cannot accept separation from the object that it is straining after.

Treating the object of desire this way involves seeing it as being everything, seeing it as if my meaning and my happiness were dependent on my relationship to it; that is, treating it as if it were God. Hence Kierkegaard claims: "Love and friendship are essentially idolatry" (69-70). (Juliet calls Romeo "the god of my idolatry" [*Romeo and Juliet* II, ii, 14].)

Kierkegaard claims that such idolatry is despair: "The despair [of spontaneous love] lies in relating oneself with infinite passion to a single individual, for with infinite passion one can relate oneself—if one is not in despair—only to the eternal" (54). He gets to this understanding of despair by beginning with a more ordinary understanding of it. According to the ordinary understanding of "despair," one despairs when it is made impossible to possess what one loves (55, 56). Hence spontaneous love despairs over *misfortune* (54); just as it was good fortune to be presented with an object that matched one's preferences, so too is it misfortune to have possession of that object be made impossible. But now Kierkegaard goes farther and claims that the lover is in despair, whether or not fortune has given the lover access to the beloved: "When spontaneous love despairs over misfortune, it only reveals that it was in despair, that in happiness it had also been in despair" (54). The fundamental problem is not the misfortune of lacking the beloved; it is the lack of the eternal: "Despair is to lack the eternal" (55). We are not merely looking for momentary happiness through a relationship with the beloved, but we are also looking to the beloved to establish us in happiness forever, something the beloved, as a transitory object, cannot do. The fundamental limitation of the beloved is that it can change. Linell E. Cady is correct when he says that Kierkegaard's position is that because the *possibility* of change remains spontaneous love is fundamentally despair.[5] The original need for the eternal is the need for something that will be capable of establishing the lover in happiness, and therefore for something that is reliable over time. Solon's understanding that "as long as he is living his happiness can change; only when he is dead and happiness had not left him while he lived, only then is it certain that he was happy" (46), drives us to want more than merely to be with our object, but also to possess it over time. The possibility of losing happiness is always there at the heart of the lover's passion. The only expression for such love is "a burning passion, whereby it is merely hinted that anxiety is hidden at the bottom" (48). What propels the lover as he or she strains in the direction of the beloved is this "anxiety over the possibility of change" (47). Even though love's passion involves "an unlimited certainty" (45) about itself as the highest, "the love is unconsciously uncertain" (48). The initial unconscious willed response to that which the lover prefers involves anxiety about whether or not the lover has really found the thing that will secure the lover in happiness, about whether or not this thing's happiness will come to an end. Thus the lover is really seeking the eternal, the only thing that will not come to an end; the eternal is what the lover is really straining after, even though he or she is not aware of it. The lover does not have what the lover truly desires, and the lover desperately reaches out to the beloved in an attempt to gain it. Hence spontaneous love "loves with the power of despair" (54); it cannot let itself remain separated from the object that it unconsciously feels it so desperately needs. Thus Kierkegaard can say: "Despair is a disrelationship in one's inmost being" (54). It is a disrelationship because one is not related to the eternal, even as one reaches out idolatrously toward the beloved as if the beloved were eternal.

Thus, in spontaneous love we are desperately reaching out, for what we feel we need, toward an object that is not capable of fulfilling that need. The idolater who despairs upon losing his idol does not realize that he did not have what he was truly desirous of, even when he possessed the idol. The fundamental problem is relating to something that is not God as if it were God.

(Jeremy Walker claims that Kierkegaard is saying: "To lack the concept of the eternal is precisely to be in despair."[6] But this is not a precise translation of "*Fortvivelse er at mingle det Evige*" [Despair is to lack the eternal]. Moreover, pagans have the concept of the eternal; for example, Kierkegaard writes, "All paganism consists in this that god is related to man directly as the obviously extraordinary to the astonished observer."[7] And Kierkegaard's position is that pagans must necessarily be in despair: "Everyone who has not undergone the transformation of duty's 'You shall' is in despair" [54].)

3. Despair in General

The formulation "Despair is to lack the eternal" (55) says much the same thing as "the despair lies in relating oneself with infinite passion to a single individual" (54). Saying that the problem is "Treating A as if it were B" is almost the same as saying that the problem is lacking B. But there also might be other ways in which one could lack B. What is added by saying that the problem is lacking the eternal is that those people who are not experiencing erotic love or friendship, but who also do not have the eternal, must *also* be in despair. They must also have this disrelationship in their inmost being.

Recall that we have seen that Kierkegaard (as well as Plato) holds that it is impossible for the lover to will that some state of affairs come into being without willing that that state of affairs be related to oneself. Here Kierkegaard is going farther and holding that all people who lack the eternal have this sort of selfish relationship with some sort of idol. He writes: "Is there anything at all for which humanity as such—is there anything for which the natural man has greater desire than for the highest!" (70). Even though we might feel that our lives are quiet enough, the reality is that we have a great desire for the highest. We are living lives of quiet desperation, desperately reaching out to this or to that petty object as if it were the highest, as if it could establish our happiness forever. As Thoreau observes, "A stereotyped but unconscious despair is concealed even under what are called the games and amusements of mankind."[8] Even if we are merely playing a game, if I start to beat you badly, you are going to want to *show* me. And then in our serious occupations, for example in our pursuit of a career, we feel that we have got to have so-and-so's approval, etc., etc. We feel that we have *got* to have; that is, we are *desperate*. As Heidegger shows, it is possible to be desperately concerned with getting the approval of the people around you without even being aware that this is what you are doing. Kierkegaard is saying that all people who do not have the eternal are necessarily treating something less than the eternal as if it were the highest, as if it were the one thing they need in order to be happy forever. And then in the next moment they might be looking for the same eternal happiness through a relationship with a different object, and on they go.

Kierkegaard indicates that the only way in which one can have the eternal (and thus the only way one can escape despair) involves obeying God's command to love one's neighbor: "Everyone who has not undergone the transformation of the eternal through duty's 'You shall' is in despair" (54). The only way to escape our desperate search for that which will make us happy is to relate to what is around us through God's command to love one's neighbor. Otherwise, my fellow travelers through a brief span of time on Earth, we are doomed to relate to what is around us, by selecting some specific thing and treating that thing as if it were God.

Notes

1. Another and earlier version of this essay was published as "Kierkegaard on Despair and the Eternal," *Sophia* 28 (1989): 21-30.
2. Søren Kierkegaard, *Works of Love*, trans. Howard Hong and Edna Hong (New York: Harper and Row, 1962), 69. All parenthetical page references are to this volume.
3. Søren Kierkegaard, *Either/Or*, vol. 2, trans. W. Lowrie (Princeton: Princeton University Press, 1971), 21.
4. Plato, *Republic*, trans. F. M. Cornford (New York: Oxford University Press, 1941).
5. Linnell E. Cady, "Alternative Interpretations of Love in Kierkegaard and Royce," *The Journal of Religious Ethics* 10 (1982), 238-63, at 242.
6. Jeremy D. B. Walker, *Kierkegaard: The Descent Into God* (Montreal: McGill-Queen's University Press, 1985), 105.
7. Søren Kierkegaard, *Concluding Unscientific Postscript*, trans. D. F. Swenson and W. Lowrie (Princeton: Princeton University Press, 1968), 219.
8. Henry David Thoreau, *Walden* (New York: New American Library of World Literature, 1942), 10.

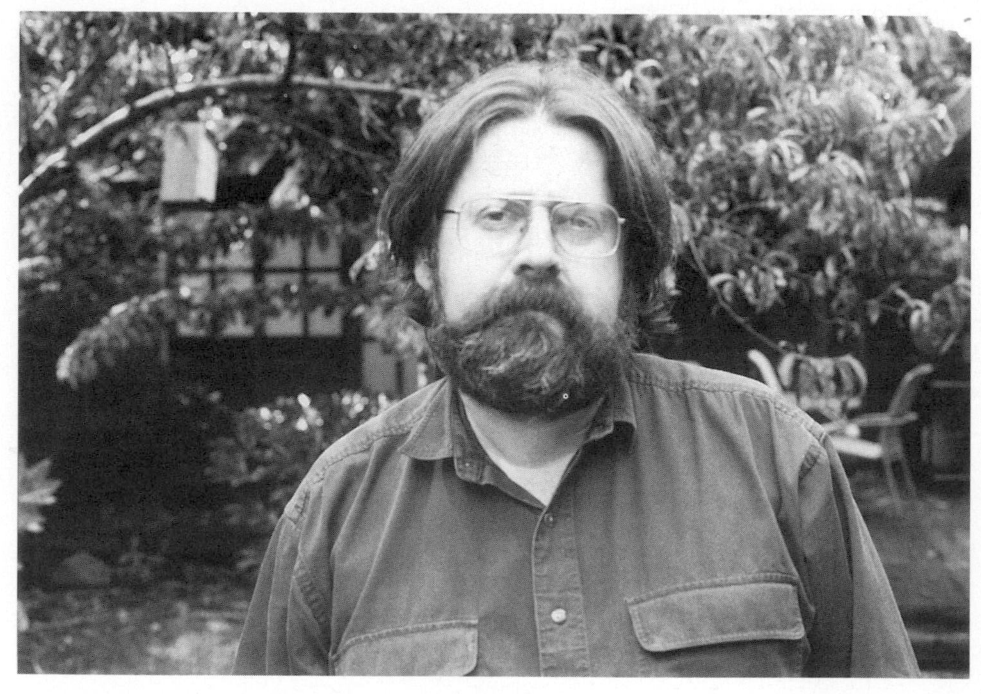

Anthony J. Graybosch
(photograph: Divna Ostojic-Graybosch)

Author of “Which One Is the Real One?”
Paper presented at the Society for the Philosophy of Sex and Love
during the
Pacific Division Meeting of The American Philosophical Association
Berkeley, Cal., 23 March 1989

Forty-Eight

WHICH ONE IS THE REAL ONE?

Anthony J. Graybosch

1. Introduction

In his prose poem "Which Is the Real One?" Baudelaire describes "a certain Benedicta who filled earth and air with the ideal, and whose eyes scattered the seeds of longing for greatness, beauty and glory, for everything that makes a man believe in immortality." But Benedicta was too beautiful to live. "I buried her with my own hands and shut her into a coffin of scented and incorruptible wood like the coffers of India." While he is still gazing on the spot where he has buried his treasure, there appears "a little creature who looked singularly like the deceased." The double, in a frenzy, stamping on the fresh grave, shrieking with laughter, says, "Look at me! I am the real Benedicta! [. . .] And to punish you for your blindness and your folly, you shall love me as I am." Baudelaire closes the poem with a scene of denial. But it is not clear whether he denies his love for the real Benedicta or that the double is Benedicta. The narrator stamps on the grave so violently that his leg sinks to the knee where, "like a wolf caught in a trap," he is "held fast, perhaps forever, to the grave of the ideal."[1]

The transition from falling in love to being in love must overcome our disappointment at the dissipation of our illusions about the beloved. And for this reason, the transition is often unsuccessful. It can also lead us to deny the reality that now presents itself as we cling to the memory of an illusion as the true beloved. Baudelaire's poem first expresses the familiar feeling of exhilaration that accompanies falling in love followed by the awareness, that we were somehow deluded, that arrives with the failure of love. An anti-romantic, he is highly skeptical of the value of love and focuses our attention on two important questions that romanticism leaves unanswered. First, suppose that Benedicta were in reality an embodiment of the lover's ideal, that the lover did have reasons for the intoxication that Baudelaire depicts so well. Any rational person should realize there are other equally good, perhaps better, exemplifications of ideal value. Why does the lover focus on an individual when the ultimate values that supposedly explain the love are universals? Thus anti-romantics avoid overvaluing the individual. In *Women in Love*, D. H. Lawrence has Ruppert remark to Ursula, "You are all women to me." Ruppert means that he does not need another female, since Ursula is an embodiment of the general feminine qualities.

The second question is why one individual is perceived as the cause of what can best be characterized as a revolution in another's life, perceived as so important that the beloved is often spoken of in terms appropriate to a deity. Other factors relevant to a radical change in the lover's life go unnoticed by the lover and are ignored by romanticism. The prevalence of the romantic interpretation of love in Western society leads lovers to focus on the beloved as the genesis of falling in love, rather than the role of their own needs and active projections. Perhaps the most obvious exception to this orientation is found in popular music. Two blues standards that are good examples of a different perspective on falling in love are "Everybody Needs Somebody to Love" and "Everybody Ought to Change Sometime."

I want to discuss these questions to introduce an anti-romantic account of falling in love. We should note that these two questions can be raised even of successful transitions to stable love. I believe that anti-romanticism provides insightful answers to the problems romanticism avoids; it supplies, as well, the basis of a nonindividualistic account of the self.

2. Love and Theories of Falling in Love

We can make believe that the meaning of love is coherent, but the truth is that theories of love relegate some strands of this rich event to the role of inferior types of love, or to what is not love at all. For instance, if love is always a "positive response to the object of love" and "love affirms the goodness of this object," then a heavy dose of romanticism has already been smuggled into the definition of love.[2] We should admit that our notion of love has a historical genesis in which incompatible elements of platonism, courtly love, romanticism, and *agape* (to name just a few influences) have become fused. Many actions motivated by love can be understood only in light of its genealogy. Perhaps what makes satisfying and successful love so difficult are the conflicting expectations derived from our incoherent concept of love. So rather than beginning with a definition of love, I offer an argument about love and the nature of the self who loves. If the argument is persuasive, then the interpretation of love endorsed will be accepted as both a definition and the way to love.

Falling in love can be explicated through exemplars such as Baudelaire's poem. Infatuation might be thought to be a better description for this experience, but the use of "infatuation" would trivialize the effect of falling in love. There might be other ways to fall in love than the one marked by the experiences of exhilaration and intoxication, but they do not capture the aspect of *falling* sufficiently. So the use of "falling in love" for this one way of entering love is warranted.

Romanticism emphasizes the feeling that accompanies falling in love as its most characteristic quality. And several aspects of the romantic account of falling in love are touched on in Baudelaire's poem. The beloved is presented as the ideal object of eros, the almost divine source of inspiration that animates the lover. Consequently, the beloved is seen as an image of a god.[3] And Baudelaire leaves the lover, having had a glimpse of the universal in the particular beloved, clinging to this recollection of a person in whom true beauty was found. But what Plato saw as divine inspiration through particular exemplars, anti-romantics (such as Baudelaire) present as an illusion that no individual can fulfill.

The romantic is committed to basing love on knowledge of another person and to finding ideal satisfaction in the beloved. For instance, Irving Singer argues that the primacy of the imagination as sympathetic identification is the key element of the romantic view of love.[4] It is only through imagination that one can comprehend another being and satisfy the universal metaphysical craving for unity: "If God and nature were the same, and if every object contained all reality within it, romanticism could easily conclude that all occurrences of love were good, and perhaps equally good. Regardless of what the beloved might be."[5]

Different theories of love can provide variant readings of the poem. The romantic theorist, Stendhal, compared falling in love to the process by which a branch thrown into the unused workings of a salt mine acquires a coat of beautiful crystals.[6] Due to the crystallization performed by imagination, "it is only in the imagination that you are certain of any particular perfection in the woman you love." Stendhal catalogs seven steps in the advance of romantic love. After the fourth step, falling in love, the first crystallization occurs. All imagined perfection is embodied in the beloved. But, in reality, the beloved is just a little twig. Doubt sets in shortly afterwards, leading the lover to develop tests of the beloved, and sometimes a second crystallization fails. But when a second crystallization occurs, love is permanent because the attempt to find a substitute for the beloved has failed. In Baudelaire's case, Stendhal's diagnosis would be that the second crystallization has failed. But the social obligations incurred to Benedicta prevent Baudelaire from finding a substitute.

Stendhal and Baudelaire both present the familiar themes of intoxication, illusion, self expansion, self completion, and fixation of attention of the lover on the beloved. But neither does much to enhance our understanding of why crystallization fails. Stendhal recommends that the beloved resist sensual love during the first crystallization, but then notes that this is incompatible with the realization of the greatest sensual pleasure. In any case, sometimes the lover continues to exalt the twig, and sometimes the lover rejects a beloved for another with even less resemblance to the ideal. The degree of illusion in romantic love might lead to the skeptical attitude that even when romantic love succeeds, it ought not to succeed.

A feminist reading of Baudelaire might focus on the rage of Benedicta. She allowed herself to be changed from a goddess into a "little creature" in order to allay Baudelaire's fear of her power and to acquire her share of derivative power from the male. In some way, he has failed her as males must, since Western society has confuted the roles of husband and god. Power can be acquired only through revenge: by subjugating, controlling, and punishing the fallen god.[7] Both males and females are deluded about the roles they can fulfill; and it is only by changing expectations that falling in love can be managed with minimal personal destruction.

Curiously, Lawrence's analysis is similar. The process by which falling in love leads to failed marriages is a series of compromises of our authentic individuality in order to satisfy our lover.[8] But Lawrence also focused on the attempt to comprehend the self of the beloved. In his view, male and female psyches are so different as to be incomprehensible to each other. Seeking for such knowledge is an attempt to fuse with the love object. And for fusion to occur, one of the lovers dies by giving up an essential difference. Lawrence believes that love can last only if the lovers remain partially mysterious to each other, and independent.[9] For Lawrence, Benedicta's lover has allowed himself to be comprehended by abandoning his male power.[10]

Disparate as these views of love are, at least one common element does bear on our problems. All three, even the romantic Stendhal, deemphasize the importance, for falling in love, of knowing the beloved's personality.

3. Falling in Love: the Social Dimension

The secondary status they attribute to the beloved allows anti-romantics to focus on the lover. But anti-romantics look at the lover in a broader social context, because they do not assume that the beloved is the primary cause of falling in love. Francesco Alberoni writes, "to fall in love is not to desire a beautiful or interesting person; it is a remaking of the social sphere, a vision of the world with new eyes."[11] Alberoni argues that what a lover requires of the beloved is not, as Singer thinks, a valued set of personality traits,[12] but only the readiness to enter into a social effort at rebirth that he calls the nascent state. Illusion and the glorification of the beloved are deemphasized as causes; they are mere symptoms of the lover's exhilaration. Alberoni's focal points are the subject who falls in love and the presuppositions that must be satisfied before a person risks falling in love.

Alberoni believes that falling in love is a reaction to extreme depression, feelings of worthlessness, and exclusion.[13]

> There is always a long preparation due to a slow change, a slow deterioration in relations with love objects. . . . Those two old mechanisms, depression and persecution, continue to function: we protect our ideal with all our strength, concealing the problem. The consequence is that the collective movement [falling in love] always strikes suddenly. . . . In the face of self-destruction, even fear is mitigated, and other things once experienced as seductions to be avoided, are now seen in a different light. . . . Two forces are freed: one—eros—violently embraces with its force new objects which it instantly transforms into ideals; the other—violence—breaks with endured and accepted restraints.[14]

The real one is the lover, not either of the Benedictas. The needs of the lover set the process in motion. All that is required of the beloved is readiness for the nascent state. As the receptive embodiment of the desires that cause us to fall in love, the beloved might seem perfect. But, as a person with projections and goals that need not match our own, it is just as possible that the illusion of perfection might not occur. This seems right to me. We can and do fall in love with people whom we perceive are less than perfect. The initial stage need not be blind.

The risks involved in building a new collective are going to cause tests on the part of the lovers. We might fall in love and also expect that some changes occur in the beloved.[15] Alberoni even argues that every lover requires full self-abandonment of the beloved. Dehumanization is not avoided by such tests, but the lover spares the beloved at the last minute.[16] Unlike Catherine in Ernest Hemingway's *The Garden of Eden*,[17] Alberoni's lover only requires the willingness to give up or to redirect writing. She does not burn the manuscripts to insure compliance.

4. Merging, Meaning, Rebirth

Falling in love is grounded in a basic metaphysical desire to merge in a small community to establish personal meaning, and involves projection of the needs of the self onto the phenomenological level. Loves should not be discriminated on the basis of their degree of apprehension of the reality of the beloved, so much as on the strength of the lover's animating desire.

Everyday life is characterized by the disappointment of not being the center of the universe. An institution such as the family might make us feel unique, but certainly not extraordinary. There are, however, people we love who are part of our identity. We do not want to fail to love them because we would lose our self identity by doing so. Ambivalence and aggression might occur because everyday life does not satisfy the need to be unique and extraordinary. Occasional crises might be needed to reawaken our knowledge of the importance of the beloved. But such events are hard to plan, at least consciously. What Alberoni calls depressive overload occurs when "continued allocation of eros to the love objects as now constituted would lead the subject to self destruction. Institutions developed to allow expansion of eros now act as impediments."[18]

Falling in love and being in a stable love both have positive and negative aspects. Falling in love has the ecstasy of fulfillment, but also torment from fear of dissolution. Being in love provides tranquility, but also boredom. Ideal love is difficult because it requires the combination of the two positive poles of ecstasy and tranquility that belong to radically different states.[19] The ambivalence is permanent. Even when all goes well, and the transition from falling in love to love is successful, the loss of the Eden-like state is felt.

The attractiveness of falling in love is countered by the risk involved in forming a new collective and rejecting established institutions. But the nascent state is attractive, at least in the West, because it promises secular rebirth. Alberoni defines falling in love as the nascent state of a collective movement involving two individuals.[20] The nascent state occurs only when our ambivalence crosses a given threshold inversely proportionate to the self's degree of emotional investment. Nascent states are always temporary; they are the transitional form taken by social states as they pass from one structured state to another.[21] The experience we undergo when we fall in love is created by the forces that lead to the nascent state, not the beloved.[22]

As a revolution, falling in love involves the construction of a new collective. People who were divided are united, and there is a rupture of past relationships. This again makes falling in love a threat to existing social institutions. And falling in love feeds on the fuel provided by the rupture of a past relationship; it needs obstacles, such as a past relationship, to fuel the founding of a new institution. A monogamous love relationship is the best solution to the nascent state because it provides the sense of being both extraordinary and unique.

Alberoni emphasizes that the couple is the only collective that ceases to exist when one member leaves.[23] So a feeling of meaning is guaranteed at least temporarily by this collective. But this is more illusion than reality. The couple never ceases to exist, but seems to reassert itself in subsequent relationships. And, where children are involved, the persistence of the couple is reinforced in shadow families. Alberoni has not sufficiently connected his metaphysics with psychology; he retains a dose of romanticism that affects his perception of the serially monogamous couple. But he correctly points out how falling in love is fueled by a joint effort to overcome obstacles and by a flight from entropy. The beloved seems perfect, partially because of the heightening of sensual pleasure that we mistakenly attribute to the beloved and not to release of blocked eros. At the same time, the lover does not feel selfish since the nascent state is a social state. The feeling of meaning can occur since a merger takes places with another "individual." And since the individual is largely unknown, there can be a great deal of faith placed in the new relationship.

Alberoni does offer insight into the two questions that romanticism leaves unanswered. The motive to fall in love originates in the lover, so the only important initial requirement placed on the beloved is tolerance of initial projections and readiness for the nascent state. The projection of the cause of the nascent state to another, new, individual is explained by the needs for meaning through merging and for release of pent up eroticism. Another benefit of the process is that needs are satisfied without the lover becoming conscious of their true nature, which might block the nascent state.

Baudelaire provided another poem, appropriately describing the nascent state. Its last lines are: "It is Time to get drunk! If you are not to be the martyred slaves of Time, be perpetually drunk! With wine, with poetry, or with virtue as you please."[24] Falling in love is just that; it is getting drunk with virtue. It is an attempt to make an entropic life feel as if it is worth living. It has little to do with intellectually motivated love and might even be hostile to it. It is no wonder that the individual does not matter, initially.

William Butler Yeats also compared falling in love to drinking.[25] His reference to wine cannot help but remind us of Plato's *Symposium*. And the vision of Socrates drinking wine but remaining sober blends with that other potion he brought to his mouth to terminate his life. Yeats plays on the double aspect of intoxication, whether it comes from wine, through the mouth, or virtue, through the eye. The lover feels more alive, more fulfilled, as the intoxicant is ingested. But, at the same time, the intoxicant moves the lover farther from life, farther from true virtue. The modern lover, unlike Plato, despairs of knowing in this life whether the beloved is an intoxicant or deserving of love. Yeats uses the sense of sight as a source of intoxication, where philosophers would associate sight with contemplation. Certainly touch and taste more commonly convey intoxication. Perhaps Yeats is playing on the intoxication that Plato claimed resulted from the contemplation of beauty.

The self in love might assert values, but during falling in love it will place minimal restrictions on the beloved. If the self's values are not actualized in the beloved to a tolerable degree, eventually love will fail. Expectations that falling in love will lead to a stable love are misguided. But the permanent value of the phenomenon of falling in love is that it can show us how love can be maintained, or refueled.

The attempt to build a love that resists entropy must take account of the needs that provoke the nascent state. It might seem that Alberoni's explanation of falling in love presents humans as automatons. But awareness of the mechanisms can provoke conscious restructuring of institutions such as marriage. The phenomenon of falling in love suggests that we should abandon the individualistic view of love as a relationship between two separate selves who merge through an intellectual knowledge of each other. Falling in love suggests that the isolated self is incomplete. And Alberoni's view supports looking at love as an attempt to complete a social organization, not an individual. Perhaps being in love is more a collective dramatic creation than an individual achievement. Unlike falling in love, being in love allows the actors to be the authors.

5. Anti-Romanticism

"Anti-romanticism" refers to any theory of love that denies at least one of the central tenets of romanticism: (1) that falling in love is a desirable state, (2) that love is appropriate only towards persons, (3) that the desire to fuse with another individual self is an integral aspect of love, (4) that the perfections, apprehended or merely imagined, exemplified in another self are the cause of the exhilaration felt by the lover, and (5) that love is a form of knowledge that allows the lover to apprehend the real or potential value of another self. For instance, Plato is an anti-romantic since he denies that love is properly directed towards persons. Love is evoked by exemplifications of perfections, by persons who possess physical or intellectual beauty. Persons are useful in awakening our memory of the Form, but love is more properly directed toward the Idea of beauty. And the platonic lover is protected from infatuation with another person since Idea and exemplification are clearly distinguished in Plato's metaphysics of love. Love can still be revolutionary and intoxicating, but not love of persons.[26]

I use "anti-romanticism" in a narrower sense. Anti-romantics provisionally accept romanticism as a theory of love and then offer an internal criticism. Their claim is not just that the romantic theory of love is conceptually deficient, but that even if it were a coherent concept it could not be realized. For instance, anti-romantics accept the romantic description of falling in love, but then argue that romantics are mistaken in the analysis they offer of the sources of love.

It could be that our earlier discussion was not completely fair to romanticism. A person could be the cause, or a cause, of falling in love, without seeming to possess the perfections that attract the lover. For instance, Singer distinguishes two forms of valuation interweaved in love, appraisal and bestowal. Appraisal is either objective or individual. Objective appraisals are those reached by fair minded appraisers who agree on the relevant circumstances. Individual appraisals of a property will vary with needs and desires peculiar to the individual lover. In addition to the valuation taking place in appraisal, there is created value.

> Bestowed value is different. It is created by the affirmative relationship itself, by the very act of responding favorably, giving an object emotional and pervasive importance regardless of its capacity to satisfy interests. Here it makes no sense to speak of verifiability; and though bestowing may often be injurious, unwise, and even immoral, it cannot be erroneous in the way an appraisal might be. For now it is the valuing alone which makes the value.[27]

Romantics need not cultivate illusion for the sake of exhilaration. Rather, in bestowal one acts as if the beloved possessed the values one admires. Perhaps we perceive deficiencies and refuse to see them or count them. Or perhaps our attributions of value are more like predictions. Falling in love would be analogous to getting drunk as a means of gaining the courage needed to act decisively. We choose to adopt an attitude of extreme care toward another. And this attitude leads to the production of the extraordinary exhilaration associated with falling in love because of the concentration of our attention.[28] Ortega argues that lovers mistake a narrowing of attention for a self-expanding sensibility. The process is analogous to how an artist like Warhol focuses attention on the banal to produce aesthetic experience more appropriately felt in the presence of real beauty. Bestowal helps us understand Stendhal's remark that it is only in the imagination that one is certain of the perfections of the beloved.

Anti-romanticism can still be directed at a romanticism that allows the lover to differentiate the beloved from the embellished image. What anti-romantics question is the wisdom of a bestowal in light of the nature of love. Anti-romanticism is an especially strong trend in twentieth-century literature (and popular music), but it is not a peculiarly modern idea. I have simply chosen my sources from contemporary literature: Lawrence, Marcel Proust, and Knut Hamsun.

Falling in love is far from a life enhancing experience in the eyes of anti-romantics. Proust called love a reciprocal torture that could only temporarily fulfill its role of satisfying the lover's need to feel.[29]

> Sometimes he [Swann] hoped that she [Odette] would die, painlessly, in some accident, since she was out of doors, in the streets, crossing busy thoroughfares, from morning to night. . . . And Swann felt a very cordial sympathy with the sultan Mahomet II whose portrait by Bellini he admired, who, on finding that he had fallen madly in love with one of his wives, stabbed her to death in order, as his Venetian biographer artlessly relates, to recover his peace of mind.[30]

Unlike the sultan, Swann embraces a different cure for love. He marries Odette despite knowing that the marriage will damage his career and cost him his place in society. Inept awareness is his peculiarly modern curse.

> To think that I've wasted years of my life, that I've longed to die, that I've experienced my greatest love, for a woman who didn't appeal to me, who wasn't even my type.[31]

Proust bases falling in love on an ontological need to feel, not to merge, which can be only temporarily satisfied by another person. Swann believes he chose Odette because she resembles a character in a painting he admires by Botticelli. Persons are independent, they tend to resist our attempts to reconstruct them in order to produce the affects we desire. So Proust suggests that a love of music or art are more appropriate ways to satisfy the need to feel. Love does not allow Swann to merge with Odette. He is unable to comprehend her in reality or imagination. She manipulates her moods and sexual life to torture him. And Swann's own good sense prevents his imagination from consistently idealizing her. Far from being life enhancing, falling in love only contributes to Swann's writer's block. Whatever the cause, falling in love induces an unrewarding, torturous state. For Proust, the only redemptive aspect of the state is the persistence of faded memories of the feelings it arouses.

Even first love does not escape the anti-romantic's skepticism:

> There's a legend about a man whose prayers God granted, so that he was given his first and only love. But that was all the joy he got out of it. Why, you're going to ask again, and if you wait I'll tell you: for the simple reason that she died immediately after—immediately after, do you hear, ha—ha—ha, instantly. It's always the same story. Naturally one doesn't get the woman one should have had; but if by some freak of reason or justice it ever does happen, then of course she dies immediately after. There's always a catch somewhere. So then the man has to find himself another love, whatever's available, and there's no need for him to die of the change.[32]

This passage is spoken by a messenger who lost his first love to another. He is now delivering a woman's deathbed note to her lover. So the younger lover is presented with his own future self in the person of one who lost his love and did not die. Hamsun's message is that even when love succeeds it fails, because the beloved dies one way or another, sooner or later. The selection of first love is especially poignant. How many of us would have survived if we had gotten our first love? Perhaps romantic love must die to be replaced with something more ordinary.

Hamsun's anti-romanticism is both less pessimistic and misogynistic than Proust's. But he has been characterized as authoritarian, misanthropic, and an anti-bourgeois who preached a naturalism that supported a feudal social order. This assumes a continuity of view in Hamsun's work produced over a sixty-year period, ignores historical contexts, and attributes to Hamsun whatever views expressed by his fictional creations fit the thesis.[33] Whatever his political views, Hamsun's early views of love are far from the romanticism prevalent in the acceptable Western thought of his time. Consider a poem addressed to a woman by a rejected lover. In the first stanza the lover expresses the hope that God will punish her. Then he says:

God give thee happiness, Alvilde!
I thank you for each moment we shared. [. . .]
You offered me your hand, your soul,
And stirred me for a little while.
God give thee hapiness, Alvilde![34]

In a short story, "The Call of Life," the narrator meets a young woman walking by the docks. Ellen is dressed in black. At first the narrator mistakes her for a prostitute. They talk, walk by the docks, then to her home where they make love. The next morning, the narrator discovers the corpse of a man in his fifties on a table in an adjoining room. As they part the couple agrees to meet the day after next. Ellen mentions that she is busy the next day; she must attend a funeral. At a nearby cafe, the narrator reads the death notices in the paper and matches one address against Ellen's. The corpse was Ellen's husband. The story ends: "A man marries. His wife is thirty years younger than he. He contracts a lingering illness. One fair day he dies. And the young widow breathes a sigh of relief."[35]

Another story, "The Ring," is a two page history of a relationship. The male narrator sees that his beloved has fallen in love with another at a party. He remarks casually that the ring she has given him as a sign of their engagement has become too tight. The beloved offers to get it enlarged and takes it back. A month later they meet again; the beloved remarks nervously that the ring has been lost. They do not meet again until a year later when she happily announces that the ring has been found. He politely tries it on, and sadly notes that it has become too large.[36]

Hamsun's poem might be an expression of ambivalence about love. But I think it is better read as an anti-romantic description of love. The lover is beset with contradictory emotions and attitudes toward the beloved, who is perceived as the source of both pain and joy. Hamsun does not condemn love so much as note what we all know about love, that falling in love is both painful and rewarding. "The Call of Life" illustrates naturalistic detachment. Hamsun does not expect the twenty-three year old widow to mourn for a day, let alone a year, for her husband. Rather, she needs a breath of life. And in "The Ring" we see anti-romanticism put into practice. The lover feels no anger at the beloved's infatuation with another. Instead, there is understanding and a willingness to accept the temporary affair. A year later, when the beloved returns, but the lover has also fallen out of love, there is still no diatribe. The lover tries on the ring and says regrettably that it is too large. The beloved has never been idealized, and there are conditions placed on the maintenance of love that have been broken. Perhaps he would like the ring to fit, he would like to love her, but he cannot. A month was not too long, but a year was.

Anti-romantics question the desirability of passionate love, and also regard emotional intimacy suspiciously. The better course is to remain partially formal, to establish limits on our behavior and emotions that maintain and preserve the ego and at the same time help preserve an important relationship from inevitable infatuations.

Lawrence also denies that there is, or should be, a need to merge with the beloved. The characters Joe and Hester of "In Love" get along fine until they become engaged. Then Joe begins treating Hester as if he were in love with her, acting as he believes he should act according to the culturally accepted interpretation of the state of love. Hester finds this behavior sickening, begins to hate Joe, and hates herself for not being normal. She believes that she must be abnormal, "because the majority of girls must like this in-love business, or men wouldn't do it."[37]

Here Lawrence is introducing his own naturalism: the male and the female are complementary, but mutually incomprehensible, selves. Joe and Hester begin to suffer when they stop acting spontaneously from their respective male and female "blood selves." It is a mistake, a socially reinforced one, to try to establish a shared self with a member of the opposite sex. Merging is possible only symbolically and temporarily in sex. The psychological self must remain separate or die. The romantic attempt to make love a fusion of male and female equals is unnatural. If it succeeds, it will be at the cost of the individuality of one of the selves. Love should not lead to happiness or death through fusion, but to greater individuality and independence as each self remains true to its peculiar nature, stays incomprehensible to the other.

But Lawrence did not believe that this type of love was possible for all couples. For instance, *Women in Love* presents several couples engaged in reciprocal torture as they work out unsatisfied needs each brought to the relationship. Only Ursula and Ruppert, having satisfied these needs in previous relationships, are capable of love. And still, Lawrence concludes the book with Ruppert's longing for a true male friend. No individual of either sex is sufficient to fulfill the goal of love, increased individuality.

Love is not the only emotion strongly expressive of self-identity, nor is being in love the only source of self-identity. Hate might be equally self-expressive, and work equally a part of one's identity. What characterizes love is the force of the initial feeling and its sensual aspect. So there is truth to the view that love is a feeling. And if that degree of feeling could be generated by political ideals, commodities, or career goals we would have to recognize that love can take impersonal objects. But all alternatives to persons, especially to the couple, fail to meet the uniqueness individualists pursue in the couple. Perhaps an anti-romanticism that devalues the individual beloved is the antidote to a romanticism that directs love primarily to persons.

In opposition to the central tenets of romanticism, anti-romantics present falling in love and being in love as precarious and challenging states. *Some* recommend satisfying the need to feel within the context of a stable, manageable, aesthetic experience. Proust's ideal lovers would not desire fusion with another, but satisfaction of a need for feeling. If a desire for fusion exists, it should be suppressed as unrealizable and destructive.

It is not clear to anti-romantics that persons are better candidates to receive love than aesthetic or intellectual ideals would be. After all, reciprocity is, in most cases, short lived. And the role of attributes, real or imagined, of the beloved in love is minimal. Lovers fall in love to satisfy a need to feel that is not being met in their current life. The motivation is the need of the lover. I do not think that we can determine that the beloved is always a mirror of the lover, an opposite, or a complement. The nature of the beloved can vary with the needs of the lover at a given point of life. But whatever the way they love at that time, it is not the particular self of the beloved that is of primary importance.

6. Love Without Individuals

Contemporary theories of love retain the romantic emphasis on individuality in the beloved. Even theorists who reject individualism and love as a form of fusion present love as a mutual self-definition and creation.[38] We are told that love as "the experience of reconceiving oneself with and through another must always be balanced by the appreciation of the importance of that individual identity and autonomy that is the presupposition of romantic love."[39] In love we find our true self, complete our self, establish self-identity.[40]

Several senses of "self" can be distinguished. A short list of the candidates must include the self as an underlying mental substance, the transcendental self and its cousin the existential empty self, the self as a bundle of impressions, and the habitual self. With the exception of the bundle theory, all share the claim that the true self is not something ephemeral and fluctuating.[41] One of the virtues of the bundle theory is the recognition that everything that occurs within our consciousness can at one time be part of the self, and yet belong to the not-self at some other time.

Falling in love is a process of separation of the self from its habitual identity. Romantics could accept this claim, and then point out that the process leads to a search for self-identity through dialogue with the beloved. Perhaps this interpretation could reconcile merging with the preservation of individuality. Falling in love might lead to establishment of new habitual selves in an institution, and perhaps a shared habitual self. But establishing a semblance of permanence, without the death of at least one individual and at the same time preserving a dialogue of growth, is difficult. Love needs refueling by periodic returns to its nascent state. The anti-romantics recognize that a love that lasts will require both reliving the nascent state and an ability to deal with separation repeatedly. Hamsun's practice of leaving his family while writing a novel is especially telling here.

What lovers desire at least initially is not to find their true separate selves or to become separate individuals. Lovers desire to establish a new collective movement, a new society, a new social self, a consciousness shared by two bodies. Perhaps Lawrence and the Freudians are correct that this new collective is based in our early emotional attachments. Romanticism is an attempt to mask the incestuous basis of love.

> The idea that love is a random event . . . was dislodged only through Freud's findings. . . . Freud has taught us that the random nature of love appeals to us precisely because we wish to deny its incestuous origins.[42]

The psychoanalytic view is that the collective desired by lovers is the family of origin, or at least one greatly influenced by that family. Anti-romanticism claims that this is only true in some cases of love. Lawrence claims that lovers must resolve family-based needs before they can love. But the ways we live out the nascent state suggests another reason for denying a retrenchment of romanticism in either a reestablishment of an earlier collective self or a dialogue of self-definition.

Lovers desire to share experiences, any experiences. The establishment of a collective is not their goal, but a presupposition of the shared experience. Lovers need various surprising, and to strain the word, inconsistent experiences to preserve or rekindle the nascent state. Proust, for instance, sees the value of love in the memories of pure emotions it leaves behind. And Hamsun wrote of the love of nature:

> My heart opens as an enchanted harbor
> With the same flowers as the island's.
> They speak together and whisper strangely,
> Like children meeting they smile and bow. [. . .]
> The night thickens across the island.
> The harbor thunders Nirvana thunder.[43]

At first, the poem suggests the Taoist acceptance of beauty through an emptying of the self. But also it urges an inner honesty in the recognition of the voices found in the true self. Our inner life accommodates and embraces many selves, and it is easier to accept love as a collective movement if we recognize that each self is also a collective. Love of nature, of another, of oneself, which seeks to establish individuality, must silence some of those selves, while their preservation is conducive to preserving love and enlarging our experience.

Love has room for a plurality of values in the selection of beloveds and the nourishing of the potentialities of the self. Don Juans, whether their concern be with sexual conquests or the emotional intensity of repeated acts of falling in love, confuse one of the aspects of love with the entire phenomenon. But the critique of falling in love does not support dismissing the event as not part of love. Rather, the ability not to reduce another self to a known quantity, to an individualized personality, allows the anti-romantic to repeatedly fall in love with the creativity of the same beloved.

The limits placed on emotional intimacy reinforce the independence of the lover and allow being in love to be conditional. If there is unconditional positive regard here, it is toward the creativity of the beloved and not toward established character traits. Some anti-romantics see unconditional love as equivalent to psychological death, but perhaps we can just conclude that it is not an appropriate way to love another equal human person.

Anti-romantics embrace the bundle theory of the self: what is the self and not-self at a given time can and should be revised. It is not that anti-romantics reject the possibility of establishing a stable individual self-identity. Rather, they emphasize the benefits of rejecting self-identity for love. "Is not a man different, utterly different, at dawn from what he is at sunset? and a woman too? And does not the changing harmony and discord of their variation make the secret music of life?"[44]

This, I think, is what anti-romanticism tells us about love. It is not so much the death that might come from fusion with another individual that is to be feared, but the death of many selves for the establishment of individuality in a person or collective. An inner society prevents identification with the habitual self and allows re-creation of the nascent state with various possible beloveds who might be within the same person. By denying the importance of the individual beloved, anti-romanticism turns us inward to recognize our potential to love and to change our lives. It is not in the necessity of another individual to our life that we find meaning, but in the knowledge of their contingency, and the freedom to love them conditionally. We truly love only those we do not need.

Notes

1. Charles Baudelaire, *Paris Spleen*, trans. Louise Varese (New York: New Directions, 1947), 81.
2. Irving Singer, *The Nature of Love*, vol. 1: *Plato to Luther*, 2nd ed. (Chicago: University of Chicago Press, 1984), 3-5.
3. Plato, *Phaedrus* 252b-252c.
4. Singer, *The Nature of Love*, vol. 2: *Courtly and Romantic* (Chicago: University of Chicago Press, 1984), 287.
5. *Ibid.*, 291.
6. Stendhal, *On Love* (New York: Grosset and Dunlap, 1967); see 5-11.
7. Simone de Beauvoir, *The Second Sex*, ed. and trans. H. M. Parshley (New York: Knopf, 1953), 655.
8. D. H. Lawrence, "On Being a Man," in John Welwood, ed., *Challenge of the Heart* (Boston: Shambhala, 1985), 117-20, at 119.
9. D. H. Lawrence, *Studies in Classic American Literature* (Garden City, N.Y.: Doubleday, 1951), 66.
10. D. H. Lawrence, "The Stream of Desire," in Welwood, *Challenge of the Heart*, 47-57, at 52.
11. Francesco Alberoni, *Falling in Love* (New York: Random House, 1983), 71.
12. Singer, *The Nature of Love*, vol. 3: *The Modern World* (Chicago: University of Chicago Press, 1987), 385.
13. Alberoni, *Falling in Love*, 69.
14. *Ibid.*, 22-3.
15. *Ibid.*, 75.
16. *Ibid.*, 94-5.
17. Ernest Hemingway, *The Garden of Eden* (New York: Macmillan, 1986), 219-20.
18. Francesco Alberoni, *Movement and Institution* (New York: Columbia University Press, 1984), 95-101.
19. *Ibid.*, 42.
20. Alberoni, *Falling in Love*, 3.
21. Alberoni, *Movement and Institution*, 85.
22. Alberoni, *Falling in Love*, 6.
23. *Ibid.*, 46.
24. Baudelaire, "Get Drunk," *Paris Spleen*, 75.
25. See W. B. Yeats, "A Drinking Song," in J. Stallworthy, ed., *A Book of Love Poetry* (Oxford: Oxford University Press, 1974), 59.
26. Gregory Vlastos, "The Individual as an Object of Love in Plato," *Platonic Studies* (Princeton: Princeton University Press, 1971), 3-34, at 26-9.

27. Singer, *Nature of Love*, vol. 1, 4-5.

28. Ortega y Gasset, *On Love: Aspects of a Single Theme* (New York: World Publishing, 1957), 48.

29. Singer, *Nature of Love*, vol. 3, 159-61.

30. Marcel Proust, *Remembrance of Things Past*, vol. 1, trans. C. K. Moncrieff and Terence Kilmartin (New York: Random House, 1981), 386.

31. *Ibid.*, 415.

32. Knut Hamsun, *Victoria*, trans. Oliver Sallybrass (New York: Farrar Strauss Giroux, 1969), 161. The original publication date was 1898.

33. Leo Lowenthal, "Knut Hamsun," in Andrew Arato and Eike Gebhardt, eds., *The Essential Frankfurt School Reader* (New York: Continuum, 1982), 319-45.

34. Knut Hamsun, "Delerium," from *Det vilde kor*, in *Samlede verker*, vol. 15 (Oslo: Gyldendal, 1963-64), 175-236, at 187. The poem was published originally in the untranslated collection *The Wild Chorus* (Copenhagen: Gyldendal, 1904). [Translation prepared by Graybosch.—A.S.]

35. Knut Hamsun, "The Call of Life," *Norway's Best Short Stories*, trans. Hanna Larsen (New York: Norton, 1927), 132. The story was written in the 1890s.

36. *Ibid.*, 133-4.

37. D. H. Lawrence, "In Love," *The Complete Short Stories*, vol. 2 (New York: Viking, 1961), 647-60, at 652.

38. Robert C. Solomon, *About Love* (New York: Simon and Schuster, 1988), 24.

39. *Ibid.*, 26.

40. *Ibid.*, 63, 194.

41. Francis Herbert Bradley, *Appearance and Reality* (Oxford: Clarendon, 1966), 65. This work was originally published in 1893.

42. Martin S. Bergmann, *The Anatomy of Loving* (New York: Columbia University Press, 1987), 33.

43. Knut Hamsun, "Skerry," in *Det vilde kor*, 190-91. This poem also appears in *The Wild Chorus*; see n. 34, above. [Translation prepared by Graybosch.—A.S.]

44. D. H. Lawrence, "Marriage and the Living Cosmos," in Welwood, *Challenge of the Heart*, 164-9, at 165.

Richard C. Richards
(photograph: Marty Richards)

Author of “Graybosch on Love”
Paper presented at the Society for the Philosophy of Sex and Love
during the
Pacific Division Meeting of The American Philosophical Association
Berkeley, Cal., 23 March 1989

Forty-Nine

LOVE IS THE REAL ONE

Richard C. Richards

Generations of human beings have experienced the phenomenon called "falling in love" and have wondered about its connection with love, or have more often accepted what their culture told them about that connection. Philosophers have occasionally entered the speculation, especially in the last thirty years. Psychologists also have had their say. My purpose here is to investigate the view of Anthony Graybosch[1] and to state my own position.

I want to emphasize a crucial distinction that many people observe. But others do not, and some who make the distinction fail to realize its implications. I believe the failure to make it, or to make it consistently, causes confusion in the philosophy of love. The distinction is between romantic love and falling in love. Those who acknowledge this distinction take falling in love to be a temporary state. Many consider falling in love to be the main, if not the only, way to reach the state of romantic love, even though in most cases falling in love does not lead to love. The experience of falling in love is fairly universal, in that descriptions of it can be found in the writings of most cultures during most periods of history. It has also been called "being in love," "infatuation," "loving," "the nascent state," "limerence," and "puppy love."

A major question, if the distinction is acknowledged, concerns the connections between falling in love, on the one hand, and loving, or genuine romantic love, on the other. Love is believed by many to be able to last a life time, though it might not. It is considered by most to be, at least, more stable than the state of falling in love. Falling in love can be accomplished without the cooperation, or even the knowledge, of the other person. Thus, falling in love need not be reciprocal. Genuine romantic love, on the other hand, is always reciprocal, and requires the effort of both people.

Some confusion arises from the tendency for the phrase "in love" to be used to denote the experience of falling in love, and by others to denote the experience of genuine romantic love. This ambiguity raises hob with attempts to understand what various thinkers are saying. To avoid this problem, I refer to the longer lasting, more stable state as "loving," "genuine love," or "romantic love," and refer to its short-lived cousin as "infatuation" or "falling in love." An account of love that does not distinguish falling in love from genuine love is subject to fundamental confusion. Graybosch and Francesco Alberoni,[2] whose terminology and hypotheses Graybosch uses occasionally, do not suffer from this confusion in any obvious way, though I still find some difficulties with their accounts and will point out where these are. No philosopher is worth his weight in tautologies if he or she cannot find something wrong with the thinking of other philosophers.

Graybosch investigates two different theories, which he labels "romanticism" and "anti-romanticism," in order to uncover several assumptions about the nature of love and the connection between falling in love and genuine love. Graybosch's view shares some similarities with both the romantic and the anti-romantic positions. He believes that romantic love is important, as do the romantics. He is unhappy with the lack of attention given to the lover by romantics, while the beloved is excessively emphasized. Anti-romantic theories, on the other hand, tend to mistrust the value of love, while Graybosch seems more sanguine about its possibilities. Graybosch deals, in particular, with two questions that a romantic account of love and falling in love tends to ignore. The first is why the lover, and also romantic love theorists, focus on an individual, the beloved, when the values that supposedly explain love are universal. The second is why one individual, the beloved, is perceived as the cause of the revolution that constitutes romantic love, while other relevant factors are unnoticed by the lover and by romantic love theorists. These factors are the role of the lover's needs and active projections. Graybosch discusses these issues in order to introduce what he calls an anti-romantic account of falling in love, which he thinks provides answers to the problems romanticism ignores.

Graybosch's own view involves a nonindividualistic account of the self. I confine my remarks to the issue of the nature of love, thorny enough by itself, and do not address the question of which theory of the nature of the self is most friendly to the theory of the nature of love that Graybosch advances. The question of the nature of the self deserves independent treatment. A recent visit to an institution in my neighborhood, suggestively labeled "Self Storage," led me to be hopeful about throwing some light on this perpetually puzzling philosophical problem. But I found only junk; bundles of junk, mostly. I am presently working on a theory that the self is a bundle of junk, but nothing startling has emerged so far.

Graybosch utilizes Francesco Alberoni's concept of the "nascent state." A nascent state, for Alberoni, is a temporary transitional form taken on by social states as they pass from one structure to another. Falling in love is the simplest form of such a state, since it involves only two people (4). Most nascent states are the beginnings of "mass movements," such as the French Revolution (3). Falling in love is like any other revolution, in that it involves the construction of a new collective. People who were divided are united, and there is a rupture of past relationships (6).

Graybosch praises anti-romantics such as Alberoni because they do not ignore the role of the lover in the development of falling in love. While romantics focus exclusively on the beloved, anti-romantics point out that the conditions in the lover are important to the development of falling in love. Alberoni specifically sees the nascent state of falling in love as developing out of a state of "extreme depression, an inability to find something that has value in everyday life . . . [,] the profound sense of being worthless and of having nothing that is valuable and the shame of not having it" (69). These seem to me to be extreme preconditions for the state of falling in love; and they cause problems for Graybosch's and Alberoni's accounts of love.

On the issue of why people fall in love, Alberoni says that falling in love is caused by a desire for release of pent up eroticism (23), a desire for fusion with another person, and a desire to be irreplaceable and unique for the other (12). While I do not necessarily question these claims, it seems to me that this answer neglects the possible beneficial social consequences that result from people falling in love and forming family units for the raising of children. This gives any society that teaches the behavior of falling in love to its children sufficient reason to do that teaching.

The anti-romantics, with the exception of Alberoni, come in for their share of criticism by Graybosch. He states that anti-romantics question the desirability of passionate love and regard emotional intimacy suspiciously. He sympathizes with neither claim. He mentions that anti-romantics have various reasons for being suspicion of intimate love, commonly on the grounds that it fails to last. But this is a true observation only of the state of falling in love, and is much less true of genuine love. Falling in love, I believe, always ends after a year or two. Genuine love can last a lifetime, though it need not in order to be genuine romantic love.

Graybosch agrees with Alberoni that falling in love is a process of separation of the self from its habitual identity. Graybosch says that establishing even the appearance of permanence without the death of one individual (by his or her becoming too much like the other), and at the same time preserving the dialogue of growth for both, is difficult. Love, he claims, "needs refueling by periodic returns to its nascent state" (514). He praises the anti-romantics for recognizing that the transition of falling in love to a state of being in love that endures requires "reliving the nascent state and an ability to deal with separation repeatedly" (514-5).

How does one do such "refueling" of love? Graybosch says we must understand that the establishment of a collective is not the lovers' goal, which is instead to share experiences; but the establishment of a collective is a presupposition of shared experience. Thus he says that lovers need "various surprising, . . . inconsistent experiences to preserve or rekindle the nascent state" (514). He does not tell us much about what these experiences are or are like. He does say that it is possible to fall in love repeatedly with the newness of the same beloved. It is my belief that the nature of the "nascent state," as presented by Graybosch and Alberoni, makes it impossible for it in any way to "refuel" or "rekindle" the genuine state of love. Love often does need revitalizing, but it is simply impossible to return to the state of falling in love and thereby to use that state to "refuel" anything. Here's why.

Returning to the nascent state, as Alberoni understands it, would require that we return to the conditions that make possible the nascent state, and those specifically are (recall) a state of "extreme depression, an inability to find something that has value in everyday life . . . [,] the profound sense of being worthless and of having nothing that is valuable and the shame of not having it" (69) That is a very negative psychological state to have to reach in order to rekindle one's romantic love relationship. Moreover, if one can easily return to those conditions, one wonders just how genuine the romantic love state is that one claims to be in, since romantic love seems, to me, to be a positive, happiness-inducing relationship. Romantic love should put the person in a state in which extreme depression, feelings of worthlessness and shame are not easily reverted to, *especially* on a regular basis and as a precondition of romantic love itself. Alberoni claims that "no one can fall in love if he is even partially satisfied with what he has or who he is" (69). This seems to suggest that if one wanted to use the nascent state to rekindle romantic love, one would have to be disenchanted with the romantic love relationship itself, which would make trying to refuel it pointless.

In addition, Alberoni claims that falling in love involves both ecstasy and torment, while the institution of love is characterized by serenity and tranquillity and, of necessity, boredom (43). That is a stark contrast between falling in love and love. The two would seem to be incompatible states by this characterization, and how one such state could assist in the establishment of the other is puzzling. Alberoni thinks that when we are in one of these two states, we are often pining for the other. In some cases, he believes, it is possible for people to be in love for a lifetime; in these "exceptional cases," the aim is to preserve the nascent state itself. This requires that neither lover has rejected the other, and in such cases love continues "in the imagination." It also helps if the other person is "inaccessible, or simply dead" (122). These would seem to be less than ideal solutions: genuine romantic love does not seem to be established, because only the nascent state is preserved. Inaccessibility can be resolved in many cases, but death is something through which one does not easily live.

Alberoni's view is apparently refuted by the experience of some people that romantic love can continue to be passionate without inaccessibility or death. Alberoni, however, apparently also accepts such a conclusion, and he offers two other accounts of what can happen. First, he insists that the "experience of falling in love can be transformed into a love that preserves the freshness of that experience for years" (128). This sounds as if falling in love has not recurred, but that something like it has been attained: genuine love with much passion attached to it. Whether we should call this genuine romantic love is hard to tell. He makes little of it. It does not fit his description of love at all. Second, he claims that for "falling in love not to disappear and love take its place, the extraordinary experience must somehow continue in everyday life." He adds that in these situations, "the experience of falling in love continues because the nascent state is reborn over and over, in a constant revision, rediscovery, renewal, self-renewal, a constant search for challenges and opportunities. Then we fall in love again with the same person" (133). From what Alberoni says, I would say that such an experience is not love at all, but only the nascent state preserved.

The two different descriptions of what happens—first, that falling in love has been transformed into some form of love that preserves the freshness of the nascent state and, second, that falling in love, either in the imagination or in reality, continues again and again without producing love—seem to me to represent a fundamental confusion in his thinking, unless he understands them as two completely separate kinds of experiences. He does not indicate any distinction between them. I find the first account, if interpreted as a belief that romantic love retains passion, acceptable. But the second account, that falling in love occurs over and over again without producing genuine love, has problems. Prior to the experience of falling in love, the requisite conditions of depression, worthlessness, and shame are either (1) experienced for their normal duration, (2) are experienced extremely briefly, or (3) are not experienced at all. I criticized the first two options earlier. In the last case, there is an important exception to the doctrine that there are always negative conditions for falling in love, which exceptions Alberoni fails to note. In addition, it seems that falling in love over and over happens because of the choice of the participants, since "it requires the initiative to come from both lovers" (133). This contradicts what Alberoni says earlier about not being able to choose to fall in love, unless we have here another unannounced exception to previous accounts.

In any case, Graybosch neither notes these difficulties in Alberoni's account nor tries to overcome them in his own. He uncritically accepts the notion that one can jump into the state of falling in love by willing it, perhaps without most of the negative preconditions, and that one can use this ability to refuel or rekindle romantic love itself. Alberoni's options seem to be a love that preserves passion without reverting to falling in love, which might be genuine romantic love (but does not sound like what Alberoni thinks love is), or a passionate state of falling in love that never becomes love. Alberoni's account of the situation thus seems unable to give sustenance to Graybosch's hope that in some way falling in love in Alberoni's sense can be used for the obviously beneficial purpose of rejuvenating a romantic love relationship. Without a modification of Alberoni's hypotheses, his account is incomplete and not up to the job to which Graybosch puts it. Graybosch might be aware of part of the problem, since he mentions that falling in love again and again requires an ability to deal repeatedly with separation.

I argue that such refueling is impossible on quite different grounds, and stress that the failure is due to the natures of falling in love and genuine romantic love. I argue for this conclusion with a different theory about the natures of falling in love and of genuine romantic love. Since Graybosch expects so much from the state of falling in love, he rejects the use of the word "infatuation" as a synonym for it. I, expecting much less from the state of infatuation, am comfortable with the synonym.

My position is that falling in love, or infatuation, is not love at all, and is different from genuine love. Falling in love does in some cases lead to the state of romantic love, but this infatuation is normally gone within a year or two of its inception. Romantic love does not start until at least a year or two after people meet, and thus infatuation is unavailable, for any length of time, for duty as an aid to romantic love. Further, the nature of infatuation makes it unsuitable for that purpose, even if it still exists. I believe infatuation is founded fundamentally on deception, while romantic love is founded on truth. Deception is not likely to be of much benefit to a relationship whose foundation is honesty and psychological openness.

Infatuation, when mutual, consists essentially of three distinct kinds of deception. First, the person who is infatuated attempts to deceive the other person about the infatuate's own characteristics, interests, and traits. This is done partly by "editing," which consists of putting his or her best foot forward, or emphasizing her or his strong points, and attempting to hide the weaknesses. Editing also consists of listening carefully to the other person to see what values that person expresses, and then convincing the other person that the editor has those values, too. The second type of deception consists of believing the line or bill of goods that we are selling to the other person, the "beloved." We come to believe our own story. We claim to love tennis, for example, just as much as the object of our infatuation claims to love it. The fact that we have not played it for years is immaterial; we have been busy, is our rationalization. We intended to get back to that wonderful game as soon as we had the time. The third type of deception consists of projecting our ideal image of the person we want to love onto the other person.

Graybosch acknowledges this last phenomenon when he talks about the lover's "active projections" (504). Active projection of an ideal explains why infatuation is blind, that is, why an infatuated person is unwilling or unable to see the other person objectively. It is said that love is blind, but this is merely to confuse infatuation with genuine romantic love. You cannot point out a blemish on the chin of an infatuated person's "beloved" without risking a fist forcefully applied to your own. When one person is busy putting another person on a pedestal, data suggesting that the pedestal is inappropriate is not appreciated. The eventual discovery that the "beloved" does not fit the image on the pedestal results in the disillusionment of the "lover." The inability to escape the truth about the "beloved" produces the disillusionment commonly associated with the end of infatuation.

I am not disparaging infatuation or falling in love. It is a temporary state whose nature it is to be destroyed by the discovery of the truth about another person and, if one is dedicated or lucky, about oneself. The problem is that people often expect more than it can deliver. Some people think it is romantic love, and then disillusionment with romantic love sets in when infatuation dies its natural death. It cannot live up to its billing as the greatest show on earth simply because it is *not* the greatest show on earth. It is a psychological roller coaster, as Alberoni documents throughout his book. It is a nice place for people to visit, but we cannot live there. In that regard, it is much like physical human life itself. Therefore, expectations that falling in love can be used to refuel genuine romantic love are misplaced. There are ways to encourage the growth of romantic love, but infatuation is not one of them.

Romantic love is a human relationship in which psychological intimacy is combined with a good sexual relationship. Psychological intimacy by itself, whether it occurs in romantic love, a good friendship, or in some other form of love, is a passionate relationship, as is infatuation. This helps explain the ease with which infatuation is confused with romantic love, and perhaps why it would seem possible to Graybosch to employ infatuation to bolster the passion of romantic love. No relationship can be passionate all the time. I doubt that any human being would want to live with nonstop passion, or biologically could live with it, if they chose to. It would be like spending a week in orgasm. A day or two, maybe; but a week?

Rather than use the metaphorical suggestions that romantic love needs "refueling" or "rekindling," I suggest that the passion of romantic love, unlike the passion of infatuation, is derived from the excitement that is essential to a psychologically intimate relationship. What keeps the passion returning to romantic love is the continuing quest for more psychological intimacy. Graybosch seems to be aware of this approach when he suggests that each person is a changing entity. This is true, even if change is not desired. There are the challenges facing us in childhood, maturity, midlife, and the long gentle decline into rigidity. Discovering the changes in oneself and in loved ones can provide the kind of passionate excitement that people in the contemporary world seem to crave (despite the excitement already provided by driveby shootings, muggings, robberies, freeway driving, and national politics). Some people want excitement in their nonpersonal lives, and want calmness and stability in their personal relationships. Others seem to want excitement in their personal relationships. Excitement is a feature of the temporary state of falling in love, but it is not within our ability to control it to any extent. Excitement is an essential part of psychologically intimate relationships, and it is well within the power of most people to learn and to use the skills that build and enhance psychological intimacy, and thereby excitement, in their personal relationships.

"Rekindling" is thus a process of choosing to learn and exercise skills. It is not a process by which to recover the passion of the infatuation that might have preceded the psychologically intimate relationship. The passion of infatuation cannot be chosen. Graybosch and I agree on the goal, which is a good loving relationship. We disagree on the means. He thinks we can return to infatuation. I believe it is neither desirable nor even possible, but that the excitement in a romantic love relationship will be renewed, *if* it diminishes, by exercising the skills necessary to build an intimate relationship. That involves some risk, as do most worthwhile human activities.

While not laying claim to being a romantic in the sense Graybosch delineates, I agree with the romantic theorists in their insistence on the importance of the beloved. I do not think, as they do, that the beloved is the sole determining factor in the genesis or course of love. I agree with Graybosch that we need to consider the needs of the lover. Yet the qualities of the beloved are also important. The beloved must want a psychologically intimate relationship. Further, if a psychologically intimate relationship is what the lover and beloved want, both must learn the skills necessary to build such a relationship. Short of the couple's having such skills and choosing to use them, relationships are not likely to become psychologically intimate and are likely doomed.

Notes

1. Anthony J. Graybosch, "Which One Is the Real One?" this volume, 503-17; page references are supplied parenthetically in the text.

2. Francesco Alberoni, *Falling in Love*, trans. Lawrence Veluti (New York: Random House, 1983); page references are supplied parenthetically in the text.

Timo Airaksinen

Author of “The Style of Sade: Sex, Text, and Cruelty”
Paper presented at the Society for the Philosophy of Sex and Love
during the
Eastern Division Meeting of The American Philosophical Association
Atlanta, Ga., 29 December 1989

Fifty

THE STYLE OF SADE: SEX, TEXT, AND CRUELTY

Timo Airaksinen

D. A. F. Sade creates a bewildering literary project in order to examine perversity and the wickedness of the human will in all its many forms.[1] His project is at least half philosophical, as the author tackles some deeply paradoxical issues, trying to relate their deeper meaning to his readers. If the subject matter tends to be paradoxical, the text themselves are enigmatic. They have the appearance of being literature, yet they really cannot be read as novels without coming to the conclusion that they are failures. Indeed, it is often said, mistakenly, that they cannot be read at all. Sade can be read, but the reader needs a key. And the key is provided by the realization that Sade is a philosopher in disguise. He produces a narrative whose style aims at ethical, theological, and metaphysical goals. Therefore, once we read Sade as a philosopher we can also appreciate his more artistic achievements. In what follows I shall start from Sade's philosophy and then return to his style and narrative technique.

The worlds of facts and values are certainly not the only playgrounds of the Divine Marquis. Sade was in prisons and mental asylums, he promoted real value change, and he wrote about such things. But his works are also fictions, where philosophical and pseudoscientific aspects are firmly embedded in the stories he wants to tell. And such stories are as weird as the hard facts and objective values he talks about. A full account of Sade's narrative technique would show how he concentrates on small repetitive vignettes and stage rehearsals of subversive acts. Here I shall only comment briefly on his stylistic devices, on his pragmatics of style. In other words, I shall focus on Sade's rhetoric, or those literary techniques by means of which he creates impressions and manipulates our reactions when we read his texts. I shall focus on the question of what those rhetorical tricks signify, in the sense of asking of what they are metaphors and from where their deep irony comes.

In Sade's philosophy, one can distinguish between the following topics: first, the level of parody, or its playful account of the social contract theory, and its related ideas of the state of nature, conventional morality, and a utopian social order. We can also find discussions on elitism and anarchism, focusing on social inequality and sexism. Second is the metaphysics of nature, where Nature is seen as the principle of death and destruction. A naturalistic ethic follows: from the principle of nature we can derive a code of conduct for the illuminated heroes who are able to appreciate real science. They ought to do unnatural acts, in the sense that law and morality do not recognize the real Nature. And, third, is ethics proper, in which virtue becomes vice and vice virtue.

Social life and the personal status are such that virtue does not pay off, vice does. At this level, Sade's anti-Epicurean hedonism appears, together with his evaluation of social success and honor. These three layers are more or less disconnected. The first deals with social philosophy, the second with metaphysical ethics, and the third with personal motivation or moral psychology. At the same time, even if the topics are disconnected, Sade's anarchistic message comes through: there are no real values or religious truths, pleasures are transient, social life is a veritable hell, and men and women are, accordingly, beasts by nature. The worldview is in its own way almost coherent, because the narrative style unifies it all.

The three main points of this paper will be (1) the repetitive structure of Sade's narrative as the structure of orgasm itself, (2) the twisted grammar of crime, or subversion as the creation of ambiguity, and (3) the ontology of an opening, or a hole, which is taken as an example of a more detailed metaphor.

First, let us look at the narrative structure of Sade's text as a metaphor of orgasmic experience, keeping in mind what can be said about orgasm. It is questionable whether Sade mentions orgasm at all. Sade uses the mechanistic term "discharge," in a wide sense, to refer to all acts of obedience to the destructive principle of nature. But at the same time its paradigmatic meaning is and must be the sexual one. Therefore we may use the slightly anachronistic term "orgasm" here, if we keep in mind the many interesting connotations of the word "discharge."

It is important that men and women achieve sexual orgasms in the same way; for instance, both are capable of ejaculating. Sexual orgasm is also diffusely located. Orgasmic feeling, even if it is paradigmatically sexual, is not restricted to the genitals. Torture results in orgasmic experiences as well, sometimes even in the passive partner. There is also a wide variety of similar, or analogous, modes of pleasant experience, like eating and drinking or philosophical discussion.

When we expand our view of orgasm to include all kinds of satisfying acts, ultimately all natural performances, what we get is a view of civilized life consisting only of orgasms. Life, as it should be, is just a series of extreme pleasures. Or if we use the word "discharge," life ought to be like a series of blasts from guns. The irony of this is that what is originally supposed to be supremely stimulating and exciting reappears now as something so dull and boring, or noisy, that we wonder why the Sadean heroes should bother. They are clearly often in difficulties: some of them are so old that they are impotent and require excess stimulation before they achieve anything like a discharge and orgasm. Some of the heroes realize that debauchery is like work or a duty that must be performed whether they like it or not. They develop mad aggressions and are extremely irritated. They hate their victims, ultimately, it seems, because what they are supposed to do to the victims is so boring.

The worshipers of natural pleasures can now be seen to be trapped by their own performances. They will flog and be flogged forever, until they are old, ugly and impotent, like the mature heroes of *The 120 Days of Sodom*. They grow more and more wicked and repulsive, which is, strangely enough, their ultimate reward. It is easy to see that the old libertines are described in the cruelest possible way. They are truly ugly, and they love ugly things, too. They are weak, and they know it.

We need to focus on the interrelation between sex and text. The basic point is that the repetitive structure of texts such as *Justine* and *Juliette* is the same as the cyclic structure of sexual orgasms. The libertines move from philosophy to debauchery and, via some more mundane acts, back to philosophy; their bodies experience arousal, orgasm, and relaxation. The structure of the scenes is also cyclic and repetitive. Therefore, the real meaning of the Sadean stage performances can be understood only though the whole body of the text of such massive works as *Juliette* and *The 120 Days*. These books should be read in their entirety.

As Sade himself says, even if the Bible claims that Sodom will burn eternally in hell, the fire has gone out a long time ago. That happens in Sade's texts all the time. Nothing is permanent, nothing is eternal; everything rises from the ashes again and again. The rhythm of the text reflects this. The novels are long because they are designed to create the impression that they are life itself. It takes a lifetime to read them through. And the heroes go through the same old routines. First philosophizing, then the initial excitement and anticipation with some more ferocious discussion, then actual love play, torture, and finally orgasms over and over again. The curtain is drawn. The same show will continue tomorrow. The texts are long and repetitive, just like the career of a libertine.

The heroes discuss questions of philosophy, history, anthropology, and religion (as well as money and professional issues, but these belong to the background). Like a traveling theater group, they also travel to other places where their performance is again a novelty and where their audience waits. But even the discussion and travel (spiritual and physical travel) is repetitive. If we read one or two accounts of them, we know exactly what is going to be said. The result is a kind of meaningless chatter. However, all this is different from the lives of their victims, and from ordinary life, because the heroes are under the spell of destructive nature, which leads to orgasms. The victims' lives are not even repetitive; they emerge and vanish into the destruction they never seem to understand. The exception is Justine, who suffers endlessly and endures it all. She is the exceptional victim in the sense that she could learn how to enjoy life, although she never does. All other victims merely perform on the stage. They arrive only in order to be disposed of. Their stories are not repetitive.

The heroes also relax and rest and discuss when they are exhausted. Their rest is a philosopher's rest, in the sense that while their bodies recuperate their minds work. As Juliette declares, she fucks like Marie Antoinette but thinks and speaks like Montesquieu and Hobbes. The result of this intellectual work can be called the theory and justification of what they are doing. For instance, much of the talk is genuinely ethical. They use moral terms in the normal sense. They also analyze and lament the unjust state of their society and the excessive power of its religious institutions. They long for a better world to live in. Yet, whatever they think of during this period, their actions will always return in the same old orgasmic form.

Travel might lead to the formation of new groups. Juliette and Justine always meet new people, but these reflect the characteristics of aggressive domination and the victim's submission and helplessness. However, the stage performances are repeated to new audiences as the heroes travel through a homogeneous medium of physical and social spacetime. This fact is related to the theatrical aspects that the text reflects. Private pleasures are turned into public performances, which are novelties to the uninitiated. Remember that Sade wanted, unsuccessfully, to be a playwright.

In all these aspects of the text, the result is as demanding as it is boring. Now, my main point is that Sade's text works unlike the way literature normally works, and also unlike a philosophical text. In Sade's text the style, rhetoric, and message are so closely connected that the text becomes almost intolerably dense. Yet the text is in its own sense enjoyable. It is certainly demanding. Its demanding features come only apparently from the repetition, deceptively from the pornographic, sadomasochistic details and labyrinthine theoretical speculations, and even more deceptively from the sheer length. To refer to any of these as the source of its alleged weaknesses is to miss the point. The text is designed to hurt its reader. This is the reader's real problem.

The main feature that concerns Sade's texts as successful rhetoric is the close connection between the message and medium. The written text and its style are so important from the point of view of the message that what is actually said becomes almost secondary. The length of the text and its repetitive nature are even more important than what Sade actually says. What needs to be done is to comprehend the structure of the text, its grammar, and its theatrical nature. Only then can we see how radical Sade is. Destructive nature promises pleasure to her followers (that is what the heroes are after), but the pleasure appears to be an infinitely tedious performance, always in the same setting, without variety, without creativity, promising the agents nothing, in the end, but ugliness. Nature destroys. Therefore, dreams of pleasure are merely rhetorical tricks. Perhaps one might suggest that they are educational tricks whose purpose is to attract new disciples to the cult of Nature; but that is too farfetched a proposition. The truth is that the text is supposed to be a violation of all that is decent in life from the social, moral, and religious points of view.

The structure of the text dominates its meaning. And wherever a message should be extracted from the structure, the task becomes tedious and difficult. The reader is normally supposed to get the message from what he understands is being said. But Sade's message does not come through reading in the sense of semantic interpretation. The reader must live through what he reads. This is why the endless descriptions of torture and the eating of filth become so nauseating. The reader cannot alienate himself from the story, so that he is forced to suffer because of it. Certainly it is a wonderful parody of French gourmandism to design meals out of excrement, but its endless repetition in *The 120 Days* makes the reader sick. Not even Gilbert Lely could avoid this effect.

We now turn to a crucially important theme, namely, the nature of what Sade calls crime, understood as the subversion of the grammar, or logic, of things. We recall that Sade is the author of theatrical plays and, moreover, as I said above, there is little distance between what he writes and what he thinks exists and is real. If his texts do not discuss a fictional world but create a reality, then its criminal ideas cannot denote things that are disconnected from the text. The text itself is the ultimate crime. The key term here is that of *subversion*. Its subtypes are blasphemy, libel, crime, pornography, torture, and perverse sex, together with a large number of similar ideas. Let us take a closer look at the umbrella term *subversion*.

The basic idea behind subversion, or what Sade himself calls crime, is that an agent's action invites an interpretation of the situation in terms that do not form a coherent context. The story remains ambiguous. In this way, Nature is destructive through the agent's action that creates ambiguity, and it might be destructive only in this sense. The idea is interesting: it might look innocent merely to break the rules of language, as if to describe things differently, but it is not. On the contrary, Sade captures an essential aspect of social control, the control of speech and imagery, which is at the core of the ideas of retribution, censorship, and hegemony. When you change the rules of grammar, he seems to think, you also change things. Therefore, something stops existing, is destroyed, dies.

In this way Sade redefines harm and injury in a more adequate way than those who think that they exist independently of our methods of grasping them. In fact, the ideas of harm and injury entail moments of surprise, inherent also in regret. What we know and predict is not a loss or harm; at the most it is a cost-related factor. What we know, we try to control. What we do not know brings about fear and terror. In that sense, our social system tries to control fear and terror more than it tries to control loss and harm. Nevertheless, we may stabilize its grammatical expressions and keep our creations intact in time. It is against such stabilizing fictions that Sade directs his most ferocious attack. He terrorizes his readers by his imagery, as much as by its repetition. Bodies are dissected in a surgical precision, although the results are ambiguous and thus imprecise: "they leave the scalpel, they plunge in a hand, they search inside her bowels and force her to shit through the cunt." In this scene, taken from *The 120 Days*, the surgical precision (the scalpel) is contrasted to the bare hand, which confuses life (cunt) with death (shit). Two levels of confusion emerge: between precision and its opposite and, following from this, between birth and waste, which is an overkill of the stability of thought.

Let me take some additional examples from Sade's text. Incest is one of Sade's favorite horror stories. A father marries his daughter and conceives a child with her. What is his crime? The crime is not violent or even overtly sexual. The crime is simply that the father is now his own child's husband and the new child's father and grandfather. The family context becomes a mess in which social identities are confused and tangled. The man creates a situation where no one knows who is who and what the social roles, duties, and virtues are. The idea of family becomes ambiguous.

Another simple example is sadomasochism and pain. When a person aims at pain, he aims at something that, through its accepted grammar, is to be avoided. Attraction and repulsion must not get confused. Sexual perversions follow the same antilogic. Normally sexual grammar distributes definite roles to the participants in sexual games. However, in Sade's world those roles vanish:

at the castle of Silling, genital sexual intercourse is almost forbidden; some of the heroes abhor even the sight of a women's breasts and vagina. Again, masturbation violates the grammar of sex because it is a solitary activity. At Silling, sex is public but violence is secret, which is the opposite of the accepted order of things. A friend of Juliette's boasts of being a coward, an act that is incomprehensible in terms of any code of virtues.

Such examples might look relatively mild today, but they have been and still are sources of considerable anxiety. And Sade claims that the anxiety results from their mysteriously twisted grammar. Male homosexuality, for instance, stops being a Sadean example of crime only when gays organize, identify themselves, and succeed in telling a convincing story of their desires and love life. In religion, Sade's blasphemy consists in his stubborn refusal to be afraid of eternal punishment in hell and to worship an infinite power.

An interesting application of this argument is the personal invulnerability that follows from one's willing acceptance of pain and harm. If one also enjoys one's own suffering, this makes one immune to all exercise of power. No threats can harm Juliette. Such a person creates a situation in which power cannot be exercised; that is another anomaly, now concerning the logic of power. And because Juliette cannot be harmed, she becomes rich and powerful, just as Hegel claims in the section on Master and Slave in his *Phenomenologie des Geistes*. You must face and risk your own death before you can rule.

In fact, most of Sade's alleged atrocities can be understood in the same manner. Sade, of course, also describes some serious tortures and some hyperactive bisexual group sex. The results are first shocking to the reader, but repetition makes such an effect soon disappear. Once the horror and excitement are gone, the analytical and interpretative problems emerge. Why is torture interesting in the special context that Sade's texts create? The answer must include the idea that such scenes are supposed to excite the reader and give him a kind a pleasure, something many writers have aimed at. But a deeper answer is that torture as something desirable and orgasmic is a goal we have great trouble in understanding. It is the opposite of those intentions we normally have and a travesty of virtuous human nature. Benevolence and kindness, and the universalization of moral norms, are what a reasonable decision maker is supposed to aim at. Their opposites defy description, and this is exactly why Sade pays attention to them. Cruelly to destroy youth and beauty is ungrammatical because the youth and beauty that are not intrinsically desirable and worth preserving are not youth and beauty.

To understand this ambiguity, we might claim that the state penal system, which has included torture and execution, is, according to Sade, inferior to private forms of cruelty. An executioner is not a heroic figure. He performs his well-defined duties. He might do horrible things, but we ignore them because everything happens according to a grammar. Therefore, Sade's cruelty is subversive and official cruelty is not. Sade's expresses human freedom and even creativity; the other expresses repression, control, and tyranny. Subversive action is uniquely individual, impossible to categorize and universalize, and also creative of new grammars and forms of life. But institutionalized state violence, or church rituals, or laws and manners, are profoundly wrong because of their restrictive nature. They are unambiguous hard facts and universal, covering laws. They bring about suffering without enjoyment, unlike Sade's own master project.

As I said, state violence is real in a different sense from Sade's. Sade tells you a story about some stage performances. But the state will imprison and kill you. And such a real fate will be yours without any reward, liberation, or enjoyment to anyone. The machine kills its nameless victims, and this is real, mad repetition, pure control without orgasm.

Sade's stories have a rhetorical message that is in direct conflict with actual repression and cruelty, like the censorship of Sade's writings for two hundred years. Cruel and evil thoughts clash, and the real system always has the upper hand. But fiction might still survive and be more enjoyable. Sade's point is, therefore, that actual cruelty does not have a subversive, or orgasmic, point. It is too well-defined for that. This is why fictional cruelty is preferable. Indeed, Sade's cruelty is always fictional, except when it hurts its reader.

My next example of the crime of ambiguity is the symbolism of the sacred openings in the human body. This is one of the central sources of metaphor in Sade. The natural orifices of the body are all functionally similar: they are forced open by penetration, and then they close again. Liquids pour in and out. Defloration is a process that actualizes a merely potential opening, but the orifice is thereby closed by the thing that enters it. The same idea occurs in *Juliette*, where the valley of Gehenna is remembered. At that ancient place of execution women strangled a criminal, forced his mouth open and poured in molten lead. The opening closes for good in an act that can be performed only once. As Sade suggests, this is what the Bible means by eternal punishment: a drastic act of violence that can be done only once, and never again. Eternity of action is created by its future impossibility. Another example can be found in *The Philosophy in the Bedroom*, where a young female apprentice is given the power over her mother, and the daughter's Electra complex makes her let a syphilitic man rape her mother, and then she sews the vagina closed so that the infected sperm can do its work. The hole was forced open and closed first by a penis, then by sewing, and finally the whole scene is destroyed by the poison trapped in the womb. As Annie Le Brun says,

> By means of this supreme outrage inflicted on woman, who gives birth in pain, Eugenie acquires the sovereignty of her own birth, becoming the first "daughter born without a mother" in our history.[2]

The extension of this idea is inevitable: just as Jesus was a man without father, Eugenie is a woman without mother.

Such is one of Sade's most complex and famous vignettes, bringing together psychology, myth, metaphor, and joke in a crazy manner. All the laws of grammar become distorted in the process. Roland Barthes writes about this act:

> Among the tortures Sade imagines (a monotonous, scarcely terrifying list, since it is most often based on the butcher shop, i.e., on abstraction),

> only one is disturbing: that which consists in sewing the viotim's anus or vagina. . . . Why? Because at first sight sewing frustrates castration: how can sewing (which is always: mend, make, repair) be equivalent to: mutilate, amputate, cut, create an empty space?[3]

The ambiguity here is between opening and closing a thing, with all its complex associations. An empty space is created, and destroyed, by utilizing a useful female art, sewing. The illustration concerns the ambiguity of nothingness, that is, metaphoric evil. The hole is in itself nothing, or a mere empty place, so that the object that closes the hole destroys a something that is nothing.

Nevertheless, the orifices of the human body are supremely interesting:

> The first cut: the rest would follow. Sharp steel met flesh. Skin parted, flesh showed below the skin, for an instant a mottled white, and then all was blinding, disfiguring blood, and Bryant could only cut at what had already been cut. She cried out in tears, in panic, in despair, "Help me Jimmy."[4]

The virgin body opened up, the clean white color is displaced by a red mess, and the surprise and shock are palpable. The rest is plain Sadean repetition.

Certainly we should not dismiss this symbolism of opening and closing holes in the human body as a mere atavistic perversion. Modern twentieth-century culture relives it all the time. A gun, that symbol of all entertainment in film and television, is nothing but a tool for opening up a human body; it is a drill or a needle; the hole is stuffed with the bullet, the blood is drawn out, instead of sperm, in an orgasmic manner. Distorted faces and bodies display the features such an allegorical intercourse needs. The grammar of shooting is, for us, a deceptively defined entertainment. Cruelty is fun when its symbolism is safely camouflaged, and yet it is capable of arousing sexual emotion. Real murder and killing is something else.

Imagine that a film shows the actual shooting of real people, and it is made clear that all this is just for the entertainment of the audience. The makers of the film really kill, and they show the film. Why is that not interesting?

The important point is that the audience understands the grammar of such real crime too well, and that is why such entertainment would not be ungrammatical or truly subversive. Crime is clearly, too clearly, wrong. The audience understands and witnesses a real killing; perhaps it enjoys fictional killing, but it will also abhor real killing as fiction. Reality and fiction do not mix. I wonder, would Sade recommend such subversive acts that confuse fiction and reality? If he did, he is really wicked in a different sense. However, he evidently never murdered anybody: if this is so, fiction is not quite the same as reality. The crucial test of Sade's texts is his own biography.[5]

Now, it can be said that there is one type of cruelty I have not yet tackled, and that is real personal cruelty: murder, rape, robbery. Certainly this is so, but its undesirability is tied to the question of control and exercise of power. There is nothing else to be said about it. Real crime and cruelty are both undesirable and immoral. But once we see that what is actually criminal and cruel is highly unclear and relative, we should resist the countercruelty practiced by the state, stop worshiping it, and appreciate the many subtle forms of fictionalized evil. At least, we must reject the idea that wickedness is a transparent set of phenomena, even if we do not accept cruelty.

When we read the Divine Marquis, we see that cruelty is not really the point. Violence, bad manners, perverse sex, and all kinds of terror can be utilized equally well. Therefore, the key word is that of a subversive fictional plan, which is the true source of anxiety and horror. Subversion as grammatical, textual, and cultural ambiguity alone presents a real threat to social power, or what is misleadingly called civilized human existence. This is Sade's favorite aesthetic crime.

Notes

1. See also Timo Airaksinen, *The Philosophy of the Marquis de Sade* (London: Routledge, 1995). Sade's main works, including *Juliette*, *Justine*, *The 120 Days of Sodom*, and *Philosophy in the Bedroom*, have been published in English by Grove Press, 1966-76.
2. Annie Le Brun, *Sade: A Sudden Abyss* (San Francisco: City Light Books, 1990), 168.
3. Roland Barthes, *Sade, Fourier, Loyola* (London: Jonathan Cape, 1976), 168.
4. V. S. Naipaul, *Guerillas* (Harmondsworth, Eng.: Penguin Books, 1987), 243.
5. Gilbert Lely, *The Marquis de Sade: A Biography* (London: Elek Books, 1961), and Maurice Lever, *Sade: A Biography* (New York: Farrar, Strauss, and Giroux, 1993).

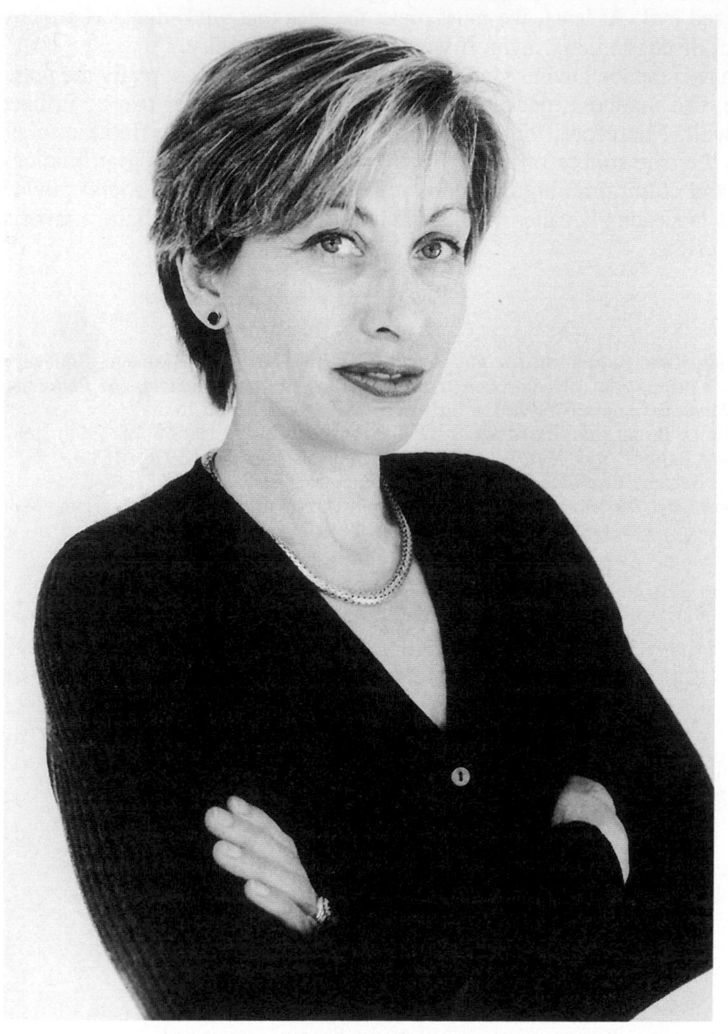

Dorothea Olkowski

Author of “Repetition and Revulsion in the Marquis de Sade”
Paper presented at the Society for the Philosophy of Sex and Love
during the
Eastern Division Meeting of The American Philosophical Association
Atlanta, Ga., 29 December 1989

Fifty-One

REPETITION AND REVULSION IN THE MARQUIS DE SADE

Dorothea Olkowski

What force is at work in the writing of Sade? Is it an active force or is it a reactive force? Is this work a desperate attempt to survive in revolutionary France, to make enough money to live and eat? Is it a philosophical narrative, a new logic or morality, an attempt to show the citizens, whom Sade despised, how a man of letters writes? In his fascinating, if overblown, biography of Sade, Maurice Lever quotes a letter written by Sade to his attorney Reinaud:

> 'They are now printing a novel of mine, but one too immoral to send to a man as pious and decent as you. I needed money, my publisher asked me for something *quite spicy*, and I made him [a book] capable of corrupting the devil. They are calling it *Justine ou les Malheurs de la Virtu*.'[1]

Lever comments that while sex was a big seller in revolutionary France and "*la foutromanie* (literally, fuckomania) was all the rage," for Sade himself, with only a few exceptions, the rush of pornography was nothing more than "'miserable brochures, conceived in cafes or bordellos, which prove that their authors suffered from two voids at once: one in the mind and the other in the stomach'."[2] While Sade often suffered from the stomach void, he would never admit to a mental void, and neither do most contemporary readers of Sade. There is no question but that this work that is capable of corrupting the devil still fascinates us today, yet we are uncertain how to approach it. Philosophy, literature, and pornography are the three categories most often alluded to in contemporary commentaries, but on what basis can such determinations be made?

Reflecting on his own reading of the works of Sade, Timo Airaksinen[3] comments, "once the horror and excitement are gone, the analytical and interpretative problems emerge" (532). Indeed, for Airaksinen, the analytical and interpretative problem has emerged forcefully, so much so that he must approach these texts as both philosophy and literature. For, according to Airaksinen, there are a variety of philosophical "issues" in Sade's narratives. First, there is the need to focus on Sade's parody or playful account of social contract theory; then, there is Sade's metaphysics of nature; and finally, Sade's ethics. However, when Airaksinen announces the three main points of his paper, they are related to Sade's rhetorical technique. These three points are: (1) narrative repetition in Sade's text as orgasm; (2) the twisted grammar of crime, which Airaksinen calls "subversion"; and (3) the ontology of the opening as a metaphor (528). These three points lead to a final distinction, which is possibly also the conclusion: that there is an important distinction between real cruelty and Sade's aesthetic, fictional cruelty.

Now, given Airaksinen's own descriptions of Sade's texts, it might well be the case that the rhetoric of narrative generates the philosophical issues. That is, Sade's rhetoric ("those literary techniques by means of which he creates impressions and manipulates our reactions when we read his texts") signifies something else, some philosophical perspective or issue. However, in spite of this, Airaksinen proceeds by listing the philosophical issues first, and then proceeds from there to Sade's rhetorical devices. What remains to be determined, it seems, is this whole question of the trajectory between the first set of philosophical concerns and the second set of rhetorical concerns. By what inner logic of Sade's text has Airaksinen arrived at these philosophical positions, as well as these rhetorical analyses? At this point, and after numerous rereadings of his paper, I cannot say, so I have decided to embark upon what might at first seem to be an arbitrary approach. I shall comment on each issue simply as it arises, in as orderly a fashion as possible in the hope that, by the end, the logic of Sade's thinking will show itself more clearly. And to ensure that I do not myself become lost in this task, I will adhere closely to a certain commentary on Sade as a guide.[4]

According to Airaksinen, the Marquis de Sade is engaged in a "bewildering literary project in order to examine perversity and the wickedness of the human will in all its many forms" (527). Unfortunately, this literary project produces a product that cannot really be read as a novel or, at least, says Airaksinen, Sade can only be read with a key. He offers us this key without, however, telling us what door, what lock, he takes it from. None the less, the key is that Sade's "failed novels" aim at ethical and metaphysical goals; that the "Divine Marquis" is a philosopher after all. If this is the case, can we not ask, what is the philosophy encompassed by this literary project?

It turns out that this philosophy follows predictable lines; those followed, in fact, by many seventeenth- or eighteenth-century philosophers. Here, I must repeat in greater detail what I only referred to superficially above. Airaksinen claims that, in Sade, there is: one, an account that parodies all the usual accounts of social contract theory; two, a metaphysics of nature accompanied by a naturalistic ethic whose code of conduct is scientifically derived from a principle of nature; and three, an ethics proper in which virtue does not pay off. Law, metaphysics, ethics. In this there is little to distinguish Sade from his contemporaries, except that, in each case, he turns the tables. He devises a contract for harm, a metaphysics of evil, an ethics of vice.

From this perspective, Sade appears as nothing more than a Locke or Hobbes forced into an irrational contract, a Hume who follows out the implications of his skepticism, or a Berkeley who listens to the devil rather than to God. So it is somewhat bewildering when Airaksinen contradicts the profile he has just laid out to claim that, in Sade's writings, these three layers are disconnected, that Sade's message is anarchistic, and that Sade lacks any real values or religious truths. Yet, Airaksinen is onto something when he says that Sade's philosophy is somehow tied up with his rhetoric, and because the narrative style unifies it all, Sade's philosophy is "almost coherent" (528). It is here, at this seeming contradiction in Airaksinen's text, that I shall finally begin.

Concerning the matter of philosophical unification provided by narrative style, I defer to my guide, the French thinker, Pierre Klossowski, who argues, in an essay titled "Sade, or the Philosopher-Villain," that the

> villain who philosophizes does not grant thought any value other than favoring the *activity of the strongest passion*. . . . If the supreme villainy consists of disguising one's passion as thought, the villain for his part never finds in the thought of an honest man anything but the disguise of an *impotent passion*.[5]

Such a "scoundrel philosophy," concludes Klossowski, puts a "sinister question mark" on the decision to think of and to describe an act "instead of committing it," since an "irreducible depth of sensibility," such as Sade's, cannot be told about except through acts that inevitably betray it.[6] Perhaps this assessment is related to Airaksinen's confusion in the face of what appears to him to be sheer anarchy. What about this apparent anarchy? Is it, following Klossowski, a function of Sade's writing, just as Airaksinen has supposed? If so, how does it operate?

It must be admitted that the very possibility of writing presupposes submitting any singular event to the medium of generality, that is, to language. Now, in Sade's situation, claims Klossowski, this medium was logically structured classical language that functions so as to reproduce and reconstitute certain normative structures, certain acts deemed normative for rational human beings.[7] Chief among these norms is the need to perpetuate oneself through reproduction; and this norm is codified in the structure of classical language. The principle of identity and the principle of noncontradiction both serve the linguistic "reciprocity of persuasion." The exchange of singularities, one identical to another, is made possible by submitting such singularities to the generalities of language, notably to identity and noncontradiction.

Thus, given the norms of classical language, it cannot be Sade's task to establish an anarchy or a subversion of norms in writing, as Airaksinen claims, but to write perversion in the form of a counter to the generality of language. Let me make the case for this. Subversion of the grammar or logic of things, says Airaksinen, is a function of the fact that there is little distance between what Sade writes and what he thinks exists and is real. Sade's texts create a reality, and so, they are themselves the ultimate crime. Such subversions, says Airaksinen, consist in the lack of a coherent context within which an agent's actions take place, so that what gets created is ambiguity (531). The story, the context, the agent's actions, and the interpretation of each of these is laden with ambiguity, because they do not conform to grammar or logic.

If this is the case, then scenes such as Juliette's admonishment to wives to always deceive their husbands are ambiguous:

> Adulterous wives, there is your portrait: lying in your husband's arms to abandon only the bodily part of yourselves, and the sensations that arise to you are never but a response to your lover. The cuckholds delude themselves, supposing they are the cause of the raptures into which their motions plunge you.[8]

There would have to be ambiguous sexual relations as well, such as when the Chancellor Zeno seeks his pleasure with the daughter of the already wronged nobleman Grimani, "thereupon, listening now to nothing but the voice of his passion, the villain has us hold Virginia and, swearing like one of the damned, with barely one hundred strokes he transforms a peerless behind into mince-meat."[9] And finally, there are sensible (as well as social) relations that must also be considered ambiguous, such as the discussions held among the Neapolitan King Ferdinand, Queen Charlotte, Clairwil, and Juliette. "Said Ferdinand, 'My aim is to revive contests between men and animals, even those pitting men against men.' . . . 'And of what account can the lives of all that trash be,' Charlotte wondered, 'when our pleasures are at stake?'."[10] My question is, are these villainous acts really just a matter of ambiguity and the subversion of grammar, or is there not something more precise going on here, another logical order, perhaps?

Let us look provisionally to the repository of semantics to begin to define these terms. The dictionary can provide a provisional account of semantics. *To subvert* is defined as to overturn or overthrow by eroding a process or state of affairs; by contrast, doing things that are wrong, improper, corrupt, wicked, and generally deviating from what is considered *normal* are all actions better defined by the term "perversion." And that is what I would suggest Sade's writing amounts to, not subversion veering towards chaos or anarchy creating ambiguous relations, but rather a perversion of reason. Concerning this, Klossowski claims:

> Sade sets out to establish a counter-generality which would obtain for the specificity of perversions, making exchanges between singular cases of perversion possible. Within the dominant classical language of normative generality, such perversions are defined merely by the lack of logical structure, that is, they remain singular while the language demands generalities.[11]

Sade's text, while not denying this, yet makes strange use of it.

Sade takes his own process of counter-generality (by which means he seeks linguistic exchanges between singular cases of perversions) as "already implicit in the existing [linguistic] generality," existing precisely in the notion of atheism, a "monstrosity," a perversion already integral to the system of reason. Klossowski argues that, for Sade, atheism is already operating within the norm of reason, it is proclaimed and necessitated by reason so that man [*sic*] may be free and sovereign. Atheism is what reverses the existing generality of logic and linguistics into a counter-generality: "This atheism, the supreme act of normative reason has to institute the reign of the total absence of norms."[12]

And, just as Airaksinen has surmised, such an act can be carried out only in writing. To follow out this line of thought, let us first look at how reason arrives at atheism, then let us see how the atheism inherent to reason produces Sadean monstrosity and perversion. Finally, since this process can be carried out only in writing, let us see how such monstrosity is produced by certain characteristic modes of description in Sade's texts, descriptions whose rhetorical and narrative structure create Sade's social contract, metaphysics, and ethics.

Atheism prevails in autonomous reason, Klossowski argues, because only a reason that demands autonomy maintains the norms of the species (that is, self-perpetuation through reproduction in life, or logical self-perpetuation through identity and noncontradiction in thought) as it determines human behavior in conformity with these norms. Reason demands, as Freud recognized a century later, that individuals subordinate their instincts and life functions to the cause of equality and freedom for all. That is the social contract. Conservation of the species (propagation, and so forth) is inherent to the structure of reason. But for Sade, the atheism of autonomous reason is nothing more than the inversion of monotheism, because, as Klossowski argues, atheism guarantees property, progeny, and individual identity to the responsible human being. Oddly enough, perverting this structure can only be accomplished in a manner reflective of how it has always been rendered null and void. If religion has threatened the autonomy of reason through the establishment of the notion of a God who is completely arbitrary, whose motives we cannot know, Sade can only demolish inverted monotheism by reinstituting Divine arbitrariness from which all arbitrary, perverse, and monstrous behavior obtains. Far from having no religious principle, Sade embodies the principle of religion. Descartes' evil genius arises like Nosferatu in the night.

French philosopher Gilles Deleuze makes a similar point when he claims, in his book on masochism, that Sade's tyrants and libertines speak the counter-language of tyranny, which is the language of absolute impersonal Evil.[13] Libertines operate in accordance with a rational and intelligible transcendence and perversion of the positive social contract, in the direction of Evil, the supreme principle of wickedness.[14] They accomplish this through a process of negation in which destruction is merely the reverse of God's creation; disorder, simply a variation of order; and death, one step in the organization of life.[15] Everything operates, concludes Klossowski, as if

> Reason would like to be freed of God. Sade—but in a very underhanded way—wishes to free thought from every pre-established normative reason: integral atheism will be the end of anthropomorphic reason.[16]

However, effecting this meets with further obstacles. Human experience and, so, human autonomous reason allow for only partial negations. Any negation within the system of reason remains, in spite of its negative character, within that system as part of its positivity. Here, Deleuze's insights are again helpful. He argues that pure human intelligibility can never be more than the "object of an Idea," a delusion of reason itself, "an exorbitance specific to reason itself."[17] Hence the rage and despair of the sadistic hero when he realizes how insignificant and slight his own crimes are in relation to the Idea of Evil, an idea that he arrives at through the omnipotence of integral atheism. The libertine dreams of a universal, impersonal crime, or as the libertine Clairwil puts it, a crime "which is perpetually effective even when I myself cease to be effective, so that there will not be a single moment of my life, even when I am asleep, when I shall not be the cause of some disturbance."[18] The problem for the libertine, Deleuze argues, is that he is forced to *demonstrate* this theorem with the partial inductive processes of experience. This has two effects: first, given the partial and incomplete nature of any demonstration in relation to the Idea of Evil, only the endless repetition of a crime can approximate the goal of absolute Evil, and it is this that accounts for the length of Sade's narratives; second, enthusiasm for crimes is not permitted, because it would make obvious the partial nature of Sadean negations in pursuit of absolute Evil, or as Klossowski calls it, integral atheism.

Still, and in spite of their dependence on reason, whenever Sade's villains carry out their vile murders, tortures, dismemberments, burnings, incestuous relations, and sexual repetitions, they do so in order to destroy reason's autonomy.[19] "'I have demonstrated it theoretically,' says Noirceuil, 'Let us now put it to the test of practice'."[20] By appealing to reason in the justification and demonstration of villainy, they deride reason insofar as it claims to guarantee positive human behavior. So, concludes Klossowski, either reason is unable to forestall monstrosity and perversion or, like God, monstrosity exceeds the realm of autonomous atheistic rationality in the coincidence of reason and sensible nature.[21]

Thus another question Airaksinen has raised emerges: that of the relation between Sade's writing and the effecting of acts independently of writing. Airaksinen is disturbed by the fictional cruelty of Sade's writing that, he says, harms the reader. Yet, he is willing, in the end, to excuse Sade's violence, claiming that the test of Sade's texts is his own biography, and since Sade never killed anyone (although he was brutal to those who worked for him, and this might be more disturbing than all his sexual escapades), Airaksinen opts for relativism with regard to crime and cruelty, while warning against cruelty perpetrated by state power:

> Real crime and cruelty are both undesirable and immoral. But once we see that what is actually criminal and cruel is highly unclear and relative, we should resist the countercruelty practiced by the state, stop worshiping it, and appreciate the many subtle forms of fictionalized evil. (535)

Airaksinen concludes that the threat represented by Sade's grammatical, textual, and cultural ambiguity is, in fact, a threat to social power or what is called civilized human existence. While this may well be the case, there is more to be said here.

Given Sade's position outside civil society, that is, as an outsider with respect to first, the French nobility, then later, with respect to the citizens of revolutionary France, and given the arguments that have been made here regarding Sade's attempt to use classical language against itself and against the norms of civil society, it does appear that, within certain limits, Sade's work was active in the creation of freedom. However, Airaksinen's reading of state cruelty is close to what Klossowski calls an "optimist" interpretation of Sade: if the whole human race were to degenerate, to become perverted, Sade's goal would be reached, and there would no longer be any necessity for monsters or sadism.[22] The "ruse" here, warns Klossowski, lies in the realization that such degeneration is *realizable only within a space composed by obstacles*, that is, within the logically structured language of norms and institutions that constitute the classical state and state power.[23] Now, what seems to occur in Sade's texts is that with the establishment of integral atheism, the principle of identity disappears, and along with this the morally and physically responsible self. The result is nothing less than the universal prostitution of all human beings. Paradoxically, cruelty, crime, and all moral transgressions oppose universal prostitution, for unless one knowingly creates rules that can be broken, that someone seeks to break (which is what happens in Sade's secret societies, Klossowski reminds us), the tension needed for sadism dissipates. Crime and cruelty are made possible by the maintenance of the norms of autonomous reason. Klossowski concludes: "Transgression presupposes the existing order, the apparent maintenance of norms, for the benefit of an accumulation of energy which makes transgression necessary."[24]

Further, universal prostitution would seem to demand a specific set of circumstances as well. Sade maintains universal prostitution as meaningful by excluding individuals from the secret or elite societies within which there is no tension, because there are no norms. With this, we find another explanation for Sade's repetitions, and the paradox pointed to in Deleuze's reading of Sade can be further articulated. Transgression seeks nothing more than self-renewal; it never gets resolved. Integral atheism demands the maintenance of the very norms it opposes in order to express itself. Klossowski argues:

> But if it [the transgressive act] is thus reiterated, in Sade it reiterates itself in principle only through one same act. This very act can never be transgressed; its image is each time represented as though it had never been carried out.[25]

As the one who carries out the act of eternal repetition, the "pervert" carries out his or her crimes, which range from simple to complicated passions, and is always forced to subordinate his/her enjoyment to the carrying out of the single transgression that serves as his/her only opportunity for self-signifying, even as this act is the act of transgressing the logic of identity.[26] Thus, the libertine's act of transgression must be one that destroys the life preserving conditions of identity in an expropriation of the pervert's own body and the bodies of others. Principle among these acts is sodomy. In Sade, sodomy is not merely, or even not at all, a question of homosexual activity, but is related to the notion of counter-generality. Sodomy denies propagation of the species and so "bears witness to the death of the species in an individual."[27]

Additionally, as I have noted, the perverse acts preformed by libertines are carried out with the aim of seeking their perfection in apathy. Enthusiasm for evil, cautions Deleuze, indicates that the good remains as a value, or, as Klossowski would argue, it indicates that reason is still operating to produce positive human behavior. However, by not allowing virtue to show itself in enthusiasm, even in enthusiasm for the negation of the good, evil, as the counterpart to the good, disappears in the eyes of the libertines. The point is not so much to hurt the reader as it is to not satisfy the reader and, instead, to satisfy the demands of the logic of classical language even while perverting it. The mechanism by which this operates is based on a particular distinction that appears in Sade's texts, a distinction that I noted at the beginning of this essay.

According to Klossowski, Sade's texts are marked by the distinction between the "actualization of the sensible in an act through writing," and "the effecting of the act independently of its description,"[28] that is, between the logical demands of classical language and the acting out of the crime. In this, Sade's writing interprets nature in the only way it can. Reading Sade's texts leaves the unmistakable conclusion that, for Sade, feeling, sensibility itself, is an irreducible element of perversion, and aberrant acts arising from the fact of that sensibility are taken to be aberrant precisely because not even atheistic reason can recognize itself in them. The result of this predicament is that the Sadean sensory experience is "obscured in the measure that discourse has to justify the act."[29] Or, to repeat what I said at the beginning, Sade's irreducible depth of sensibility cannot be told about except through acts that inevitably betray it.

If Sade's libertines commit crimes, it is because that is the perversion classical language permits. If they bore or assault the reader with endless repetitions, this is to meet the demands of language. If they display apathy, coldness, and cruelty, it is because to do otherwise would be to affirm positive reason and linguistic generality. I do not believe that we can claim that Sade's texts create a new reality. Rather, Sade's sensibilities can find expression only within linguistic generality and integral atheism as repetition and revulsion.

While Sade's perversion is unquestionably a protest against positive reason and linguistic generality, it seems to me that we must also be careful about to what extent we valorize this outcome. Leo Bersani and Ulysse Dutoit point out in their essay on Sade that fascism is the political system best suited to Sadean sex because it allows for the elimination of partners. Sadean sex translates the agony in the bodies of the libertine's victims into the sexual vibrations of the executioners.[30] Sexuality, in Sade's texts, is inherently destabilizing, a consequence of psychic pain. The best sexuality is when pain is inflicted on another so that their destabilized commotion can be appropriated by the libertine. This is not the creation of new forms of sexuality, nor is it the creation of new logics or grammars; rather, such sexuality is the equivalent of sadism and masochism in social relations, and fascism in politics. In short, it is the violence of Western rationality that Sade writes, and to read him is to begin to read ourselves.

Notes

1. Maurice Lever, *Sade: A Biography* (New York: Farrar, Strauss, Giroux, 1993), 382-3.
2. *Ibid.*, 383.

3. Timo Airaksinen, "The Style of Sade: Sex, Text, and Cruelty," this volume, 527-35; page references to this essay are supplied parenthetically in the text.
4. Pierre Klossowski, "Sade, or the Philosopher-Villain," trans. Alphonso Lingis, *SubStance* 15: 2 (1986): 5-25.
5. *Ibid.*, 5.
6. *Ibid.*
7. *Ibid.*, 6.
8. Marquis de Sade, *Juliette*, trans. Austryn Wainhouse (New York: Grove Press, 1968), 1005-6.
9. *Ibid.*, 1144.
10. *Ibid.*, 999.
11. Klossowski, "Sade, or the Philosopher-Villain," 6.
12. *Ibid.*
13. Gilles Deleuze, *Masochism. An Interpretation of Coldness and Cruelty. Together With the Entire Text of Venus in Furs by Leopold von Sacher-Masoch*, trans. Jean McNeil and Aude Willm (New York: Braziller, 1971). See also Dorothea Olkowski, "Monstrous Reflection: Sade and Masoch—Rewriting the History of Reason," in Arleen Dallery and Charles E. Scott, eds., *Crisis in Continental Philosophy: Selected Studies in Phenomenology and Existential Philosophy* (Albany: State University of New York Press, 1990), 189-200.
14. Deleuze, *Masochism*, 76.
15. *Ibid.*, 24.
16. Klossowski, "Sade, or the Philosopher-Villain," 7.
17. Deleuze, *Masochism*, 25.
18. *Ibid.*, 25-6.
19. Klossowski, "Sade, or the Philosopher-Villain," 7.
20. Deleuze, *Masochism*, 19.
21. Klossowski, "Sade, or the Philosopher-Villain," 7.
22. *Ibid.*, 10.
23. *Ibid.*
24. *Ibid.*, 9.
25. *Ibid.*, 11.
26. *Ibid.*, 12.
27. *Ibid.*
28. *Ibid.*, 8.
29. *Ibid.*
30. Leo Bersani and Ulysse Dutoit, "Merde Alors," *October* 13 (1979): 23-35, at 26.

Steven G. Smith
(photograph: Kay Barksdale)

Author of "The Attractions of Gender"
Paper presented at the Society for the Philosophy of Sex and Love
during the
Central Division Meeting of The American Philosophical Association
New Orleans, La., 26 April 1990

Fifty-Two

THE ATTRACTIONS OF GENDER

Steven G. Smith

"Genders" are sex-related ways of being human. Thus, whatever else they are, they are ways of valuing and implications for valuing. To be masculine, for example, is to have a man-associated way of liking, preferring, and approving, and also to have a man-associated way of being pleasing, preferable, or approvable. The possibility of distinguishing masculine and feminine styles of moral valuation is much discussed lately, especially in connection with Carol Gilligan's work; I propose to bring the two parts of the valuation question into one picture, gender ethics together with gender aesthetics, and specifically to ask about the attractiveness that a moral style or character has within a gender system and what the role of that attractiveness is in constituting the gender system. In doing this, I hope to make some headway on old questions of moral psychology, such as the role of feeling in morality and the relation between virtue and happiness.

Immanuel Kant opens up an approach to our subject in his 1764 essay "Observations on the Feeling of the Beautiful and the Sublime."[1] Two lines of thinking were running together in his mind when he wrote this essay, which I fancy were stimulated by two books that had just appeared. One of the books was Rousseau's *Emile*, which would have provoked him to reflect on norms for the sexes. The other was Burke's essay on the beautiful and the sublime, which showed the possibilities in mapping the universe of pleasing qualities around the two polar reference points of the beautiful and the sublime.[2] The *beautiful* delights, charms, and makes us feel lively and gay, while the *sublime* causes pleasure in exceeding our ordinary scale. The "noble" is the type of sublimity that occasions a quiet wonder. Nobility, both the feeling for it and the exemplification of it, turns out to be the key quality recommended for judging the attractiveness of men, while beauty is the prescribed leading quality for women. Neither sex is totally lacking in the quality assigned to the other, but in some sense each sex is defined by its cultivation of one rather than the other.

Kant's topic is clearly what we would call gender. What's at issue are modes of consciousness and practical styles linked to sex, not sexual anatomy as such. Furthermore, his depictions of femininity and masculinity are faithful in a general way to modern Western gender norms; while they call for challenge and revision, for present purposes they suffice to illustrate the sort of valuational content that our gender scheme has, or rather is. Kant says he is reporting on these valuations "more with the eye of an observer than of a philosopher" (45), and that his subject is feelings rather than moral rules (83); yet a normative edge frequently appears in his remarks. While his characterizations of the genders are not purely normative in the way that moral principles are, they pertain to a specially important set of empirically given feelings called the "*finer* feelings" that "fit the soul for virtuous impulses" (46). These feelings tend toward steadiness and universality, such that Kant calls them "principles" in contrast with "impulses" (60, 65). They lie on the boundary of the aesthetic and the ethical. Kant is studying the attractiveness of moral character—the "beauty and dignity of human nature," as he calls it (60)—and at the same time organizing human attractions in relation to moral principles. This is the central ambiguity of the essay. From the ambiguous crux of the so-called "finer feelings," one can think one's way to moral principles proper, on the one side, and to sexual desires, on the other (the so-called "coarser feelings").

A closely related ambiguity in Kant's thinking is that men's nobility and women's beauty are simultaneously what men and women have special feeling for, respectively, and what any and all observers specially feel in them, respectively. For example, it is said to be beautiful in a woman both to love merriment in others and to be lovably merry. One would expect being merry to go together with enjoying merriment; the two are not really separate. Would we not generally agree, however, that what is centrally valuable in a person is just the way she or he values? This proposition is hard to reject, but it poses a problem when we line it up next to the proposition that the different genders are different ways of valuing. Can a noble valuer value the valuing of a beautiful valuer? If feelings of attraction, as Kant says, rest "not so much upon the nature of the external things that arouse them as upon each person's disposition to be moved by these to pleasure" (45), and if gender is a determining feature of one's disposition, then how could one appreciate someone of a different gender (except peripherally, that is, in spite of gender)? Are the gender dispositions complementary only in the sense that they fill different niches in the ensemble of human nature, or are they complementary also in the sense that they call for each other, want each other, as is commonly thought?

To see what is thinkable from a starting point like Kant's (which, I think, is also the ordinary starting point), we need to inquire into what it is to value valuing.

First, let us say that to value a thing is to feel that one is living well (at least in principle) in relation to the thing. (The subject of this life is an intentional being, so let us say that "living well" always means that a subject's aims are being furthered.) In valuing, I virtually qualify my position with respect to something (either approaching nearer to it or tarrying in its presence) in such a way that my intending prospects are furthered. Now, when I value valuing, I position myself with respect to another intender in order to realize the happiness that inheres in interintentional relationship. Some sort of teamwork is stipulated in this valuing. The other intending might team with mine in different ways; it might echo mine, or elaborate on mine in a certain direction, or contribute a quite different but somehow complementary quality of its own. But in all cases the event of the intentional togetherness is the foundational level in the flourishing involved, and the sense of this, whether triumphant or trusting, is the foundational pro-feeling in the valuing.

To value a particular valuing is to value a particular relationship, and vice versa. A gender system is a system of relationships of a particular kind, centrally, for us, a relationship of one kind between masculine and feminine beings, of another kind among masculine beings, and of yet another kind among feminine beings. (Note that there are significant subtypes within these main types of relationship as well as significant "noncentral" relationships like those between gays and straights.) A gender system is therefore a scheme of valuing valuing in which we enjoy the experience of particular kinds of interintentional teamwork or at least orient ourselves to the prospect of such teamwork. The implication for one's understanding of others in an interintentional scheme is that one posits them not merely as members playing individual and class roles but as representatives of the whole. Otherwise they would not be *fellow subjects*, or not fully. Thus a failure of the other to act consistently with the requirements of the scheme is more than an occasion of cognitive dissonance: it is a betrayal of trust. We do not feel this betrayal when we adopt the detached social scientific perspective in which valuing becomes something other than our own actual living and all we see is someone's observed "behavior" changing patterns. But betrayal or faith keeping is the inside of the interintentional reality, and that goes toward determining the *stakes* of gendered conduct in an inescapably commanding way, that is, in directly shaping our valuing.

The others represent the whole team, including me; accordingly, I represent the whole team and each of them. My identity is staked to this interintentional project; I have promised and trusted *myself* to it, to the extent that my existence goes into this sort of valuing and relationship. I like, approve of, and prefer the version of myself that belongs to the team. Thus a fellow subject's betrayal not only lets down the larger enterprise, it wounds my selfhood (which indeed is the sharp point of all real betrayal). But how I am liable to be wounded depends on how I am invested. (We can joke about wounds to masculinity but not to femininity. This might reveal a distance between masculine selfhood and where we locate the real self. Or perhaps, as is sometimes suggested, masculinity is more a *venture*, an enterprise more intrinsically liable to fail.)[3]

Within the larger range of possible schemes of relationship, moral character and moral community figure as *perfectly trustworthy* forms. The evolution of such ideals is driven by the problem of trusting others and trusting oneself. Seen one way, Kant's essay responds to uncertainty and discomfort in the gender system by linking gender norms to moral ideals through the "finer feelings." The genders would not be arbitrary or oppressive if they could be shown to anchor in the two great principles of perfect community, love (the feeling for the beautiful) and respect (the feeling for the noble). In the perspective of cultural history, then, the essay serves as a good specimen of eighteenth-century gender ideology. But we can also turn Kant's line of thinking back around and see it as a response to uncertainty about a rationalistic moral ideal that perhaps hangs in the air without solid connections to empirical human nature. (This is to take the perspective determined by the problematic of ethical theory in general and Kant's theory in particular.) The "finer feelings" then show a way from the more abstractly attractive moral ideal to the more concretely attractive human gender qualities, and beyond. A continuum of "fineness" is established along which one's "feelings" or valuations move up, toward the universal, or down, toward the selfish, from "the beauty and dignity of human nature" all the way to sexual desires and trepidations.

Valuing is not usually a single intentional episode, like shooting an arrow at a target, but rather a continuing stream of dense life, like driving down a highway at varying speeds, in this lane or that, in light or heavy traffic, with turns and branches always coming into view. The sort of valuing we are investigating here can range in various ways over this dimension of universal-to-selfish or moral-to-sexual, according to the extent of the interintentional system in which human attraction is appreciated. The frame of reference might be the Kantian Kingdom of Ends or it might be the supremely particular and concrete prospect of carnal relation. Or it might be both, oscillating or ambiguously superimposed. I suspect that valuing another person *always* actualizes *all* of these possibilities, sounds all the notes on the scale, however much the relative prominence of certain notes might vary. But whether or not this is true in general, an essential feature of gender is that it unites the more universal attractiveness of a human subject as such with the more particular attractiveness of the sexed body type, and likewise unites the more disinterested mode of valuation, the admiration of the subject who judges as anyone ideally should judge, with the personally interested mode of valuation, the actually being drawn. I intentionally sound these two chords whenever I say, with the normal appreciative force, "X is feminine" or "Y is masculine"; to set up this intriguing resonance is one of the main points of gender valuing.

We wondered how masculine subjects qua masculine and feminine subjects qua feminine could appreciate each other, given that they are defined by their different valuing orientations; we now have resources for constructing possible answers.

First, since to value valuing is always to affirm someone as a member and representative of an interintentional team, X in valuing Y has to admit that Y belongs to and represents the team as a complement to X; X must also take responsibility for being Y's complement and representative, in spite of Y's difference. In this case the felicitation of intention that occurs through affirming X's participation in a larger life would transcend X's gender quality rather than expand it. One affirms something opaque because one is capable of enjoying the spaciousness of an intentional world with alien inhabitants. How is it that one can do this? Does a generic human Z valuing exist—say, a valuing of personal expression as such and fellowship as such—on the basis of which one feels the inadequacy of gender specializations if they try to stand on their own? (Perhaps so, but let's not shift out of gendered valuing.) Might the character of every X contain Y-qualities that stay hidden in the regime of the X gender but still provide the necessary receptivity or motivation for affirming the Y gender? Or do X and Y perhaps like each other as foils, realizing that their capacities are exercised to best advantage when set in contrast? (That is, when the feminine has the challenging noble to attract, and the noble has the challenging feminine to administer.) On this scenario, X and Y can value their cross-gender relations as expressive of their own leading qualities. That would mean that affirming the other-than-noble can be seen as noble, and affirming the other-than-beautiful can be seen as beautiful. The Kantian husband is noble to indulge his wife (up to a point); he says of his marriage, by way of enunciating an especially sublime principle, a most strenuous obligation: "It takes all kinds." Meanwhile his wife is especially charming to put up with her husband's plain ways; she gracefully concedes a diversity of kinds. One is *blindly* noble, the other *blindly* charming. Their toleration of mutual opacity will perennially degrade into misunderstanding and distrust, what Dorothy Dinnerstein (with a different analysis) calls the "malaise" intrinsic to a gender system.[4] Nobility and charm are realized in such a way that they suffer defeats to themselves, but insofar as they suffer defeat nobly and gracefully, they excel.

The second dimension wherein there is room to appreciate the alien gender in spite of oneself lies in the distance between ideal judgment and personal attraction. That which I cannot lucidly approve of, I may yet be moved by. Kant says quaintly that a "single sly glance" from a woman sets a man "more in confusion than the most difficult problem of science" (79). Feminine attraction reaches a masculine subject from the blind side of sexual susceptibility or some other dispositional aspect not featured in the project of nobility. A similar attraction pulls in the other direction, too: "In pain you shall bring forth children, yet your desire shall be for your husband" (Genesis 3:16). Gender teaming does not make good sense, for at certain points one not only does not understand it, one suffers from it palpably.

While none of these interintentional structures will necessarily obtain in relations between men and women, all of them are admitted by the *concept* of gender or sex-inflected humanity, which means that any of them *might* play an important part in gender attraction at a given moment. Attraction might actually come about in one or more of the ways I have outlined or, while arising for whatever underlying reason, might be interpreted by the subject in one of these ways, the interpretation having its own effect on the course of relationship.

As is well known, Kant later detaches moral motivation from "feelings" (no matter how "fine") and prefers to speak of "reason becoming practical"; the special feeling of "respect" is then the mysterious aesthetic trace left by the direct self-assertion of reason, and also the one trace left of the masculine roots of Kant's interpretation of morality. In Kant's critical ethics, virtue is no longer divided into the beautiful and the noble, and the link between moral attractiveness and other kinds of human attractiveness disappears. One might expect, then, that any return to the premise of gendered moral experience would at the same time make possible a restored connection between the different human attractions. Indeed, I see this implication in the gender ethic sketched in Carol Gilligan's *In a Different Voice* and will close by trying to demonstrate it.[5]

Gilligan defines two complementary styles of moral reasoning, or "voices": an "ethic of care" more prominent in women and an "ethic of rights" more prominent in men. The "ethic of care" is primarily oriented to protecting and enhancing actual persons and relationships. In its most mature form, it "reflects a cumulative knowledge of human relationships [and] evolves around a central insight, that self and other are interdependent" (74). Gilligan speaks of a woman-associated "psychological logic of relationships" in contrast to the "formal logic of fairness" that flourishes among men (73), whose main personal concern is individuation. This division of moral styles is bound to remind us of the categories of Kant's *Observations*. Kant had allowed a feminine virtue and moral understanding that he called "beautiful" (78, 81); this moral femininity had an aesthetic sort of parity with moral masculinity; it was, however, kept subordinate in "strict" moral perspective, designated "adoptive" rather than "genuine" virtue (61), and this foreshadowed its complete suppression later in the moral theory of Kant's critical period. Now Gilligan is bringing feminine virtue to the fore again. By deploying evidence from psychological research that an ethic of care has as long and rich a development as the ethic of rights, and that it engages choice situations just as thoughtfully and responsively as does its masculine counterpart, she implicitly argues for moral parity.

Gilligan does not take up the question of masculine and feminine attractiveness. She does, however, relate moral style to the construction and maintenance of selfhood, and the question of what the gendered self wants and fears for itself is a crucial piece of our puzzle.[6] Broadly speaking, the masculine self wants a secure individual identity and is threatened by affiliation; masculine imagery (in daydreaming and storytelling) tends to be violent, explosive. Strength is highly valued, and strength means getting along by oneself and not having to impose on others. The feminine self, on the other hand, wants to be secure in relationship and is threatened by separation. Sensitivity is highly valued and hurting someone else is the chief sin.

These psychological claims take us back, with a vengeance, to our old problem of cross-gender valuation. How can feminine and masculine subjects value each other if—and this is worse than merely being tuned to different wavelengths—they actively threaten each other? Relatedness and individuatedness seem antipathetic.

Gilligan's solution is to argue that the feminine and masculine modes *need* each other, not only for the sake of rounding out the whole of human nature, but for the development of each on its own path.[7] A more maturely feminine subject is one who has learned to let self count as an object of care equally with others; masculine maturity, in turn, has learned the truth of interdependence. The genders do not converge on a single postgendered humanity, but they refract through each other so that each comes to represent more adequately the whole of human possibility. The tension between the two is the basis of a dialogue (174).

On this conception of the development of self, we are led to interpret the attractiveness of the other gender at least partly as the allure of one's own enriched gender identity. X is not exactly blind in valuing Y and the larger human reality to which X and Y jointly belong; X sees a prospective development of X's own gender wherein present dangers will be reduced and present capacities will be exercised to better effect. Y holds the key to that higher grade of X's happiness. The move to maturity *removes* blindness inasmuch as the later X, the X that *has* appreciated Y, is aware of a wider range of valuation consistent with its own gender. (X would also attain *virtue* in this way insofar as the valuations have anything to do with conduct. X is, in ideal terms, a more welcome fellow subject.) Such could be precisely Kant's orientation in the *Observations* where, with an explicitly masculine attitude, he adopts feminine value in a subordinate place (and his text almost asks aloud to be complemented by a feminine view in which an alternative to this subordination would appear). His formula for moral sense, that "feeling for the beauty and dignity of human nature," could be an androgynous composite fitting Gilligan's recipe for a mature gendered view. (In Kant's later moral theory, the feminine will become invisible, dignity will entirely supersede beauty, willing will supersede feeling, and one will have to seek the valuations of beauty and care in what he calls the duties of benevolence.)[8]

I have suggested that a gender system is a system of trust. A certain kind of interdependence and teamwork is at stake in gendered conduct, a certain realization of the human as interintentionally extended. By way of provisional conclusion, we can say that feminine and masculine beings count on each other not only to round out a larger human ensemble, not only to cover certain practical bases respectively, and not only to provide certain pleasures (sexual or otherwise), but to teach each other and draw each other on to types of human excellence that remain connected with our body types. All this belongs to the *concept* of gender as an attraction.

Notes

1. Immanuel Kant, *Observations on the Feeling of the Beautiful and Sublime*, trans. J. Goldthwait (Berkeley: University of California Press, 1960). Page references to this text are supplied parenthetically in the text.

2. According to J. T. Boulton (apparently relying on G. Candrea, *Der Begriff des Erhabenen bei Burke und Kant* [Strassburg, 1984]), Kant, in 1764, probably knew Burke's book only from Mendelssohn's review, but had read the original by the time of writing the *Critique of Judgment*. See the "Editor's Introduction" to Edmund Burke, *A Philosophical Enquiry Into the Origin of Our Ideas of the Sublime and Beautiful* [1759] (London: Routledge and Kegan Paul, 1958), cxxv.

3. See Walter J. Ong, *Fighting for Life: Contest, Sexuality, and Consciousness* (Ithaca, N.Y.: Cornell University Press, 1981).

4. Dorothy Dinnerstein, *The Mermaid and the Minotaur: Sexual Arrangements and Human Malaise* (New York: Harper and Row, 1976).

5. Carol Gilligan, *In a Different Voice: Psychological Theory and Women's Development* (Cambridge, Mass.: Harvard University Press, 1982).

6. In what follows, I summarize from chs. 2 and 3 of Gilligan, *In a Different Voice.*

7. *Ibid.*, ch. 6.

8. See Kant, *Groundwork of the Metaphysic of Morals*, Ak. 423, and *The Doctrine of Virtue*, Ak. 392, 401, 447 *et seq.*

Nancy E. Snow

Author of "Comment on 'The Attractions of Gender'"
Paper presented at the Society for the Philosophy of Sex and Love
during the
Central Division Meeting of The American Philosophical Association
New Orleans, La., 26 April 1990

Fifty-Three

ARE THE ATTRACTIONS OF GENDER REALLY ATTRACTIONS?

Nancy E. Snow

The problem, suggested by Kant,[1] on which Steven Smith's essay focuses is this: how is it possible for persons of opposite genders to attract?[2] Gender attraction is interpreted by Kant and Smith as a complex mode of valuing in which moral valuation, sexual attraction, and aesthetic valuing can coalesce. Kant identifies two polar aesthetic qualities, the beautiful and the sublime (or noble), which he associates with the feminine and masculine genders, respectively. Kant believes that "men's nobility and women's beauty are simultaneously what men and women have special feeling for, respectively, and what any and all observers specially feel in them, respectively" (548). According to Smith, the question of how it is possible for opposite genders to attract is generated by the conjunction of the belief that the way he or she values is centrally valuable in a person, and the claim that the different genders are different ways of valuing. Smith asks, "can a noble valuer value the valuing of a beautiful valuer?" (548). Similarly, can a beautiful valuer value the valuing of a noble valuer? In short, "if gender is a determining feature of one's disposition, then how could one appreciate someone of a different gender?"

Smith proposes three ways in which someone might appreciate another of a different gender. According to the first, persons of different genders can appreciate one another through what Smith calls "their toleration of mutual opacity" (551). By this he means that "affirming the other-than-noble can be seen as noble, and affirming the other-than-beautiful can be seen as beautiful" (551). Smith claims that "the Kantian husband is noble to indulge his wife (up to a point)" and "his wife is especially charming to put up with her husband's plain ways" (551).

The difficulty with this as a solution to the problem of gender attraction is that *toleration* is different from *attraction* or *appreciation*. Joseph Raz has argued that toleration implies disapproval of that which we tolerate.[3] This disapproval can be aesthetic or moral. For example, a parent might tolerate his or her child's loud rock music while finding it perfectly repulsive. In a society committed to freedom of religion, members of one religious faith might tolerate the beliefs of another faith, yet consider them false beliefs and disapprove of them on moral grounds. Consequently, to argue that members of different genders can *tolerate* the qualities of the opposite gender does not establish Smith's point, which is that members of different genders can appreciate or be attracted by the qualities exhibited by their opposites. But perhaps Smith believes that we can tolerate something yet regard it positively. For example, he writes, "one affirms something opaque because one is capable of enjoying the spaciousness of an intentional world with alien inhabitants" (550). But then one enjoys a world characterized by toleration, and not by the alien qualities of others. Even conceding that we can tolerate something while viewing it positively instead of negatively, this is not strong enough to make Smith's point conclusively. That we affirm something does not show that we are attracted by it or are appreciative of it. We might affirm it simply because we are forced to live with it. The wife, for example, might tolerate her husband's plain ways because, after all, that is how he is; he cannot be changed. Though it could be charming of the wife to tolerate her husband, she is not necessarily appreciating his characteristics. She might simply be coping with them.

Smith makes his second proposal by arguing that "there is room to appreciate the alien gender in spite of oneself" and that this room "lies in the distance between ideal judgment and personal attraction. That which I cannot lucidly approve of, I may yet be moved by" (551). The difficulty with this approach is that it makes being attracted to persons of the opposite gender seem irrational. If ideal judgment is that of which I can lucidly approve, it must be that to which I can rationally assent. If I can be moved by personal attraction, but cannot lucidly approve of it, I cannot rationally assent to it. That means that personal attraction, including gender attractions, must be irrational in some sense. Smith's examples bear this interpretation out. Discussing the attraction of the feminine to the masculine, he quotes Genesis 3:16: "In pain you shall bring forth children, yet your desire shall be for your husband." This makes gender attraction sound a lot like the desire for another cigarette: you want it, but you know it will hurt you. One cannot rationally approve of such self-destructive desires. Unlike Smith's first proposal, this second attempt does establish a way in which persons of opposite genders can be attracted by each other, but it is an unattractive attraction, irrational and possibly self-destructive.

Smith's third explanation of how opposite genders can attract relies on the work of Carol Gilligan, which associates the different genders not with different aesthetic qualities, but with different psychological orientations.[4] The masculine self seeks "a secure individual identity and is threatened by affiliation. . . . Strength is highly valued, and strength means getting along by oneself and not having to impose on others." By contrast, "the feminine self . . . wants to be secure in relationship and is threatened by separation. Sensitivity is highly valued and hurting someone else is the chief sin" (552).

Smith realizes that this way of understanding gender identities seems at first sight to exacerbate the problem of gender attractiveness. Not only are the different genders characterized by opposing qualities, but each gender threatens the identity of the other. However, he finds the resources for a resolution in Gilligan's claim that persons of different genders need each other for their own gender development. He writes:

> X is not exactly blind in valuing Y and the larger human reality to which X and Y jointly belong; X sees a prospective development of X's own gender wherein present dangers will be reduced and present capacities

> will be exercised to better effect. Y holds the key to that higher grade of X's happiness. The move to maturity *removes* blindness inasmuch as the later X, the X that *has* appreciated Y, is aware of a wider range of valuation consistent with its own gender. (552-3)

This proposal does not generate a satisfying account of gender attraction. Smith's second proposal makes gender attraction sound a bit extreme: blindly irrational and potentially self-destructive. His present attempt takes us to the opposite extreme. We can and do value members of the opposite gender, but *because* and *insofar as* they enhance the development of our own gender identities. Our appreciation is not blind, but calculating and manipulative. X recognizes that she can improve herself through relating to Y, that Y "holds the key" to her happiness. This implies that X values Y primarily as a means to her gender development. This fails to explain the sense in which gender attractions are genuinely other-regarding. It does not tell us how X can value Y for Y's own sake, nor how, as a consequence of that valuing, both X and Y can grow as separate, yet consciously and willingly interdependent, individuals.

Smith's essay leaves us with a more refined version of the question with which we started. How is it possible for members of opposite genders to attract, in a way that reduces neither to blindly irrational and possibly self-destructive desire on the one hand, nor, on the other, to a self-centered attraction that uses another as a means to one's gender development? If there is a mean between these two extremes, we have yet to find how it is possible.

Notes

1. Immanuel Kant, *Observations on the Feeling of the Beautiful and Sublime*, trans. J. Goldthwait (Berkeley: University of California Press, 1960).
2. Steven G. Smith, "The Attractions of Gender," this volume, 547-53; page references are supplied parenthetically in the text.
3. Joseph Raz, *The Morality of Freedom* (Oxford: Oxford University Press, 1986), 401-3.
4. Carol Gilligan, *In a Different Voice: Psychological Theory and Women's Development* (Cambridge, Mass.: Harvard University Press, 1982).

Natalie Dandekar
(photograph: D. P. Dandekar)

Author of "Eros, Romantic Illusion, and Political Opportunism (*Symposium* 178-180)"
Paper presented at the Society for the Philosophy of Sex and Love during the
Eastern Division Meeting of The American Philosophical Association
Boston, Mass., 29 December 1990

Fifty-Four

EROS, ROMANTIC ILLUSION, AND POLITICAL OPPORTUNISM (*Symposium* 178-180)

Natalie Dandekar

1. The Wonder of Eros Reduced to Romanticized Illusions

Phaedrus praises Eros in terms that describe the God of Love as a wondrous being: unborn, unbegotten, wholly without parents—Eros appears. The origin of Eros is held to be entirely independent of procreation. More surprisingly, the power of Eros is, throughout Phaedrus's encomium, described without reference to any form of reproduction. Instead, the God's power is singular. In a world where most people fear death and try to preserve their own life, Eros transforms the motivational structure of human beings. The devotees of Eros, lovers and beloved alike, act in accordance with an other-regarding motive: shame. While a person is erotically inspired, Death is no longer that which is most fearsome. Erotically-inspired shame thus promotes a disdain for death that issues in a willing defiance of death's power.

The poets lovingly detail erotically-inspired individuals who show disdain for death. In his encomium, Phaedrus cites three such stories. Achilles and Alcestis both choose death in ways that prove the strength of their devotion. Even the poet Orpheus is so powerfully motivated by Eros that he willingly confronts death in order to win back his Eurydice.

I argue here that Phaedrus portrays a singularly reductive understanding of Eros that reflects a singularly unpleasant relationship between poetry and politics. Phaedrus's encomium to Eros illustrates graphically the way in which poetic license issues in stories that reduce an immortal divinity to a political tool. Any polis in which Phaedrus's construct of Eros functions will have a plentiful supply of erotically-inspired heroes energetically willing to die as uncritical, willing sacrifices to a militaristic state bent on world conquest.

Poets transform the romantic *Liebestod* into an erotically driven triumph over death itself. In the opportunistic polis, this poetic formula, love-leads-to-death [but true lovers never really die], can be used for the benefit of the political order in its drive toward world conquest.

I argue that Phaedrus's encomium naively reveals an unpleasant dynamic between political opportunism and poetic license. The polis provides poets to sing deathless paeans in praise of the undying fame of dead heroes. These poetic renditions then inspire emotionally susceptible humans to imitate their heroes without realizing the extent to which these heros are the product of poetic illusion. After socially-constructed poetic illusions have transformed Eros, the god of love functions as a servant of the polis, producing politically useful, self-sacrificing deaths.

My argument consists of four parts: first, I consider why Plato uses Phaedrus as the putative voice for this particular speech; second, I analyze what Phaedrus says in his encomium; third, I consider other perspectives on Eros readily available to Phaedrus but which contradict his thesis and go unmentioned. Among these perspectives is the critical realization that the poets lie. Finally, I explore the respect in which an unexamined poetically-inspired disdain for death differs from the philosophical disdain for death that Plato puts in the mouth of Socrates.

2. Why Phaedrus?

Phaedrus epitomizes the callow lover of rhetoric. Especially at *Phaedrus* 228, he is depicted as an unreflective lover of charming speeches. As depicted by Plato, Phaedrus is an enthusiast, a fan of composition, committed to hearing and repeating as many charming examples of poetic composition as he can. Because his "love" is so obvious, Phaedrus is an example of someone with an eroticized response to the play of poetic genius expressed in words. Phaedrus personally embodies the phenomenon later described by Agathon (*Symp*. 196e 197a). Phaedrus represents all those who come to a performance, hoping for an experience so compelling that when the performance has ended, they can truthfully report that they loved it. Thus, Phaedrus represents the perfect target audience.

Phaedrus apparently takes it to be his function to urge (more gifted) others into creativity. In one dialogue, Socrates describes Phaedrus's relationship with discourse as well beyond the ordinary: "Of the discourses pronounced during your lifetime no one . . . has been responsible for more than you, whether by delivering them yourself or by compelling others to do so by one means or another."[1] In the *Symposium* (177d), Eryximachus credits Phaedrus as "the father of our subject."[2] Phaedrus is held responsible for Eryximachus's proposal that the symposiasts entertain each other with impromptu encomia to Eros.

Loving rhetoric uncritically, Phaedrus's grasp of Eros illustrates a mind formed, in terms of *Republic* 509, from psychological constructs available at the lowest level of Plato's divided line. Phaedrus's understanding is limited by the level of his grasp and the focus of his attention. He therefore identifies Eros with those portrayals provided by poets whose genius leads them to construct potent imaginative tales graspable at the lowest level of the divided line, *eikasia*.

Phaedrus readily accepts the challenge of setting out his own encomium to Eros first among the party. He confidently calls upon the resources of his well stocked memory and constructs his speech so that it reflects what he takes to be the most praiseworthy aspects of that god from among the verbal depictions he has, as we might say, learned by heart. His encomium is thus about what Phaedrus holds praiseworthy on the basis of an education that uncritically values the informative power of poetry and fine speech as a source of knowledge.

3. What Phaedrus Says

Significantly, Phaedrus begins his encomium by praising Eros for his amazing unborn origin, the quality of appearing apparently without cause. Phaedrus describes this quality as *thaumastos*, a word generally translated as "wonderful," but which also carries connotations of conjuring tricks. In Book X of the *Republic*, the *thaumatopoiia* produce amazement and delight both in children and in those adults who are ignorant and foolish. But reasonable men take "care against falling back again into this love which is childish."[3] By the standard of Book X of the *Republic* (608), Phaedrus ranges himself with the children, the ignorant and the foolish, for he is unashamedly prone to admire wonders. Among the wonders Phaedrus admires are those conjurers of speech who transform mere words into wonders and thus become themselves something wonderful as well.

It is Phaedrus's admiration of the wonder worker that first sets the parameters within which he praises Eros. In Stanley Rosen's phrase,

> The wonderful thing about Eros is that no one . . . tells of his having been born of parents: he has a genesis but not a generation.[4]

To prove the wondrous nature of Eros as the ultimate conjurer who appears amazingly on the world stage (Ta da!) without any geneology at all, Phaedrus refers to mysterious private (*idiotou*) sources. Bury discusses the possibility that *idiotou* in this context represents no more than a distinction between the prose writer and the poet. Plato uses the word *idiotou* to distinguish prose composition at *Phaedrus* 258d, *Laws* 890a, and *Republic* 366e. Bury comments:

> the term ἰδιώτης [idiotes] may be taken as a survival of the time when the poet alone had his work published at religious festivals, theatrical shows, etc.[5]

But even if this is all Phaedrus means, he nevertheless heightens the mystery of these mysterious private sources, for they go unquoted. Three published works are offered, instead, as further support for his point that Eros is most wonderful in having an ungenerated genesis. Phaedrus cites Hesiod's *Theogony* as testimony:

> Chaos first appeared, and then from Chaos rose broad-bosomed Earth, the sure and everlasting seat of all that is, and after, Eros. (*Symp*. 178b)

A summary reference to Acusileus further emphasizes the unborn origin of Eros as a primordial principle. Earth and Eros emerge from Chaos as a pair. The primacy of Earth is reduced to merely ordinal priority. Earth happens to have been mentioned first. Finally, Phaedrus cites Parmenides. In this citation, the amazing quality of Eros's ungenerated genesis becomes clear, for Parmenides holds that the abstract Genesis "devised Eros first of all the gods" (*Symp*. 178b).

Primordial Eros is older than Aphrodite. Eros therefore must have some initial function that precedes acting as the erotic complement of Aphrodite in her role of joining lovers together. In the initial scenario, the principles from which the cosmos derives produce the later phases by independent activity. Earth and Chaos never couple with each other. As Jean-Pierre Vernant reminds us, Chaos is neuter.[6] From Chaos others come into being (*ek Khaeos . . . egenonto*).[7] The Greek language uses the phrase "come into being" in a careful avoidance of any phrase that could suggest either begetting or bearing children. Gaia, a female principle, does bear children: *geinomai*. Gaia also brings forth *tikto* (*Theogony*, 126, 129, 131, 139) and without need of coupling. This reflects the mythic understanding of Gaia as fecund mother, parthenogenetically bringing forth offspring.[8] But it also reinforces the presumption that Eros does not couple. Before Gaia can couple, she must draw forth from within herself her future male partners, Ouranos the sky and Pontos the sea.

Gaia does bring forth. From Chaos, other principles come into being. Chaos and Gaia do not couple. Whatever power Eros provides, it cannot consist in promoting the union of two sexes for the creation of a new generation. Nor does Eros bring forth. No principle issues from Eros. In this initial stage, Eros merely appears. It is hard to imagine in what way Eros has or displays any special power.

Yet Eros is. Why should Eros appear third on the world stage if Eros has no functional necessity in this arrangement? If Eros has a functional necessity, of what does it consist? Vernant plausibly suggests that whatever is posited as the function of Eros in this triad, it must be appropriate to the characters present.[9] Surprisingly, this simple premise serves to specify the function of primordial Eros. After Eros appears, Erebos and Night come into being from within Chaos. Gaia brings forth otherness in Ouranos and Pontos. Eros thus functions to disturb the apparent integrity of the other two, promoting the disclosure of that which each contains within itself.

In Parmenides, neither Chaos nor Gaia are mentioned as pre-existing principles. Here, too, primordial Eros, old as the world, simply appears wondrously. Using Vernant's approach to the function of Eros in Hesiod as a basis reveals that the Eros of Parmenides functions first to provoke its own emergence from the abstract Genesis. Then it continues to function in its own unique capacity to promote other emergences as well. Eros creates by promoting the discovery of otherness hidden within the apparent integrity of self. Eros functions to bring that which is originally hidden and unrecognized out onto the world stage.

By the fifth century, Eros seems to have succeeded too well. Otherness is everywhere. The human population is organized into increasingly militant, threatening, conquest-oriented political structures. Yet Phaedrus holds that the primordial principle of Eros continues to provide an important function. Phaedrus praises Eros for unique beneficence, claiming that Eros alone can "light the beacon which a man must steer by when he sets out to live the better life"

(*Symp*. 178c). Does this mean that Eros now has a different function? How does Phaedrus's praise for this fifth-century function connect to the earlier primal function of the primordial God? According to Rosen,

> Phaedrus's words . . . deviate from the traditional Greek view. In effect, Phaedrus is sanctioning the subordination of political institutions to the gratification of individual desire.[10]

Although, in general, Rosen's views on the speakers in the *Symposium* are persuasive, I think it is hard to support the contention that Phaedrus's idea of the better life (*kalos biosesthai*) subordinates the political to the individual. Rather, Phaedrus portrays the better life as worthwhile because it promotes a singular political focus. Love's efficacy at shaming lovers into laudable behaviors is pictured by Phaedrus as functioning most appropriately on a battlefield, in the service of military conquest.

This is not immediately apparent. At first, Phaedrus seems to be claiming that Eros has equal commitment to promote every laudable act and to dissuade devotees from any shameful public behavior:

> What I say is this: if a man in love is found doing something shameful, or accepting shameful treatment because he is a coward and makes no defense, then nothing would give him more pain than being seen by the boy he loves—not even being seen by his father or his comrades. We see the same thing also in the boy. . . . He is especially ashamed before his lover when he is caught in something shameful. (*Symp*. 178d-e)

Here Phaedrus apparently claims that the social value of erotic love is its widespread effectiveness at producing shame, which serves to deter inglorious cowardly behavior. But immediately following, Phaedrus reveals his own reductive identification of glorious behavior with valor resulting in death:

> If only there were a way to start a city or an army made up of lovers and the boys they love. . . . Even a few of them in battle side by side would conquer all the world. . . . No one is so base that true love could not inspire him with courage and make him as brave as if he'd been born a hero. (*Symp*. 179a-b)

Phaedrus's subsequent selection of meaningful love stories reveals how completely his understanding of Eros is identified with this singularly reductive function. As he says, "no one will die for you but a lover, and a lover will do this even if she's a woman" (*Symp*. 179b).

Indeed, Phaedrus first describes the love-motivated death of a woman. According to the myth, Admetus "the Pious" is told that although he is destined to die, the gods will accept a substitute if anyone voluntarily dies in his place. Desperate, he asks his aged parents and then his friends, but only his bride Alcestis willingly offers to give up her life to save his. He happily accepts her sacrifice.

Yet as Phaedrus recounts the tale, the same erotic self-sacrifice that brings her to die in place of Admetus wins her reprieve from death itself. "The gods . . . sent her soul back from the dead" (*Symp*. 179d). In Phaedrus's story, Alcestis and Admetus share a "happily ever after" ending. The understanding of death as final is contravened.

This contravention puzzled the fifth-century Greeks, for the myth provides two alternative explanations. In what is taken to be the matriarchal variant, recounted by Apollodorus, Persephone refuses to allow a wife to die in place of her husband and therefore sends Alcestis back into the world of the living. In what is presumably the patriarchal version of the same tale, Euripides has Heracles wrestle Death to restore Alcestis to life. Heracles' motivation is especially noteworthy, since he describes his intent as the desire to return good to Admetus who had been hospitable to him. Alcestis in Euripides' variant is simply a means to Admetus's good.

Phaedrus seems to offer a third explanation: Death's dominion fails to hold in this case precisely because Eros is so deeply implicated in Alcestis's act. Alcestis returns to life because her behavior demonstrates the driving force of love as motivating a pure altruism, a hopeless self-sacrifice so willing that the God of Love rewards his acolyte's devotion with a return to the life that devotion interrupted.

Phaedrus contrasts the strength and purity of Alcestis's love with the less successful example set by Orpheus. Inspired by his love, Orpheus is willing to defy Death. But in Phaedrus's terms, Orpheus loves less fully than does Alcestis:

> lacking the courage to die as Alcestis died for love, and choosing rather to scheme his way, living, into Hades. (*Symp*. 179d)

Orpheus is willing to defy death only to the extent of entering Hades. Because he is unwilling to die to prove his love, Phaedrus judges that Orpheus is not fully inspired by Eros, not a true devotee of the God who motivates self-sacrificing deaths.

The third example, Achilles, most fully realizes Phaedrus's ideal of love-inspiring death. "And this I say is why [the gods] paid more honor to Achilles than to Alcestis" (*Symp*. 180b). Taken together, these examples reveal a pattern suggesting that Phaedrus identifies Eros with the service of a singular purpose: motivating mortals to sacrifice their lives willingly. No alternatives, not generation, not intimacy, not caring or creativity has any place in this ultimately reductive monistic understanding of the power of love. Stripped of rhetorical flourishes, the telos of the erotic impulse is death.

In particular, the pattern of Phaedrus's encomium makes it clear that for him the best possible death results from hopeless courage expended in battle. As Kenneth Dover has observed, the Greeks found that

> homosexual eros can inspire as much unselfish devotion as heterosexual. It was certainly exploited for military purposes and to good military effect,

> the erastes and eromenons displaying to each other their readiness to endure pain and death.[11]

Phaedrus makes himself a spokesperson for precisely this exploitation, arguing that pairing lovers within sight of each other in a single army unit will best promote that willingness to die that he equates with military courage. The political implications are spelled out in a straightforward claim

> If a city or an army could be composed of none but lover and beloved . . . [they] might conquer . . . the whole world in arms. (*Symp*. 178-179)

On the basis of the stories told, the erotic implications are equally straightforward. Those who truly die for love do not truly die. Alcestis returns to life and gains immortality through poetic retellings as well. Through the poetic rendering of his story in the *Iliad*, Achilles achieves undying fame, and an immortality in which he is worshiped as a cult hero across Greece.

4. What Has Gone Unsaid?

The organization of Phaedrus's encomium as a whole imitates, in certain important respects, what Phaedrus depicts as the pattern of erotic inspiration. For Phaedrus, Eros is the ultimate conjurer who brings forth that which is hidden in such a way as to amaze the onlookers. Beginning with Eros's amazing origin, Phaedrus imitatively practices the conjurer's techniques of suppressing alternatives and misdirecting audience attention. As Rosen (1968) points out, the initial quote from Hesiod (*Theogony* 116-22) is traditionally taken to read

> Indeed Chaos first came to be, and next broad-bosomed Earth, always steadfast seat of all the deathless ones who hold the peaks of snowy Olympus and murky Tartarus.[12]

Suppression of Hesiod's reference to the deathless Gods shuts both immortality and its contrasting counterpart, mortality, away from verbal depiction. Moreover, Phaedrus speaks as though one can reasonably conclude that Eros has no genealogy because three authorities mention none. This might be called sleight of tongue, since Phaedrus must know full well that other authorities have proclaimed Eros to be the offspring of parents. Alcaeus, for example, makes Eros the son of Zephyros and Iris. For Simonides, Aphrodite is impregnated by Ares and gives birth to Eros. In the *Hippolytus*, Euripides calls Eros the son of Zeus. Sappho considers Eros son of Uranus and Earth. Fifth-century Orphic cosmogony apparently held the theory that "black winged Night, a goddess . . . courted by the Wind . . . laid a silver egg in the Womb of Darkness; and that Eros whom some call Phanes (revealer) was hatched from this egg and set the Universe in motion."[13] Since this myth is expounded in Aristophanes' play "The Birds,"[14] and since Aristophanes is among those present while Phaedrus praises Eros as unborn, Phaedrus's suppressions could not possibly go unnoticed. They merely go unremarked.

When Phaedrus describes the social utility of Eros, he again practices techniques that force attention in a way that seems to parallel the power of Eros over the erotic devotee. Thus, human devotees of Eros focus on one idea alone: life without the one they love is not worth living. Dominated by Eros, so that one chooses self-sacrifice over self-preservation, the devotee proves in circular fashion that life can hold no value without the continued presence of the lost love. Yet Phaedrus has chosen stories that describe the erotic hero beyond the moment of death. Thus Eros is portrayed as the great trickster who can pull off the ultimate trick. For the devotee of Eros, death has no dominion. Or so the storytellers say, for both Achilles and Alcestis live on through poetic tales. Foremost among the possibilities that Phaedrus has suppressed is the possibility that the poets lie.

The political import of Phaedrus's encomium to Eros involves another suppression. Phaedrus claims that love inspires successful military campaigns. He does not dwell upon the fact that the military heroes who presumably make victory possible by their energetic willingness to die will not return to enjoy their city's triumph. The logic of military victory through courage that leads to death requires that the death-inducing ideal of Eros promotes world conquest only if the ideal lovers, those most fully inspired by Eros, die gallantly on the field of battle. Thus, the Sacred Band of Thebes, an army composed entirely of pairs of homosexual lovers, died to a man at Khaironea in 338.[15] Their deaths, like the deaths Phaedrus suggestively depicts, follow from the internalization of the romantic ideal brought forth by poetic retellings that construct a conventional understanding of what it is to truly love.

The monolithic conquest oriented implications of this romantic view of Eros reflect a reductive stereotype of manliness. Peggy Reeves Sanday found the equation of masculine courage with violent mindless aggression evolves under conditions of threat. When once courage is defined as violently aggressive, a culture might even embrace mass slaughter in defense of threatened traditions.[16] Phaedrus's false and misleading universalization promotes one response to threat as if it were the only response to threat. The telos of politics is reduced to world conquest. Eros is valuable only as it serves this aggressive political ideal. The value of Eros is falsely reduced to the production of willing death, preferably upon a battlefield.

5. Poetically-Based Disdain for Death Distinguished from the Philosophically-Based

Phaedrus's encomium to Eros reveals itself as a reductive, one-sided, militaristic and death-inducing understanding of Eros. In this section, I discuss the possibility that such a distortion of the erotic is fostered by Phaedrus's habit of uncritically assuming that poetry can provide an easily accessible grasp of truth, whether about Eros or anything else. To do this, I contrast the philosopher's disdain for death with the disdain that Phaedric lovers come to feel.

Plato (*Phaedo* 64a) consistently asserts that philosophers,

> those who really apply themselves in the right way to philosophy are directly and of their own accord preparing themselves for dying and death.[17]

In the *Apology*, Socrates insists that "in every kind of danger there are plenty of devices for avoiding death if you are unscrupulous. . . . The difficulty is not so much to escape death as to escape from doing wrong" (39a).[18] In the *Crito*, Socrates accepts the imperative "do not think more of your children or your life or of anything else than you think of what is right" (54b).[19] In the *Republic* (429c), courage is defined as a kind of steadfast holding of right and lawful opinion about what is terrible in the face of pleasures, pains, fears, and desires.[20]

Philosophers disdain death. Yet their disdain must be distinguished from the willingness to die that Phaedrus holds to be the benefit Eros confers upon the polis. One important difference focuses on the way in which poetically idealized lovers are unshakably immune to reasoning once they begin their drive toward death. For the Phaedric lover, the romantically idealized protagonist of poetic license, life is worth living only when attachment with the beloved other makes life worth living. Deprived of the special erotic object, life so lacks redemptive value that these Phaedric devotees of eros are eager to sacrifice their lives in the service of some militaristic political aim. In Phaedrus's account, once a lover is motivated to sacrifice, any contingent cause will do, so long as poets enhance the illusion that such deaths are romantic.

Nothing could be further from the motivations that Socrates seeks to inspire. For philosophers, continual exercise of judgment remains essential. Death is chosen where the only choice is to die rather than engage in wrongdoing that will corrupt the rational part of the soul.

Both Socrates and Phaedrus agree that the loving attachment to something beyond one's own mere life is that which makes life worth living, that without which life is not worth living. But Phaedrus accepts the poetic assumption, that the crucial "something" is provided by one's attachment to another person. Socrates insists that the quality of life depends upon the possibility of philosophic inquiry as expressed in the claim "the unexamined life is not worth living" (*Apology* 38a).[21]

The romantic convention that true love consists in self-sacrifice, with death as its appropriate expression, can readily be turned to the service of unworthy political goals. Phaedrus celebrates Eros, in which love leads to death, for the benefit of the political order. Grateful to those who died in order to make victory possible, the conquering polis provides poets to sing deathless paeans in praise of the undying fame of these dead heroes. As Rosen noted, "It is . . . dramatically appropriate that the last word of Phaedrus's speech should be 'the dead.'"[22] Phaedrus depicts Eros as the great conjurer, but it is the romantic illusions created by the poets that reduce Eros to the service of political opportunism. Through the good offices of praise singers, Eros serves to produce politically useful, philosophically unwarranted, self-sacrificing deaths.

6. Conclusion

The political import of Phaedrus's encomium to Eros runs deeper than its militaristic message to include three less obvious points.

1. Individuals like Phaedrus imitate that which they love to the extent and in the way they understand love; Phaedrus, the callow lover of the amazing, who loves speeches simply because they are wonderful, relies uncritically upon the techniques of conjury to describe a trickster god.

2. Eros, as a concept, is distorted and deformed by socially constructed understandings such as are fostered by poetry. The primordial function of Eros is thus tamed and turned to the service of producing socially useful shame. Ultimately this usefulness reduces to the service of producing lovers and beloveds willing to emulate romantic heroes in their energetic willingness to die rather than be shamed before the one to whom they are erotically attached. This distorted Eros is itself the product of poetic license, uncritically practiced to bring forth a philosophically unenlightened vision of beauty, co-opted by a political order bent upon world conquest.

3. The psyche grasps different levels of reality in accordance with the functions set out on the divided line. At least in the case of Phaedrus, the level of one's grasp promotes different forms of political functioning. Phaedrus's grasp of reality is conditioned by his reliance on *eikasia*, a poetically based understanding of the good life. That such an understanding can support a politics of unlimited militarism aiming at world conquest offers philosophers in more modern democracies an important challenge. We should attend to the ways in which our own poets are licensed to construct our contemporary understandings of Eros, in the awareness that our most romantic aspirations can be co-opted to politically corrupt ends.[23]

Notes

1. Plato, *Phaedrus* (224b), in Edith Hamilton and Huntington Cairns, eds., *The Collected Dialogues of Plato* (New York: Random House, 1959), 489.

2. πατὴρ τοῦ λογοῦ [pater tou logou]; R. G. Bury, ed., *The Symposium of Plato* (Cambridge, Eng.: W. Heffer and Sons, 1909), 20; *Symposium*, trans. Alexander Nehamas and Paul Woodruff (Indianapolis: Hackett, 1989), 8.

3. Plato, *Republic*, in Hamilton and Cairns, *Collected Dialogues*, 833.

4. Stanley Rosen, *Plato's Symposium* (New Haven: Yale University Press, 1968), 45.

5. Bury, *Symposium*, 22.

6. Jean-Pierre Vernant, "One . . . Two . . . Three: EROS," trans. Deborah Lyons, in David M. Halperin, John J. Winkler, and Froma I. Zeitlin, eds., *Before Sexuality* (Princeton: Princeton University Press, 1990), 465-78, at 465.

7. Hesiod, *Theogonia*, ed. Friedrich Solmsen, in *Works* (Oxford: Clarendon Press, 1970), 10.

8. Page Du Bois, *Sowing the Body: Psychoanalysis and Ancient Representations of Women* (Chicago: University of Chicago Press, 1988).

9. Vernant, "One . . . Two . . . Three: EROS," 465-6.

10. Rosen, *Plato's Symposium*, 51.

11. Kenneth James Dover, *Greek Homosexuality* (Cambridge, Mass.: Harvard University Press, 1978), 192.

12. Hesiod, *Theogony*, 10.

13. Robert Graves, *The Greek Myths*, vol. 1 (New York: Penguin, 1955), 30.

14. Aristophanes, "The Birds," trans. Patric Dickinson, in *Plays*, vol. 2 (New York: Oxford University Press, 1970), 34.

15. Dover, *Greek Homosexuality*, 192.

16. Peggy Sanday, *Female Power and Male Dominance* (Cambridge, Eng.: Cambridge University Press, 1981), 181, 231.

17. In Hamilton and Cairns, *Collected Dialogues*, 46.

18. *Ibid.*, 24.

19. *Ibid.*, 39.

20. *Ibid.*, 671.

21. *Ibid.*, 23.

22. Rosen, *Plato's Symposium*, 59.

23. I want to thank Alan Soble for a sympathetic and helpful reading of the first draft of this paper, and Carol S. Gould for the close critical reading she gave as commentator on the version presented at the Society for the Philosophy of Sex and Love.

Carol S. Gould
(photograph: Michael A. Taylor)

Author of "Response to Professor Dandekar's
Analysis of Phaedrus's Praise of Eros"
Paper presented at the Society for the Philosophy of Sex and Love
during the
Eastern Division Meeting of The American Philosophical Association
Boston, Mass., 29 December 1990

Fifty-Five

ROMANTIC AND PHILOSOPHICAL VIEWS OF EROS IN PLATO'S *SYMPOSIUM*

Carol S. Gould

Natalie Dandekar presents an interpretation of Phaedrus's speech,[1] a welcome gesture given the scarcity of such treatments in the secondary literature on the *Symposium*.[2] Though Phaedrus is the "father of the discussion" and will become the eponymous character of Plato's next major work on eros, scholars tend to ignore this speech, perhaps because it seems so insubstantial and so remote from Plato's philosophical concerns. But in taking a closer glance, one cannot help but notice that Phaedrus introduces a crucial philosophical theme in the dialogue, that of eros as a source of courage and virtue more generally. Phaedrus considers eros the most powerful and reliable motivational source of virtuous (especially courageous) action. Plato agrees that eros leads to virtue, but he rejects Phaedrus's romantic notion of eros[3] and his conventional notion of virtue. Because Plato tacitly rejects Phaedrus's ideas in developing his own, Phaedrus's speech has more significance than it might initially appear. Moreover, Phaedrus brings to light, as we shall see, a penetrating insight about romantic love. We must be grateful to Dandekar for riveting our attention to this passage.

1.

Dandekar finds much of interpretative and philosophical interest in Phaedrus's speech. Phaedrus, she tells us, represents the person susceptible to poetry, rhetoric, and images. As a lover of poetry, he has internalized the values of the poets, including that which they attach to poetry itself. As such, he is the product of "an education that uncritically values the informative power of poetry and fine speech as a source of knowledge" (561). Dandekar insinuates that Plato, with his well-known contempt for poetry and rhetoric, chose Phaedrus to express Platonically objectionable ideas. What are these ideas that Dandekar finds embedded in Phaedrus's speech?

As Dandekar has it, Phaedrus defends a "singularly reductive" account of eros. By "singularly reductive," she must mean that he reduces the essence of eros to one property or function. Moreover, she avers, this concept "reflects a singularly unpleasant relationship between poetry and politics" (559). She makes it difficult for the reader to accept her claim that this account is "reductive," because she never specifies exactly what this one property or function is, whether it is being the source of shame, the source of the human willingness to die, the source of otherness in either the individual or the political arena, or the source of poetic service to a militaristic state. Whatever her view, Phaedrus's eros makes one desire to appear noble or worthy in the eyes of the loved one, and thus willing to die in battle. Dandekar tacitly suggests that the poets can make us "disdain death" by exploiting the immature human inclination to preserve the erotic relationship at *any* cost. Thus, the poets, by glamorizing death in the cause of eros, can serve the interests of a militaristic state (such as Athens). Such conceptions of eros as this, Dandekar maintains, show us that erotic ideals are socially constructed and potentially dangerous, given the priority of eros in human life. Therefore, she argues in her conclusion, responsible intellectuals must attend to those potentially nefarious myths in their own cultures. Thus, as she has it, Phaedrus's speech directs us anew to the dangers of poetry and to the special perils of erotic poetry.

Before analyzing Dandekar's treatment, let us recall the basic structure of Phaedrus's speech. It divides neatly into three parts, excluding the epilogue: (1) Phaedrus's praise of eros's wondrousness and antiquity (178a6-c2); (2) his praise of eros's power to guide us through life by giving us a sense of shame and pride (178c2-179b3); (3) his claim that eros can make a person willing to die for the one he loves (179b4-180b5), a view in support of which he adduces three examples. Later we shall see that Dandekar's interpretation turns in part on how she construes the relation between (2) and (3). Let us look more closely at the details of her interpretation.

Dandekar's interpretation is rich and provocative, but basically she endeavors to prove the following three interpretative theses: (1) eros, for Phaedrus, is wonderful in his power and nature, but most remarkable in his power to deceive: eros is the "ultimate conjurer." As such, he can make death seem desirable, even prudent, and thus eros can be exploited by the poets in the militaristic interests of the state. (2) Phaedrus himself is a conjuror; like a poet, he makes his audience believe one set of propositions in part by suppressing evidence for another, perhaps more plausible, set of propositions. (3) Phaedrus identifies virtue (so felicitously inspired by eros) with willingness to die.

2.

Let us consider Dandekar's first thesis. Dandekar takes Phaedrus to focus on eros's wondrousness right from the start where he remarks on eros's great antiquity and what is arguably his unborn origin.[4] Phaedrus describes eros as *thaumastos* in this regard. Dandekar finds great significance in Phaedrus's use of *thaumastos*, which can indeed mean "wonderful" or "marvelous." In support of her thesis (1), she connects this to Plato's use of the compound cognate *thaumatopoioi* in *Republic* X, which refers to those who produce wonders and illusions. Plato uses the term also at the start of Book VII (*Republic* 514b5) to mean "maker of an illusion," which does indeed have the connotations Dandekar suggests. The term *thaumastos*, like our "wonderful," can convey other senses.[5] One such meaning is "admirable" or "excellent." Given that Phaedrus promptly moves to the subject of virtue, might he not be using it with such moral connotations here? This seems to be the way Eryximachus uses it at the start of his speech (*Symp*. 186b1).[6]

Moreover, Dandekar makes far too much of Phaedrus's negative theogony. Phaedrus wants to praise eros for his great antiquity, a proof (*tekmērion*) of which is that no one speaks of his parents. He does not say that eros had no parents (though this might be a reasonable inductive inference from what he does say), but that no one mentions them. It might seem odd to connect his advanced age with his benefits to humanity, yet it is simply a rhetorical way of praising someone for his long, august lineage. This might be all Phaedrus means to do. But even without the support of linguistic usage or genealogy, Dandekar's (1) has plausibility. Phaedrus does see eros as a conjurer, and arguably with good reason. On Dandekar's view, Phaedrus depicts an eros that (a) infuses a lover with virtue, (b) makes a lover willing to die and, therefore, (c) inspires courageous action in even the most physically perilous of situations and (d) reveals otherness, especially that "otherness hidden within the apparent integrity of self" (562). The conjuring trick, on Dandekar's construal, is to make death appear not only desirable, but also a form of life. So, Phaedrus would be making eros a handmaiden to, rather than an enemy of, thanatos. Dandekar does not specify whether the revelation of otherness is one of his conjuring tricks, but here Phaedrus does seem to be on to something important. Putting aside until later some of the issues involved with (a)-(c), let us consider what Phaedrus might be saying and why it might be Platonically reprehensible.

Eros does, in an important sense, make one willing to die in that those in love, at least in Phaedrus's sense of romantic infatuation, will feel inclined to do anything for a beloved. Euripides' portrayal of Alcestis shows us a person willing to abandon everything for her loved one, as does his portrayal of Phaedra. Examples from literature abound. Love, on Phaedrus's conception, does deceive us into seeing the world, or at least one constituent (the loved person) as it is not. This illusion is one of the most powerful motifs in poetry. Phaedrus is here anticipating Stendhal's crystallization,[7] a process painted by poets as diverse in sensibility as Euripides, Chaucer, George Eliot, Proust, and Nabokov.

This illusion of the beloved's perfection, without which all else in life pales, can lead to an abnegation of one's obligations to the self, as Alcestis so poignantly exemplifies. Eros can bring a death to the self as one knows it,[8] and bring to light a fault at the core of an apparently integral self. For Plato, only one with a loosely formed philosophical and emotional identity could be vulnerable to Phaedrean eros. It is Phaedrean eros that reveals the "hidden otherness" of which Dandekar speaks. Platonic eros, possible only for a unified self, would disclose the integrity of the self.

Platonic eros directs us not to other individuals. It might involve another individual who accompanies the lover in his quest for understanding. But that individual is not the object of love. This kind of eros, not the Phaedrean, improves us ethically, for Plato. As Martha Nussbaum has powerfully shown in her analysis of the *Symposium*,[9] Plato is not insensitive to the appeal of romantic love (which Nussbaum finds embodied in Alcibiades, not Phaedrus). But, to return to our earlier focus, Phaedrean love is an intoxication that imperils our judgment and annihilates the ego. Platonic love clarifies our mental vision and fortifies the ego.

Phaedrus's eros is, then, a wizard who can make us think that love for another person is life affirming rather than suicidal, morally invigorating rather than enervating. And Dandekar rightly intimates that Phaedrean eros, with its many emotional and epistemological facets, has a glittering allure for the poetic sensibility. A skillful poet can make even the most common person assume the aspect of a god when viewed through a lover's eyes. More dangerously, a poet with certain motivations might make Phaedrean love seem the most valuable goal in human life, as might a skillful rhetorician who has been duped by such poets. Is Dandekar right in describing Phaedrus himself as either a poetical or rhetorical conjurer, as implied by her thesis (2)?

3.

Her second thesis brings to mind the self-reference in the various speeches that other commentators have noticed: some of the portrayals of eros, most saliently those of Agathon and Socrates, describe the speaker as well. On Dandekar's reading, Phaedrus "imitatively [of eros] practices the conjurer's techniques of suppressing alternatives and misdirecting audience attention" (565). Phaedrus, she alleges, deceives his listeners with regard to several matters. Her frequent use of "suppresses" makes clear that she views these deceptions as intentional. Phaedrus must therefore be sly rather than inept or benighted. She pays Phaedrus a compliment in saying that his discourse is fallacious by design. But Phaedrus is no Aristophanes or Socrates. Let us examine the suppressions she ascribes to him, which she sets forth in the penultimate section of her essay.

First of all, she charges Phaedrus with suppressing the mythical accounts of eros's parentage, such as those of Alcaeus, Simonides, Euripides, Sappho, and Aristophanes himself. These "suppressions," she says, must have been noticed, even though they go unremarked. Interestingly, each of the accounts she mentions attributes a different lineage to eros. But none of these accounts is a suppression; rather, each is a mythic account, which is why none of the speakers takes umbrage. Alternative myths about eros or any other mythic figure were in the air. Any myth, by its nature, has some elasticity, as these various genealogies of eros show. Thus, the poets offer conflicting accounts of one and the same subject. Perhaps it would be more helpful to think of a myth as more of a general formula so that fashioning a mythic account would be like playing a figured bass line in a baroque musical score.[10] So, on this matter of eros's parentage, Phaedrus is not suppressing alternatives. His audience's silence indicates not some nefarious collusion, but simply their cultural expectations.

Phaedrus's second alleged suppression is that death is preferable to losing either the devotion or respect of the loved one. Yet, Phaedrus's poetic authorities depict the "erotic hero beyond the moment of death" (566). So, in a sense, death does not affect the true Phaedrean lover. Phaedrus not only suppresses the unfortunate finality of death, but more seriously "that the poets lie." Here we find a contradiction in Dandekar's account: in the second section of her paper ("Why Phaedrus?"), she argues that Phaedrus exemplifies the reliance on *eikasia*. A lover of images, he "uncritically values the informative power of poetry and fine speech as a source of knowledge" (561). If her depiction of Phaedrus is apt, then Phaedrus could not possibly commit this second set of suppressions. If Phaedrus knew, even inchoately, that the poets lie and had he reflected on the implications of the stories he had chosen, he would not be a lover of images. Such a suppression would require epistemic processes at a much higher level than Dandekar ascribes to Phaedrus. Either she has misjudged his epistemological faculties or he is not suppressing the poets' prevaricating tendencies.

Phaedrus's third supposed suppression, related to the second, is that love is valuable for inspiring courage in battle. The problem here is that it is not of value to the one who dies fighting bravely, for he will not benefit from the victory. To romanticize military courage, then, is to dupe those who have to fight, or as Dandekar would have it, to "suppress" an alternative valuation. Dandekar here leads us to an important issue, namely the paradox of valuing courage within a eudaimonistic ethical system. Courage does seem to conflict with the eudaimonistic aim of human flourishing. But Plato takes it to be crucial for actualizing the best human potentials. He demonstrates this in his various portraits of Socrates, who, Dandekar points out, expresses a philosophical contempt for valuing life under any circumstances. As she emphasizes, he conveys almost a "disdain for death." Nowhere does Plato underscore Socrates' physical courage as vividly as at the end of the *Symposium* in Alcibiades' moving speech about Socrates (220a-221c). If Socrates embodies Platonic virtue, then Plato sees great value in courageous behavior in battle, a subject to which we shall return shortly.

If Phaedrus is "suppressing" the truth about the value of courage, then Plato would be eager to reveal that alternative later. But evidently, Plato accepts the ethical merits of risking one's life in battle. While Plato does not validate such action by appealing to the importance of appearing noble to the object of one's infatuation, he would not object to presenting such an appeal to those for whom romantic love has priority over philosophy. This is, after all, the point of Plato's noble lie in his *Republic* (414c). If some people cannot follow a philosophical justification for their civic obligations, then political leaders will have to appeal to fictional tales to induce those people to act responsibly. Thus, Plato allows that the poets in a sense can tell falsehoods without suppressing the truth, because some people are responsive only to images (as Dandekar indicates) and images can have their own sort of truth. Plato has intriguingly presented two poetic defenses of military courage in the *Symposium*, in the first and the last speech. Each account includes an exemplar of courage: the first of courage born from romantic infatuation, the second from philosophical eros. If Phaedrus has suppressed a truth about the value of courage, Plato does not disapprove, for he deems such suppressions pragmatically necessary. Whether *we* should disapprove is another issue, one to which Dandekar has admirably drawn our attention.

4.

Let us turn now to Dandekar's thesis (3), that Phaedrus reduces virtue to the willingness to die. Eros, Phaedrus tells us, inspires virtue. A person in love wants nothing more than to be admired by the one he loves. The more vividly he imagines how he appears to his beloved, the stronger will be his sense of shame and pride. Phaedrean love therefore can fortify one's resolve to act according to one's principles. Though Phaedrus does not explicitly articulate this, one thing that can undermine our resolve is the anticipation of pain or the perception of danger. A lover, if Phaedrus is right, will be more likely to resist the inclination to avoid pain if he feels himself under the eyes of his loved one. This is why Phaedrus exclaims that an army of amorous couples would be triumphant: its soldiers could be counted on not to desert or to subordinate the interests of the cause to their own individual interests. (Phaedrus does not divulge how the lover should adjudicate a conflict between the interests of the polis and the interests of his boyfriend.)

At this point in the speech, which is the second part, Phaedrus invokes this example not in order to reduce virtue to fighting bravely, but to present the strongest case of a person acting against inclination. As Diotima emphasizes, self-preservation and the avoidance of pain are among our strongest drives. The Phaedrean lover has at best a fragile sense of self, but nonetheless can be relied upon to perform virtuous acts, *even* when they threaten his life.

Phaedrus moves to the third part of his speech to argue that an inamorato will die for his beloved. He adduces three examples familiar to his audience: Alcestis, Orpheus, and Achilles. Dandekar links this with the second part of the speech, so that eros's capacity to make us virtuous amounts to the willingness to die, and as her remarks on the masculine ideals of courage suggest, to die in battle. She thus takes the third part of Phaedrus's speech as illustrative and supportive of the second. Are the two parts conceptually related in this way? Or does Phaedrus make an entirely distinct point in the third part?

Arguably, Phaedrus is making here an independent claim. In the second part, he contends that eros improves us morally (or at least our moral behavior). In the third part, with his contention that a lover will do anything for you, even die, he shows the utility of eros. Phaedrus begins the third part of his speech with the transitional *kai mēn*, an expression that often introduces a new idea.[11] Given the difference between the ideas in the second and third parts of Phaedrus's speech, we must view the expression as bringing out yet another advantage of eros, especially since Alcestis is a woman and one who dies peacefully.

Phaedrus's conception of virtue, then, does not reduce to willingness to die in military glory. This is not to say that it is unflawed. Phaedrus sees virtue in terms of a set of conventionally sanctioned acts that one should perform in order to find favor in the eyes of others. This could elicit only antipathy from Plato, who considers virtue a motivational force dependent on the interior justice of the agent. Is Phaedrus tacitly urging us to reject self-value and psychic integrity as ethical goals? Or, is he adding his voice to those of Proust, Euripides and the others who suggest we recoil from the seductive delights of romantic love? This leads to new problems about the nature of poetry.[12]

Notes

1. Natalie Dandekar, "Eros, Romantic Illusion, and Political Opportunism (*Symposium* 178-180)," this volume, 559-69; page references to this essay are supplied in the text.
2. In preparing this essay I used Kenneth Dover's edition of the Greek text, *Plato: Symposium* (Cambridge, Eng.: Cambridge University Press, 1982).
3. Alexander Nehamas makes this point in his introduction to the translation of *Symposium* he did with Paul Woodruff. See Nehamas and Woodruff, *Plato: Symposium* (Indianapolis: Hackett, 1989), xvi.
4. Dandekar's interpretation is in the tradition of Stanley Rosen, with its focus on eros's questionable parentage (or lack thereof). See Rosen, *Plato's Symposium* (New Haven: Yale University Press, 1968), 45-50.
5. As Henry George Liddell and Robert Scott indicate, in *A Greek-English Lexicon*, revised by Henry Stuart Jones with the assistance of Roderick McKenzie (Oxford: Clarendon Press, 1968), 786.
6. Dover seems to agree in his note on the passage; he translates *hōs megas kai thaumastos* as "how great and wonderful" (*Plato: Symposium*, 106).
7. Anne Carson connects Stendhal's crystallization to Greek thought in her splendid *Eros the Bittersweet: An Essay* (Princeton: Princeton University Press, 1986), 63-4. She does not relate it to the speech of Phaedrus, however.
8. Carson also has some compelling remarks on the death of the self inherent in eros, but along different lines than those offered here. See *ibid.*, esp. the chapter "Losing the Edge," 39-45.
9. See Nussbaum's chapter on the speech of Alcibiades in *The Fragility of Goodness* (Cambridge, Eng.: Cambridge University Press, 1986), 165-99.
10. I am grateful to Professor Christy Sorum (Union College) for many discussions on the nature of myth.
11. See Herbert Weir Smyth, *Greek Grammar* (Cambridge, Mass.: Harvard University Press, 1956), 659; J. D. Denniston, *The Greek Particles* (Oxford: Clarendon, 1954), 351-8.
12. This essay is a revision of my comments on Natalie Dandekar's presentation (at a meeting of the Society for the Philosophy of Sex and Love). For helpful remarks, I am grateful to the members of the audience, especially Irving Singer and Josiah B. Gould.

Joseph Kupfer

Author of “The Power of Love, the Impotence of Infatuation”
Paper presented at the Society for the Philosophy of Sex and Love
during the
Central Division Meeting of The American Philosophical Association
Chicago, Ill., 25 April 1991

Fifty-Six

ROMANTIC LOVE

Joseph Kupfer

This essay examines romantic love, a subject deserving more philosophical attention than it has received. The romantic relationship is culturally conditioned and historically bound, since most cultures have not had any conception of romantic love. But romantic love is still important, especially in light of the growing emphasis it receives throughout the world today. I will describe an ideal, realized less frequently than we wish but sought after by most. My discussion focuses on the way romantic love involves positive redefinition of the lovers. I begin by distinguishing romantic love from infatuation, and conclude by showing how it is aligned with falling in love.

1.

When infatuated, we are not just attracted to another, but are preoccupied with him or her, overwhelmed by the frequency and force of our daydreams and pipe-dreams. However, we are not truly absorbed in the beloved; we are, instead, taken up by an unrealistic image. We have an incomplete perception, glossing over or missing unattractive traits. Infatuation tends to focus on apparent rather than underlying qualities of the beloved. Looks, charm, and wit, for instance, enthrall us. Infatuation usually hits quickly, but to appreciate qualities such as sensitivity or wisdom takes time.

Infatuation is also unrealistic in that its object is as much the product of the infatuate's imagination as his or her perceptions. The infatuate embroiders what is perceived, adds characteristics not even there to be embroidered on, and fantasizes. Just as this fantasizing is tailored to what has been selectively perceived, so, too, is selective perception dictated by the readiness to fantasize. We seize on those features that lend themselves to our penchant for imaginative embellishment: our beloved's voice, grace, cleverness, or spontaneous warmth.

Distance and ignorance keep infatuation alive by giving the infatuate's imagination room to take flight, preventing the hard reality of the beloved from intruding. This is corroborated by the way infatuation evaporates under prolonged or demanding interaction with the real person. The reality of the other, combined with our real needs, destroys the fantastic overlay in all but the most insulated and determined of the smitten. Infatuation is intense but fragile. It can evolve into romantic love, but only if the disillusionment is not too disappointing and enough of the infatuate's love-construct can accommodate the other's real personality.

Infatuation might be additionally unrealistic if the infatuate wishes or expects the beloved to fulfill needs and solve problems he or she cannot. The fabricated object of infatuation can shape our conception of happiness. This might skew the lovers' understanding of themselves, promoting an unrealistic conception of their needs and what will satisfy them. The distortion of the beloved thereby invites distortion in our self-understanding, and we risk becoming victims of our fantasies. The insulation of infatuation prevents the self-examination and discovery that results from having our self-conceptions challenged. Illusions about ourselves can persist when not subject to the interrogation of sustained interaction.

Writers like Stendhal advocate infatuation,[1] calling it love because they see no alternative. He sees elaborating on selective perception as the only way to avoid the boredom of loving a real person. For Stendhal, the person is but a stimulus for a stream of fantasies. Being finite, real people's selves are exhaustible because comprehendible, and infatuation hinges on the excitement of novelty. Since this novelty can be provided only by our imaginations, reality is denigrated in favor of fantasy's plasticity.

In contrast to infatuation is romantic love, which develops in realistic perception of the beloved. Where infatuation feeds on a fantastic image to satisfy our needs, real and imagined, love is driven by appreciation of the other's individuality. Instead of being absorbed in our fantastic creation, we are focused on a real personality. Now Stendhal's problem arises. Once we fathom our beloveds, once we know them "inside out," how can we avoid boredom? Shirley Robin Letwin argues that fantasy is not needed for love to persist, because its object is "constantly creating itself" and so "cannot be used up."[2] This contention should first be qualified and then extended. Not everyone is "constantly creating" the self. Some stop growing, jeopardizing love the way Stendhal predicts. What Letwin probably means is that we all have the distinctively human potential to keep growing.

Lack of growth or self-creation does cause love's decay. An extension of Letwin's thought, however, also provide a response to this threat. We do not create ourselves exclusively by our efforts. Because lovers mutually foster their growth, the object of romantic love need not remain the same. The beloved discovers and appreciates qualities in us that we did not know, or only dimly, that we possessed. This is an impetus for us to develop worthwhile qualities and a challenge to remedy flaws. The lover also evokes and develops new traits through interaction. The newness of these traits ranges from those just waiting to be summoned—a latent talent—to those requiring prolonged encouragement—the capacity for a virtue.

2.

Sexuality further distinguishes love from infatuation. Sexual knowledge of the beloved easily extinguishes infatuation by smothering the imagination, leaving nothing to it. However, sexual relations should not demolish or diminish romantic love. "As the desire of such lovers does not cause their love but is created by it, the satisfaction of such desire cannot bring love to an end."[3] We might sexually desire someone before loving him or her. But once we love, sexual desire stems from that. Because love engenders and fuels sexual desire, satisfying the desire does not threaten the love, unless what is disclosed or developed in sexuality is itself antagonistic to love.

We might be tempted by a reductive view, that romantic love is nothing but lust within friendship, because it is parsimonious and clear. We need not populate our moral universe with an additional kind of love, one that has seemed murky to many. But Letwin's insight that romantic love is the basis of sexual desire should keep us from yielding to this temptation. When we desire sexual gratification with a friend, the desire isn't aroused because this person is our friend. We desire sexual gratification and friendship makes this person a preferable sexual partner by virtue of familiarity, warmth, or security. The friendship is incidental to our lust; it does not define the desire. As C. S. Lewis expresses the difference between love and lust, "Without Eros sexual desire, like every other desire, is a fact about ourselves. Within Eros it is rather about the Beloved."[4]

In romantic love, our sexual desire is instigated by loving the other. Sexuality becomes a context for mutually expressing emotion and deepening intimacy. We seek sexual interaction to experience the other more fully and to disclose ourselves more completely. Sexuality can be a mode of intimate communion, communication and unity with another at the deepest level. Sex is more than a medium for intimacy; it breeds intimacy, encouraging the exchange of ideas as well as bodily sensations.[5] Physical closeness, self-exposure, an inevitable feeling of vulnerability, all conspire to make us want to share other aspects of ourselves. We want to share what exposes us, what is important to us. This is because our bodies are not instruments or material to manipulate. They are us; we are embodied beings.

Robert Solomon observes that "sexuality is not a specific desire so much as it is part of our basic bodily being—the way we comport ourselves, the way we move and the way we feel as well as the way we sense ourselves with others."[6] Our bodies express and define us in sex. We experience the other in terms of our bodies even as we experience ourselves by virtue of our bodily involvement with the other. When we present ourselves sexually to and for another, we invite mutual exploration and redefinition.

In sexual intimacy, we perceive the beloved's individuality and express ours. Sex can be motivated by need for expression and communication since love is a concern for and appreciation of one another's personality. Our hunger is not merely for sex, but is for physical and sexual intimacy with this individual. Sexuality is an intense context for the mutual self-creation that more generally characterizes romantic love.

3.

We are constituted by our interactions and relations with others, especially our romantic partners whose lives we share. Solomon stresses the mutual melioration of romantic love. It is "the mutual creation of self-identity," not just any identity, but a good one. "Love embodies a reflective desire for self-improvement."[7] Self-esteem propels romantic love because we desire to be good, perhaps as a concomitant of self-love. The redefining of self has an ontological and an epistemological side. Ontologically, the lover collaborates in our transformation. Epistemologically, the lover inspires us to imagine ourselves better than we are. This is no infatuate's imagination, fantasizing about beloveds with no projection of how they might improve.

A beloved helps us see our potential goodness and promotes its actuality. The entwining of the ontological and epistemological aspects of self-creation in romantic love is captured in this passage by Russell Banks:

> Wade Whitehouse and Lillian Pittman, through their openness and intimacy with one another, had separated themselves, by the age of sixteen, from the kids and adults around them and had protected each other while they made themselves more sensitive and passionate than those kids, until they came to depend on one another for an essential recognition of their more tender qualities and their intelligence.[8]

No guarantee exists that the redefinition lovers accomplish will be for the good; they might recreate each other badly, fostering tendencies destructive to themselves or others.[9] This is a serious problem, but does not undermine my view of love. The lover's conception of himself or herself as enhanced by the beloved need not be accurate for such redefinition to characterize romantic love. Even where our ideal is genuinely good, the beloved might fail to facilitate its realization. Love involves reaching for positive self-transformation with another, however mistaken or abortive the attempt.

The effort required in loving does provide a hedge against destructive relationships. In more subtle ways than how we consciously see ourselves, love makes us better. Because loving involves actively helping the other, it fosters our virtue. M. Scott Peck defines love as "the will to extend one's self for the purpose of nurturing one's own or another's spiritual growth."[10] (I interpret this as a generic definition; specific loves are differentiated by other defining features.) To extend ourselves for another's growth enlarges our capacities and develops our virtues as well.

We cannot work for the growth of our beloveds unless we notice what they do. Iris Murdoch describes the link between love and attention:

> love . . . is an exercise of . . . really *looking*. The difficulty is to keep the attention fixed upon the real situation and to prevent it from returning surreptitiously to the self with consolations of self-pity, resentment, fantasy.[11]

Paying attention to what is really going on, instead of to what we imagine or want to see, requires patience; what is really occurring might be concealed. We might have to wait watchfully to learn what our beloved needs or what we are able to do for him or her.

Patience is also needed to help our loved ones develop their abilities and talents. They need to change at their pace, not ours. Helping them grow includes "building up" their capacity for love itself. As Kierkegaard epigrammatically phrases it, "to build up is to build up love, and it is love which builds up."[12] Although Kierkegaard is speaking about neighbor love, *agape*, it is an ingredient of romantic love. Encouraging neighbor love in our beloveds requires patience to refrain from making demands on them. Kierkegaard points out that "self-constraint" is needed since we might wish to do too much for or impose our ideas on the beloved. Self-constraint involves an effort to control our emotion and conduct, but it seems inseparable from patience.

For reasons specific to his philosophy, Kierkegaard also maintains that genuine loving is not possessive; the lover must "not confuse love with possession of the beloved."[13] We need not subscribe to Kierkegaard's theology or practical psychology to agree that when we extend ourselves for the other's spiritual growth, we do not worry about our needs. We use our help neither to manipulate the other nor to further our interests. Consequently, becoming less possessive is another meliorating component of romantic love. This distinguishes romantic love from mutually destructive or one-sided relationships.

Interacting and forming loving relationships with people outside the romantic union is necessary for lovers to grow:

> By myself I am not large enough to call the whole man into activity; I want other lights than my own to show all his facets. Now that Charles is dead, I shall never again see Ronald's reaction to a specifically Caroline joke. Far from having more of Ronald . . . I have less of Ronald.[14]

Lovers can evolve in creative ways by virtue of outside relationships, enabling them to replenish the romantic relationship with new viewpoints and sensitivities. When lovers assist one another's growth by encouraging outside interests and friendships, they risk growing apart. Involvement with work, causes, and people can move the lovers in incompatible directions. But denying other interests or loved ones also denies their recreative power. Preserving the relationship by withdrawing into it dooms it to stagnate.

Exerting ourselves on behalf of the other broadens us through identification. We invest the beloved with energy, "as if . . . [he or she] were a part of ourselves."[15] We incorporate our lovers' interests and desires, suffering their failures and rejoicing in their triumphs apart from their effects on us. By identifying with our lovers' main goals and concerns, their experience becomes part of our own. This widens how and what we think, feel, and desire. Shulamith Firestone describes this feature of love as looking through an extra window on the world. Enrichment of self results from "each enlarging himself through the other: instead of being one, locked in the cell of himself with only his own experience and view, he could participate in the existence of another."[16] The enlargement of identification can also be cast in terms of caring. "Love may be a matter of self, but what defines the self in love is first of all *caring* for another person. Love is an expansion of self to include—and even to favor—the other."[17] We grow because our perspective and sympathies are expanded through caring.

4.

Falling in love is different from loving, but intimates it. Where love is a gradual process, demanding effort and interaction, falling in love is quick and easy. And just as quick and easy does the self change when it falls. As with love, the change is uplifting, and has both an ontological and epistemological dimension.

The ontological dimension of falling in love involves an abrupt dissolution of "ego boundaries," the cognitive, emotional structures that define the self, setting it off from the rest of the world. Our bodies, needs, thoughts, and emotions delimit the territories of the self. They remind us of the difference and distance between ourselves and others. Ego structure is the culmination of the gradual process by which the infant is individuated from its mother. Although normal, necessary, and healthy, separation gives rise to a feeling of loneliness from which we would like to escape.

> Falling in love is a sudden collapse of a section of an individual's ego boundaries, permitting one to merge his or her identity with that of another person. The sudden release of oneself from oneself, the explosive pouring out of oneself into the beloved, and the dramatic surcease of loneliness accompanying this collapse of ego boundaries is experienced by most of us as ecstatic.[18]

This merging must be temporary; lovers cannot satisfy one another's desires all the time. When desires are frustrated, we see ourselves as distinct from the beloved, whose interests and needs might differ, even conflict, with ours. With the return of ego boundaries, the stage of falling in love is ended. Falling in love weaves the illusion that the lovers will always and effortlessly be able to meet each other's needs. They are not prepared for love's labors, having to work for each other when they do not feel like it.

The epistemological aspect of falling in love is the shining vision of ourselves ennobled by the beloved. Imagining the wonderful things possible with this new person, the lovers experience "a rapid conceptual transformation of the self."[19] Flooded with the story of what their new life can be, they are exhilarated. Each is viewed as someone with whom he or she can realize the new and improved self of love, and a rosy future is narratively woven (a "romance"). The ontological and epistemological aspects of falling in love are complementary. When our ego boundaries collapse (the ontological), we feel at one with someone envisioned (the epistemological) as transforming us. And imagining ourselves made better by our beloveds arouses the desire to unite with them, physically, emotionally, intellectually.

The image of a redefined self and the collapse of ego boundaries intimate love's transforming power. Imagining ourselves happily recreated presages love's potential to rework our selves. Similarly, the ecstatic dissolution of ego boundaries suggests the expansion of self that results from exerting ourselves on behalf of another. The thrill of the collapse of ego-boundaries is a precursor to the steady joy of the enlargement of ego boundaries. In the film *African*

Queen, Charlie Allnut and Rosie Sayer can foresee their mutual transformation because they have begun to taste love's edifying power. He is becoming less callous and more caring; she, more tender and less prissy and rigid. Each shows off for the other with feats of bravery and generosity of spirit. They've fallen in love.

Falling in love, therefore, should be valued as an epiphany, foreshadowing the transforming power of love. Applying Simone Weil's metaphor, "there is a resemblance between the lower and the higher. . . . Humiliation [for example, is] an image of humility."[20] Infatuation holds out no possibilities for self-transformation because it feeds on a fantasy spun to satisfy only the infatuate's needs. Because it does nothing to prepare us for loving a real person, infatuation is usually dissolved by realistic perception.

Falling in love does tempt us with the illusion that we will remain merged, satisfying forever each other's needs seamlessly. Unlike infatuation, however, this illusion harbors truth: the truth that exerting ourselves for our beloved will expand our ego boundaries and horizon of care. Although collapse of ego boundaries must be transitory, their expansion through identification with the beloved can endure. Falling in love can be a precursor to genuine love because it points to this reality. The fantastic, self-centered nature of infatuation is more of an obstacle to overcome, that we might get on with the attention and effort of loving.

Notes

1. Stendhal, *De L'Amour* (Paris: Gallimard, 1980).
2. Shirley Robin Letwin, "Romantic Love and Christianity," *Philosophy* 52 (1977): 131-45, at 139.
3. *Ibid.*
4. C. S. Lewis, *The Four Loves* (New York: Harcourt, Brace, Jovanovich, 1960), 136.
5. Robert Solomon, *About Love* (New York: Simon and Schuster, 1988), 212.
6. *Ibid.*, 195.
7. *Ibid.*, 203-6.
8. Russell Banks, *Affliction* (New York: Harper and Row, 1989), 300.
9. Lee Horvitz made this and other helpful observations in his comments on the version of this essay read at a meeting of the Society for the Philosophy of Sex and Love.
10. M. Scott Peck, *The Road Less Traveled* (New York: Simon and Schuster, 1978), 81.
11. Iris Murdoch, *The Sovereignty of Good* (New York: Shocken Books, 1971), 91.
12. Søren Kierkegaard, *Works of Love*, trans. Howard Hong and Edna Hong (New York: Harper and Row, 1962), 205.
13. *Ibid.*, 52.
14. Lewis, *The Four Loves*, 92.
15. Peck, *The Road Less Traveled*, 117.
16. Shulamith Firestone, "Love in a Sexist Society," in Alan Soble, ed., *Eros, Agape, and Philia* (New York: Paragon House, 1989), 29-39, at 30.
17. Solomon, *About Love*, 256.
18. Peck, *The Road Less Traveled*, 87.
19. Solomon, *About Love*, 148.
20. Simone Weil, *The Simone Weil Reader*, ed. George Panichas (Mt. Kisco, N.Y.: Moyer Bell Ltd., 1977), 352.

Art Stawinski
(photograph: Joy D. Fisher)

Author of "Comments on Joseph Kupfer's 'The Power of Love, the Impotence of Infatuation'"
Paper presented at the Society for the Philosophy of Sex and Love
during the
Central Division Meeting of The American Philosophical Association
Chicago, Ill., 25 April 1991

Fifty-Seven

SOLVING STENDHAL'S PROBLEM

Art Stawinski

Romantic love is one of the most widely discussed but poorly understood human experiences. Joseph Kupfer has attempted to make this complex subject manageable by focusing on one element of romantic love, the positive redefinition it creates in the character of the lovers.[1] He contrasts romantic love with infatuation, which lacks love's transforming power, and applies his elucidation of love to the experience of "falling in love." I will attempt to expand Kupfer's distinction between infatuation and romantic love, especially as it relates to his solution of Stendhal's problem, and to raise some questions I hope will advance the discussion of romantic love.

Kupfer distinguishes romantic love from infatuation in part by the objects toward whom they are directed. The object of an infatuation is partly fictional. Although a real person provides a focus for the infatuate, that person serves only as an ontological hook on which to hang fantasies. One might weave complex fantasies, sexual and nonsexual, about a person one has only glimpsed, and then become obsessed with this image, possibly pathologically. Infatuation, as Kupfer understands it, is fundamentally self-directed. The embellished, semi-fictional person created by the infatuate is going to meet the infatuate's every need, satisfy every desire, and bring him or her true happiness. Thus the object of infatuation is regarded not as an autonomous person, but as a means to the infatuate's own welfare. Kupfer points out that intimacy, particularly sexual intimacy, "extinguishes infatuation by smothering the imagination, leaving nothing to it" (580).

By contrast, the object of genuine romantic love, the lover's beloved, is experienced as a person. To the lover, the beloved is not the realization of a fantasy or a means to an end. Rather, the beloved is cherished, respected, and understood in his or her own right. "Instead of being absorbed in our fantastic creation," writes Kupfer, "we are focused on a real personality" (580). The differing objects of infatuation and love, one fantasy, the other real, lay the foundation for Stendhal's problem. Love for a real person, for Stendhal, leads to boredom once all aspects of the beloved have been understood. The fantasy object of infatuation, however, can be continually recreated and thus remains novel and interesting.

Kupfer solves Stendhal's problem by arguing that people involved in a romantic love relationship are continually growing and redefining themselves. Citing Robin Letwin and Robert Solomon, Kupfer offers an account of how love leads lovers to redefine themselves for each other through helping realize each other's potential goodness. This mutual quest for a better self-identity has, for Kupfer, an ontological and an epistemological aspect. Ontologically, it makes the lovers better people; epistemologically, it transforms their self-perception, so that they perceive themselves and each other as better people. The continual personal growth and self-realization that the love relationship creates is why lovers can love without becoming bored with each other. As the lovers grow, they discover and explore new aspects of each other. As they identify with each other and nurture each other's development, they expand their awareness of the world through each other's experiences. It seems that love could never be boring.

Appealing as this solution to Stendhal's problem is, I see some difficulties with it. For one, the experiences of lovers do not always match the description Kupfer offers. Many couples have been able to maintain long-term love relationships accompanied by little personal growth of the sort Kupfer envisions. At the same time, many love relationships have ended because the lovers "grew apart" as their evolving identities took them in different directions. Some love relationships are mutually self-destructive, fostering unhealthy codependencies instead of personal growth. Kupfer might claim that such relationships are not cases of romantic love, even though the participants believe that they are. Yet these types of relationships do exhibit at least some of the aspects of romantic love Kupfer mentions, including a regard for the beloved as a person and a motivation to act from a concern for him or her.

Kupfer's solution also presupposes a specific cultural context for love. He acknowledges that many cultures do not have a conception of romantic love. It appears, however, that for love in Kupfer's sense to flourish and survive, the lovers must live in a culture that not only conceives of romantic love, but values personal growth and self-realization as well. It is through helping each other attain these valuable things that the lovers sustain their love. The pursuit of self-realization has only recently become a widely held value in Western culture and is not universal. Yet love relationships seem to occur in almost all human cultures, even if they do not possess all the characteristics usually ascribed to romantic love.

One other way in which Kupfer distinguishes infatuation from romantic love actually offers a better solution to Stendhal's problem. Love, unlike infatuation, is other-centered. The lover is acting out of concern for the happiness of his or her beloved, rather than acting from self-interest. The lover's feelings, of boredom or otherwise, cannot threaten true love because the lover is not motivated by those feelings but by concern for the beloved. If lovers feel that novelty, excitement, or advancing each other's personal development will enhance their relationship by increasing each other's happiness, they can act to realize these values for each other. But any feelings of boredom they might have do not threaten their love because neither loves the other in order to feel good. If an important part of my love for you is my benevolent concern, then, unless you are or become, like God, perfectly self-sufficient, I will *always* have something to do to make you better off than you are. Hence, if boredom threatens love, it's not really love.

Kupfer hints at this solution in his discussion of falling in love. Falling in love, he says,

> involves an abrupt dissolution of "ego boundaries," the cognitive, emotional structures that define the self, setting it off from the rest of the world. (584)

When I fall in love, I no longer act out of self-interest. My beloved assumes an importance that transcends my own concerns; my life becomes motivated by the needs, desires, and happiness of my beloved. If my love is reciprocated and my beloved falls in love with me, ego dissolution is complete. We now live for each other and not for ourselves alone. Kupfer points out that this state of falling in love cannot sustain itself; it is not yet love, but an intimation of it. The responsibilities of everyday life gradually require a redefinition of our egos. As the "falling in love" stage of our relationship passes, either the reassertion of ego becomes complete and the relationship ends, or we transform our sense of self to include one another, our relationship evolving into romantic love.

The ontological transformation that falling in love presages makes the lover a different person. The lover's ego boundaries are reconstructed in a new form: the lover *becomes* someone who loves another specific person. Love is something one *is*, rather than something one *does*. While love expresses itself in the behavior of the lovers, it is not itself behavior. Love is a reason for acting, but does not itself require a reason: love is *nonrational*. The question often asked of lovers, "Why do you love this person?" makes no sense. There can be reasons for what one does, but not for what one is. This is another reason love can never be boring. Because love is not an activity, one cannot become bored doing it. Apparently Stendhal never experienced true love.

Note

1. Joseph Kupfer, "Romantic Love," this volume, 579-85. All references to this essay are supplied parenthetically in the text.

Lee Horvitz

Author of "Commentary on Kupfer"
Paper presented at the Society for the Philosophy of Sex and Love
during the
Central Division Meeting of The American Philosophical Association
Chicago, Ill., 25 April 1991

Fifty-Eight

IMAGINATION, AND OTHER, MATTERS

Lee Horvitz

I will discuss Joseph Kupfer's essay, "Romantic Love,"[1] on two levels, focusing on the significance of the matter under discussion and the persuasiveness of his arguments. As for the significance of the issues concerning romantic love and the differences between it and infatuation, they are all worthy of sustained philosophical attention. To say completely why I believe so would take us too far afield, but I want to give four general reasons: the place love holds in a conception of the valuable human life; the place love holds in a conception of the self; the place love holds in a conception of moral agency; and the role love might play as a critical category of philosophy as itself the love of wisdom. Distinguishing love from its rivals and pretenders is therefore important. Kupfer makes meaningful contributions to that philosophical task.

I enthusiastically endorse Kupfer's approach to the nature of love: he emphasizes the *power* of love, by which he means its creative, generative capacities for producing characteristic effects, forms of development, or growth. His method is like Socrates' in the *Republic*, who, in order to understand the natures of justice and injustice, creates narratives of the kinds of lives to which each leads. From this perspective, we understand the nature of love, as well as the nature of its pretenders and rivals, in terms of capacities for bringing about and sustaining identifiable forms of life. Kupfer's guiding questions, then, are these: To what forms of life does infatuation give birth? To what forms does love? In other words, what are the general structures of each and what sustains them? Someone schooled in philosophy might well think such an approach is pragmatic, even given my comparison to the *Republic*. However, this approach is not pragmatic at all in the Rortian sense, and only partially so in a Jamesian sense. Rather, the approach is existential and phenomenological. The approach is particularly appropriate for understanding the nature of love, for love in general is paradigmatically generative and the approach makes normative considerations central by highlighting the concept of the good through the focus on differing forms of life.

In general, Kupfer does a good, thought-provoking job. On the whole I agree with his views, so I will focus on ways in which his thinking might be modified or supplemented, draw out some implications and assumptions of his views, and correct points that are especially important. To do this, I must first summarize the main points of his argument. Kupfer begins by analyzing the inevitable failure of infatuation and then turns to the potential successes of love, each at two stages: the initial stage (the first rush of infatuation and first blush of falling in love), and the continuing stage (the futile attempt to sustain infatuation and the ongoing work of being in love).

Kupfer begins with infatuation. Infatuation cannot generate anything because the power of romantic, erotic relations depends on knowing the other, which is not part of infatuation. The infatuate, while preoccupied, even overwhelmed, by the object of his or her desire, is not truly absorbed by, does not truly perceive, the admired; therefore, the infatuate cannot know the other. The reason is that infatuation makes up, ignores, and exaggerates features of the other. This analysis of infatuation is true and not controversial, I would think. However, I do have a problem with Kupfer's claim that the imagination is the basic mechanism of infatuation. According to Kupfer, the imagination drives infatuation by distorting perception, infecting it with unreality. By contrast, love "develops in realistic perception of the beloved" (580). This point is true, but by articulating it the way he does Kupfer misrepresents the relation of imagination to veridical perception and does not give sufficient credit to the affirmative role imagination can play in love.

The root of the problem is revealed in the following quote, in which Kupfer claims that the role the imagination plays in infatuation is "corroborated by the way infatuation evaporates under prolonged or demanding interaction with the *real* person" (579, emphasis added). Kupfer is partially correct here. In fact, infatuation often needs much less of "the hard reality of the beloved" (579) to make it evaporate than Kupfer seems to think: one remark or incident, if sufficiently telling, objectionable, or inconsistent with the infatuate's construct, can undermine infatuation. Once, a person with whom I was infatuated, on hearing that an African-American girl's name was "Keisha," turned to me with the knowing grin and slightly lowered voice reserved for club members only, and asked, "Why do *they* give their children such funny names?" With this moment infatuation vanished. As frustrating as the loss was, the infatuation simply could no longer hold up, a fact that points to its hollowness. Apart from how much of the other person is needed for infatuation to evaporate, note how for Kupfer the faculty of imagination directs us to the unreality of the other, while the faculty of perception directs us to his or her reality.

There are four reasons I balk at identifying the distorted with the imagination and the real with perception. First, perception itself can be mistaken, without being pushed into distortion by the imagination. Second, the imagination can provide insight into reality, often a reality that lies beneath what appears to perception. Third, Western philosophy has always tended to conceive of the imagination as a power of deception, and this way of viewing the imagination might derive from philosophy's bias against the body and its desires. Finally, locating the mechanism of infatuation in the imagination does not tell us enough; it does not inform us about the motivations for infatuation and thus what would cause the imagination to distort. The old connection of the imagination with unreality comes through in Kupfer's passages on infatuation. The reason, I suspect, is that Stendhal is in the background of his analysis. Kupfer objects to Stendhal's view that love is only infatuation, but he seems to accept Stendhal's view that imagination's chief role in love is to serve the infatuate's fantasies, which are needed to combat the boredom that besets love of a finite being.

Kupfer has a more important point concerning the unreality of infatuation: it leads to distortions in *self*-understanding. The distortions come from expecting the admired to fulfill needs she or he cannot. This hapless condition distorts how the infatuate understands her or his needs and their satisfaction. The sorry upshot is that the infatuate misses the kind of self-discovery love can bring. The ways that infatuation defeats and confuses love's possibilities for expanding understanding, expressed so poignantly by Oscar Wilde in *De Profundis*,[2] are aspects of infatuation that should be stressed, and I welcome Kupfer's discussion of infatuation's tendency to promote or sustain alienation. Indeed, this point about infatuation and self-distortion is among the more important ones of Kupfer's essay. It opens a possibility for powerful cultural criticism: a good case can be made that our culture functions to a significant extent through a systematic denial or misconception of the differences between infatuation and love. In this sense, our culture tragically inhibits living within the power of love.

Further, recognizing the deleterious effects of infatuation on the infatuate raises the issue of its motivation Why do we so easily fall into infatuation if it is sterile and blinding? No doubt more than one motivation can come into play, but there is one in particular that I want to mention here. Infatuation often comes from some need that is narcissistically egoistic and possessive. Kupfer makes this kind of point about infatuation by noting its solipsism; it "feeds on a fantasy spun to satisfy only the infatuate's needs" (585). I think he might develop this point by wondering why human beings are susceptible to such fantasies; doing so is particularly important because an answer would help illuminate the power of love. My suspicion is that infatuation often tries to avoid the demands of love through its inability to suffer the vulnerabilities that make love both terrifying and transforming. The power of love, then, lies in large measure in its relation to vulnerability, for love transforms through disclosure, and disclosure is exposure. Such exposure, as the etymology of "vulnerable" indicates, puts lovers at risk for wounding and being wounded.

Let me turn to Kupfer on the power of love. Its power, on his view, is transformative and educative, and lies in love's relation to self-discovery and self-development, what Kupfer calls the "positive redefinition of the lovers" (579). It is worth spelling out how, for Kupfer, love has this power. (1) The power is rooted in the ontological fact that the self is dialogical. (2) The power is rooted in the psyche-logical fact that our loved ones are particularly important "interlocutors." "We are constituted by our interactions and relations with others, especially our romantic partners whose lives we share" (581). (3) Love focuses our attention on the reality of the individual being of the other, not our self. (4) This focus has a particular structure or color to it. "Love is a concern for and appreciation of one another's personality" (581). This kind of *participative attention* makes mutual redefinition possible. How so? (5) It reveals possibilities; being loved by another allows us to see what we could be. But love does not reveal just any possibilities, for (6) true romantic love is inherently meliorative. Quoting Solomon (Robert, not the Hebrew King), Kupfer claims that "love embodies a reflective desire for self-improvement" (581).[3] Kupfer explains this view when he asserts that falling in love and love both have an epistemological and an ontological side: the beloved "inspires us to imagine ourselves better than we are"; "the lover collaborates in our transformation" (582). Love helps us know ourselves as what we can and should be, and aids the realization of these possibilities.

Consider the "should be." Kupfer claims that genuine love connects essentially to goodness and the development of virtue. This meliorative, normative feature of forms of love has often been noted, but thinkers have not typically ascribed it to romantic, erotic love. In recent work on such love, this connection is being made with increasing frequency. I applaud this trend, because of the importance of considering how love might help fill a normative void, the lack of foundation Werner Marx calls the "loss of measure."[4] Love might go far in providing a measure for valuable action on earth in secular times. It might do this in two ways: by providing a locus for affirming meaningfulness and so the point of valuable action, and by providing an immediate context for the revealing of value.

Another reason Kupfer's points about love and value are important is that in them he *does* give a positive role to the imagination. "Epistemologically, the lover inspires us to imagine ourselves better than we are" (582). An imaginative relation with the other that serves knowledge and love well emerges here. I believe, however, that the role of imagination in nondeceived, romantic relations is wider than this, albeit important, role. Imagination aids perception in seeing the whole person in the appearance of the other, as the imagination aids perception in interpreting a work of art. Imagination helps reveal the meaningful and valuable in the actual. Consider Goethe's Werther. Imagination allows Werther to be enthralled by the sight of Lotte's arms as he is about to join her in a dance; when Werther loses Lotte, he feels a loss of imagination.[5]

One more reason Kupfer's point about the power of love to redefine the lovers in terms of the good is important is that it places love within what I call "the practice of personhood." A vital implication of locating love within a practice of personhood is that *to be a self is to be a lover*, although just what place love has in the structure of the self, and just what its relation to other aspects of the self (for example, self as producer) is, remains to be considered. Here Kupfer gets to a fundamental point about the power of love: it is a principle of self and agency. This is a view found within the history of philosophy when talking about nonromantic love, for example, in the thinking of Plato and Kierkegaard. It needs to be revived and extended to romantic love. To put the point in more contemporary language—loving is part of the practice of selfhood. This point has profound consequences: it affects how ethics should conceive of the good life, for it provides us with a kind of primary virtue as a basis for normative judgment; it grounds the cultural criticism mentioned earlier; it provides an important way to test concepts of the self, most significantly, nowadays, deconstructive theories of the subject.

Reflecting on just why love is inherently normative is worthwhile, even though the profundity and mystery of such a matter is close to overwhelming. Kupfer addresses this matter to some extent by noting that love is essentially participative. This fact perhaps entails a shared *telos* and shared responsibility. However, what lovers participate in must be inherently good if genuine love is inherently normative. Perhaps life in the (admittedly vague) Nietzschean sense is the inherently good matter love participates in, and the meliorative aspect of love provides an example of the joyous innocence that Nietzsche claimed characterizes becoming and that constitutes the reevaluation of values. Kupfer addresses the matter by claiming that "self-esteem propels romantic love because we desire to be good, perhaps as a concomitant of self-love" (581). Out of self-love, lovers strive to develop each other and themselves in order to be good. A problem with this view is that it connects love and value through self-love. But there is already love, then, before the connection. Kupfer might argue that he connects love and value through romantic love, and self-love is not the same as romantic love. But then I wonder why being directed to the good is not a feature of *all* forms of love, even self-love. Further, self-love will not connect love and value because the relation to the other might be prior to or equal to the self-relation. Perhaps the reality is more like what Levinas describes as the relation of the face, in which the presence of the other calls us to ourselves by calling us out of ourselves to show ourselves in a shared responsibility.[6] I am hardly certain about this weighty matter of love's seemingly inherent relation to the normative, but I am sure that further reflection on the source of love's movement toward the good is worthwhile.

I had once claimed that Kupfer slips too easily between the creative and meliorative;[7] after all, not everything we have an interest in becoming is valuable or good. He thereby misses the opportunity to show how love connects the two. His response is that "love involves reaching for positive self-transformation with another, however mistaken or abortive the attempt" (582). This response is correct; love might err in both of these ways. But it is also incomplete, for it omits a crucial issue for understanding the power of love: love tends to (it need not) clarify our interests in the light of value. It not only directs us to the good but also focuses our capacity to grasp it and helps develop the virtues necessary for doing so.

Is this meliorative, normative structure of love necessary? As with all phenomenological structures, the answer is "yes," in the sense of a constitutive existential possibility. Why does love have this uplifting and enhancing power? That question is hard, maybe impossible to answer; this feature of love likely escapes knowledge, which is why it so often has been thematized as a gift and blessing. Thus we come to another feature of Kupfer's analysis: the degree to which love is subsumed under knowing.

Kupfer analyzes the impotence of infatuation and the power of love in terms of capacities for knowing the real and the good, and acting on the basis of that knowledge. I endorse this idea. However, I wonder if Kupfer has not neglected another dimension of love, one that might even underlie its capacity to help us come to know our best possibilities. Consider that when falling in love we do not want the beloved to be better, but to be who she or he is, and we do not want to be loved for whom we might be, but for whom we are. I suggest, then, that romantic love rests on a unique revelation of being through a generative and redeeming combination of values, freedom, and beauty in the figures of the individuals in love, a refreshing and uplifting innocence of need. Indeed, the power of love probably does rest on something like what Nietzsche called the affirmation of life (which is not a matter of reason) or something like the Levinasian face that calls us to our responsibility (which is not a matter of knowledge). Kupfer makes this kind of point in discussing how falling in love tears down ego boundaries, but he goes astray by asserting that falling in love intimates the higher stage of being in love. I take him to be assuming that falling in love and love share a basic structure, which means that falling in love, too, is basically about knowledge. To an extent this is right; however, falling in love is based more on the presence of the other person and how the revealing of that presence reveals us, together, *to be* known. Perhaps we can learn something here from the old saw that the answer to "Why do you love me?" is "Because you are you."

I now want to address a piece of reasoning that has become part of the new canon but which seems problematic to me. Kupfer says, "the romantic relationship is culturally conditioned and historically bound, since most cultures have not had any conception of romantic love" (579). There is an argument squeezed into this one sentence that goes like this:

P: Most cultures have not had any conception of romantic love.
C: Our conception of romantic love is culturally conditioned and historically bound.

I want to raise two objections to this argument, one about the truth of its premise and another about the logical support it could provide for the conclusion. There are exceptions to Kupfer's premise. His premise is general and not universal, so providing such counterexamples will not be entirely telling. My point with the counterexamples is that the phenomenon of romantic love might be more widespread than Kupfer believes. As counterexamples, think about Sappho's poetry, Ibn Hazm's *The Ring of the Dove*, and numerous texts from the Old Testament. My conceptual point is that while our conception of romantic love grew out of the tradition of courtly love, there might be other versions of such love, just as the Western half-tone musical scale is a variation of the musical scale, different in degree but not kind, from the East Indian quarter-tone scale. Any phenomenon distinct to persons, such as romantic love, will emerge within history and culture because it will emerge within time and place. But this fact does not mean that there were not other instances or variations of the same phenomenon. I want to raise the possibility, then, that the current position about historicizing knowledge and concepts, might be wrong in its tendency to restrict concepts to their history alone.

Even if the argument's premise were true, it would not follow that our conception was historically bound or culturally conditioned in any sense beyond that it emerged in a particular place at a particular time. Kupfer is making a stronger claim, expressing skepticism about knowledge based on the historically and culturally embedded concepts. While there might not be universals, because concepts and ideas must emerge within a particular context it does not follow that said concepts are true, false, applicable or inapplicable only within that context. In this regard, concepts might not be historically or culturally conditioned at all. Therefore, that a conception is limited to a few cultures, or even one, does not mean that it is historically bound and culturally conditioned in any way that is philosophically meaningful. Unless we take Kupfer's conclusion to mean only that the concept emerged within time and place (as all phenomena of existence do) the premise does not support the conclusion.

The thought arises naturally here that Kupfer should consider feminist and post-structuralist objections to the idea that love has this capacity of positive transformation. That love has this power is a reigning cultural assumption. However, this assumption is sufficiently suspicious ideologically to warrant at least acknowledging the suspicions. As Michel Foucault says, "The irony of this deployment is in having us believe that our 'liberation' is in the balance."[8] By "this deployment," Foucault means any discourse about the deep secrets of sexuality that promises special truths about ourselves. Such discourses extend beyond love, but our discourse about love is a prime example. It is true, as Kupfer claims, that romantic love is one significant area for love's power of redefinition. But why not find this power in the love of God, justice, or nature? Why not find it in all or some of these as well as in romantic love? Kupfer's investigating romantic love does not commit him to the view that romantic love is the only area for love's power. But given that our culture assumes it is, and given that this view is untenable, Kupfer should acknowledge the issue and should address why he focuses on romantic love. Not incidentally, in doing so he would meaningfully engage a way in which our notion of romantic love is culturally conditioned and historically bound.

Finally, I want to consider an aspect of Kupfer's analysis of sexuality that suffers from the reductivism I already noted; sex appears to be only about learning and communicating knowledge, yet it is also a matter of release, pleasure, and ecstasy. Kupfer emphasizes the epistemological dynamics of sexuality. More importantly, he holds this position for the ontological reason that "our bodies are not instruments or material to manipulate. They are us; we are embodied beings" (581). Sexuality, then, encompasses our entire being. I emphasize this point because while seemingly obvious, the current avalanche of discussions about sex often woefully ignores this crucial understanding of sexuality. This oversight is especially egregious in postmodern discussions of sex, gender, and identity. The problem with the oversight is that sexuality is taken as an independent force or material accompaniment, giving it what Heidegger called a "free-floating" (*freischwebend*) status.[9] The price of doing so is that sexuality is not understood as what it is, an integral human phenomenon, a revealing, existential phenomenon. So while Kupfer might stress the epistemological character of sexuality too much, he provides a strong voice for righting an imbalance by insisting that we understand sexuality as an integral existential phenomenon that is importantly about knowing. I do have what might be only a nitpick about how he expresses the point about embodiment. Kupfer cites Solomon to express it. Continental philosophy is not given its due. Nietzsche, Merleau-Ponty, Sartre, and de Beauvoir all had this view of sexuality long before the current discussions in American philosophy about sex and love.

Notes

1. Joseph Kupfer, "Romantic Love," this volume, 579-85. All page references to this essay are supplied parenthetically in the text.

2. Oscar Wilde, *De Profundis* (New York: G. P. Putnam's Sons, 1909).

3. See Robert Solomon, *About Love* (New York: Simon and Schuster, 1988), 203.

4. Werner Marx, *Is There a Measure on Earth? Foundations for a Non-Metaphysical Ethics*, trans. Reginald Lilly and Thomas J. Nenon, Jr. (Chicago: University of Chicago Press, 1987).

5. Johann Wolfgang von Goethe, *The Sorrows of Young Werther*, trans. Elizabeth Mayer and Louise Brogan (New York: Modern Library, 1984), 26.

6. Emmanuel Levinas, *Totality and Infinity*, trans. Alphonso Lingis (Pittsburgh: Duquesne University Press, 1969), 187-240.

7. In the earlier version of my commentary read at a meeting of the Society for the Philosophy of Sex and Love.

8. Michel Foucault, *The History of Sexuality,* vol. 1: *An Introduction* (New York: Vintage Books, 1980), 159.

9. Martin Heidegger, *Being and Time*, trans. John Macquarrie and Edward Robinson (New York: Harper and Row, 1962), 160.

Justin Leiber
(photograph: M. C. Valada)

Author of “Pornography, Art, and the Origins of Consciousness”
Paper presented at the Society for the Philosophy of Sex and Love
during the
Eastern Division Meeting of The American Philosophical Association
New York, N.Y., 29 December 1991

Fifty-Nine

PORNOGRAPHY, ART, AND THE ORIGINS OF CONSCIOUSNESS

Justin Leiber

Guy de Maupassant remarked that he composed his stories with one hand while maintaining an erection with the other. Did the writing hand contribute to the project of the stroking hand; was there a contribution the other way round, *vice versa*? Since the answer to both questions seems to be yes, since both hands seem mutually supportive, both contributing manually, though by different routes, to his state of sexual arousal, certain questions naturally arise. Because successful prose fiction and related forms of depiction are likely to, even ought to, recreate in the audience the author's compositional intentions and emotions, much the same questions arise, *mutatis mutandis*, for the audience. Is the activity of either of Maupassant's hands inartistic, immoral, or harmful to society, women particularly, through degradation, objectification, and incitement to physical abuse of women by men? Similarly, are Maupassant's sympathetic auditors inartistic, immoral, or harmful to society, women particularly, through imaginatively enjoying women's degradation and objectification, priming themselves for actual physical abuse if they, like Maupassant, experience sexual arousal or enhance it through manipulations of their own genitalia?

Someone might add, "Of course it's pornography, of course, pornographic violence, and of course the answer to all these questions is yes." While I agree with the first *of course*, I want to convince you that the rest of the *of course* doesn't follow a priori, nor, perhaps, *a posteriori*.

Yes, Maupassant's ironic and heart-rending stories are often about prostitutes, particularly if we also include related "unrespectable" women: entertainers, bar maids, dancers. In other words, Maupassant writes about whores, which is what "pornography" literally, or at least etymologically, means. But, equally, Maupassant's short stories are superb works of art. Frank O'Connor finds that a leitmotif of his work is the celebration of a "submerged population," which O'Connor compares to Turgenev's serfs and Chekhov's clerks, teachers, and country doctors.[1] In my early teens, when I read Maupassant's "*Boule de Suif*" (ball of fat), I received my first vivid realization that men, occasionally with shrill subordinate support from "respectable" women, could be horribly cruel, and hypocritically unfair, to women. (As a boy of the 1950s U.S., I was in a position to observe a pervasive pattern of male cruelty and hypocrisy toward women. But it took Maupassant to begin to get me to see what was going on.) I say "women" because, at the time, I did not recognize the category of prostitute but that of a woman who did not have a male owner and protector, who could not submit herself to an official position in a brutishly dominating male order. I recall myself in worshipful tumescence to the cheerful, healthy, male-compliant beauty of Esther Williams and Debbie Reynolds: though I felt a frisson of dangerous sexuality flowing around the poor boule de suif, I felt more her puzzled decency and good will, her subjectivity against the backdrop of organized male manipulation and contempt. Perhaps it is pornographic, but not a clear enough case. When Wallace Stegner says that "over and over again . . . Maupassant persuades us to accept his illusion that cunning, ferocity, greed, and coarseness are more common among men than we hope they are," by *men* he clearly means *males*.[2]

Might "hard-core porn movies" provide the clear-cut case? Here, it is often assumed, we find the essence of male fantasies of violent exploitation and objectification of women, the really bad stuff of which the surrounding male-dominated softcore and network TV culture is a partly softened reflection. *Here*, one might suggest, *is the real out and out dirt*, unrelieved by claims of artistry, realism, androgyny, or any other sort of redeeming value; this stuff is indefensible except for bare First Amendment claims that we defend, if at all, with our noses clamped, like the ACLU defending the American Nazi demonstration march through Skokie. So let's take a look at typical, professional (as opposed to amateur) hard-core porn movies.

Not a single person gets killed in 99% of hard-core pornographic movies. Unlike virtually all TV and movie forms, natural death is more common in pornography, perhaps approaching point four percent, though the death usually occurs before and premises the movie: memoirs of the legendary sex goddess, the comic conflicts of the claimants to the deceased's will. Nor is the percentage any better so far as threatened or active employment of guns, knives, axes, or poisons go; bloodless, perfunctory fist fights or threats of such might reach a half a percent level; rape or even the hint of physical compulsion is possibly even more rare. That hard-core porn is terribly unAmerican is further suggested by the field's own term for the tiny number of pornographic movies that do have mild physical violence; these attempts to season pornographic movies with elements of the ubiquitous violence of the other popular art forms of our culture are called "crossovers." In contrast to virtually all TV and movie genres, from cop to real crime shows, from news to soap operas, kid shows to mainstream movies, hard-core porn's level of violence is comparable only to that of cooking shows, aerobic exercise shows, and dance presentations like ballet's *pas de deux* and its ice skating equivalent. (If gymnastics produced such an art form, it might even more closely resemble hard-core porn movies.)

For most of us, certainly for me, the pornographic movie (along with exercise, dance, and skating shows) is like real life, as against other genres, in the following respects. I have never killed anyone, nor seen anyone killed in my presence. I have never attacked, or been attacked, with a gun, knife, axe, or more exotic weapon, though I once saw someone threatened with a knife. I did have a few fist fights in the intermediate grades and high school, but I have not had a physical fight as an adult, though I was on the peripheries of a few. I have had the good luck never to have been raped (a man nearly managed it when I was six). Most women I know well enough to know that they have been raped once or twice or close to it see these atrocious assaults as isolated intolerable catastrophes, not everyday sexist irritants.

On the other hand, over the past 40 years I have had sexual intercourse thousands of times, often violating Aquinas' missionary-position-only rule, masturbated in like numbers, and looked at my own and my spouse's naked body on a daily basis. You might argue that while pornographic movies are more realistic than other genres about violence in our daily, middle-class U.S. lives over the past few decades, nonetheless such movies exaggerate the frequency, variety, and ecstasy of sex by comparison with our actual lives. If we are to trust Kinsey and his work, we have to conclude that pornographic movies are not far from the normal with respect to frequency and variety, though few of us have the strength or grace to carry off the ballet-like lifts and related gymnastics, which in any case do not approach the exotic, apparatus-ridden fancies of the *Kama Sutra*. There is one notable exception to the realism of pornography: Kinsey's interviews suggest that something more than half of U.S. males have, as adults, experienced climax with a male partner; you would not get this impression from straight pornographic movies, which leave this human possibility out as rigorously as physical violence.[3] Regarding frequency, the similarity to ordinary life might in part reflect a convention of realism that is nearly mandatory in the genre: the man must be seen to ejaculate, in proof positive closeup, at the end of every act of intercourse, and he is not shown recommencing after a few minutes, though in fact this is well within the range of male variability.

In the accounts given in their pornographic sex manuals, perhaps the primary form of literature of ancient Islam, India, and China, we find the male of an evening having several ejaculations or practicing withdrawal so as to satisfy several or even scores of partners before depositing his supposedly enriched seed in his primary wife. Do not bridle at the word "satisfy," for these manuals also emphasize the great importance of female orgasm, suggesting that lack of female satisfaction brings well-deserved disasters on the family or the community, causing infertility, discord, worms, illness, and vengeful demons and goddesses. In traditional Hinduism, it was commonly assumed that if a woman should have an intact hymen when she marries, she will do her husband serious damage.[4] After a nineteenth century in which the male physicians of our civilization maintained that no normal, unperverted female could experience or enjoy sex in any way, Masters and Johnson had but to conduct the first actual laboratory study of sexual technology to discover that human females, given half a chance, can often be multiply orgasmic and more easily, and physiologically more intensely so, with dildos or vibrators.[5]

Masters and Johnson could well have suspected this after reading the ancient manuals, in which such claims are commonplace (note *mien-ling* balls as a kind of vibrator). Our pornography is the reappearance of the ancient sex manuals, erotic art, and technology. Maybe the most archetypical plot of our hardcore movies is this: wife and husband are frustrated. Husband desires physical variations that Aquinas interdicted. He is unable to present his desires well or attractively. He is inept at foreplay, doesn't realize this, and doesn't pick up on his shy wife's attempt to explain. Neither can communicate with the other. (Masters and Johnson confirmed this about married couples who volunteered to perform before them and who thought, mistakenly on the male's part, that they communicated well.)[6] The husband storms off to have affair in which he learns emotional understanding and technique. The wife discovers the affair and storms off to have her own, from which she, too, learns. The couple are reunited and become satisfied together sexually. The End. The plot is not unlike some of the ancient sex manuals; both sincerely aim at simple satisfactions. The banality and simplicity of the plot reminds me of ballet, where one equally needs a pretextual structure within which to display the taut beauty of the human body in decorous, yet inescapably sexual, postures. The greater portion of hard-core movies have no plot at all, simply picturing athletic and stunningly beautiful partners in a series of *pas de deux*, a moving and technically enhanced version of those delightful ancient Greek vases.

In short, our civilization, not the pornographic movie, is out of step with reality and ecstasy. We have made a religion of violence in which sex is only allowed as violence's handmaiden and object, explicitly left out or pervertedly let in. Aphrodite, and the larger Goddesses that proceeded her, are not to be mocked. They have taken and will take their toll, as Ares, shamed, beaten, and mocked in the *Iliad*, came to know full well.

I expect you can see my deconstructionist project already. (1) Along with weapons and agriculture, humanity's first technologies were erotic. Artificial male and female organs, erotic foods, drugs, art, narratives and practices, erotic training and educational programs for male and female, and the use of professional initiators, are ubiquitous in early civilizations. As with preliterate societies, the less of these practices, the more violence will abound and be praised. Ancient Greek art celebrated the human body, finding it, as did Plato, the essential exemplification of the beautiful. Open acceptance of lovers, of sexual variation, and public nudity in athletics, dance, and even on the street (Pausanias suggests in Plato's *Symposium*), is the mark of civilization, opposed by despots and barbarians alike. This Greek civilization disdained even the most abstract simulation of violence on stage. Jocasta hangs, and Oedipus pokes his eyes out, offstage.

(2) Given that the alphabet is the first information-processing technology, we must realize that its first widespread use over the Indian subcontinent and throughout southeast Asia is as erotica, as combination manuals and stimulants, decorated with religious flourishes that suggest that religion itself was largely erotic. Sei Shonagun, writing *Pillow Talk* in eleventh-century Heian Japan, gives us a witty, helpful, and stimulating guide to good conduct in a lover. Murasaki Shikabu, who authored the world's first romantic novel, *Tale of Genji*, Japan's equivalent of Cervantes' *Don Quixote* and Dante's *Inferno*, was Sei's younger and more romantic, though more reserved, critic in the Heian court. Both unquestionably shared the view that sexual love (and writing and reading about it) is the most fulfilling and exciting of all life's possibilities. Only males were allowed to write in the Chinese ideograms, so Sei and Murasaki were the first to write, significantly and foundationally, in the Japanese syllabary, hirigana. Indeed, Julian Jaynes suggests a relatively recent and analogous origin in general for human consciousness, our ability to maintain, savor, and often

direct an inner, subjective life (and hence to fantasize or at leisure recall possible actions).[7] He supposes this acquisition of a full, conscious, subjective life first came to classical Greece around the ninth century B.C., roughly between the oldest oralist passages of the *Iliad*, in which no inner subjectivity is supposed, and the later, more sophisticated *Odyssey*. Similarly, E. H. Gombrich proposes that the interacting development of Homeric point-of-view narrative and Greek perspectival visual art made possible, for the first time, the representation of a subjective inner life, of the world *as it looks and feels* to the individual eye and mind.[8] Also at this time, we find the chaste and wooden images of Mycenaean pre-Homeric art giving way to the erotically-charged vase painting and ubiquitous phallic statuary of the first millennium B.C. After noting "the modest, innocent murals from [preconscious] Thera," Julian Jaynes continues:

> With the coming of consciousness, particularly in Greece, where the evidence is most clear, the remains of these early Greek societies are anything but chaste. Beginning with seventh-century B.C. vase paintings, with depictions of ithyphallic tatyrs, new, semidivine beings, sex indeed seems a prominent concern. . . . When human beings can be conscious about their mating behavior, can reminisce about it in the past and imagine it in the future, we are in a very different world, . . . one that seems more familiar to us. Try to imagine what your "sexual life" would be if you could not fantasize about sex.[9]

Pornography is more the fount from which art and literature arise than a modern decadent departure from it.

(3) Though cultures lay interpretive filigrees over it, the ideally-healthy and athletic, fresh and flawless human form is naturally beautiful and, as Plato explicitly suggests in *Phaedrus*, a form that naturally produces literal sexual swelling and lubrication. (It would be fair to say that Plato took the swelling—which Plato analogizes to sprouting and development—as properly a form of perception or knowledge, though one that may grow false and strange if reason and the spirited elements are wrenched aside and dissolved in exploitive, delusive rut, discordantly twisted with violence, like Ares in the net with Aphrodite.) If I swell or lubricate when I see my beloved without veils, have I debased or abused him? If I do so looking at my spouse's photograph or a video tape we playfully made, have I debased or abused her? Or she, me, *mutatis mutandis*, if she is doing the looking? What of the lawyer, recently reported in the *New York Times*, who enjoys making amateur pornographic videos of herself to share with others similarly inclined and has lately gotten some chuckles and spare change from allowing porn distributors to carry her stuff?[10] Did the woman I once knew who lubricated while watching Baryshnikov dance debase and abuse him? And what of the one who had the same psychophysiological perception of ice skating pairs?

Someone might say, "I won't for the moment dispute that lawyer's right to distribute pictures of herself for free, but the real evil is in the commercial distribution, by a large number of predatory, profit-seeking males, who exploit the women they compel and sell." Now, I reply, we are at the perverse nub of the matter, shades of *boule de suif*. Hard-core movie acting is perhaps the single occupation in which women make substantial money and more money, considerably more money, than do men. And because pornography is legal, the women, with some exceptions, control and choose their working conditions, and they keep and control the considerable money they can make. In sharp contrast to nonpornographic movies and television, a substantial proportion of hard-core porn is directed and produced by women. When porn was illegal, all this was reversed and if we made it illegal again men (as they did prior to legalization) would coerce women and cash in.

Here one sees a quite general deconstructionist point hove into view. Our paternal, chauvinist culture makes all the valuable occupations that women alone can perform illegal, so women have to do them for free or expect, if paid, to be victim to the pimp, the serial killer, or the police. The most obvious examples of this are prostitution and marriage (traditionally, and mostly still in fact, adultery is a wife's crime, and marriage is ownership and restraint on a woman). But one also notes that some well paid male lawyers make their money arranging, prior to birth, adoptions for which highly paid, invariably male, obstetricians also receive their fees: the one person who cannot, legally, make any money out of the transaction is the mother, the woman.

In *Too Many Women?*, Marcia Guttentag and Paul Secord chart the effect of ratios between marriageable males and females on the value ascribed to marriage and the relative bargaining value of prospective brides and grooms.[11] Simply put, if there are less marriageable females than males, brides will be valued more highly as, for example, in a bridal price and (given Guttentag and Secord's reasonable, albeit depressing, claim that all human cultures have been male dominated) marriage itself will be regarded as highly desirable. Conversely, if (as has been true the last two decades in the United States) there are "too many women," then there might be a dowry or the like required, and marriage will not be as highly prized a state. Guttentag and Secord also point out, however, that when the ratio shifts to several, or tens, of men to every woman, the women become so valuable that they are taken over by pimps, who sell them to the other men, taking the profit for themselves. Guttentag and Secord note one exception to their generalizations, a community in which women, individually, earned much more money and controlled much more wealth than did men. This was an African community, under British colonial rule, in which there was one woman for every four or five men; the women were highly valued and often both married and carried on prostitution as well. (The colonial administration maintained laws that did not allow the men to take the women's money and power away from them, as they undoubtedly would have otherwise.)

(4) I cannot here say much more about that much vexed and often ferociously obscure topic of objectification. But imagine *boule de suif* transmogrified and transmigrated into Madonna. I quote Judith Williamson:

> Giles Smith of the *Independent* is certain that Madonna "intended to titillate"—but tells us precisely how she didn't titillate him. In other words, she failed to turn him on. But the show I saw—along with the cheering

> crowd—was about female desire. That, boys, isn't about whether you find Madonna sexy, it's about whether she/we find *you* sexy, geddit? Poor John Sweeny of the *Observer* felt that in Madonna's masturbatory act to Like a Virgin "she was dearly enjoying herself but it seemed something was missing. . . ." You, Big Boy? . . . Letting what you want show, for women, has always been taboo. In the last decade, men have increasingly—in popular imagery—become objects of desire, but this hasn't been matched by women—or gay men for that matter—becoming more accessible as subjects of desire, i.e., the ones doing the desiring.[12]

Hard-core porn is illegal in Britain, so Ms Williamson may be pardoned for not mentioning that, in hard-core gay movies in the United States, there is plenty of presentation of gay men as subjects of desire. More importantly, perhaps, nongay hard-core movies frequently present both men, in all their naked vulnerability, as objects of desire and women, often gracefully in command, as subjects desiring them.

Notes

1. Frank O'Connor, *The Lonely Voice: A Study of the Short Story* (New York: Simon and Schuster, 1966), 18.
2. Wallace Stegner, "Guy de Maupassant," in Louis Kronenberger, ed., *Brief Lives* (Boston: Little, Brown, 1971), 509-11, at 511.
3. Alfred C. Kinsey, Wardell B. Pomeroy, and Clyde E. Martin, *Sexual Behavior in the Human Male* (Philadelphia: W. B. Saunders, 1948), 650ff.
4. Vern L. Bullough, *Sexual Variance in Society and History* (New York: John Wiley, 1976), 261.
5. William H. Masters and Virginia E. Johnson, *Human Sexual Response* (Boston: Little, Brown, 1966), 133.
6. William H. Masters and Virginia E. Johnson, *Homosexuality in Perspective* (Boston: Little, Brown, 1979), 67-8, 84-6.
7. Julian Jaynes, *The Origins of Consciousness in the Breakdown of the Bicameral Mind* (New York: Houghton-Mifflin, 1982).
8. E. H. Gombrich, *Art and Illusion: A Study in the Psychology of Pictorial Representation* (Princeton: Princeton University Press, 1960), 131ff.
9. Jaynes, *The Origins of Consciousness*, 466.
10. Michael deCourcy Hinds, "Starring in Tonight's Video: The Couple Down the Street," *New York Times*, 22 March 1991, A14.
11. Marcia Guttentag and Paul Secord, *Too Many Women? The Sex-Ratio Question* (Beverly Hills, Cal.: Sage, 1983).
12. Judith Williamson, "What Men Miss About Madonna," *Guardian*, 2 August 1990.

Sylvia Walsh
(photograph: Stetson University)

Author of “Desire and Love in Kierkegaard’s *Either/Or*”
Paper presented at the Society for the Philosophy of Sex and Love
during the
Eastern Division Meeting of The American Philosophical Association
Washington, D. C., 28 December 1992

Sixty

DESIRE AND LOVE IN KIERKEGAARD'S *EITHER/OR*

Sylvia Walsh

Love is a major theme in Kierkegaard's writings, forming a central concern of *Either/Or, Repetition, Stages on Life's Way, Two Ages,* and *Works of Love*. These works establish Kierkegaard as a major thinker and perhaps the most penetrating and profound modern Christian philosopher of love. In the present paper, however, I shall limit my examination to *Either/Or* (1843), and within this work I shall focus on three sections from Part I ("The Immediate Erotic Stages or the Musical Erotic," "The First Love," and the infamous "The Seducer's Diary") and on the first essay in Part II entitled "The Esthetic Validity of Marriage."[1]

The first thing that should be noted about *Either/Or* is that it is made up of a collection of writings by an anonymous esthete referred to as "A" (Part I) and by a civil judge named William who is designated as "B" (Part II). These writings were supposedly discovered and published by a pseudonymous "editor" named Victor Eremita. The work is thus deliberately twice removed from Søren Kierkegaard as its author and should not be interpreted as setting forth his own viewpoints on love, which are spelled out more directly in writings published under his own name, for example, *Works of Love*. Rather, *Either/Or* should be understood as presenting only the viewpoints of the esthete and the judge, whose writings are intended as representations of an esthetic-romantic and a bourgeois-ethical life view, respectively. By allowing the representative authors to speak for themselves and to criticize one another, Kierkegaard himself stands in the background as an indirect critic of both. This is not to say, however, that Kierkegaard is entirely opposed to everything written by the esthete and the judge in *Either/Or*. The knowledgeable reader can find many points of agreement with both authors, although Kierkegaard's own standpoint is much closer to the ethical perspective of Judge William than to the hedonistic viewpoint of the romantic esthete.

That a characterization and critique of romanticism are intended in Part I of *Either/Or* is not self-evident but is suggested by the *form* of the work, which takes the shape of a romantic novel in the form of an arabesque or mixture of genres, and also by the *content* of A's thought, which reflects an ironic and esthetic standpoint typical of the German romantic movement as understood and criticized by Kierkegaard in his academic dissertation, *The Concept of Irony* (1841). In this work, the estheticism of the German romantics is identified with irony understood not merely as a rhetorical device but as a negative standpoint toward existence, which they find to be meaningless, inadequate, and boring. Thus they seek to transcend actuality by way of the imagination and a recovery of esthetic or sensuous immediacy in their lives and art in an effort to create themselves and their environment via experimentation with an infinity of possibilities. It is this romantic-ironic mentality and its fascination with the erotic as an expression of sensuous immediacy, on the one hand, and as a reflective, seductive, manipulative sensuality, on the other, that we find reflected in the writings of A in Part I of *Either/Or*. Kierkegaard seeks to expose and counteract this negative standpoint in a twofold fashion, first by depicting the irony, despair, illusion, fragmentation, and moral bankruptcy of the romantic-esthetic lifestyle in and through an artistic portrayal of its erotic moods, attitudes, viewpoints and actions; and second through a direct critique of the romantic esthete from an ethical standpoint by the pseudonym Judge William.

1. Desire and Love as Seduction: "The Immediate Erotic Stages or The Musical-Erotic"

Turning now to an examination of selected sections from the romantic esthete's collage of writings, let us look first at his interpretation of desire and love as represented by the figure of Don Juan, a perennial character in Western drama, music, and literature since the Middle Ages. According to A, Don Juan is a product of the Middle Ages' unconscious penchant for representing single aspects of life in figurative form. The aspect or idea Don Juan represents is that of the sensuous-erotic in its abstract or elemental originality qualified as desire. As A understands it, the sensuous-erotic constitutes the elementary passion or primitive life force in humanity manifested as an insatiable desire for enjoyment through an immediate gratification of the senses, especially in the form of sexual desire. As such, the sensuous-erotic or desire characterizes the esthetic stage of human life at its most immediate level, or that stage in which we live primarily on the basis of our natural drives and inclinations.

A views the expression of desire or the sensuous-erotic as developing in three stages, which he finds artistically represented in several of Mozart's operas. The first stage is portrayed by the Page in *The Marriage of Figaro*; the second by Papageno in *The Magic Flute*; and the third is epitomized by the opera *Don Giovanni*, the whole of which "is essentially the expression of the idea" of desire, though that idea is represented more specifically in the opera by the figure of Don Juan (*EO*, 1: 84). According to A, the first stage consists in a state of dreaming or intoxication in erotic love, in which there is still a substantial unity between desire and the desired and only a presentiment of a deeper desire separated from its object. The second stage is one in which desire actively seeks to discover its object in the multiplicity of particularity, but without actually having an object or desiring it. The third stage is characterized by desire of the particular absolutely in a unity of the two previous stages, the one and multiplicity or the particular and the universal (*EO*, 1: 75-85). This last stage is the only one that concerns us here. A claims that desire is manifested in Don Juan as a *principle*, not as an element in a particular individual, although it is personified in the opera in a figure who appears to be an individual, or more accurately, who is "continually being formed but is never finished" as an individual, so that he hovers between being an individual and an idea, that is, a power or life force (*EO*, 1: 92).

As a power or life force, Don Juan is the embodiment of the sensuous-erotic determined as a *demonic* principle in opposition to spirit. Being an aspect of our given nature, sensuousness is not intrinsically immoral or sinful, but A claims that with the coming of Christianity into the world sensuousness was excluded in favor of a spiritual form of existence. The sensuous-erotic then began to assert itself in its raw, pristine form as an independent power or force in esthetic indifference to the spiritual, whereas previously in the Greek psyche it had been harmoniously integrated as an element in the beautiful personality. Being the representative of sensuousness in this demonic form, Don Juan thus represents, on a spiritless level, the rebel in us, the desire to gratify our natural inclinations without constraints, without regard for others, in total freedom and total enjoyment of the senses. In his kingdom, where "everything is only one giddy round of pleasure," we hear "only the elemental voice of passion, the play of desires, the wild noise of intoxication" (*EO*, 1: 90).

It is the romantic esthete's contention that the sensuous-erotic in its immediacy, and especially in all its demonic force as represented in the figure of Don Juan, can be artistically represented only in music, for music is the only medium that is capable of expressing the immediate *in its immediacy* (*EO*, 1: 70). Other media either destroy immediacy by bringing it under the power of reflection in language or else give the sensuous static expression, as in painting and sculpture (*EO*, 1: 67, 70). Music is essentially a sensuous medium and has the sensuous as its absolute subject. Moreover, like the principle of sensuousness, it is also abstract and demonic, being essentially a medium for the expression of that which is general or indeterminate and which lies outside the realm of spirit (*EO*, 1: 65, 73).

As a representative of the immediate or sensuous-erotic in demonic form, Don Juan was given classic expression, A claims, in Mozart's opera *Don Giovanni*, for in this work there is achieved a perfect unity of form and content or medium and idea (*EO*, 1: 57). Being the embodiment of sensuous desire, Don Juan deceives and seduces women, but in the romantic esthete's opinion he is not, strictly speaking, a seducer, since that requires a level of consciousness and cunning that is lacking in Don Juan, who always acts with a passion, energy, and exuberance that is completely spontaneous and unreflective. Rather, he desires and therein acts seductively to obtain the satisfaction of his desire. As soon as he has enjoyed it, however, he seeks a new object in a repetitive process that goes on indefinitely (*EO*, 1: 99). His love for a woman, therefore, is always momentary and faithless. As soon as he has had one woman, he desires another, for it is not a particular woman but all women or more precisely the ideal of total femininity in every woman that he desires indiscriminately in all (*EO*, 1: 95, 100). Thus it is not the extraordinary woman but the ordinary woman who constitutes the object of his desire, since every woman is ordinary by virtue of the fact that she is a woman (*EO*, 1: 97).

The fact that Don Juan is a male figure and the preceding stages of the immediate-erotic are also represented by male figures raises an interesting question as to whether the immediate-erotic qualified as desire is gender specific, and more specifically whether the seductiveness of demonic desire is limited to males. In his analysis of the stages of desire the romantic esthete identifies desire with the male and the desired with the female, and in all three stages the object of desire is femininity (*EO*, 1: 77-8, 100). But if the sensuous-erotic is to be understood as an aspect of human existence in its esthetic condition or "elemental originality," then desire and the seductive character of desire would have to be a feature of women as well as men. Either the romantic esthete has committed the male chauvinist sin of identifying humanity solely with males or else he clearly intends to identify demonic desire and seduction as a male tendency. This is a point of view that runs contrary to the traditional stereotyped view of woman as a seductress derived from the biblical story of Adam and Eve, but which is consistent with A's philosophy of male dominance elsewhere in the text.

That the second alternative is intended is supported by a passage from another book, *The Concept of Anxiety*, published under the pseudonym Vigilius Haufniensis, in which Haufniensis says:

> So when the Genesis story, contrary to all analogy, represents the woman as seducing the man, this is on further reflection quite correct, for this seduction is precisely a feminine seduction, because only through Eve could Adam be seduced by the serpent. In every other place where there is a question of seduction, linguistic usage (delude, persuade, etc.) always attributes superiority to man.[2]

And in an earlier draft of this passage, Haufniensis writes:

> In a way it has always seemed remarkable to me that the story of Eve has been completely opposed to all later analogy, for the expression "to seduce" used for her generally refers in ordinary language to the man, and the other related expressions all point to woman as weaker (easier to infatuate, lure to bed, etc.). This, however, is easy to explain, for in Genesis it is a third power that seduces the woman, whereas in ordinary language the reference is always only to the relationship between man and woman and thus it must be the man who seduces the woman.[3]

Although this passage is by another pseudonym, one who stands much closer to Kierkegaard's own thought than does the romantic esthete, it reflects a point of view that is compatible with the esthete's practice of associating desire and seduction with the male and in fact provides a rationale for understanding the biblical story and feminine seduction as atypical, since in this instance the seduction of both the man and the woman is carried out by a third power, namely the serpent, and woman is simply the intermediary or instrument by which the male is seduced by the serpent. In ordinary situations, however, Haufniensis seems to be saying that seduction is generally perpetrated by man, since woman is the weaker sex. The possibility of woman being a seducer is not ruled out, but the phenomenon is primarily associated with males, or in the case of the figure of Don Juan, with male fantasy life.

This leads to a consideration of why the romantic esthete is so infatuated with Mozart's opera and the figure of Don Juan in the first place. Being highly reflective by nature or training, A seeks to lose himself in fantasy and to expand his own erotic moods by rediscovering them artistically in the music of Mozart. Finding Mozart's music tempting and irresistible as a stimulus and medium for fantasizing in this manner, A asks:

> where is the young man who has not had a moment in his life when he would have given half his kingdom to be a Don Juan, or perhaps all of it, when he would have given half his lifetime for one year of being Don Juan, or perhaps his whole life? But that was as far as it went. The more profound natures, who were moved by the idea, found everything, even the softest breeze, expressed in Mozart's music; in its grandiose passion, they found a full-toned expression for what stirred in their own inner beings, they perceived how every mood strained toward that music just as the brook hurries on in order to lose itself in the infinitude of the sea. (*EO*, 1: 104)

The point A is making here is not that men should be inspired by the Mozartian Don Juan to act out their male fantasy life and become Don Juans themselves. This is made clear as he goes on to say:

> The bunglers, who think themselves a Don Juan because they have pinched a peasant girl's cheek, put their arms around a waitress, or made a young girl blush, of course understand neither the idea nor Mozart, or how to produce a Don Juan themselves, except as a ludicrous freak, a family idol, who perhaps to the misty, sentimental eyes of some cousins would seem to be a true Don Juan, the epitome of all charm. (*EO*, 1: 104)

It is not the indulgence in *actual sensuousness* in comic imitation of Don Juan (who, being a mythic figure larger than life and the symbol of a power or force rather than an individual, is not a role model for virile males), but rather a *poetic sensuousness* that A and all the "more profound natures" moved by the idea seek to enjoy. As a romantic ironist, A has essentially rejected actuality and taken flight into the realm of fantasy as a way of recovering a lost immediacy or eroticism that can never be regained in actuality but might be momentarily, that is, *illusively* recaptured and enjoyed in an infinity of erotic moods stimulated by music and the imagination. Thus, while A claims that the essay on Don Juan "is written only for those who have fallen in love" (*EO*, 1: 58), he does not really believe in love, not even the sensuous love of Don Juan in any real sense. That love is an illusion nourished by the wrong sort of fantasy life, that is, by the conception of love portrayed in romantic novels, is the subject of another esthetic essay by A, "The First Love," to which we shall now turn.

2. Love as an Illusion: "The First Love"

"The First Love" is a review of a play by that title written by a nineteenth-century French dramatist, Augustin Eugène Scribe, a playwright little remembered today but one who enjoyed immense popularity in his own time, especially in the tiny country of Denmark, where his works were performed over 900 times (almost twice as often as Shakespeare) during Kierkegaard's lifetime (1813-55).[4] *Les Premières Amours* or *The First Love*, a modern situation comedy in one act, was the most popular of Scribe's plays in Denmark. Just as A praises Mozart's *Don Giovanni* as an unparalleled masterpiece of music, in agreement with popular opinion he lauds *The First Love* as "a flawless play, so consummate that it alone is bound to make Scribe immortal" (*EO*, 1: 248).

The First Love centers around two characters, Emmeline and Charles, who according to A's interpretation illustrate respectively the results of having been nurtured on romantic novels: either a sinking into a state of illusion in which one is hidden from oneself, as in the case of Emmeline, or a gaining of a talent for mystification by which one can hide oneself from others, as in the case of Charles. Emmeline espouses the romantic dictum that "the first love is the true love, and one loves only once" (*EO*, 1: 254). She is convinced that she loves her cousin Charles, whom she has not seen since she was eight years old, and she holds fast to this illusion during the course of a comic mix up in which Charles courts her under another name and is roundly rejected. When it is at last revealed to her who he is and that he is already married, she agrees to marry another man who had pretended to be Charles. She will marry him, however, not out of love (for an "ideal" Charles remains her first and only love), but to be obedient to her father's wish and to get even with the real Charles for having been untrue to her. For his part, Charles, who has squandered all his money and become dissolute, thinks he can hide his identity and ingratiate himself to his uncle in the disguise of a respectable man. The man whose identity he assumes is the man who is passing himself off as Charles in order to court Emmeline. In the end both Charles and Emmeline effect the opposite of what they sought, so that the play ends in irony. Emmeline's illusion, however, remains intact, as she looks to the future still in love with the ideal Charles who was her first and only love. Thus it is not a real man but an ideal one created in her own imagination whom she thinks she loves.

A uses the occasion of a performance of Scribe's play as an occasion for poetically recollecting and reliving his own first love, or what he thought was his first and only love. Although he seeks in this manner to renew his first love, confident that "the poetic power of this play will prompt the love in my breast to spring forth," he does not actually want to renew his relation to his first love but prefers instead to feel the beauty of loving her at a distance (*EO*, 1: 241-2). Even when he was experiencing love for the first time, he admits, they saw each other infrequently and felt more comfortable and closer when they were apart (*EO*, 1: 240). In this he sees a similarity between his situation and that of heroes in novels and comedies and thus thinks of himself as a poetic character and as leading a poetic life (*EO*, 1: 241). What he really hopes to recover and reexperience poetically is his youth and the spontaneous passion of love, which he expects to burst forth forcefully like the snap of a passion flower or the popping of the cork on a bottle of champagne (*EO*, 1: 241).

But while A seeks to recapture and enjoy the illusion of first love, he is under no illusion about the illusory nature of romantic love (*EO*, 1: 244). Although A admits that as a young man he went through a period of illusion in which he believed in first love, he later lost faith in it so as to "believe no more in the first" (*EO*, 1: 244). This disillusionment is further confirmed by the fact that his former first love informed him upon a later chance meeting at a performance of the play that she had never loved him and that her present love was her first love. This prompts him to undertake a review of the play in order to determine what first love really means. The thesis adhered to by Emmeline and his own "first love" (and other women as well, since in A's opinion "[a] girl is more likely to become immersed in illusion" than is a man) A finds sophistical in that it confuses what is supposed to be a qualitative category, "the first," which is thought to be essentially different from later loves, with a numerical category inasmuch as it is possible to love more than once (*EO*, 1: 250, 254). The typical way of conflating these categories, illustrated by A's former first love, is to maintain that though we might love several times, each time is really the first time, thus negating the validity of the previous times. Emmeline is not guilty of this sort of confusion, since her first love is Charles and she has loved only him since she was eight years old. Her confusion consists in the fact that "[s]he understands the thesis numerically and so conscientiously that she believes that an impression in her eighth year is decisive for her whole life" (*EO*, 1: 254).

A finds such a sentimental view of love ridiculous though representative of "a large class of people" (*EO*, 1: 254). Contending that Scribe presents "an infinitely witty mockery of Emmeline's sentimentality" in almost every situation in the play, he concludes that the drama should be interpreted ironically, that is, as a parody that negates romantic love rather than affirms it (*EO*, 1: 261, 273, 277). Having contended that A is himself a representative of romanticism, we are thus required to make a distinction between two forms of romanticism, a sentimental kind that naively believes in romantic love, and a pessimistic brand characterized by romantic irony that regards love as an illusion. This second form of romanticism, reflecting A's own view of love, is developed to its logical conclusion in "The Seducer's Diary," the final section from *Either/ Or* Part I to be considered here.

3. The Irony of Erotic Love: "The Seducer's Diary"

In "The Seducer's Diary," A brings before us another esthete by the name of Johannes, who specializes in the seduction of young girls. A character of A's own creation and perhaps a reflection of his own darker nature (although he claims to be only the editor of the seducer's diary, which he supposedly found in a secretary drawer), the seducer figure portrayed here is designed as an analogue to the immediate Don Juan at the reflective level; that is, he is a conscious seducer and thus constitutes a genuine seducer, whereas the immediate Don Juan merely acts seductively in the process of desiring. Unlike the musical Don Juan, this seducer is much more interested in the art of seduction, the method of conquering, than in the act of seduction or the sensuous experience itself. The mode of treatment in this instance, therefore, centers on a portrayal of the craftiness with which the seducer wins over his victim and carries out the seduction. We might find an analogy, and possibly even a model, for the seducer figure and his diary in several works of the eighteenth century: Samuel Richardson's epistolary novel *Clarissa. Or, The History of a Young Lady* (1747-8), recently cast for television on Masterpiece Theatre; Choderlos de Laclos's epistolary novel *Les Liaisons dangereuses* (1782), brilliantly made into a film starring Glenn Close and John Malkovich a few years ago; the Marquis de Sade's *La philosophie dans le boudoir* (1795), a tale of seduction in dialogue form; and Friedrich Schlegel's *Lucinde* (1799), a romantic novel considered to be "obscene" by Kierkegaard and widely regarded as pornographic in the early nineteenth century.[5] There is no evidence that Kierkegaard was familiar with Richardson, de Sade, or Laclos, but a Danish translation of Laclos's novel was published in Copenhagen in 1832, making it at least possible that Kierkegaard read it.[6]

Unlike the figures in these writers' works, however, Kierkegaard's Johannes is more than a master seduction artist; indeed, he claims not to be a seducer at all but rather an *eroticist*, that is, a person who, according to his definition, "has grasped the nature and the point of love, who believes in love and knows it from the ground up," and who also knows that "the highest enjoyment imaginable is to be loved, loved more than anything else in the world" (*EO*, 1: 368). For an eroticist, love is the absolute, but in Johannes' view it is a short-lived experience that must be carefully cultivated and controlled for maximum enjoyment. In his opinion, "no love affair should last more than a half year at most and . . . any relationship is over as soon as one has enjoyed the ultimate" (*EO*, 1: 368). Unlike "vulgar seducers" who deceptively entice girls with false promises of marriage, the eroticist makes no promises but receives everything as a gift of freedom (*EO*, 1: 367-68). "Only in freedom is there love; only in freedom are there diversion and everlasting amusement," he proclaims, for otherwise the girl will fall "like a heavy body" as a burden and obligation upon him (*EO*, 1: 360-1). To bring about this freedom requires a special kind of artfulness, a "discerning touch" that knows how to evoke devotedness along with freedom (*EO*, 1: 342). "The majority enjoy a young girl as they enjoy a glass of champagne, at one effervescent moment" that, in Johannes' view, corresponds to rape (*EO*, 1: 341-2). By contrast, the eroticist is able to enjoy more and to make the experience more interesting for himself by artfully developing a young girl within herself. As techniques in this educative process, he employs deception, dissimulation, psychological conflict, irony, erotic stimulation, anything that will aid her development. Essentially, however, his method is passive in nature, relying on and being alert to making the right impression on her. Johannes writes:

> The art is to be as receptive as possible to impressions, to know what impression one is making and what impression one has of each girl. In that way, one can be in love with many girls at the same time, because

> one is in love in a different way with each one. To love one girl is too little, to love all is superficiality; to know oneself and to love as many as possible, to let one's soul conceal all the powers of love inside itself so that each receives its specific nourishment while the consciousness nevertheless embraces the whole—that is enjoyment, that is living. (*EO*, 1: 361)

To this end Johannes undertakes, and recollects in his diary, the education of a young girl of seventeen, named Cordelia Wahl, in the art of erotic love. Unlike other young girls he has loved in the past, Johannes senses something special about this one. She is lovely, lively, passionate, innocent, imaginative, proud, full of confidence, ripe for an awakening of love. Much to his surprise, she also stirs up in him the passion and rapture of erotic love, which he had not expected to experience again and which necessitates all the more breaking the relationship to her once he has accomplished his objective with her. That consists, first of all, in implanting himself into her life and becoming engaged to her even though she does not yet love him. Then her education begins in earnest as she learns to love him with all the powerful force of erotic love, and in learning to love comes to love him doubly so because she has learned to love from him (*EO*, 1: 377). Patiently, cautiously, Johannes cultivates love in her through a series of letters, which he uses to develop the power of imagination in her by which she can discover and make a leap into the infinite. Johannes writes: "What she must learn is to make all the motions of infinity, to swing herself, to rock herself in moods, to confuse poetry and actuality, truth and fiction, to frolic in infinity. Then when she is familiar with this tumult, I shall add the erotic; then she will be what I want and desire" (*EO*, 1: 392). To evoke the erotic in her, he switches from letters to notes and with these arouses her to the level of a naive erotic passion.

But the eroticist has a higher form of the erotic than this in mind for his pupil. What he wants to develop in her is a reflected passion that is bold and free as well as "definite, energetic, determined, dialectical" in character (*EO*, 1: 412). Having cultivated her passion within the bounds of the universal through an engagement, he now seeks to make her bored and dissatisfied with this convention and thus lead her to break the engagement in order to go beyond the universal in the expression of a devoted yet free love that recognizes no earthly bounds. As Johannes puts it:

> The point now is to guide her in such a way that in her bold flight she entirely loses sight of marriage and the continent of actuality, so that her soul, as much in pride as in her anxiety about losing me, will destroy an imperfect human form in order to hurry on to something that is superior to the ordinarily human. (*EO*, 1: 428)

Here we have a clear statement of the ironic standpoint toward actuality that the romantic esthete and his alter ego Johannes espouse in the pitting of free love against marriage, the unconventional against convention, the exception against the universal. With ironic detachment, Johannes transcends and cuts himself off from actuality, its only significance for him being to serve as a temporary stimulus to sensual experimentation and reproduction of the same in poetic form. But Johannes' irony extends beyond this to love itself. The moment Cordelia gives herself to him in freedom and total devotion everything is over. He is rejuvenated and ready to move on to another young girl in waiting; she is relativized and made weak and insignificant by her deflowering. For as the eroticist interprets woman's existence, she is a "being-for-others" whose value is instantly deflated in the moment of her birth and baptism as a woman (*EO*, 1: 429). From Johannes Cordelia has learned to love, but through him she has also learned the irony of erotic love, which is what he ultimately sought to teach her.

As an eroticist, then, Johannes is the consummate esthete and diabolical seducer, a prospect so terrifying in its ultimate implications that even A is frightened by the shadowy, dreamlike relation of this character to his own being. We find him repulsive too, whether we identify with the victims of his psychological manipulation and subliminal control or with the perpetrator of these actions who has gone so far astray in his inner being that there is little or no chance of exit from the self-entrapment in irony and moral bankruptcy concealed there. Yet the flight into boundless freedom that Johannes and Cordelia take is an alluring one that constitutes the essence of the romantic-esthetic view of life and love as Kierkegaard sees it. In a letter to A that likens him to a "matchless instrument" of music (an appropriate medium for expressing "the demonic," we might recall), Cordelia describes her reaction to Johannes: "With an indescribable but cryptic, blissful, unnameable anxiety, I listened to this music I myself had evoked and yet did not evoke; always there was harmony, always I was enraptured by him" (*EO*, 1: 310).

In emphasizing the sensuous, illusory, and temporary character of romantic love, Kierkegaard's portrayal of it in Part I of *Either/Or* is consonant with the usual understanding of this form of love. But his figurative analysis of the romantic esthete's philosophy of love goes further in revealing it to be *anti-sensuous* in its desire for a poetic rather than actual recovery and indulgence in the sensuous-erotic; *anti-woman* in its characterization of woman as the object and victim of male seduction, on the one hand, and as a silly, sentimental believer in the illusion of love, on the other; and finally, *anti-love* in its ironic negation of any real and lasting erotic relationship between a man and a woman. At the end of Part I we are left wondering, then, whether erotic love can be given expression in actuality in such a way as to preserve and enhance its sensuous nature without negating the existence of woman and ultimately of love itself. For a possible answer to that question, let us turn finally to Judge William's view of love in Part II.

4. The Ennoblement of Erotic Love in Marriage: "The Esthetic Validity of Marriage"

Part II of *Either/Or* consists of two long epistles (only the first of which will be considered here) written by Judge William to A, whom the judge claims to love as a son, brother, and friend. The judge seeks to help A secure an ethical-religious center for his life by confronting him with a well-meaning critique of his esthetic-ironic lifestyle and countering it in the first letter with a strong defense of love and marriage (*EO*, 2: 6-7). Judge William believes in first love just as adamantly as does Emmeline, claiming that his wife is "the only one I have ever loved, the first," a sentiment that, according to him, is mutually shared by his wife (*EO*, 2: 9; see also 37, 39, 41, 60). But for Judge William love is "not a venture in the imaginary erotic" as it is for Emmeline, A, and Johannes the Seducer; rather, it is "the earnestness of life," which in his view does not make it "cold, unbeautiful, unerotic, unpoetic" but more beautiful, more deeply erotic, and truly poetic (*EO*, 2: 10). As his marriage has gained stability over the years, first love, the judge claims, has been continually rejuvenated in it in such a way as to acquire religious as well as esthetic meaning. For him, however, rejuvenation is not a "sad looking back" or a "poetic recollecting of past experience" as it is for A but rather an action that is situated in striving (*EO*, 2: 10).

Although the judge does not presume to set forth his own marriage as normative, he finds esthetic treatments of love and marriage in literature generally untrue and unsatisfactory. On the one hand, he claims, novels about love tend to glorify marriage by having the story end in a happy marriage, as if all the struggles and difficulties of life were now over. On the other hand, in his view modern literature no longer really believes in love; thus love is ridiculed and shown to be an illusion, as in the works of Scribe (*EO*, 2: 18-19). Working against the literary stream, therefore, Judge William seeks to establish not only the esthetic validity of marriage, that is, the possibility of preserving erotic love in marriage, but also the validity of love itself.

Beginning with an analysis of the nature of erotic or romantic love, the judge emphasizes first of all its immediate, sensuous quality but goes on to point out that erotic love is not merely sensuous, since it contains a consciousness of the eternal, which gives it nobility and distinguishes it from lust (*EO*, 2: 21). Whereas the merely sensuous is momentary and in its more refined expression makes the moment of enjoyment into a "little eternity" or a "sensuous eternity" in "the eternal moment of the embrace," the true eternal factor in romantic love "rescues it first out of the sensuous," he claims (*EO*, 2: 22). Thus, while the judge admits that "romantic love is rather overworked these days," he has "a certain faith in the truth of it" and "a certain respect for it" (*EO*, 2: 20). However, in partial agreement with the modern literary viewpoint, the judge regards the eternal factor in romantic love as illusory and presumptive, since in his view it is based on nothing more than the conviction of the lovers that their love will last forever (*EO*, 2: 21). This is the weakness, the fatal flaw in romantic love against which modern literature has unleashed its devastating and sometimes amusing ironic polemic. But in the judge's considered opinion modern literature has nothing to put in its place, or rather, goes off reflectively in two directions, neither of which is acceptable to him because the first is immoral and the second "misses out on what is more profound in love" (*EO*, 2: 22). The first path is one of indulging in a transitory sensuality that is antithetical to marriage or else enters into marriage as a temporary civil arrangement until someone more attractive comes along (*EO*, 2: 23).

The other path moves in the opposite direction toward a neutralization of the sensuous in a marriage of convenience based on calculation and involving only the "prose of love," that is, social and economic considerations (*EO*, 2: 23, 27). In contrast to these paths, both of which effectively annihilate love, Judge William holds that romantic love can be delivered from its "illusory eternal" or transient nature and given a deeper erotic or sensuous expression by being assumed, transfigured, and ennobled in a marriage that has its center and authority in the divine (*EO*, 2: 29-30, 43).

The notion of a "higher concentricity" in which love and marriage are oriented in a religious perspective is central to Judge William's doctrine of love (see *EO*, 2: 43, 47, 55, 57, 89, 94). For it is not marriage *per se* that secures and ennobles romantic love, as he has already shown in his critique of secular forms and motives for marriage. Only those marriages that take their point of departure in the saying of vows before God, in the recognition of the authority and power of the divine in their lives, have the possibility of doing so. In the higher concentricity of the religious, marital love becomes a unity of contrasting elements: sensuous yet spiritual, necessary (bound) yet free, momentarily present yet eternal (*EO*, 2: 30, 60).

In Judge William's view there exists, then, a close bond between the erotic and the religious and between marriage and the religious. In this regard he is particularly concerned to point out the essential relation between Christianity, marriage, and the erotic. In an apparent reference to A's claim in his essay on the musical erotic that the sensuous is "excluded" by Christianity (*EO*, 1: 61-62), Judge William denies that sensuousness is negated or annihilated in Christianity (*EO*, 2: 48-9). While admitting that the Christian God is spirit and that spirit and the flesh stand in discord with one another in this religion, he stresses that the flesh is not identical to the sensuous but rather is to be understood as selfishness (*EO*, 2: 36, 49). Thus Judge William avers: "the joy and fullness that are in the sensuous in its innocence can very well be caught up in Christianity" (*EO*, 2: 49). In another passage he notes that "it would indeed be beautiful if the Christian dared to call his God the God of love in such a way he thereby thought of that inexpressibly blissful feeling, that neverending force in the world: earthly love" (*EO*, 2: 30). And he concludes that "if marital love has no place within itself for the eroticism of first love, then Christianity is not the highest development of the human race" (*EO*, 2: 31). In Judge William's opinion, however, marriage provides the connecting link between the erotic and the religious inasmuch as it contains, or should contain, both of these elements. Furthermore, in his view "marriage belongs essentially to Christianity," more so than in paganism and Judaism, because sex differences are more deeply reflected in Christianity than in these other religions, enabling woman to attain her full right as a separate and independent being (*EO*, 2: 29). Although, somewhat contradictorily, the judge declares himself against female emancipation, regarding it as a male plot to corrupt and exploit woman, marriage oriented in the religious is viewed as emancipating both man and woman from a patriarchal mentality (*EO*, 2: 22, 52, 61). By referring marriage to God, man is freed from a false pride that leads him to try to conquer and assert superiority over woman; and woman is freed from a false humility that causes her to surrender and submit herself to him as if she were nothing.

Marriage oriented in the religious also has a historical character lacking in immediate love that enables it to gain continuity and the eternal in time. Marital love is historical in the sense that it is a process of inward blossoming in which such qualities as humility, patience, constancy and faithfulness are acquired and possessed through daily repetition and a steady acquisition over the years. The ideal husband or wife, therefore, is not one who is that once in his or her life but who is that every day (*EO*, 2: 135). This form of repetition is not identical with habit, which Judge William regards as evil and thus something that ought to be changed (*EO*, 2: 127). The way to counteract boredom and habit in marriage, he claims, is not by changing partners or distancing oneself from the beloved so as to maintain interest, mystery, and secretiveness, but by developing a shared history and a shared consciousness or mutual understanding characterized by sincerity, self-giving, and openness. For Judge William, understanding is "the life principle of marriage" and "the absolute condition for preserving the esthetic [or love] in marriage" (*EO*, 2: 116-17). Without it marriage is neither beautiful nor moral. With it repetition in the ethical sphere becomes a forward movement in which one constantly repeats what one already possesses in the form of love, faithfulness, patience, and so forth, and thereby gains content and continuity in the midst of the ongoing flux of life. In this way marital love preserves eternity in time and time in eternity, for the qualities acquired through daily repetition constitute the eternal in the individual and have within them the qualification of time, that is, the condition that their veracity consists in being continually realized in time rather than once and for all (*EO*, 2: 139).

From Judge William's standpoint, therefore, every individual has a duty to marry. Capitalizing on the possibility of a play on words in Danish to make this point with respect to men, Judge William claims that it is only as a married man (*Ægtemand*) that one proves oneself to be a "genuine man" (*ægte mand*) in the trials of life (*EO*, 2: 125). Although, in his opinion, it is not sinful for a person to remain single unless that individual is responsible for it, he regards marriage as advantageous and superior to the single life and to any erotic relationship outside of marriage, for several reasons. First of all, from an ethical standpoint, marriage must be understood as an expression of the universal rather than the accidental; that is, it puts an emphasis on the ordinary, what might be said of or experienced by every couple, rather than the extraordinary, the differences that set an individual or couple apart from others. Although differences are not canceled in marriage, they become transfigured in the relationship so that one is able to see the universal in the differences and to appreciate differences as differences without making them determinative for the relation. A second advantage of marriage, therefore, is that it makes the universal, that is, the marital relationship itself, not differences, the absolute. Whether or not a person is uncommonly beautiful or handsome is thus inconsequential in marriage, as there is essentially no difference from others at the fundamental level. On the matter of beauty, however, a third advantage shows itself in that marriage reveals the true beauty of love, which consists not in the accidental beauty of the lover's or loved one's good looks but in an "historical beauty" of freedom, whose task is to fashion something great and beautiful out of the ordinary, not merely to develop the differences or out-of-the-ordinary features that distinguish a marriage or the parties in a marriage (*EO*, 2: 304-5).

Although *Either/Or* ends without validating either the judge's or the romantic esthete's view of love and marriage, requiring us to reflect upon and make a fundamental choice between them, we know from a journal entry of Kierkegaard that he regarded the judge as "unconditionally the winner" of the contest between their contrasting life views (*JP*, 5: 5804). But this does not mean that he viewed Judge William's perspective as final or without shortcomings. Indeed, the parson's sermon on the theme that "in relation to God we are always in the wrong" at the conclusion of the book is intended to suggest just the opposite. In particular, one can detect in Judge William vestiges of the patriarchal mentality that a religious orientation of marriage is supposed to overcome, and he assumes a natural compatibility between the erotic and the religious that will later be questioned and reformulated in *Works of Love* in a more strictly Christian perspective that makes spiritual love the center of both the erotic and the religious. It is to this later work, therefore, that one must turn for a full account of Kierkegaard's philosophy of love.[7]

Notes

1. All references to this work in the present paper are from Søren Kierkegaard, *Either/Or*, 2 vols., ed. and trans. Howard V. Hong and Edna H. Hong (Princeton: Princeton University Press, 1987). References will be placed in parentheses in the text, using the sigla *EO* followed by volume and page numbers.

2. Søren Kierkegaard, *The Concept of Anxiety*, ed. and trans. Reidar Thomte (Princeton: Princeton University Press, 1980), 66.

3. *Søren Kierkegaard's Journals and Papers*, 7 vols., ed. and trans. Howard V. Hong and Edna H. Hong, assisted by Gregor Malantschuk (Bloomington: Indiana University Press, 1967-78), vol. 5, entry 5730; hereafter cited in the text by the sigla *JP*, followed by volume and entry number.

4. Ronald Grimsley, *Søren Kierkegaard and French Literature* (Cardiff, Wales: University of Wales Press, 1966), 112-14.

5. For Kierkegaard's critique of Schlegel's novel, see *The Concept of Irony with Constant Reference to Socrates*, ed. and trans. Howard V. Hong and Edna H. Hong (Princeton: Princeton University Press, 1989), 286-301. On the hostile reception of Schlegel's novel, see the "Introduction" to *Friedrich Schlegel's "Lucinde" and the "Fragments"*, trans. Peter Firchow (Minneapolis: University of Minnesota Press, 1971), 3-8. On Kierkegaard and the Marquis de Sade, see Henning Fenger, *Kierkegaard, the Myths and Their Origins: Studies in the Kierkegaardian Papers and Letters*, trans. George C. Schoolfield (New Haven: Yale University Press, 1980), 204-12.

6. Grimsley, *Søren Kierkegaard and French Literature*, 27.

7. On *Works of Love*, see my article, "Forming the Heart: The Role of Love in Kierkegaard's Thought," in Richard H. Bell, ed., *The Grammar of the Heart: New Essays in Moral Philosophy and Theology* (San Francisco: Harper and Row, 1988), 234-56.

Contributors

TIMO AIRAKSINEN (Ph.D., Turku, Finland, 1975) is Professor of Philosophy (ethics, social philosophy, philosophy of law) at the University of Helsinki. During 1994-96, he was Visiting Professor of Philosophy at Texas A&M University in Corpus Christi. He is a life member of Clare Hall, Cambridge, England, the former Vice-President of the International Society for Value Inquiry, and an honorary member of the Praxeological Society (Warsaw, Poland). He has published extensively on epistemology, history of philosophy (Berkeley, Hobbes, and Hegel), and ethics; his work has appeared in *American Philosophical Quarterly*, *Logique et Analyse*, *Philosophy and Phenomenological Research*, *Philosophia*, *Synthèse*, and *Journal of Applied Philosophy*. Two of his books are *Ethics of Coercion and Authority* (University of Pittsburgh Press, 1988) and *The Philosophy of the Marquis de Sade* (Routledge, 1995). He is the managing editor of the journal *Hobbes Studies*.

NEERA KAPUR BADHWAR is Associate Professor of Philosophy at the University of Oklahoma, where she has taught since 1987. She received her Ph.D. from the University of Toronto in 1986 and was a Killam Postdoctoral Fellow at Dalhousie University in 1986-87. Her areas of interest include ethical theory, moral psychology, and political and legal theory, and she is working on a book on the connection between virtue and self-interest. Her articles on friendship, self-interest and altruism, virtue, communitarianism and liberalism, and contemporary moral theory have appeared in *Ethics*, *Noûs*, *American Philosophical Quarterly*, *Social Philosophy and Policy*, *Philosophy and Phenomenological Research*, and *Journal of Political Philosophy*. Her anthology, *Friendship: A Philosophical Reader* (Cornell University Press), was published in 1993. In 1996-97 she was a Laurance S. Rockefeller fellow at the University Center for Human Values at Princeton University.

STEVEN BARBONE holds his B.S. from the University of Scranton and a diploma as *Pensionnaire Scientifique* from the Ecole Normale Supérieure at Fontenay-Saint Cloud in France. He is presently completing thesis work at Sorbonne, Paris IV, under a Smith Family Fellowship through Marquette University in Milwaukee. He has written on Spinoza and seventeenth-century philosophy, and also has interests in aesthetics and the philosophy of sexuality. His published works have appeared in *Idealistic Studies*, *Augustiniana*, *Iyyun* (*Jerusalem Philosophical Quarterly*), *International Philosophical Quarterly*, *Journal of Homosexuality*, *Studia Spinozana*, *Philosophy Today*, *Dialogue*, and *Lyceum*. He is one of the coeditors of a new translation of Spinoza's letters (Baruch Spinoza, *The Letters*, trans. Samuel Shirley, Introduction and Notes by Steven Barbone, Lee Rice, and Jacob Adler [Hackett, 1995]); has served as a consultant to the French research group that is preparing the new edition and translation of the complete works of Spinoza; and has been the Executive Secretary of the North American Spinoza Society (1994-96).

LEONARD J. BERKOWITZ is Associate Professor of Philosophy at the Pennsylvania State University at York, where he has taught since 1972. He received a B.A. in psychology from Duke University and his M.A. and Ph.D. in Philosophy from Johns Hopkins University. He has published articles in the areas of the philosophy of science, social ethics, critical thinking, and general education, which have appeared in *Philosophy of Science*, *Journal of General Education*, *Informal Logic*, and *Philosophical Forum*. He is a member of the Executive Council of the Association for General and Liberal Studies and associate editor of its journal, *Perspectives*.

DANA E. BUSHNELL holds a B.A. in philosophy from the University of New Orleans and the M.A. and Ph.D. from Tulane University. She has been teaching philosophy and women's studies at Edinboro University of Pennsylvania since 1990, and is now a tenured assistant professor. She is the editor of *"Nagging" Questions: Feminist Ethics in Everyday Life* (Rowman and Littlefield, 1995). Her essays have appeared in *Journal of Philosophical Research* and *Philosophy and Theology*.

CAROL CARAWAY has been President of the Society for the Philosophy of Sex and Love since 1992. Educated at the University of Oklahoma (Ph.D., 1982), she taught at the University of Wisconsin at Oshkosh, Chatham College, and Converse College, and is now Professor of Philosophy at Indiana University of Pennsylvania. Her interests include epistemology, philosophy of mind, and the later Wittgenstein. She has published in these and other areas in *Philosophical Investigations*, *Southern Journal of Philosophy*, *Teaching Philosophy*, *Philosophy and Theology*, *Metaphilosophy*, and *Informal Logic*.

CLAUDIA CARD is the author of *Lesbian Choices* (Columbia University Press, 1995) and editor of *Feminist Ethics* (University Press of Kansas, 1991) and *Adventures in Lesbian Philosophy* (Indiana University Press, 1994). She received the Ph.D. in philosophy from Harvard University in 1969, and since 1966 has been a member of the Philosophy Department of the University of Wisconsin. She is also affiliated with Wisconsin's Women's Studies Program and Institute for Environmental Studies.

MARY ANN CARROLL received her Ph.D. from the University of North Carolina in 1973. She is Professor of Philosophy in the Department of Philosophy and Religion and serves as Director of the Humanities Program at Appalachian State University in Boone, North Carolina. She has coauthored three books, including *Ethics in the Practice of Psychology* (Prentice-Hall, 1987). She is the author of papers in applied ethics that have appeared in *Journal of Medicine and Philosophy* and *Metaphilosophy*, and has written book reviews for *Journal of Value Inquiry* and *Teaching Philosophy*. She is the writer and editor of the column "Out of the Mouths of Babes . . . or, Quotable Quotes," which appears in the American Association of Philosophy Teachers Newsletter. A fancier of Borzoi and cats, she and her husband Galen Lutz are owned by three Borzoi and six cats.

JOHN CHRISTMAN received the B.A. from the University of New Orleans, where he was a student of Dr. Deborah Rosen. He received the M.A. (1982) and Ph.D. (1985) from the University of Illinois at Chicago. He has since been on the faculty at Virginia Polytechnic and State University and is now Associate Professor of Philosophy. While on leave in 1990-91, he spent a year at the University of California at San Diego as a Visiting Assistant Professor. His articles have appeared in *Ethics*, *Philosophy and Public Affairs*, *Political Theory*, *Social Philosophy and Policy*, and *Canadian Journal of Philosophy*. He is the editor of *The Inner Citadel: Essays on Individual Autonomy* (Oxford University Press, 1989) and the author of *The Myth of Property: Toward an Egalitarian Theory of Ownership* (Oxford, 1994).

NATALIE DANDEKAR earned her Ph.D. at the University of Chicago. Her most recent teaching experience has been five years at the University of Rhode Island. She is interested in the relationship between political systems and the possibility of personal autonomy. She is working on a book tentatively titled *International Justice: A Feminist Perspective*.

M. C. DILLON is Distinguished Teaching Professor of Philosophy at Binghamton University. He is author of *Merleau-Ponty's Ontology* (Indiana University Press, 1988), *Semiological Reductionism: A Critique of the Deconstructionist Movement in Postmodern Thought* (State University of New York Press, 1995), and essays on phenomenology, psychology, literature, and the philosophy of love and sexuality. He is editor of *Merleau-Ponty Vivant* (SUNY Press, 1991), *Écart & Différance: Merleau-Ponty and Derrida on Seeing and Writing* (Humanities Press, 1996), and is writing a book on the philosophy of love. Dillon is General Secretary of the Merleau-Ponty Circle and a founding member of the International Association for Philosophy and Literature.

STEVEN M. EMMANUEL was born on 22 July 1959 in Boston. He was admitted in 1977 to Boston University, where he read for the B.A. in philosophy and German. Realizing that an undergraduate philosophy degree would not get him far in life, he continued the study of philosophy in the doctoral program at Brown University. During his first year of graduate study he developed an interest in the thought of Kierkegaard, and spent two of the next four years as a visiting scholar at the University of Copenhagen (1982-83, 1985-86), where he attended lectures on Kierkegaard and pursued independent research. Upon completing the degree, he accepted a teaching appointment at the University of California at Riverside. Later, he held positions at Grinnell College and Kenyon College before moving into his present appointment as Assistant Professor of Philosophy at Virginia Wesleyan College. He resides in Virginia Beach with his Danish wife, Henriette, and their sons Daniel, Nicholas, and Marcus.

GENE FENDT teaches philosophy at the University of Nebraska at Kearney. He has published two books, *Works of Love? Reflections on* Works of Love (Scripta Humanistica, 1990) and *For What May I Hope? Thinking with Kant* *and Kierkegaard* (Peter Lang, 1990). He has published articles on Augustine, Shakespeare, Pinter, Kant, and Kierkegaard, as well as on topics in philosophy and literature and literary theory. Over the last several years his poetry has appeared regularly in *Aethlon*, *Anglican Theological Review*, *Puerto del Sol*, and *Theology Today*. He shares a birthday with Karl Marx and Søren Kierkegaard.

STEPHEN M. FISHMAN is Professor in the Philosophy Department, the University of North Carolina at Charlotte. Since attending his first Writing Across the Curriculum workshop in 1983, he has been studying student writing in his classes. This research has led to articles in *Teaching Philosophy*, *Research in the Teaching of English*, *College Composition and Communication*, and *College English*. One of his articles (with co-researcher Lucille P. McCarthy) won the 1993 James N. Britton award for inquiry in the English language arts. His short stories have appeared in *Sing Heavenly Muse*, *Crescent Review*, *Crucible*, *Emrys Journal*, *St. Andrews Review*, and *Carolina Literary Companion*.

ANN GARRY is Chair and Professor of Philosophy at California State University, Los Angeles. She coedited *Women, Knowledge, and Reality: Explorations in Feminist Philosophy* with Marilyn Pearsall (Routledge; 1st edn., 1989; 2nd edn., 1996). Her publications range from traditional philosophy of mind to abortion and pornography ("Pornography and Respect for Women," which appeared in *Social Theory and Practice* in 1978, has been widely reprinted), but most recently she has been interested in the intersection of feminist and traditional philosophy. She has long been active in the community of feminist philosophers. She is an associate editor of *Hypatia: A Journal of Feminist Philosophy*, a past member of the American Philosophical Association Committee on the Status of Women, and a founding member of the Pacific Division of the Society for Women in Philosophy. In the wider world, she has served on the California Council for the Humanities.

CAROL S. GOULD is Associate Professor of Philosophy, Florida Atlantic University, where she teaches aesthetics and philosophy of literature. She publishes in these areas and in Greek Philosophy; her essays have appeared in *Phronesis*, *British Journal of Aesthetics*, *Philosophy and Literature*, *Journal of Aesthetics and Art Criticism*, and *History of Philosophy Quarterly*. In aesthetics, she focuses on the ontological problem of aesthetic properties, and she is working on an extensive defense of aesthetic realism. She received her Ph.D. from the State University of New York at Buffalo, writing a dissertation on Plato's theory of reference in the middle theory of the Forms. She is deeply involved in the arts, especially as a musician and an observer of Greek vases and contemporary painting.

ANTHONY J. GRAYBOSCH, born on Long Island in 1949, is Professor of Philosophy at California State University, Chico. He has also taught at Mount Senario College in Wisconsin and the University of Central Oklahoma. During 1990-91, he was a Fulbright lecturer at Tel-Aviv University in Israel and

Eötvös Loránd University in Budapest, Hungary. He is a graduate of Fordham University and received his Ph.D. from the Graduate Center of the City University of New York. He has published essays on children's rights, friendship between parents and adult children, and love in the blues. His other areas of interest are social philosophy, pragmatism, and criminal justice ethics. His work has appeared in *Journal of Social Philosophy*, *Journal of Value Inquiry*, *The Monist*, *Philosophia*, *Southern Journal of Philosophy*, and a number of collections. Married with two sons, he dragged the family, in the summer of 1992, two hundred fifty miles north of the Arctic Circle in Norway, to Hamory and the Lofoten Islands, to see the landscapes Knut Hamsun wrote about in his early novels.

SANDRA HARDING is Professor of Philosophy at the University of Delaware and Adjunct Professor of Philosophy and Women's Studies at the University of California, Los Angeles. She is the author or editor of seven books, including *Discovering Reality: Feminist Perspectives on Metaphysics, Methodology and Philosophy of Science* (with Merrill Hintikka; Reidel, 1983); *The Science Question in Feminism* (Cornell University Press, 1986); *Whose Science? Whose Knowledge?* (Cornell, 1991), which includes the essay "Thinking From the Perspective of Lesbian Lives"; and *The "Racial" Economy of Science: Toward a Democratic Future* (Indiana University Press, 1993). She is completing a book on decolonizing science studies.

ERIC HOFFMAN received his Ph.D. in philosophy from the University of Pennsylvania in 1978, having written a dissertation on John Rawls's theory of justice. He taught from 1978 to 1980 at the State University of New York at Fredonia. His research focused on ethics, social and political philosophy, moral education, and the philosophy of personal relationships. In 1981, he entered law school and, in 1984, received the J.D. from the University of Pennsylvania Law School, where he served as Articles Editor for the law review. After clerking for Judge Sloviter on the U. S. Court of Appeals for the Third Circuit, he practiced employment law until 1993 with the Philadelphia law firm of Schnader, Harrison, Segal, and Lewis. In 1990, he and his wife, JoAnne Fischer, became local coordinators of the Essential Experience Workshop, an intensive program in support of personal development. In 1993, Hoffman left the active practice of law. He now serves as Executive Director of the American Philosophical Association and Assistant Professor of Philosophy at the University of Delaware.

LEE HORVITZ was an actor and now tries to be a philosopher. He teaches philosophy at Miami University in Ohio. He has lived in New York and Chicago and wants to live in both again. Love, justice, and the arts seem to him to be the most important things going, and he would like to write poetry and drama with the depth and vitality of Shakespeare.

CHARLES W. JOHNSON attended the U. S. Military Academy at West Point, DePaul University (B.A.), and Michigan State University (M.A. and Ph.D.).

He has taught philosophy at Utah State University since 1972. His main professional interests include philosophy of mind, philosophical methods, and Wittgenstein. He was active in the peace movement of the 1960s and now remains active in the American Civil Liberties Union. He enjoys playing drums and classical guitar but not both at the same time. He lives in Smithfield Canyon with three very strange cats.

EDWARD JOHNSON has published essays on ethics, both theoretical and applied, including such topics as animal rights, environmental ethics, philosophy of technology, philosophy of education, and philosophy of sex and love. His work has appeared in, among other places, *Ethics and Animals*, *Environmental Ethics*, *Between the Species*, *Philosophy of the Social Sciences*, *Ethics*, and *Philosophical Review*. He received his Ph.D. from Princeton University in 1976, and since then has taught at the University of New Orleans, where he is Professor and Chair.

JOSEPH KUPFER is Professor of Philosophy at Iowa State University, where he teaches ethics, aesthetics, medical ethics, and philosophy of law. He has written on privacy, violence, architecture and politics, lying, and the parent-child relationship, his work appearing in *The Personalist*, *Review of Metaphysics*, *Metaphilosophy*, *Social Theory and Practice*, *American Philosophical Quarterly*, and other journals. He has published two books with State University of New York Press, *Experience as Art* (1983) and *Autonomy and Social Interaction* (1990).

JUSTIN LEIBER (Ph.D., Chicago; B.Phil., Oxford) is Professor of Philosophy at the University of Houston. His books include *Noam Chomsky: A Philosophic Overview* (Twayne, 1975); *Structuralism* (Twayne, 1978); *Can Animals and Machines Be Persons?* (Hackett, 1985); *An Invitation to Cognitive Science* (Blackwell, 1991); *Paradoxes* (Duckworth, 1993); and his trilogy of novels, which investigates issues of cognition, consciousness, and personhood: *Beyond Rejection* (Ballantine, 1980), *Beyond Humanity* (TOR, 1987), and *Beyond Gravity* (TOR, 1988). His home page URL is http://bentley.uh.edu/philosophy/leiber/jleiber.html.

FLO LEIBOWITZ (Ph.D., The Johns Hopkins University) is Professor and Director of Graduate Studies in the Department of Philosophy at Oregon State University. She teaches and writes on issues in aesthetics and is particularly interested in art and rationality. Her work has appeared in *Philosophy and Literature*, *Journal of Aesthetics and Art Criticism*, *Jump Cut*, and *Film Quarterly*. Recent publications include "Movie Colorization and the Expression of Mood," reprinted in Alex Neill and Aaron Ridley, eds., *Arguments About Art: Contemporary Philosophical Debates* (McGraw-Hill, 1994) and "Apt Feelings, or Why Women's Films Aren't Trivial," in David Bordwell and Noël Carroll, eds., *Post-Theory* (University of Wisconsin Press, 1996).

LINDA LeMONCHECK received her Ph.D. in philosophy in 1981 from the University of California, Los Angeles. She writes and teaches at California State University, Long Beach, in the areas of feminist philosophy and applied ethics. She is the author of *Dehumanizing Women: Treating Persons as Sex Objects* (Rowman and Littlefield, 1985), and her book *Loose Women, Lecherous Men: A Feminist Philosophy of Sex* is being published by Oxford University Press. Her current project is a book on sexual harassment for Rowman and Littlefield, coauthored with Mane Hajdin. She lives in Seal Beach, California, where she supports the local battered women's shelter as well as feminist bookstores and organic produce markets in the surrounding area.

DONALD LEVY, Professor of Philosophy, Brooklyn College, City University of New York, was born in New York, 17 June 1936. He was educated at the Bronx High School of Science, Cornell University (B.A., 1957; Ph.D., 1980), and the University of Washington. He served as an associate editor for *The Encyclopedia of Philosophy*, 1961-65. His essays and reviews have appeared in *Inquiry*, *Analysis*, *Journal of Social Philosophy*, *Journal of the History of Ideas*, *Ethics*, *International Review of Psycho-Analysis*, *Philosophical Psychology*, and *Canadian Philosophical Reviews*. His book *Freud Among the Philosophers* (Yale University Press) was published in 1996.

HILDE LINDEMANN NELSON is Director of the Center for Applied and Professional Ethics at the University of Tennessee at Knoxville, where she also teaches courses in biomedical ethics. She is the coauthor of *The Patient in the Family* (Routledge, 1995), general coeditor of the Routledge series, "Reflective Bioethics," and editor of *Feminism and Families* (Routledge, forthcoming). Her articles have appeared in *Hypatia*, *Bioethics*, *Journal of Clinical Ethics*, *Utah Law Review*, the *Encyclopedia of Bioethics*, and *Hastings Center Report*, as well as in many anthologies. She has previously taught at St. John's University in Minnesota, Michigan State University, and Vassar College, and was Research Associate at The Hastings Center and Associate Editor of the *Hastings Center Report*.

JAMES LINDEMANN NELSON is Professor of Philosophy at the University of Tennessee at Knoxville, where he teaches and conducts research in bioethics and ethical theory. He has collaborated with Hilde Lindemann Nelson on *The Patient in the Family* (Routledge, 1995), the "Reflective Bioethics" series, and on several shorter publications. His own research has appeared in, among other places, *Hastings Center Report*, *Journal of Medicine and Philosophy*, *Bioethics, Journal of the American Geriatrics Society*, *Public Affairs Quarterly*, *Dialogue*, *Journal of Medical Ethics*, *American Philosophical Quarterly*, and *Journal of Law, Medicine, and Ethics*. Prior to his appointment at the University of Tennessee, he was Associate for Ethical Studies at The Hastings Center.

DAVID J. MAYO is Professor in the Philosophy Department and a member of the Center for Ethics and Public Policy at the University of Minnesota,

Duluth. He is also Faculty Associate of the Center for Biomedical Ethics at the University of Minnesota, Twin Cities. He received his B.A. from Reed College and his Ph.D. from the University of Pittsburgh. His primary area of interest is medical ethics, in particular, issues involving privacy, AIDS, and physician-assisted suicide. He has published widely in these areas, including an anthology with M. Pabst Battin, *Suicide: The Philosophical Issues* (St. Martin's Press, 1980), and a book, *AIDS: Privacy and Testing* (University of Utah Press, 1989) with Martin Gunderson and Frank Rhame. His essays have appeared in *Journal of Clinical Ethics*, *Journal of Homosexuality*, *Journal of Medicine and Philosophy*, and *Teaching Philosophy*.

JOHN McMURTRY is Professor of Philosophy at the University of Guelph. He is also Joint Ph.D. Programme Professor of Philosophy at McMaster University and Adjunct Professor of International Development at the University of Guelph. He received his B.A. (English) and M.A. (Philosophy) from the University of Toronto and his Ph.D. from University College, University of London. He is the father of four children, a widower, and is now living in an unmarried partnership. He is the author of three books, *The Dimensions of English* (Holt, Rinehart, and Winston, 1970), *The Structure of Marx's World-View* (Princeton University Press, 1978), and *Understanding War* (Science for Peace and Samuel Stevens, 1989). His academic articles have appeared in *Inquiry*, *The Monist*, *Canadian Journal of Philosophy*, *Journal of Applied Philosophy*, *Praxis International*, *Journal of Philosophy of Education*, *Journal of Business Ethics*, *Journal of Speculative Philosophy*, *Social Justice*, and *Informal Logic*. He has been a regular columnist for the *Toronto Telegram* and *Canadian Social Studies*, and his feature articles have appeared in *Atlantic*, *Nation*, *Macleans*, *Globe and Mail*, *Toronto Star*, *Canadian Forum*, *In These Times*, and the *Literary Review of Canada*.

DIANE P. MICHELFELDER received her Ph.D. in philosophy at the University of Texas at Austin. Since 1981, she has been a member of the Philosophy Department at California Polytechnic State University, San Luis Obispo, and is now Professor and Chair. She is coeditor of *Dialogue and Deconstruction: The Gadamer-Derrida Encounter* (State University of New York Press, 1989) and, as Diane Michelfelder Wilcox, *Applied Ethics in American Society* (Harcourt Brace, forthcoming). Her primary areas of philosophical interest are twentieth-century European philosophy (especially Heidegger and Gadamer), ethics, and philosophy of art, including philosophy of architecture.

RICHARD D. MOHR (B.A., University of Chicago; Ph.D., University of Toronto) is Professor of Philosophy, University of Illinois-Urbana. He had a secret early life as a classicist, but for the last decade has chiefly been writing on social issues affecting gay Americans. He is the author of *Gays/Justice: A Study of Ethics, Society, and Law* (Columbia University Press, 1988). In 1989 he founded for Columbia the book series *Between Men, Between Women: Lesbian and Gay Studies*, which was the first institutionalized form of gay studies in the U. S. A. In 1992, Beacon Press brought out his book *Gay Ideas:*

Outing and Other Controversies, which won the Lambda Literary Awards' "Editors' Choice" Award. In 1994 Beacon published his latest book, *A More Perfect Union: Why Straight America Must Stand Up for Gay Rights*. A public intellectual, Mohr has also written for magazines and newspapers, including *Chronicle of Higher Education*, *Advocate*, *Christopher Street*, *Nation*, *Reason*, *Chicago Tribune*, and *Boston Globe*.

T. F. MORRIS. The first step was recognizing that I needed to do first things first, and figure out how I should live. The second step was not forgetting Godard's principle: "If I lose my money I lose nothing, if I lose my character I lose everything." I managed to get through the terribly corrupting experience known as graduate school, but I have not been so intense about it as to ask, when the dice fall my way, "Am I then a crooked gambler?" (*Thus Spoke Zarathustra* 4). I teach philosophy part-time at four different colleges. I have published exegetical studies of Kierkegaard, Paul, and Plato in journals as "good" as *Apeiron*, *Sophia*, *Interpretation*, *Ancient Philosophy*, *International Journal for the Philosophy of Religion*, and *Heythrop Journal*. In most of these I manage to talk about Shakespeare as well. I am completing *Is Plato Dumb or What? A Commentary on the Apology and the Crito,* which takes seriously the (obvious) fact that Plato makes many mistakes on purpose.

DOROTHEA OLKOWSKI is Associate Professor of Philosophy and former Director of Women's Studies (1991-95) at the University of Colorado at Colorado Springs. She is coeditor, with Constantin Boundas, of *Gilles Deleuze and the Theatre of Philosophy* (Routledge, 1994), and has written numerous articles on aesthetics, feminism, and continental philosophy. Her current project is a book, *Materiality and Language*, that combines these interests with the philosophy of Deleuze.

ROGER PADEN is a specialist in social and political philosophy and in environmental ethics. In the first area, he has published papers on the limits of the liberal conception of justice, the nature of democracy, and practical reasoning. In the second, he has published papers on animal welfare, the nature of conservationism, and grand theory in environmental ethics. His essays and reviews have appeared in *Hobbes Studies*, *Agriculture and Human Values*, *International Journal of Applied Philosophy*, *Environmental Ethics*, *Metaphilosophy*, *Teaching Philosophy*, *Philosophy and Social Criticism*, *Social Theory and Practice*, *Journal of Value Inquiry*, and *Review of Metaphysics*. He received a Ph.D. from the University of Illinois in 1981. He is an Associate Professor at George Mason University, and has taught at the Universities of Connecticut, Maryland, and Florida.

ROBERT PIELKE, a native of Baltimore, lives in Claremont, California. He earned a B.A. at the University of Maryland, an M.Div. at the Lutheran Theological Seminary in Gettysburg (thereby escaping the draft), and a Ph.D. at the Claremont Graduate School in California. He has taught philosophy at George Mason University in Virginia and California State Polytechnic University in Pomona. He now teaches at El Camino College, where he specializes in logic, ethics, and on-line distance education. Aside from his academic writings, he has published short stories, feature articles, film reviews, screenplays, and a book on rock music in American culture. He is also a firm believer in the truth and efficacy of "sex, drugs, and rock and roll."

CHRISTINE PIERCE is Professor of Philosophy at North Carolina State University. She is the author of numerous essays in ethics and feminist philosophy; most recently she has written on the topic of gay marriage. Her work has appeared in *Journal of Social Philosophy*, *Signs*, *Journal of Medicine and Philosophy*, *Philosophical Studies*, *Southern Journal of Philosophy*, and *Analysis*. She has edited three books with Donald VanDeVeer, *AIDS: Ethics and Public Policy* (Wadsworth, 1988), *The Environmental Ethics and Policy Book: Philosophy, Ecology, Economics* (Wadsworth, 1994), and *People, Penguins, and Plastic Trees: Basic Issues in Environmental Ethics* (Wadsworth, 1986, 1995).

JO-ANN PILARDI is Associate Professor of Philosophy and Women's Studies at Towson State University in Maryland, where she is Coordinator of the Women's Studies Program. A Pittsburgh native, Pilardi received her B.A. at Duquesne University, holds an M.A. in Philosophy from Pennsylvania State University and a Ph.D. from Johns Hopkins University's Humanities Center. She specializes in continental thought, and has published articles on feminist philosophy and Simone de Beauvoir, which have appeared in *Hypatia*, *Feminist Studies*, *Feminist Interpretations of Simone de Beauvoir* (Margaret Simons, ed.; Pennsylvania State University Press, 1995), and *History of Women Philosophers*, vol. 4 (M. E. Waithe, ed.; Kluwer, 1995). Active for many years in the Baltimore women's movement and in creating a feminist philosophy curriculum at Towson State, she has worked to integrate feminist scholarship into the regular philosophy curriculum and to redesign introductory level philosophy courses to include attention to issues of race, class, and gender. Her most recent papers include one on Nietzsche and another on racism in the United States.

LEE RICE is Associate Professor of Philosophy at Marquette University, and a former Fulbright, Danforth, and Woodrow Wilson Fellow at the University of Paris and Saint Louis University. He is the author of over forty articles on Spinoza's thought, and one of the coeditors of a new translation of Spinoza's letters (Baruch Spinoza, *The Letters*, trans. Samuel Shirley, Introduction and Notes by Steven Barbone, Lee Rice, and Jacob Adler [Indianapolis: Hackett, 1995]). He is interested also in both human sexuality and artificial intelligence, and has published articles in these areas as well. His works have appeared in *Journal of the History of Philosophy*, *Iyyun* (*Jerusalem Philosophical Quarterly*), *International Philosophical Quarterly*, *Southern Journal of Philosophy*, *Studia Spinozana*, *Modern Schoolman*, *Philosophiques* (Montréal), *Journal of Homosexuality*, and *Canadian Journal of Philosophy*.

RICHARD C. RICHARDS is Professor of Philosophy at California State Polytechnic University, Pomona. He received the B.A. from the University of California, Santa Barbara; the M.A. from the University of California, Los Angeles; and the C. Phil. from UCLA in 1968. He and Marty C. Richards edited *Love: A Philosophical Perspective* (Ginn Press, 1987), and he is the author of *It Looks Like Love—Sometimes It Is* (Ginn Press, 1993). In 1968, he received the Outstanding Teacher award from California State Polytechnic University and was named Distinguished Professor.

DEBORAH ROSEN. I was born in 1944 (after the Normandy invasion) in Orangeburg, South Carolina. In my struggles to make sense of my religious beliefs and in trying vainly to win arguments with my father, who was a lawyer, philosophy first took root in me. I received a B.A. in philosophy at Agnes Scott College, with major hours in religion. I took all the logic I could understand while in graduate school at Stanford, but I still never remember my father conceding any argument (or card game). When I received my Ph.D. at Stanford in 1970, I was the first woman to have done so in that department. No one knew what I was supposed to wear to my dissertation orals. I bought the tallest heels I could walk in, which was the last time my growing feminist beliefs would allow such subterfuge. Patrick Suppes was a patient dissertation advisor who taught me to argue more rigorously and to love the puzzles involved in giving a probabilistic account of causality. This became the basis of my first published papers. I taught philosophy at the University of New Orleans from 1970 to 1986, and helped start their honors awards program, their women's studies program, and their general studies program. From 1982 to 1994 I was appointed a medical ethicist to Louisiana State University Medical Center, and helped to start an Ethics Review Committee for their teaching hospital. From 1993 I have made my living as a professional investor, using the marketplace of stocks as a focus of research into probabilistic causality.

MICHAEL RUSE is Professor of Philosophy and Zoology at the University of Guelph. He is founder and editor of *Biology and Philosophy*, and is on the editorial boards of the journals *Zygon*, *Philosophy of Science*, *Science and Education*, *Quarterly Review of Biology*, and *Episteme*. He is also the general editor of Cambridge Studies in Philosophy and Biology. Among his books are *Sociobiology: Sense or Nonsense* (Reidel, 1979), *Is Science Sexist?* (Reidel, 1981), *Taking Darwin Seriously* (Blackwell, 1986), *Homosexuality: A Philosophical Inquiry* (Blackwell, 1988), *Philosophy of Biology Today* (State University of New York Press, 1988), *The Darwinian Paradigm* (Routledge, 1989), and *Evolutionary Naturalism* (Routledge, 1994).

JEROME A. SHAFFER was born in Brooklyn in 1929, received a B.A. in Philosophy from Cornell University in 1950, and then a Ph.D. from Princeton University in 1952. In 1953 he was a Fulbright Scholar at Magdalen College, Oxford. Following a stint in the Army (1953-55), he joined the faculty at Swarthmore College, where he taught for twelve years. In 1967, he moved to the University of Connecticut and was instrumental in developing its graduate program in philosophy. He served as chair of the department from 1977 until retirement, June 1994. He is now a practicing marital and family therapist. Among his publications are *The Philosophy of Mind* (Prentice-Hall, 1968) and *Reality, Knowledge, and Value* (Random House, 1971).

STEVEN G. SMITH, a native of South Florida, moved to the American South in 1968. He majored in religion at Florida State University and combined graduate studies in philosophy and Western religious thought at Vanderbilt and Duke. He has taught in philosophy and religious studies programs since 1980, first at North Carolina Wesleyan College and, since 1985, at Millsaps College. His published articles are predominantly in philosophy of religion and philosophical anthropology; they have appeared in *Kant-Studien*, *American Philosophical Quarterly*, *Philosophy and Theology*, *Religious Studies*, *Journal of Religious Ethics*, and *Journal of Value Inquiry*. His books are *The Argument to the Other* (Scholars Press, 1983), a comparative study of Karl Barth and Emmanuel Levinas; *The Concept of the Spiritual* (Temple University Press, 1988), a first philosophy keyed to the primacy of the issue of how beings who transcend each other's comprehension shall live in relationship; and *Gender Thinking* (Temple, 1992), an exploration of conceptual issues relating to sex differences.

NANCY E. SNOW is Assistant Professor of Philosophy at Marquette University. She received her B.A. from Marquette in 1980, her M.A. in philosophy from Marquette in 1982, and her Ph.D. in philosophy from the University of Notre Dame in 1988. Her research interests are in ethical theory and practical ethics. Her publications include articles on compassion, self-forgiveness, humility, drug legalization, and self-blame and blame of rape victims, and have appeared in *Journal of Value Inquiry*, *American Philosophical Quarterly*, *Philosophy and Phenomenological Research*, and *Between the Species*. She is editing a book, *In the Company of Others: Perspectives on Community, Family, and Culture*, forthcoming from Rowman and Littlefield, and is working on an article on the moral significance of vulnerability.

ALAN SOBLE is Professor and Research Professor of Philosophy at the University of New Orleans. He is the author of *The Philosophy of Sex and Love: An Introduction* (Paragon House, 1997), *Sexual Investigations* (New York University Press, 1996), *The Structure of Love* (Yale University Press, 1990), and *Pornography: Marxism, Feminism, and the Future of Sexuality* (Yale, 1986). He has edited *The Philosophy of Sex* (Rowman and Littlefield, 1st ed., 1980; 2nd ed., 1991; 3rd ed., 1997) and *Eros, Agape, and Philia* (Paragon House, 1989). In 1977 he founded the Society for the Philosophy of Sex and Love and served as its director until 1992. He received the B.S. in biology from Albright College (1969), and the M.A. in pharmacology (1972) and the Ph.D. in philosophy (1976) from the State University of New York at Buffalo. His essays in ethics, philosophy of the social sciences, and love and sex have appeared in *Metaphilosophy*, *Social Epistemology*, *The Monist*, *Philosophy of the Social Sciences*, *Social Theory and Practice*, *Apeiron*, *Philosophy* *and Phenomenological Research*, *Pacific Philosophical Quarterly*, *Canadian Journal of Philosophy*, and *International Journal of Applied Philosophy*; his reviews have appeared in *Ethics*, *Journal of Value Inquiry*, *Canadian Philosophical Reviews*, and *Teaching Philosophy*. He wrote the "Sexuality and Sexual Ethics" entry for the *Encyclopedia of Ethics* (Garland, 1992; 2nd ed., forthcoming), the "La Morale Sexuelle" entry for the *Dictionnaire de philosophie morale* (Presses Universitaires de France, 1996), and the "Sexuality, Philosophy of" entry for the *Routledge Encyclopedia of Philosophy* (forthcoming, 1998). The recipient of a Fulbright Teaching grant for 1991-92, he spent the year in Hungary teaching philosophy of science, social philosophy, and philosophy of love and sex at Eötvös Loránd University and the Budapest Technical University. During that time, he wrote two essays: "A Szexualitás Filozófiájáról" ["The Philosophy of Sex"], *Magyar Filozófiai Szemle* [Hungarian Philosophical Review] (1992), and "Egyesülés és Jóakarat" ("Union and Concern"), *Athenaeum* (1994); both were translated into Hungarian by Módos Magdolna, and the latter has been revised for publication in Roger Lamb, ed., *Love Analyzed* (Westview, 1997). He is currently writing *The Limits of Feminist Scholarship: Sex, Rape, and Pornography*, to be published by Rowman and Littlefield. The URL of his home page is http://www.uno.edu/~phil/soble.html, and he welcomes comments on this book at AGSPL@jazz.ucc.uno.edu.

ART STAWINSKI received a Ph.D. in philosophy from Northwestern University, with a dissertation on Wittgenstein's discussion of perception in the *Philosophical Investigations*. While a member of the philosophy faculty at Illinois Institute of Technology, his interests turned to ethics and social philosophy. He developed a course in the philosophy of sexuality, and joined the staff of the Center for the Study of Ethics in the Professions, where he taught and researched issues in engineering and computer ethics. After leaving academic employment in 1986, he has continued research in ethics and has presented workshops for community organizations. Now he is an independent consultant in business and professional ethics.

JOHN P. SULLIVAN, the classicist and specialist in the literature of the early Roman Empire, was born in 1930 in Liverpool, England, and died in Santa Barbara, California, in 1993. He studied at St. John's College, Cambridge University, receiving the B.A. (Starred Double First in Classics) in 1953 and the M.A. (Cantab.) and M.A. (Oxon.) in 1957. In the United States, he held appointments at the University of Texas at Austin (where he co-founded *Arion* in 1961), the State University of New York at Buffalo, and the University of California at Santa Barbara. Among his books are *Ezra Pound and Sextus Propertius: A Study in Creative Translation* (University of Texas Press, 1964); *Petronius: The* Satyricon *and the Fragments* (Penguin, 1965); *The* Satyricon *of Petronius: A Literary Study* (Faber, 1968); *Propertius: A Critical Introduction* (Cambridge University Press, 1976); *Literature and Politics in the Age of Nero* (Cornell University Press, 1986); *Epigrams of Martial Englished by Divers Hands* (edited with Peter Whigham; University of California Press, 1987); *Martial: The Unexpected Classic. A Literary and Historical Study*

(Cambridge University Press, 1991); and *Modern Critical Theory and Classical Literature* (edited with Irene J. F. de Jong; Brill, 1994).

RUSSELL VANNOY was born in 1933 and raised in a small Missouri town near Mark Twain's Hannibal. In college he was converted to philosophy by reading John Dewey and Bertrand Russell; but in graduate school (M.A., Illinois; M.A., Harvard; Ph.D., Rochester) his initial enthusiasm began to diminish. Finding this philosophy dry and technical, he turned to Nietzsche and Sartre for solace. In the Philosophy Department of the State University of New York College at Buffalo, he taught the philosophy of sex and love as early as 1973, and in 1980 his book *Sex Without Love: A Philosophical Exploration* (Prometheus) appeared. He is the author of the "Philosophy of Sex" entry in *Human Sexuality: An Encyclopedia* (Vern Bullough and Bonnie Bullough, eds., Garland, 1994). Now retired ("on permanent sabbatical"), he is working on a book that develops his theory of sexual perversity.

SYLVIA WALSH has been an adjunct professor of philosophy at Stetson University since 1989, teaching courses in the history of Western philosophy and feminist philosophy. Prior to 1989 she taught in Atlanta, in the Department of Religion and Philosophy at Clark College and the Department of Religion at Emory University. She holds the A.B. degree from Oberlin College, the M.A. in religion from Yale University, and the Ph.D. from Emory, where she did a dissertation on Kierkegaard. She is the author of *Living Poetically: Kierkegaard's Existential Aesthetics* (Pennsylvania State University Press, 1994), and is coediting a collection of essays, *Feminist Interpretations of Kierkegaard*, for the "Rereading the Canon" series published by Penn State Press. She has presented numerous scholarly papers at regional, national, and international meetings and has published over thirty articles and reviews in scholarly journals and books. In 1985 she was Director of a NEH Summer Seminar for College Teachers on Kierkegaard. She is serving a two-year term as President of the Søren Kierkegaard Society and is a member of the Advisory Board for the *International Kierkegaard Commentary*.

HUGH T. WILDER is Professor and Chair of the Philosophy Department, College of Charleston, Charleston, South Carolina. His B.A. is from Denison University, and his M.A. and Ph.D. are from the University of Western Ontario. His philosophical interests are in aesthetics and philosophy of mind; his essays have appeared in *Metaphilosophy*, *Canadian Journal of Philosophy*, *Australasian Journal of Philosophy*, *Philosophical Studies*, *Social Epistemology*, and *Philosophy and Literature*. With Judith de Luce, he edited *Language in Primates* (Springer-Verlag, 1983).

Index

Pages bearing photographs are indicated in ***boldface italics***.

VIBS

The **Value Inquiry Book Series** is co-sponsored by:

American Maritain Association
American Society for Value Inquiry
Association for Personalist Studies
Association for Process Philosophy of Education
Center for East European Dialogue and Development,
Rochester Institute of Technology
Centre for Cultural Research, Aarhus University
College of Education and Allied Professions, Bowling Green State University
Concerned Philosophers for Peace
Conference of Philosophical Societies
Conference on Value Inquiry
International Academy of Philosophy of the Principality of Liechtenstein
International Society for Universalism
International Society for Value Inquiry
Natural Law Society
Philosophical Society of Finland
Philosophy Seminar, University of Mainz
R.S. Hartman Institute for Formal and Applied Axiology
Society for Iberian and Latin-American Thought
Society for the Philosophic Study of Genocide and the Holocaust
Yves R. Simon Institute.

Titles Published

1. Noel Balzer, *The Human Being as a Logical Thinker.*

2. Archie J. Bahm, *Axiology: The Science of Values.*

3. H. P. P. (Hennie) Lötter, *Justice for an Unjust Society.*

4. H. G. Callaway, *Context for Meaning and Analysis: A Critical Study in the Philosophy of Language.*

5. Benjamin S. Llamzon, *A Humane Case for Moral Intuition.*

6. James R. Watson, *Between Auschwitz and Tradition: Postmodern Reflections on the Task of Thinking.* A volume in **Holocaust and Genocide Studies.**

7. Robert S. Hartman, *Freedom to Live: The Robert Hartman Story,* edited by Arthur R. Ellis. A volume in **Hartman Institute Axiology Studies.**

8. Archie J. Bahm, *Ethics: The Science of Oughtness.*

9. George David Miller, *An Idiosyncratic Ethics; Or, the Lauramachean Ethics.*

10. Joseph P. DeMarco, *A Coherence Theory in Ethics.*

11. Frank G. Forrest, *Valuemetrics: The Science of Personal and Professional Ethics.* A volume in **Hartman Institute Axiology Studies.**

12. William Gerber, *The Meaning of Life: Insights of the World's Great Thinkers.*

13. Richard T. Hull, Editor, *A Quarter Century of Value Inquiry: Presidential Addresses of the American Society for Value Inquiry.* A volume in **Histories and Addresses of Philosophical Societies.**

14. William Gerber, *Nuggets of Wisdom from Great Jewish Thinkers: From Biblical Times to the Present.*

15. Sidney Axinn, *The Logic of Hope: Extensions of Kant's View of Religion.*

16. Messay Kebede, *Meaning and Development.*

17. Amihud Gilead, *The Platonic Odyssey: A Philosophical-Literary Inquiry into the* Phaedo.

18. Necip Fikri Alican, *Mill's Principle of Utility: A Defense of John Stuart Mill's Notorious Proof.* A volume in **Universal Justice.**

19. Michael H. Mitias, Editor, *Philosophy and Architecture.*

20. Roger T. Simonds, *Rational Individualism: The Perennial Philosophy of Legal Interpretation.* A volume in **Natural Law Studies.**

21. William Pencak, *The Conflict of Law and Justice in the Icelandic Sagas.*

22. Samuel M. Natale and Brian M. Rothschild, Editors, *Values, Work, Education: The Meanings of Work.*

23. N. Georgopoulos and Michael Heim, Editors, *Being Human in the Ultimate: Studies in the Thought of John M. Anderson.*

24. Robert Wesson and Patricia A. Williams, Editors, *Evolution and Human Values.*

25. Wim J. van der Steen, *Facts, Values, and Methodology: A New Approach to Ethics.*

26. Avi Sagi and Daniel Statman, *Religion and Morality.*

27. Albert William Levi, *The High Road of Humanity: The Seven Ethical Ages of Western Man,* edited by Donald Phillip Verene and Molly Black Verene.

28. Samuel M. Natale and Brian M. Rothschild, Editors, *Work Values: Education, Organization, and Religious Concerns.*

29. Laurence F. Bove and Laura Duhan Kaplan, Editors, *From the Eye of the Storm: Regional Conflicts and the Philosophy of Peace.* A volume in **Philosophy of Peace.**

30. Robin Attfield, *Value, Obligation, and Meta-Ethics.*

31. William Gerber, *The Deepest Questions You Can Ask About God: As Answered by the World's Great Thinkers.*

32. Daniel Statman, *Moral Dilemmas.*

33. Rem B. Edwards, Editor, *Formal Axiology and Its Critics.* A volume in **Hartman Institute Axiology Studies.**

34. George David Miller and Conrad P. Pritscher, *On Education and Values: In Praise of Pariahs and Nomads.* A volume in **Philosophy of Education.**

35. Paul S. Penner, *Altruistic Behavior: An Inquiry into Motivation.*

36. Corbin Fowler, *Morality for Moderns.*

37. Giambattista Vico, *The Art of Rhetoric* (*Institutiones Oratoriae,* 1711-1741), from the definitive Latin text and notes, Italian commentary and introduction by Giuliano Crifò, translated and edited by Giorgio A. Pinton and Arthur W. Shippee. A volume in **Values in Italian Philosophy.**

38. W. H. Werkmeister, *Martin Heidegger on the Way,* edited by Richard T. Hull. A volume in **Werkmeister Studies.**

39. Phillip Stambovsky, *Myth and the Limits of Reason.*

40. Samantha Brennan, Tracy Isaacs, and Michael Milde, Editors, *A Question of Values: New Canadian Perspectives in Ethics and Political Philosophy.*

41. Peter A. Redpath, *Cartesian Nightmare: An Introduction to Transcendental Sophistry.* A volume in **Studies in the History of Western Philosophy.**

42. Clark Butler, *History as the Story of Freedom: Philosophy in Intercultural Context,* with Responses by sixteen scholars.

43. Dennis Rohatyn, *Philosophy History Sophistry.*

44. Leon Shaskolsky Sheleff, *Social Cohesion and Legal Coercion: A Critique of Weber, Durkheim, and Marx.*

45. Alan Soble, Editor, *Sex, Love, and Friendship: Studies of the Society for the Philosophy of Sex and Love, 1977-1992.* A volume in **Histories and Addresses of Philosophical Societies.**